Real World Enterprise Reports Using VB6 and VB .NET

CARL GANZ, JR.

Apress™

Real World Enterprise Reports Using VB6 and VB .NET
Copyright ©2003 by Carl Ganz, Jr.

ISBN (pbk): 1-59059-064-3

Printed and bound in the United States of America 12345678910

Trademarked names may appear in this book. Rather than use a trademark symbol with every occurrence of a trademarked name, we use the names only in an editorial fashion and to the benefit of the trademark owner, with no intention of infringement of the trademark.

Editorial Directors: Dan Appleman, Gary Cornell, Simon Hayes, Martin Streicher, Karen Watterson, John Zukowski

Assistant Publisher: Grace Wong

Project Managers: Sofia Marchant, Laura Cheu, Nate McFadden

Copy Editor: Ami Knox

Production Editor: Laura Cheu

Compositor and Proofreader: Impressions Book and Journal Services, Inc.

Indexer: Lynn Armstrong

Artist and Cover Designer: Kurt Krames

Production Manager: Kari Brooks

Manufacturing Manager: Tom Debolski

Distributed to the book trade in the United States by Springer-Verlag New York, Inc., 175 Fifth Avenue, New York, NY, 10010 and outside the United States by Springer-Verlag GmbH & Co. KG, Tiergartenstr. 17, 69112 Heidelberg, Germany.

In the United States: phone 1-800-SPRINGER, email orders@springer-ny.com, or visit http://www.springer-ny.com.

Outside the United States: fax +49 6221 345229, email orders@springer.de, or visit http://www.springer.de.

For information on translations, please contact Apress directly at 2560 Ninth Street, Suite 219, Berkeley, CA 94710. Phone 510-549-5930, fax 510-549-5939, email info@apress.com, or visit http://www.apress.com.

The source code for this book is available to readers at http://www.apress.com in the Downloads section.

To the memory of my three thousand fellow Americans murdered by terrorists on September 11, 2001, at the World Trade Center, the Pentagon, and in Shanksville, Pennsylvania.

God bless the United States of America.

World Trade Center

Gordon McCannel Aamoth Jr.
Edelmiro (Ed) Abad
Maria Rose Abad
Andrew Anthony Abate
Vincent Abate
Laurence Abel
William F. Abrahamson
Richard Anthony Aceto
Alicia Acevedo Carranza
Heinrich B. Ackermann
Paul Andrew Acquaviva
Donald L. Adams
Patrick Adams
Shannon Lewis Adams
Stephen Adams
Ignatius Adanga
Christy A. Addamo
Terence E. Adderley Jr.
Sophia B. Addo
Lee Adler
Daniel Thomas Afflitto
Emmanuel Afuakwah
Alok Agarwal
Mukul Agarwala
Joseph Agnello
David Agnes
Joao A.D. Aguiar Jr.
Lt. Brian G. Ahearn
Jeremiah J. Ahern
Joanne Ahladiotis
Shabbir Ahmed
Terrance Andre Aiken
Godwin Ajala
Gertrude M. Alagero
Andrew Alameno
Margaret Ann (Peggy) Jezycki Alario
Gary Albero
Jon L. Albert
Peter Craig Alderman
Jacquelyn Delaine Aldridge
Grace Alegre-Cua

David D. Alger
Boutros al-Hashim
Ernest Alikakos
Edward L. Allegretto
Eric Allen
Joseph Ryan Allen
Richard Dennis Allen
Richard Lanard Allen
Christopher Edward Allingham
Janet M. Alonso
Anthony Alvarado
Antonio Javier Alvarez
Juan Cisneros Alvarez
Telmo Alvear
Cesar A. Alviar
Tariq Amanullah
Angelo Amaranto
James Amato
Joseph Amatuccio
Christopher Charles Amoroso
Kazuhiro Anai
Calixto Anaya Jr.
Joseph Peter Anchundia
Kermit Charles Anderson
Yvette Anderson
John Andreacchio
Michael Rourke Andrews
Jean A. Andrucki
Siew-Nya Ang
Joseph Angelini Jr.
Joseph Angelini Sr.
Laura Angilletta
Doreen J. Angrisani
Lorraine D. Antigua
Peter Paul Apollo
Faustino Apostol Jr.
Frank Thomas Aquilino
Patrick Michael Aranyos
David Gregory Arce
Michael G. Arczynski
Louis Arena
Adam Arias
Michael J. Armstrong

Jack Charles Aron
Joshua Aron
Richard Avery Aronow
Japhet J. Aryee
Carl Asaro
Michael A. Asciak
Michael Edward Asher
Janice Ashley
Thomas J. Ashton
Manuel O. Asitimbay
Lt. Gregg Arthur Atlas
Debbie S. Attlas-Bellows
Gerald Atwood
James Audiffred
Frank Louis Aversano
Ezra Aviles
Samuel (Sandy) Ayala
Arlene T. Babakitis
Eustace (Rudy) Bacchus
John James Badagliacca
Jane Ellen Baeszler
Robert J. Baierwalter
Andrew J. Bailey
Brett T. Bailey
Tatyana Bakalinskaya
Michael S. Baksh
Julio Minto Balanca
Sharon Balkcom
Michael Andrew Bane
Kathy Bantis
Gerard Jean Baptiste
Walter Baran
Gerard A. Barbara
Paul V. Barbaro
James W. Barbella
Ivan Kyrillos Fairbanks Barbosa
Victor Daniel Barbosa
Colleen Ann Barkow
David Michael Barkway
Matthew Barnes
Sheila Patricia Barnes
Evan J. Baron
Renee Barrett-Arjune

Arthur T. Barry
Diane G. Barry
Maurice Vincent Barry
Scott D. Bart
Carlton W. Bartels
Guy Barzvi
Inna Basina
Alysia Basmajian
Kenneth William Basnicki
Lt. Steven J. Bates
Paul James Battaglia
W. David Bauer
Ivhan Luis Carpio Bautista
Marlyn C. Bautista
Jasper Baxter
Michele (Du Berry) Beale
Paul F. Beatini
Jane S. Beatty
Larry I. Beck
Manette Marie Beckles
Carl John Bedigian
Michael Beekman
Maria Behr
Yelena Belilovsky
Nina Patrice Bell
Andrea Della Bella
Stephen Elliot Belson
Paul Michael Benedetti
Denise Lenore Benedetto
Domingo Benilda
Bryan Craig Bennett
Eric L. Bennett
Oliver Duncan Bennett
Margaret L. Benson
Dominick J. Berardi
James Patrick Berger
Steven Howard Berger
John P. Bergin
Alvin Bergsohn
Daniel D. Bergstein
Michael J. Berkeley
Donna Bernaerts-Kearns
Dave Bernard
William Bernstein
David M. Berray
David S. Berry
Joseph J. Berry
William Reed Bethke
Timothy D. Betterly
Edward F. Beyea
Paul Michael Beyer
Anil T. Bharvaney
Bella Bhukhan
Shimmy D. Biegeleisen
Peter Alexander Bielfeld
William Biggart
Ralph Bijoux
Brian Bilcher
Carl Vincent Bini
Gary Bird
Joshua David Birnbaum
George Bishop

Jeffrey D. Bittner
Balewa Albert Blackman
Christopher Joseph Blackwell
Susan L. Blair
Harry Blanding Jr.
Janice L. Blaney
Craig Michael Blass
Rita Blau
Richard M. Blood Jr.
Michael A. Boccardi
John Paul Bocchi
Michael L. Bocchino
Susan Mary Bochino
Bruce Douglas (Chappy) Boehm
Mary Katherine Boffa
Nicholas A. Bogdan
Darren C. Bohan
Lawrence Francis Boisseau
Vincent M. Boland Jr.
Alan Bondarenko
Andre Bonheur Jr.
Colin Arthur Bonnett
Frank Bonomo
Yvonne L. Bonomo
Sean Booker
Juan Jose Borda Leyva
Sherry Ann Bordeaux
Krystine C. Bordenabe
Martin Boryczewski
Richard E. Bosco
John Howard Boulton Jr.
Francisco Bourdier
Thomas H. Bowden Jr.
Kimberly S. Bowers
Veronique (Bonnie) Nicole Bowers
Larry Bowman
Shawn Edward Bowman Jr.
Kevin L. Bowser
Gary R. Box
Gennady Boyarsky
Pamela Boyce
Michael Boyle
Alfred Braca
Sandra Conaty Brace
Kevin H. Bracken
David Brian Brady
Alexander Braginsky
Nicholas W. Brandemarti
Michelle Renee Bratton
Patrice Braut
Lydia Estelle Bravo
Ronald Michael Breitweiser
Edward A. Brennan III
Frank H. Brennan
Michael Emmett Brennan
Peter Brennan
Thomas M. Brennan
Capt. Daniel Brethel
Gary L. Bright
Jonathan Eric Briley
Mark A. Brisman
Paul Gary Bristow

Victoria Alvarez Brito
Mark Francis Broderick
Herman C. Broghammer
Keith Broomfield
Janice J. Brown
Lloyd Brown
Capt. Patrick J. Brown
Bettina Browne
Mark Bruce
Richard Bruehert
Andrew Brunn
Capt. Vincent Brunton
Ronald Paul Bucca
Brandon J. Buchanan
Greg Joseph Buck
Dennis Buckley
Nancy Bueche
Patrick Joseph Buhse
John E. Bulaga Jr.
Stephen Bunin
Matthew J. Burke
Thomas Daniel Burke
Capt. William F. Burke Jr.
Donald James Burns
Kathleen A. Burns
Keith James Burns
John Patrick Burnside
Irina Buslo
Milton Bustillo
Thomas M. Butler
Patrick Byrne
Timothy G. Byrne
Jesus Cabezas
Lillian Caceres
Brian Joseph Cachia
Steven Cafiero Jr.
Richard M. Caggiano
Cecile M. Caguicla
Michael John Cahill
Scott W. Cahill
Thomas J. Cahill
George Cain
Salvatore B. Calabro
Joseph Calandrillo
Philip V. Calcagno
Edward Calderon
Kenneth Marcus Caldwell
Dominick E. Calia
Felix (Bobby) Calixte
Capt. Frank Callahan
Liam Callahan
Luigi Calvi
Roko Camaj
Michael Cammarata
David Otey Campbell
Geoffrey Thomas Campbell
Jill Marie Campbell
Robert Arthur Campbell
Sandra Patricia Campbell
Juan Ortega Campos
Sean Canavan
John A. Candela

Vincent Cangelosi

Stephen J. Cangialosi

Lisa B. Cannava

Brian Cannizzaro

Michael R. Canty

Louis A. Caporicci

Jonathan N. Cappello

James Christopher Cappers

Richard M. Caproni

Jose Cardona

Dennis M Carey

Edward Carlino

Michael Scott Carlo

David G. Carlone

Rosemarie C. Carlson

Mark Stephen Carney

Joyce Ann Carpeneto

Jeremy M. Carrington

Michael T. Carroll

Peter Carroll

James J. Carson Jr.

Christopher Newton Carter

James Marcel Cartier

Joel Cartridge

Vivian Casalduc

John F. Casazza

Paul Cascio

Margarito Casillas

Thomas Anthony Casoria

William Otto Caspar

Alejandro Castano

German Castillo Galicia

Arcelia Castillo

Leonard M. Castrianno

Jose Ramon Castro

Richard G. Catarelli

Christopher Sean Caton

Robert J. Caufield

Mary Teresa Caulfield

Judson Cavalier

Michael Joseph Cawley

Jason D. Cayne

Juan Armando Ceballos

Marcia G. Cecil-Carter

Jason Cefalu

Thomas J. Celic

Ana M. Centeno

Joni Cesta

Jeffrey M. Chairnoff

Swarna Chalasini

William Chalcoff

Eli Chalouh

Charles Lawrence (Chip) Chan

Mandy Chang

Mark L. Charette

Gregorio Manuel Chavez

Pedro Francisco Checo

Douglas MacMillan Cherry

Stephen Patrick Cherry

Vernon Paul Cherry

Nestor Chevalier

Swede Joseph Chevalier

Alexander H. Chiang

Dorothy J. Chiarchiaro

Luis Alfonso Chimbo

Robert Chin

Wing Wai (Eddie) Ching

Nicholas P. Chiofalo Jr.

John Chipura

Peter A. Chirchirillo

Catherine E. Chirls

Kyung (Kaccy) Cho

Abdul K. Chowdhury

Mohammed Salahuddin Chowdhury

Kirsten L. Christophe

Pamela Chu

Steven Paul Chucknick

Wai-ching Chung

Christopher Ciafardini

Alex F. Ciccone

Frances Ann Cilente

Elaine Cillo

Edna Cintron

Nestor Andre Cintron

Lt. Robert Dominick Cirri

Benjamin Keefe Clark

Eugene Clark

Gregory A. Clark

Mannie Leroy Clark

Thomas R. Clark

Christopher Robert Clarke

Donna Clarke

Michael Clarke

Suria R.E. Clarke

Kevin Francis Cleary

James D. Cleere

Geoffrey W. Cloud

Susan M. Clyne

Steven Coakley

Jeffrey Coale

Patricia A. Cody

Daniel Michael Coffey

Jason Matthew Coffey

Florence Cohen

Kevin Sanford Cohen

Anthony Joseph Coladonato

Mark J. Colaio

Stephen J. Colaio

Christopher M. Colasanti

Kevin Nathaniel Colbert

Michel Paris Colbert

Keith Eugene Coleman

Scott Thomas Coleman

Tarel Coleman

Liam Joseph Colhoun

Robert D. Colin

Robert J. Coll Jr.

Jean Marie Collin

John Michael Collins

Michael L. Collins

Thomas J. Collins

Joseph Collison

Patricia Malia Colodner

Linda M. Colon

Soledi Colon

Ronald Comer

Jaime Concepcion

Albert Conde

Denease Conley

Susan Clancy Conlon

Margaret Mary Conner

Cynthia L. Connolly

John E. Connolly

James Lee Connor

Jonathan (J.C.) Connors

Kevin P. Connors

Kevin Francis Conroy

Brenda E. Conway

Dennis Michael Cook

Helen D. Cook

John A. Cooper

Joseph J. Coppo Jr.

Gerard J. Coppola

Joseph Albert Corbett

Alejandro Cordero

Robert Cordice

Davids Vargas Cordoba

Ruben D. Correa

Danny A. Correa-Gutierrez

James Corrigan

Carlos Cortes

Kevin M. Cosgrove

Dolores Marie Costa

Digna Alexandra Rivera Costanza

Charles Gregory Costello Jr.

Michael S. Costello

Conrod K.H. Cottoy Sr.

Martin Coughlan

Sgt. John Gerard Coughlin

Timothy John Coughlin

James E. Cove

Andre Cox

Frederick John Cox Jr.

James Raymond Coyle

Michelle Coyle-Eulau

Anne M. Cramer

Christopher Seton Cramer

Denise Crant

James L. Crawford Jr.

Robert James Crawford

Joanne Mary Cregan

Lucia Crifasi

Lt. John Crisci

Daniel Hal Crisman

Dennis A. Cross

Helen Crossin-Kittle

Kevin Raymond Crotty

Thomas G. Crotty

John Crowe

Welles Remy Crowther

Robert L. Cruikshank

Francisco Cruz Sr.

John Robert Cruz

Kenneth John Cubas

Francisco C. Cubero

Richard Joseph Cudina

Neil James Cudmore
Thomas Patrick Cullen III
Joan McConnell Cullinan
Joyce Cummings
Brian Thomas Cummins
Nilton Albuquerque Fernao Cunha
Michael Joseph Cunningham
Robert Curatolo
Laurence Curia
Paul Dario Curioli
Beverly Curry
Sgt. Michael Curtin
Gavin Cushny
Manuel Da Mota
Caleb Arron Dack
Carlos S. DaCosta
John D'Allara
Vincent D'Amadeo
Thomas A. Damaskinos
Jack L. D'Ambrosi Jr.
Jeannine Marie Damiani-Jones
Patrick W. Danahy
Mary D'Antonio
Vincent G. Danz
Dwight Donald Darcy
Elizabeth Ann Darling
Annette Andrea Dataram
Lt. Edward Alexander D'Atri
Michael D. D'Auria
Lawrence Davidson
Michael Allen Davidson
Scott Matthew Davidson
Niurka Davila
Clinton Davis Sr.
Wayne Terrial Davis
Anthony Richard Dawson
Calvin Dawson
Edward James Day
Jayceryll M. de Chavez
Nataly de la Cruz
Emerita (Emy) De La Pena
Azucena de la Torre
Cristina de Laura
Oscar de Laura
Francis (Frank) Albert De Martini
William T. Dean
Robert J. DeAngelis Jr.
Thomas P. Deangelis
Tara Debek
Anna Debin
James V. DeBlase
Paul DeCola
Simon Dedvukaj
Jason Christopher DeFazio
David A. Defeo
Jennifer DeJesus
Monique E. DeJesus
Nereida DeJesus
Manuel Del Valle Jr.
Donald A. Delapenha
Vito Joseph Deleo
Danielle Delie

Joseph A. Della Pietra
Palmina Delli Gatti
Colleen Ann Deloughery
Anthony Demas
Martin DeMeo
Francis X. Deming
Carol K. Demitz
Kevin Dennis
Thomas F. Dennis
Jean C. DePalma
Jose Nicholas Depena
Robert J. Deraney
Michael DeRienzo
David Paul DeRubbio
Jemal Legesse DeSantis
Christian D. DeSimone
Edward DeSimone III
Lt. Andrew Desperito
Michael Jude D'Esposito
Cindy Ann Deuel
Melanie Louise DeVere
Jerry DeVito
Robert P. Devitt Jr.
Dennis Lawrence Devlin
Gerard Dewan
Simon Dhanani
Michael L. DiAgostino
Lourdes Galletti Diaz
Matthew Diaz
Nancy Diaz
Obdulio Ruiz Diaz
Michael Diaz-Piedra III
Judith Belguese Diaz-Sierra
Patricia F. DiChiaro
Joseph Dermot Dickey Jr.
Lawrence Patrick Dickinson
Michael David Diehl
John DiFato
Vincent F. DiFazio
Carl DiFranco
Donald J. DiFranco
Alexandra Costanza Digna
Debra Ann DiMartino
Stephen P. Dimino
William J. Dimmling
Christopher Dincuff
Jeffrey M. Dingle
Anthony DiOnisio Jr.
George DiPasquale
Joseph DiPilato
Douglas Frank DiStefano
Ramzi A. Doany
John J. Doherty
Melissa C. Doi
Brendan Dolan
Neil Dollard
James Joseph Domanico
Benilda P. Domingo
Charles Dominguez
Geronimo (Jerome) Mark Patrick Dominguez
Lt. Kevin W. Donnelly

Jacqueline Donovan
Stephen Dorf
Thomas Dowd
Lt. Kevin Christopher Dowdell
Mary Yolanda Dowling
Ray M. Downey
Frank Joseph Doyle
Joseph M. Doyle
Randy Drake
Stephen Patrick Driscoll
Mirna A. Duarte
Luke A. Dudek
Christopher Michael Duffy
Gerard Duffy
Michael Joseph Duffy
Thomas W. Duffy
Antoinette Duger
Sareve Dukat
Christopher Joseph Dunne
Richard A. Dunstan
Patrick Thomas Dwyer
Joseph Anthony Eacobacci
John Bruce Eagleson
Robert D. Eaton
Dean P. Eberling
Margaret Ruth Echtermann
Paul Robert Eckna
Constantine (Gus) Economos
Dennis Michael Edwards
Michael Hardy Edwards
Christine Egan
Lisa Egan
Capt. Martin Egan Jr.
Michael Egan
Samantha Egan
Carole Eggert
Lisa Caren Weinstein Ehrlich
John Ernst (Jack) Eichler
Eric Adam Eisenberg
Daphne F. Elder
Michael J. Elferis
Mark J. Ellis
Valerie Silver Ellis
Albert Alfy William Elmarry
Edgar H. Emery Jr.
Doris Suk-Yuen Eng
Christopher S. Epps
Ulf Ramm Ericson
Erwin L. Erker
William J. Erwin
Sarah (Ali) Escarcega
Jose Espinal
Fanny M. Espinoza
Brigette Ann Esposito
Francis Esposito
Lt. Michael Esposito
William Esposito
Ruben Esquilin Jr.
Sadie Ette
Barbara G. Etzold
Eric Brian Evans
Robert Edward Evans

Meredith Emily June Ewart
Catherine K. Fagan
Patricia M. Fagan
Keith G. Fairben
William F. Fallon Jr.
William Fallon
Anthony J. Fallone Jr.
Dolores B. Fanelli
John Joseph Fanning
Kathleen (Kit) Faragher
Capt. Thomas Farino
Nancy Carole Farley
Elizabeth Ann (Betty) Farmer
Douglas Farnum
John G. Farrell
John W. Farrell
Terrence Patrick Farrell
Capt. Joseph Farrelly
Thomas P. Farrelly
Syed Abdul Fatha
Christopher Faughnan
Wendy R. Faulkner
Shannon M. Fava
Bernard D. Favuzza
Robert Fazio Jr.
Ronald C. Fazio
William Feehan
Francis J. (Frank) Feely
Garth E. Feeney
Sean B. Fegan
Lee S. Fehling
Peter Feidelberg
Alan D. Feinberg
Rosa Maria Feliciano
Edward T. Fergus Jr.
George Ferguson
Henry Fernandez
Jose Manuel Contreras Fernandez
Judy H. Fernandez
Elisa Giselle Ferraina
Anne Marie Sallerin Ferreira
Robert John Ferris
David Francis Ferrugio
Louis V. Fersini Jr.
Mike Ferugio
Bradley James Fetchet
Jennifer Louise Fialko
Kristen Fiedel
Samuel Fields
Michael Bradley Finnegan
Timothy J. Finnerty
Michael Curtis Fiore
Stephen J. Fiorelli
Paul M. Fiori
John Fiorito
Lt. John R. Fischer
Andrew Fisher
Bennett Lawson Fisher
John Roger Fisher
Thomas J. Fisher
Lucy Fishman
Ryan D. Fitzgerald

Thomas Fitzpatrick
Richard P. Fitzsimons
Salvatore A. Fiumefreddo
Christina Donovan Flannery
Eileen Flecha
Andre G. Fletcher
Carl Flickinger
John Joseph Florio
Joseph W. Flounders
David Fodor
Lt. Michael N. Fodor
Steven Mark Fogel
Thomas Foley
David Fontana
Chih Min (Dennis) Foo
Del Rose Forbes-Cheatham
Godwin Forde
Donald A. Foreman
Christopher Hugh Forsythe
Claudia Alicia Martinez Foster
Noel J. Foster
Ana Fosteris
Robert J. Foti
Yolette Fouchet
Jeffrey L. Fox
Virginia Fox
Joan Francis
Pauline Francis
Virgin (Lucy) Francis
Gary J. Frank
Morton Frank
Peter Christopher Frank
Richard K. Fraser
Kevin Joseph Frawley
Clyde Frazier Jr.
Lillian I. Frederick
Andrew Fredericks
Jamitha Freemen
Brett O. Freiman
Lt. Peter L. Freund
Arlene E. Fried
Alan Wayne Friedlander
Andrew K. Friedman
Gregg J. Froehner
Peter Christian Fry
Clement Fumando
Steven Elliot Furman
Paul James Furmato
Fredric Gabler
Richard S. Gabrielle
James Andrew Gadiel
Pamela Gaff
Ervin Vincent Gailliard
Deanna L. Galante
Grace Galante
Anthony Edward Gallagher
Daniel James Gallagher
John Patrick Gallagher
Tomas Gallegos Linares
Cono E. Gallo
Vincenzo Gallucci
Thomas Edward Galvin

Giovanna (Genni) Gambale
Thomas Gambino Jr.
Giann F. Gamboa
Peter J. Ganci Jr.
Claude Michael Gann
Lt. Charles William Garbarini
Cesar Garcia
David Garcia
Jorge Luis Morron Garcia
Juan Garcia
Marlyn C. Garcia
Christopher Gardner
Douglas B. Gardner
Harvey J. Gardner III
Jeffrey B. Gardner
Thomas A. Gardner
William Arthur Gardner
Francesco Garfi
Rocco Gargano
James M. Gartenberg
Matthew David Garvey
Bruce Gary
Boyd A. Gatton
Donald Richard Gavagan Jr.
Terence D. Gazzani
Gary Geidel
Paul Hamilton Geier
Julie M. Geis
Peter Gelinas
Steven Paul Geller
Howard G. Gelling Jr.
Peter Victor Genco
Steven Gregory Genovese
Alayne F. Gentul
Edward F. Geraghty
Suzanne Geraty
Ralph Gerhardt
Robert J. Gerlich
Denis P. Germain
Marina R. Gertsberg
Susan M. Getzendanner
James Gerard Geyer
Joseph M. Giaccone
Lt. Vincent Francis Giammona
Debra L. Gibbon
James A. Giberson
Craig Neil Gibson
Ronnie Gies
Laura A. Giglio
Andrew Clive Gilbert
Timothy Paul Gilbert
Paul Stuart Gilbey
Paul John Gill
Mark Y. Gilles
Evan H. Gillette
Ronald Gilligan
Sgt. Rodney C. Gillis
Laura Gilly
Lt. John F. Ginley
Donna Marie Giordano
Jeffrey Giordano
John Giordano

Steven A. Giorgetti
Martin Giovinazzo
Jinny Lady Giraldo
Kum-Kum Girolamo
Salvatore Gitto
Cynthia Giugliano
Mon Gjonbalaj
Dianne Gladstone
Keith Alexander Glascoe
Thomas I. Glasser
Harry Glenn
Barry H. Glick
Steven Lawrence Glick
John T. Gnazzo
William (Bill) Robert Godshalk
Michael Gogliormella
Brian Fredric Goldberg
Jeffrey Grant Goldflam
Michelle Herman Goldstein
Monica Goldstein
Steven Goldstein
Andrew H. Golkin
Dennis James Gomes
Enrique Antonio Gomez
Jose Bienvenido Gomez
Manuel Gomez Jr.
Wilder Gomez
Ana Irene Medina Gonzalez
Jenine Gonzalez
Joel Guevara Gonzalez
Mauricio Gonzalez
Rosa J. Gonzalez
Calvin J. Gooding
Harry Goody
Kiran Reddy Gopu
Catherine Carmen Gorayeb
Kerene Gordon
Sebastian Gorki
Kieran Gorman
Thomas E. Gorman
Michael Edward Gould
Yugi Goya
Jon Richard Grabowski
Christopher Michael Grady
Edwin John Graf III
David M. Graifman
Gilbert Granados
Elvira Granitto
Winston Arthur Grant
Christopher Stewart Gray
James Michael Gray
Linda Mair Grayling
John Michael Grazioso
Timothy Grazioso
Derrick Arthur Green
Wade Brian Green
Elaine Myra Greenberg
Gayle R. Greene
James Arthur Greenleaf Jr.
Eileen Marsha Greenstein
Elizabeth (Lisa) Martin Gregg
Denise Gregory

Donald H. Gregory
Florence M. Gregory
Pedro (David) Grehan
John M. Griffin
Tawanna Griffin
Joan D. Griffith
Warren Grifka
Ramon Grijalvo
Joseph F. Grillo
David Grimner
Kenneth Grouzalis
Joseph Grzelak
Matthew J. Grzymalski
Robert Joseph Gschaar
Liming (Michael) Gu
Jose A. Guadalupe
Yan Zhu (Cindy) Guan
Geoffrey E. Guja
Lt. Joseph Gullickson
Babita Guman
Douglas B. Gurian
Janet H. Gustafson
Philip T. Guza
Sabita Guzman
Barbara Guzzardo
Peter Gyulavary
Gary Robert Haag
Andrea Lyn Haberman
Barbara M. Habib
Philip Haentzler
Nizam A. Hafiz
Karen Hagerty
Steven Hagis
Mary Lou Hague
David Halderman Jr.
Maile Rachel Hale
Richard Hall
Vaswald George Hall
Robert John Halligan
Lt. Vincent Gerard Halloran
James D. Halvorson
Mohammed Salman Hamdani
Felicia Hamilton
Robert Hamilton
Frederic Kim Han
Christopher James Hanley
Sean Hanley
Valerie Joan Hanna
Thomas Hannafin
Kevin James Hannaford
Michael L. Hannan
Dana Hannon
Vassilios G. Haramis
James A. Haran
Jeffrey P. Hardy
Timothy John Hargrave
Daniel Harlin
Frances Haros
Lt. Harvey L. Harrell
Lt. Stephen Gary Harrell
Aisha Harris
Stewart D. Harris

John Patrick Hart
John Clinton Hartz
Emeric J. Harvey
Capt. Thomas Theodore Haskell Jr.
Timothy Haskell
Joseph John Hasson III
Leonard William Hatton Jr.
Capt. Terence S. Hatton
Michael Helmut Haub
Timothy Aaron Haviland
Donald G. Havlish Jr.
Anthony Hawkins
Nobuhiro Hayatsu
Philip Hayes
William Ward Haynes
Scott Hazelcorn
Lt. Michael K. Healey
Roberta Bernstein Heber
Charles Francis Xavier Heeran
John Heffernan
Howard Joseph Heller Jr.
JoAnn L. Heltibridle
Mark F. Hemschoot
Ronnie Lee Henderson
Janet Hendricks
Brian Hennessey
Michelle Marie Henrique
Joseph P. Henry
William Henry
John Henwood
Robert Allan Hepburn
Mary (Molly) Herencia
Lindsay Coates Herkness III
Harvey Robert Hermer
Anabel Hernandez
Claribel Hernandez
Eduardo Hernandez
Norberto Hernandez
Raul Hernandez
Gary Herold
Jeffrey A. Hersch
Thomas Hetzel
Capt. Brian Hickey
Ysidro Hidalgo-Tejada
Lt. Timothy Higgins
Robert D. Higley II
Todd Russell Hill
Clara Victorine Hinds
Neal Hinds
Mark D. Hindy
Katsuyuki Hirai
Heather Malia Ho
Tara Yvette Hobbs
Thomas A. Hobbs
James L. Hobin
Robert Wayne Hobson III
DaJuan Hodges
Ronald George Hoerner
Patrick Aloysius Hoey
Frederick J. Hoffman
Joseph Hoffman
Marcia Hoffman

Michele L. Hoffman
Stephen G. Hoffman
Judith Florence Hofmiller
Thomas Warren Hohlweck Jr.
Jonathan R. Hohmann
John Holland
Joseph Francis Holland III
Elizabeth Holmes
Thomas P. Holohan Jr.
Bradley Hoorn
James P. Hopper
Montgomery McCullough Hord
Michael Horn
Matthew D. Horning
Robert L. Horohoe Jr.
Aaron Horwitz
Charles J. Houston
Uhuru G. Houston
George Howard
Michael C. Howell
Steven L. Howell
Jennifer L. Howley
Milagros Hromada
Marian Hrycak
Stephen Huczko Jr.
Kris R. Hughes
Melissa Harrington Hughes
Paul R. Hughes
Robert T. "Bobby" Hughes Jr.
Thomas F. Hughes
Timothy Robert Hughes
Susan Huie
Mychal Lamar Hulse
Kathleen (Casey) Hunt
William C. Hunt
Joseph G. Hunter
Robert Hussa
Thomas E. Hynes
Capt. Walter Hynes
Joseph Anthony Ianelli
Zuhtu Ibis
Jonathan Lee Ielpi
Michael Patrick Iken
Daniel Ilkanayev
Capt. Frederick Ill Jr.
Abraham Nethanel Ilowitz
Anthony P. Infante Jr.
Louis S. Inghilterra
Christopher N. Ingrassia
Paul Innella
Stephanie V. Irby
Douglas Irgang
Kristin A. Irvine-Ryan
Todd A. Isaac
Erik Hans Isbrandtsen
William Iselepis Jr.
Taizo Ishikawa
Aram Iskenderian Jr.
John Iskyan
Kazushige Ito
Aleksandr Valeryerich Ivantsov
Virginia Jablonski

Brooke Alexandra Jackman
Aaron Jacobs
Ariel Louis Jacobs
Jason Kyle Jacobs
Michael Grady Jacobs
Steven A. Jacobson
Ricknauth Jaggernauth
Jake Denis Jagoda
Yudh V.S. Jain
Maria Jakubiak
Ernest James
Gricelda E. James
Mark Jardim
Mohammed Jawara
Francois Jean-Pierre
Maxima Jean-Pierre
Paul E. Jeffers
Joseph Jenkins Jr.
Alan K. Jensen
Prem N. Jerath
Farah Jeudy
Hweidar Jian
Fernando Jimenez Molina
Eliezer Jimenez Jr.
Luis Jimenez Jr.
Charles Gregory John
Nicholas John
LaShawana Johnson
Scott M. Johnson
William Johnston
Allison Horstmann Jones
Arthur Joseph Jones III
Brian L. Jones
Christopher D. Jones
Donald T. Jones
Donald W. Jones
Linda Jones
Mary S. Jones
Andrew Jordan
Robert Thomas Jordan
Albert Joseph
Ingeborg Joseph
Karl Henri Joseph
Stephen Joseph
Jane Eileen Josiah
Lt. Anthony Jovic
Angel Luis Juarbe Jr.
Karen Susan Juday
Rev. Mychal Judge
Paul W. Jurgens
Thomas Edward Jurgens
Shashi Kiran Lakshmikantha Kadaba
Gavkharoy Mukhometovna Kamardinova
Shari Kandell
Howard Lee Kane
Jennifer Lynn Kane
Vincent D. Kane
Joon Koo Kang
Sheldon R. Kanter
Deborah H. Kaplan
Alvin Peter Kappelmann Jr.

Charles Karczewski
William A. Karnes
Douglas G. Karpiloff
Charles L. Kasper
Andrew Kates
John Katsimatides
Sgt. Robert Kaulfers
Don Jerome Kauth Jr.
Hideya Kawauchi
Edward T. Keane
Richard M. Keane
Lisa Kearney-Griffin
Karol Ann Keasler
Paul Hanlon Keating
Leo Russell Keene III
Joseph J. Keller
Peter Rodney Kellerman
Joseph P. Kellett
Frederick H. Kelley
James Joseph Kelly
Joseph A. Kelly
Maurice Patrick Kelly
Richard John Kelly Jr.
Thomas Michael Kelly
Thomas Richard Kelly
Thomas W. Kelly
Timothy C. Kelly
William Hill Kelly Jr.
Robert C. (Bob) Kennedy
Thomas J. Kennedy
John Keohane
Lt. Ronald T. Kerwin
Howard L. Kestenbaum
Douglas D. Ketcham
Ruth E. Ketler
Boris Khalif
Sarah Khan
Taimour Firaz Khan
Rajesh Khandelwal
Bhowanie Devi Khemraj
SeiLai Khoo
Michael Kiefer
Satoshi Kikuchihara
Andrew Jay-Hoon Kim
Lawrence Don Kim
Mary Jo Kimelman
Andrew Marshall King
Lucille T. King
Robert King Jr.
Lisa M. King-Johnson
Takashi Kinoshita
Chris Michael Kirby
Howard (Barry) Kirschbaum
Glenn Davis Kirwin
Richard J. Klares
Peter A. Klein
Alan D. Kleinberg
Karen J. Klitzman
Ronald Philip Kloepfer
Andrew Knox
Thomas Patrick Knox
Yevgeny Knyazev

Rebecca Lee Koborie
Deborah Kobus
Gary Edward Koecheler
Frank J. Koestner
Ryan Kohart
Vanessa Lynn Kolpak
Irina Kolpakova
Suzanne Kondratenko
Abdoulaye Kone
Bon-seok Koo
Dorota Kopiczko
Scott Kopytko
Bojan Kostic
Danielle Kousoulis
John J. Kren
William Krukowski
Lyudmila Ksido
Shekhar Kumar
Kenneth Kumpel
Frederick Kuo Jr.
Patricia Kuras
Nauka Kushitani
Thomas Joseph Kuveikis
Victor Kwarkye
Kui Fai Kwok
Angela R. Kyte
Amarnauth Lachhman
Andrew LaCorte
Ganesh Ladkat
James P. Ladley
Joseph A. Lafalce
Jeanette LaFond-Menichino
David LaForge
Michael Patrick LaForte
Alan Lafranco
Juan Lafuente
Neil K. Lai
Vincent A. Laieta
William David Lake
Franco Lalama
Chow Kwan Lam
Stephen LaMantia
Amy Hope Lamonsoff
Robert T. Lane
Brendan M. Lang
Rosanne P. Lang
Vanessa Langer
Mary Lou Langley
Peter J. Langone
Thomas Langone
Michele B. Lanza
Ruth Sheila Lapin
Carol Ann LaPlante
Ingeborg Astrid Desiree Lariby
Robin Larkey
Christopher Randall Larrabee
Hamidou S. Larry
Scott Larsen
John Adam Larson
Gary E. Lasko
Nicholas C. Lassman
Paul Laszczynski

Jeffrey Latouche
Charles Laurencin
Stephen James Lauria
Maria Lavache
Denis F. Lavelle
Jeannine M. LaVerde
Anna A. Laverty
Steven Lawn
Robert A. Lawrence
Nathaniel Lawson
Eugen Lazar
James Patrick Leahy
Lt. Joseph Gerard Leavey
Neil Leavy
Leon Lebor
Kenneth Charles Ledee
Alan J. Lederman
Elena Ledesma
Alexis Leduc
David S. Lee
Gary H. Lee
Hyun-joon (Paul) Lee
Jong-min Lee
Juanita Lee
Kathryn Blair Lee
Linda C. Lee
Lorraine Lee
Myung-woo Lee
Richard Y.C. Lee
Stuart (Soo-Jin) Lee
Yang Der Lee
Stephen Lefkowitz
Adriana Legro
Edward J. Lehman
Eric Andrew Lehrfeld
David Ralph Leistman
David Prudencio LeMagne
Joseph A. Lenihan
John J. Lennon Jr.
John Robinson Lenoir
Jorge Luis Leon
Matthew Gerard Leonard
Michael Lepore
Charles Antoine Lesperance
Jeffrey Earle LeVeen
John D. Levi
Alisha Caren Levin
Neil D. Levin
Robert M. Levine
Robert Levine
Shai Levinhar
Adam J. Lewis
Margaret Susan Lewis
Ye Wei Liang
Orasri Liangthanasarn
Daniel F. Libretti
Ralph M. Licciardi
Edward Lichtschein
Steven B. Lillianthal
Carlos R. Lillo
Craig Damian Lilore
Arnold A. Lim

Darya Lin
Wei Rong Lin
Nickie L. Lindo
Thomas V. Linehan Jr.
Robert Thomas Linnane
Alan Linton Jr.
Diane Theresa Lipari
Kenneth P. Lira
Francisco Alberto Liriano
Lorraine Lisi
Paul Lisson
Vincent Litto
Ming-Hao Liu
Joseph Livera
Nancy Liz
Harold Lizcano
Martin Lizzul
George A. Llanes
Elizabeth Claire Logler
Catherine Lisa Loguidice
Jerome Robert Lohez
Michael W. Lomax
Laura M. Longing
Salvatore Lopes
Daniel Lopez
George Lopez
Luis Lopez
Manuel L. Lopez
Joseph Lostrangio
Chet Louie
Stuart Seid Louis
Joseph Lovero
Michael W. Lowe
Garry Lozier
John Peter Lozowsky
Charles Peter Lucania
Edward (Ted) H. Luckett II
Mark G. Ludvigsen
Lee Charles Ludwig
Sean Thomas Lugano
Daniel Lugo
Marie Lukas
William Lum Jr.
Michael P. Lunden
Christopher Lunder
Anthony Luparello
Gary Lutnick
Linda Luzzicone
Alexander Lygin
Farrell Peter Lynch
James Francis Lynch
Louise A. Lynch
Michael F. Lynch
Michael Francis Lynch
Michael Lynch
Richard Dennis Lynch Jr.
Robert H. Lynch
Sean Patrick Lynch
Sean Lynch
Michael J. Lyons
Monica Lyons
Patrick Lyons

Robert Francis Mace
Jan Maciejewski
Catherine Fairfax MacRae
Richard B. Madden
Simon Maddison
Noell Maerz
Jeannieann Maffeo
Joseph Maffeo
Jay Robert Magazine
Brian Magee
Charles Wilson Magee
Joseph Maggitti
Ronald E. Magnuson
Daniel L. Maher
Thomas Anthony Mahon
William Mahoney
Joseph Maio
Takashi Makimoto
Abdu Malahi
Debora Maldonado
Myrna T. Maldonado-Agosto
Alfred R. Maler
Gregory James Malone
Edward Francis (Teddy) Maloney III
Joseph E. Maloney
Gene E. Maloy
Christian Maltby
Francisco Miguel (Frank) Mancini
Joseph Mangano
Sara Elizabeth Manley
Debra M. Mannetta
Marion Victoria (vickie) Manning
Terence J. Manning
James Maounis
Joseph Ross Marchbanks Jr.
Peter Edward Mardikian
Edward Joseph Mardovich
Lt. Charles Joseph Margiotta
Kenneth Joseph Marino
Lester Vincent Marino
Vita Marino
Kevin D. Marlo
Jose J. Marrero
John Marshall
James Martello
Michael A. Marti
Lt. Peter Martin
William J. Martin Jr.
Brian E. Martineau
Betsy Martinez
Edward J. Martinez
Jose Martinez
Robert Gabriel Martinez
Lizie Martinez-Calderon
Lt. Paul Richard Martini
Joseph A. Mascali
Bernard Mascarenhas
Stephen F. Masi
Nicholas G. Massa
Patricia A. Massari
Michael Massaroli
Philip W. Mastrandrea Jr.

Rudolph Mastrocinque
Joseph Mathai
Charles William Mathers
William A. Mathesen
Marcello Matricciano
Margaret Elaine Mattic
Robert D. Mattson
Walter Matuza
Charles A. (Chuck) Mauro Jr.
Charles J. Mauro
Dorothy Mauro
Nancy T. Mauro
Tyrone May
Keithroy Maynard
Robert J. Mayo
Kathy Nancy Mazza-Delosh
Edward Mazzella Jr.
Jennifer Mazzotta
Kaaria Mbaya
James J. McAlary Jr.
Brian McAleese
Patricia A. McAneney
Colin Richard McArthur
John McAvoy
Kenneth M. McBrayer
Brendan McCabe
Michael J. McCabe
Thomas McCann
Justin McCarthy
Kevin M. McCarthy
Michael Desmond McCarthy
Robert Garvin McCarthy
Stanley McCaskill
Katie Marie McCloskey
Tara McCloud-Gray
Charles Austin McCrann
Tonyell McDay
Matthew T. McDermott
Joseph P. McDonald
Brian G. McDonnell
Michael McDonnell
John F. McDowell Jr.
Eamon J. McEneaney
John Thomas McErlean
Katherine (Katie) McGarry-Noack
Daniel F. McGinley
Mark Ryan McGinly
Lt. William E. McGinn
Thomas H. McGinnis
Michael Gregory McGinty
Ann McGovern
Scott Martin McGovern
William J. McGovern
Stacey S. McGowan
Francis Noel McGuinn
Patrick J. McGuire
Thomas M. McHale
Keith McHeffey
Ann M. McHugh
Denis J. McHugh III
Dennis P. McHugh
Michael Edward McHugh Jr.

Robert G. McIlvaine
Donald James McIntyre
Stephanie McKenna
Barry J. McKeon
Evelyn C. McKinnedy
Darryl Leron McKinney
George Patrick McLaughlin Jr.
Robert C. McLaughlin Jr.
Gavin McMahon
Robert Dismas McMahon
Edmund M. McNally
Daniel McNeal
Walter Arthur McNeil
Christine Sheila McNulty
Sean Peter McNulty
Robert William McPadden
Terence A. McShane
Timothy Patrick McSweeney
Martin E. McWilliams
Rocco A. Medaglia
Abigail Medina
Anna Iris Medina
Deborah Medwig
Damian Meehan
William J. Meehan Jr.
Alok Mehta
Raymond Meisenheimer
Manuel Emilio Mejia
Eskedar Melaku
Antonio Melendez
Mary Melendez
Yelena Melnichenko
Stuart Todd Meltzer
Diarelia Jovannah Mena
Charles Mendez
Lizette Mendoza
Shevonne Mentis
Steve Mercado
Wesley Mercer
Ralph Joseph Mercurio
Alan H. Merdinger
George C. Merino
Yamel Merino
George Merkouris
Deborah Merrick
Raymond J. Metz III
Jill A. Metzler
David Robert Meyer
Nurul Huq Miah
William Edward Micciulli
Martin Paul Michelstein
Luis Clodoaldo Revilla Mier
Peter T. Milano
Gregory Milanowycz
Lukasz T. Milewski
Corey Peter Miller
Craig James Miller
Douglas C. Miller
Henry Miller Jr.
Joel Miller
Michael Matthew Miller
Phillip D. Miller

Robert Alan Miller
Robert C. Miller Jr.
Benjamin Millman
Charles M. Mills Jr.
Ronald Keith Milstein
Robert Minara
William G. Minardi
Louis Joseph Minervino
Thomas Mingione
Nana Akwasi Minkah
Wilbert Miraille
Domenick Mircovich
Rajesh A. Mirpuri
Joseph Mistrulli
Susan Miszkowicz
Lt. Paul Thomas Mitchell
Richard Miuccio
Frank V. Moccia Sr.
Capt. Louis Joseph Modafferi
Boyie Mohammed
Lt. Dennis Mojica
Manuel Mojica
Kleber Rolando Molina
Manuel Dejesus Molina
Carl Molinaro
Justin J. Molisani Jr.
Brian Patrick Monaghan
Franklin Monahan
John Gerard Monahan
Kristen Montanaro
Craig D. Montano
Michael Montesi
Cheryl Ann Monyak
Capt. Thomas Moody
Sharon Moore
Krishna Moorthy
Abner Morales
Carlos Morales
Paula Morales
John Christopher Moran
John Moran
Kathleen Moran
Lindsay S. Morehouse
George Morell
Steven P. Morello
Vincent S. Morello
Arturo Alva Moreno
Yvette Nicole Moreno
Dorothy Morgan
Richard Morgan
Nancy Morgenstern
Sanae Mori
Blanca Morocho
Leonel Morocho
Dennis G. Moroney
Lynne Irene Morris
Seth A. Morris
Stephen Philip Morris
Christopher M. Morrison
Ferdinand V. Morrone
William David Moskal
Marco Motroni Sr.

Chung Mou
Iouri A. Mouchinski
Jude J. Moussa
Peter C. Moutos
Damion Mowatt
Christopher Mozzillo
Stephen V. Mulderry
Richard Muldowney Jr.
Michael D. Mullan
Dennis Michael Mulligan
Peter James Mulligan
Michael Joseph Mullin
James Donald Munhall
Nancy Muniz
Carlos Mario Munoz
Theresa (Terry) Munson
Robert M. Murach
Cesar Augusto Murillo
Marc A. Murolo
Brian Joseph Murphy
Charles Murphy
Christopher W. Murphy
Edward C. Murphy
James F. Murphy IV
James Thomas Murphy
Kevin James Murphy
Patrick Sean Murphy
Lt. Raymond E. Murphy
Robert Eddie Murphy Jr.
John Joseph Murray
John Joseph Murray
Susan D. Murray
Valerie Victoria Murray
Yuriy Mushynskyi
Richard Todd Myhre
Lt. Robert B. Nagel
Takuya Nakamura
Alexander J.R. Napier
Frank Joseph Naples III
John Napolitano
Catherine A. Nardella
Mario Nardone Jr.
Manika Narula
Narender Nath
Karen S. Navarro
Joseph M. Navas
Francis J. Nazario
Glenroy Neblett
Marcus R. Neblett
Jerome O. Nedd
Laurence Nedell
Luke G. Nee
Pete Negron
Ann Nicole Nelson
David William Nelson
James Nelson
Michele Ann Nelson
Peter Allen Nelson
Oscar Nesbitt
Gerard Terence Nevins
Nancy Yuen Ngo
Jody Tepedino Nichilo

Martin Niederer
Alfonse J. Niedermeyer III
Frank John Niestadt Jr.
Gloria Nieves
Juan Nieves Jr.
Troy Edward Nilsen
Paul R. Nimbley
John Ballantine Niven
Curtis Terrence Noel
Daniel R. Nolan
Robert Walter Noonan
Daniela R. Notaro
Brian Novotny
Soichi Numata
Brian Felix Nunez
Jose R. Nunez
Jeffrey Nussbaum
James A. Oakley
Dennis Oberg
James P. O'Brien Jr.
Michael O'Brien
Scott J. O'Brien
Timothy Michael O'Brien
Lt. Daniel O'Callaghan
Jefferson Ocampo
Dennis J. O'Connor Jr.
Diana J. O'Connor
Keith K. O'Connor
Richard J. O'Connor
Amy O'Doherty
Marni Pont O'Doherty
Douglas Oelschlager
Takashi Ogawa
Albert Ogletree
Philip Paul Ognibene
James Andrew O'Grady
Joseph J. Ogren
Lt. Thomas O'Hagan
Samuel Oitice
Patrick O'Keefe
Capt. William O'Keefe
Gerald Michael Olcott
Gerald O'Leary
Christine Anne Olender
Elsy Carolina Osorio Oliva
Linda Mary Oliva
Edward K. Oliver
Leah E. Oliver
Eric T. Olsen
Jeffrey James Olsen
Maureen L. Olson
Steven John Olson
Matthew Timothy O'Mahoney
Toshihiro Onda
Seamus L. O'Neal
John P. O'Neill Sr.
Peter J. O'Neill Jr.
Sean Gordon Corbett O'Neill
Michael C. Opperman
Christopher Orgielewicz
Margaret Orloske
Virginia A. Ormiston-Kenworthy

Kevin O'Rourke
Juan Romero Orozco
Ronald Orsini
Peter K. Ortale
Alexander Ortiz
David Ortiz
Emilio (Peter) Ortiz Jr.
Pablo Ortiz
Paul Ortiz Jr.
Sonia Ortiz
Masaru Ose
Patrick J. O'Shea
Robert W. O'Shea
James Robert Ostrowski
Timothy O'Sullivan
Jason Douglas Oswald
Michael Otten
Isidro Ottenwalder
Michael Ou
Todd Joseph Ouida
Jesus Ovalles
Peter J. Owens Jr.
Adianes Oyola
Angel M. Pabon
Israel Pabon
Roland Pacheco
Michael Benjamin Packer
Deepa K. Pakkala
Jeffrey Matthew Palazzo
Thomas Anthony Palazzo
Richard (Rico) Palazzolo
Orio Joseph Palmer
Frank A. Palombo
Alan N. Palumbo
Christopher M. Panatier
Dominique Pandolfo
Paul Pansini
John M. Paolillo
Edward J. Papa
Salvatore Papasso
James N. Pappageorge
Vinod K. Parakat
Vijayashanker Paramsothy
Nitin Parandkar
Hardai (Casey) Parbhu
James Wendell Parham
Debra (Debbie) Paris
George Paris
Gye-Hyong Park
Philip L. Parker
Michael A. Parkes
Robert Emmett Parks Jr.
Hasmukhrai Chuckulal Parmar
Robert Parro
Diane Marie Moore Parsons
Leobardo Lopez Pascual
Michael J. Pascuma Jr.
Jerrold H. Paskins
Horace Robert Passananti
Suzanne H. Passaro
Victor Antonio Martinez Pastrana
Avnish Ramanbhai Patel

Dipti Patel
Manish K. Patel
Steven B. Paterson
James Matthew Patrick
Manuel Patrocino
Bernard E. Patterson
Cira Marie Patti
Robert Edward Pattison
James R. Paul
Patrice Paz
Sharon Cristina Millan Paz
Victor Paz-Gutierrez
Stacey L. Peak
Richard Allen Pearlman
Durrell Pearsall Jr.
Thomas E. Pedicini
Todd D. Pelino
Michel Adrian Pelletier
Anthony Peluso
Angel Ramon Pena
Jose D. Pena
Richard Al Penny
Salvatore F. Pepe
Carl Allen Peralta
Robert David Peraza
Jon A. Perconti
Alejo Perez
Angel Perez Jr.
Angela Susan Perez
Anthony Perez
Ivan Perez
Nancy E. Perez
Joseph John Perroncino
Edward J. Perrotta
Emelda Perry
Lt. Glenn C. Perry
John William Perry
Franklin Allan Pershep
Daniel Pesce
Michael J. Pescherine
Davin Peterson
William Russel Peterson
Mark Petrocelli
Lt. Philip S. Petti
Glen Kerrin Pettit
Dominick Pezzulo
Kaleen E. Pezzuti
Lt. Kevin Pfeifer
Tu-Anh Pham
Lt. Kenneth John Phelan
Eugenia Piantieri
Ludwig John Picarro
Matthew Picerno
Joseph O. Pick
Christopher Pickford
Dennis J. Pierce
Bernard T. Pietronico
Nicholas P. Pietrunti
Theodoros Pigis
Susan Elizabeth Ancona Pinto
Joseph Piskadlo
Christopher Todd Pitman

Josh Piver
Joseph Plumitallo
John M. Pocher
William Howard Pohlmann
Laurence M. Polatsch
Thomas H. Polhemus
Steve Pollicino
Susan M. Pollio
Joshua Poptean
Giovanna Porras
Anthony Portillo
James Edward Potorti
Daphne Pouletsos
Richard Poulos
Stephen E. Poulos
Brandon Jerome Powell
Shawn Edward Powell
Tony Pratt
Gregory M. Preziose
Wanda Ivelisse Prince
Vincent Princiotta
Kevin Prior
Everett Martin (Marty) Proctor III
Carrie B. Progen
David Lee Pruim
Richard Prunty
John F. Puckett
Robert D. Pugliese
Edward F. Pullis
Patricia Ann Puma
Hemanth Kumar Puttur
Edward R. Pykon
Christopher Quackenbush
Lars Peter Qualben
Lincoln Quappe
Beth Ann Quigley
Lt. Michael Quilty
James Francis Quinn
Ricardo Quinn
Carol Rabalais
Christopher Peter A. Racaniello
Leonard Ragaglia
Eugene J. Raggio
Laura Marie Ragonese-Snik
Michael Ragusa
Peter F. Raimondi
Harry A. Raines
Ehtesham U. Raja
Valsa Raju
Edward Rall
Lukas (Luke) Rambousek
Julio Fernandez Ramirez
Maria Isabel Ramirez
Harry Ramos
Vishnoo Ramsaroop
Lorenzo Ramzey
A. Todd Rancke
Adam David Rand
Jonathan C. Randall
Srinivasa Shreyas Ranganath
Anne Rose T. Ransom
Faina Rapoport

Robert Arthur Rasmussen
Amenia Rasool
Roger Mark Rasweiler
David Alan James Rathkey
William Ra;ph Raub
Gerard Rauzi
Alexey Razuvaev
Gregory Reda
Sarah (Prothero) Redheffer
Michele Reed
Judith A. Reese
Donald J. Regan
Lt. Robert M. Regan
Thomas M. Regan
Christian Michael Otto Regenhard
Howard Reich
Gregg Reidy
James B. Reilly
Kevin O. Reilly
Timothy E. Reilly
Joseph Reina Jr.
Thomas Barnes Reinig
Frank B. Reisman
Joshua Scott Reiss
Karen Renda
John Armand Reo
Richard Rescorla
John Thomas Resta
Eduvigis (Eddie) Reyes
Bruce A. Reynolds
John Frederick Rhodes
Francis S. Riccardelli
Rudolph N. Riccio
AnnMarie (Davi) Riccoboni
David Rice
Eileen Mary Rice
Kenneth F. Rice III
Lt. Vernon Allan Richard
Claude D. Richards
Gregory Richards
Michael Richards
Venesha O. Richards
James C. Riches
Alan Jay Richman
John M. Rigo
James Riley
Theresa (Ginger) Risco
Rose Mary Riso
Moises N. Rivas
Joseph Rivelli Jr.
Carmen A. Rivera
Isaias Rivera
Juan William Rivera
Linda Rivera
David E. Rivers
Joseph R. Riverso
Paul Rizza
John Frank Rizzo
Stephen Louis Roach
Joseph Roberto
Leo A. Roberts
Michael Edward Roberts

Michael Roberts
Donald Walter Robertson Jr.
Catherina Robinson
Jeffrey Robinson
Michell Lee Robotham
Donald Robson
Antonio Augusto Tome Rocha
Raymond J. Rocha
Laura Rockefeller
John M. Rodak
Antonio Jose Carrusca Rodrigues
Anthony Rodriguez
Carlos Cortez Rodriguez
Carmen Milagros Rodriguez
Gregory E. Rodriguez
Marsha A. Rodriguez
Richard Rodriguez
David B. Rodriguez-Vargas
Matthew Rogan
Karlie Barbara Rogers
Scott Rohner
Keith Roma
Joseph M. Romagnolo
Efrain Franco Romero Sr.
Elvin Santiago Romero
James A. Romito
Sean Rooney
Eric Thomas Ropiteau
Wendy Alice Rosario Wakeford
Aida Rosario
Angela Rosario
Mark H. Rosen
Brooke David Rosenbaum
Linda Rosenbaum
Sheryl Lynn Rosenbaum
Lloyd D. Rosenberg
Mark Louis Rosenberg
Andrew I. Rosenblum
Joshua M. Rosenblum
Joshua A. Rosenthal
Richard David Rosenthal
Daniel Rossetti
Norman Rossinow
Nicholas P. Rossomando
Michael Craig Rothberg
Donna Marie Rothenberg
Nick Rowe
Timothy A. Roy Sr.
Paul G. Ruback
Ronald J. Ruben
Joanne Rubino
David Michael Ruddle
Bart Joseph Ruggiere
Susan Ann Ruggiero
Adam K. Ruhalter
Gilbert Ruiz
Stephen P. Russell
Steven Harris Russin
Lt. Michael Thomas Russo Sr.
Wayne Alan Russo
Edward Ryan
John J. Ryan

Jonathan Stephan Ryan
Matthew Lancelot Ryan
Tatiana Ryjova
Christina Sunga Ryook
Thierry Saada
Jason E. Sabbag
Thomas E. Sabella
Scott Saber
Joseph Sacerdote
Francis J. Sadocha
Jude Elias Safi
Brock Joel Safronoff
Edward Saiya
John Patrick Salamone
Hernando R. Salas
Juan Salas
Esmerlin Salcedo
John Salvatore Salerno Jr.
Richard L. Salinardi
Wayne John Saloman
Nolbert Salomon
Catherine Patricia Salter
Frank Salvaterra
Paul R. Salvio
Samuel R. Salvo Jr.
Carlos Samaniego
Rena Sam-Dinnoo
James Kenneth Samuel Jr.
Michael V. San Phillip
Sylvia San Pio Resta
Hugo Sanay-Perafiel
Alva J. Sanchez
Erick Sanchez
Jacquelyn P. Sanchez
Eric Sand
Stacey Leigh Sanders
Herman Sandler
James Sands Jr.
Ayleen J. Santiago
Kirsten Santiago
Maria Theresa Santillan
Susan G. Santo
Christopher Santora
John Santore
Mario L. Santoro
Jorge Octavio Santos Anaya
Rafael Humberto Santos
Rufino Conrado F. (Roy) Santos III
Kalyan K. Sarkar
Chapelle Sarker
Paul F. Sarle
Deepika Kumar Sattaluri
Gregory Thomas Saucedo
Susan Sauer
Anthony Savas
Vladimir Savinkin
Jackie Sayegh Duggan
John Sbarbaro
Robert L. Scandole Jr.
Michelle Scarpitta
Dennis Scauso
John A. Schardt

John G. Scharf
Fred Claude Scheffold Jr.
Angela Susan Scheinberg
Scott M. Schertzer
Sean Schielke
Steven Francis Schlag
Jon S. Schlissel
Karen Helene Schmidt
Ian Schneider
Thomas G. Schoales
Marisa Di Nardo Schorpp
Frank G. Schott
Gerard P. Schrang
Jeffrey Schreier
John T. Schroeder
Susan Lee Kennedy Schuler
Edward W. Schunk
Mark E. Schurmeier
Clarin Shellie Schwartz
John Schwartz
Mark Schwartz
Adriane Victoria Scibetta
Raphael Scorca
Randolph Scott
Christopher J. Scudder
Arthur Warren Scullin
Michael Seaman
Margaret Seeliger
Anthony Segarra
Carlos Segarra
Jason Sekzer
Matthew Carmen Sellitto
Howard Selwyn
Larry John Senko
Arturo Angelo Sereno
Frankie Serrano
Alena Sesinova
Adele Sessa
Sita Nermalla Sewnarine
Karen Lynn Seymour-Dietrich
Davis (Deeg) Sezna Jr.
Thomas Joseph Sgroi
Jayesh Shah
Khalid M. Shahid
Mohammed Shajahan
Gary Shamay
Earl Richard Shanahan
Shiv Shankar
Neil G. Shastri
Kathryn Anne Shatzoff
Barbara A. Shaw
Jeffrey J. Shaw
Robert J. Shay Jr.
Daniel James Shea
Joseph Patrick Shea
Linda Sheehan
Hagay Shefi
Terrance H. Shefield
John Anthony Sherry
Atsushi Shiratori
Thomas Shubert
Mark Shulman

See-Wong Shum
Allan Shwartzstein
Johanna Sigmund
Dianne T. Signer
Gregory Sikorsky
Stephen Gerard Siller
David Silver
Craig A. Silverstein
Nasima H. Simjee
Bruce Edward Simmons
Arthur Simon
Kenneth Alan Simon
Michael John Simon
Paul Joseph Simon
Marianne Simone
Barry Simowitz
Jeff Simpson
George V. Sims
Khamladai K. (Khami) Singh
Roshan R. (Sean) Singh
Thomas Sinton III
Peter A. Siracuse
Muriel F. Siskopoulos
Joseph M. Sisolak
John P. Skala
Francis J. Skidmore Jr.
Toyena Corliss Skinner
Paul A. Skrzypek
Christopher Paul Slattery
Vincent R. Slavin
Robert Sliwak
Paul K. Sloan
Stanley S. Smagala Jr.
Wendy L. Small
Catherine T. Smith
Daniel Laurence Smith
George Eric Smith
James G. Smith
Jeffrey Randall Smith
Joyce Smith
Karl Trumbull Smith
Kevin Smith
Leon Smith Jr.
Moira Smith
Rosemary A. Smith
Sandra Fajardo Smith
Bonnie S. Smithwick
Rochelle Monique Snell
Leonard J. Snyder Jr.
Astrid Elizabeth Sohan
Sushil Solanki
Ruben Solares
Naomi Leah Solomon
Daniel W. Song
Michael C. Sorresse
Fabian Soto
Timothy P. Soulas
Gregory T. Spagnoletti
Donald F. Spampinato Jr.
Thomas Sparacio
John Anthony Spataro
Robert W. Spear Jr.

Maynard S. Spence Jr.
George E. Spencer III
Robert Andrew Spencer
Mary Rubina Sperando
Frank J. Spinelli
William E. Spitz
Joseph P. Spor
Klaus Johannes Sprockamp
Saranya Srinuan
Fitzroy St. Rose
Michael F. Stabile
Lawrence T. Stack
Capt. Timothy Stackpole
Richard James Stadelberger
Eric A. Stahlman
Gregory M. Stajk
Alexandru Liviu Stan
Corina Stan
Mary D. Stanley
Joyce Stanton
Patricia Stanton
Anthony M. Starita
Jeffrey Stark
Derek James Statkevicus
Craig William Staub
William V. Steckman
Eric Thomas Steen
William R. Steiner
Alexander Robbins Steinman
Andrew Stergiopoulos
Andrew Stern
Martha Stevens
Michael James Stewart
Richard H. Stewart Jr.
Sanford M. Stoller
Lonny J. Stone
Jimmy Nevill Storey
Timothy Stout
Thomas S. Strada
James J. Straine Jr.
Edward W. Straub
George Strauch Jr.
Edward T. Strauss
Steven R. Strauss
Steven F. Strobert
Walwyn W. Stuart
Benjamin Suarez
David S. Suarez
Ramon Suarez
Yoichi Sugiyama
William Christopher Sugra
Daniel Suhr
David Marc Sullins
Lt. Christopher P. Sullivan
Patrick Sullivan
Thomas Sullivan
Hilario Soriano (Larry) Sumaya Jr.
James Joseph Suozzo
Colleen Supinski
Robert Sutcliffe
Selina Sutter
Claudia Suzette Sutton

John F. Swaine
Kristine M. Swearson
Brian Edward Sweeney
Kenneth J. Swensen
Thomas F. Swift
Derek O. Sword
Kevin T. Szocik
Gina Sztejnberg
Norbert P. Szurkowski
Harry Taback
Joann Tabeek
Norma C. Taddei
Michael Taddonio
Keiichiro Takahashi
Keiji Takahashi
Phyllis Gail Talbot
Robert R. Talhami
Sean Patrick Tallon
Paul Talty
Maurita Tam
Rachel Tamares
Hector Tamayo
Michael Andrew Tamuccio
Kenichiro Tanaka
Rhondelle Cherie Tankard
Michael Anthony Tanner
Dennis Gerard Taormina Jr.
Kenneth Joseph Tarantino
Allan Tarasiewicz
Ronald Tartaro
Darryl Taylor
Donnie Brooks Taylor
Lorisa Ceylon Taylor
Michael M. Taylor
Paul A. Tegtmeier
Yeshavant Moreshwar Tembe
Anthony Tempesta
Dorothy Temple
David Tengelin
Brian J. Terrenzi
Lisa Marie Terry
Goumatie T. Thackurdeen
Harshad Sham Thatte
Thomas F. Theurkauf Jr.
Lesley Thomas-O'Keefe
Brian T. Thompson
Clive Thompson
Glenn Thompson
Nigel Bruce Thompson
Perry Anthony Thompson
Vanavah Alexi Thompson
Capt. William Harry Thompson
Eric Raymond Thorpe
Nichola A. Thorpe
Sal Tieri Jr.
John Patrick Tierney
William R. Tieste
Kenneth F. Tietjen
Stephen Edward Tighe
Scott C. Timmes
Michael E. Tinley

Jennifer M. Tino
Robert Frank Tipaldi
John J. Tipping II
David Tirado
Hector Luis Tirado Jr.
Michelle Titolo
John J. Tobin
Richard J. Todisco
Vladimir Tomasevic
Stephen K. Tompsett
Thomas Tong
Doris Torres
Luis Eduardo Torres
Amy E. Toyen
Christopher M. Traina
Daniel Patrick Trant
Abdoul Karim Traore
Glenn J. Travers
Walter (Wally) P. Travers Jr.
Felicia Traylor-Bass
Lisa L. Trerotola
Karamo Trerra
Michael Trinidad
Francis Joseph Trombino
Gregory J. Trost
William Tselepis Jr.
Zhanetta Tsoy
Michael Patrick Tucker
Lance Richard Tumulty
Ching Ping Tung
Simon James Turner
Donald Joseph Tuzio
Robert T. Twomey
Jennifer Tzemis
John G. Ueltzhoeffer
Tyler V. Ugolyn
Michael A. Uliano
Jonathan J. Uman
Anil Shivhari Umarkar
Allen V. Upton
Diane Maria Urban
John Damien Vaccacio
Bradley H. Vadas
William Valcarcel
Mayra Valdes-Rodriguez
Felix Antonio Vale
Ivan Vale
Benito Valentin
Santos Valentin Jr.
Carlton Francis Valvo II
Erica Van Acker
Kenneth W. Van Auken
Richard Bruce Van Hine
Daniel M. Van Laere
Edward Raymond Vanacore
Jon C. Vandevander
Frederick T. Varacchi
Gopalakrishnan Varadhan
David Vargas
Scott C. Vasel
Azael Ismael Vasquez

Santos Vasquez
Arcangel Vazquez
Peter Anthony Vega
Sankara S. Velamuri
Jorge Velazquez
Lawrence Veling
Anthony M. Ventura
David Vera
Loretta A. Vero
Christopher Vialonga
Matthew Gilbert Vianna
Robert A. Vicario
Celeste Torres Victoria
Joanna Vidal
John T. Vigiano II
Joseph Vincent Vigiano
Frank J. Vignola Jr.
Joseph B. Vilardo
Sergio Villanueva
Chantal Vincelli
Melissa Vincent
Francine A. Virgilio
Lawrence Virgilio
Joseph G. Visciano
Ramsaroop Vishnu
Joshua S. Vitale
Maria Percoco Vola
Lynette D. Vosges
Garo H. Voskerijian
Alfred Vukuosa
Gregory Wachtler
Gabriela Waisman
Courtney Wainsworth Walcott
Victor Wald
Benjamin Walker
Glen J. Wall
Mitchel Scott Wallace
Peter G. Wallace
Lt. Robert F. Wallace
Roy Wallace
Jean Marie Wallendorf
Matthew Blake Wallens
John Wallice Jr.
Barbara P. Walsh
James Walsh
Jeffrey Patrick Walz
Ching H. Wang
Weibin Wang
Lt. Michael Warchola
Stephen Gordon Ward
James A. Waring
Brian G. Warner
Derrick Washington
Charles Waters
James Thomas (Muddy) Waters Jr.
Capt. Patrick J. Waters
Kenneth Watson
Michael H. Waye
Todd C. Weaver
Walter E. Weaver
Nathaniel Webb

Dinah Webster
Joanne Flora Weil
Michael Weinberg
Steven Weinberg
Scott Jeffrey Weingard
Steven Weinstein
Simon Weiser
David M. Weiss
David T. Weiss
Vincent Michael Wells
Timothy Matthew Welty
Christian Hans Rudolf Wemmers
Ssu-Hui (Vanessa) Wen
Oleh D. Wengerchuk
Peter M. West
Whitfield West
Meredith Lynn Whalen
Eugene Whelan
Adam S. White
Edward James White
James Patrick White
John S. White
Kenneth W. White
Leonard Anthony White
Malissa White
Wayne White
Leanne Marie Whiteside
Mark Whitford
Michael T. Wholey
Mary Lenz Wieman
Jeffrey David Wiener
William J. Wik
Allison M. Wildman
Lt. Glenn Wilkinson
John C. Willett
Brian Patrick Williams
Crossley Williams Jr.
David Williams
Deborah Lynn Williams
Kevin Michael Williams
Louie Anthony Williams
Louis Calvin Williams III
Lt. John Williamson
Cynthia Wilson
Donna Wilson
William E. Wilson
David H. Winton
Glenn J. Winuk
Thomas Francis Wise
Alan L. Wisniewski
Frank T. Wisniewski
David Wiswall
Sigrid Charlotte Wiswe
Michael R. Wittenstein
Christopher W. Wodenshek
Martin P. Wohlforth
Katherine S. Wolf
Jennifer Y. Wong
Jenny Seu Kueng Low Wong
Siu Cheung Wong
Yin Ping (Steven) Wong

Yuk Ping Wong
Brent James Woodall
James J. Woods
Patrick Woods
Richard Herron Woodwell
Capt. David Terence Wooley
John Bentley Works
Martin Michael Wortley
Rodney James Wotton
William Wren
John Wright
Neil R. Wright
Sandra Wright
Jupiter Yambem
Suresh Yanamadala
Matthew David Yarnell
Myrna Yaskulka
Shakila Yasmin
Olabisi L. Yee
Edward P. York
Kevin Patrick York
Raymond York
Suzanne Youmans
Barrington L. Young
Jacqueline (Jakki) Young
Elkin Yuen
Joseph Zaccoli
Adel Agayby Zakhary
Arkady Zaltsman
Edwin J. Zambrana Jr.
Robert Alan Zampieri
Mark Zangrilli
Ira Zaslow
Aurelio Zedillo
Kenneth Albert Zelman
Abraham J. Zelmanowitz
Martin Morales Zempoaltecatl
Zhe (Zack) Zeng
Marc Scott Zeplin
Jie Yao Justin Zhao
Ivelin Ziminski
Michael Joseph Zinzi
Charles A. Zion
Julie Lynne Zipper
Salvatore J. Zisa
Prokopios Paul Zois
Joseph J. Zuccala
Andrew Steven Zucker
Igor Zukelman

American Airlines Flight 11

John Ogonowski
Thomas McGuinness
Barbara Arestegui
Jeffrey Collman
Sara Low
Karen Martin
Kathleen Nicosia
Betty Ong
Jean Roger

Dianne Snyder
Madeline Sweeney
Anna Williams Allison
David Angell
Lynn Angell
Seima Aoyama
Myra Aronson
Christine Barbuto
Berry Berenson
Carolyn Beug
Carol Bouchard
Robin Caplin
Neilie Casey
Jeffrey Coombs
Tara Creamer
Thelma Cuccinello
Patrick Currivan
Andrew Curry Green
Brian Dale
David DiMeglio
Donald Ditullio
Albert Dominguez
Alex Filipov
Carol Flyzik
Paul Friedman
Karleton D.B. Fyfe
Peter Gay
Linda George
Edmund Glazer
Lisa Fenn Gordenstein
Paige Farley Hackel
Peter Hashem
Robert Hayes
Ted Hennessy
John Hofer
Cora Holland
Nicholas Humber
John Jenkins
Charles Jones
Robin Kaplan
Barbara Keating
David Kovalcin
Judy Larocque
Jude Larson
Natalie Larson
N. Janis Lasden
Daniel John Lee
Daniel C. Lewin
Susan MacKay
Chris Mello
Jeff Mladenik
Antonio Montoya
Carlos Montoya
Laura Lee Morabito
Mildred Naiman
Laurie Neira
Renee Newell
Jacqueline Norton
Robert Norton
Jane Orth
Thomas Pecorelli

Sonia Morales Puopolo
David Retik
Philip Rosenzweig
Richard Ross
Jessica Sachs
Rahma Salie
Heather Smith
Douglas Stone
Xavier Suarez
Michael Theodoridis
James Trentini
Mary Trentini
Mary Wahlstrom
Kenneth Waldie
John Wenckus
Candace Lee Williams
Christopher Zarba

American Airlines Flight 77

Charles Burlingame
David Charlebois
Michele Heidenberger
Jennifer Lewis
Kenneth Lewis
Renee May
Paul Ambrose
Yeneneh Betru
M.J. Booth
Bernard Brown
Suzanne Calley
William Caswell
Sarah Clark
Asia Cottom
James Debeuneure
Rodney Dickens
Eddie Dillard
Charles Droz
Barbara Edwards
Charles S. Falkenberg
Zoe Falkenberg
Dana Falkenberg
Joe Ferguson
Wilson "Bud" Flagg
Dee Flagg
Richard Gabriel
Ian Gray
Stanley Hall
Bryan Jack
Steven D. "Jake" Jacoby
Ann Judge
Chandler Keller
Yvonne Kennedy
Norma Khan
Karen A. Kincaid
Norma Langsteuerle
Dong Lee
Dora Menchaca
Christopher Newton
Barbara Olson
Ruben Ornedo
Robert Penniger

Lisa Raines
Todd Reuben
John Sammartino
Diane Simmons
George Simmons
Mari-Rae Sopper
Bob Speisman
Hilda Taylor
Leonard Taylor
Leslie A. Whittington
John Yamnicky
Vicki Yancey
Shuyin Yang
Yuguag Zheng

United Airlines Flight 175

Alona Avraham
Garnet "Ace" Bailey
Mark Bavis
Graham Berkeley
Touri Bolourchi
Klaus Bothe
Daniel Brandhorst
David Brandhorst
John Cahill
Christoffer Carstanjen
John Corcoran
Dorothy Dearaujo
Gloria Debarrera
Lisa Frost
Ronald Gamboa
Lynn Goodchild
Rev. Francis E. Grogan
Carl Hammond
Peter Hanson
Susan Hanson
Christine Hanson
Gerald Hardacre
Eric Hartono
James E. Hayden
Herbert Homer
Robert Jalbert
Ralph Kershaw
Heinrich Kimmig
Brian Kinney
Robert LeBlanc
Maclovio "Joe" Lopez Jr.
Marianne MacFarlane
Louis Neil Mariani
Juliana Valentine McCourt
Ruth McCourt
Wolfgang Menzel
Shawn Nassaney
Patrick Quigley
Frederick Rimmele
James M. Roux
Jesus Sanchez
Kathleen Shearer
Robert Shearer
Jane Simpkin
Brian D. Sweeney

Timothy Ward
William Weems

United Airlines Flight 93

Jason Dahl
Leroy Homer
Lorraine Bay
Sandra Bradshaw
Wanda Green
CeeCee Lyles
Deborah Welsh
Christian Adams
Todd Beamer
Alan Beaven
Mark Bingham
Deora Bodley
Marion Britton
Thomas E. Burnett Jr.
William Cashman
Georgine Corrigan
Joseph Deluca
Patrick Driscoll
Edward Felt
Colleen Fraser
Andrew Garcia
Jeremy Glick
Lauren Grandcolas
Donald F. Green
Linda Gronlund
Richard Guadagno
Toshiya Kuge
Waleska Martinez
Nicole Miller
Mark Rothenberg
Christine Snyder
John Talignani
Honor Wainio

Pentagon

Spc. Craig Amundson
Melissa Rose Barnes
Master Sgt. Max Beilke
Kris Romeo Bishundat
Carrie Blagburn
Lt. Col. Canfield D. Boone
Donna Bowen
Allen Boyle
Christopher Lee Burford
Daniel Martin Caballero
Sgt. First Class Jose Calderon
Angelene C. Carter
Sharon Carver
John J. Chada
Rosa Maria (Rosemary) Chapa
Julian Cooper
Lt. Cmdr. Eric Allen Cranford
Ada Davis
Capt. Gerald Francis Deconto
Lt. Col. Jerry Don Dickerson
Johnnie Doctor

Capt. Robert Edward Dolan
Cmdr. William Howard Donovan
Cmdr. Patrick S. Dunn
Edward Thomas Earhart
Lt. Cmdr. Robert Randolph Elseth
Jamie Lynn Fallon
Amelia V. Fields
Gerald P. Fisher
Matthew Michael Flocco
Sandra N. Foster
Capt. Lawrence Daniel Getzfred
Cortz Ghee
Brenda C. Gibson
Ron Golinski
Diane M. Hale-McKinzy
Carolyn B. Halmon
Sheila Hein
Ronald John Hemenway
Maj. Wallace Cole Hogan
Jimmie Ira Holley
Angela Houtz
Brady K. Howell
Peggie Hurt, Crewe
Lt. Col. Stephen Neil Hyland
Robert J. Hymel
Sgt. Maj. Lacey B. Ivory
Lt. Col. Dennis M. Johnson
Judith Jones
Brenda Kegler
Lt. Michael Scott Lamana
David W. Laychak
Samantha Lightbourn-Allen
Maj. Steve Long
James Lynch
Terrance M. Lynch

Nehamon Lyons
Shelley A. Marshall
Teresa Martin
Ada L. Mason
Lt. Col. Dean E. Mattson
Lt. Gen. Timothy J. Maude
Robert J. Maxwell
Molly McKenzie
Patricia E. (Patti) Mickley
Maj. Ronald D. Milam
Gerard (Jerry) P. Moran
Odessa V. Morris
Brian Anthony Moss
Ted Moy
Lt. Cmdr. Patrick Jude Murphy
Khang Nguyen
Michael Allen Noeth
Diana B. Padro
Spc. Chin Sun Pak
Lt. Jonas Martin Panik
Maj. Clifford L. Patterson
Lt. J.G. Darin Howard Pontell
Scott Powell
Capt. Jack Punches
Joseph John Pycior
Deborah Ramsaur
Rhonda Rasmussen
Marsha Dianah Ratchford
Martha Reszke
Cecelia E. Richard
Edward V. Rowenhorst
Judy Rowlett
Robert E. Russell
William R. Ruth
Charles E. Sabin

Marjorie C. Salamone
Lt. Col. David M. Scales
Cmdr. Robert Allan Schlegel
Janice Scott
Michael L. Selves
Marian Serva
Cmdr. Dan Frederic Shanower
Antoinette Sherman
Don Simmons
Cheryle D. Sincock
Gregg Harold Smallwood
Lt. Col. Gary F. Smith
Patricia J. Statz
Edna L. Stephens
Sgt. Maj. Larry Strickland
Maj. Kip P. Taylor
Sandra Taylor
Karl W. Teepe
Sgt. Tamara Thurman
Lt. Cmdr. Otis Vincent Tolbert
Willie Q. Troy
Lt. Cmdr. Ronald James Vauk
Lt. Col. Karen Wagner
Meta Waller
Staff Sgt. Maudlyn A. White
Sandra L. White
Ernest M. Willcher
Lt. Cmdr. David Lucian Williams
Maj. Dwayne Williams
Marvin Woods
Kevin Wayne Yokum
Donald McArthur Young
Lisa Young
Edmond Young

Now let's roll!

Contents at a Glance

Contents

About the Author

Carl Ganz, Jr. is president of Seton Software Development, Inc., a provider of software design and development services located in Raritan, New Jersey. He earned an M.B.A in Finance from Seton Hall University and is the author of two other books on software development as well as the author of several dozen technical articles on Visual Basic and Microsoft .NET technology. Carl is the president/founder of the New Jersey Visual Basic User Group and has been a featured speaker at software development conferences in both the U.S. and Germany. Carl and his wife, Wendy, live in Raritan, New Jersey, with their cats Jack and Jake. Contact him at seton.software@verizon.net.

Acknowledgments

THERE ARE SEVERAL PEOPLE whom I would like to thank for their assistance in writing this book:

Issam Elbaytam of DataDynamics, Inc., for reviewing the chapters on ActiveReports for technical accuracy and completeness. Likewise, Rob Duncan of ComponentOne, Inc., for checking the chapters on VS-View and Preview.

Dan Carr, Aric Rosenbaum, Ryan Follmer, and Chuck Cage for their advice, guidance, and technical assistance on various chapters.

Karen Watterson, my editor at *Hardcore Visual Basic* magazine, who helped develop the initial idea for this book, proofread every chapter, and steered this ship through some very troubled waters.

Sofia Marchant, Laura Cheu, and Nate McFadden, project managers; Laura Cheu and Kari Brooks, production editors; and Ami Knox, copy editor, for their invaluable contributions and hard work (much of it over the Christmas holidays) that drove this project to completion.

My clients, whose many challenges over the years provided the foundation of literally all that is contained within these pages.

My wife, Wendy, for providing me with the love, affection, and support that makes all these efforts worthwhile.

Most important, thanks be to God for the ability to do this kind of intellectually demanding work.

Introduction

REPORT WRITING HAS ALWAYS BEEN a thorn in the side of software developers. Like all other tools for software development, report writing technologies have evolved dramatically over the past several years. When Visual Basic was first released, there were only two viable ways of building reports: 1) Using an interactive report writing tool like Crystal Reports or R&R Report Writer, or 2) hand-coding using the VB Print object. The more adventurous addressed the Windows Printer API directly, calling functions such as OpenPrinter and TextOut. The VB Printer object was (and still is) rather weak, especially in its lack of an event-driven interface, and most developers had neither the time nor the expertise to deal with the API approach. This left interactive report writers as the only viable possibility. In time, many developers became experts in their chosen report writer and, overall, these tools have served their purpose very well.

Times have changed and scores of other tools have emerged into the marketplace. Today, the way I see things, there are three categories of report writing tools:

- The now-classic interactive report writers like Crystal Reports

- Source code–only alternatives like VS-View and Preview, both from ComponentOne, Inc.

- Tools that are a cross between an interactive report writer and source code like ActiveReports from DataDynamics, Inc., and VS-View Reporting Edition from ComponentOne, Inc.

There's also a wide assortment of other not-so-standard report writers that seem to defy categorization. Some even come with source code. Which tool is best is a long-running philosophical discussion among software professionals, and strong opinions vary from developer to developer. I personally prefer the VS-View/Preview approach, whereas many of my colleagues prefer ActiveReports. Both of these products are consistently among the top sellers at VBXtras.com. I also have many experienced colleagues who prefer Crystal Reports. There are even some users of R&R Report Writer (http://www.livewarepub.com) out there, although the market has been dominated by Crystal Reports for the past several years. We each have very specific reasons why we have chosen the tools that we use and, to be honest, familiarity has a lot to do with it.

Other developers have their choices and reasons as well. In August 2002, I suggested a survey question to the Webmasters of VBWire.com, a Web site dedicated to providing updated technical and product information to users of VB and .NET technologies. The question was, "If you had your choice, what tool would you use for report development?" I gave five possible responses: Crystal Reports, ComponentOne's VS-View/Preview for .NET, Data Dynamics ActiveReports, Actuate, and Other. With 1297 people responding, the response percentage breakdown was as follows:

Crystal Reports	42%
VS-View/Preview for .NET	16%
ActiveReports	20%
Actuate	10%
Other	12%

Since the first word of this book's title is "Enterprise," rest assured that I intend to show you how to make reports available to the enterprise by hosting report engines on servers. Because Crystal Decisions has the largest market share of any report development tool, as evidenced by the results of the preceding Web poll, I'll concentrate on the Crystal Enterprise technology as an example of enterprise-wide report distribution. Nevertheless, I'll also discuss the advantages of creating your own report server (it's not difficult) using tools such as ActiveReports and VS-View/Preview. There are certainly other alternatives to these approaches such as Actuate, Cognos, Business Objects, and WebFocus, but detailed coverage of these tools is beyond the scope of this book.

Reporting is as much a philosophy as a technology. It's fundamentally an issue of getting the right information (not too much and not too little) to the right people quickly and efficiently. There are a myriad of ways to accomplish this: e-mail; Web availability; output format options such as PDF, HTML, Excel, RTF, or Word; options of interactive reports that allow drilldown to subreports or even the raw database information itself; and graphing. Of course, paper printouts will be with us forever. It's been said that the paperless office is about as likely as the paperless bathroom.

In 1995, I was at a technology conference where the keynote speaker was an expert in virtual reality. He spoke of a future day where users could don virtual reality goggles and view their data in a virtual world where data would be plotted and graphed in three dimensions or even one where an artificially intelligent virtual person would respond to natural language questions as to what the data meant. While such *Star Trek* scenarios are certainly far-fetched, it shows the extent to which people are thinking about meeting reporting requirements.

While there are certainly differences in technology for report delivery, there are also differences in methodology as well. One is just as important as the other. By "methodology," I refer to the processes and procedures of building a report, designing a criteria screen, and deploying it to the user. It is the rule, not the exception, at most companies I've worked with that developers often reinvent the wheel every time a simple report is needed. It often takes days and weeks to deliver a report that should be done in a few hours. Often, no one knows what version of which reporting tools are on what workstations, where to deploy the report, and who has the documentation. Like any other aspect of software development, these problems need to be addressed, or every new report a client requests becomes a project unto itself.

The idea for this book grew out of an e-mail I sent to my long-time *Visual Basic Developer* (now *Hardcore Visual Basic*) newsletter editor at Pinnacle Publishing, Karen Watterson, way back in February 2002. After suggesting an article idea for the Crystal Report Creation API, she suggested that the advanced developer's features of Crystal would make a good book topic. I thought that this topic had been exhaustively covered by other authors and that I couldn't add much to the existing field of knowledge. I thought, however, that a book on other reporting tools such as VS-View and ActiveReports and the entire range of report-related technologies would be appropriate. In fact, after researching the market, I couldn't find another book that had ever been written specifically on the subject of report writing. I found this to be very strange, as report writing is such a vital part of application development.

My goal in this book is to discuss report writing from a developer's perspective. I plan to discuss the programming of reports using such tools as VS-View / Preview and ActiveReports, as well as the programmatic interface offered by Crystal Reports, and even delivery of reports to handheld wireless devices. In addition, I'll cover how to design reports and what items to consider when creating a specification document. Then, I'll discuss the SQL and ADO/ADO.NET issues you'll need to understand to extract the data necessary for the reports you are building. From there, I'll show you how to create effective and easy-to-maintain criteria screens. You'll learn about the role played by the Microsoft Office XP suite. Since reports will often be exported to both Excel and Word, as well as transmitted throughout the enterprise by Outlook, we'll explore these technologies in depth together. Since both Lotus Notes and Adobe Acrobat also play an important role in the creation and dissemination of reports, I'll explain the parts they can play as well. Then, you'll learn how to deliver reports over the Internet using both ASP and ASP.NET, paying careful attention to the role played by XML Web services. Finally, I'll conclude by showing you the new Palm and Windows CE technologies for Pocket PCs and remote wireless connections.

This book isn't intended either as an endorsement or a manual replacement for any particular product. For those reporting products covered, it's not the goal to exhaustively explain every property, method, and event. If you are already a user of these products, you will find in these pages much helpful information on how to use these products to their fullest potential. For those of you new to report development, this book will help you decide which tools and methodologies are right for you. My goal is to focus on the programming necessary to use these tools to develop "real-world" reports and to integrate these reports into your applications. All of the techniques that I describe—and most of the code examples that I use (with the exception of some of the .NET examples, as this technology is so new)—are taken from production applications that I have delivered to paying customers over the past few years.

All in all, I hope this book provides you with some fresh (or forgotten) ideas about delivering reports. Enjoy, and let me know what you think.

Carl Ganz, Jr.
seton.software@verizon.net
Raritan, New Jersey

CHAPTER 1

Reporting in a Nutshell

REPORT WRITING HAS EVOLVED over the years as radically as the tools for software development itself. Those of us who are a little older remember the days when a central computer system would produce the formerly ubiquitous "green-bar" reports. Large, continuous-feed data outputs were distributed by hand throughout the organization by a clerk who carried these monstrosities to individual managers. Mercifully, technology has evolved beyond all that so that now the same report can be served up automatically, usually by e-mail or even wireless transmission to a personal digital assistant (PDA). Moreover, the trend is toward better "just in time" information (often in the form of exception or summary reports instead of comprehensive ones) so that only those individuals who require certain data receive it and those individuals can get timely "bites" of data instead of only large monthly or yearly reports.

Because information technology has evolved so rapidly over the past few years, the definition of what constitutes a report has undergone a dramatic transformation. Traditionally, reports were only thought of as something that printed on paper. This definition has since become blurred as there are multiple ways information can be disseminated throughout the enterprise. Today, paper reports are largely used only as working copies to be carried to meetings or as written notes or archives. Given the use of Web technology, e-mail, PDAs, and Adobe Acrobat PDF files, paper has—mercifully for the environment—fallen to a tertiary position as a means of conveying information.

Report development is often one of the last processes in developing an application when, practically speaking, it should be one of the first steps when performing a system design. By starting with the reports and other data outputs that are required, you can better determine what the inputs should be. In fact, when all is said and done, if a data element that is used in the application is not found on any of the reports, the need for that data element should be questioned.

Certain standards govern the format of reports. Text and date information, for example, should be left justified in their respective columns along with their column titles. Numeric amounts and their column titles, however, should be right justified so that decimal points and digits line up. Margins can be adjusted as necessary given the amount of data you intend to print on a page, but remember that users may want to hold printed output in a binder, so take this into consideration when sizing margins.

To make sure that no information is lost, it is judicious to evaluate whether the page numbers should read "Page x of y". Also, the phrase "End of Report" should appear after the last row of data on the last page. For reports that contain sensitive data, it is often a good practice to include a phrase on each page footer to this effect: "The information contained in this report is internal corporate information only and should not be distributed outside of the organization." Highly sensitive reports can be printed with the label "Copy x of y" so as to account for all printed copies. Moreover, special paper can be used that will preclude photocopying the printed documents.

As a rule, users should be provided with the option to print a criteria page at the beginning of each report that indicates the criteria used to filter the data contained within it. If possible, these criteria can also appear on the first page of the report before the data itself.

Report distribution has made huge leaps since the introduction of the Internet and corporate intranets. Since many reports are built into applications (compiled EXEs), a user would normally need a copy of that application installed on his or her desktop in order to access the report. Now, the reporting functionality can be completely Web-based. Using Web-based technology, the comparatively finite number of desktop users can still have access to report functionality, while the often much larger number of Web users can access a Web-based application that will provide them with report criteria screens to allow them to run and export reports.

Security

Of course, all these means of disseminating information bring with them numerous security issues. While a comprehensive discussion of computer security is beyond the scope of this book, a brief mention of report-and document-related security issues is appropriate. There are different levels of security related to report information. It could be simply that the ability to print certain reports is available only to specified users. This fails, of course, when one of these users sends a report to a shared printer to which anyone on the floor has access. I once had a user print a list of salary and bonus information that was fortunately found by the human resources director before any damage was done. It was the last time that user ever made that mistake. It is difficult to employ any kind of security measures on a computer system without incurring significant expense. All it takes is one user to write their password on their keyboard and the most elaborate security system is immediately compromised. One way to track who is being careless is to create a log entry in an audit trail table every time a report is run.

You can record what report was run, the criteria, at what date and time, by whom, and on what machine. You could also print the ID of the user who ran the report on all output so that when the salary report is carelessly left on a table in the lunchroom you'll know who to blame.

Another form of data access restriction is to allow multiple users permission to run the same report but restrict the set of criteria. Thus, one user could run a compensation report for Departments A, B, or C, whereas another user might only be able to run it for Department B. Optionally, any user could be allowed to run the report, but the Compensation column could be suppressed for those users who don't have authorization to view this information.

Some of the technology for securing documents lies in the forms upon which they are printed. Checks are a common example. Most checks have numerous security devices to deter fraud. First, they can be printed on paper that has various color tones throughout the document as well as a distinctive watermark to prevent photocopying. Then, the check amount is printed in several locations on the check itself. I've even seen checks that have heat-sensitive logos on the reverse side that will disappear for a few seconds when heat, say, from your thumb, is applied to them. Taken together, these security devices may not completely prevent fraud, but they'll at least make it very difficult for the culprits and show that you've done due diligence.

Magnetic ink character recognition (MICR) allows you to print the entire check—logo, check and account numbers, signature, etc.—directly on blank paper rather than maintain preprinted check stock, which is easier to steal. In this way there is no need to constantly void preprinted checks that are destroyed in printing.

Security threads are polyester or plastic bands embedded into paper just beneath the surface. The new U.S. currency employs this device as an anticounterfeiting measure. Security threads restrict visibility in reflected light while permitting visibility in transmitted light. They offer protection against photocopying, as copiers see documents only in reflected light. Also, the presence of threads in a document provides for easy authentication. You can obtain more information on the different products and techniques for document security from your forms manufacturer.

Aesthetics

Effective report presentation requires also that you consider your audience's background. Many of my clients are investment banking and pharmaceutical companies. While there is certainly a remarkable difference in the corporate cultures between the two industries, there is also a vast difference in the average age of the staff. The majority of the users at the investment banking firms are under 35, whereas the opposite is true of the pharmaceutical clients. This age difference manifests itself in the way reports are produced. Younger people can generally see reports printed in a smaller font and in fact often prefer it as there is more information printed on one page. Older people have a much harder time viewing this information, and the font size for your reports needs to reflect this.

Font size can also come into play when there is a significant need to conserve paper. I have a client who is a reseller of telecommunication service. His company works on a multilevel marketing model. A person becomes a dealer in the organization and recruits other people as dealers, who in turn recruit others, and so on. Dealers receive commissions from their sales as well as the sales of all the dealers in their sales organization. Because telecommunication sales is such a high-volume, low-margin industry, cost efficiency is a far more sensitive issue than it is in many other industries, and this sensitivity affects reporting. Each month, commission reports need to be mailed to individual dealers, along with a statement of which dealers in the downline produced what sales. Since some of these commission reports run to several pages, and anything more than four $8^1/_2 \times 11$ sheets in an envelope will push the letter into the next postage bracket, it behooves the client to cram as much information as possible onto one sheet of paper. The result is a commission report that uses a 6-point Arial font with a line spacing of .75, meaning that the space between printed lines is 75 percent of the spacing required by a printed line. The result looks something like this:

```
Name  Sales  Comm.  Bonus  Total
John Smith   100.00   10.00   4.00   14.00
Jane Jones   200.00   20.00   8.00   28.00
```

Naturally, this is not an easy read without the use of a ruler and a magnifying glass. But, since the reports were printed duplex (note that not all printers support duplexing), that is, printed on both sides of the paper, a lot of paper was saved and only rarely did the letter get pushed into the next postage level. Most importantly, the client was happy.

Such exacting requirements for report presentation are normally not an overriding issue for most business reports. Presenting data in a clear and organized way, usually some form of a table structure, is all that is required (although I do have clients who have an official font that is used for all their reports, documents, and correspondence so as to create a more uniform look for the firm as a whole). Be careful about using too many different fonts in a report, as this could cause memory overflow errors on older printers (of course, so could too many graphics). Variations in the bold and size attributes of the same font are most appropriate to highlight important areas of the report. The right font can make all the difference in building an effective report presentation. Font selection can be so important that many books have a paragraph in the front matter describing the font used to print the pages within. Serif fonts are the most popular fonts to use for printed reports, but sans serif fonts such as Arial are preferred for screen viewing. Serif fonts have small lines at the top and bottom of the characters that research has proven makes text easier to read. Sans serif fonts do not have these lines ("sans" is simply French for "without"). Take a look at these examples:

This is a serif font.
This is a sans serif font.

Examine your favorite books, magazines, and newspapers, and you'll see that as a rule they use serif fonts. When viewing reports on a computer screen, however, studies have shown that sans serif fonts are easier to read than serif fonts. Because Arial is a sans serif font, it is often used for screen displays. Since most reports are viewed on screen and not printed, Arial may be your best bet for font selection.

You can make the layout easier to read by shading alternate rows of data on reports, especially those that print landscape, and most especially those that print landscape on legal-size paper. Though alternating shading is especially good when reading rows of figures and distinguishing between lines with similar kinds of data, consider that the report may be put through a fax machine. If this is the case, you may need to rethink shading, or at least use a very light shade, as shaded text often can't be read on a fax. When you design a report to print for legal-size paper, you need to consider that the user may or may not have an ample supply of legal-size paper available. While legal-size paper can typically be fed into a printer via the manual feed, this method usually only allows a small number of sheets at a time. If you expect the report to print a large number of pages, recommend that the client obtain a legal-size paper bin. Also, before printing the report, display a message box reminding the user that legal-size paper is required in order for the report to print.

Some reports require a far greater level of fine-tuning. I have a client who develops financial sales software that produces printed sales presentations. The reports for this project were the most complex and involved of any I have ever done. There are a number of forces at play here. First, each phrase, word, and even punctuation mark had to be carefully crafted by the legal department in order to meet regulatory compliance requirements. Then, the marketing department had to be satisfied that it was an effective sales tool. Finally, I had the issue of making sure that the reports were simple to understand for both the financial clients as well as the sales reps because as my client politely tells me, "Carl, they're idiots."

International Considerations

If you plan to deliver your applications outside the United States, there is one very important issue you must consider. The United States is one of the few countries that uses letter-size paper ($8^1/_2 \times 11$). Almost everyone else uses A4 paper, which is a bit longer and a bit narrower than letter-size, specifically 8.27×11.69 inches. (The staff at my client's European offices are only mildly amused when I refer to "regular" paper and "foreign" paper.) If you don't take this width difference into consideration, then your data will print off the right side of the page.

You can determine the paper size setting of the currently selected printer via the Visual Basic Printer object. Simply querying the PaperSize property as follows

```
iPaperSize = Printer.PaperSize
```

will return a constant value indicating the paper size setting for the currently selected printer. You can find a list of all the different PaperSize settings in the Visual Basic documentation.

The Windows Regional Settings, known as Regional Options in Windows 2000 and later, are important for determining the formatting of dates, times, decimals, currency, days of the week, and months of the year. Dates are probably the greatest area of confusion. Many countries use the dd/mm/yyyy format, while the United States uses the mm/dd/yyyy style. In China and some Asian countries, dates appear as yyyy/mm/dd. Therefore, if a date on a report reads 04/01/02, you cannot be certain if it is referring to January 4, 2002, or April 1, 2002. To eliminate all confusion without consuming much extra space, I usually write the date as 04-Jan-2002 on all reports that are used internationally.

Any of the Windows Regional Settings are only an API call away. The GetLocaleInfo API function, shown in Listing 1-1, receives a hexadecimal value as a parameter. This value equates to the setting you wish to retrieve.

Listing 1-1. GetLocaleInfo API Syntax

```
Function LocaleInfo(lDataNeeded As Long) As String
    Dim cBuffer As String
    Dim lResult As Long
    Dim iBuffer As Integer

    iBuffer = 255

    cBuffer = String$(iBuffer - 1, 0)

    lResult = GetLocaleInfo(LOCALE_USER_DEFAULT, lDataNeeded, _
        cBuffer, iBuffer)
```

```
    If lResult <> 0 Then
        LocaleInfo = Left$(cBuffer, lResult - 1)
    End If

End Function
```

The book's downloadable source code, which is available at the Apress Web site (`http://www.apress.com`), has a list of the Regional Settings values expressed as an enumerator. The example shown in Listing 1-2 illustrates what some of the values are.

Listing 1-2. Some of the Valuable Data Returned by GetLocaleInfo

```
Dim cSettings As String

cSettings = "Abbrev. Country: " & _
    LocaleInfo(Locale.AbbrevCountry) & vbCrLf

cSettings = cSettings & "Country: " & _
    LocaleInfo(Locale.CountryEnglish) & vbCrLf

cSettings = cSettings & "Currency Decimal Separator: " & _
    LocaleInfo(Locale.CurrDecimalSep) & vbCrLf

cSettings = cSettings & "Language: " & _
    LocaleInfo(Locale.Language) & vbCrLf

cSettings = cSettings & "Currency Symbol: " & _
    LocaleInfo(Locale.IntlCurrencySymbol) & vbCrLf

cSettings = cSettings & "Long Date: " & _
    LocaleInfo(Locale.LongDateFormat) & vbCrLf

cSettings = cSettings & "Short Date: " & _
    LocaleInfo(Locale.ShortDateFormat) & vbCrLf

cSettings = cSettings & "Time Format: " & _
    LocaleInfo(Locale.TimeFormat) & vbCrLf

cSettings = cSettings & "First Day of week: " & _
    LocaleInfo(Locale.DayName1)

MsgBox cSettings
```

This code produces the message box depicted in Figure 1-1.

Figure 1-1. Regional Settings—United States

If you open the Regional Settings dialog box under the Control Panel and change the settings to Germany, you'll see the message box shown in Figure 1-2.

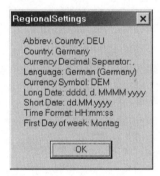

Figure 1-2. Regional Settings—Germany

Of course, you are in no way bound to use the regional settings. Most applications—both in-house and off-the-shelf—have (or at least should have) a security module that manages the names of authorized users and their access levels. This same module can also assign a regional setting as well. The regional setting can refer to a collection of predefined settings—either user-defined or hard-coded—that specify the date format, currency format, etc., regardless of the regional settings specified through the Control Panel. However, if your New York user logs on to a workstation during his trip to the London office, he'll get an

"Insert Letter Size" printer error when he tries to print a report to a printer that is expecting A4.

Report Design

The design stage of any application is the most crucial part of the software development process. My experience has been that almost all projects that go over budget are the result of poor planning, or worse, the complete absence of it. I have had several clients give me a rough idea of their projects and then tell me to begin programming. I would sit at a desk next to a client and work. During the workday the client would tell me to add this or that feature as often as he or she had new and sudden insights about the application. As a junior programmer, I accepted this from clients. As an experienced professional, I no longer tolerate it, although I still see this practice throughout the corporate world. (Note to my clients reading this book: You know if you're a past offender, so take time out now to feel guilty and then continue reading.)

Creating a Report Specification

The principles discussed here for report design apply as well to the remainder of your application. Screens, logic and workflow, business rules, and database design all need to be prototyped and documented so that the client and the developers understand the mission and objective. Since this book focuses on reports, that is what this design section will focus on.

Report design is often a balancing act of having either too much or not enough information. You have only so much room on a page and a limited amount of time to read it. Therefore, you want to display no less, but no more, than is necessary. First, you'll need to specify the objective of the report. Is it primarily a summary or a detail? Then determine what columns from what tables will provide the data. This type of design needs to be done working closely with the client. My experience has been that clients have a better understanding of the reports they want from the system than they do of any other feature of the application. Once the purpose and fields have been determined, you can use a tool like Microsoft Word or Excel to lay out the structure of the report. (I personally find Excel easier to work with.) Figure 1-3 illustrates an example of what this layout may look like, using the same fonts and attribute settings that will appear in the final product.

Figure 1-3. Report layout

Sales by Group Report

GROUP	PRODUCT	ON HAND	QTY SOLD	SALE AMOUNT
Group 1	Product 1	4	6	300
	Product 2	3	4	500
	Product 3	6	2	200
Group 1 Totals		*13*	*12*	*1000*
Group 2	Product 5	7	9	600
	Product 6	7	4	800
	Product 8	11	5	500
Group 2 Totals		*25*	*18*	*1900*
Grand Totals		38	30	2900

This layout takes about 5 minutes to create and clearly illustrates to the client exactly how the report will appear. Populating it with sample data is a helpful technique and is better than simply listing the fields or a straight description of the layout. Use paper of the same size as is intended for the final report, even if this means attaching legal-size paper to your specification document. Try to take a what-you-see-is-what-you-get (WYSIWYG) approach and keep all the fonts and font attributes the same as in the final output. Don't make clients use their imagination.

Anticipate client needs by suggesting summary levels that they may not be thinking about. Do they require averages as well as subtotals? Would the report be too difficult to read if there were too many subtotal groupings? Do they want certain parts boldfaced, italicized, or underlined? Are graphs needed? I once used a strikethrough attribute on an employee recruitment report so the client could easily see cancelled interviews. Mention *drilldowns* to clients, that is, paths to get from summary information to detail information. This can occur by having "interactive" reports on a Web page that allow you to click a summarized figure or a bar on a graph to open another report that breaks down detail. These are very intuitive to managers and often elicit "oohs" and "aahs."

The next step in the design process is to create a list of the criteria for the report. I generally recommend being generous in this area as you can't really have too many criteria unless the users would literally be confused by the sheer number of them. For each criteria you'll need to know if the user can select one or many options, a date range, yes/no options, and different sorting options. Also, you'll need to indicate if certain criteria are mandatory in order to run the report. For example, the criteria description of the Sales by Group Report shown in Figure 1-3 may be

- Sale date from-to range (mandatory)

- Group (one or multiple)

- Product (one or multiple)

- Include discontinued products? Yes/No

- Sort options: On hand, Quantity Sold, Sale Amount

Generally, date criteria should be expressed as a range. If the user only needs one day's worth of information, the "from" and "to" dates are set to the same value. The option of selecting one or multiple criteria, as in the case of the group or product, is expressed in the user interface as a combo box or a multiselect list box, respectively. Finally, the Yes/No options, such as whether or not to include discontinued products in the sales summary, can be expressed with a check box. Sort options belong in a combo box as there is usually only one sort option per report, unless you really need to allow primary, secondary, or even tertiary sorts. When multiple sort options are necessary, you may wish to consider adding Ascending/Descending options next to each sort selection. Often what the client thinks of as a distinct report is simply the same report sorted a different way. Chapter 3 completely explains the technical implementation of these criteria screens.

Report headers are another design element the client needs to approve. Generally, headers will display the name of the company (and, optionally, the company logo), the date and time the report is run, and the page number. Normally, the title of the report is displayed in a larger font in the center. You may wish to display the name of the user who ran the report or even a disclaimer stating that the material included within the report is confidential. Report headers should be consistent across all reports in an application. How critical it is to agree upon report headers at the beginning of the process depends in large part on the report development tool you are using. Crystal Reports, for example, has no easy way of centralizing headers in one location such that a change in one is reflected in all reports. If you are using VS-View or Preview for .NET, report headers can be centralized in one function call that will enable you to change them as needed.

Make sure the report specs are made available to everyone who could possibly have a comment on their final appearance and data composition. Any changes can be discussed at meetings without you, the developer, present. Let the clients fight it out amongst themselves. Doing so will keep you largely insulated from the often excruciating debates as to how data should be organized and presented. In addition, by involving users and management at all levels who wish to participate, no one can truthfully say "I was never consulted" when they end up with a product that isn't exactly what they want. A technically savvy product or project manager, if not the developer, should be at meetings to handle immediate questions about the technical feasibility of including certain data items and explaining and clarifying often complex relationships between data items. Failing to capture these requirements early on can cause distorted user expectations and ill will between development teams and customers.

Generally, tables that support the various data entry screens in the application need some facility to print out their contents. Since many of these tables consist of simply a primary key value and a verbal description, a generic print routine is easy to create. Usually these dictionary prints don't even warrant the entry of filter criteria. Other dictionaries are either more complicated and require customization or have a rather large number of records, at which point a criteria screen may be appropriate. These criteria should be discussed with the client during the design stage.

Report aesthetics are also an important topic for discussion. Are there times when color would be appropriate in the report? If so, there are two things to consider. First, color printers are not yet ubiquitous and you cannot depend on one always being available. PDF and Excel files, however, handle color easily, and if your report will largely be disseminated in one of these formats, you are in good shape. The second issue is that of color blindness. About eight percent of men and one half of one percent of women have some type of color-deficient vision. The genes that affect color deficiency belong to the X chromosome, hence the preponderance of male color blindness. Therefore, that sharp-looking grand total of red letters on a green background may be completely invisible to some of your users. For a complete explanation of the various issues regarding color deficiency, see the article "Can Color-Blind Users See Your Site?" at `http://msdn.microsoft.com`.

Export Options

Export options are another point to be decided upon. Normally, reports should print directly to the screen, that is, in "Print Preview," and from there the client has the option to send the data to the printer or export the data to Excel, ASCII, HTML, or Adobe Acrobat. You could also offer the option of exporting to an Access database. Find out if there are any special report export requirements.

Of course, the report itself could be entirely an export process. Several of my clients have asked me for reports that present a criteria screen and then simply export the results to Excel. They have no interest at all in printed output.

Preprinted Forms

Oftentimes you may need to print a report on a preprinted form, like an IRS 1040 or a W-2. If this is the case, you should examine whether the application really needs to print specific pieces of data at specific locations on the preprinted page, or simply reprint the entire form itself on blank paper. I have a client who was once spending $7,000 per year on preprinted forms. When I showed him that the same result could be achieved if he performed a mail-merge with a document composed in Microsoft Word, he was naturally elated at the annual savings. Moreover, he now has the flexibility of being able to change the document at will.

High-Volume Printing

High-volume printing raises issues that must be examined for cost efficiency. I have a client who is a New Jersey councilman who printed his constituent reports on an ink-jet printer. Ink-jet printers are relatively cheap, and a decent one can be purchased for about $100. The hidden costs here are the ink cartridges. With cartridges costing about $40 each, you don't want to do high-volume printing on an ink-jet printer. In fact, ink-jet printers are loss leaders for the printer industry, as the real profits are in the replacement ink cartridges. Since they are used up at a much faster rate than laser toner cartridges that cost twice as much, you'll end up spending more on ink-jet replacements than you will on toner. There are companies that also sell recycled toner cartridges at a sizable discount compared to new cartridges. In addition to this, ink-jet printers operate at only a fraction of the speed of laser printers. When my client indicated he wanted to print an annual newsletter to send to his 5,000 constituents, I recommended a laser printer. He now prints the text of the newsletter and merges the addresses as well.

Mass mailing can be a science unto itself. If your client needs do customized high-volume mailing pieces—for example, a monthly telephone bill as opposed to a supermarket circular where every recipient receives the same one—you may wish to examine an automated mailing solution. I have another long distance reseller client who sent thousands of telephone bills every month. The billing software creates print images of the bills and sends them to a Pitney Bowes machine that prints the bill, folds it, places it into a postage-paid window envelope, and seals it. Machines such as those sold by Pitney-Bowes are designed specifically for this type of high-volume mailing, and the staff are experts on how to sort and organize the letters to achieve the maximum bulk rate postage. If you have a requirement for customized high-volume mailing, examine the product solutions at `http://www.pb.com`.

If your volume of mail is so great that it cannot be realistically done in house, consider the services of a bulk mailing company. These firms have the computers and printing equipment to print millions of documents and mail them within a few days. Mailing firms are large, high-volume facilities, some of which print and mail several hundred million documents per year. You can use your software to produce print images according to specifications given to you by the mailing company and then e-mail the data to their facility. Optionally, you can simply give them the raw data, and they will create the print routines for you. Depending on cost, you can work out with them where your work will leave off and theirs will begin. Because it doesn't matter where the mailing company is located, you can contract with virtually any one in the country to obtain the most reasonable rates. Consider this option carefully—you could very easily become overwhelmed with printing and mailing tasks in a high-volume environment.

External Data

You'll need to make sure you can access all the data necessary for your report. A client may want to display sales figures by zip code and then match the zip code to a sales rep roster that you are not maintaining in your application's database. You then need to contact the folks who are the keepers of the sales rep roster and see about joining your tables with theirs or possibly inquire about an export from their system and an import into yours. Be careful here. The machinations you may need to undertake to satisfy a client's seemingly simple request to display sales rep names via a zip code join could add a day or two to the project. Also, going forward you are at the mercy of the owners of the source system. They may change their data structures without warning you, and you'll then need to scramble to adjust your applications to handle the change. I have had this happen to me on several occasions.

Legal Issues

One often overlooked area of report design is the legal implications of system output. Usually, data that is intended for internal corporate use is not an issue. Output that is intended for use external to the organization can often bring with it significant legal liability. As a rule, every report, certificate, fax, statement, or letter that is intended for use outside the organization should be passed by legal counsel for approval. Seemingly innocuous documents may have enormous legal ramifications, and these ramifications may be different from industry to industry.

For example, one of the first systems I ever built was a target market mailing system for the sales agents of a leading U.S. insurance company. A sales agent would buy a list of names, and my system would merge these names with a marketing letter. As I made the system more flexible, I allowed the users to create their own letters. They gladly did so without ever consulting with in-house legal counsel. There were no safeguards in place preventing an agent from sending out a letter promising, say, a guaranteed 20 percent return on a particular product. In the past, courts have ruled that such statements are binding on the company who issued them.

Documents as simple as account statements or even invoices can be potential traps for legal liability. Alert counsel to the format of these documents and exactly what information they contain. Counsel may create a disclaimer that accompanies the text of the document as a safeguard. Even these disclaimers have potential pitfalls, as some states do not recognize this proverbial "fine print" if the print is, literally, too fine. This means by law that if the font is too small, the courts will disregard the existence of the text as having been too small for someone to reasonably read.

Copyright is also a property right that must be guarded. The summarization of even publicly available data has long been held to be copyrightable. Therefore, a company like Dun & Bradstreet, which compiles business information on millions of business entities worldwide, has an intellectual property interest in the data it has collected and in the unique way it presents it. Therefore, it is necessary for any reports that may present this data to individuals outside the organization to affix a copyright notice declaring the information in the report to be proprietary. Absence of a copyright notice can make prosecuting a case for infringement difficult to impossible, as it is incumbent on the copyright owner to make a clear and visible declaration of ownership.

A good rule of thumb is to contact corporate counsel before distributing any information to the outside. The attorneys (and your client) will be impressed by your foresight on these legal issues and will appreciate the fact that you consulted them.

Availability and Distribution

The final design issue is to determine who needs to run the reports. Traditionally there is a Report option on the main menu of desktop-based applications from which criteria screens are launched and reports printed, displayed, and exported. While there may be only 20 users of your application, there may be 100 users of the reports. This is where hybrid application development comes into play. The past few years have seen an explosion in the development of applications for the Web, and the future will offer more opportunities as ASP.NET takes root. Therefore, it may make sense to select some or all of the reports that are needed by users who are not users of the application itself and create them as Web reports. Chapter 9 explains this process in more detail.

The Web is no longer the only way to make reports available to the masses. As PDAs become more prevalent, more users will want to access their data remotely via a wireless connection to the server. Due to the current state of PDA and wireless technology, you'll need to deal with a number of limitations when allowing reports to be transmitted to a PDA. Because of the slow connection speed, you'll need to limit the amount of data you can transmit between the server and the PDA. Note that this speed problem occurs with wireless modems. People using PDAs with wireless LAN cards enjoy speeds above 10 mbps. This will affect the way you design your reports, especially the HTML exports that PDA devices often use. Chapters 10 and 11 explain these concerns in more detail.

In many instances, users are more interested in receiving reports on a regular basis than they are in running them individually. This is known as the "push" versus "pull" approach. One of my clients has a personnel headcount report that lists the incoming, outgoing, and current employees and temps working in their respective groups. The managing director calls this the "Warm Cushion" report, as it tracks the number of warm cushions, or occupied seats, in the organization. The definitions of these groups are maintained in an organizational hierarchy table. Each Friday, an unattended process is run that loops through the names of each manager, determines what departments ultimately report to him or her, and then produces a report for those departments as a PDF file that is then automatically e-mailed to the manager for review. Chapter 7 explains how to use the VBA interface of such e-mail packages as Outlook and Lotus Notes to send these files.

Report Servers

Report servers are machines and software dedicated to the purpose of running reports. The decision as to whether or not you'll need a report server is the same as whether or not you'll need a fax server. If your automated reporting requirements are so great that they would interfere with an individual workstation user's productivity, then a dedicated machine needs to be considered.

NOTE   *See Chapter 9 for a discussion of using Crystal Reports with a report server.*

We'll take a look at a report server developed by AR Consulting, Inc. (http://www.arconsultinginc.com/rptsvr) to explain how a report server operates. A workstation connects to an ASP page on a Web server and indicates what report should be run and with what criteria. An example of this criteria screen is shown in Figure 1-4.

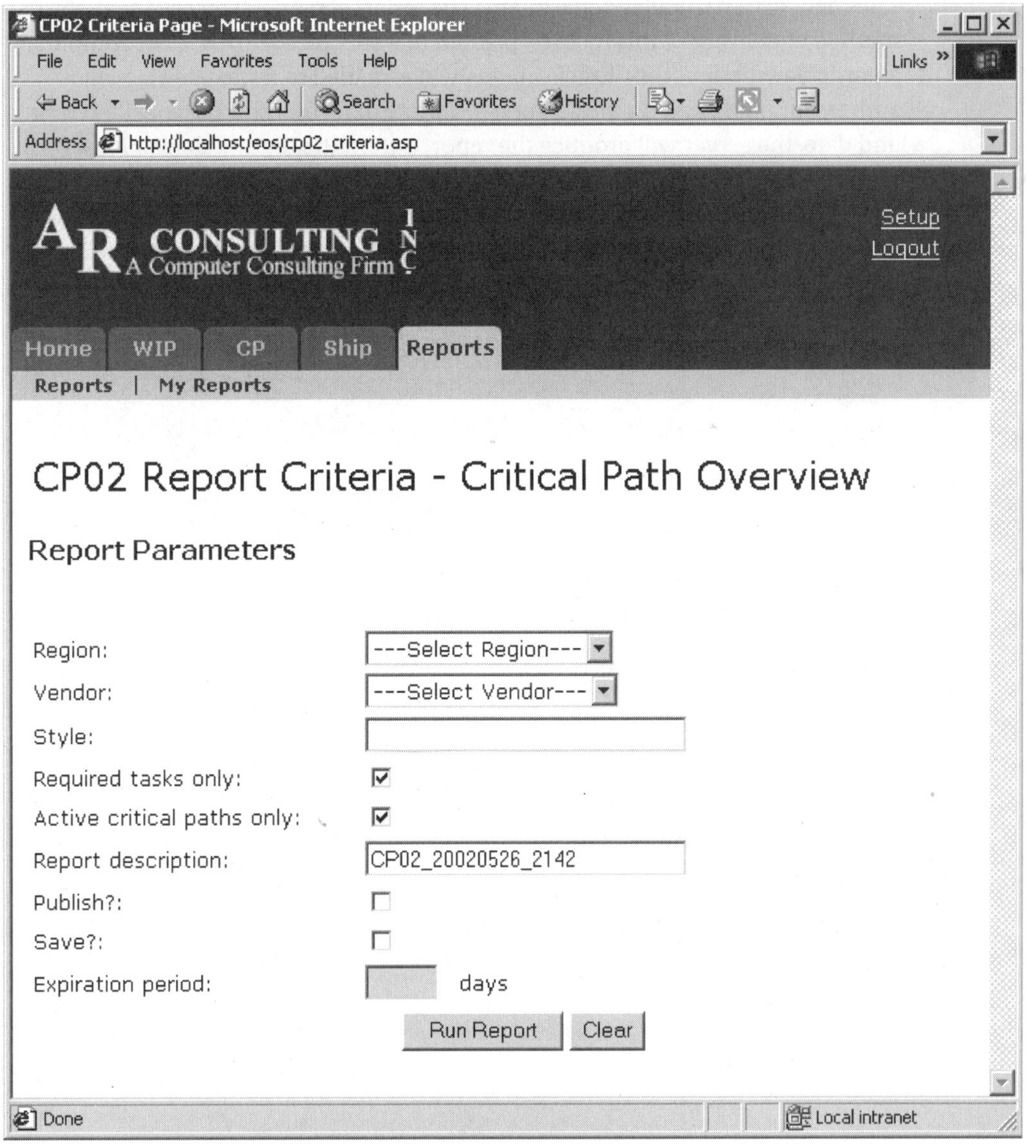

Figure 1-4. Criteria ASP page

This information is then appended to a table in the application's database located on a report server machine. It is this database that serves as the report queue. A report server–based ActiveX EXE continually monitors this queue and runs the requested report.

Report servers are often used to store a queue of those reports that need to run on a periodic basis. For example, a user may wish to request that the Sales by Product report be run every Friday at 3:00 p.m. and contain the previous week's sales data for a particular department. The report server will record the preferred method of delivery of this report—printed to a specified printer, PDF dump to a particular subdirectory, Excel spreadsheet e-mailed to a specified e-mail address, or published on the server in a variety of formats. At the specified time and date, the server will produce the report automatically and deliver it as requested, up through the expiration date of the report.

Most users request that the report, which can consist of a PDF, Excel, Word, or PowerPoint file, be stored on the server for later retrieval (see Figure 1-5).

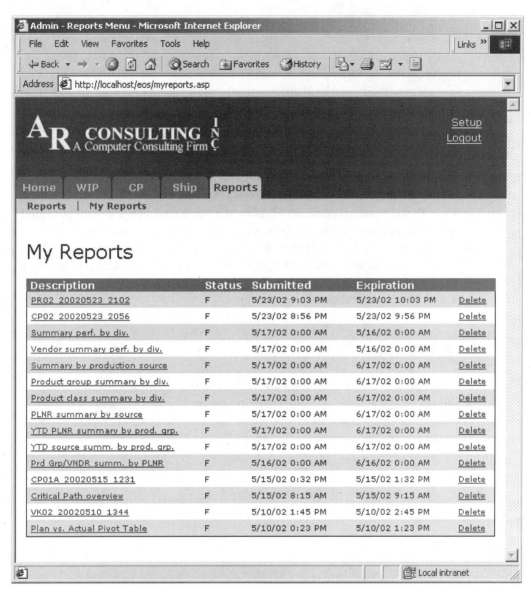

Figure 1-5. List of published reports

One of the great benefits of publishing reports to the server is that individual users don't need to run the same report from different workstations, wasting their time and putting an increased load on the server. Moreover, since users can view reports in the requested format, such as Excel XLS or Adobe PDF, these users can save them to their local hard disk using Microsoft Excel or Acrobat and take them on the road.

Security features allow the report owner to make the file available only to the user who requested it, a specific workgroup, or to all users. Since the queue is never erased, a log is kept of who ran what report, when, and with what criteria. Each report has an expiration period after which it will disappear from the list. The report queue itself stores the start and end times of each individual report job so that the system administrator might determine if jobs are taking too long and more memory or processors may be required. Several factors affect the length of time needed to generate a report, including the database server, database design, indexing, and performance tuning; the physical RAM and hardware performance characteristics of a server, such as RAID; and other loads on the server, if it's not a dedicated report server.

Conclusion

Proper report design is fundamental to the success of any application. Once you've completed your due diligences in selecting the reporting tools and presenting the layout and criteria options to the client, then you've paved the way for the actual development of the report.

CHAPTER 2

Introducing SQL and ADO

STRUCTURED QUERY LANGUAGE (SQL) is the lingua franca of relational databases, and a solid understanding of it is not optional. SQL is also the ultimate report writer and usually allows you to extract your data exactly in the format that you want it to print. This chapter reviews general SQL syntax and how it varies from one relational database management system (RDBMS) to another. Though most of the SQL examples in this chapter are run against the Northwind database that ships both with Microsoft SQL Server 2000 and Microsoft Access, we'll also examine dialects of SQL particular to Microsoft Access 2000, Oracle 8, and Sybase 12.

What Is SQL?

SQL, pronounced "sequel," was first developed in the late 1970s by IBM for a precursor of today's DB2 database. Since then, it has evolved into the de facto standard for RDBMSs. The good news about SQL is that even if you don't know it yet, it's easy to master the basics within a few hours. The syntax is very understandable and easy to follow. True mastery of SQL, though, can require years of experience, because different implementations of the same statement, though syntactically correct, perform with varying efficiencies on different databases of different sizes.

 TIP *For a good online SQL tutorial, check out* `http://www.geocities.com/SiliconValley/Vista/2207/sql1.html`.

What made SQL unique for its time was that it's a nonprocedural language. This means that SQL merely states what information is required but not how to obtain it. The database engine makes the decisions on how to best accomplish this. The beauty of SQL lies in the intelligence of the database server. Unlike so-called flat file databases such as dBase with its DBF files or spreadsheet databases that access records sequentially using a navigational approach, you do not need to explicitly specify the indices used to accelerate a search. Each RDBMS engine is programmed with the smarts to know what indices are needed from the context of the query and uses them automatically. For example, if an index existed for the EmployeeID column, the RDBMS would automatically use it to facilitate the following query:

```
SELECT EmployeeID
FROM Employees
WHERE Country = 'USA'
```

When you find it necessary to optimize your SQL queries for maximum performance, remember that you do have the ability to specify what indices should be used. The RDBMS doesn't take all the power away from you.

Each RDBMS implements its own dialect of SQL. Microsoft SQL Server 2000 and Sybase are the most syntactically similar to each other, as both implement a flavor called Transact-SQL, often abbreviated T-SQL. Oracle uses PL/SQL, and Access uses its own slightly different flavor of Transact-SQL. Fortunately, the data extraction commands of the different versions are about 90 percent the same.

Inline (Embedded) SQL Versus Stored Procedures

The question of whether to use inline SQL (using SQL within your own code, often as a string) versus stored procedures is one of the many philosophical questions in the profession of software development. The examples in this book use inline SQL merely because it serves to make the examples more readable. There are pros and cons to both approaches.

Some development shops use stored procedures exclusively so as to delineate application development from database development. After the software specification is approved, the database developer determines what SQL statements and parameters will be needed to support each screen and report in the software. He or she then creates these as stored procedures. The programmer can then access the database only via these stored procedures. It is often dangerous to give an application access to table objects directly, and it is more secure to limit access solely to stored procedures. Stored procedures are less prone to security violations and destructive actions. Plus, granting EXECUTE rights on a procedure is simpler than granting SELECT, UPDATE, INSERT, and DELETE rights for each table object based on users.

Inline SQL is easier to manage in some cases, as the developer has the freedom to change SQL statements at will, recompile the application, and distribute an updated version of the software without being concerned about obtaining the necessary security permissions to make changes directly to the database. Often my clients will request that a new feature be added to a production application. I build this feature into the software on my development machine and then e-mail the compiled EXE to the client, who deposits it on the network. Presto: all users have the change immediately. While I could e-mail them a CREATE PROCEDURE script, this would take more work on their part, and in some companies only DBAs can make even the simplest changes to the database. You have the same freedom of maneuver in n-tier applications as well. In these cases, the data access code resides in a separate component. Provided no methods are added and no interfaces change, altering inline SQL inside a data access component insulates the main application from recompilation.

Stored procedures allow the SQL statements to be managed (centrally) on the database server itself. One of the most significant advantages is that stored procedures are precompiled and therefore preoptimized to the task at hand. When a stored procedure is executed, the RDBMS determines the most efficient use of indices and other resources required to execute the statement. This optimization path is then stored in the database so that the next time the stored procedure is called, the server engine doesn't need to "rethink" the best way to execute it. With inline SQL, the statement is recompiled each time it is executed, as the database engine has no memory of ever having run it before. Another advantage is that you can make changes to the stored procedures without having to recompile and distribute another EXE. On multiprogrammer projects, the discipline of documented stored procedures will prevent multiple developers from re-creating the same SQL statement in different areas of the program. A further advantage is that a stored procedure allows you to use the full power of the underlying SQL language, whether it be T-SQL or PL/SQL (Oracle's dialect of SQL), to shape and form the resulting data set to that which most closely meets your system requirements. True, you could always do this in the language in which the application is written, but if the same stored procedure returns result sets to more than one application, you'll save yourself a lot of coding by having all the work done once for all data consumers by the RDBMS.

If you need to meet halfway between inline SQL and a stored procedure, you could always pass a SQL statement to a stored procedure and execute it. The following code will do the trick for Microsoft SQL Server 2000:

```
CREATE PROCEDURE sp_ExecSQL

@SQL varchar(2000)

AS

EXEC(@SQL)
```

Of course, any SQL statement passed to sp_ExecSQL will not be precompiled. There is a security issue here as well. While users will not have rights to the tables, they will still need rights to the stored procedures. If they find out the names of these stored procedures, they could always invoke them from the database. One additional layer of security here is to send a password parameter to each stored procedure. If the password is not the correct one, the stored procedure won't execute.

NOTE *Triggers are essentially event handlers in a database that are fired whenever a specified action such as an INSERT, UPDATE, or DELETE statement is executed against a table. Often triggers handle complex data integrity logic, which, if it fails, causes the latest change to be rolled back.*

Data Manipulation Language

SQL is sometimes broken down into three sublanguages: Data Manipulation Language (DML), Data Definition Language (DDL), and Data Control Language (DCL), but it's DML that you'll use most often—particularly the warhorse SQL SELECT command. In the following sections, you'll learn the commands and components of DML. In total, there aren't a lot of DML commands to learn, but how they interact with one another is a science unto itself.

SELECT, FROM, and WHERE

SELECT and FROM are the two most fundamental parts of any SQL statement that extracts data. For example, the statement

```
SELECT *
FROM Employees
```

returns every column and every row from a table called Employees. Of course, there very easily could be thousands of records in a table, and it isn't usually desirable to deal with all of a table's rows and columns at once. As a rule, you should limit your search by using a WHERE clause and specifying only those columns that you need. For example, the statement

```
SELECT LastName, FirstName
FROM Employees
WHERE Country = 'USA'
```

returns the last name and first name of only those employees who live in the United States. As a rule, all columns containing dissimilar data (where the values aren't all 0, 1, or 2, for example) that are used in WHERE clauses should be indexed.

Case-Sensitive Naming

You'll discover that most "high end" RDBMSs are installed either as case-sensitive or case-insensitive by default—though you'll generally have the option of overriding the default for specific databases, perhaps even for individual tables or other database objects. The point is, you need to, well, be sensitive to case sensitivity. When SQL statements are run, the table and field names referenced must be in the proper case or an error may result. For example, without case sensitivity the following statement is perfectly valid and creates a table with three distinct columns:

```
CREATE TABLE CaseTest(
CaseSensitive varchar(30),
casesensitive varchar(30),
CASESENSITIVE varchar(30))
```

In order to avoid any problems with case, it makes sense to agree upon all upper- or lowercase object names. Consult with your DBA to determine if your organization has a naming standard.

Having Trouble with the Irish?

The presence of single quotes within a search string can be a bit tricky. Suppose you were looking for Mr. O'Conner. Would the presence of a single quote cause a problem? It depends. If you enclose the search string in double quotes as follows, you won't have a problem:

```
SELECT * FROM student WHERE last = "O'Conner"
```

However, the use of all single quotes like the example shown next will generate a syntax error:

```
SELECT * FROM student WHERE last = 'O'Conner'
```

To overcome this problem, you can replace the single quote with two single quotes—not a double quote. For example:

```
SELECT * FROM student WHERE last = 'O''Conner'
```

ORDER BY

Once you specify row criteria using the WHERE clause, you'll usually find it desirable to view the rows in a certain order. This is where the ORDER BY clause comes in. The statement

```
SELECT LastName, FirstName
FROM Employees
WHERE Country =  'USA'
ORDER BY LastName, FirstName
```

returns only the LastName and FirstName columns for those employees who live in the United States, and sorts the returned columns first by LastName and then by FirstName.

By default, ORDER BY returns data in ascending (alphabetical) order. SQL has a keyword for descending order, DESC, which can be applied individually to each column specified in the ORDER BY clause. To use the DESC keyword, adjust the previous query to appear as follows:

```
SELECT LastName, FirstName
FROM Employees
WHERE Country =  'USA'
ORDER BY LastName, FirstName DESC
```

In this case, the LastName column is returned in ascending (alphabetical) order, but the FirstName within each LastName is returned in descending order. For example:

```
LastName          FirstName
Jones             Fred
Smith             William
Smith             John
Smith             Abner
```

WARNING   *DESC is a reserved word. You may be tempted to abbreviate the name of a column called "Description" as "Desc"—Don't do it! Oracle, Sybase, and Microsoft SQL Server will generate an error. Access 2000 will allow you to create the column but will generate a syntax error when you try to reference the field name in a SQL statement.*

TIP   *If your report has multiple user-selected sort orders, one way to accomplish this in a stored procedure is to pass a value indicating the sort order and then change the ORDER BY clause using a CASE . . . END statement. The following example illustrates this technique using Microsoft SQL Server 2000:*

```
Declare @SortCol int

SET @SortCol = 2

SELECT CompanyName, ContactName, ContactTitle
FROM Customers
ORDER BY CASE
    WHEN @SortCol=1 THEN CompanyName
    WHEN @SortCol=2 THEN ContactName
END
```

Mathematical Operators

SQL SELECT statements use mathematical operators as well, creating in effect a virtual column. The following statement determines what life would be like if every order had its freight charges increased by ten percent.

```
SELECT OrderID, CustomerID, Freight, Freight * 1.10
FROM Orders
ORDER BY CustomerID, Freight DESC
```

This code returns the following:

OrderID	CustomerID	Freight	(No column name)
10835	ALFKI	69.5300	76.483000
10692	ALFKI	61.0200	67.122000
10952	ALFKI	40.4200	44.462000
10643	ALFKI	29.4600	32.406000
10702	ALFKI	23.9400	26.334000
11011	ALFKI	1.2100	1.331000
10625	ANATR	43.9000	48.290000
10926	ANATR	39.9200	43.912000
10759	ANATR	11.9900	13.189000
10308	ANATR	1.6100	1.771000

LIKE

Sometimes the data you are searching for doesn't always have an exact match. For example, a user may not know the exact spelling of a person's last name. By using the LIKE clause, the user can enter the first few letters of a string, and SQL will perform a partial search for that string using a wildcard—in this example an asterisk. For instance, the statement

```
SELECT EmployeeID, LastName, FirstName
FROM Employees
WHERE LastName LIKE 'Call%'
```

will return all columns for every row in which the last name begins with Call:

EmployeeID	LastName	FirstName
8	Callahan	Laura

The LIKE clause has many other options as well. For example, to find all last names where the third letter of the last name is "l," use the following statement:

```
SELECT LastName
FROM Employees
WHERE LastName LIKE '__l%'
(That's two underscores, the letter 'l', and a percent sign)
```

This returns

```
LastName
Callahan
Fuller
```

Similarly, the next statement returns those last names that have at least two letter a's:

```
SELECT LastName
FROM Employees
WHERE LastName LIKE  '%a%a%'
```

This code produces the following:

```
LastName
Buchanan
Callahan
Suyama
```

There are many other wildcard options that are listed in the documentation for the RDBMS you are using.

Column Concatenation (AS clause)

Often, you'll want to display fields from records in a certain format. Rather than create this format using additional lines of source code, the concatenation of fields can be accomplished directly in the SQL statement via the use of the AS clause. A common use of this technique is the concatenation of first and last names. The statement

```
SELECT LTrim(LastName) + ', ' + FirstName AS name
FROM Employees
```

which works with Access, SQL Server, and Sybase, will return every row in the student table similar to this format:

```
name
Davolio, Nancy
Fuller, Andrew
Leverling, Janet
Peacock, Margaret
Buchanan, Steven
Suyama, Michael
King, Robert
Callahan, Laura
Dodsworth, Anne
```

With Oracle, use of the plus sign (+) would return an error because it's employed to add numerics. Oracle uses the double pipe characters to concatenate strings, as follows:

```
SELECT LTrim(LastName) ||', '|| FirstName AS name
FROM Employees
```

NOTE   *AS is not simply for column concatenation; it is most often used for more descriptive column names or to identify an aggregate function or computed column.*

Nulls

A Null value is a data type that means specifically that no value has been entered into a particular field. There are many advantages to Nulls and many disadvantages as well. Mostly, the disadvantages lay in the confusion that they cause. For example, some data entry screens may have check boxes that default to a gray value. If the user does not manually click the check box to specify either yes or no, the underlying value can remain Null to indicate that the question was never answered as opposed to defaulting to, say, 0 for yes or -1 for no. To avoid confusion, you could always use a value of perhaps 1 to indicate an unknown value. Business rules for some applications often impose legal requirements that a user specifically click a check box, and this is one way to ascertain that this manual intervention happens.

A Null value must not be confused with an empty string (vbNullString). It is good practice to check the value of a control or object property before saving data. If the data is an empty string, you can then save a Null value to the field to indicate that no data was actually entered by the user. For example:

```
cSQL = "UPDATE Employees " & _
            "SET LastName = " & Iif(txtLastName = vbNullString, "Null", txtLastName)
```

To check for a Null value, simply use the IS NULL statement. For example:

```
SELECT LastName
FROM Employees
WHERE Region IS NULL
```

Conversely, this statement has the opposite effect:

```
SELECT LastName
FROM Employees
WHERE Region IS NOT NULL
```

Nulls can cause type-mismatch errors when running reports, so you need to check for their presence in your code. If you're printing the contents of a LastName column, the following syntax will work for a row with a value but will cause an error for a row with a Null:

```
VSPrinter.Table = oRS("LastName")
```

One way to avoid this trap is to prepend the column reference with a NullString value either on the print line or set it to a variable beforehand. Doing so will cause an automatic type conversion from a Null to a zero-length string. For example, use either this

```
VSPrinter.Table = "" & oRS("LastName")
```

or this

```
Dim cLastName As String
cLastName = "" & oRS("LastName")
VSPrinter.Table = cLastName
```

Be careful when you are working with numerics, however. You can prepend a column value with a zero in the same fashion as a string, but if the column value contains a negative number, you'll end up with an error. It's usually best to use an IsNull function to determine if there's a value or not. If not, you could always return a zero, an N/A, or whatever is appropriate. For example:

```
cLastName = Iif(IsNull(oRS("LastName"), vbNullSting, oRS("LastName"))
```

SELECTing Dates

Date manipulation is the one area where the different databases vary slightly. For example, the following statement works just fine with Sybase and Microsoft SQL Server:

```
SELECT *
FROM Employees
WHERE BirthDate = '12/08/1948'
```

Access and Oracle are a bit different. Access requires that the date be enclosed by pound (#) signs rather than quotes. For example:

```
SELECT *
FROM Employees
WHERE BirthDate = #12/08/1948#
```

However, with Oracle you'll need to format the date to the default system date format as follows:

```
SELECT *
FROM Employees
WHERE BirthDate = '08-DEC-1948'
```

Logical Operators (AND, OR, and NOT)

Just as with the logical operators in any programming language, SQL syntax allows the use of AND, OR, and NOT. For example, the statement

```
SELECT *
FROM Employees
WHERE Country = 'USA'
OR Country = 'UK'
```

returns all employees who live in either the United States or England, whereas

```
SELECT *
FROM Employees
WHERE Country = 'USA'
AND FirstName = 'Andrew'
```

returns all employees named Andrew who live in the United States. By comparison, the statement

```
SELECT *
FROM Employees
WHERE (Country = 'USA'
OR Country = 'UK')
AND FirstName = 'Andrew'
```

returns anyone named Andrew who lives in either the United States or England. Note how the OR condition is enclosed in parentheses. The reason is that this part of the statement is intended to be treated as one unit so that there are really only two criteria in this statement, not three. The SQL engine only returns rows that meet these two criteria: first, the country must be

```
Country = 'USA' OR Country = 'UK'
```

And second, the first name must be

```
FirstName = 'Andrew'
```

NOTE *In many RDBMSs, it's better to put the most restrictive criterion first in the WHERE clause order. In this example, if there are only three instances of Andrew and a thousand people who live in the United States, it's faster for the query engine to grab all instances of Andrew and then filter on the United States portion. Many RDBMSs will perform this optimization for you, but it doesn't hurt to set it up that way anyway.*

UNION

The UNION clause returns a data set that contains a combination of rows that meet the criteria of two SELECT statements. For example, given that the statement

```
SELECT Country
FROM Employees
WHERE Country = 'USA'
```

returns the following data:

```
Country
USA
USA
USA
USA
USA
```

And the statement

```
SELECT Country
FROM Employees
WHERE Country = 'UK'
```

returns this data:

```
Country
UK
UK
UK
UK
```

The UNION statement

```
SELECT Country
FROM Employees
WHERE Country = 'USA'
UNION
SELECT Country
FROM Employees
WHERE Country = 'UK'
```

returns the following unique values between the two statements:

```
Country
UK
USA
```

To return a nondistinct list, use the UNION ALL clause. For example, the statement

```
SELECT Country
FROM Employees
WHERE Country = 'USA'
UNION ALL
SELECT Country
FROM Employees
WHERE Country = 'UK'
```

returns these results:

```
Country
USA
USA
USA
USA
USA
UK
UK
UK
UK
```

In order for a UNION/UNION ALL to execute, the two statements must be structurally similar. This means that they must both pull the same number of columns of the same data type, though these columns may exist in two separate tables. The following SQL statement will return an error:

```
SELECT Country, LastName, FirstName
FROM Employees
WHERE Country = 'USA'
UNION ALL
SELECT Country, FirstName
FROM Employees
WHERE Country = 'UK'
```

And this one will return a data type conversion error:

```
SELECT Country, LastName, FirstName
FROM Employees
WHERE Country = 'USA'
UNION ALL
SELECT Country, FirstName, BirthDate
FROM Employees
WHERE Country = 'UK'
```

If you really need a dissimilar column set, substitute Null for the missing column name like this:

```
SELECT Country, LastName, FirstName
FROM Employees
WHERE Country = 'USA'
UNION ALL
SELECT Country, FirstName, Null
FROM Employees
WHERE Country = 'UK'
```

Or simply substitute another value like this:

```
SELECT Country, LastName, FirstName
FROM Employees
WHERE Country = 'USA'
UNION ALL
SELECT Country, FirstName, 'Missing First Name'
FROM Employees
WHERE Country = 'UK'
```

And you'll see results similar to this:

```
Country    LastName     FirstName
USA        Davolio      Nancy
USA        Fuller       Andrew
USA        Leverling    Janet
USA        Peacock      Margaret
USA        Callahan     Laura
UK         Steven       Missing First Name
UK         Michael      Missing First Name
UK         Robert       Missing First Name
UK         Anne         Missing First Name
```

BETWEEN

The BETWEEN clause is an alternative to using the greater than or equal to (>=) and less than or equal to (<=) operators when searching for data that falls within a certain range of values. The following two statements are identical:

```
SELECT ProductName, UnitPrice
FROM Products
WHERE UnitPrice BETWEEN 40 AND 50

SELECT ProductName, UnitPrice
FROM Products
WHERE UnitPrice >= 40 AND UnitPrice <= 50
```

IN

Similar to the BETWEEN clause, the IN clause retrieves records that have a column value found in a specified list of values. For example, the statement

```
SELECT *
FROM Customers
WHERE Country IN ('Germany', 'Sweden')
```

returns only those customers located in either Germany or Sweden.

A common use of the IN clause is to extract data that matches a set of values selected by the user in a list box as would be found on a report criteria screen. This usage is explained fully in Chapter 3.

> **NOTE** *You can only specify one column name with the IN keyword. The following statement would return an error:*
>
> ```
> SELECT *
> FROM Customers
> WHERE ID, Country IN ('Germany', 'Sweden')
> ```

DISTINCT

The DISTINCT clause returns unique values for the columns specified by eliminating any duplicates. For example, suppose you want to populate a combo box with the abbreviations of only those countries in which you have customers. You may wish to load a combo box that allows users to select from a list of existing countries before entering their own. Doing so will assist with maintaining—but will not guarantee—consistent spellings. Such a feature would be more appropriate to a data set that is finite but cannot realistically be assembled for storage in a comprehensive dictionary or display to the user—for example, the list of every city and town or every high school in the nation.

The following statement would retrieve a distinct list of countries:

```
SELECT DISTINCT Country
FROM Customers
ORDER BY Country
```

This statement returns the following list:

```
Country
Canada
Denmark
Finland
France
Germany
Ireland
Italy
Mexico
Norway
Poland
Portugal
Spain
Sweden
Switzerland
UK
USA
Venezuela
```

You could also achieve the same results via a GROUP BY clause:

```
SELECT Country
FROM Customers
GROUP BY Country
ORDER BY Country
```

GROUP BY clauses will be discussed later in the chapter.

Functions Within SQL

Every flavor of SQL offers a function set that can be used within SQL statements. One of the more commonly used is the UPPER() function, which returns the referenced field in uppercase. For example, the statement

```
SELECT UPPER(LastName)
FROM Employees
```

returns

```
(No column name)
BUCHANAN
CALLAHAN
DAVOLIO
DODSWORTH
FULLER
KING
LEVERLING
PEACOCK
SUYAMA
```

Note that because of the UPPER() function, the LastName column is returned with a default virtual name, not the actual column name. To assign a name to a virtual column, use the AS clause. For example:

```
SELECT UPPER(LastName) AS UpperLastName
FROM Employees
```

Functions Can Slow Down Searches

Take a look at the following two statements that were run against a 375,000 record Oracle table:

```
SELECT COUNT(*)
FROM requestor
WHERE UPPER(LastName) = 'SMITH'

SELECT COUNT(*)
FROM requestor
WHERE LastNameCap = 'SMITH'
```

The first statement forced each LastName field to be uppercase and compared it to the string SMITH. Its execution took 18 seconds. The second statement searched the LastNameCap field where all the data is already uppercase and its execution took about 1 second. Be careful when using functions against an entire table's worth of data.

Most RDBMSs allow you to create user-defined functions as database objects and then use them in SQL statements—essentially building an extension of SQL. For example, suppose you wanted to select the ages of a list of patients from an Oracle table. The following PL/SQL function would do the trick:

```
CREATE FUNCTION GetAge(birthdate IN date)
  RETURN NUMBER
  IS
    patientage number(5,2);
  BEGIN
    SELECT MONTHS_BETWEEN(patientdob, sysdate)/12 AS Age
    INTO patientage
    FROM adverseevent
    WHERE patientdob IS NOT NULL;
RETURN(patientage);
END;
```

Then to extract the ages, run the following SQL statement:

```
SELECT GetAge(patientdob) AS Age
FROM adverseevent
WHERE patientdob IS NOT NULL;
```

Use of RDBMS functions invokes the philosophical discussion of just how much data processing you wish to place on the server and how much in the application code. More data intensive calculations are best placed on the server using the database functions just discussed. See the sidebar "Inline (Embedded) SQL Versus Stored Procedures" at the beginning of this chapter for the pluses and minuses of server-side versus application-side processing.

SQL Aggregate Functions

SQL provides a number of aggregate functions, so called because they return aggregate statistics for a particular data set. In other words, aggregate functions return a summary of data in a table, but they do not return the actual data. You'll most likely want to use the AS clause with aggregate functions in order to provide a more English-like name for the summary column. For example, the statement

```
SELECT COUNT(*) AS ExpensiveFreight
FROM Orders
WHERE Freight > 400
```

will return the following aggregate result, displaying ExpensiveFreight as the column name followed by the number of orders where the shipping costs were greater than $400.

```
ExpensiveFreight
20
```

Aggregate functions return the total of non-Null values. For example, the statement

```
SELECT COUNT(*)
FROM Employees
```

returns 9, which is the total number of records in the Employee table. However, the statement

```
SELECT COUNT(Region)
FROM Employees
```

returns 5, the number of records where the Region column has a non-Null value. Adding a DISTINCT clause like the following returns 1, as there's only one unique non-Null value in the column:

```
SELECT COUNT(DISTINCT Region)
FROM Employees
```

TIP   *When possible, use COUNT(*) rather than COUNT(ColumnName). COUNT(*) executes much faster.*

COUNT is often used to determine how many records will be returned from a query. In executing a SQL statement, performance degradation generally does not come from finding the requested records—assuming your indices are structured appropriately—but from transporting them in the long haul across the network. The last thing you want to do is allow users to specify report criteria that would result in pulling the entire database down to their client machine. Because COUNT returns only one value, it can be used to determine if the main SQL query will take an inordinate amount of time to execute. For example, Listing 2-1 shows an instance of using the COUNT(*) function to warn a user if a specified criteria will return more than 1,000 records.

Listing 2-1. Determining the Number of Records Before Retrieving Them

```
cSQLCount = "SELECT COUNT(*) FROM Employees WHERE "
cSQL = "SELECT * FROM Employees WHERE "
cWhere = " LastName = " + Chr(34) + txtLastName  + Chr(34)
cSQL = cSQL + cWhere + " ORDER by LastName, FirstName "
cSQLCount = cSQLCount + cWhere
Set oRS = oConn.Execute cSQLCount
If oRS.Fields(0) > 1000 Then
    MsgBox "This query will return too many records. " & _
    "Please narrow the search criteria.", vbOKOnly, PROGNAME
    Screen.MousePointer = vbDefault
    Exit Sub
End If
'If no more than 1000 records will be returned, then go get the actual data
Set oRS = oConn.Execute cSQL
```

Restrict Record Access

In every application I release, I add in a management module that allows the system administrator to specify two values to control data access. The first value indicates the number of records that may be returned from any query without warning. The second indicates the maximum number of records that may be returned in total. Commonly, users will set these values at 500 and 1,000, respectively. This is important for several reasons. First, you don't want to allow a user to run any query, whether it be a report filter or a browser filter, that would return such a large amount of data that the server would overload or, worse, crash. Likewise, you don't want queries that would overload the client either, as when using a browser-based application and sending a large number of records such that the browser crashes or client system resources are completely used. Nor would you want a user to print a report, go to lunch, and then find out that the report was several hundred pages long. This is one of the reasons I always display all reports to the screen first, and then if the user wants to print it from there he or she can.

Second, there is the security consideration of having a user specify a report criteria that dumps the entire database to an export file, effectively making a copy of the entire system's data. Ordinarily, I would wrap the code in Listing 2-1 in a function that returns a Boolean value. If this function returns false, the maximum records message is displayed, and the report will not execute.

There are a number of other aggregate functions, including SUM, AVG, MIN, and MAX. I present a brief introduction to each aggregate function in the following sections.

SUM

SUM returns the sum of a specified column. For example, you could add up the only numeric column in the test table using the following statement:

```
SELECT SUM(Freight) AS TotalFreight
FROM Orders
```

AVG

AVG returns the average of a specified column. For example, you could use AVG to return the average shipping costs per order by using the following statement:

```
SELECT AVG(Freight) AS TotalFreight
FROM Orders
```

MIN and MAX

MIN and MAX return the minimum and maximum values for a data set. The statements

```
SELECT MAX(Freight) AS MaxFreight
FROM Orders
```

and

```
SELECT MIN(Freight) AS MinFreight
FROM Orders
```

return the minimum and maximum shipping charges for all orders in the system.

Mixing Aggregate Functions

Aggregate functions can also be used simultaneously within the same SQL query to return a statistical summary of the database. For example, the statement

```
SELECT MIN(Freight) AS MinFreight,
MAX(Freight) AS MaxFreight,
AVG(Freight) AS AvgFreight,
SUM(Freight) as SumFreight
FROM Orders
```

returns this data:

MinFreight	MaxFreight	AvgFreight	SumFreight
.0200	1007.6400	78.2442	64942.6900

GROUP BY

The GROUP BY clause returns summary values for a specified field or group of fields. This clause is usually used in combination with an aggregate function. If you're ever asked to create a frequency distribution report, you'll need the GROUP BY clause. For example, the statement

```
SELECT Country, COUNT(Country) AS CountryCount
FROM Customers
GROUP BY Country
ORDER BY Country
```

returns a list of every unique country in the Customers table and shows the number of customers located in each country:

Country	CountryCount
Argentina	3
Austria	2
Belgium	2
Brazil	9
Canada	3
Denmark	2
Finland	2

```
France        11
Germany       11
Ireland       1
Italy         3
Mexico        5
Norway        1
Poland        1
Portugal      2
Spain         5
Sweden        2
Switzerland   2
UK            7
USA           13
Venezuela     4
```

A GROUP BY clause must contain all the nonaggregate columns referenced by the SELECT statement or an error will occur. For example, examine the following SQL statement:

```
SELECT CompanyName, Address, City, Region, Country, COUNT(Country)
FROM Customers
GROUP BY CompanyName, Address, City, Region, Country
ORDER BY Country
```

Because the CompanyName, Address, City, Region, and Country columns are referenced in the SELECT statement, they must be referenced in the GROUP BY clause as well. Make sure that your GROUP BY clause only groups the minimum number of fields necessary. The more columns you specify, the longer your query will take to execute.

HAVING

HAVING is used to further restrict the summary records returned from a GROUP BY statement, similar to a WHERE clause. For example, to refine the preceding statement to show only those countries having two customers, use a HAVING clause as follows:

```
SELECT Country, COUNT(Country) AS CountryCount
FROM Customers
GROUP BY Country
HAVING COUNT(Country) = 2
ORDER BY Country
```

This statement returns the following list:

Country	CountryCount
Austria	2
Belgium	2
Denmark	2
Finland	2
Portugal	2
Sweden	2
Switzerland	2

Or, you can examine the results for Sweden. Note the use of the WHERE clause, as the name of the country is not part of the aggregate. HAVING only operates on the aggregated portion of the query.

```
SELECT Country, COUNT(Country) AS CountryCount
FROM Customers
WHERE Country = 'Sweden'
GROUP BY Country
ORDER BY Country
```

This statement returns the following:

Country	CountryCount
Sweden	2

Joins

The true power of SQL lies in its ability to relate data between tables via join statements. This is where the relational part of a relational database is clearly seen and where you'll first start to suffer if your tables aren't normalized. Joins are usually created by choosing two or more tables and linking them on a common column. (We say "usually" because you could execute a self join, which joins a table to itself.) The columns involved in joining tables should be indexed, or the performance degradation could be severe depending on the size of the tables. It's best to join tables on numeric columns rather than strings, as numeric comparisons evaluate faster. Note that you can't join binary large object (BLOB) fields.

Primary Keys, Foreign Keys, and Relationships

Each row in a table must be unique; that is, there must be some way to distinguish one row from any other row in the same table. This is done via the primary key. The *primary key* is a single column or combination of columns that holds a unique value to identify each row in the table. Therefore, a primary key can never contain a Null value. Even part of a multicolumn primary key cannot contain a Null. In Microsoft SQL Server, if you choose to make a nondescriptive sequentially numbered column a primary key, you can execute a Column Constraint in DDL or use Enterprise Manager to assign it as the primary key. To make it automatically generate a new key value, you can set the AutoIncrement property of the column. In Oracle, you would create a column of type numeric and feed from a sequence incrementor established in the database. Either way, the row is uniquely identified.

There are other ways to create a primary key. Some developers use one of the columns in the table that would, by virtue of company business rules and the kind of data the column stores, contain a unique value. All columns, or combination of columns, that contain unique values are called *candidate keys* from which the primary key is derived. The primary key can be a simple one; that is, composed of one column only or a composite composed of multiple columns. Whichever type of primary key you choose, keep two points in mind: First, try to choose the minimum number of columns necessary, and second, choose a key that seldom, if ever, changes. Social Security numbers, for example, or student numbers could uniquely identify each student. This approach, though, assumes that the Social Security Administration or the registrar's office did not inadvertently assign the same number to two individuals. Just to be safe, use an AutoIncrement column and let the system generate the unique number. It will be transparent to the user. Using an AutoIncrement field as a primary key is generally done to increase join speeds and account for the fact that columns that are thought to be unique often aren't. As business rules change and duplicate values are found to be perfectly valid, primary keys based on real data often become invalid. As a rule, I use an AutoIncrement field as a primary key and create a unique index on any combinations of fields that comprise candidate, or alternate, keys. This enforces the business rule and guarantees uniqueness. It's also easier to deal with, since foreign keys store the AutoIncrement field, which is *always* unique, not the "real value" key, which can change.

Foreign keys are columns in one table that reference the primary keys in another table. In the example shown in Figure 2-1, the Hcountry column in the Student table is a foreign key, as it references the Code column in the Country table, which is a primary key.

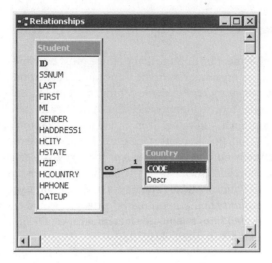

Figure 2-1. Primary and foreign keys

Relationships

There are three types of relationships between tables: one-to-many, many-to-many, and one-to-one.

One-to-many: *One-to-many relationships* are the most common type of relationship in any RDBMS. The classic example given in database primers is that of an accounts receivable system. Every row in the Invoice Header table has one or more related rows in the Invoice Detail table. This relationship is also known as a *parent/child* or *master/detail relationship*. The Student table in Figure 2-1 has a one-to-many relationship to the Country table. Here Country is the parent and Student is the child. One row in the Country table can have zero, one, or many rows in the Student table that reference that particular unique ID for country.

Many-to-many: In a *many-to-many relationship*, every row in the first table can relate to many rows in the second table. Likewise, every row in the second table can relate to many rows in the first table. Continuing the school example, a student can take many exams, and one exam—for example, a history final,—can be taken by many students. To accomplish this structurally, use a third table that links the student codes with the test codes. This table, StudentTest, acts as the parent table to its two children—Student and Test (see Figure 2-2).

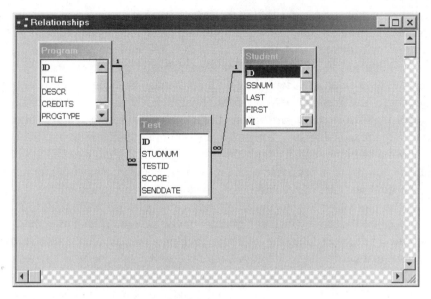

Figure 2-2. Many-to-many relationship

One-to-one: *One-to-one relationships* link a row in one table to only one row in another. These relationships are less common, as it would normally make more sense to eliminate the second table and include the second table's columns in the first table. One-to-one relationships are usually established to overcome limitations on the number of available columns allowed in one table. This practice was more common to xBase systems where file bloat could become a problem due to the static allocation of disk space. In an xBase file, a 100-character text field would consume 100 characters of disk space whether the field was empty or not. Therefore, many systems that had comment fields would often create a comment table in a one-to-one relationship so as not to bloat the main file if comments were not used in every record. Modern RDBMSs use dynamic allocation of disk space for data storage. If a field needs only 10 out of the 100 bytes available for it, then only 10 bytes are consumed. Practically, you should not have much need for one-to-one relationships anymore.

There are two main types of joins: inner and outer. First, let's look at how joins work.

RDBMSs use a cost-based query optimizer to determine the most efficient strategy to use when joining tables. The optimizer analyzes several statistics in determining how to proceed and treats base tables and nonbase tables differently.

For base table inputs, the optimizer analyzes the total number of records, the number of data pages (the more data pages that need to be read from disk, the more costly the query is), the location of the table, and the indices available. Indices are the key to carrying out a join efficiently, and they can affect a join based on several elements, including the level of duplicated values, number of index pages, and presence of Null values. Highly selective indices—indices that have few duplicate values—are the most efficient indices to use in joins. Unique indices are the most highly selective. Because your joins will almost invariably occur using a unique primary key index, duplicate values should not be a problem. The number of index pages is also important. Like data pages, the more index pages that must be read from disk, the less efficient a query will be.

For nonbase table inputs, the optimizer looks at record counts and input costs. Because the input consists of another query, the cost of executing that query must be factored into the total cost. Each possible join combination is then examined to determine which join will offer the least costly execution. To accomplish this, the RDBMS first selects a base table access strategy. The optimizer then stores the estimated number of records returned and generates all combinations of pairs of tables—the *Cartesian join*, also known as a *cross join*—and determines the cost of each combination. This method takes every row in every table and matches it with every other row. In the SQL Server example, the Customers table (91 rows) is joined with the Orders table (830 rows) and the Products table (77 rows). This forms a join of 5,815,810 unique permutations, ($91 \times 830 \times 77 =$ 5,815,810). To view this record set, simply execute the statement

```
SELECT *
FROM Customers, Orders, Products
```

Better yet, don't execute this statement, as you'll be waiting quite a long time—just take my word for it. Cross joins are something you usually execute by accident only to be yelled at by the DBA. Try this statement instead:

```
SELECT COUNT(*)
FROM Customers, Orders, Products
```

Once the Cartesian product has been formed, the conditions in the WHERE clause are then applied, and the rows that do not satisfy the join are eliminated.

Now that you have an idea of how joins work, let's take a look at the different types of joins. We'll kick off our discussion by looking at inner joins.

INNER JOIN

An *inner join*, also known as an *equi-join*, links records from two tables where both tables have a match in a common field. If matching records don't exist in both tables, no records will be returned. Since there are no examples of this in the Northwind database (at least that I could find), I added a fake Employee table entry—Fred Flintstone—to illustrate the point. As a new employee, Fred has not made any sales. Therefore, the following Transact-SQL statement will not return his name:

```
SELECT LastName, FirstName, OrderID
FROM Employees e INNER JOIN Orders o
ON e.EmployeeID = o.EmployeeID
```

Or, in the older syntax:

```
SELECT LastName, FirstName, OrderID
FROM Employees e, Orders o
WHERE e.EmployeeID = o.EmployeeID
```

See the sidebar "Old Versus ANSI SQL-92 JOIN Syntax" later in this chapter for a discussion of the old versus the new JOIN syntax.

Alias Those Table Names!

In the interest of brevity, table names can be aliased. When you are dealing with columns from multiple tables, it's good practice to prefix those columns with an identifier that indicates to which table a column belongs. In cases where two tables have identically named columns, aliasing is mandatory so as not to confuse the SQL engine and trigger some form of an ambiguous field reference error. In the SQL statement

```
SELECT LastName, FirstName, OrderID
FROM Employees e INNER JOIN Orders o
ON e.EmployeeID = o.EmployeeID
```

using e and o yields a much shorter SQL statement than writing out the full table name. Note that aliases can be case sensitive.

OUTER JOIN

Outer joins come in two varieties: left and right. "Left" and "right" refer to the direction the join is heading relative to the position of the table in the FROM clause. A *left join* returns a row from a table on the left side of the FROM clause, whether or not a matching record exists on the right side. Conversely, a *right join* returns a row from a table on the right side of the JOIN statement, whether or not a matching record exists on the left side. This concept is a little tricky to express verbally, so let's look at some examples. The following statement displays the use of a left join in Transact-SQL:

```
SELECT LastName, FirstName, OrderID
FROM Employees e LEFT OUTER JOIN Orders o
ON e.EmployeeID = o.EmployeeID
```

You may also see such a join expressed using the *= operator in a WHERE clause in older systems as follows:

```
SELECT LastName, FirstName, OrderID
FROM Employees e, Orders o
WHERE e.EmployeeID *= o.EmployeeID
```

In Oracle's PL/SQL, you indicate a left join like so:

```
SELECT LastName, FirstName, OrderID
FROM Employees e, Orders o
WHERE e.EmployeeID = o.EmployeeID(+)
```

Either way, these statements partially return the following:

LastName	FirstName	OrderID
Dodsworth	Anne	11017
Dodsworth	Anne	11022
Dodsworth	Anne	11058
Flintstone	Fred	NULL

The following statement returns the same result set as the preceding statement except that the position of the table names is reversed:

```
SELECT LastName, FirstName, OrderID
FROM Employees e, Orders o
WHERE o.EmployeeID =* e.EmployeeID
```

This partially returns the following:

LastName	FirstName	OrderID
Dodsworth	Anne	11017
Dodsworth	Anne	11022
Dodsworth	Anne	11058
Flintstone	Fred	NULL

Suppose you want to return a list of all employees who do not yet have any sales. The SQL statement

```
SELECT LastName, FirstName, OrderID
FROM Employees AS e FULL OUTER JOIN Orders AS o
ON o.EmployeeID = e.EmployeeID
WHERE o.OrderID IS NULL
```

would do the trick:

LastName	FirstName	OrderID
Flintstone	Fred	NULL

Let's look at a slightly more complex example that joins multiple tables using the older syntax. The following statement lists every employee in the table (whether they have made any sales or not), the company they sold to, the name of who shipped the order, and the order number:

```
SELECT e.LastName, e.FirstName, c.CompanyName AS CustomerName,
s.CompanyName AS ShipperName, o.OrderID
FROM Employees e, Orders o, Customers c, Shippers s
WHERE e.EmployeeID = o.EmployeeID
AND o.CustomerID = c.CustomerID
AND o.ShipVia = s.ShipperID
ORDER BY e.LastName, CustomerName
```

A portion of the output appears below:

LastName	FirstName	CustomerName	ShipperName	OrderID
Buchanan	Steven	Berglunds snabbköp	Speedy Express	10654
Buchanan	Steven	Berglunds snabbköp	Speedy Express	10866
Buchanan	Steven	Blondesddsl père et fils	United Package	10297
Buchanan	Steven	Bon app'	Speedy Express	10730
Buchanan	Steven	Chop-suey Chinese	United Package	10254
Buchanan	Steven	Familia Arquibaldo	Federal Shipping	10650
Buchanan	Steven	Folk och fä HB	Federal Shipping	10378

Self Join

A *self join* allows a table to be joined with itself. In order to accomplish this, the table must be given two aliases to distinguish the two instances of the table within the SQL statement. In the following example, we are looking for employees who live in the same city within the United States. The statement

```
SELECT e1.LastName, e1.FirstName, e2.LastName, e2.FirstName
FROM Employees e1, Employees e2
WHERE e1.Country = 'USA'
AND e1.City = e2.City
AND e1.EmployeeID < e2.EmployeeID
ORDER BY e1.LastName, e1.FirstName
```

returns

LastName	FirstName	LastName	FirstName
Davolio	Nancy	Callahan	Laura

The last clause, AND e1.EmployeeID < e2.EmployeeID, eliminates rows in the result set where the employee IDs match themselves.

A similar instance where a table needs two aliases is when multiple joins are being made to the same table. In the following simplified statement taken from a pharmaceutical quality assurance application using Access SQL, the report will display the study number, director name, and monitor name. Both the director and monitor names are taken from the Personnel table to which the StudInfo table is joined via the director and monitor personnel IDs stored in StudInfo. At first, you may try something like this:

```
SELECT s.studnum,  p.last & ', ' & p.first AS monitor,
p.last & ', ' & p.first AS director
FROM studinfo s, personnel p
WHERE s.moncode =  p.persid
AND s.dircode =  p.persid
ORDER BY s.studnum
```

However, this query will try to simultaneously match both instances of the personnel IDs to the Personnel table and return a result set similar to the following:

A-001	,	,

This next statement creates two aliased references to the Personnel table, so the joins are now distinct and successful, as follows:

```
SELECT s.studnum,  pmon.last & ', ' & pmon.first AS monitor,
pdir.last & ', ' & pdir.first AS director
FROM studinfo s, personnel pmon, personnel pdir,
s LEFT JOIN pmon ON s.moncode =  pmon.persid,
s LEFT JOIN pdir ON s.dircode =  pdir.persid
ORDER BY s.studnum
```

This statement returns the following list:

Studnum	monitor	director
A-001	Kilburn, Jon	Huebsch, Wendy

....

Old Versus ANSI SQL-92 JOIN Syntax

In this section you've seen references to the "older" syntax and several examples of how joins are performed by the WHERE clause instead of the FROM clause. Use of the WHERE clause for joins and the *= syntax for outer joins is a leftover from the days when Sybase and Microsoft were the joint developers of SQL Server. While this legacy approach is somewhat easier to read and work with, it also has some limitations, especially at times when you're joining multiple tables, and the use of JOINs in the FROM clause is the recommended method moving forward. You can see an example of this limitation in the following SQL statements, which can be run against SQL Server's Northwind database. This first SQL statement will return the requested data:

```
SELECT LastName, FirstName, OrderDate, Quantity, UnitPrice
FROM Employees LEFT OUTER JOIN Orders ON Employees.EmployeeID = Orders.EmployeeID
LEFT OUTER JOIN [Order Details] ON Orders.OrderID = [Order Details].OrderID
```

This second one uses the older join syntax

```
SELECT LastName, FirstName, OrderDate, Quantity, UnitPrice
FROM Employees, Orders, [Order Details]
WHERE Employees.EmployeeID *= Orders.EmployeeID
AND Orders.OrderID *= [Order Details].OrderID
```

and returns the following error:

```
Query contains an outer-join request that is not permitted.
```

Subqueries

A *subquery* is a query that is passed as a parameter to another query. Effectively, you are nesting one query within another. For example, suppose you wanted to list the names of all employees who report to the same person employee number 3—Janet Leverling—reports to. The following SQL statement would execute the subquery first to return Janet Leverling's report to ID and then proceed to retrieve the detail information for the report to ID:

```
SELECT LastName, FirstName
FROM Employees
WHERE ReportsTo =
(SELECT ReportsTo
FROM Employees
WHERE EmployeeID = 3)
```

This statement results in the following:

LastName	FirstName
Davolio	Nancy
Leverling	Janet
Peacock	Margaret
Buchanan	Steven
Callahan	Laura

In the following example, we are using a subquery to retrieve the name and country of all rows in the employee table where there are at least five employees in the same country:

```
SELECT LastName, FirstName, Country
FROM Employees
WHERE Country IN
(SELECT Country
FROM Employees
GROUP BY Country
HAVING Count(*) > 4)
ORDER BY Country
```

As you'd expect, this statement returns

LastName	FirstName	Country
Davolio	Nancy	USA
Fuller	Andrew	USA
Leverling	Janet	USA
Peacock	Margaret	USA
Callahan	Laura	USA

As mentioned earlier, subqueries can be nested several levels deep, but there is a limit. Eventually, the database engine will inform you when a query is too complex to process. At that point, you will need to break the statement into smaller parts, write the results to a temporary table, and apply the remainder of the query against the temporary table.

Correlated Subqueries

A *correlated subquery* is one that references the tables of the query that contains it. These types of queries are used to mimic a loop because for each row in the outer queries, the subquery is invoked with different parameters. The downside here is that the subquery is evaluated once for every row in the outer query, resulting in a performance hit.

The following example is from a human resources application that stores personnel names in a Personnel table and the start dates that a person had for each department in which they ever worked in a departmental history table called DeptHist. This statement returns the names and departments of all persons who have a departmental start date that is after January 1, 2003, where the department is not also their current department. The current department is stored in the DeptID column in the Personnel table. True, this is not a normalized relationship, but it was necessary to more efficiently support other functionality in the system.

```
SELECT DISTINCT g1.PersonnelID, g1.DeptID, g1.DateFrom, p.LastName
FROM DeptHist g1, Personnel p
WHERE g1.PersonnelID = p.ID
AND DateFrom =
(SELECT MAX(DateFrom)
FROM DeptHist g2
AND PersonnelID IN
(SELECT g.PersonnelID
FROM DeptHist g,  Personnel p
WHERE g.DateFrom > "01/01/2003"
AND g.PersonnelID = p.ID
AND g.DeptID <> p.DeptID)
GROUP BY g1.PersonnelID, g1.DeptID,  g1.DateFrom, p.LastName
ORDER BY PersonnelID, DateFrom DESC
```

Be careful not to use a correlated subquery when a join will suffice, as joins execute faster. The documentation for Microsoft SQL Server gives an example of a correlated subquery for returning all authors who earn 100 percent of royalties on a book as follows:

```
SELECT au_lname, au_fname
FROM authors
WHERE 100 IN
    (SELECT royaltyper
    FROM titleauthor
    WHERE titleauthor.au_ID = authors.au_id)
```

The following join statement will accomplish the same result:

```
SELECT DISTINCT au_lname, au_fname
FROM authors INNER JOIN titleauthor
ON titleauthor.au_ID = authors.au_id
AND royaltyper = 100
```

N-Level Trees

One of the coolest—and often the most complicated—sets of data relationships that you can define are *n-level trees*, also referred to as *hierarchies*. The two most common business examples of n-level trees are the organizational chart and the multilevel marketing model. Since I have a client who does multilevel marketing, let's take an example from his application. This client is a reseller of long-distance phone service. Sales reps receive a commission on their sales as well as the sales of the people they sponsor, and the people in turn sponsored by those people, and so on, down a maximum of seven levels. This means that each sales rep record has both a sales rep ID and a sponsor ID. At commission time, the application must create the often-labyrinthine downlines for each sales rep in the database. Take a look at the following set of sample data:

ID	LASTNAME	FIRSTNAME	SPONSORID
2	Rubble	Barney	1
3	Rubble	Betty	1
4	Flintstone	Wilma	1
5	Rockhead	Joe	2
6	Bunny	Bugs	2
7	Duck	Daffy	5
8	Fudd	Elmer	7
9	Coyote	Wile E.	6
1	Flintstone	Fred	0

Here we have a set of dealers and their sponsors. Fred Flintstone is the anchor dealer and is effectively unsponsored. By looking at the sponsor IDs, you can see that Fred (ID = 1) has sponsored three dealers (Barney, Betty, and Wilma). Using the following Oracle-specific SQL statement, we can extract the hierarchy for this downline. The command COL name FORMAT a20 and Oracle's LPAD function are used here only to make the output more readable when run from the SQL Plus command line:

```
COL name FORMAT a20;
SELECT lpad(' ', (level-1) * 4) || LastName||', '|| FirstName name,
level, ID, SponsorID
FROM Dealers
START WITH SponsorID = 0
CONNECT BY PRIOR ID = SponsorID;
```

This statement will produce the following output. The level column is a virtual column returned by the SQL statement and does not actually exist in the table.

NAME	LEVEL	ID	SPONSORID
Flintstone, Fred	1	1	0
Rubble, Barney	2	2	1
Rockhead, Joe	3	5	2
Duck, Daffy	4	7	5
Fudd, Elmer	5	8	7
Bunny, Bugs	3	6	2
Coyote, Wile E.	4	9	6
Rubble, Betty	2	3	1
Flintstone, Wilma	2	4	1

Transact-SQL unfortunately does not provide specific syntax for n-level hierarchies as Oracle does. The same effect is obtained by utilizing a temporary table and looping through each level as shown in Listing 2-2.

Listing 2-2. Transact-SQL N-Level Tree

```
DROP TABLE  #Dealer, #temp

CREATE TABLE #temp (level int, ID int)
CREATE TABLE #Dealer (seq int identity, level int, ID int)

DECLARE @level int, @curr int
SELECT TOP 1 @level=1, @curr=ID
FROM Dealer
WHERE ID=SponsorID

INSERT INTO #temp (level, ID)
VALUES (@level, @curr)

WHILE (@level > 0) BEGIN

  IF EXISTS(SELECT *
      FROM #temp
      WHERE level=@level)
BEGIN
```

```
        SELECT TOP 1 @curr=ID
        FROM #temp
        WHERE level=@level

        INSERT #Dealer (level, ID)
        VALUES (@level, @curr)

        DELETE #temp
        WHERE level=@level
        AND ID=@curr

        INSERT #temp
        SELECT @level+1, ID
        FROM Dealer
        WHERE SponsorID=@curr
        AND SponsorID <> ID

        IF (@@ROWCOUNT > 0) SET @level=@level+1
    END ELSE
        SET @level=@level-1

END

SELECT REPLICATE(CHAR(9),level)+i.LastName + ', ' +
i.FirstName AS DealerName, level
FROM #Dealer d JOIN Dealer i ON d.ID = i.ID
ORDER BY seq
```

This statement produces the results shown here:

DealerName	Level
Flintstone, Fred	1
Rubble, Barney	2
Flintstone, Wilma	3
Rockhead, Joe	3
Bunny, Bugs	4
Fudd, Elmer	5
Rubble, Betty	2

> **NOTE** *SQL can get rather complex, and there are many gray areas as to what constitutes the most efficient method of extracting data. I've personally seen SQL statements as perfectly crafted as a Shakespearean sonnet, and it is very easy to get caught up in writing the most elegant logic. Remem-ber, there are no Nobel prizes for literature awarded to the most profound SQL statement, but there are signifi-cant financial awards to those developers who deliver their client applications on time and within budget. If you can achieve your ship date by using a slightly less efficient SQL statement (without, of course, seriously compromising sys-tem performance or client development standards), then it is often best to do so rather than delay the project.*

DDL and DCL

As mentioned previously, in addition to DML, which we just covered, there are also DDL and DCL to consider. DDL deals primarily with the INSERT, UPDATE, and DELETE aspects of SQL programming, whereas DCL handles the command to create and modify database objects like tables, indices, or sequences. To learn more, check out the books recommended in the next section or visit http://www.sqlcourse.com.

Recommended Reading

Following are a few SQL books that I highly recommend:

- *Joe Celko's SQL for Smarties: Advanced SQL Programming,* by Joe Celko (Morgan Kaufmann Publishers. ISBN: 1-55860-576-2): Honestly, any book by Joe Celko is worth many times the purchase price. You can read his many articles dealing with advanced SQL issues at http://www.intelligententerprise.com.

- *The Guru's Guide to Transact-SQL,* by Ken Henderson (Addison-Wesley Publishing Co. ISBN: 0-201-61576-2)

- *Code Centric: T-SQL Programming with Stored Procedures and Triggers,* by Garth Wells (Apress. ISBN: 1-89311-583-6)

- *Advanced Transact-SQL for SQL Server 2000,* by Itzik Ben-Gan and Tom Moreau (Apress. ISBN: 1-89311-582-8)

These volumes have proven invaluable to me in my database development work over the last several years.

Database Access

No discussion of data retrieval and manipulation would be complete without covering Microsoft's ActiveX Data Objects (ADO) and ADO.NET. ADO is a vast subject and requires an entire book to cover all its features. Several excellent tomes have already been written on this subject. Personally, I would recommend *ADO.NET and ADO Examples and Best Practices for VB Programmers,* by William Vaughn (Apress. ISBN: 1-89311-568-2). Since this book deals with report writing, the discussion that follows covers those aspects of ADO that are most appropriate to this endeavor.

As a rule, most report routines extract data from a data source into a data object. The stored procedure name and parameters necessary to extract this data are often encapsulated in Command objects. Then, this data object is navigated through to the end, involving invariably a forward-only Recordset. You'll learn about these Command and Recordset objects in the following sections. But first, we'll look at the Connection object, which is needed to originate the others.

Connection Objects

The ADO Connection object is your first stop for any type of database access using ADO. Often, Connection objects are commonly kept in existence for the lifetime of the application. However, this approach often fails when working with high-concurrency applications. For these situations, you'll need to be aware of connection pooling. *Connection pools* are a collection of connections that are made available on an as-needed basis. Therefore, when you open and close connections only for the duration of the time you need them, a connection can be freed from the pool and made available to another user. You don't need one connection for every user on the system. Your data provider handles connection pooling for you automatically.

You can instantiate a Connection object by setting the ConnectionString property and invoking the Open method. For example:

```
Dim oConn As New ADODB.Connection
Dim cConnect As String
```

```
cConnect = "Provider=Microsoft.Jet.OLEDB.4.0;Data
Source=C:\Reports\SampleDatabase.mdb;Persist Security Info=False"
oConn.ConnectionString = cConnect
oConn.Open
```

If you are unsure of the text needed by the ConnectionString property, a quick way to construct it is to drop a Microsoft ADO data control onto a VB form and, using the wizard associated with the ConnectionString property, select your data source and build the string. Rather than hard-code your connection string, you could store it in a Universal Data Link (UDL) file. This UDL file is set as the value of the ConnectionString property. The negative aspect of using UDLs is that every time a connection is established, the UDL file needs to be opened, and this could slow performance a bit.

Command Objects

Command objects encapsulate the information needed to create a Recordset. Using a Command object, you can specify the type of data source you're dealing with, the data source itself, and any parameters that need to be passed. The two most common CommandType settings are represented by the enums adCmdStoredProc and adCmdText. As the name would suggest, adCmdStoredProc indicates that the text stored in the CommandText property is the name of a stored procedure, whereas adCmdText indicates that it's an inline SQL statement. The CommandTimeout property indicates the number of seconds to wait to execute the command before returning an error. The default value is 30. Look at the code in Listing 2-3.

Listing 2-3. ADO Command Object of CommandType = adCmdText

```
Dim oCmd As New ADODB.Command
Dim oRS As New ADODB.Recordset
Dim cSQL As String

cSQL = "SELECT * FROM Product"

With oCmd
    Set .ActiveConnection = oConn
    .CommandText = cSQL
    .CommandType = adCmdText
    .CommandTimeout = 20
    Set oRS = .Execute
End With
```

This very basic example creates a Recordset object from a SQL statement using the Command object's Execute method. In Listing 2-4, you'll see how to call a stored procedure with parameters using a Command object. For each parameter in your stored procedure, you'll need to add a corresponding entry in the Command object's Parameters collection. To do this, call the CreateParameter method of the Command object. This method requires a name, data type, direction, and value. The name is identical to the database parameter name used in your stored procedures. If using Microsoft SQL Server or Sybase, remember to preface each parameter name with the @ sign. The data type is commonly specified by using an enumerator, which loosely corresponds to a database field data type. The direction enumerator indicates whether the parameter is only sent to the procedure, or whether it is a value returned. A full discussion of Parameter Direction Enumerators can be found in the MSDN library.

Listing 2-4. ADO Command Object of CommandType = adCmdStoredProc

```
Dim oCmd As New ADODB.Command
Dim oRS As New ADODB.Recordset
Dim cSQL As String

cSQL = "sp_GetProduct"

With oCmd
    Set .ActiveConnection = oConn
    .CommandText = cSQL
    .CommandType = adCmdStoredProc
    .CommandTimeout = 20
    .Parameters.Append .CreateParameter("ID", adInteger, adParamInput, , 1)
    Set oRS = .Execute
End With
```

The code in Listing 2-4 executes the following stored procedure:

```
CREATE PROCEDURE sp_GetProduct

@ID integer

AS

SELECT *
FROM Product
WHERE ID = @ID
```

Recordset Objects

A forward-only Recordset (also known as a "firehose" cursor because it goes very fast in one direction only) is created by setting the CursorType property of the ADODB.Recordset object to the enum adOpenForwardOnly. As a general rule, you should be as kind as possible to the server. Therefore, a disconnected Recordset is usually the most appropriate type for use in reports. A disconnected Recordset is one where the CursorLocation property is set to adUseClient (as opposed to adUseServer) and the ActiveConnection property is set to Nothing after the Open method is invoked. Because a report requires only a static data set that moves only in one direction, there is no need to maintain an active connection to the server for this Recordset object. The code in Listing 2-5 illustrates this approach.

Listing 2-5. Forward-Only ADO Recordset

```
Dim oRS As New ADODB.Recordset
Dim cSQL As String

cSQL = "SELECT * FROM Product"

With oRS
    Set .ActiveConnection = oConn
    .CursorLocation = adUseClient
    .CursorType = adOpenForwardOnly
    .Open cSQL
End With

Set oRS.ActiveConnection = Nothing

Do While Not oRS.EOF

    Debug.Print oRS("descr")

    oRS.MoveNext

Loop

oRS.Close
Set oRS = Nothing
```

NOTE *If you're running a clustered environment with connection pooling, it might be more appropriate to run a server-side cursor and not a disconnected one. If the client machine is weak, disconnected recordsets are not appropriate because of the potential for large record retrievals.*

The RunCommand function shown in Listing 2-6 illustrates how both Command objects and Recordset objects work together. This function takes as parameters an open Connection object, a command to be executed, a value for the CommandType property, and a value for the CursorType property. In addition, it can take a column name and a value to create a parameter for a stored procedure. Because many of the stored procedures you will use have only one parameter, the RunCommand function will serve its purpose in many situations.

Listing 2-6. RunCommand Function

```
Function RunCommand(ByRef oConn As ADODB.Connection, cSQL As String, _
        iCommandType As Integer, iCursorType As Integer, _
        Optional vntColumn As Variant, _
        Optional vntID As Variant) As ADODB.Recordset

    Dim oRS As New ADODB.Recordset
    Dim oCmd As New ADODB.Command

    oConn.CursorLocation = adUseClient

    With oCmd

        Set .ActiveConnection = oConn

        .CommandText = cSQL
        .CommandType = iCommandType
        .CommandTimeout = 1200

        If iCommandType = adCmdStoredProc And _
            Not IsMissing(vntColumn) And _
            Not IsMissing(vntID) Then
```

```
        If IsNumeric(vntID) Then
            oCmd.Parameters.Append _
            oCmd.CreateParameter(vntColumn, adInteger, adParamInput, 9, vntID)
        Else
            oCmd.Parameters.Append _
            oCmd.CreateParameter(vntColumn, adVarChar, adParamInput, 50, vntID)
        End If

    End If

End With

With oRS
    .CursorType = iCursorType
    .LockType = adLockReadOnly
    .CursorLocation = adUseClient
    .Open oCmd
End With

Set RunCommand = oRS

End Function
```

ADO.NET

Though the name is similar, ADO.NET is a very different technology from COM-based ADO. In order to use any of ADO.NET's data access technology, you'll need to import the appropriate namespace into your application. This is similar to setting Project | References in Visual Basic 6. The System.Data.SqlClient namespace handles classes that access Microsoft SQL Server 7.0 and 2000 databases and are optimized for that purpose, whereas System.Data.OleDb handles all other OLE DB data sources. The System.XML namespace offers objects to handle XML data sources.

There are no Recordset objects as such in ADO.NET. Rather, you have DataSet, DataTable, and DataReader objects. DataSet objects are similar to memory-resident databases. They store information on the structure, constraints, and relationships of and between the various tables. Relationships that do not already exist in the database can be established between DataTables in a DataSet. For the purpose of creating a specialized report, you can create relationships and references that exist only during the runtime of the program.

Each DataSet object in turn contains a collection of DataTable objects, which usually encapsulate the results of a query but can be populated from any source, including tables, XML documents, and strings, and through directly accessing members in code. ADO.NET provides the DataReader object to access data in a forward-only fashion, much like the "firehose" cursor in an ADO Recordset. DataSets have their own Update, Delete, and Add methods to synchronize with the underlying data source.

Connection Objects

The syntax for instantiating a Connection object in ADO.NET is almost the same as it is for COM-based ADO. Examine the following code:

```
Dim oConn As New OleDb.OleDbConnection()
Dim cConnectString As String

cConnectString = "Provider=Microsoft.Jet.OLEDB.4.0;Data
Source=C:\Reports\SampleDatabase.mdb"

oConn.ConnectionString = cConnectString
oConn.Open()
```

The only variation between ADO and ADO.NET when creating a Connection object is that you must specify the type of connection you are interested in. What you are creating is an instance of a specific Data Provider. This example uses a OleDbConnection object. If you were working with Microsoft SQL Server, you would use a SQLConnection object.

Command Objects

The ADO.NET Command object is very similar to its ADO counterpart. Its primary purpose is to encapsulate a SQL statement or a stored procedure. Examine the code in Listing 2-7.

Listing 2-7. Command Object of CommandType = Text

```
Dim objDR As OleDbDataReader
Dim objCommand As New OleDbCommand()
Dim cSQL As String

cSQL = "SELECT * FROM Source"
```

```
With objCommand
    .Connection = oConn
    .CommandText = cSQL
    .CommandType = CommandType.Text
    .CommandTimeout = 60
    objDR = .ExecuteReader()
End With
```

The first step is to declare an object variable (objCommand) as type OleDbCommand. Then, the various properties are set. The Connection property holds the existing Connection object. The CommandText property stores the SQL statement, stored procedure name, or table name that the Command object will ultimately execute. It is the CommandType property that distinguishes what the text stored in CommandText represents. CommandType can contain one of three enum values: CommandType.StoredProcedure, CommandType.TableDirect, or CommandType.Text. For example, the code in Listing 2-8 specifies only a table name as the value of the CommandText property, yet the entire contents of the table will be extracted when the ExecuteReader method is invoked. This is the equivalent of specifying SELECT * FROM Source as the CommandText property and setting the CommandType to CommandType.Text.

Listing 2-8. Command Object of CommandType = TableDirect

```
Dim objDR As OleDbDataReader
Dim objCommand As New OleDbCommand()
Dim cSQL As String

cSQL = "Source"

With objCommand
    .Connection = oConn
    .CommandText = cSQL
    .CommandType = CommandType.TableDirect
    .CommandTimeout = 60
    objDR = .ExecuteReader()
End With
```

You may frequently be working with stored procedures that will require you to pass parameters to the variables embedded within them. If so, you'll need the Parameters method to specify those values along with an enum indicating their data type. The code in Listing 2-9 illustrates how this is done.

Listing 2-9. Command Object of CommandType = StoredProcedure

```
Dim objDR As OleDbDataReader
Dim objCommand As New OleDbCommand()
Dim cSQL As String

cSQL = "sp_GetProduct"

With objCommand
    .Connection = oConn
    .CommandText = cSQL
    .CommandType = CommandType.StoredProcedure
    .CommandTimeout = 60
    .Parameters.Add("ProductID", OleDbType.Integer).Value = 1
    objDR = .ExecuteReader()
End With
```

The Prepare method will compile the SQL statement or the stored procedure as shown in Listing 2-10. Note that this method will have no effect if CommandType is set to CommandType.TableDirect.

Listing 2-10. Command Object Using Prepare Method

```
Dim objDR As OleDbDataReader
Dim objCommand As New OleDbCommand()
Dim cSQL As String

cSQL = "sp_GetProduct"

With objCommand
    .Connection = oConn
    .CommandText = cSQL
    .CommandType = CommandType.StoredProcedure
    .CommandTimeout = 60
    .Parameters.Add("ProductID", OleDbType.Integer).Value = 1
    .Prepare()
    objDR = .ExecuteReader()
End With

Console.WriteLine(objDR.Item("Descr"))

objDR.Close()
```

```
With objCommand
    .Connection = oConn
    .CommandText = cSQL
    .CommandType = CommandType.StoredProcedure
    .CommandTimeout = 60
    .Parameters(0).Value = 2
    .Prepare()
    objDR = .ExecuteReader()
End With


Console.WriteLine(objDR.Item("Descr"))
```

DataReader Objects

In all the examples given in the preceding section on Command objects, you may have noticed that the DataReader objects were created via the ExecuteReader method. The reason is that the ADO.NET DataReader object most closely resembles the type of ADO Recordset object best used for report development. DataReader objects are read-only, forward-only data objects and are the .NET version of the "firehose" cursor. As a result, they are the most efficient type of result set you can create. The difference between DataReaders and their COM equivalents is that DataReaders cannot be disconnected. If you specifically need a disconnected data source, create an instance of the DataSet object instead. Because there are three separate namespaces that deal with Microsoft SQL Server databases, other OLEDB databases, and XML data sources, respectively, there are also three types of DataReader objects—SqlDataReader, OleDbDataReader, and XMLReader. SqlDataReader and OleDbDataReader are very similar to one another. Syntactically, the primary difference is in their names. Take a look at the code in Listing 2-11.

Listing 2-11. DataReader Example

```
Dim objDR As OleDbDataReader
Dim objCommand As OleDbCommand
Dim cSQL As String

cSQL = "SELECT * " & _
       "FROM Source " & _
       "ORDER BY descr"
```

```
objCommand = New OleDbCommand(cSQL, oConn)

objDR = objCommand.ExecuteReader()

While objDR.Read

    Console.WriteLine(objDR.GetInt32(0))
    Console.WriteLine(objDR.GetString(1))

End While

objDR.Close()
```

As you can see, the DataReader object is created from a Command object. The Read method then accesses the next available row of data by way of the MoveNext method. The GetInt32 and GetString methods allow you to retrieve the underlying data in the native data type, which refers to the data type of the column stored in the underlying data source as opposed to its equivalent in VB .NET. There are, of course, other type-specific methods such as GetByte, GetDecimal, GetDouble, etc., which are listed in the VB.NET documentation. These *Get* methods only take the ordinal position of the column as a parameter. The following lines of code illustrate the Item method, which does take a string description:

```
Console.WriteLine(objDR.Item("ID"))
Console.WriteLine(objDR.Item("Descr"))
```

You can check for Null values by using the IsDBNull method of the DataReader object as shown here:

```
If objDR.IsDBNull(0) Then
    MsgBox("This is null")
End If
```

Like the type-specific *Get* methods, IsDBNull takes the ordinal position of the column as a parameter.

If you only need to return one value, say, the result from a SQL aggregate such as SUM(), use the ExecuteScalar method. ExecuteScalar is faster than ExecuteReader and uses less overhead (see Listing 2-12).

Listing 2-12. ExecuteScalar Method

```
cSQL = "SELECT COUNT(*) " & _
              "FROM Source"

objCommand = New OleDbCommand(cSQL, oConn)

Console.WriteLine(objCommand.ExecuteScalar)
```

ExecuteXMLReader returns results expressed in XML format. This method is only available for the SQLCommand object, which supports the Microsoft SQL Server databases.

Conclusion

This chapter covers most of what you need to know about SQL and ADO in both VB and .NET. You'll need to become familiar with the subtleties and nuances of your database server's particular flavor of SQL in order to properly optimize the effectiveness of your particular RDBMS. In the next chapter, you'll learn about building effective report criteria screens.

CHAPTER 3

Creating Criteria Screens

REGARDLESS OF THE KIND OF reporting tool you use, you'll generally need to collect criteria data from your users. Before building a report, you must first know what criteria the user will require in order to limit the data that will be displayed in the report. Creating criteria screens without the proper tools or methodologies can be a rather time-consuming process and may result in an application that is difficult to maintain. The purpose of this chapter is to illustrate how to quickly produce effective criteria screens that will provide the user maximum flexibility to filter report output while offering you, the developer, the most easily maintainable application possible. I cover criteria screen issues for the Web in Chapter 9 and those for PDA devices in Chapter 11.

User Interface Considerations

Whatever style you use for your criteria screens, they should above all be consistent in both appearance and operation. Nothing makes a user more comfortable with an application than consistency. Start by finding out if the organization for which you're building the application has any user interface (UI) standards in place. If you're lucky enough to be able to create the standard "look and feel" yourself, try to use a set of editing controls in a standard fashion, supported by a common code base.

The controls required for criteria screens in any Windows or Web application are text/numeric input boxes, date controls, check boxes, list boxes, and combo boxes. Radio buttons are not necessary, as combo boxes handle these choices just as well. (Radio buttons are also more difficult to work with when using data-driven programming techniques.)

Date criteria should be set up in a "from/to" layout and specified by the user as a range. If a user only needs one day's worth of information, the "from/to" dates can be set to the same date. If the particular parameter requires only a single date, then certainly offer the user only one date box. Programmatic validation, including such techniques as bounds checking and regular expressions, can be used to catch user selections that are not appropriate (i.e., March 33, or February 29 outside of a leap year). Likewise, the user should not be able to enter a "from" date that is later than the "to" date. Optionally, the "to" date can be defaulted to the system date as user needs require. Since there's very little free-form data that you would normally pass to a report engine, most of the error checking can occur client side rather than server side.

> **NOTE** *You may wish to consider performing both client-AND server-side validation, especially if you're writing a Web application. A malicious user could edit an HTML page, remove any client-side validations, and easily route bad data to the server, causing a server error.*

List boxes provide the most flexible criteria control. Use of a list box implies that the user may select more than one option. Each list box will have a button underneath it that allows the user to clear the choices made. This way if a user wishes to run a report for Departments A, D, and G, it is rather easy to do so (see Figure 3-1 later in this chapter). In those cases where the user is permitted to select only one out of a set of options, use a combo box. In both cases, each control has two columns. The first is invisible to the user and contains the unique ID of the table that contains the filter options. The second column contains the text description that the user would recognize. See the LoadTable routine in the source code, which is available at the Apress Web site (`http://www.apress.com`).

Check boxes handle Boolean values. By default, they can be set to the "gray" option, rather than a specific checked or unchecked value. Doing so will instruct the SQL WHERE clause builder routines, discussed later in the chapter, to ignore this criteria completely. Finally, text boxes can allow the user to restrict the output based on free-form text—a last name, for example. Often you may wish to treat all entries in the text box as partial search criteria. For example, if in filtering by last name the user enters "Sm", the report could return "Smoot", "Smith", "Smythe", etc. Depending upon the flavor of SQL you are using, this can be accomplished by using the LIKE keyword and appending a percent sign to the end of the search value. For example:

```
SELECT *
FROM Employees
WHERE LastName LIKE 'Sm%'
```

UI in Visual Basic 6

In order to implement these user interface guidelines in a completely reusable fashion, your criteria screen must consist of one form that has one copy of all the possible controls available on it to create filters. Each control is set as the zero element of a control array with a Visible property set to False. Before you cringe at this slightly outdated (VB5) approach, read the sidebar "Data-Driven Programming in VB6" and you'll see why I'm doing it. (Note also that control arrays don't exist with VB .NET, but you'll learn how to handle this later in the chapter.) Using data-driven programming techniques, you can create criteria collection forms that accept date ranges and use list boxes, combo boxes, check boxes, and text/numeric input boxes to collect criteria information and pass this data into a report. The form can contain as many of each type of control as you require that you can position anywhere. Of course, not all criteria forms are generic enough to be created dynamically. If two or more controls depend on each other, or need to follow special rules (populating one combo box with respect to another's current value), then dynamic programming can be quite complex since this "generic" framework must be built to handle elaborate inter-actions between controls. Though the techniques explained in this chapter will handle the majority of report criteria screens, you'll need to do custom program-ming on occasion.

Data-Driven Programming with VB6

Data-driven programming is a software development technique whereby some or all of the attributes of an application are set at runtime. Data-driven develop-ment is particularly useful if all or part of your program is user-definable or if you want to make changes to the application without having to recompile every time. Implementation of these techniques is vastly different between VB6 and VB. NET.

Data-driven design can be a challenge at first. It requires you to think of your application from a completely different angle. Many of the traditional design assumptions are no longer valid. For experienced programmers, thes as-sumptions are often second nature. As you're developing a data-driven applica-tion, you'll sometimes attempt to refer to a control, table, or column and realize, "Oh yeah, I don't have access to that yet." Data-driven programming is like designing a program from the inside out.

First, let's take a look at how data-driven programming is done in VB6. If you've ever examined a Visual Basic 6 FRM file, you're already familiar with data-driven development. When you lay out a form in VB and assign properties to the forms and controls, this information is stored in an ASCII file with an FRM extension. Listing 3-1 shows a segment of an FRM.

Listing 3-1. FRM Control Definition

```
Begin VB.CheckBox chkCheckBox
      Caption  = "Check1"
      Height = 495
      Index = 0
      Left = 1800
      TabIndex = 5
      Top = 2760
      Width = 1215
End
```

Here, VB is storing the definition for a CheckBox control. The FRM entry contains the caption, height, width, and several other properties of the check box that the IDE will need to display the control again at runtime. (Remember, design time for you is actually runtime for Visual Basic.) When the form is loaded for further modifications, these definitions are read from the FRM file, and the screen is repainted to look just the way you left it. The examples that follow do exactly the same thing, except that the definitions are stored in an Access database rather than an ASCII file.

There are two ways you can perform data-driven programming in VB6—by using control arrays or by wrapping a class around each control type you wish to dynamically create and adding each new control to a collection. While control arrays were the only way to accomplish this in versions of VB prior to 6, the class wrapper approach is 6.0 specific. Because control arrays are simpler and accomplish our objective well for purposes of creating criteria screens, we'll use them to illustrate the examples in this chapter. However, in the interest of completeness, let's examine the class wrapper approach first.

The class wrapper approach to data-driven programming is very similar to the way it needs to be done in VB. NET, given VB .NET's lack of control arrays. First, you'll need to create Collections to track the various types of objects. For example:

```
Dim colListBoxes As New Collection
Dim colListBoxButtons As New Collection
```

Then, you'll need to create a class module to encapsulate each individual object on the criteria form. The code in Listing 3-2 handles Microsoft's ListView control as a tool for implementing a multiselection list box.

Listing 3-2. ListView Control Wrapper Class

```
Option Explicit

Dim WithEvents objList As MSComctlLib.ListView
```

```vb
Public frmOwner As Form
Public iIndex As Integer

Public Sub CreateControl(iIndex As Integer, iTop As Integer, iLeft As Integer, _
iWidth As Integer, iHeight As Integer)
    Dim clmX As ColumnHeader
    Dim itmX As ListItem

    Set objList = frmOwner.Controls.Add("MSComctlLib.ListViewCtrl.2", _
                            "objList" & iIndex, frmOwner)

    With objList
        Set clmX = objList.ColumnHeaders.Add()
        clmX.Width = iWidth
        Set clmX = objList.ColumnHeaders.Add()
        clmX.Width = 0

        .Top = iTop
        .Left = iLeft
        .Width = iWidth
        .Height = iHeight
        .View = lvwReport
        .Checkboxes = True
        .Visible = True
    End With

End Sub

Public Sub AddItem(vntcDescr As Variant, vntID As Variant)
    Dim itmX As ListItem

    Set itmX = objList.ListItems.Add()
    itmX.Text = vntcDescr
    itmX.SubItems(1) = vntID

End Sub

Public Function ListCount() As Integer
    ListCount = objList.ListItems.Count
End Function

Public Sub DeselectAll()
    Dim iCount As Integer
  Dim x As Integer
```

```
        iCount = objList.ListItems.Count


    For x = 1 To iCount
        objList.ListItems(x).Selected = False
    Next x
End Sub


Public Function GetCodes() As String
    Dim cResult As String
    Dim iCount As Integer
    Dim x As Integer


    iCount = objList.ListItems.Count


    For x = 1 To iCount


        If objList.ListItems(x).Checked Then
            cResult = cResult & objList.ListItems(x).SubItems(1) & ","
        End If


    Next x


    If cResult <> vbNullString Then
        cResult = Mid$(cResult, 1, Len(cResult) - Len(","))
        cResult = "(" & cResult & ")"
    End If


    GetCodes = cResult


End Function
```

This class uses the Add method of the Controls collection of the owner form to add a control of type MSComctlLib.ListViewCtrl.2 with the unique name "objList" plus the index number. Once instantiated, you can set the positional and column properties on the control and make it visible. In the criteria form itself, you'll need to invoke a subroutine similar to the one in Listing 3-3 that instantiates an object of the DynamicListBox class and invokes the CreateControl method.

Listing 3-3. Instantiate ListBox at Runtime

```
Sub CreateListBox(iIndex As Integer, iTop As Integer, iLeft As Integer, _
iWidth As Integer, iHeight As Integer)
    Dim objListBox As DynamicListBox

    Set objListBox = New DynamicListBox
    Set objListBox.frmOwner = Me
    objListBox.iIndex = iIndex
    Call objListBox.CreateControl(iIndex, iTop, iLeft, iWidth, iHeight)
    colListBoxes.Add objListBox
End Sub
```

By contrast, a control array is a collection of controls of the same type that share the same name and event procedures. The controls are differentiated from one another by their Index property, which can hold a number from zero to 32767. Numbering does not need to start at zero, but for the examples in this chapter it will.

Control arrays are normally created at design time to handle a group of controls with a similar purpose. By doing this, the same event handler can respond to events for a set of controls rather than have one event procedure for each. Radio buttons, for example, are almost always created as part of a control array. Control arrays are needed in a data-driven application primarily as they are the easiest way to instantiate controls dynamically. They also allow a finite number of controls to be instantiated as needed without having to track the names of the new controls because all of the new controls have the same name, just a different index. All control names may now be known at design time. All you need to do is refer to the dynamically created controls through their Index property, as shown in this example:

```
txtText(1).Height = 375
txtText(2) = "Hello World"
```

frmReportCriteria must contain one copy of every control used in the application with an Index property set to zero and a Visible property set to False. It does not matter how these controls are positioned or sized on frmReportCriteria, as these attributes will be set at runtime before the Visible property is set to True. Almost every other attribute may be set at runtime as well. The code in Listing 3-4 shows a simplified example of this technique.

Listing 3-4. Instantiating Controls in VB6

```
' The Form_Load event of frmMainForm instantiates and
' loads a new instance of frmReportCriteria
```

```
Private Sub Form_Load()

    Dim frmForm1 As New frmReportCriteria

    frmForm1.Show

    Unload Me

End Sub

' Once loaded, frmReportCriteria uses the Load statement to add
' another member to the Text1 control array. The Visible property
' of the new member is then set to True and the control appears
' on the screen

Private Sub Form_Load()
    Dim iCnt As Integer

    iCnt = 1

    Load Text1(iCnt)

    Text1(iCnt).Visible = True

End Sub
```

Designing the Criteria Form

The first step in building a criteria form is to make an assessment of all the criteria for all the reports in your application. You will undoubtedly notice that there is a great deal of commonality in criteria across the many reports you need to build, and many reports will have the exact same set of criteria. Let's look at an example from a pharmaceutical product inquiry system. The code appearing in Listing 3-5 shows the Click event of the menu item for a series of duration reports. These reports will show how long it took to close a case as grouped by the staff member who entered the case, the product involved in the case, or the source from which the case originated. The constant values used for each Case statement refer to the Index value of the menu item selected. These constants are defined in the declarations section of the MainMenu form.

Listing 3-5. Click Event of Report Menu

```
Private Sub mnuReport_Click(Index As Integer)

    objReport.ReportTitle = mnuReport.Item(Index).Caption

    Select Case Index

        Case DURATION_EDIT_BY_STAFF
            objReport.HelpContext = 101
            objReport.Report = "DurationByStaffRpt"

        Case DURATION_EDIT_BY_PRODUCT
            objReport.HelpContext = 102
            objReport.Report = "DurationByProductRpt"

        Case DURATION_EDIT_BY_SOURCE
            objReport.HelpContext = 103
            objReport.Report = "DurationBySourceRpt"

    End Select

    frmReportCriteria.Show vbModal

End Sub
```

Each report option needs two pieces of information—the name of the class method (it is a good programming practice to store all your report-related code in a separate report class, or even in an ActiveX DLL) that contains the report code and the Help identifier to link to the CHM file that will explain the report when the user clicks the Help button on the criteria screen.

The form frmReportCriteria is the criteria screen itself. This form contains all the code needed to configure and display a criteria screen to the user. The controls used for the list boxes and combo boxes on this form are FarPoint Technology's ListPro 3.0 (http://www.fpoint.com). You should be able to modify this code to easily fit whatever list and combo box controls you may be using. Take a look at the Form_Load event of frmReportCriteria as shown in Listing 3-6.

Listing 3-6. Form_Load Event

```
Private Sub Form_Load()

    Me.Caption = "Criteria for " & objReport.ReportTitle
```

```
Select Case objReport.Report

    Case "DurationBySourceRpt"
        Call ShowDates(SELECT_ENTER_DATE, 120, 100, "Enter Date Range:")
        Call ShowListBox(SELECT_PRODUCT, 1400, 100, 3000, "Product")
        Call ShowListBox(SELECT_SOURCE, 1400, 3500, 3000, "Source")
        Call ShowComboBox(SELECT_DEPARTMENT, 4300, 100, 3000, "Department")
        Call ShowCheckBox(SELECT_COMPLEX_QUESTION, 4300, 4500, _
                                        "Complex Question")

        Call LoadTable(oConn, lstListBox(SELECT_PRODUCT), _
                    "product", "ID", "Descr")
        Call LoadTable(oConn, lstListBox(SELECT_SOURCE), _
                    "source", "ID", "Descr")
        Call LoadTable(oConn, cboComboBox(SELECT_DEPARTMENT), _
                    "department", "ID", "Descr")

        Me.Width = 7000
        Me.Height = 6000


    Case "DurationByProductRpt", "DurationByStaffRpt"
        Call ShowDates(SELECT_ENTER_DATE, 120, 100, "Enter Date Range:")
        Call ShowDates(SELECT_RECEIVE_DATE, 700, 100, "Enter Receive Range:")
        Call ShowListBox(SELECT_PRODUCT, 1500, 100, 3000, "Product")

        Call LoadTable(oConn, lstListBox(SELECT_PRODUCT), _
                    "product", "ID", "Descr")

        Me.Width = 7000
        Me.Height = 4500

End Select

Call PositionButtons

Call FormCenter(frmMainMenu, Me)

End Sub
```

This code—and its VB .NET counterpart, which is very similar—calls a series of subroutines that display the necessary controls using data-driven programming techniques. You can see that the Duration by Product and the Duration by Staff reports both have the same set of criteria.

When the Duration by Source report is selected from the main menu, the criteria screen will look like Figure 3-1.

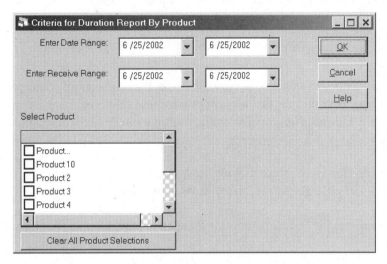

Figure 3-1. Criteria screen for the Duration by Source report

Yet when the Duration by Product report is selected from the main menu, the criteria screen will look like Figure 3-2.

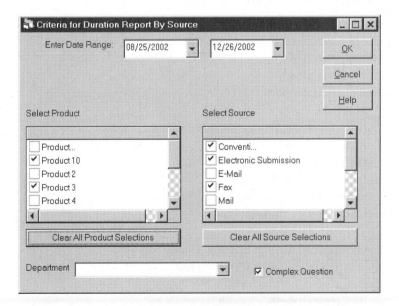

Figure 3-2. Criteria screen for the Duration by Product report

List Boxes

Each control is represented by a constant value that identifies its ordinal position within the control array. Since the user has the option to select both a product and a source, these controls are represented by the following constant values:

```
Const SELECT_PRODUCT = 1
Const SELECT_SOURCE = 2
```

There is no zero element, as zero comprises the base control of any given control type. For example, the following subroutine calls create two list boxes that offer the user the option of selecting multiple sources and/or multiple products:

```
Call ShowListBox(SELECT_PRODUCT, 1400, 100, 3000, "Product")
Call ShowListBox(SELECT_SOURCE, 1400, 3500, 3000, "Source")
```

A few lines later the LoadTable routine is called to populate these list boxes with data:

```
Call LoadTable(oConn, lstListBox(SELECT_PRODUCT), "product", "ID", "Descr")
Call LoadTable(oConn, lstListBox(SELECT_SOURCE), "source", "ID", "Descr")
```

The code for the ShowListBox routine is shown in Listing 3-7.

Listing 3-7. ShowListBox Routine

```
Sub ShowListBox(iIndex As Integer, iTop As Integer, iLeft As Integer, _
                iWidth As Integer, cCaption As String)
    Load lblListBox(iIndex)
    Load lstListBox(iIndex)
    Load cmdListBox(iIndex)

    lstListBox(iIndex).MultiSelect = MultiSelectExtended

    lblListBox(iIndex).Top = iTop
    lblListBox(iIndex).Left = iLeft
    lblListBox(iIndex).Width = iWidth
    lblListBox(iIndex) = "Select " & cCaption

    lstListBox(iIndex).Top = lblListBox(iIndex).Top + _
                             lblListBox(iIndex).Height + 100
    lstListBox(iIndex).Left = iLeft
    lstListBox(iIndex).Width = iWidth
```

```
cmdListBox(iIndex).Left = iLeft
cmdListBox(iIndex).Width = iWidth
cmdListBox(iIndex).Top = lstListBox(iIndex).Top + _
                            lstListBox(iIndex).Height + 100
cmdListBox(iIndex).Caption = "Clear All " & cCaption & " Selections"

lblListBox(iIndex).Visible = True
lstListBox(iIndex).Visible = True
cmdListBox(iIndex).Visible = True
```

End Sub

The first task is to instantiate the specified numeric element in the control array for the list box description label, the list box itself, and the command button that clears the selected items as follows:

```
Load lblListBox(iIndex)
Load lstListBox(iIndex)
Load cmdListBox(iIndex)
```

Since control array elements do not need to be added in a specific order, you do not need to worry about which of the control sets are instantiated first. After this, the remainder of the code simply sizes and positions the individual controls. The MultiSelect property is always set to MultiSelectExtended, as the use of a list box always means that the user can make multiple selections. Finally, once all the controls have been created, sized, and positioned, their respective Visible properties are set to True.

Combo Boxes

Combo boxes work in much the same way. The code shown in Listing 3-8 illustrates how individual combo boxes are created.

Listing 3-8. ShowComboBox Routine

```
Sub ShowComboBox(iIndex As Integer, iTop As Integer, iLeft As Integer, _
                iWidth As Integer, cCaption As String)

    Load lblComboBox(iIndex)
    Load cboComboBox(iIndex)

    cboComboBox(iIndex).Style = StyleDropDownList
```

```
      lblComboBox(iIndex) = cCaption
      lblComboBox(iIndex).AutoSize = True

      cboComboBox(iIndex).Top = iTop
      cboComboBox(iIndex).Left = lblComboBox(iIndex).Width + 200
      cboComboBox(iIndex).Width = iWidth

      lblComboBox(iIndex).Top = iTop
      lblComboBox(iIndex).Left = iLeft
      lblComboBox(iIndex).Width = lblComboBox(iIndex).Width
      lblComboBox(iIndex) = cCaption

      lblComboBox(iIndex).Visible = True
      cboComboBox(iIndex).Visible = True

End Sub
```

The main difference here is that the Label control, which holds the description of the combo box, is displayed to the left of the control instead of on top, as is the case with the list box. Because of this, you need to know the width, measured in pixels, of the text used by the caption in order to adjust the width of the Label control so that the combo box can be positioned directly to the right of the caption describing it. By setting the Label control's AutoSize property to True, the Label control will automatically adjust its width to contain the text of the caption.

Check Boxes

The routine that displays the CheckBox control is a bit different. Because a CheckBox control does not have an AutoSize property, you'll need to use an invisible Label control that receives the Font and the caption of the Label control and has its AutoSize property set to True. Then, you can compute the width of the CheckBox control based on the width of this invisible Label control as shown in Listing 3-9.

Listing 3-9. ShowCheckBox Routine

```
Sub ShowCheckBox(iIndex As Integer, iTop As Integer, _
                 iLeft As Integer, cCaption As String)
      Dim iTextWidth As Integer

      Load chkCheckBox(iIndex)
```

```
Set lblWidthChecker.Font = chkCheckBox(iIndex).Font
lblWidthChecker = cCaption
lblWidthChecker.AutoSize = True

iTextWidth = lblWidthChecker.Width + 300

With chkCheckBox(iIndex)
    .Top = iTop
    .Left = iLeft
    .Width = iTextWidth
    .Caption = cCaption
    .Visible = True
End With

End Sub
```

 TIP   *Before creating a criteria form of any complexity, you may wish to lay out the various controls on a rough draft of the form. Doing so will allow you to preview the resulting screen design and retrieve the position values before you code all the routines to display the same controls dynamically.*

Now that you understand how to dynamically create a criteria entry screen, let's examine how to turn the selections made by the user into a report filter.

Building the SQL WHERE Clause

Once the user has selected all the criteria for the report, you can build the WHERE clause that filters the data. The code for this is found in the Click method of the OK button on the criteria screen as shown in Listing 3-10.

Listing 3-10. cmdOK_Click Event

```
Private Sub cmdOK_Click()
    Dim iDateCnt As Integer
    Dim cDateFrom As String
    Dim cDateTo As String
    Dim cDescr As String
    Dim cSQL As String
```

```
Dim cCriteria As String
Dim x As Integer

iDateCnt = txtDateFrom.Count - 1

For x = 0 To iDateCnt

    cDateFrom = txtDateFrom(x)
    cDateTo = txtDateTo(x)

    If cDateFrom <> vbNullString Or cDateTo <> vbNullString Then

        If Not IsDate(cDateFrom) Or Not IsDate(cDateTo) Then

            MsgBox "You must enter both a valid 'from' and a 'to' date.", _
                vbOKOnly

            Exit Sub

        End If

    End If


    If IsDate(cDateFrom) And IsDate(cDateTo) Then

        If DateValue(cDateFrom) > DateValue(cDateTo) Then

            MsgBox "The 'from date' cannot be greater than the 'to date'.", _
                vbOKOnly

            txtDateFrom(x).SetFocus

            Exit Sub

        End If

    End If

Next x
```

```
Select Case objReport.Report

    Case "DurationBySourceRpt"
        cSQL = GetDateSQL("createdate", cDateFrom, cDateTo)
        cSQL = cSQL & GetListBoxSQL(SELECT_PRODUCT, "productid")
        cSQL = cSQL & GetListBoxSQL(SELECT_SOURCE, "sourceid")
        cSQL = cSQL & GetComboBoxSQL(SELECT_DEPARTMENT, "deptid")
        cSQL = cSQL & GetCheckBoxSQL(SELECT_COMPLEX_QUESTION, "questiontype")

        cCriteria = GetDateCriteria("Create Date", cDateFrom, cDateTo)
        cCriteria = cCriteria & GetListBoxCriteria(SELECT_PRODUCT, "Product")
        cCriteria = cCriteria & GetListBoxCriteria(SELECT_SOURCE, "Source")
        cCriteria = cCriteria & GetComboBoxCriteria(SELECT_DEPARTMENT, _
                                "Department")
        cCriteria = cCriteria & GetCheckBoxCriteria(SELECT_COMPLEX_QUESTION,_
                                "Complex Question")

End Select

If cSQL <> vbNullString Then
    cSQL = Mid$(cSQL, 1, Len(cSQL) - 4)
End If

If cCriteria <> vbNullString Then
    cCriteria = Mid$(cCriteria, 1, Len(cCriteria) - 6)
End If

With objReport
    .PrintCriteriaPage = IIf(chkCriteriaPage = vbChecked, True, False)
    .ReportCriteria = cCriteria
    .ReportSQL = cSQL
    .ShowPrint
End With

End Sub
```

This code takes the criteria entered into the dynamically created controls and converts it into segments of a WHERE clause that will complete the SQL statement used to extract the report data. Each function that returns a section of the WHERE clause also has a companion function that returns the English-language criteria that may be optionally printed at the top of the report. Take a look at the GetListBoxSQL and the GetListBoxCriteria functions shown in Listing 3-11.

Listing 3-11. GetListBoxSQL and GetListBoxCriteria Functions

```
Function GetListBoxSQL(Index As Integer, cColumn As String) As String
    Dim cSQL As String
    Dim cList As String

    If lstListBox(Index).SelCount > 0 Then

        cList = ParseIt(lstListBox(Index), True, False)

        cSQL = cColumn & " IN " & cList & " AND "

    End If

    GetListBoxSQL = cSQL

End Function

Function GetListBoxCriteria(Index As Integer, cDescr As String) As String
    Dim cResult As String
    Dim cNames As String

    If lstListBox(Index).SelCount > 0 Then

        cNames = ParseIt(lstListBox(Index), True, False, 1)

        cResult = cResult & "the " & cDescr & " is among " & _
                        cNames & " and " & vbCrLf

    End If

    GetListBoxCriteria = cResult

End Function
```

The GetListBoxSQL function receives the Index value of the list box and the name of the column in the WHERE clauses as parameters. Then, GetListBoxSQL calls the ParseIt function, which returns a string containing all the primary key values of the items used in the database—for example, "(342, 534, 132)". The SQL IN keyword then uses this value. Taking all the SQL building functions together will produce a WHERE clause similar to the following:

createdate BETWEEN '03/11/2002' AND '03/25/2002'
AND productid IN (10,3,6)
AND sourceid IN (3,1,6)
AND deptid = 3
AND questiontype = -1

Likewise, the GetListBoxCriteria function will return what all this means in English:

the Create Date is between 03/13/2002 and 03/26/2002 and
the Product is among (Product 10, Product 3, Product 6,) and
the Source is among (Electronic Submission, Mail, Sales Rep,) and
the Department is Department D and
the Complex Question is True

Once you have created the SQL WHERE clause and its English counterpart, you can invoke the Report Viewer form (frmReportViewer). The Load event of frmReportViewer then uses the CallByName function to invoke the method of the Report class that is stored as a string in the Report property, as shown in Listing 3-12.

Listing 3-12. GetListBoxSQL and GetListBoxCriteria Functions

```
Private Sub Form_Load()

    Screen.MousePointer = vbHourglass

    Set objReport.ReportViewer = Me

    objReport.LocalPath = App.Path

    Me.Caption = objReport.ReportTitle + " Report"

    If objReport.PrintDestination = SCREEN_VIEW Then
        VSPrinter1.Preview = True
    Else
```

```
        VSPrinter1.Preview = False
    End If


    Call CallByName(objReport, objReport.Report, VbMethod)


    If Dir$(objReport.LocalPath, vbDirectory) = vbNullString Then
        MkDir objReport.LocalPath
    End If


    VSPDF1.ConvertDocument VSPrinter1, objReport.LocalPath & _
                "\" & objReport.Report & ".pdf"


    Screen.MousePointer = vbDefault


    If objReport.PrintDestination <> SCREEN_VIEW Then
        Unload Me
    End If


End Sub
```

That's it! You now have a fully data-driven criteria form that can be reused again and again across applications. Now let's take a look at how to accomplish the same task in VB .NET.

UI with VB .NET

Criteria screens in VB .NET utilize the same overall architecture as VB6. Of course, the programmatic implementation is considerably different. Because so much of the criteria form is created via data-driven programming techniques, it is imperative that you understand the unique way these techniques are implemented in VB .NET (see the sidebar "Data-Driven Programming with VB .NET).

....

Data-Driven Programming with VB .NET

Now that you understand what it takes to do data-driven programming with VB6, you can leverage the class wrapper approach previously discussed as you learn data-driven programming with VB .NET. VB .NET takes the runtime instantiation of objects to an entirely new metaphysical plane. There is no concept of control arrays. Any controls you'll need can be instantiated via a derived class that inherits from the appropriate System.Windows.Form base class. Nevertheless, control arrays still make it easier to manage dynamically created objects and track the existence of individual controls. Though the result is the same as in VB6, implementing these simulated control arrays is somewhat more complicated.

To accomplish all this using VB .NET, you must take an entirely different approach than you did in VB6. The data previously stored in the FRM files is now directly available to you in the system-generated source code of your .NET application. In many ways, data-driven programming is easier and less of a kludge in .NET, as you can instantiate controls and display them on the form without requiring a preexisting control on the form.

If you open a form in the VB .NET IDE and drag a TextBox control onto it, you'll see the code for the instantiation of the TextBox directly in the form's code window as shown in Listing 3-13.

Listing 3-13. Runtime Instantiation of Objects in VB .NET

```
Me.TextBox1 = New System.Windows.Forms.TextBox()

Me.TextBox1.Location = New System.Drawing.Point(176, 104)
Me.TextBox1.Name = "TextBox1"
Me.TextBox1.Size = New System.Drawing.Size(128, 20)
Me.TextBox1.TabIndex = 2
Me.TextBox1.Text = "TextBox1"
```

This code is generated automatically by VB .NET, and while you can edit it directly, I would not recommend that you do so. In VB6, this same type of object definition is found in the FRM file.

In order to more easily manage an unknown number of different controls using the familiar VB6 control array metaphor, you can use a Collection as shown here:

```
Dim objCheckBoxColl As New Collection()
```

New instances of the object are added to this Collection by invoking a subroutine that sets the size, screen position, and caption of the check box you wish to create as shown in Listing 3-14.

Listing 3-14. Runtime Instantiation of CheckBox Object

```
Private Sub AddDynamicCheckBox(ByVal iIndex As Short, ByVal iLeft As Short, _
        ByVal iTop As Short,  ByVal iHeight As Short, _
        ByVal cCaption As String)
    Dim objLabel As New Label()
    Dim iWidth As Short
```

```
objCheckBoxColl.Add(New CheckBox())

With objLabel
    .Visible = False
    .Font() = objCheckBoxColl.Item(iIndex).Font
    .Text = cCaption
    .AutoSize = True
    iWidth = .Width + 25
End With


objLabel = Nothing

With objCheckBoxColl.Item(iIndex)
    .Name = "CheckBox" & iIndex
    .Size = New Size(iWidth, iHeight)
    .Location = New Point(iLeft, iTop)
    .ThreeState = True
    .CheckState = CheckState.Indeterminate
    .Text = cCaption
End With

Me.Controls.AddRange(New _
  System.Windows.Forms.Control() {objCheckBoxColl(iIndex)})

End Sub
```

The code in Listing 3-14 is the heart of data-driven development in
VB .NET. The first step is to add a new item to the Collection that contains the
CheckBox object. Then, you need to create a Label object to determine how
wide to size the check box. By setting the Text property of the label to the
caption intended for the check box, you can set the label's AutoSize property to
True. Doing so will adjust the width of the label to a size just wide enough to
accommodate the caption text. Then, by assigning the Width property of the
check box to the width of the label (and adding 25 to accommodate the width of
the check itself), the resulting check box will be sized appropriately. Finally, the
AddRange method of the owner form's Control collection will add the newly
instantiated CheckBox object to the collection of controls owned by the form.

Event handlers in VB .NET are associated with their owner control via the
Handles keyword. Name-based linkage is no longer a consideration as in VB6,
where an event handler for the cmdCancel button is named, for example,
cmdCancel_Click. In VB .NET the Handles keyword is what determines the
linkage between a subroutine and a control. For example, in the following code,
it is the Handles keyword that associates the subroutine cmdCancel_Click with
the Click event of the button named cmdCancel:

```
Private Sub cmdCancel_Click(ByVal sender As System.Object, _
          ByVal e As System.EventArgs) Handles cmdCancel.Click
     Me.Close()
End Sub
```

Though the name of the event handler subroutine defaults to the familiar <objectname>_<eventname> format, any name will suffice. It's a good idea to stick to the default naming to have a familiar standard.

The Form_Load event for the VB .NET criteria screen is very similar to that of the Form_Load event in VB6. First, routines must be invoked to display the needed controls on the form, and then LoadTable routines will populate certain ones with data. Listing 3-15 illustrates this point.

Listing 3-15. VB .NET Form_Load Event

```
Dim oConn As New OleDb.OleDbConnection()
Dim cConnectString As String

cConnectString = _
"Provider=Microsoft.Jet.OLEDB.4.0;Data Source=C:\Ganz\SampleDatabase.mdb"

oConn.ConnectionString = cConnectString
oConn.Open()

SuspendLayout()

ShowDateRange(SELECT_ENTER_DATE, 8, 32, 20, "Enter Date")
ShowListBox(SELECT_PRODUCT, 8, 82, 180, 20, "Product")
ShowListBox(SELECT_SOURCE, 300, 82, 180, 20, "Source")
ShowComboBox(SELECT_DEPARTMENT, 8, 340, 180, 20, "Department")
ShowCheckBox(SELECT_COMPLEX_QUESTION, 300, 340, 20, "Complex Question")

LoadTable(oConn, aListBox(SELECT_PRODUCT), "Product", "ID", "Descr")
LoadTable(oConn, aListBox(SELECT_SOURCE), "Source", "ID", "Descr")
LoadTable(oConn, aComboBox(SELECT_DEPARTMENT), "Department", "ID", "Descr")

Me.Height() = 400
Me.Width() = 600

PositionButtons()

ResumeLayout()
```

Date Ranges

The ShowDateRange subroutine invokes three additional subroutines that instantiate the three controls comprising a date range entry—the descriptive label, a "from" date, and a "to" date. This code is shown in Listing 3-16.

Listing 3-16. ShowDateRange Routine

```
Private Sub ShowDateRange(ByVal iIndex As Short, ByVal iLeft As Short, _
    ByVal iTop As Short, ByVal iHeight As Short, ByVal cCaption As String)

    Call AddDynamicDateRangeLabel(iIndex, iLeft, iTop, iHeight, cCaption)

    Call AddDynamicDateFrom(iIndex, objDateRangeLabelColl(iIndex).Left + _
        objDateRangeLabelColl(iIndex).Width + 5, iTop, iHeight)

    Call AddDynamicDateTo(iIndex, objDateFromColl(iIndex).Left + _
        objDateFromColl(iIndex).Width + 5, iTop, iHeight)

End Sub
```

Each of the three individual *AddDynamic* routines, illustrated in Listing 3-17, displays one of the individual elements needed to create a date range. These subroutines all require an Index number, corresponding to a declared constant value, to later identify their position in the simulated control array encapsulated by the Collection that manages them. In the case of the Date From and Date To controls, the Left property is determined by the Left property of the control preceding it plus that control's Width property. Using this formula will align the controls proportionately without leaving any gaps between them.

Listing 3-17. Date Range AddDynamic Routines

```
Private Sub AddDynamicDateRangeLabel(ByVal iIndex As Short, ByVal iLeft As Short, _
    ByVal iTop As Short, ByVal iHeight As Short, ByVal cCaption As String)

    objDateRangeLabelColl.Add(New Label())

    With objDateRangeLabelColl(iIndex)
        .AutoSize = True
        .Name = "DateRangeLabel" & iIndex
        .Height = iHeight
        .Location = New Point(iLeft, iTop)
        .Text = cCaption
    End With
```

```
    Me.Controls.AddRange(New _
        System.Windows.Forms.Control() {objDateRangeLabelColl(iIndex)})


End Sub

Private Sub AddDynamicDateFrom(ByVal iIndex As Short, ByVal iLeft As Short, _
    ByVal iTop As Short, ByVal iHeight As Short)

    objDateFromColl.Add(New DateTimePicker())

    With objDateFromColl(iIndex)
        .Name = "DateFrom" & iIndex
        .Size = New Size(90, iHeight)
        .Location = New Point(iLeft, iTop)
        .Format = DateTimePickerFormat.Custom
        .CustomFormat = "MM/dd/yyyy"
    End With

    Me.Controls.AddRange(New _
        System.Windows.Forms.Control() {objDateFromColl(iIndex)})


End Sub

Private Sub AddDynamicDateTo(ByVal iIndex As Short, ByVal iLeft As Short, _
    ByVal iTop As Short, ByVal iHeight As Short)

    objDateToColl.Add(New DateTimePicker())

    With objDateToColl(iIndex)
        .Name = "DateTo" & iIndex
        .Size = New Size(90, iHeight)
        .Location = New Point(iLeft, iTop)
        .Format = DateTimePickerFormat.Custom
        .CustomFormat = "MM/dd/yyyy"
    End With

    Me.Controls.AddRange(New _
        System.Windows.Forms.Control() {objDateToColl(iIndex)})

End Sub
```

List Boxes

Just as in VB6, list boxes are a bit trickier, as they also need to be populated with data. Instantiating list boxes is accomplished in a fashion very similar to the date controls we have just examined. The code in Listing 3-18 illustrates how to populate list boxes.

Listing 3-18. LoadTable Subroutine

```
Sub LoadTable(ByVal oConn As OleDb.OleDbConnection, ByRef oControl As Object, _
        ByVal cTable As String, ByVal cID As String, ByVal cDescr As String)
        Dim oDS As New DataSet()
        Dim oDA As OleDb.OleDbDataAdapter
        Dim cSQL As String

        cSQL = "SELECT * " & _
                "FROM " & cTable & _
                " ORDER BY " & cDescr

        oDA = New OleDb.OleDbDataAdapter(cSQL, oConn)
        oDA.Fill(oDS, cTable)

        With oControl
            .DataSource = oDS.Tables(0)
            .DisplayMember = cDescr
            .ValueMember = cID
        End With

    End Sub
```

A Click event needs to be associated with the button to clear all the selections made by the user. You can accomplish this by using the AddHandler method once the new ListBox is created. You need to pass the event name and the AddressOf for the subroutine that serves as the event handler. This approach is shown in Listing 3-19.

Listing 3-19. DynamicListBoxButton Class

```
Private Sub AddDynamicListBoxButton(ByVal iIndex As Short, ByVal iLeft As Short, _
    ByVal iTop As Short, ByVal iWidth As Short, ByVal iHeight As Short, _
    ByVal cCaption As String)
    Dim objButton As Button
```

```
        objListBoxButtonColl.Add(New Button())

        With objListBoxButtonColl(iIndex)
            .Name = "ListBoxButton" & iIndex
            .Size = New Size(iWidth, iHeight)
            .Location = New Point(iLeft, iTop)
            .Text = "Clear Selected " & cCaption
        End With

        objButton = CType(objListBoxButtonColl(iIndex), Button)

        AddHandler objButton.Click, AddressOf objListBox_Click

        Me.Controls.AddRange(New _
          System.Windows.Forms.Control() {objListBoxButtonColl(iIndex)})

End Sub

Private Sub objListBox_Click(ByVal sender As Object, ByVal e As
System.EventArgs)
        Dim objListbox As ListBox
        Dim objButton As Button
        Dim iIndex As Integer

        For Each objButton In objListBoxButtonColl

            iIndex += 1

            If objButton Is sender Then
                Exit For
            End If

        Next

        objListbox = CType(objListBoxColl(iIndex), ListBox)

        objListbox.ClearSelected()

End Sub
```

Building the SQL WHERE Clause

Now that you know how to create criteria screens in VB .NET, let's take a look at how the selections made by the user are harvested and turned into a WHERE clause that you can feed to the report engine. This section of code is far more similar to its VB6 counterpart than the preceding dynamic control creation section was. All the examples use the list and combo boxes provided by Microsoft in VB .NET. As of this writing, FarPoint Technologies plans to release the VB .NET version of their excellent ListPro controls in the second quarter of 2003.

Let's begin by looking at what happens when the user clicks the OK button to run the report as shown in Listing 3-20.

Listing 3-20. OK Button Click Event

```
Private Sub cmdOK_Click(ByVal sender As System.Object, _
    ByVal e As System.EventArgs) Handles cmdOK.Click
    Dim objSQL As New StringBuilder()
    Dim cSQL As String
    Dim objCriteria As New StringBuilder()
    Dim cCriteria As String
    Dim cDateFrom As String
    Dim cDateTo As String
    Dim iDateCnt As Short
    Dim x As Short

    iDateCnt = objDateFromColl.Count

    For x = 1 To iDateCnt

        cDateFrom = objDateFromColl(x).Text
        cDateTo = objDateToColl(x).Text

        If cDateFrom <> String.Empty Or cDateTo <> String.Empty Then

            If Not IsDate(cDateFrom) Or Not IsDate(cDateTo) Then

                MsgBox("You must enter both a valid 'from' and a 'to' date.", _
                    vbOKOnly)

                Exit Sub

            End If
```

```
            End If


        If IsDate(cDateFrom) And IsDate(cDateTo) Then

            If DateValue(cDateFrom) > DateValue(cDateTo) Then

                MsgBox("The 'from date' cannot be greater than the 'to date'.", _
                        vbOKOnly)

                objDateFromColl(x).Focus()

                Exit Sub

            End If

        End If

    Next x

    cDateFrom = objDateFromColl(SELECT_ENTER_DATE).Text
    cDateTo = objDateToColl(SELECT_ENTER_DATE).Text

    With objSQL
        .AppendFormat (GetDateSQL("createdate", cDateFrom, cDateTo))
        .AppendFormat (GetListBoxSQL(objListBoxColl(SELECT_PRODUCT), "productid"))
        .AppendFormat (GetListBoxSQL(objListBoxColl(SELECT_SOURCE), "sourceid"))
        .AppendFormat (GetComboBoxSQL(SELECT_DEPARTMENT, "deptid"))
        .AppendFormat (GetCheckBoxSQL(SELECT_COMPLEX_QUESTION, "questiontype"))
    End With

    With objCriteria
        .AppendFormat (GetDateCriteria("createdate", cDateFrom, cDateTo))
        .AppendFormat (GetListBoxCriteria(objListBoxColl(SELECT_PRODUCT), _
                                "Product"))
        .AppendFormat (GetListBoxCriteria(objListBoxColl(SELECT_SOURCE), "Source"))
        .AppendFormat (GetComboBoxCriteria(SELECT_DEPARTMENT, "Department"))
        .AppendFormat (GetCheckBoxCriteria(SELECT_COMPLEX_QUESTION, _
                                "Complex Question"))
    End With

    cSQL = objSQL.ToString
    cCriteria = objCriteria.ToString
```

```
    If objSQL.ToString <> String.Empty Then
        cSQL = Mid(cSQL, 1, cSQL.Length - 4)
    End If


    If objCriteria.ToString <> String.Empty Then
        cCriteria = Mid$(cCriteria, 1, objCriteria.Length - 5)
    End If


    MsgBox (cSQL.ToString)


    MsgBox (cCriteria.ToString)


End Sub
```

First make sure that all the date controls have valid dates in them. Then, the SQL statement and the criteria statement can be concatenated by invoking the subroutines that deal with the individual controls containing their data. The code for these individual subroutines is almost exactly the same as their VB6 counterparts and can be found on the Apress Web site. The main difference lies in the subroutines that handle combo and list boxes. Since both controls are bound to their data source via the ValueMember and DisplayMember properties, the methods of extracting the selected data from them are different. For the combo box, the unique ID data stored in the ValueMember property is extracted as follows:

```
lChoiceID = objComboBoxColl(Index).SelectedValue()
```

while the text description is extracted like this:

```
cChoice = objComboBoxColl(Index).Text
```

List boxes, however, are another story. Microsoft's documentation for them is rather poor, and very few examples are provided as to how data is extracted from them. The code shown in Listing 3-21 illustrates how both the unique ID values and the descriptions are extracted via the ParseIt function.

Listing 3-21. List Box Code

```
    Function GetListBoxSQL(ByRef objListBox As ListBox, _
                            ByVal cColumn As String) As String
        Dim cSQL As String
        Dim cList As String
```

```
        If objListBox.SelectedItems.Count > 0 Then

            cList = ParseIt(objListBox, True, False, 0)

            cSQL = cColumn & " IN " & cList & " AND "

        End If

        GetListBoxSQL = cSQL

    End Function

    Function GetListBoxCriteria(ByRef objListBox As ListBox, _
                            ByVal cDescr As String) As String
        Dim cResult As String
        Dim cNames As String

        If objListBox.SelectedItems.Count > 0 Then

            cNames = ParseIt(objListBox, True, False, 1)

            cResult = cResult & "the " & cDescr & " is among " & _
                        cNames & " and " & vbCrLf

        End If

        GetListBoxCriteria = cResult

    End Function

Function ParseIt(ByVal oList As ListBox, ByVal bTagged As Boolean, _
            ByVal bQuotes As Boolean, _
    ByVal iCol As Short) As String
    Dim objResult As New StringBuilder("(")
    Dim cResult As String = String.Empty
    Dim cQuotes As String
    Dim cData As String
    Dim oTemp As Object
    Dim oCollection As Object

    If bQuotes Then
        cQuotes = Chr(39)
    Else
```

```
            cQuotes = String.Empty
        End If

        If bTagged Then
            oCollection = oList.SelectedItems
        Else
            oCollection = oList.Items
        End If

        For Each oTemp In oCollection

            cData = oTemp.Item(iCol)

            objResult.AppendFormat (cQuotes & cData & cQuotes & ",")

        Next

        cResult = objResult.ToString

        If bQuotes Then
            cResult = Mid$(cResult, 1, Len(cResult) - 2) & cQuotes & ")"
        Else
            cResult = Mid$(cResult, 1, Len(cResult)) & cQuotes & ")"
        End If

        cResult = Replace(cResult, ",)", ")")

        cResult = Replace(cResult, ",,", String.Empty)

        If cResult = "()" Then
            cResult = String.Empty
        End If

        ParseIt = cResult

    End Function
```

Conclusion

By now you should have an understanding of what it takes to build report criteria screens in both VB6 and VB .NET that are as easy for your clients to use as they are for you to maintain. By utilizing dynamically created controls, you need only one form to encapsulate all your criteria screen functionality regardless of how many reports will ship with your application, as long as your criteria screens are very similar in functionality and don't have any interdependencies between controls. Coming up, you'll learn how to integrate reports into your applications using Crystal Reports Developer's Edition.

CHAPTER 4

Crystal Reports 9

CRYSTAL DECISIONS' CRYSTAL REPORTS has been the market leader for report writing tools for many years and has been exhaustively covered in many excellent books. It has so many rich features that proper coverage of its visual design-time functionality truly requires an entire book. The focus of this chapter is to discuss the developer features of the Crystal Reports Engine offered only in Crystal Reports 9's Developer's and Advanced Editions.

Pros and Cons of Crystal Reports

Crystal Reports has come a long way in the past several years. In its current versions for both VB and .NET, Crystal allows seamless integration with your applications. It is one of the most popular tools on the market and the de facto standard for report writing for several reasons. It is a product with a large installed user base—eleven million licenses worldwide—and a stable company behind it. Of course, a licensing agreement with Microsoft, which has been shipping Crystal Reports with VB since version 2 and now with .NET, hasn't hurt either.

> **NOTE**   *Of course, the version that ships with VB 6 and .NET is only the "teaser" version of Crystal Reports. If you want the full functionality, you'll need to license the Developer's Edition, and if you want to deploy these reports on the Web, you'll need Crystal Enterprise, which is discussed in Chapter 9.*

Pros

Using a visual report writer has many advantages. First, you have wizards that will do most of the work for you. While this may not seem like much when building simple columnar reports, it is a huge time-saver on reports with such items as labels and cross tabs. Since report writers allow you to paint your reports visually, you can at least see the final appearance of the product simply by switching between the design and preview tabs. Moreover, if you like what you see and wish to have it available in every report created in your application, you can save the common "look and feel" as a template. Future reports opened with this template will inherit all the settings of the template document—fonts, colors, logos, page headers, disclaimer notices, etc. Crystal Reports' templates function very much like Microsoft Word templates for guaranteeing consistency of appearance between reports.

Because Crystal Reports is so heavily entrenched as a development tool and is the official standard in many development shops, there are many developers available who have the expertise to staff your projects in comparison with other tools that are not as well known or widely used. Since it is not necessary to be a developer to use Crystal Reports, many of your end users will have already created their own RPTs (RPT is the extension Crystal Reports gives to its report files), which you can then link to a compiled application. I often recommend Crystal Reports to my clients as it liberates them from needing me to create reports and perform data analysis.

Cons

Report writers have their downsides as well. If you are blessed to have a client who makes changes to his or her original program specification every other day for the entire project lifecycle, your report writer can easily work against you. Suppose you must calculate a certain result using a complex algorithm created in your report file. If your client changes the algorithm, the only way to back up the original is to back up the entire report writer file or place it under version control. If you are doing the work in VB, however, you can simply comment out that section of code, annotate when and why you changed it, and still have it readily available when the client calls you one month and eight revisions later asking that the original calculation be put back in because that is what he or she really wanted to begin with. Also, the algorithm you need to produce a certain number may be compiled into an EXE or ActiveX DLL. Unfortunately, Crystal Reports cannot access this code. In this case, you may need to create a temporary table and then report from this table.

Applications often have several sets of reports that differ from one another only marginally. An internal invoice may show terms of sale but a bill of lading may not, though in all other aspects the two reports are identical. While a report writer can easily decide whether or not to print a field based upon parameters that are passed, it falls short if this requires realignment of the other fields. If the report existed as source code, parameters could easily handle this realignment by setting the Top and Left properties of the individual fields. Moreover, when you have similar reports in a report writer, the change of an algorithm in one report requires that you make the change in all reports. Then, when you have a problem, it can be quite difficult to find, as the report writer doesn't offer the luxury of a source code debugger.

While you do have the ability to create subroutines with the Crystal Reports Designer utilizing VB-compatible source code, you still do not have the full power of a programming language. This can cause some limitations when you need to implement something nonstandard. For example, you couldn't use Crystal Reports to direct some pages of a report to one paper bin and other pages to another paper bin. If this were necessary, the solution would require you to create two separate reports. One report would print the first part of the data and send it to one bin, and then the second report would print the rest of the data and send it to another bin. Most likely, this would require the use of temporary tables. Obviously, such a solution is a massive kludge.

Probably the biggest drawback of using Crystal Reports—or any of the higher-end report development tools like Cognos, Actuate, BusinessObjects, and WebFocus—is the licensing. If you have plans to make your reports available to a large number of users via the Internet or a report server, you'll find that Crystal Decisions' licensing requirements can send your deployment costs to the stratosphere. See Chapter 9 for a discussion of Crystal Reports licensing.

Runtime

Crystal Reports' runtime can be rather large. The Report Designer Component (craxdrt.dll) is 5MB and the Embeddable Designer Control requires the ActiveX Designer Design and Runtime Support DLL (craxddrt9.dll), which is 10.5MB. Craxddrt9.dll combines the runtime capabilities of craxdrt.dll with the design-time capabilities of the ActiveX Designer Design Time Library (craxddt.dll). The viewer control itself adds an extra 753K. In addition, each export format requires its own support DLL. While these are small (generally less than 200K), you still need to make sure these files are all present and accounted for. Of course, don't forget the database drivers.

Crystal Reports 9 Object Model

Like the Microsoft Office suite, Crystal Reports exposes its object model so that developers may make full use of its features via ActiveX Automation. Starting with the Application object, the developer can move down the tree to the Report object as well as to other objects that encapsulate the different areas of a report—header, footer, body, grouping, summary fields, subreport, etc. A developer therefore can programmatically manipulate individual field objects, running totals, and formulas. On the back end, objects are available to set the report's database connection, sort options, and individual parameter fields. Taken together, you can create reports entirely at runtime using the Report Designer Component (RDC). The RDC is an ActiveX Designer that offers three main components:

- *Report Designer:* This component lets your users create, view, and modify reports directly in the IDE.

- *Automation Server:* An object model with approximately 800 properties and methods you can use to program a report. Depending on the Automation Server features you use, you may need a separate runtime license.

- *Report Viewer:* Allows you to preview reports on a form and offers properties to customize appearance and toolbar options.

Though Crystal Reports still continues to support the older OCX technology and the Crystal Report Print Engine APIs, this is done primarily for backward compatibility purposes. The RDC is the way all Crystal Reports' new developer technology is going, so I recommend that you do all new development using this tool.

TIP   *Crystal Decisions has an RDC object browser that is available free for download from their Web site. This allows you to view the documentation for the RDC via a treeview hierarchy of all the objects, properties, and methods.*

Report Designers vs. RPT files

Using the Developer's Edition, you can create your reports in one of two ways: either using the traditional RPT file format or using a VB Designer. The one major drawback to using a VB Designer is that since the report is compiled into the application, you'll need to deploy a new EXE every time a change is made to a report. Using separate RPT files, you can distribute updates to existing reports to the server without needing to register DLLs or fight with the change control manager.

Getting Started with the RDC Automation Server

The RDC Automation Server provides a powerful object model to create and modify reports at runtime as well as programmatically display and print reports. The example in Listing 4-1 shows how a VB form with a Viewer control (crviewer.dll) can open an RPT and display it to the user.

Listing 4-1. Displaying an RPT File with Viewer Control

```
Dim WithEvents CRViewer91 As CRVIEWER9LibCtl.CRViewer9
Dim objApplication As New CRAXDRT.Application
Dim objReport As New CRAXDRT.Report


Private Sub Form_Load()


    ' Dynamically add the CRVIEWER control to the form
    Set CRViewer91 = Me.CRViewer91


    'Set the report object
    Set objReport = objApplication.OpenReport(App.Path & "\requestor.rpt")


    objReport.DiscardSavedData


    With CRViewer91
        .DisplayGroupTree = False
        .EnableGroupTree = False
        .EnableNavigationControls = True
        .EnableSearchControl = True
        .EnableExportButton = True
        .EnableRefreshButton = False
        .ReportSource = objReport
        .ViewReport
    End With


    'maximizes the window
    Me.WindowState = vbMaximized


End Sub
```

If you've ever programmed the Microsoft Office suite using ActiveX Automation, this code will look very familiar to you structurally. First, you'll need to declare object variables to represent the report viewer as well as to reference the Application and Report objects themselves—objApplication and objReport, respectively. The Report object is created using the OpenReport method of the Application object, and the physical location of the report file is passed as a parameter. Then, any data already existing in the report—such as preset parameters values—is cleaned out by invoking the DiscardSavedData method. After this, a series of settings on the viewer for various features such as whether or not to display a search or export button are turned on or off as needed. Finally, the Report object is set to the ReportSource property of the viewer control and the ViewReport method is invoked. Voila!—you're now looking at your report.

Reports are rarely this simple, of course, as you'll undoubtedly need to pass parameters to the report. If the preceding report had parameters, they could be set programmatically by creating a ParameterFieldDefinitions object, which is a collection to hold parameters represented by individual ParameterFieldDefinition objects. The code in Listing 4-2 illustrates how parameters can be set at runtime.

Listing 4-2. Parameters Collection

```
Dim objApplication As New CRAXDRT.Application
Dim objReport As New CRAXDRT.Report
Dim objParameterFields As CRAXDRT.ParameterFieldDefinitions
Dim objParameterField1 As CRAXDRT.ParameterFieldDefinition

' Dynamically add the CRVIEWER control to the form
Set CRViewer91 = Me.CRViewer91

'Set the report object
Set objReport = objApplication.OpenReport(App.Path & "\requestor.rpt")

objReport.DiscardSavedData

Set objParameterFields = objReport.ParameterFields

Set objParameterField1 = objParameterFields.Item(1)
objParameterField1.AddCurrentValue ("SC")
```

As you can see, this code is similar to Listing 4-1, only a parameters object called objParameterFields is instantiated and set equal to the collection of parameters encapsulated by objReport.ParameterFields. Then, an object representing a single parameter, objParameterField1, is instantiated and set equal to the first element in the parameter collection object. The AddCurrentValue method then assigns a parameter value to filter the report.

Since all the parameter fields are stored within the RPT files, you can even create dynamic criteria screens for each report using data-driven programming techniques. For a full explanation of data-driven programming using both VB and .NET, see the sidebars "Data-Driven Programming with VB6" and "Data-Driven Programming with VB .NET" in Chapter 3. Listing 4-3 shows how criteria screens can be dynamically created for Crystal Reports.

Listing 4-3. Dynamic Criteria Screens

```
Dim objApplication As New CRAXDRT.Application
Dim objReport As New CRAXDRT.Report
Dim objParameterFields As CRAXDRT.ParameterFieldDefinitions
Dim objParameterField1 As CRAXDRT.ParameterFieldDefinition

Sub RunReport(cFileName As String)

    Set objReport = objApplication.OpenReport(cFileName)

    objReport.DiscardSavedData

    Set objParameterFields = objReport.ParameterFields
    Set objParameterField1 = objParameterFields.Item(1)

    Call CreateLabel(1, 100, 100, 1800, 285, objParameterField1.Prompt)
    Call CreateComboBox(1, 100, 1900, 900, 285)

    Call LoadComboBox(1)

    objReport.PaperOrientation = crLandscape
    objReport.PaperSize = crPaperLegal
    objReport.ReportTitle = "Ex-presidents list to be printed on " & _
                                        objReport.PrinterName
    objReport.PaperSource = crPRBinUpper

End Sub
```

The Prompt property returns the descriptive text embedded in the RPT file for the referenced parameter field. Finally, the PaperSize, ReportTitle, PrinterName, and PaperSource properties are set with values that could easily be user configured. The remainder of this example can be found on the source code available on the Apress Web site (http://www.apress.com). This code will produce the criteria screen shown in Figure 4-1.

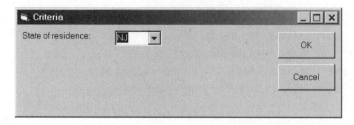

Figure 4-1. Dynamically created criteria screen

The code for the form invoked by the criteria screen OK button is shown in Listing 4-4. It simply receives the configured Report object in the Viewer control and displays the filtered output to the screen. The process is similar to that for the code in Listing 4-1.

Listing 4-4. Display Parameterized Report to Screen

```
Public objReport As New CRAXDRT.Report

Dim WithEvents CRViewer91 As CRVIEWERLibCtl.CRViewer

Private Sub Form_Load()

    ' Dynamically add the CRVIEWER control to the form
    Set CRViewer91 = Me.CRViewer91

    With CRViewer91
        .DisplayGroupTree = False
        .EnableGroupTree = False
        .EnableNavigationControls = True
        .EnableSearchControl = True
        .EnableExportButton = True
        .EnableRefreshButton = False
        .ReportSource = objReport
        .ViewReport
    End With

        'maximizes the window
    Me.WindowState = vbMaximized

End Sub
```

Crystal Reports Repository

Crystal Reports 9 advertising states that the main focus of this release of the product is productivity. Arguably, then, the greatest feature introduced in version 9 is the Crystal Reports repository. Often objects such as text boxes, formulas, SQL commands, and images need to be shared among different reports. In the past, each formula, for example, that was used previously had to be copied into a new report from an existing one. Not only was it difficult to find the previous instance of the formula needed, but if the formula had to be universally changed, the change had to be made in every report in which it was used. The repository now eliminates this problem. By centralizing all formulas in a common library and linking them to reports, a change to a formula in the central repository will be reflected in all reports in which the formula is used and is connected to the repository.

The repository is any ODBC database that you select. It could be Access (and is by default), SQL Server, Oracle, or whatever your company standard is. Crystal Reports' orMap.ini file contains the reference to the System DSN that is connected to the name of the repository. For example, to create a repository called the Seton Software Crystal Repository and set it to a System DSN named Seton Software CR Repository, enter the following line in orMap.ini:

```
Seton Software Crystal Repository=Crystal Repository
```

When Crystal Reports first connects to the specified database, it will create two tables—OR_OBJECTS and OR_TYPE_SCHEMA—to hold references to the objects stored there. Crystal Reports 9 currently doesn't offer any programmatic access to the repository through its object model. But this doesn't mean that you can't access the repository yourself. After all, it's only a set of database tables to which you have access, just like any other database.

The details of the repository objects are stored in XML format, and there is no reason you couldn't edit this XML and write it back to the repository database without using Crystal Reports. Suppose you wish to allow your users to modify a Crystal Reports text object called Disclaimer from within your application. The XML block stores such attributes as the position, text, and font of the text object. The XML that describes this object would look something like Listing 4-5.

Listing 4-5. Text Object XML Description

```
<CrystalReports.TextObject xmlns="http://www.crystaldecisions.com/report"
xmlns:xsi="http://www.w3.org/2001/XMLSchema-instance"
xmlns:xsd="http://www.w3.org/2001/XMLSchema" xsi:type="CrystalReports.TextObject"
version="2">
  <SectionCode>0</SectionCode>
```

```
<SectionName />
<Top>0</Top>
<Left>0</Left>
<Width>1931</Width>
<Height>226</Height>
<Kind>Text</Kind>
<ObjectName />
<Border xsi:type="CrystalReports.Border" id="1" version="2">
<LeftLineStyle>NoLine</LeftLineStyle>
<RightLineStyle>NoLine</RightLineStyle>
<TopLineStyle>NoLine</TopLineStyle>
<BottomLineStyle>NoLine</BottomLineStyle>
<HasDropShadow>false</HasDropShadow>
<BackColor>-1</BackColor>
<BorderColor>0</BorderColor>
<TightHorizontal>false</TightHorizontal>
<ConditionFormulas />
</Border>
<ObjectFormat xsi:type="CrystalReports.ObjectFormat" id="2" version="2">
<CanGrow>false</CanGrow>
<Suppress>false</Suppress>
<CloseAtPageBreak>false</CloseAtPageBreak>
<KeepTogether>true</KeepTogether>
<HorizontalAlignment>Default</HorizontalAlignment>
<ToolTipText />
<CssClass />
<ConditionFormulas />
<HyperlinkText />
<HyperlinkType>Undefined</HyperlinkType>
<TextRotationAngle>Rotate0</TextRotationAngle>
</ObjectFormat>
<LinkedURI />
<ReportPartBookmark />
<Paragraphs xsi:type="CrystalReports.Paragraphs" id="3" version="2">
<Paragraph xsi:type="CrystalReports.Paragraph" id="4" version="2">
<TabStops />
<Elements xsi:type="CrystalReports.ParagraphElements" id="5" version="2">
<Element xsi:type="CrystalReports.ParagraphTextElement" id="6" version="2">
<FontColor xsi:type="CrystalReports.FontColor" id="7" version="2">
<Color>0</Color>
<Font xsi:type="CrystalReports.Font" id="8" version="2">
<Name>Arial</Name>
<Size.Low>100000</Size.Low>
```

```
  <Size.High>0</Size.High>
  <Bold>false</Bold>
  <Italic>false</Italic>
  <Underline>false</Underline>
  <Strikethrough>false</Strikethrough>
  <Weight>400</Weight>
  <Charset>1</Charset>
  </Font>
  <ConditionFormulas />
  </FontColor>
  <Kind>Text</Kind>
  <Text>This information is for internal use only</Text>
  <CharacterSpacing>0</CharacterSpacing>
  </Element>
  </Elements>
 <IndentAndSpacingFormat xsi:type="CrystalReports.IndentAndSpacingFormat" id="9"
version="2">
  <FirstLineIndent>0</FirstLineIndent>
  <LeftIndent>0</LeftIndent>
  <RightIndent>0</RightIndent>
  <LineSpacingType>Multiple</LineSpacingType>
  <LineSpacing>65536</LineSpacing>
  </IndentAndSpacingFormat>
  <Alignment>Left</Alignment>
  <ReadingOrder>LeftToRight</ReadingOrder>
  </Paragraph>
  </Paragraphs>
  <MaxNumberOfLines>0</MaxNumberOfLines>
 <TextObjectFormat xsi:type="CrystalReports.TextObjectFormat" id="10"
version="2">
  <SuppressIfDuplicated>false</SuppressIfDuplicated>
  <SuppressEmbedBlankLines>false</SuppressEmbedBlankLines>
  </TextObjectFormat>
  </CrystalReports.TextObject>
```

There is another XML block that describes the registry key information for
the text object that looks something like this:

```
 <CrystalReports.PropertyBag xmlns="http://www.crystaldecisions.com/report"
xmlns:xsi="http://www.w3.org/2001/XMLSchema-instance"
xmlns:xsd="http://www.w3.org/2001/XMLSchema" xsi:type="CrystalReports.PropertyBag"
version="2">
```

```
<Property>
 <Name>Author</Name>
 <Value VariantType="String">Administrator</Value>
</Property>
<Property>
 <Name>Description</Name>
 <Value VariantType="String" />
</Property>
<Property>
 <Name>ObjectDescriptor</Name>
 <Value VariantType="String">contentSize=1931,226 fullSize=1931,226
contentOffset=0,0 cursorOffset=182,0 baselineOffset=0 analysisObjectType=12
analysisGroupLevel=0 objectType=1 isSummaryObject=0 canCopyObject=2145907280
isFieldObject=10435464</Value>
</Property>
<Property>
 <Name>Type</Name>
 <Value VariantType="String">{08FE72BD-FD24-485E-B3B0-6C43B7D07208}</Value>
</Property>
</CrystalReports.PropertyBag>
```

When Crystal Reports writes an object to the repository, it makes a GUID entry into the registry of the local machine. This registry key is used to uniquely identify the entry for the object in the repository database. Using the XML DOM, you can manipulate these XML blocks to change their properties outside of Crystal Reports using your own custom interface.

Dynamic Report Creation

Crystal Reports' programmatic interface is so powerful that you can use it to create entire reports at runtime, not just view and manipulate existing ones. The RDC exposes an object model that allows you as much flexibility for runtime report creation as you have with the user interface at design time. Table 4-1 lists the individual objects that are exposed by the RDC.

Table 4-1. Crystal Report Objects

Application	OlapGridObject
Area	OleObject
BlobFieldObject	Page
BoxObject	PageEngine
CrossTabGroup	PageGenerator
CrossTabObject	ParameterFieldDefinition
Database	PrintingStatus
DatabaseFieldDefinition	Report
DatabaseTable	ReportAlert
ExportOptions	ReportAlertInstance
FieldElement	ReportObjects
FieldMappingData	RunningTotalFieldDefinition
FieldObject	Section
FormattingInfo	SortField
FormulaFieldDefinition	SpecialVarFieldDefinition
GraphObject	SQLExpressionFieldDefinition
GroupNameFieldDefinition	SubreportLink
FieldDefinition	SubreportObject
IReportObject	SummaryFieldDefinition
LineObject	TableLink
MapObject	TextObject

Table 4-2 lists the various collection objects of the Crystal model.

Table 4-2. Crystal Report Collections

Areas	ReportAlerts
CrossTabGroups	ReportAlertInstances
DatabaseFieldDefinitions	RunningTotalFieldDefinitions
DatabaseTables	Sections
FieldDefinitions	SortFields
FieldElements	SQLExpressionFieldDefinitions
ObjectSummaryFieldDefinitions	SubreportLinks
Pages	SummaryFieldDefinitions
ParameterFieldDefinitions	TableLinks

NOTE   *The Crystal Reports object model offers you a powerful interface to report programming that allows you to do almost everything at runtime that you can at design time. While the object model for Crystal Reports offers most of the features you'll need, it is not as rich or as mature as that of the Microsoft Office suite. The Report Creation API was only recently released in Crystal 8, but new features are being added with each version as it continues to grow in popularity.*

Suppose you want to create a report at runtime that displays in a columnar fashion the results of a query. You also want to display the results grouped by state with the total count of all records printed in a summary at the end of the report. You could accomplish this with the code in Listing 4-6.

Listing 4-6. Dynamic Report Creation

```
Dim objApplication As New CRAXDRT.Application
Dim objReport As New CRAXDRT.Report
Dim objText As CRAXDRT.TextObject
Dim objField As CRAXDRT.FieldObject
Dim objFieldDef As CRAXDRT.DatabaseFieldDefinition
Dim objSection As CRAXDRT.Section
Dim oConn As ADODB.Connection
```

```
Dim oCmd As ADODB.Command
Dim cConnectString As String
Dim cSQL As String
Dim cCaption As String
Dim cFieldName As String
Dim iFieldCnt As Integer
Dim iLeft As Integer
Dim x As Integer

'Create ADO Connection object
Set oConn = New ADODB.Connection
cConnectString = "Provider=Microsoft.Jet.OLEDB.4.0;" & _
                 "Data Source=C:\Reports\SampleDatabase.mdb;" & _
                 "Persist Security Info=False"
oConn.Open cConnectString


cSQL = "SELECT LastName, FirstName, Address1, City, State " & _
       "FROM Requester " & _
       "WHERE State IN ('NJ', 'NY', 'SC')"


'Create ADO Command object
Set oCmd = New ADODB.Command
Set oCmd.ActiveConnection = oConn
oCmd.CommandText = cSQL
oCmd.CommandType = adCmdText

'Instantiate new Crystal Application object
Set objApplication = New CRAXDRT.Application

'Instantiate a blank report object
Set objReport = objApplication.NewReport

'Set the data source of the new report
Call objReport.Database.AddADOCommand(oConn, oCmd)
objReport.PaperSize = crPaperLetter
objReport.TopMargin = 200
objReport.BottomMargin = 200


cCaption = "US Presidents - Where are they now?"
```

```
'Create report title section
objReport.Sections(1).Height = objReport.Sections(1).Height + 300
Set objText = objReport.Sections(1).AddTextObject(cCaption, 1700, 0)

With objText
    .HorAlignment = crHorCenterAlign
    .BorderColor = vbBlack
    .Font.Size = 18
    .Font.Bold = True
    .TextColor = vbBlue
    .Height = 600
    .Width = 7500
End With


With objReport

    'How many fields in data source
    iFieldCnt = .Database.Tables(1).Fields.Count


    'Loop through each field and add it to the report

    For x = 1 To iFieldCnt

        cFieldName = .Database.Tables(1).Fields(x).Name

        Set objField = .Sections(3).AddFieldObject(cFieldName, iLeft, 0)

        objField.Font.Name = "Arial"
        objField.Font.Size = 10

        iLeft = iLeft + (.Database.Tables(1).Fields(x).NumberOfBytes * 60)

    Next x

    'Group by state field
    Set objFieldDef = .Database.Tables(1).Fields(5)

    Call objReport.AddGroup(0, objFieldDef, crGCAnyValue, crAscendingOrder)
```

```
    Set objSection = objReport.Sections.Item("GH1")
    Call objSection.AddFieldObject(objFieldDef, 100, 0)



    'Add a subtotal count
    Set objSection = objReport.Sections.Item("RF")

    objSection.BackColor = vbCyan

    cCaption = "Total US Presidents listed:"

    Set objText = objSection.AddTextObject(cCaption, 100, 0)

    objText.Font.Name = "Arial"
    objText.Font.Size = 10
    objText.Font.Bold = True
    objText.Width = 3000

    Set objFieldDef = .Database.Tables(1).Fields(1)

    Call objSection.AddSummaryFieldObject(objFieldDef, crSTCount, 2500, 0)

End With

'Display the report
With CRViewer91
    .ReportSource = objReport
    .Zoom (100)
    .ViewReport
End With
```

In this example, straight VB/ADO code is used to establish a connection to a database and instantiate a Command object. Then, an object reference to the Crystal application is instantiated and the AddADOCommand method connects the ADO Connection object and the ADO Command object to the report.

After this, the header area is sized and a TextObject is added to display the title of the report:

```
cCaption = "US Presidents - Where are they now?"
objReport.Sections(1).Height = objReport.Sections(1).Height + 300
Set objText = objReport.Sections(1).AddTextObject(cCaption, 1700, 0)
```

Since the goal is to create as many data columns in the body of the report as there are fields in the result set, the For...Next loop moves through the field count and creates, sizes, and positions a FieldObject for each column found. Finally, a subtotal represented as an AddSummaryFieldObject counts the number of records found for each group—in this example each state—and displays the number in the report footer area, which gets referenced through the Section object.

This code produces the output shown in Figure 4-2.

Preview				
NJ				
NY				
SC				

US Presidents – Where are they now?

NJ

| Bush | George | 123 Main Street | Anytown | NJ |
| Nixon | Richard | 7834 Main Street | Princeton | NJ |

NY

| Clinton | Bill | 210 Little Rock Lane | Starrville | NY |
| Roosevelt | Franklin | 56 Fifth Street | Elmira | NY |

SC

| Johnson | Andrew | 35 Eighteenth Street | Charleston | SC |

| Total US Presidents listed: | 5 |

Figure 4-2. Dynamic report output

Using any of the report creation features of the Report Creation API requires special licensing. You'll know you've invoked a routine that requires this license when you receive the message box shown in Figure 4-3.

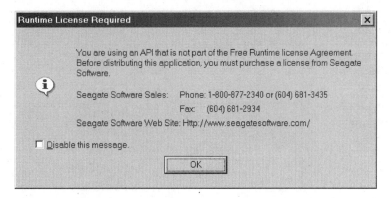

Figure 4-3. Runtime license message box

Approximately 100 of the 800 different Report Creation API calls available require licenses that are sold on a per-seat basis. These licenses are $199 per single named user and are sold in packs of 1, 5, and 25. Visit Crystal Decisions' Web site at `http://www.crystaldecisions.com/products/crystalreports/licensing/default .asp` for full information about runtime Report Creation API license options.

Advanced Dynamic Report Creation

Next we'll study a more complicated example by dynamically creating a one-to-many relationship as shown in Figure 4-4. In this report, taken from SQL Server's Northwind database, the Customer table is joined with the Order table to determine the total freight costs each customer is incurring. The freight charge for each individual order is displayed under each customer and then the subtotal for that customer is displayed. Finally, the grand total of all freight costs is displayed at the end of the report. Because the length of the entire source code output would consume 15 book pages, we'll only examine the most significant areas here. The entire source code can be found with the downloadable code on the Apress Web site (`http://www.apress.com`).

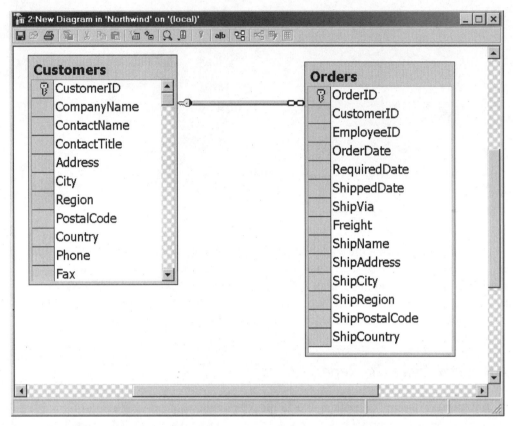

Figure 4-4. One-to-many relationship

The first step in creating this report dynamically is to declare a series of variables to reference the various Crystal Reports objects—Application, Report, FieldObject, TextObject, etc.—and the different database connectivity objects. These declarations are shown in Listing 4-7.

Listing 4-7. Crystal Declarations

```
Dim objApplication As CRAXDRT.Application
Dim objReport As CRAXDRT.Report
Dim objSpecialField As CRAXDRT.FieldObject
Dim objTextObject As CRAXDRT.TextObject
Dim objFieldObject As CRAXDRT.FieldObject
Dim objDBTables As CRAXDRT.DatabaseTables
Dim objOneDBTable As CRAXDRT.DatabaseTable
Dim objManyDBTable As CRAXDRT.DatabaseTable
Dim objOneDBField As CRAXDRT.DatabaseFieldDefinition
```

```
Dim objManyDBField As CRAXDRT.DatabaseFieldDefinition
Dim objDBlinks As CRAXDRT.TableLinks
Dim objDBLink As CRAXDRT.TableLink
```

The next steps are to instantiate the Application and Report objects and establish database connectivity. In this example, the connection is being made through an ODBC DSN called SQLServerNorthwind, and the name of the first table is called Customers. This information is added to the Tables collection of the Database object that is owned by the Report object. The parameter value p2sodbc.dll indicates which Crystal database driver to use and depends on the data source and method of connectivity. Some of the other database drivers available include p2sora7.dll for the Oracle 7.x series; p2smon.dll for ADO, RDO, or DAO connections; and p2soutlk.dll for Microsoft Outlook. Listing 4-8 illustrates the setup of the database connectivity objects.

Listing 4-8. Database Connectivity

```
Set objApplication = New CRAXDRT.Application
Set objReport = objApplication.NewReport

' Add a table.
Set objDBTables = objReport.Database.Tables
objReport.Database.Tables.Add "Northwind.dbo.Customers", "", , , "p2sodbc.dll", _
    "SQLServerNorthwind.dsn", "", "dbo", , ""
objReport.Database.Tables(1).Name = "Customers"

' Add a table.
Set objDBTables = objReport.Database.Tables
objReport.Database.Tables.Add "Northwind.dbo.Orders", "", , , "p2sodbc.dll", _
    "SQLServerNorthwind.dsn", "", "dbo", , ""
objReport.Database.Tables(2).Name = "Orders"
```

The next step is to establish the data relationships between the two tables. The object variables objOneDBTable and objManyDBTable refer to the Customers table and the Orders table, respectively. Likewise, objOneDBField and objManyDBField refer to the primary and foreign key columns that create the referential link between the two tables. In this case, their names are {Customers.CustomerID} and {Orders.CustomerID}, respectively. The references to these items in both the Table and Fields collections of the Database object are made by passing the ordinal position within the collection. Once the individual table and field references have been established, the objDBLink object cements the link together by receiving as parameters the two table objects and the two field objects required to complete the join. The parameter crJTEqual indicates the type of join to use. The parameters indicating the other types of joins are shown in Table 4-3.

Table 4-3. TableLink Object Join Parameters

CONSTANT	VALUE
crJTEqual	4
crJTGreaterOrEqual	10
crJTGreaterThan	8
crJTLeftOuter	5
crJTLessOrEqual	11
crJTLessThan	9
crJTNotEqual	12
crJTRightOuter	6

The code establishing the table links is shown in Listing 4-9.

Listing 4-9. Database Connectivity

```
' Set database link.
Set objOneDBTable = objReport.Database.Tables.Item(1)
Set objManyDBTable = objReport.Database.Tables.Item(2)
Set objOneDBField = objReport.Database.Tables.Item(1).Fields.Item(1)
Set objManyDBField = objReport.Database.Tables.Item(2).Fields.Item(2)
Set objDBlinks = objReport.Database.Links
Set objDBLink = objDBlinks.Add(objOneDBTable, objManyDBTable, objOneDBField, _
    objManyDBField, crJTEqual, crLTLookupParallel, False, True)
```

At this point, the individual report areas and sections of the report can be created. Crystal Reports has five default report areas in design mode: Report Header, Page Header, Details, Report Footer, and Page Footer. Group Headers and Group Footers are areas as well, and you may add multiple groups to a report. To each of these areas, you may add additional sections.

Since the purpose of the report is to list the freight costs by company, you need to group the report by Company Name. The code shown in Listing 4-10 illustrates how a new group is added to the groups collection as section GH1.

Listing 4-10. Group Heading

```
' Add group Object. - "{Customers.CompanyName}"
objReport.AddGroup 0, objReport.Database.Tables.Item(1).Fields(3), _
    crGCAnyValue, crAscendingOrder


' Set group options.
With objReport.Areas("GH1")
    .Suppress = False
    .HideForDrillDown = False
    .DiscardOtherGroups = False
    .KeepGroupTogether = False
    .RepeatGroupHeader = False
    .EnableHierarchicalGroupSorting = False
    .GroupIndent = 0
End With
```

Note that the KeepGroupTogether property is set to False. This option allows data within the group—in this example, the individual freight charges per order—to print across onto the next page. If KeepGroupTogether were set to True, each company's freight information would print on the same page and leave white space at the bottom if the next company's data could not fit.

Once the areas and sections have been established, the column captions can print in the section of the Page Header area. You can accomplish this by instantiating a series of TextObjects and setting the Text, Left, and Top properties using the AddTextObject method (see Listing 4-11).

Listing 4-11. Company Column Caption

```
' Add a text object.
Set objTextObject = objReport.Sections("PHa").AddTextObject("Company", 60, 697)

With objTextObject
    .Height = 230
    .Width = 2648

    .TextColor = vbBlack
    .Font.Italic = False
    .Font.Name = "Arial"
    .Font.Size = 10
    .Font.Strikethrough = False
    .Font.Underline = True
    .Font.Bold = True
```

```
        .Suppress = False
        .HorAlignment = crLeftAlign
        .KeepTogether = True
        .CanGrow = False
        .LeftLineStyle = crLSNoLine
        .RightLineStyle = crLSNoLine
        .TopLineStyle = crLSNoLine
        .BottomLineStyle = crLSNoLine
        .BackColor = vbWhite
        .SuppressIfDuplicated = False
End With
```

Add the remainder of the column captions in the same fashion. To add
the individual data fields, use the AddFieldObject as shown in Listing 4-12.
objFieldObject refers to every data element, in this example Customer Name,
that will print in a column. Thus, the properties set for a FieldObject apply to
every row on which a FieldObject prints.

Listing 4-12. Company Column Data

```
Set objFieldObject = objReport.Sections("GH1a")._
        AddFieldObject("{Customers.CompanyName}", 60, 0)


With objFieldObject
        .Height = 230
        .Width = 2648
        .TextColor = vbBlack
        Set .Font = objFont
        .Suppress = False
        .HorAlignment = crDefaultAlign
        .KeepTogether = True
        .CanGrow = False
        .LeftLineStyle = crLSNoLine
        .RightLineStyle = crLSNoLine
        .TopLineStyle = crLSNoLine
        .BottomLineStyle = crLSNoLine
        .BackColor = vbWhite
        .SuppressIfDuplicated = False
        .UseSystemDefaults = True
End With
```

Since the goal is to subtotal the freight charges for each customer, you'll need to use the AddSummaryFieldObject method (Listing 4-13) to create a subtotal counter and display it in the Group Footer that mirrors the Group Header defined by the Customer Name. Remember, a report may have multiple group headers and footers, each with their own subtotal. Note the constant value crSTSum to indicate the sum of the values. Crystal Reports offers options to print the average, count, minimum value, maximum value, standard deviation, median, and most frequent, among other statistics.

Listing 4-13. Group Summary Field

```
Set objFieldObject = objReport.Sections("GF1a")._
    AddSummaryFieldObject("{Orders.Freight}", crSTSum, 6960, 0)

With objFieldObject
    .TextColor = vbBlack
    Set .Font = objFont
    .Height = 240
    .Width = 986
    .Suppress = False
    .HorAlignment = crDefaultAlign
    .KeepTogether = True
    .CanGrow = False
    .LeftLineStyle = crLSNoLine
    .RightLineStyle = crLSNoLine
    .TopLineStyle = crLSNoLine
    .BottomLineStyle = crLSNoLine
    .BackColor = vbWhite
    .SuppressIfDuplicated = False
    .UseSystemDefaults = True
    .SuppressIfZero = False
    .NegativeType = crBracketed
    .ThousandsSeparators = True
    .UseLeadingZero = True
    .DecimalPlaces = 2
    .RoundingType = crRoundToHundredth
    .CurrencySymbolType = crCSTFloatingSymbol
    .UseOneSymbolPerPage = False
    .CurrencyPositionType = crLeadingCurrencyOutsideNegative
    .ThousandSymbol = ","
    .DecimalSymbol = "."
    .CurrencySymbol = "$"
End With
```

Finally, when the body of the report finishes printing, the grand total of all the freight costs across all companies must display. A method call very similar to the one illustrated in Listing 4-11 that shows a group summary will accomplish this. In both cases, you're still creating a summary field, but it's where you're placing it that counts. Since this field is going into a section of the Report Footer area, it will act as a subtotal for the entire report, not just for one customer. This method call is shown here:

```
Set objFieldObject = objReport.Sections("RFa")._
    AddSummaryFieldObject("{Orders.Freight}", crSTSum, 6697, 0)
```

Finally, having created all the attributes of the report programmatically, you can save it to an RPT file using the following syntax:

```
objReport.Save "c:\Crystal\MyReport.rpt"
```

Section Format Event

The Section Format event allows you to change the format of a section before it is printed. This event doesn't maintain state, so do not try to use it to maintain running totals, as you never know the exact sequence in which the event will be fired.

The code for a Section Format event doesn't lie within the RPT file itself. Rather, it is external to the report code and is often included in the form that contains the report viewer. Suppose you wanted to format the freight subtotal field in the Orders report created previously so that all subtotal amounts greater than $200 displayed with a red background. First, you would declare a section option using the WithEvents keyword in the Global Declarations section of the form like this:

```
Dim WithEvents objSectionGF1a As CRAXDDRT.Section
```

Then you'll need to create a section object to reference the section of the report that contains the subtotal field. Do this before you display the report in the viewer. For example:

```
Set objReport = objApplication.OpenReport(cFileName)
```

```
Set objSectionGF1a = objReport.Sections("GF1a")
```

```
CRDesignerCtrl1.ReportObject = objReport
```

The final step is to create a section event handler. In it, you'll create a reference to the exact subtotal field being printed at the moment and check the current value of that field. If the value is greater than 200, display the background color in red; otherwise, display it in black. Listing 4-14 illustrates this point.

Listing 4-14. Section Format Event

```
Private Sub objSectionGF1a_Format(ByVal pFormattingInfo As Object)
    Dim objFieldObject As CRAXDDRT.FieldObject

    Set objFieldObject = objReport.Sections("GF1a").ReportObjects.Item(1)

    If objFieldObject.Value > 200 Then
        objFieldObject.BackColor = vbRed
    Else
        objFieldObject.BackColor = vbWhite
    End If

End Sub
```

NOTE *If you're so excited by these examples of the Crystal Report Creation API that you want still more, see Chapter 8 for an example of how to dynamically create a cross tab report. Then, go get a life!*

Embeddable Designer Control

You may wish to embed the functionality of the Crystal Reports Designer itself into your applications. This can be accomplished with the Embeddable Designer Control (crdesignerctrl.dll). Using this tool, your users have the ability to create and modify reports at runtime. Of course, you'll need a runtime license in order to distribute this functionality, and you'll need users who have the technical expertise to use Crystal Reports. The screen shown in Figure 4-5 serves as a simple report writer interface that you can easily add to any application.

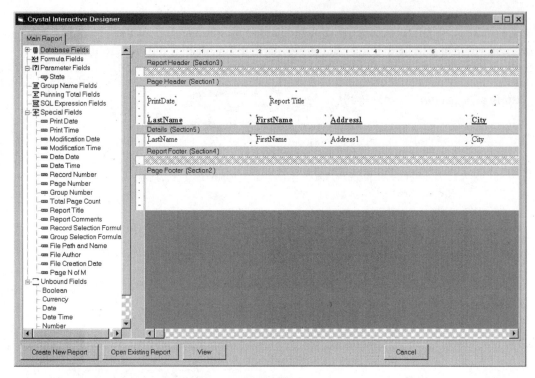

Figure 4-5. Embeddable Designer Control interface

The code example in Listing 4-15 illustrates how simple it is to allow a user to create a new report or edit an existing one, as well as switch between design and preview modes.

Listing 4-15. Embeddable Designer Control Properties

```
Dim objApplication As New CRAXDDRT.Application
Dim objReport As CRAXDDRT.Report
Dim cFileName As String

Private Sub cmdCreateNew_Click()

    Set objReport = objApplication.NewReport

    With CRDesignerCtrl1
        .ReportObject = objReport
        .DisplayToolbar = True
        .DisplayGrid = True
    End With
```

```
End Sub

Private Sub cmdDesignView_Click()

    If cmdDesignView.Caption = "Design" Then
        cmdDesignView.Caption = "View"
        CRDesignerCtrl1.Visible = True
        CRViewer91.Visible = False
    Else
        cmdDesignView.Caption = "Design"
        CRDesignerCtrl1.Visible = False
        CRViewer91.Visible = True

        If Not objReport Is Nothing Then
            CRViewer91.ReportSource = objReport
            CRViewer91.ViewReport
        End If

    End If

End Sub

Private Sub cmdOpenExisting_Click()

    With CommonDialog1
        .Filter = "Crystal Reports|*.rpt"
        .ShowOpen
    End With

    cFileName = CommonDialog1.FileName

    If cFileName = vbNullString Then
        Exit Sub
    End If

    Set objReport = objApplication.OpenReport(cFileName)

    CRDesignerCtrl1.ReportObject = objReport

End Sub
```

Exporting Data

Crystal Reports' data export ability is one of its main advantages over competing report development tools, offering a wide range of export options. Crystal Reports can output report data to ASCII files, HTML, Excel, Lotus, RTF, Word, XML, and ODBC data sources, to name just a few. The full list of export constants can be seen in Table 4-4.

Table 4-4. Export Options

ENUMERATED TYPE	VALUE
crEFTCharSeparatedValues	7
crEFTCommaSeparatedValues	5
crEFTCrystalReport	1
crEFTCrystalReport70	33
crEFTDataInterchange	2
crEFTExactRichText	35
crEFTExcel50	21
crEFTExcel50Tabular	22
crEFTExcel70	27
crEFTExcel70Tabular	28
crEFTExcel80	29
crEFTExcel80Tabular	30
crEFTExplorer32Extend	25
crEFTHTML32Standard	24
crEFTHTML40	32
crEFTLotus123WK1	12
crEFTLotus123WK3	13
crEFTLotus123WKS	11
crEFTNoFormat	0
crEFTODBC	23
crEFTPaginatedText	10
crEFTPortableDocFormat	31

(continued)

Table 4-4. Export Options (continued)

ENUMERATED TYPE	VALUE
crEFTRecordStyle	3
crEFTReportDefinition	34
crEFTTabSeparatedText	9
crEFTTabSeparatedValues	6
crEFTText	8
crEFTWordForWindows	14
crEFTXML	36

The actual process of exporting the report data is rather simple. Export functionality is encapsulated in the ExportOptions object, which is obtained via the property of the same name in the Report object. You'll then need to specify a destination filename. For such export options as PDF, Excel, and Word, use the DiskFileName property, but for XML, use the XMLFileName property; for HTML, use the HTMLFileName property; and for RTF, use the RTFFileName property. The specific export format is determined by the FormatType property, which is set to one of the options listed in Table 4-4. Then, the Export method of the Report object is invoked and the data is exported. Listing 4-16 illustrates the export to Adobe PDF, XML, Microsoft Word, Microsoft Excel, and HTML.

Listing 4-16. Export Options

```
With objReport.ExportOptions
    .DiskFileName = App.Path & "\myreport.pdf"
    .DestinationType = crEDTDiskFile
    .PDFExportAllPages = True
    .FormatType = crEFTPortableDocFormat
End With


objReport.Export False


With objReport.ExportOptions
    .XMLFileName = App.Path & "\myreport.xml"
    .DestinationType = crEDTDiskFile
    .FormatType = crEFTXML
End With
```

```
objReport.Export False



With objReport.ExportOptions
    .DiskFileName = App.Path & "\myreport.xls"
    .DestinationType = crEDTDiskFile
    .FormatType = crEFTExcel80
End With

objReport.Export False



With objReport.ExportOptions
    .DiskFileName = App.Path & "\myreport.doc"
    .DestinationType = crEDTDiskFile
    .FormatType = crEFTWordForWindows
End With

objReport.Export False



With objReport.ExportOptions
    .HTMLFileName = App.Path & "\myreport.html"
    .DestinationType = crEDTDiskFile
    .FormatType = crEFTHTML40
End With

objReport.Export False
```

The Excel export formats listed in Table 4-4 marked as "Tabular" will create a spreadsheet where the subtotals are stored as formulas rather than simply numbers. This feature only works with summary fields, which are in group headers or footers. Therefore, the grand total of freight charges across all customers will not export at all using this option, as this total is located in the report footer.

Passing ADO Recordsets Directly to Crystal Reports 9

Rather than use Crystal Reports' parameter objects, you may wish to use stored procedures or inline SQL to retrieve your data from within your application and then pass it into Crystal Reports. Since you may have a rather complex set of criteria that is already set up as a stored procedure, it can often be better to rely solely on this approach than to use the Crystal Reports tools to set table relationships and create a parameterized data extraction query.

There are several advantages to passing ADO Recordsets to Crystal Reports programmatically. The same SQL queries used for reports often are employed in the application for extracting data for use in edit screens or browsers. Since reports are sometimes executed when a particular Recordset object is still in scope, there is no reason to execute the same query twice. You need only pass the existing Recordset to Crystal Reports, which will loop through the existing data set. Moreover, SQL statements that are pieced together from a diverse set of user-selectable criteria would need to have the same criteria options defined again in Crystal Reports, which would in turn pass the data through to the stored procedure before it is executed.

The first step in getting your Crystal report and VB-based ADO Recordset to communicate is to create a TTX file. This file is simply a structural listing of your data source as shown in the example in Listing 4-17.

Listing 4-17. TTX Output File

```
; Field definition file for table: ADORecordset
ID              long            1
UserID          long            1
ApplicationID   long            1
DateTime        datetime        Jan 5, 1994 1:23:45 PM
DataAction      byte            1
NewData         string          100             string sample value
OldData         string          100             string sample value
TableName       string          30              string sample value
FieldName       string          30              string sample value
MachineName     string          20              string sample value
UserName        string          52              string sample value
AppName         string          50              string sample value
```

You can create a TTX file manually by selecting Database | Add Database to Report. In the Data Explorer dialog box, select More Data Sources | Active Data | Active Data (Field Definitions Only). When the Select Data Source dialog box appears, select New and add the fields yourself to the Database Definition Tool dialog box.

You can also create a TTX file by adding the following function declaration to your project:

```
Public Declare Function CreateFieldDefFile Lib "p2smon.dll" (x As Object, _
ByVal fieldDefFilePath$, ByVal bOverWriteExistingFiles%) As Integer
```

and invoke the code shown in Listing 4-18. Note that this function is considered obsolete in Crystal Reports 9 but is supported for backward compatibility purposes.

Listing 4-18. Creating the TTX Output File

```
Dim oRS As ADODB.Recordset

Set oRS = RunCommand(oConn, "sp_GetAuditTrail", adCmdStoredProc,
adOpenForwardOnly)

Call CreateFieldDefFile(oRS, App.Path & "\struct.ttx", True)
```

I have used my RunCommand function in the example and included it in the downloadable source code available on the Apress Web site (http://www.apress.com), as I think you'll find it rather useful. Essentially you need to pass in a Connection object, the name of the stored procedure, the CommandType of adCmdStoredProc (or you could also pass in a fully formatted inline SQL statement and a CommandType parameter of adCmdText), and finally the cursor type. This Recordset is then passed to Crystal Reports' CreateFieldDefFile function, which in turn extracts the structure into a TTX file.

Once you have created your TTX file, you may then use it in the Crystal Reports Designer as shown in the following steps:

1. Start up Crystal and choose to create a blank report.

2. The Data Explorer window is then presented to you. From here select More Data Sources, then Active Data, and finally Active Data (Field Definitions Only).

3. A Select Data Source dialog box appears from which you can use the Browse button to locate the Data Definition file.

4. Close the Select Data Source dialog box, and a blank report with a Field Explorer window will appear. Under the Database Fields option in the tree view, you will see the TTX file that you have selected, under which all the columns from the stored procedure will be listed. At this point you may select individual fields from the Field Explorer, lay out your report, and save and name the RPT file.

5. From the Visual Basic menu, select Project | Components to display the Components dialog box. Select the Designers tab and choose Crystal Reports 9. This will add the Crystal Reports Designer to VB's Project menu.

6. Select Project | Add Crystal Reports 9. You will then be presented with a Crystal Report Gallery dialog box. Choose the option to create from an existing report and, using the file dialog box, select the RPT file you saved earlier. When the Report Expert asks you to add a form containing the Crystal Reports Viewer control, say yes. A form is created with some base code in it. Add the code in Listing 4-19 to create and pass in the ADO Recordset and allow your report to display.

Listing 4-19. Passing the Recordset and Displaying the Crystal Reports Designer

```
' CrystalReport1 is the default name of the report designer
Dim Report As New CrystalReport1

Dim oRS As ADODB.Recordset

' Execute the Recordset. ApplicationID and lApplicationID
'are parameters which can be
'passed into the RunCommand function and sent to the stored procedure
Set oRS = RunCommand(oConn, "sp_GetAuditTrail",_
adCmdStoredProc, adOpenDynamic, "ApplicationID", lApplicationID)

' Defensive code - make sure there is no data stored with the report
Report.DiscardSavedData

Set CRViewer91 = Me.CRViewer91

'The second parameter indicates the type of data being passed in the first parameter.
'Currently, the 'only possible value allowed is 3 which must be used for all
'Active data sources including DAO, 'ADO, RDO, and CDO.
Report.Database.SetDataSource oRS, 3, 1

CRViewer91.DisplayGroupTree = False
CRViewer91.ReportSource = Report
CRViewer91.ViewReport
```

If you wish to avoid using the designer and instead use a traditional Crystal RPT file, study Listing 4-20 to see how this is accomplished.

Listing 4-20. Passing the Recordset and Displaying an RPT File

```
Dim WithEvents CRViewer91 As CRVIEWERLibCtl.CRViewer
Dim crApplication As New CRAXDRT.Application
Dim crReport As New CRAXDRT.Report
```

```
Set oRS = RunCommand(oConn, " sp_GetAuditTrail", _
    adCmdStoredProc, adOpenDynamic, "ApplicationID", lApplicationID)

Set crReport = crApplication.OpenReport("c:\ AuditTrail.rpt")
crReport.DiscardSavedData
crReport.Database.Tables.Item(1).SetLogOnInfo "Server", _
"ApplicationSecurity", "uid", "pwd"

Set CRViewer91 = Me.CRViewer91

crReport.Database.SetDataSource oRS, 3, 1
CRViewer91.ReportSource = crReport
CRViewer91.ViewReport
```

 TIP *If you're working with existing data-bound reports, you can retrieve the SQL statement used to populate them by selecting Database | Show SQL Query from the main menu. In VB .NET, right-click over the Database Fields entry in the Fields Explorer and select Show SQL Query. Either way, you'll be presented with a dialog box similar to the one in Figure 4-6.*

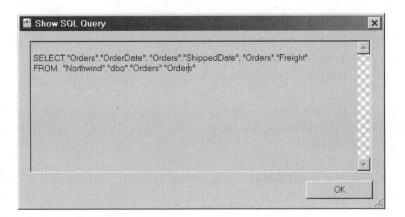

Figure 4-6. Show SQL Query dialog box

Controlling the Data Source via a COM Driver

Beginning with version 9, you can connect your data source to a report via a COM driver. You can also accomplish this in Crystal Reports 8.x using a special multithreaded version of the Active Data Reporting DLL—P2SMON.dll—designed to recognize COM drivers.

When you create a report using Crystal Reports Developer, select More Data Sources | Active Data, and you'll see a new entry for COM Data as shown in Figure 4-7.

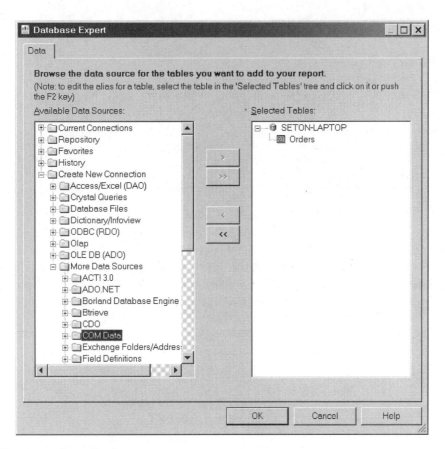

Figure 4-7. Data Explorer

The moment you click the COM Data option, you'll be presented with another dialog box prompting you for the ProgID of the ActiveX DLL class that handles access to the data. This dialog box is shown in Figure 4-8.

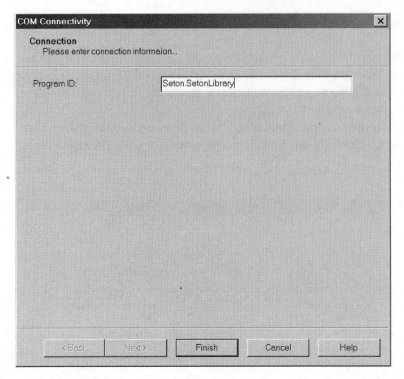

Figure 4-8. ProgID prompt

Once you enter the ProgID, Crystal Reports instantiates the object and connects to the data source specified in the Initialize event of the class. Crystal will then access all the methods within the class indicated and return a list of those that have the type ADO.Recordset as a return value as shown in Figure 4-9.

Figure 4-9. Methods with ADO.Recordset as a return value

Simply select one of these methods as the data source for your report, and all the fields extracted by the SQL statement or stored procedure called by this method will be made available to you. If the method has any parameters associated with it, Crystal will prompt you to enter values for them. In the example shown in Listing 4-21, the entire SQL statement itself is the sole parameter. This example is intended to handle SQL statements that are processed by criteria screens that build WHERE clauses external to stored procedures. By entering this SQL statement in the Crystal parameter dialog box, the names of the data columns extracted by this SQL statement will be offered in the field selection list.

Listing 4-21. COM Driver Class

```
Dim oConn As ADODB.Connection

Private Sub Class_Initialize()

    Set oConn = New ADODB.Connection
    oConn.ConnectionString = "DSN=SampleDSN"
    oConn.Open

End Sub

Private Sub Class_Terminate()

    oConn.Close
    Set oConn = Nothing

End Sub

Public Function GetReportData(cSQL As String) As ADODB.Recordset

    Set GetReportData = oConn.Execute(cSQL)

End Function
```

Crystal Reports for Visual Studio .NET

Crystal Reports for Visual Studio .NET, like its previous incarnations, ships with the .NET package from Microsoft. Unfortunately, it is not quite as full featured as Crystal Developer 9. At the time of this writing, it has no Embeddable Designer Control that you can release to your users nor a Report Creation API. Many other features are not available for this version of Crystal Reports. Check out a file on Crystal's Web site, called cr9feat_ver.pdf, which itemizes the feature differences among the various versions of Crystal Reports 9 (Advanced, Developer, Professional, and Standard) as well as the .NET version. In this section, you'll learn how to implement Crystal Reports in your .NET applications as well as how to modify them at runtime.

Integrating Reports

In spite of all the code conversion you'll need to do to migrate your VB6 applications to VB .NET, you'll be happy to learn that integrating your existing RPT files is a rather painless exercise. To add an existing RPT file to your project, select Project | Add Existing Item from the VB .NET menu. Use the file dialog box to select an RPT; in this example, Orders.RPT has been selected. Select the Solutions Explorer window and click the Show All Files button. Then, drill down on the Orders.rpt option. The result should look like Figure 4-10.

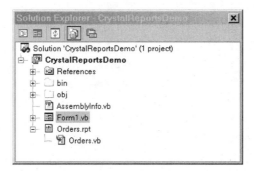

Figure 4-10. Solutions Explorer

An Orders class is automatically created to encapsulate the RPT file you've just added. To manipulate it in code, simply declare a variable of the Orders class and all the properties and methods of the report are exposed to you. For example, the following will display the Orders report in the viewer:

```
Dim objOrders As New Orders()

CrystalReportViewer1.ReportSource = objOrders
```

ReportDocument Object

The lack of a Report Creation API in Crystal Reports for Visual Studio .NET doesn't mean that you do not have any programmatic access to your reports at all. The starting point for any development with Crystal Reports for Visual Studio .NET is the ReportDocument object. Through ReportDocument you can access any of the objects, properties, and methods of the Crystal object hierarchy and create reports dynamically. You can make ReportDocument available to your application by referencing the CrystalDecisions.CrystalReports.Engine namespace.

Viewing Reports

Achieving seamless integration between your application and Crystal Reports is very easy. Simply select the CrystalReportsViewer control from the Windows Forms tab on the ToolBox and paint it on your form. Then add code similar to that shown in Listing 4-22.

Listing 4-22. CrystalReportsViewer Code

```
Private Sub CrystalReportViewer1_Load(ByVal sender As System.Object, _
    ByVal e As System.EventArgs) Handles CrystalReportViewer1.Load

    With CrystalReportViewer1
        .ShowExportButton = True
        .ShowGroupTreeButton = False
        .ShowGotoPageButton = True
        .ShowTextSearchButton = True
        .ShowPageNavigateButtons = True
        .ReportSource = "C:\Reports\CrystalDemo\Requestor.rpt"
        .Zoom(150)
    End With

End Sub
```

To accomplish the same thing by encapsulating the RPT in a ReportDocument object, use the code in Listing 4-23.

Listing 4-23. CrystalReportsViewer with ReportDocument Object

```
Imports CrystalDecisions.CrystalReports.Engine

Private Sub CrystalReportViewer1_Load(ByVal sender As System.Object, _
    ByVal e As System.EventArgs) Handles CrystalReportViewer1.Load

    Dim objReport As New ReportDocument()

    objReport.Load("C:\Reports\CrystalDemo\Requestor.rpt")
```

```
With CrystalReportViewer1
    .ShowExportButton = True
    .ShowGroupTreeButton = False
    .ShowGotoPageButton = True
    .ShowTextSearchButton = True
    .ShowPageNavigateButtons = True
    .ReportSource = objReport
    .Zoom(150)
End With

End Sub
```

Either way, you'll end up with a result similar to that shown in Figure 4-11.

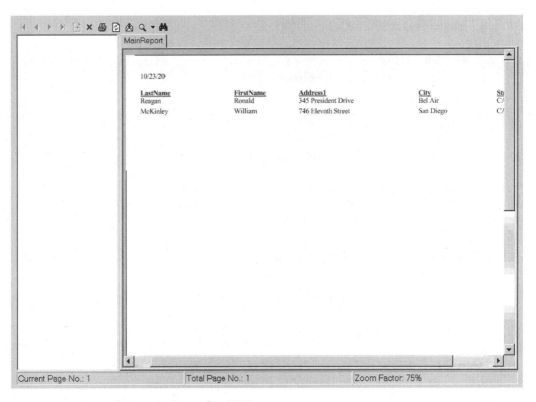

Figure 4-11. Crystal Reports viewer for .NET

As you'll see in Chapter 9, displaying reports in your ASP.NET applications is just as easy as displaying them in VB .NET.

Passing Parameters

Handling parameters in Crystal Reports for Visual Studio .NET is similar as well to VB, but there are more options available. Parameters are encapsulated in one of two classes, ParameterDiscreteValue or ParameterRangeValue, depending on whether you are passing one value or a from/to range. There is even a ParameterValues object designed to hold the actual values you are passing in as parameters. When dealing with a range of values, you would use the StartValue and EndValue properties of the ParameterValues object as follows:

```
objRangeParamValues.StartValue = 1
objRangeParamValues.EndValue = 20
```

whereas the Value property handles single, discrete values like this:

```
objDiscreteParamValue.Value = "CA"
```

The code shown in Listing 4-24 illustrates how the sample report can be filtered for the presidents living in California.

Listing 4-24. Passing Parameters

```
Dim objReport As New ReportDocument()
Dim objParameterField As New ParameterField()
Dim objParameterFields As New ParameterFields()
Dim objParameterDiscreteValue As New ParameterDiscreteValue()

objReport.Load ("C:\BookCode\Chapter4\Requestor.rpt")

objParameterField.ParameterFieldName = "State"

objParameterDiscreteValue.Value = "SC"

objParameterField.CurrentValues.Add (objParameterDiscreteValue)

objParameterFields.Add (objParameterField)

With CrystalReportViewer1
    .ParameterFieldInfo = objParameterFields
    .ReportSource = objReport
    .Zoom (150)
End With
```

Exporting Data

Exporting data is a bit simpler in Crystal Reports for Visual Studio .NET, but the export options are more limited as well. You can only export to Crystal Reports, Excel, HTML, PDF, RTF, and Microsoft Word. Syntactically, all of these export options follow the same pattern as shown in Listing 4-25.

Listing 4-25. Export to PDF

```
Imports CrystalDecisions.Shared
Imports CrystalDecisions.CrystalReports.Engine

Dim objReport As New ReportDocument()
Dim objExport As New ExportOptions()
Dim objDiskFile As New DiskFileDestinationOptions()

objReport.Load("C:\Reports\CrystalDemo\Requestor.rpt")

objExport = objReport.ExportOptions

objDiskFile.DiskFileName = "c:\temp\myreport.pdf"

With objExport
    .ExportFormatType = ExportFormatType.PortableDocFormat
    .ExportDestinationType = ExportDestinationType.DiskFile
    .DestinationOptions = objDiskFile
End With

objReport.Export()
```

In this example, the content of the specified report is being exported to a PDF file. You'll need to create objects of the ExportOptions and DiskFileDestinationOptions classes, objExport and objDiskFile, respectively. Then, you need to set the DiskFileName property of objDiskFile to the name of the output file. The ExportOptions object receives the ExportFormatType enumerator to indicate an export to PDF, and the ExportDestinationType property receives the ExportDestinationType enumerator to indicate that the PDF is a disk file. Finally, the Export method is invoked and the PDF file is created.

Passing ADO.NET Data Directly to Crystal Reports for .NET

Crystal Reports for Visual Studio .NET allows you to create the data set needed to populate your report within your VB .NET application and then pass it in to the report at runtime. To accomplish this, you'll need to first create an XML Schema Definition (XSD) language file that contains the structure of the data source and all the data types of the component fields used in the report. You can create this schema by instantiating a DataSet object that is populated from the SQL statement needed to provide these fields. A DataSet object stores data in a disconnected state, as opposed to a DataReader object (see Chapter 2), which stores it in a connected state. Moreover, where a DataReader contains only the data itself, a DataSet contains the structure, constraint rules, and relationship rules. It is, in effect, a copy of the database in memory.

The data moves between the DataSet object and the database with the assistance of a DataAdapter object. A DataAdapter object acts as a communication object between a DataSet and any kind of data source, whether it be a traditional RDBMS, an Excel spreadsheet, or an ASCII file. As is the pattern with the other ADO.NET data objects, there is an OLE DB version, OleDbDataAdapter, and a SQL Server (7.0+) version, SqlDataAdapter. The data adapter's Fill method populates the DataSet object. Then, the WriteXmlSchema method of the DataSet outputs the schema to the XSD file. The code for this is shown in Listing 4-26.

Listing 4-26. Creating an XSD File

```
Dim objOleDBConnection As OleDbConnection
Dim objOleDBDataAdapter As OleDBDataAdapter
Dim objDS As DataSet
Dim cConnectString As String
Dim cPath As String
Dim cSQL As String

cPath = System.Reflection.Assembly.GetExecutingAssembly.Location

cPath = Mid$(cPath, 1, InStrRev(cPath, "\"))

cConnectString = "Provider=Microsoft.Jet.OLEDB.4.0;" & _
                 "Data Source=C:\Reports\SampleDatabase.mdb;" & _
                 "Persist Security Info=False"

objOleDBConnection = New OleDbConnection(cConnectString)
```

```
cSQL = "SELECT * FROM requester"

'Execute SQL statement and store results in DataAdapter  object
objOleDBDataAdapter = New OleDBDataAdapter(cSQL, objOleDBConnection)

objDS = New DataSet()

'Populate the DataSet object from the DataAdapter object.
'The table name passed as the second parameter must be the
'same as the table name in the report.
objOleDBDataAdapter.Fill(objDS, "requester")

'Create XSD file from the DataSet object
objDS.WriteXmlSchema(cPath & "\Requester.xsd")
```

Then, instead of connecting your report directly to the database, you connect it to the XSD schema as shown in Figure 4-12.

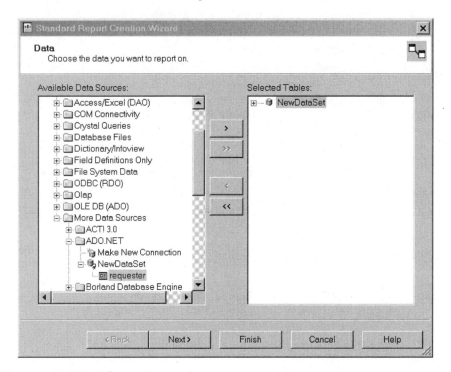

Figure 4-12. XSD Schema Connection

The same fields will be made available to you in the Database Fields object selector when you are designing your report. Finally, the code shown in Listing 4-27 will create the data source of the report and pass it to Crystal Reports at runtime.

Listing 4-27. Passing DataSet at Runtime

```
Dim objReport As New ReportDocument()
Dim objOleDBConnection As OleDbConnection
Dim objOleDBDataAdapter As OleDbDataAdapter
Dim objDS As DataSet
Dim cConnectString As String
Dim cSQL As String

cConnectString = "Provider=Microsoft.Jet.OLEDB.4.0;" & _
                 "Data Source=C:\Reports\SampleDatabase.mdb;" & _
                 "Persist Security Info=False"

objOleDBConnection = New OleDbConnection(cConnectString)

cSQL = "SELECT * FROM requester"

'Execute SQL statement and store results in DataAdapter object
objOleDBDataAdapter = New OleDbDataAdapter(cSQL, objOleDBConnection)

objDS = New DataSet()

'Populate the DataSet object from the DataAdapter object.
'The table name passed as the second parameter must be the
'same as the table name in the report.
objOleDBDataAdapter.Fill(objDS, "requester")

objReport.Load("C:\Reports\CrystalDemo\Requestor.rpt")

'Set the DatSet object as the data source for the report
objReport.SetDataSource(objDS)

CrystalReportViewer1.ReportSource = objReport
```

Conclusion

You can see that Crystal Reports provides a wide array of tools for developers as well as a user interface that justifies its popularity with end users. The user interface provides a familiar way to create reports visually, and the developer tools allow you to go a long way toward automating report distribution. In the next chapter, you'll learn how to build reports using ComponentOne's VS-View and Preview for .NET.

CHAPTER 5

VS-View/Preview

COMPONENTONE, INC., created by the merger of Videosoft, Inc. and Apex Software, Inc., is the publisher of both VS-View for Visual Basic and Preview for .NET. These two products share a common purpose: to allow the developer to create reports via hand coding rather than using a GUI-based product (like Crystal Reports, for example); in this way, they're unique relative to other report writing products. In other words, VS-View and Preview aren't report writers. Rather, they're wrappers for the Windows Printer API.

VS-View

VS-View 1.0 was first released in 1994. It is in its 8.0 version (as of November 2002) and has been a sales leader for quite some time. The VSPrint8.OCX is a visual component that encapsulates both the report viewer and the object model used for programming those reports. Since it uses ATL technology, there are no dependency files you need to worry about.

TIP *VS-View—and its .NET counterpart, Preview—relies heavily on the currently selected printer driver for proper formatting of the output. While your development machine will certainly have a printer driver selected, you cannot expect that the client machine will as well. If there are no installed printer drivers, VS-View will return poorly formed output or will generate an error. Preview will simply generate an error. Be sure to check for the existence of a current printer before running any reports. Printer drivers can be funny things. When debugging strange-looking output, always try changing printer drivers to see if this makes a difference. You don't need to physically have the printer for which the driver was intended, as you can always display the output to the screen. Many problems called into ComponentOne's tech support turn out to be printer driver issues.*

One of the main objections I've heard from developers about using VS-View and Preview is that it is so much easier to create your reports using the wizards offered by Crystal Reports. For the first round of reports, this is true. My experience has been that there are four reports that comprise 98 percent of all business reporting styles—columnar, labels, free-form text, and cross tabs. Of these, the overwhelming majority are columnar. The advantage of using tools like VS-View and Preview is that once you have a base report, you can simply copy over the code to a new subroutine, change the column designations, and you're done. This approach does not work with Crystal Reports, as the field selection list comes from binding to a data source. Since the work is done visually, you'll need to change the properties of the painted fields one by one. Because you will most likely already have a stored procedure SELECT written to support other parts of the application, you can reuse this to obtain the data needed for your report. Moreover, because you'll already have a report viewer form created, the new report subroutine simply snaps into this structure without any further modification.

Getting Started

The basic tools for developing reports in VS-View are the StartTable/TableCell/EndTable and AddTable methods. These methods are multi-featured tools for formatting and printing data. Taken together, they form the cornerstone of VS-View report writing. If you've ever worked with HTML tables, these concepts will be familiar to you. Listing 5-1 shows a simple report example.

Listing 5-1. Simple Columnar Report

```
Sub SampleRpt()
    Dim x As Integer

    With VSPrinter1

        .StartDoc
```

```
       .StartTable

       .TableCell(tcCols) = 2
       .TableCell(tcColWidth, , 1) = 3900
       .TableCell(tcColWidth, , 2) = 3900

       For x = 1 To 1000

           .TableCell(tcInsertRow) = x
           .TableCell(tcText, x, 1) = "Column 1 - Data Element " & x
           .TableCell(tcText, x, 2) = "Column 2 - Data Element " & x

       Next  x

       .EndTable

       .EndDoc

   End With
End Sub

Private Sub VSPrinter1_NewPage()
    VSPrinter1.AddTable "3900|3900", "Header 1|Header 2", vbNullString
End Sub
```

This code produces the output shown in Figure 5-1.

Header 1	Header 2
Column 1 - Data Element 1	Column 2 - Data Element 1
Column 1 - Data Element 2	Column 2 - Data Element 2
Column 1 - Data Element 3	Column 2 - Data Element 3
Column 1 - Data Element 4	Column 2 - Data Element 4
Column 1 - Data Element 5	Column 2 - Data Element 5
Column 1 - Data Element 6	Column 2 - Data Element 6
Column 1 - Data Element 7	Column 2 - Data Element 7
Column 1 - Data Element 8	Column 2 - Data Element 8
Column 1 - Data Element 9	Column 2 - Data Element 9
Column 1 - Data Element 10	Column 2 - Data Element 10
Column 1 - Data Element 11	Column 2 - Data Element 11
Column 1 - Data Element 12	Column 2 - Data Element 12
Column 1 - Data Element 13	Column 2 - Data Element 13
Column 1 - Data Element 14	Column 2 - Data Element 14
Column 1 - Data Element 15	Column 2 - Data Element 15
Column 1 - Data Element 16	Column 2 - Data Element 16
Column 1 - Data Element 17	Column 2 - Data Element 17
Column 1 - Data Element 18	Column 2 - Data Element 18
Column 1 - Data Element 19	Column 2 - Data Element 19
Column 1 - Data Element 20	Column 2 - Data Element 20
Column 1 - Data Element 21	Column 2 - Data Element 21
Column 1 - Data Element 22	Column 2 - Data Element 22
Column 1 - Data Element 23	Column 2 - Data Element 23
Column 1 - Data Element 24	Column 2 - Data Element 24
Column 1 - Data Element 25	Column 2 - Data Element 25
Column 1 - Data Element 26	Column 2 - Data Element 26
Column 1 - Data Element 27	Column 2 - Data Element 27
Column 1 - Data Element 28	Column 2 - Data Element 28
Column 1 - Data Element 29	Column 2 - Data Element 29
Column 1 - Data Element 30	Column 2 - Data Element 30
Column 1 - Data Element 31	Column 2 - Data Element 31
Column 1 - Data Element 32	Column 2 - Data Element 32
Column 1 - Data Element 33	Column 2 - Data Element 33
Column 1 - Data Element 34	Column 2 - Data Element 34
Column 1 - Data Element 35	Column 2 - Data Element 35
Column 1 - Data Element 36	Column 2 - Data Element 36
Column 1 - Data Element 37	Column 2 - Data Element 37
Column 1 - Data Element 38	Column 2 - Data Element 38
Column 1 - Data Element 39	Column 2 - Data Element 39
Column 1 - Data Element 40	Column 2 - Data Element 40
Column 1 - Data Element 41	Column 2 - Data Element 41
Column 1 - Data Element 42	Column 2 - Data Element 42
Column 1 - Data Element 43	Column 2 - Data Element 43
Column 1 - Data Element 44	Column 2 - Data Element 44
Column 1 - Data Element 45	Column 2 - Data Element 45
Column 1 - Data Element 46	Column 2 - Data Element 46
Column 1 - Data Element 47	Column 2 - Data Element 47
Column 1 - Data Element 48	Column 2 - Data Element 48

Figure 5-1. Simple columnar report

NOTE *Though the TableCell method is far more flexible than the original Table method, bear in mind that the Table method is faster. This can make a significant difference when users are running reports that are hundreds of pages long.*

Before you run this code, you must open the Components list from the Project menu in the IDE. Choose ComponentOne VSPrinter 8.0. You'll see a VSPrinter icon on the toolbar. Drag it onto the page and use the control handles to make it bigger. Voila! You now have a Print Preview window. By default, the component name is VSPrinter1.

The first step is to invoke the StartDoc method. Doing so will reset the VSPrinter control and prepare it for a new report. Certain VS-View properties need to be set before invoking StartDoc, unless, of course, the default settings are acceptable. Page size is one of them, as this property cannot change while the report is being created. Orientation is another property that should be set up before StartDoc; otherwise, any changes made won't apply until the next page is printed.

Most reports—and not merely columnar reports—are usually structured such that they fit into a table format, that is, they are composed of rows and columns. The StartTable method is used to initialize that table. At this point, you can specify how many columns the report will require. In most cases you'll know this ahead of time. Since you probably won't know how many rows will be needed, these can be added one at a time using the TableCell method's tcInsertRow parameter. Row and column numbers are one-based, not zero-based, and a particular cell is identified by a row and column offset. The tcText parameter represents the cell contents. The EndTable method notifies the VSPrinter object that the table definition is complete. The EndDoc method indicates that the document is complete and should be displayed either to the printer or to the screen, depending on the value of the VSPrinter object's Preview property. A setting of True shows the Preview window, while False prints the report directly without displaying it first.

NOTE *It is important to apply global formatting changes to columns and rows* before *you have specified the number of columns and rows. Global formatting changes occur when no row and column offsets are passed to the TableCell method. Therefore, the code .TableCell(tcFontBold, , 1) = True will make all text in the first column appear in bold.*

In order to print the column headers that appear on every page, the AddTable method is called from within the NewPage event. You cannot use another StartTable/EndTable combination, as calls to these methods cannot be nested with an existing StartTable/EndTable combinations like this:

```
.StartTable
.StartTable
.EndTable
.EndTable
```

The NewPage event fires after StartDoc is called. This event also fires when the report is rendered to the VSPrinter object each time enough data has been added to an individual page. Since the NewPage event will position the current print line at the top of the newly created page, it is generally the best place to invoke the code that displays the column headers.

The AddTable method uses a number of formatting symbols to control the alignment of the text within the table. By placing these symbols before the column width designations, you can align the text in the specified cells. For example, in the following statement, the greater-than character (>) indicates that both headers will print right justified:

```
VSPrinter1.AddTable ">3900|>3900", "Header 1|Header 2", vbNullString
```

The available formatting symbols are listed in Table 5-1.

Table 5-1. Formatting Symbols

CHARACTER	EFFECT
<	Aligns column contents to the left
^	Aligns column contents to the center
>	Aligns column contents to the right
=	Justifies column contents
+	Aligns column contents vertically to the center
_	Aligns column contents vertically to the bottom
*	Aligns column contents according to the TextAlign property
~	Prevents word wrapping on this column
!	Draws a vertical border to the right of the column

> **TIP** *Pay close attention to the sample applications that ship with both VS-View and Preview. In addition to offering an introduction to the products, they explain the more esoteric features rather well. Check out the Index Generation utility that accepts a text file containing keywords in which you are interested and produces an index showing on which pages these words appear.*

TableCell Method Features

Listing 5-1 illustrated a very simple use of the TableCell method, but there is much more that this method can do. The various parameters that you can pass to TableCell will permit you full customization of your reports. You can specify text alignment, color, row height, column width, and font characteristics. You can even allow individual cells to span multiple columns. Take a look at the example is Listing 5-2. Here, the code prints an address block.

Listing 5-2. Address Report

```
With VSPrinter1

    .StartDoc

    .StartTable

    .TableCell(tcCols) = 3
    .TableCell(tcRows) = 3

    .TableCell(tcColWidth, , 1) = 2000
    .TableCell(tcColWidth, , 2) = 600
    .TableCell(tcColWidth, , 3) = 1400

    .TableCell(tcAlign, 1) = taCenterMiddle
    .TableCell(tcRowHeight, 1) = 1000
    .TableCell(tcFont, 1, 1) = "Times New Roman"
    .TableCell(tcFontSize, 1, 1) = 24
    .TableCell(tcFontBold, 1, 1) = True
    .TableCell(tcFontItalic, 1, 1) = True
```

```
    .TableCell(tcBackColor, 1, 1) = vbRed
    .TableCell(tcColSpan, 1, 1) = 3
    .TableCell(tcText, 1, 1) = "Joe Smith"

    .TableCell(tcColSpan, 2, 1) = 3
    .TableCell(tcText, 2, 1) = "123 Main Street"

    .TableCell(tcText, 3, 1) = "Anytown"
    .TableCell(tcText, 3, 2) = "NJ"
    .TableCell(tcText, 3, 3) = "12345"

    .EndTable

    .EndDoc

End With
```

This example defines a table with three columns and three rows. The first column is set to a width of 2000 twips, the second column to 900 twips, and the third column to 1800 twips. A *twip* is 1/1440 of an inch. Since the name and address rows need to span the city, state, and zip columns, the tcColSpan parameter is used. The font for the name cell is set to 24-point Times New Roman, bold, italic, centered to the middle of the cell, with a yellow background color and red text. The result can be seen in Figure 5-2.

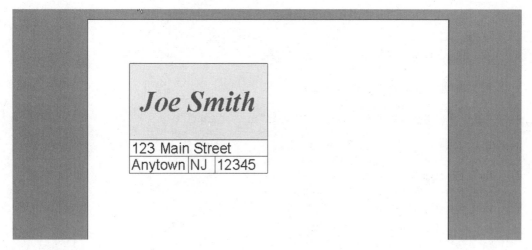

Figure 5-2. TableCell method features

You can see that there are a number of constant values used to describe the data being passed to the TableCell method. These constants are defined in Table 5-2. Size settings are by default measured in twips, but you can specify the units if you wish (e.g., "3in").

Table 5-2. TableCell Constant Values

CONSTANT	VALUE	DESCRIPTION
tcIndent	0	Returns or sets the indent for the table.
tcRows	1	Returns or sets the number of rows in the table. The header row is not included in this count. If you change the number of rows, rows are added or deleted from the bottom of the table.
tcCols	2	Returns or sets the number of columns in the table. If you change the number of columns, columns are added or deleted from the right of the table.
tcInsertRow	3	Inserts a row at the specified position.
tcInsertCol	4	Inserts a column at the specified position.
tcDeleteRow	5	Deletes the row at the specified position.
tcDeleteCol	6	Deletes the column at the specified position.
tcRowHeight	7	Returns or sets the height of the rows. The header row has index zero.
tcRowBorder	8	Returns or sets whether the rows will have a border drawn above them.
tcRowData	9	Returns or sets a Variant associated with the row. This value is for your own use and is not used by the control.
tcRowSource	10	Returns or sets the array row used as a data source for the table row. This setting only applies if the table was bound to an array (with the AddTableArray method). Note that array indices are zero-based, unlike table indices, which are one-based.

(continued)

Table 5-2. TableCell Constant Values (continued)

CONSTANT	VALUE	DESCRIPTION
tcRowKeepWithNext	11	Returns or sets whether the control should prevent page breaks after the rows.
tcRowIsSubHeader	12	Returns or sets whether the row should become the table header after it is rendered (useful for subtitles).
tcColWidth	13	Returns or sets the width of the columns.
tcColBorder	14	Returns or sets whether the columns will have a border drawn on their right-hand side.
tcColData	15	Returns or sets a Variant associated with the column. This value is similar to VB's Tag property and is not used by the control.
tcColSource	16	Returns or sets the array column used as a data source for the table column. This setting applies only if the table was bound to an array (with the AddTableArray method). Note that array indices are zero-based, unlike table indices, which are one-based.
tcColSpan	17	Returns or sets the number of columns that the cell should span.
tcText	18	Returns or sets the cell text.
tcAlign	19	Returns or sets the alignment of text in the cells. See Table 5-3 for possible values.
tcBackColor	20	Returns or sets the background color for the cell.
tcForeColor	21	Returns or sets the foreground (text) color for the cell.
tcFont	22	Returns or sets the cell font.
tcFontName	23	Returns or sets the name of the cell font.
tcFontSize	24	Returns or sets the size of the cell font.
tcFontBold	25	Returns or sets the bold attribute.

(continued)

Table 5-2. TableCell Constant Values (continued)

CONSTANT	VALUE	DESCRIPTION
tcFontItalic	26	Returns or sets the italic attribute.
tcFontUnderline	27	Returns or sets the underline attribute.
tcFontStrikethru	28	Returns or sets the strikethrough attribute.
tcPicture	29	Returns or sets the cell picture.
tcPictureAlign	30	Returns or sets the alignment of pictures in the cells. See Table 5-3 for possible values.

Table 5-3. Constants for Cell Data Alignment

CONSTANT	VALUE	DESCRIPTION
taLeftTop	0	Text is aligned to the left and to the top.
taCenterTop	1	Text is aligned to the center and to the top.
taRightTop	2	Text is aligned to the right and to the top.
taLeftBottom	3	Text is aligned to the left and to the bottom.
taCenterBottom	4	Text is aligned to the center and to the bottom.
taRightBottom	5	Text is aligned to the right and to the bottom.
taLeftMiddle	6	Text is aligned to the left and to the middle.
taCenterMiddle	7	Text is aligned to the center and to the middle.
taRightMiddle	8	Text is aligned to the right and to the middle.
taJustTop	9	Text is fully justified and aligned to the top.
taJustBottom	10	Text is fully justified and aligned to the bottom.
taJustMiddle	11	Text is fully justified and aligned to the middle.

Setting Up the Page

To format reports for printing, you can set properties like paper orientation, margins, text size, cursor position, current printer, paper bin, and text styles. These can be set programmatically at runtime, or at design time.

Margins

Set report margins using the MarginLeft, MarginRight, MarginTop, and MarginBottom properties. The spacing for these properties is measured in twips from the edge of the page. Since most of your reports will have consistent margin settings, these properties are best set in a subroutine that you can invoke before each report executes.

Page orientation is, of course, also a must. The Orientation property receives one of two constants as settings: orLandScape (width-oriented) or orPortrait (height-oriented). You can even change the orientation as the report is being built. For example, the code that follows alternates pages between portrait and landscape:

```
Private Sub VSPrinter1_NewPage()

    If VSPrinter1.PageCount Mod 2 = 1 Then
        VSPrinter1.Orientation = orLandscape
    Else
        VSPrinter1.Orientation = orPortrait
    End If

End Sub
```

Paper Bins

You can also change specific paper bin settings during the creation of reports. The PaperBins property first determines if a specific paper bin is available based on the selected printer driver. Then, the PaperBin property accepts your selection and directs output toward the specified bin. Table 5-4 lists all the available paper bin constants.

Table 5-4. PaperBin/PaperBins Property Bin Constants

CONSTANT	VALUE	DESCRIPTION
binUpper	1	Use paper from the upper bin.
binLower	2	Use paper from the lower bin.
binMiddle	3	Use paper from the middle bin.
binManual	4	Wait for manual insertion of each sheet of paper.
binEnvelope	5	Use envelopes from the envelope feeder.
binEnvManual	6	Use envelopes from feeder, but wait for manual insertion.
binAuto	7	Use paper from the current default bin.
binTractor	8	Use paper fed from the tractor feeder.
binSmallFmt	9	Use paper from the small paper bin.
binLargeFmt	10	Use paper from the large paper bin.
binLargeCapacity	11	Use paper from the large capacity feeder.
binCassette	14	Use paper from the attached cassette cartridge.
binFormSource	15	Use paper from form source.
binUser	256	Use Custom bin.

One situation where paper bin control comes in handy is when you have a report that needs to print on two different types of paper. For example, suppose you have a form letter whose first page prints from one bin that contains company letterhead and all other pages print on plain white paper from another bin. This switch could be easily be accomplished by the following code that changes the PaperBin setting in the EndPage event:

```
Private Sub vsPrinter1_EndPage()

    If VSPrinter1.CurrentPage = 1 Then
        VSPrinter1.PaperBin = binUpper
    End If

End Sub
```

Cursor Position

Cursor position on the page is referenced by CurrentY and CurrentX properties that determine the distance in twips from the top of the page and from the left of the page, respectively. You can use these properties to position printing at any location on the page. CurrentY and CurrentX come in handy when working with snaked reports. You can record the CurrentY position at the start of a column and then reset it before you begin printing the next column.

Printer Selection

The Device Property is used to set the current printer. The *Devices* property, on the other hand, is an array that contains a list of printers whose drivers are installed on the system. See Listing 5-3 for an illustration of how the available printers are loaded into a list box and a new setting is chosen by a command button.

Listing 5-3. Devices Property

```
Sub GetPrinterList()
    Dim x As Integer

    For x = 0 To VSPrinter1.NDevices - 1 ' Iterate through entire printer list
        lstPrinters.AddItem VSPrinter1.Devices(x)  ' add printer name to list box
    Next

End Sub


Private Sub cmdSelectPrinter_Click()
    VSPrinter1.Device = lstPrinters.Text    'Make selected printer active
End Sub
```

Styles

Text styles contain all the attributes—font, bold, underline, size, color, alignment, etc.—that printed text will use. They are similar to the style settings you can define in Microsoft Word. By creating a series of styles to define your text, you can easily standardize how text will display throughout your report without much concern that you'll inadvertently change the formatting. Take a look at the code in Listing 5-4.

Listing 5-4. Styles

```
With VSPrinter1
    .FontName = "Arial"
    .FontSize = 48
    .FontBold = True
    .SpaceAfter = 2000
    'vpsAll indicates that all the settings just made
    'should be saved to the new style
    .Styles.Add "Chapter Title", vpsAll

    .FontName = "Arial"
    .FontSize = 16
    .FontBold = False
    .LineSpacing = 250
    .Styles.Add "Intro Text", vpsAll


    .StartDoc

    .Styles.Apply "Chapter Title"
    .Paragraph = "Chapter 1"

    .Styles.Apply "Intro Text"
    .Paragraph = "It was the best of times, it was the worst of times. " & _
                "It was the age of wisdom, it was the age of foolishness..."

    .EndDoc
End With
```

This example creates two styles, one defining chapter titles and another defining intro text. SpaceAfter adds an amount of blank space, here specified as 2000 twips, after the text is printed. LineSpacing determines how much space will appear between printed lines measured as a percentage of the space consumed by a single line in the current font. This example produces the output shown in Figure 5-3.

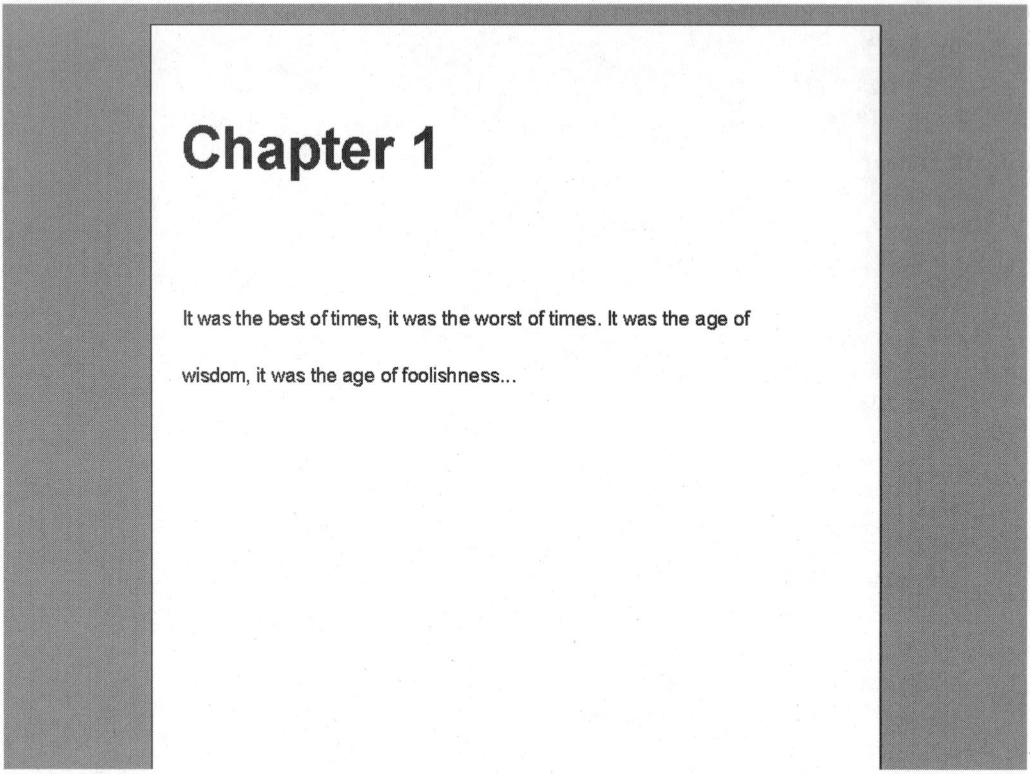

Chapter 1

It was the best of times, it was the worst of times. It was the age of

wisdom, it was the age of foolishness...

Figure 5-3. Output showing different styles

Hyperlinks

New to version 8.0 of VS-View are hyperlinks that can link items in a report to a Web page or permit a drilldown to a detail report. Hyperlinks can also assist in creating navigable document reports. These navigable links also carry over to the PDF and HTML files exported from VS-View.

To make your document aware of hyperlinks, you must first set the AutoLinkNavigate property to True. You may add two types of hyperlinks: those allowing you to jump to a Web site, and those allowing you to navigate within the document. To create a link to a Web site, use the AddLink method as shown here:

```
Call .AddLink("George Washington", "www.microsoft.com", True)
```

The first parameter contains the text of the link that is shown to the user, the second parameter contains the URL launched by clicking the link, and the final parameter indicates if the link should display underlined in blue text, the standard format for displaying hyperlinks. The main drawback to this method is that you can only position the placement of the hyperlink by setting the CurrentX and CurrentY properties. Ordinarily, features such as this would allow you to provide "More information" links for the topics mentioned to create drilldown reports. For example, you could create a report showing the amount sold per sales rep and make the name of each sales rep a hyperlink. Then, when a user clicks one of these links, they would be taken to a report showing the details of each sale made by that rep. Unfortunately, you cannot place these links within a TableCell or control their display via use of the Table property.

The AddLinkTarget method allows you to embed navigation links within your document to enable the user to move around more easily. One common use of this functionality is to create a detailed table of contents at the beginning of a long document and set up each chapter or section entry as a hyperlink. In this way the user can simply find the topic he or she is looking for and by clicking the associated link can jump dozens or even hundreds of pages to find that topic immediately. Like the AddLink method, you can only position the hyperlink by setting the CurrentX and CurrentY properties, but this type of link is far less likely to be used in a columnar report so this drawback isn't as noticeable.

Examine the following code, which illustrates how both types of links are used:

```
With VSPrinter1

    .AutoLinkNavigate = True

    .StartDoc

    .Preview = True

    .StartTable

    .TableCell(tcCols) = 2
    .TableCell(tcColWidth, , 1) = 3900
    .TableCell(tcColWidth, , 2) = 3900

    Call .AddLinkTarget("US Presidents", "TopOfFirstPage")

    .Text = "" & vbCrLf
    .Text = "" & vbCrLf

    Call .AddLink("George Washington", "www.microsoft.com", True)

    .Text = "" & vbCrLf
```

```
    For x = 1 To 75

        .Text = "More text" & vbCrLf

    Next x

    .EndTable

    Call .AddLink("Go to the beginning of the document", "#TopOfFirstPage", True)

    .EndDoc

End With
```

Headers and Footers

In order to establish a consistency in your application, report headers and footers should adhere to the same format across all reports. VS-View has both Header and Footer properties so that header and footer text can be set and automatically printed at the top and bottom, respectively, of each page. Each property has three sections delimited by pipe symbols (|) that print on the right, center, and left of the page. For example, to print a header that displays the company name to the left, the name of the report in the center, and the date printed to the right, use the following line of code:

```
VSPrinter1.Header = "Seton Software|Sample Report|" & Format(Date, "mm/dd/yyyy")
```

The Footer property works exactly the same way. Should you wish to display a page number, the symbol %d is used. For example, if you want the footer to display the page number in the lower-right corner of the page, the following property setting would accomplish this:

```
.Footer = "||Page %d"
```

You can specify special formatting options for the header and footer through the use of the following properties: HdrColor, HdrFont, HdrFontBold, HdrFontItalic, HdrFontUnderline, HdrFontName, HdrFontSize, HdrFontStrikethru, and HdrFontUnderline. The Footer property uses the same attributes that are specified for the Header property. If you wish to use different attributes for the footer, you can modify headers and footers before printing by writing code in the BeforeFooter and AfterFooter events as shown in Listing 5-5.

Listing 5-5. BeforeFooter and AfterFooter Events

```
'Declare module variables
Dim cHdrFontName As String
Dim bHdrFontBold As Boolean
Dim iHdrFontSize As Integer


Private Sub VSPrinter1_AfterFooter()
  With VSPrinter1
        .HdrFontName = cHdrFontName
        .HdrFontBold = bHdrFontBold
        .HdrFontSize = iHdrFontSize
  End With
End Sub


Private Sub VSPrinter1_BeforeFooter()

    With VSPrinter1
        cHdrFontName = .HdrFontName
        bHdrFontBold = .HdrFontBold
        iHdrFontSize = .HdrFontSize

        .HdrFontName = "Courier"
        .HdrFontBold = False
        .HdrFontSize = 14
    End With


End Sub
```

By declaring variables to store the current settings of the header, you can change the Hdr* property attributes in the BeforeFooter event and then restore them in the AfterFooter event once the footer has been printed.

Creating Reports in VS-View

Now that you understand the basics of report writing with VS-View, let's take a look at how to create various types of reports. Since most reports will fit into one of the categories discussed in this section, you will find yourself creating most of your new reports simply by copying over the code from an existing report that matches it. You then simply change your data source references and you're done.

We'll start by examining standard columnar reports and move on to looking at labels, snaked column reports, and form letters. Cross tab reports are examined in Chapter 8.

Standard Columnar

You saw an example of a standard columnar report in the "Getting Started" section at the beginning of the chapter. Let's now examine one that extracts data from a database and displays the output. You'll see that the process is quite simple—create a forward-only ADO Recordset from an inline SQL statement or stored procedure that shapes your data to fit the report, and then loop through that Recordset, printing the data as you go. It's that simple. Listing 5-6 illustrates how this is done.

Listing 5-6. Standard Columnar Report

```
Sub StandardColumnarRpt()
    Dim oRS As ADODB.Recordset

    Dim cSQL As String
    Dim x As Long

    With VSPrinter1

        .HdrFontName = "Arial"
        .HdrFontBold = True
        .HdrFontSize = 12

        .Footer = "||Page %d"

        .Header = "Seton Software|Sample Report|" & Format(Date, "mm/dd/yyyy")

        .FontName = "Arial"
        .FontBold = False
        .FontSize = 10

        cSQL = "SELECT LastName, FirstName, State " & _
               "FROM Requester " & _
               "ORDER BY LastName"

        Set oRS = oConn.Execute(cSQL)

        If oRS.EOF Then
          .KillDoc
            MsgBox "The report criteria you have selected contains no data"
            Exit Sub
        End If
```

```
        x = 1

        .StartDoc

        .StartTable

        .TableCell(tcCols) = 3
        .TableCell(tcColWidth, , 1) = 2500
        .TableCell(tcColWidth, , 2) = 2000
        .TableCell(tcColWidth, , 3) = 900

        Do While Not oRS.EOF

            .TableCell(tcInsertRow) = x
            .TableCell(tcText, x, 1) = oRS("LastName")
            .TableCell(tcText, x, 2) = oRS("FirstName")
            .TableCell(tcText, x, 3) = oRS("State")

            x = x + 1

            oRS.MoveNext

        Loop

        .EndTable

        .EndDoc

    End With

    oRS.Close
    Set oRS = Nothing

End Sub

Private Sub VSPrinter1_NewPage()
    Dim bFontBold As Boolean

    bFontBold = VSPrinter1.FontBold

    VSPrinter1.FontBold = True

    VSPrinter1.AddTable "2500|2000|900", "Last Name|First Name|State", vbNullString
```

```
        VSPrinter1.FontBold = bFontBold

End Sub
```

Labels

Labels are a bit trickier than standard columnar reports, and your first time
through you'll miss having a report writer's label creation wizard. However,
once you have the layout working, it's a snap to reuse the code again and again.
Essentially, you need to print each individual label as its own one-column table.
The only question is how many columns per page you'll be printing and how
many labels per column. Listing 5-7 prints labels that match Avery standard 5163,
that is, two columns of five labels each.

Listing 5-7. Code for Printing Labels

```
Sub Labels()
    Dim oRS As ADODB.Recordset
    Dim cSQL As String
    Dim cName As String
    Dim cAddress1 As String
    Dim cAddress2 As String
    Dim cCSZ As String
    Dim iLine As Integer
    Dim iLabels As Integer
    Dim iCol As Integer
    Dim iCurrentY As Integer
    Dim x As Integer

    cSQL = "SELECT LastName, FirstName, Address1, " & _
            "Address2, City, State, Zip " & _
            "FROM Requester " & _
            "WHERE Address1 IS NOT NULL " & _
            "ORDER BY LastName"

    Set oRS = oConn.Execute(cSQL)

    ' Tracks which column is being printed
    iCol = 1

    ' Counter to track the number of labels
```

```
' printed in a particular column
iLabels = 0



With VSPrinter1

    .TableBorder = tbNone
    .PageBorder = pbNone
    .Orientation = orPortrait
    .FontName = "Arial"
    .FontSize = 14
    .MarginTop = 900
    .MarginLeft = 600
    .MarginBottom = 300
    .StartDoc

    ' The CurrentY property measures the cursor position in twips
    ' from the top of the page. Because there are 2 columns to
    ' this label style, we will need to return to this
    ' spot when the second columns begin.
    iCurrentY = .CurrentY

Do While Not oRS.EOF

        cName = oRS("firstname") & " " & oRS("lastname")
        cAddress1 = "" & oRS("Address1")
        cAddress2 = "" & oRS("Address2")
        cCSZ = ("" & oRS("city")) & ", " & oRS("state") & " " & oRS("zip")



        'Print an address as a table
        .StartTable

        .TableCell(tcCols) = 1
        .TableCell(tcColWidth) = 4000

        .TableCell(tcRows) = 7
        .TableCell(tcRowHeight) = 410


        .TableCell(tcText, 2, 1) = cName
        .TableCell(tcText, 3, 1) = cAddress1

        If cAddress2 = vbNullString Then
```

```
                        .TableCell(tcText, 4, 1) = cCSZ
            Else
                        .TableCell(tcText, 4, 1) = cAddress2
                        .TableCell(tcText, 5, 1) = cCSZ
            End If

            .EndTable


            iLabels = iLabels + 1

            ' If ten labels have been printed, it's time to move
            ' to the top of the page and begin another column
            If iLabels = 5 Then

                iLabels = 0

                Select Case iCol

                        ' If the first has just completed,
                        ' move to the top of the page but go 3900 twips
                        ' to the right
                        Case 1
                            iCol = iCol + 1
                            .CurrentY = iCurrentY
                            .MarginLeft = .MarginLeft + 6000

                        ' If the second column just completed, reset
                        ' the cursor position and eject the page
                        Case 2
                            iCol = 1
                            .MarginLeft = 600
                            .NewPage
                            .CurrentY = iCurrentY

                End Select

            End If

            oRS.MoveNext

    Loop
```

```
        .EndDoc

    End With

    oRS.Close
    Set oRS = Nothing

End Sub
```

This code will produce the output shown in Figure 5-4.

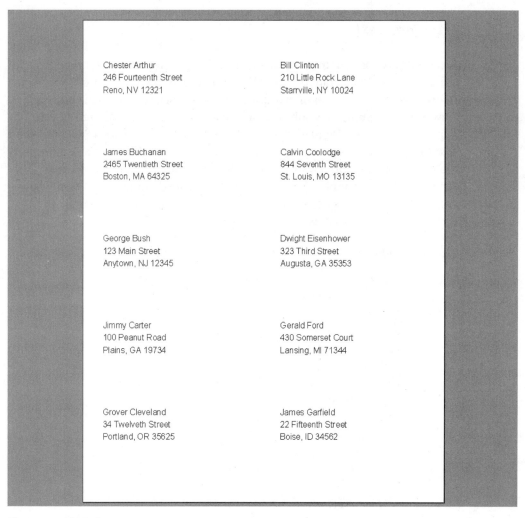

Figure 5-4. Label output

> **NOTE** *ComponentOne has a tool called vsLabeler that generates label format files for the most popular Avery styles. It is an open source utility written in Visual Basic that allows you to select the Avery number and the data source and then lay out the fields to appear on the label. The interface is similar to the Microsoft Access Label Wizard. You'll need to link the vsLabeler source code to your applications in order for the format files to be read. vsLabeler is available upon request by e-mailing* support.vsview@componentone.com.

Free-Form Text

Sometimes you'll want to merge database information with free-form text stored as a form letter. You could use ActiveX Automation to direct Microsoft Word's mail merge object to do this task for you, and this approach is covered in Chapter 7. However, this approach is only feasible if you are certain that all users of your application will have Word installed on their workstations. Using VS-View to print free-form text and create a mail merge is very simple. VS-View has a Text property that will accept and print a string. By adding your own merge fields to this string—in these examples the merge parameters are delimited by percent signs—you can use Visual Basic's Replace function to substitute values from the database in the text as illustrated by Listing 5-8.

Listing 5-8. Free-Form Text/Mail Merge

```
Sub FreeFormText()
    Dim oRS As ADODB.Recordset
    Dim cSQL As String
    Dim cName As String
    Dim cSalutation As String
    Dim cLastName As String
    Dim cAddress1 As String
    Dim cAddress2 As String
    Dim cCSZ As String
    Dim cCaseNumber As String
    Dim cLetterText As String
    Dim cText As String

    cSQL = "SELECT LetterText " & _
           "FROM FormLetters " & _
           "WHERE ID = " & 1
```

```
Set oRS = oConn.Execute(cSQL)


If Not oRS.EOF Then
    cLetterText = oRS("LetterText")
Else
    Exit Sub
End If


cSQL = "SELECT ID, Salutation, LastName, FirstName, " & _
       "Address1, Address2, City, State, Zip " & _
       "FROM Requester " & _
       "WHERE Address1 IS NOT NULL " & _
       "ORDER BY LastName"

Set oRS = oConn.Execute(cSQL)

With VSPrinter1

    .TableBorder = tbNone
    .PageBorder = pbNone
    .Orientation = orPortrait
    .FontName = "Arial"
    .FontSize = 11
    .StartDoc

    Do While Not oRS.EOF

        cText = cLetterText

        cCaseNumber = oRS("id")
        cSalutation = "" & oRS("Salutation")
        cLastName = "" & oRS("lastname")
        cName = oRS("firstname") & " " & oRS("lastname")
        cAddress1 = "" & oRS("Address1")
        cAddress2 = "" & oRS("Address2")

        If cAddress2 <> vbNullString Then
            cAddress1 = cAddress1 & vbCrLf & cAddress2
        End If

        cCSZ = ("" & oRS("city")) & ", " & oRS("state") & " " & oRS("zip")
```

```
cText = Replace(cText, "%Name%", cName)
cText = Replace(cText, "%Address%", cAddress1)
cText = Replace(cText, "%CSZ%", cCSZ)
cText = Replace(cText, "%Salutation%", cSalutation)
cText = Replace(cText, "%LastName%", cLastName)
cText = Replace(cText, "%CaseNumber%", cCaseNumber)

.CurrentY = 4320

.Text = cText

oRS.MoveNext

If Not oRS.EOF Then
    .NewPage
End If

    Loop

    .EndDoc

End With

oRS.Close
Set oRS = Nothing

End Sub
```

This subroutine will produce the output shown in Figure 5-5.

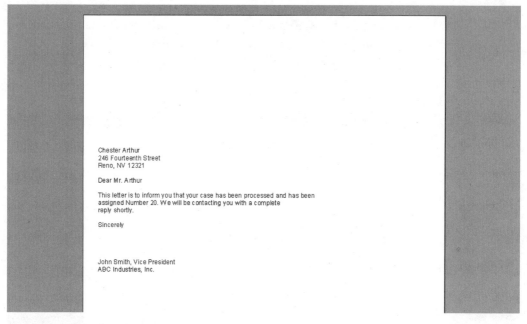

Chester Arthur
246 Fourteenth Street
Reno, NV 12321

Dear Mr. Arthur

This letter is to inform you that your case has been processed and has been
assigned Number 20. We will be contacting you with a complete
reply shortly.

Sincerely

John Smith, Vice President
ABC Industries, Inc.

Figure 5-5. Free-form text output

Of course, you may also wish to work with formatted text. Fortunately, VS-View has a TextRTF property that receives a string containing RTF-encoded information and displays it according to the formatting codes. The code to do this is the same as shown in Listing 5-8 except that the line

```
.Text = cText
```

is replaced by

```
.TextRTF = cText
```

where cText contains an RTF-encoded string.

By formatting your text document in a word processor—or if you're really sick you can program the RTF codes yourself—you can save the document to an RTF file and then insert the text into your database. Merging the RTF data in the same fashion as Listing 5-8 did with the plain data will produce the output shown in Figure 5-6.

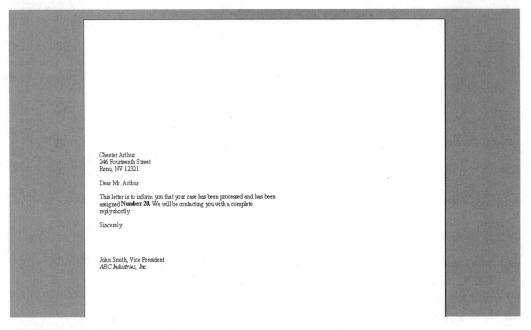

Chester Arthur
246 Fourteenth Street
Reno, NV 12321

Dear Mr. Arthur

This letter is to inform you that your case has been processed and has been assigned **Number 20.** We will be contacting you with a complete reply shortly.

Sincerely

John Smith, Vice President
ABC Industries, Inc.

Figure 5-6. Free-form text output

Be advised that rendering RTF text is much slower than working with plain text.

Snaked Column Reports

Snaked column reports are very similar to labels but can have their own idiosyncrasies that need to be understood. A snaked column report begins printing data at the top of one column and continues this data at the top of a second column. This path is shown in Figure 5-7.

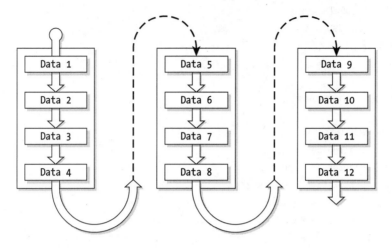

Figure 5-7. Snaked column data flow

Listing 5-9 shows a snaked column report that prints summary information for all the conventions scheduled for a particular range of dates.

Listing 5-9. Snaked Column Report

```
Sub SnakedColumnRpt()
    Dim oRS As ADODB.Recordset
    Dim cSQL As String
    Dim iCol As Integer
    Dim iCurrentY As Integer
    Dim iLeft As Integer
    Dim iMarginLeft As Integer
    Dim cMonth As String
    Dim cCoordinator As String
    Dim cDateRange As String
    Dim cConventionName As String
    Dim cCityState As String
    Dim cConvNumber As String

    cSQL = "SELECT ID, ConventionName, StartDate, " & _
           "EndDate, City, State, Coordinator " & _
           "FROM Convention " & _
           "ORDER BY StartDate"

    Set oRS = oConn.Execute(cSQL)
```

```
If oRS.EOF Then
    Exit Sub
End If

iCol = 1
iLeft = iMarginLeft

With VSPrinter1
    .TableBorder = tbNone
    .PageBorder = pbNone
    .Orientation = orLandscape
    .FontName = "Arial"
    .FontSize = 12
    .MarginLeft = 500
    .StartDoc

    iCurrentY = .CurrentY
    iMarginLeft = .MarginLeft
    iLeft = .MarginLeft

    cMonth = Format(oRS("StartDate"), "mmmm")

    Call PrintMonth(iLeft, cMonth)

    Do While Not oRS.EOF

        cCoordinator = oRS("Coordinator")
        cDateRange = Format(oRS("StartDate"), "mm/dd")
        cConventionName = UCase$(oRS("ConventionName"))
        cCityState = oRS("City") & ", " & oRS("State")
        cConvNumber = "#" & oRS("id")

        With VSPrinter1

            .MarginLeft = iLeft

            .StartTable

            .TableCell(tcFontSize) = 12
            .TableCell(tcFontBold) = True

            .TableCell(tcCols) = 2
            .TableCell(tcRows) = 4
```

```
        .TableCell(tcColWidth, 1, 1) = 2000
        .TableCell(tcColWidth, 1, 2) = 1500

        .TableCell(tcAlign, 1, 2) = taRightMiddle

        .TableCell(tcColWidth, 3, 1) = 2500
        .TableCell(tcColWidth, 3, 2) = 1000

        .TableCell(tcAlign, 3, 2) = taRightMiddle

        .TableCell(tcFontBold, 2, 1) = True
        .TableCell(tcColSpan, 2) = 2

        .TableCell(tcText, 1, 1) = cCoordinator
        .TableCell(tcText, 1, 2) = cDateRange
        .TableCell(tcText, 2, 1) = cConventionName
        .TableCell(tcText, 3, 1) = cCityState
        .TableCell(tcText, 3, 2) = cConvNumber

        .EndTable

End With


oRS.MoveNext

If oRS.EOF Then

    Exit Do

End If

If Format(oRS("StartDate"), "mmmm") <> cMonth Then

    If .CurrentY > 9300 Then

        If iCol < 4 Then
            iCol = iCol + 1
            iLeft = iMarginLeft + 3500 * (iCol - 1)
            .CurrentY = iCurrentY

        Else
            iCol = 1
```

```
                            iLeft = iMarginLeft
                            .NewPage
                    End If

            End If

            cMonth = Format(oRS("StartDate"), "mmmm")

            Call PrintMonth(iLeft, cMonth)

        End If

        If .CurrentY > 9300 Then

            If iCol < 4 Then
                iCol = iCol + 1
                iLeft = iMarginLeft + 3500 * (iCol - 1)
            Else
                iCol = 1
                iLeft = iMarginLeft
                .NewPage
            End If

            .CurrentY = iCurrentY

        End If

    Loop

    .EndDoc

    oRS.Close
    Set oRS = Nothing

    End With

End Sub
```

```
Sub PrintMonth(iLeft As Integer, cMonth As String)

    With VSPrinter1

        .MarginLeft = iLeft

        .TableBorder = tbAll

        .StartTable

        .TableCell(tcCols) = 1
        .TableCell(tcRows) = 1

        .TableCell(tcFontSize) = 14
        .TableCell(tcFontBold) = True

        .TableCell(tcColWidth, , 1) = 3500

        .TableCell(tcText, 1, 1) = cMonth

        .EndTable

        .TableBorder = tbNone

    End With

End Sub
```

The PrintMonth routine prints the name of the current month in a 14-point font whenever the month changes. If the CurrentY position is greater than 9300 twips from the top of the page, the column counter (iCol) is incremented by one and the left margin variable (iLeft) is incremented by 3500 twips. If the column count is four, the maximum number allowed on a page, the counter is reset to one and a NewPage method is invoked to move to the next page. The output of this code is shown in Figure 5-8.

March		Joe Smith	04/09	Mr. Spock	07/01	November	
John Hawkins	03/09	MICROSOFT TECH-ED		STAR TREK CONVENTION		Bill Gates	11/01
ADVISOR DEVCON		New Orleans, LA	#11	New York, NY	#1	VISUAL BASIC SUMMIT	
Redmond, WA	#29					Los Angeles, CA	#18
		May		Mr. Spock	07/01		
John Hawkins	03/09	Scott McNealy	05/10	STAR TREK CONVENTION		Bill Gates	11/01
ADVISOR DEVCON		JAVA PROGRAMMING		New York, NY	#9	VISUAL BASIC SUMMIT	
Redmond, WA	#5	CONVENTION				Los Angeles, CA	#10
		Butte, MO	#4	Mr. Spock	07/01		
John Hawkins	03/09			STAR TREK CONVENTION		Bill Gates	11/01
ADVISOR DEVCON		Scott McNealy	05/10	New York, NY	#17	VISUAL BASIC SUMMIT	
Redmond, WA	#13	JAVA PROGRAMMING				Los Angeles, CA	#26
		CONVENTION		Joe Smith	07/04		
John Hawkins	03/09	Butte, MO	#28	ADOBE ACROBAT		Bill Gates	11/01
ADVISOR DEVCON				CONFERENCE		VISUAL BASIC SUMMIT	
Redmond, WA	#21	Scott McNealy	05/10	San Francisco, CA	#8	Los Angeles, CA	#2
		JAVA PROGRAMMING					
April		CONVENTION		Joe Smith	07/04	Jon Kilburn	11/13
Joe Smith	04/09	Butte, MO	#12	ADOBE ACROBAT		PALM DEVELOPER	
MICROSOFT TECH-ED				CONFERENCE		CONFERENCE	
New Orleans, LA	#3	Scott McNealy	05/10	San Francisco, CA	#16	Dallas, TX	#23
		JAVA PROGRAMMING					
Joe Smith	04/09	CONVENTION		Joe Smith	07/04	Jon Kilburn	11/13
MICROSOFT TECH-ED		Butte, MO	#20	ADOBE ACROBAT		PALM DEVELOPER	
New Orleans, LA	#27			CONFERENCE		CONFERENCE	
		July		San Francisco, CA	#32	Dallas, TX	#7
Joe Smith	04/09	Mr. Spock	07/01				
MICROSOFT TECH-ED		STAR TREK CONVENTION		Joe Smith	07/04	Jon Kilburn	11/13
New Orleans, LA	#19	New York, NY	#25	ADOBE ACROBAT		PALM DEVELOPER	
				CONFERENCE		CONFERENCE	
				San Francisco, CA	#24	Dallas, TX	#31

Figure 5-8. Snaked column output

Variable Length Columns

The snaked column example is rather easy because, like labels, no information will print across pages or columns. If it is determined that there is insufficient room to print all of a convention's data, the next information block will carry to the next column or the next page. Things get rather complicated once you have a report that consists of multiple columns of data that do not wrap to another column. For example, suppose you had a report that listed summary information in the following format:

Column 1	Column 2	Column 3
Convention Name	Exhibit 1	Attendee 1
Coordinator	Exhibit 2	Attendee 2
Location	Exhibit 3	Attendee 3
	Exhibit 4	

Though the number of columns is fixed, you never know how many data rows each column will have. You cannot simply move down the page and then up again, as any given column could span a page. Once the NewPage event fires, you cannot move the current print line back to a previous page. Since the down-and-up approach taken by labels will not work here, you'll need to print left to right. An easy approach to handle this is to extract all the data needed to populate the report and to traverse the ADO Recordsets and load up an array with the data. To handle formatting codes for bolding, underlining, etc., use another array of the same structure. Thus, one array stores the data and another stores the formatting. If you wish, you could also store the formatting codes in a third dimension of the data array. The code shown in Listing 5-10 illustrates printing an array-based report.

Listing 5-10. Array-Based Report

```
Sub ArrayBasedRpt()
    Dim oRS As ADODB.Recordset
    Dim oExhibitRS As ADODB.Recordset
    Dim oAttendeeRS As ADODB.Recordset
    Dim cSQL As String
    Dim iRow As Integer
    Dim iRowThisPage As Integer
    Dim iMaxPos As Integer
    Dim iTableRow As Integer
    Dim iStart As Integer
    Dim x As Integer
    Dim y As Integer
    Dim lConventionID As Long
    Dim aData(2000, 3) As Variant
    Dim aFormat(2000, 3) As Variant

    Const COL_CONVENTION = 1
    Const COL_EXHIBIT = 2
    Const COL_ATTENDEE = 3
```

```
cSQL = "SELECT * " & _
       "FROM Convention " & _
       "WHERE ID IN " & _
       "(SELECT ConventionID " & _
       "FROM Attendee)"

Set oRS = oConn.Execute(cSQL)

With VSPrinter1

    .TableBorder = tbNone
    .PageBorder = pbNone
    .Orientation = orLandscape
    .MarginBottom = 500
    .StartDoc

    iRowThisPage = 1

    Do While Not oRS.EOF

        lConventionID = oRS("ID")

        'Clear out arrays before beginning new convention
        Erase aData
        Erase aFormat

        'After each column is printed, record the maximum
        'value of iRow so the printing logic knows
        'how far down the array to print
        iMaxPos = 0

        'Start every convention block at array element 0
        'regardless of where it may begin to print on the page
        iRow = 0

        'Convention name should be bold
        aFormat(iRow, COL_CONVENTION) = "b"
        aData(iRow, COL_CONVENTION) = oRS("ConventionName")
```

```
'Get convention information
cSQL = "SELECT * " & _
        "FROM Exhibit " & _
        "WHERE ConventionID = " & lConventionID


Set oExhibitRS = oConn.Execute(cSQL)


If Not oExhibitRS.EOF Then
    aFormat(iRow, COL_EXHIBIT) = "b"
    aData(iRow, COL_EXHIBIT) = "EXHIBITS"
    iRow = iRow + 1
End If


Do While Not oExhibitRS.EOF

    aData(iRow, COL_EXHIBIT) = oExhibitRS("Descr")

    iRow = iRow + 1

    oExhibitRS.MoveNext

Loop


If iMaxPos < iRow Then
    iMaxPos = iRow
End If



'Now get attendee information
iRow = 0

cSQL = "SELECT * " & _
        "FROM Attendee " & _
        "WHERE ConventionID = " & lConventionID


Set oAttendeeRS = oConn.Execute(cSQL)


If Not oAttendeeRS.EOF Then
    aFormat(iRow, COL_ATTENDEE) = "b"
    aData(iRow, COL_ATTENDEE) = "ATTENDEES"
```

```
                    iRow = iRow + 1
            End If


            Do While Not oAttendeeRS.EOF

                aData(iRow, COL_ATTENDEE) = oAttendeeRS("name")

                iRow = iRow + 1

                oAttendeeRS.MoveNext

            Loop

            If iMaxPos < iRow Then
                iMaxPos = iRow
            End If

            oRS.MoveNext



            If .CurrentY > 10000 Then

                iRowThisPage = 1

                Call DrawLines(iStart, .CurrentY)

                .NewPage

            End If

            .TableBorder = tbNone

            .StartTable
            .TableCell(tcCols) = 3

            'Count what row we're on for the convention currently being
            'printed. This is the row counter for the StartTable/EndTable
            'set and is reset for each convention regardless
            'of how many conventions print on a single page
            iTableRow = 1
```

```
iStart = .CurrentY

For x = 0 To iMaxPos


    'Avoid printing a blank line at the top of the next
    'page just before beginning a new convention
    If IsEmpty(aData(iMaxPos, COL_CONVENTION)) And _
        IsEmpty(aData(iMaxPos, COL_EXHIBIT)) And _
        IsEmpty(aData(iMaxPos, COL_ATTENDEE)) And _
        iRowThisPage = 1 And _
        x = iMaxPos Then

        Exit For

    End If


    .TableCell(tcInsertRow) = iTableRow

    .TableCell(tcFontSize, iTableRow) = 10

    .TableCell(tcColWidth, iTableRow, COL_CONVENTION) = 3500
    .TableCell(tcColWidth, iTableRow, COL_EXHIBIT) = 3500
    .TableCell(tcColWidth, iTableRow, COL_ATTENDEE) = 3500

    For y = COL_CONVENTION To COL_ATTENDEE

        If InStr(aFormat(x, y), "b") <> 0 Then
            .TableCell(tcFontBold, iTableRow, y) = True
        End If

        .TableCell(tcText, iTableRow, y) = "" & aData(x, y)

    Next y

    iTableRow = iTableRow + 1
    iRowThisPage = iRowThisPage + 1

    'No more than 36 rows per page
    If iRowThisPage > 36 Then
        .EndTable
```

```
                         iTableRow = 1
                         iRowThisPage = 1

                         Call DrawLines(iStart, .CurrentY)

                         .NewPage

                         iStart = .CurrentY

                         .StartTable
                         .TableCell(tcCols) = 3

                   End If

              Next x

              .EndTable

              Call DrawLines(iStart, .CurrentY)

         Loop

         .EndDoc

         oRS.Close
         Set oRS = Nothing

      End With

End Sub

Sub DrawLines(iStart As Integer, iEnd As Integer)

    With VSPrinter1
        .PenWidth = 15
        .BrushStyle = bsTransparent
        .DrawRectangle .MarginLeft, iStart, 10505, iEnd
        .DrawRectangle 3500 + .MarginLeft, iStart, 3505 + .MarginLeft, iEnd
        .DrawRectangle 7000 + .MarginLeft, iStart, 7005 + .MarginLeft, iEnd
    End With

End Sub
```

The output of this code is shown in Figure 5-9.

Star Trek Convention	EXHIBITS	ATTENDEES
	Star Trek Booth 1	Washington, George
	Star Trek Booth 1	Adams, John
	Star Trek Booth 1	Jefferson, Thomas
		Madison, James
		Monroe, James
		Adams, John Quincy
		Jackson, Andrew
		van Buren, Martin
Visual Basic Summit	EXHIBITS	ATTENDEES
	VB Booth 1	Bush, George W
	VB Booth 2	Clinton, Bill
	VB Booth 3	Bush, George
	VB Booth 4	Reagan, Ronald
		Carter, Jimmy
		Ford, Gerald
		Nixon, Richard
		Johnson, Lyndon
Microsoft Tech-Ed	EXHIBITS	ATTENDEES
	Microsoft Booth 1	McKinley, William
	Microsoft Booth 2	Roosevelt, Theodore
	Microsoft Booth 3	Taft, William Howard
	Microsoft Booth 4	Wilson, Woodrow
	Microsoft Booth 5	Coolidge, Calvin
	Microsoft Booth 6	Hoover, Herbert
	Microsoft Booth 7	
	Microsoft Booth 8	
	Microsoft Booth 9	

Figure 5-9. Array-based report

What really gets tricky with this type of array-based approach is that within a column any given data element, say, an attendee name, could wrap within the cell it is printing. If this happens, there will be a gap in that row across all the columns that comprise it. Therefore you'll need to first determine if each data element has sufficient space to print without wrapping. This can be accomplished with the TextWidth method. TextWidth returns the number of twips required to print a string at the current font settings. If the string is too long, then the SplitLine function, which is found in the source code available at the Apress

Web site (http://www.apress.com), will break the string at a space or a linefeed and place each part in the next element of the data array.

Report Preview Screen

The VS-View report preview screen consists solely of the visual interface of the VSPrinter control as shown in Figure 5-10.

Figure 5-10. Report preview screen

Of course, no report viewing form would be complete unless a few enhancements were made to the existing layout. Note the Find and Find Next buttons adjacent to the navigation bar. This custom feature allows you to search for a specific string within the report and highlight the first occurrence of it. The code to locate and highlight text within the output—admittedly adapted from the VS-View documentation—can be found in Listing 5-11.

Listing 5-11. Find and FindNext Code

```
Private Sub cmdFind_Click(Index As Integer)
  Static iStartPage As Integer
  Static iStartY As Integer

  With VSPrinter1
    .PenWidth = 20
    .PenColor = vbRed
    .PenStyle = psSolid
    .BrushStyle = bsTransparent
  End With

  If Index = 0 Then
    iStartPage = 0
    iStartY = 0
  End If

  iStartPage = VSPrinter1.FindText(txtFind, , iStartPage, , iStartY)

  If iStartPage <= 0 Then
    MsgBox "Text not found: " & txtFind, vbOKOnly, "Not Found"
    iStartY = 0
    Exit Sub
  End If

  iStartY = VSPrinter1.Y2

  With VSPrinter1
    .StartOverlay iStartPage
    .DrawRectangle .X1, .Y1, .X2, .Y2
    .EndOverlay
    .PreviewPage = iStartPage
    .ScrollIntoView .X1, .Y1, .X2, .Y2
  End With

End Sub
```

The display screen is also a good place to offer an Export to ASCII and an Export to Excel button. The source code to perform these exports is discussed later in the chapter.

Using Graphics

VS-View can display graphical images as well as text. The code that follows prints a signature image stored in a GIF file. A Picture control is required to contain the image.

```
With VSPrinter1
    .StartDoc
    .DrawPicture Picture1, 6000, 4000, "50%", "50%"
    .EndDoc
End With
```

Here, the DrawPicture method is displaying a graphic at a specified offset—4000 twips down the page and 6000 twips from the left. The percentage parameters indicate that the width and height of the graphic should be scaled to half its natural size.

You can use the DrawRectangle and DrawCircle methods to create boxes, lines, and circles. The following code draws the boxes around the text shown in Listing 5-10.

```
Sub DrawLines(iStart As Integer, iEnd As Integer)

    With VSPrinter1
        .PenWidth = 15
        .BrushStyle = bsTransparent
        .DrawRectangle .MarginLeft, iStart, 10505, iEnd
        .DrawRectangle 3500 + .MarginLeft, iStart, 3505 + .MarginLeft, iEnd
        .DrawRectangle 7000 + .MarginLeft, iStart, 7005 + .MarginLeft, iEnd
    End With

End Sub
```

Exporting Data

VS-View unfortunately does not have many data export options. It natively handles exports to HTML, DHTML, and RTF. With an add-on control—VSPDF8.OCX—it can export to Adobe Acrobat as well. ASCII and Excel dumps need to be handled manually.

By setting the ExportFile property, you can specify the name of the file to receive the export information. Then, by passing one of the constants shown in Table 5-5 to the ExportFormat property, you can export your report data to RTF or one of the flavors of HTML/DHTML.

Table 5-5. ExportFormat Constants

CONSTANT	VALUE	DESCRIPTION
vpxPlainHTML	0	Generates plain HTML. Results in compact HTML files, but some paragraph formatting options are lost.
vpxDHTML	1	Generates HTML with style tags. Results in larger HTML files, but all paragraph formatting is included in the document.
vpxPagedHTML	2	Similar to vpxPlainHTML, but creates several hyperlinked HTML files.
vpxPagedDHTML	3	Similar to vpxDHTML, but creates several hyperlinked DHTML files.
vpxRTF	4	Generates RTF output.

VSPDF8.OCX allows you to create tagged PDF files that contain metadata information for title, creator, author, subject, and keywords. Simply set these properties, invoke the ConvertDocument method, and pass the name of the VSPrinter control and the destination filename as shown here:

```
With VSPDF81
    .Title = "PDF Export"
    .Creator = "Your Name"
    .Author = "My Name"
    .Subject = "Enterprise Reports with VB6 and VB.NET"
    .Keywords = "VB VB.NET Reports"
    .ConvertDocument VSPrinter1, App.Path & "\myreport.pdf"
End With
```

TIP *Because the PDF export occurs so fast, I usually export all reports to PDF automatically and don't offer the user a separate PDF option. I found that after introducing the PDF export feature to my applications, users have created elaborate archive systems around it. They rename PDF reports to the report run date and refer back to them as the database is updated in the future. Optionally, you could name the export file to the current date and time so the files won't overwrite each other and the users can have copies of every report they have ever run.*

Exporting data to ASCII and Excel is a bit tougher. Because VS-View does not provide methods to export to these file formats, you'll need to program this functionality yourself. Fortunately, there are two simple methods of accomplishing this. Since most of your reports will be columnar, you need only pass the VSPrinter object and an indicator of the destination file type—ASCII or Excel—to a data dumping routine. Then, by looping through the rows and columns of the one table that comprises the report, you can print the data as comma/quote-delimited records of an ASCII file or as individual cells of an Excel spreadsheet. Listing 5-12 illustrates how this is accomplished.

Listing 5-12. TableCell Data Dump

```
Sub DumpTable(oPrinter As VSPrinter, iDumpType As DumpType)
    Dim objExcel As Excel.Application
    Dim objWorkBook As Excel.Workbook
    Dim objWS As Excel.Worksheet
    Dim x As Integer
    Dim y As Integer
    Dim iRows As Integer
    Dim iCols As Integer
    Dim cLine As String
    Dim cFileName As String
    Dim cData As Variant

    Screen.MousePointer = vbHourglass

    If iDumpType = dtASCII Then
        cFileName = App.Path & "\ASCIIDump.txt"
```

```
        Open cFileName For Output As #1
    Else
        Set objExcel = CreateObject("Excel.Application")
        objExcel.Visible = False

        Set objWorkBook = objExcel.Workbooks.Add
        Set objWS = objExcel.Worksheets.Add

        cFileName = App.Path & "\ASCIIDump.xls"

    End If

    With VSPrinter1

        iRows = .TableCell(tcRows)
        iCols = .TableCell(tcCols)

        For x = 1 To iRows

            cLine = vbNullString

            For y = 1 To iCols

                cData = .TableCell(tcText, x, y)

                If iDumpType = dtASCII Then

                    cLine = cLine & Chr(34) & cData & Chr(34) & ","

                Else

                    If Not IsNull(cData) Then

                        If IsNumeric(cData) And _
                            cData <> Empty And InStr(cData, ")") = 0 Then

                            objWS.Cells(x, y) = CDbl(cData)

                        Else

                            If IsNumeric(Mid(cData, 1, 1)) And _
                                Occurs(cData, "/") = 2 Then
```

```
                            If IsDate(CStr("" & cData)) Then
                                objWS.Cells(x, y) = _
                                    Format(CStr(cData), "mm/dd/yyyy")
                            Else
                                objWS.Cells(x, y) = Chr(39) & cData
                            End If

                    Else

                        objWS.Cells(x, y) = Chr(39) & cData

                    End If

                End If

            End If

        Next y

        If iDumpType = dtASCII Then
            Print #1, Mid$(cLine, 1, Len(cLine) - 1)
        End If

    Next x

End With

If iDumpType = dtASCII Then

    Close #1

Else

    If Dir(cFileName) <> vbNullString Then
        Kill cFileName
    End If

    objWS.Cells.ColumnWidth = 40

    objWS.SaveAs cFileName
```

```
            objWorkBook.Close

            objExcel.Quit

        End If

        MsgBox "Report has been exported to " & cFileName, vbOKOnly

        Screen.MousePointer = vbDefault

End Sub
```

Most of your users will use the Excel dump to perform numerical analysis on the data. Because Excel will make certain assumptions about the type of each piece of data, the code for the Excel dump needs to examine each element individually to determine if it is a string, a date, or a number. If everything were saved as a string value, your users would not be able to use it for mathematical computations.

Since some of your reports will not fit so neatly into one TableCell, you can collect your data in an array and print each coordinate in the same fashion as shown in Listing 5-12. The code for this routine can be found in the source file for the book, available at the Apress Web site (`http://www.apress.com`).

ComponentOne Preview for .NET

ComponentOne's Preview offers the same programmatic report writing functionality for .NET as VS-View does for Visual Basic. Whereas VS-View 8.0 combined both its report building and displaying functionality into one OCX control called VSPrinter, Preview divides these tasks into two main components: C1PrintDocument and C1PrintPreview. C1PrintDocument represents the report document object and C1PrintPreview is the report viewer.

As you've no doubt discovered, VB .NET relies heavily on namespaces. The namespace for the PrintPreview control is C1.Win.C1PrintPreview and for PrintDocument it is C1.C1PrintDocument. The .NET runtime is larger than its OCX incarnation, consisting of three DLLs—C1.C1PrintDocument.dll, C1.Win.C1PrintPreview.dll, and C1.PrintUtil.dll—totaling 1.5 megabytes. Of the three, the first two are written in C#, and the third is written in managed C++. There is no OCX code involved (or ported from VS-View for that matter).

Because .NET is an OOP development environment, you'll need to use some of .NET's internal printer classes in conjunction with Preview's C1PrintDocument and C1PrintPreview components. For example, to set the paper bin, the margins of a document, or the number of copies to print, use the appropriate properties in the Printing namespace. It's a bit disconcerting at first looking for these properties in the Preview help file and not finding them. This is because they're handled by .NET and documented by Microsoft.

Differences Between Preview and VS-View

While familiarity with VS-View will afford you a head start, there are enough differences between the two products to present a bit of a learning curve. Many of these differences are inherent in the dissimilarities between VB6 and VB .NET, not necessarily between VS-View and Preview. Conceptually, the two products are very much the same. Though the table is still the basic structure of all reports, you still need to manage headers and footers, and you still need to set margins and page orientation. Still, not every feature between the two products has an obvious translation. Table 5-6 lists some of the more commonly used properties, methods, and events in VS-View and indicates their counterpart in Preview.

Table 5-6. VS-View Properties, Methods, and Events, and Preview Counterparts

VS-VIEW FEATURE	PREVIEW EQUIVALENT
AddTable	Handled by the Table object
AddTableArray	Handled by the Table object
BrushColor	Use the Style object
BrushStyle	Use the Style object
Collate	C1PrintPreview1.PrinterSettings.Collate
Copies	C1PrintPreview1.PrinterSettings.Copies
CurrentColumn	C1PrintDocument.CurrentColumn
CurrentPage	C1PrintDocument.CurrentPage
Device	C1PrintPreview1.PrinterSettings.PrinterName
Devices	C1PrintPreview1.PrinterSettings.InstalledPrinters
Draw methods	Use the Render methods
Duplex	C1PrintPreview1.PrinterSettings.Duplex
EndDoc	C1PrintDocument.EndDoc()
EndTable	C1PrintDocument.RenderBlock(objTable), where objTable is a RenderTable object
Footer	C1PrintDocument.PageFooter.RenderObject = objTable, where objTable is a Table object designed to print on the bottom of every page

(continued)

Table 5-6. VS-View Properties, Methods, and Events, and Preview Counterparts (continued)

VS-VIEW FEATURE	PREVIEW EQUIVALENT
Header	C1PrintDocument.PageHeader.RenderObject = objTable, where objTable is a Table object designed to print on the top of every page
LineSpacing	C1PrintDocument.Style.LineSpacing
Margin properties	C1PrintDocument.PageSettings.Margins. Left C1PrintDocument.PageSettings. Margins.Right C1PrintDocument.PageSettings. Margins.Top C1PrintDocument.PageSettings. Margins.Bottom
Orientation	C1PrintDocument.PageSettings.Landscape = True / False
PageCount	C1PrintDocument.PageCount
PaperBin	C1PrintDocument.PageSettings.PaperSource = PaperSourceKind.
PaperBins	C1PrintDocument.PageSettings. PrinterSettings.PaperSources
PaperSize	C1PrintPreview1.PageSettings.PaperSize = PaperKind.
Paragraph	C1PrintDocument.RenderBlockText
PenColor	Use the Style object
PenStyle	Use the Style object
PenWidth	Use the LineDef object
Preview	N/A—document is rendered and then the Print method is invoked
PrintDoc	C1PrintPreview1.Print()
PrintQuality	C1PrintDocument.PageSettings. PrinterResolution.Kind

(continued)

Table 5-6. VS-View Properties, Methods, and Events, and Preview Counterparts (continued)

VS-VIEW FEATURE	PREVIEW EQUIVALENT
SpaceAfter, SpaceBefore	objStyle.Spacing.Bottom
	objStyle.Spacing.Left
	objStyle.Spacing.Top
	objStyle.Spacing.Right
StartDoc	C1PrintDocument.StartDoc()
StartTable	N/A, see EndTable
TableBorder	objTable.StyleTableCell.Borders
	objTable.StyleTableCell.BorderTableHorz.Empty
	objTable.StyleTableCell.BorderTableVert.Emptywhere
	objTable is a RenderTable object
TableCell	objTable.Body.Cell, where
	objTable is a RenderTable object
Text	C1PrintDocument.RenderInlineText
TextRTF	RTF text not supported

Getting Started

Like its COM predecessor, Preview uses Table objects as its basic unit of report construction. Tables are comprised of three horizontal table bands—header, body, and footer. Each band, in turn, may contain multiple table rows. Tables are also divided into vertical columns. Individual cells can be accessed either via the band they are contained in using row and column offsets or through their row using the column index. Individual cells may contain anything—text, graphics, or even another table.

Let's examine a simple columnar report in Preview, as illustrated by the code in Listing 5-13, that draws from the book's sample database.

Listing 5-13. Columnar Report

```
Private Sub GettingStarted(ByVal oConn As OleDbConnection)
    Dim objDR As OleDbDataReader
    Dim objCommand As OleDbCommand
    Dim objTable As New RenderTable(Doc)
    Dim iRow As Integer
    Dim cSQL As String
```

```
cSQL = "SELECT * " & _
        "FROM Source " & _
        "ORDER BY descr"


objCommand = New OleDbCommand(cSQL, oConn)
objDR = objCommand.ExecuteReader()

With objTable.Columns
    .AddSome(2)
    .Item(0).Width = 1.7
    .Item(1).Width = 3
End With


With Doc
    .StartDoc()

    While objDR.Read

        With objTable.Body
            .Rows.Add()
            .Cell(iRow, 0).RenderText.Text = objDR.Item("ID")
            .Cell(iRow, 1).RenderText.Text = objDR.Item("Descr")
        End With

        iRow += 1

    End While

    .RenderBlock(objTable)

    .EndDoc()

End With

End Sub
```

This code produces the output shown in Figure 5-11.

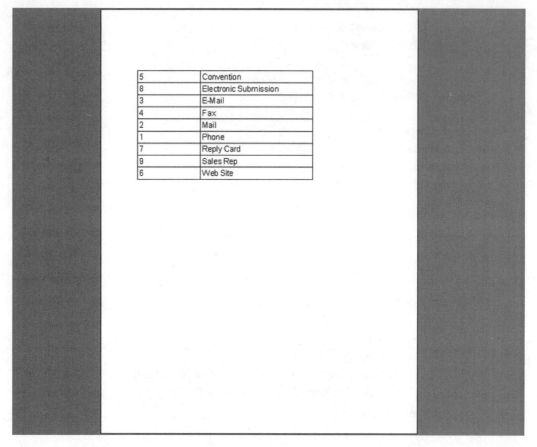

5	Convention
8	Electronic Submission
3	E-Mail
4	Fax
2	Mail
1	Phone
7	Reply Card
9	Sales Rep
6	Web Site

Figure 5-11. Columnar report output

The first step in creating this report is to declare a variable to encapsulate the Table object of the class RenderTable, where Doc is the name of the C1PrintDocument engine:

```
Dim objTable As New RenderTable(Doc)
```

Next, add two columns to this Table object—one 1.7 inches wide and the other 3 inches wide.

```
With objTable.Columns
    .AddSome(2)
    .Item(0).Width = 1.7
    .Item(1).Width = 3
End With
```

The remainder of the code loops through the DataReader object, and for each record encountered, a new row is added to the table. Then, each cell in the newly added row is populated with the data from the DataReader object. Finally, the table is rendered via the RenderTable method.

Setting Up the Page

All of your reports will need to be set up for printing. Such attributes as paper orientation, margins, text size calculations, cursor position, current printer, paper bin, and text styles all need to be controlled and manipulated throughout the project. While it is the PrintDocument component that encapsulates this functionality, it is .NET that offers these features through the hierarchy of the System class. The printing-related subclasses of the System namespace are listed in Table 5-7.

Table 5-7. System.Drawing.Printing Class Hierarchy

CLASS TREE

System.Drawing.Printing.Margins

System.Drawing.Printing.PageSettings

System.Drawing.Printing.PaperSize

System.Drawing.Printing.PaperSource

System.Drawing.Printing.PreviewPageInfo

System.Drawing.Printing.PrintController

System.Drawing.Printing.PrinterResolution

System.Drawing.Printing.PrinterSettings

System.Drawing.Printing.PrinterSettings.PaperSizeCollection

System.Drawing.Printing.PrinterSettings.PaperSourceCollection

System.Drawing.Printing.PrinterSettings.PrinterResolutionCollection

System.Drawing.Printing.PrinterUnitConvert

Margins

You'll need to establish the margins of your report via the Left, Right, Top, and Bottom properties. In .NET, the default spacing for these properties is measured in units of one hundredths of an inch. For example, the code that follows sets the top and left margins to 3 inches and the bottom and right margins to 2 inches:

```
With Doc
    With .PageSettings
        .Margins.Top = 300
        .Margins.Bottom = 200
        .Margins.Right = 200
        .Margins.Left = 300
    End With
End With
```

Page orientation is, of course, also a must and is handled by setting the Landscape property to a Boolean value as follows:

```
Doc.PageSettings.Landscape = True
```

Paper Bins

Specific paper bin settings can also be changed during the creation of reports. The PrinterSettings.PaperSources property returns a collection of all the paper sources available based on the settings of the current printer driver. Then, the PaperSource property accepts your selection and directs output toward the specified bin as shown in the following example:

```
Doc.PageSettings.PaperSource = _
Doc.PageSettings.PrinterSettings.PaperSources(PaperSourceKind.Upper)
```

Printer Selection

You can select printers via the PrinterName property. The PrinterSettings.InstalledPrinters property contains all the printers recognized by Windows. See Listing 5-14 for an illustration of how the available printers are loaded into a list box.

Listing 5-14. Selecting Current Printer

```
Sub GetPrinterList()
    Dim cPrinter As String

    For Each cPrinter In PrinterSettings.InstalledPrinters
        lstPrinters.Items.Add(cPrinter)
    Next
```

```
End Sub

Private Sub cmdSelectPrinter_Click(ByVal sender As System.Object, _
    ByVal e As System.EventArgs) Handles cmdSelectPrinter.Click

    Doc.PageSettings.PrinterSettings.PrinterName = lstPrinters.Text

End Sub
```

Styles

Like their counterparts in Microsoft Word, Style objects contain all the attributes—font, bold, underline, size, color, alignment, etc.—that printed text will use. By creating a series of Style objects to define your text, you can easily standardize how text will display throughout your report without much concern that you'll inadvertently change the formatting. Take a look at the code in Listing 5-15.

Listing 5-15. Style Objects

```
Dim objStyleName As New C1DocStyle(Doc)
Dim objStyleQuotation As New C1DocStyle(Doc)

With objStyleName
    .Font = New Font("Arial", 20, FontStyle.Bold)
    .TextColor = Color.Black
    .BackColor = Color.Red
    With .Borders
        .All = New LineDef(Color.Black, 5)
    End With
    .TextAlignHorz = AlignHorzEnum.Center
End With

With objStyleQuotation
    .Font = New Font("Arial", 10, FontStyle.Italic)
    .TextColor = Color.Black
    With .Spacing
        .TopUnit.Value = 0.2
        .BottomUnit.Value = 0.1
    End With
End With
```

```
With Doc
    .StartDoc()

    .RenderBlockText("Abraham Lincoln", objStyleName)
    .RenderBlockText("With malice toward none, " & _
    "with charity toward all...", objStyleQuotation)

    .RenderBlockText("Bill Clinton", objStyleName)
    .RenderBlockText("I swear I thought she " & _
    "was over eighteen.", objStyleQuotation)

    .EndDoc()
End With
```

Much as you can do with headers and footers, you can also create a class library of Styles that can be reused throughout your project and across all applications in your development group.

This example produces the output shown in Figure 5-12.

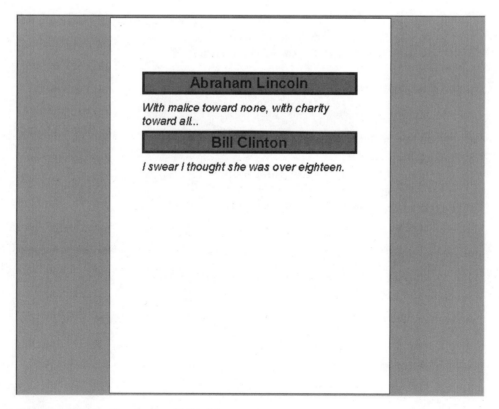

Figure 5-12. Results of using Style objects

Borders and LineDefs

Borders and the lines that comprise them are a complicated subject. Preview gives you complete control over the lines that comprise a table and the individual cells within a table. Since the header and footer are distinct tables from the body of the report, they can have their own unique table and cell line settings.

Code to control the various border settings can be seen in Listing 5-16. I have not included a screen shot showing the output of this listing, as this book is not printed in color, so it's best to run and experiment with this code yourself to see all the garish colors set up for the examples. LineDef objects are, as the name suggests, definitions of lines. Their properties allow you to set the color and point width of the line. These objects can then be assigned to the Bottom, Left, Right, and Top properties of Border objects.

Listing 5-16. Borders and LineDefs

```
Sub BorderDemo()
    Dim objTable As New RenderTable(Doc)
    Dim objHeader As New RenderTable(Doc)
    Dim objFooter As New RenderTable(Doc)
    Dim objTableBottomLineDef As New LineDef(Color.Red, 10)
    Dim objTableLeftLineDef As New LineDef(Color.Green, 10)
    Dim objTableRightLineDef As New LineDef(Color.RoyalBlue, 10)
    Dim objTableTopLineDef As New LineDef(Color.Gold, 10)
    Dim objCellBottomLineDef As New LineDef(Color.Silver, 3)
    Dim objCellLeftLineDef As New LineDef(Color.SeaShell, 3)
    Dim objCellRightLineDef As New LineDef(Color.SeaGreen, 3)
    Dim objCellTopLineDef As New LineDef(Color.Salmon, 3)
    Dim x As Short

    With objHeader
        .Columns.AddSome(3)
        .Columns(0).Width = 2
        .Columns(1).Width = 2
        .Columns(2).Width = 2

        .Style.Borders.AllEmpty = False
        .StyleTableCell.BorderTableHorz.Empty = True
        .StyleTableCell.BorderTableVert.Empty = True

        .Body.Rows.Add()
```

```
        .Body.Cell(0, 0).RenderText.Style.TextAlignHorz = AlignHorzEnum.Center
        .Body.Cell(0, 1).RenderText.Style.TextAlignHorz = AlignHorzEnum.Center
        .Body.Cell(0, 2).RenderText.Style.TextAlignHorz = AlignHorzEnum.Center

        .Body.Cell(0, 0).RenderText.Text() = "Header 1"
        .Body.Cell(0, 1).RenderText.Text() = "Header 2"
        .Body.Cell(0, 2).RenderText.Text() = "Header 3"

End With

With objFooter
    .Columns.AddSome(3)
    .Columns(0).Width = 2
    .Columns(1).Width = 2
    .Columns(2).Width = 2

    .Style.Borders.AllEmpty = True
    .StyleTableCell.BorderTableHorz.Empty = True
    .StyleTableCell.BorderTableVert.Empty = True

    .Body.Rows.Add()

    .Body.Cell(0, 0).RenderText.Style.TextAlignHorz = AlignHorzEnum.Center
    .Body.Cell(0, 1).RenderText.Style.TextAlignHorz = AlignHorzEnum.Center
    .Body.Cell(0, 2).RenderText.Style.TextAlignHorz = AlignHorzEnum.Center

    .Body.Cell(0, 0).RenderText.Text() = "Footer 1"
    .Body.Cell(0, 1).RenderText.Text() = "Footer 2"
    .Body.Cell(0, 2).RenderText.Text() = "Footer 3"

End With

objTable.Style.Borders.AllEmpty = False

With objTable.StyleTableCell.BorderTableHorz
    .Empty = False
    .Color = Color.Indigo
    .WidthPt = 20
End With

With objTable.StyleTableCell.BorderTableVert
    .Empty = False
    .Color = Color.DarkGreen
```

```
            .WidthPt = 20
        End With


        With objTable.StyleTableCell.Borders
            .Bottom = objCellBottomLineDef
            .Left = objCellLeftLineDef
            .Right = objCellRightLineDef
            .Top = objCellTopLineDef
        End With


        With objTable.Style.Borders
            .Bottom = objTableBottomLineDef
            .Left = objTableLeftLineDef
            .Right = objTableRightLineDef
            .Top = objTableTopLineDef
        End With


        With objTable.Columns
            .AddSome(4)
            .Item(0).Width = 1.5
            .Item(1).Width = 1.5
            .Item(2).Width = 1.5
            .Item(3).Width = 1.5
        End With


        With Doc


            .PageHeader.RenderObject = objHeader
            .PageFooter.RenderObject = objFooter


            .StartDoc()


            For x = 0 To 10


                With objTable.Body
                    .Rows.Add()
                    .Cell(x, 0).RenderText.Text = "Col 0 - Row " & x
                    .Cell(x, 1).RenderText.Text = "Col 1 - Row " & x
                    .Cell(x, 2).RenderText.Text = "Col 2 - Row " & x
                    .Cell(x, 3).RenderText.Text = "Col 3 - Row " & x
                End With


            Next x
```

```
            .RenderBlock(objTable)

            .EndDoc()

        End With

    End Sub
```

objTable.StyleTableCell.Borders determines the LineDef object for the cells that comprise a table, whereas objTable.Style.Borders make the same determination for the borders of the table itself.

Headers and Footers

Preview handles headers and footers in a far more sophisticated fashion than VS-View. Each header and footer is created as a Table object, just like the body of the report. Then, these Table objects are assigned to the PrintDocument object as shown here:

```
Doc.PageHeader.RenderObject = objHeader
Doc.PageFooter.RenderObject = objFooter
```

Since you'll most likely utilize the same header and footer format throughout the report—the name of the report itself being the only variable element—you can create your own header and footer classes. Doing so will allow you to establish consistency between reports and across applications. Examine the code in Listing 5-16 for examples of setting the header and footer tables.

Rendering Layers

Another one of Preview's cool features is page rendering layers. There are three rendering layers in Preview—Main, Background, and Overlay. By default, your usual report text will be rendered to the Main layer. By setting the PageLayer property, you can print to any of the three layers. Suppose you need to print invoices that have the company logo as a watermark. You can display this logo on the Background layer while printing the text of the invoice on the Main layer. If the invoice is paid, the Overlay layer can handle display of the *Paid in Full* graphic. Examine the code in Listing 5-17 to see how this is done.

Listing 5-17. RenderingLayers Demo

```
Private Sub RenderingLayers()
    Dim objCompanyLogo As New C1DocStyle(Doc)
    Dim dblHeight As Double
    Dim dblWidth As Double
    Dim cPath As String

    cPath = System.Reflection.Assembly.GetExecutingAssembly.Location

    cPath = Mid$(cPath, 1, InStrRev(cPath, "\"))

    With objCompanyLogo

        .BackgroundImage = Image.FromFile(cPath & "setonsoftware.jpg")

        With .BackgroundImageAlign
            .StretchHorz = False
            .StretchVert = False
            .TileHorz = True
            .TileVert = True
        End With

    End With


    With Doc
        .PageHeader.Height = 0

        .StartDoc()

        dblWidth = .BodyAreaSize.Width
        dblHeight = .BodyAreaSize.Height

        .PageLayer = DocumentPageLayerEnum.Overlay
        .RenderDirectImage(dblWidth / 10, dblHeight / 10, _
            Image.FromFile(cPath & "paidinfull.jpg"))

        .PageLayer = DocumentPageLayerEnum.Main

        .Style.TextColor = Color.Red
```

```
            .RenderBlockText("Invoice for consulting services rendered")
            .RenderBlockText("Project Management:")
            .RenderBlockText("Development:")
            .RenderBlockText("Documentation:")
            .RenderInlineEnd()

            .PageLayer = DocumentPageLayerEnum.Background
            .RenderDirectText(0, 0, " ", dblWidth, dblHeight, objCompanyLogo)

            .EndDoc()
        End With
    End Sub
```

This code will produce the rather hideous output shown in Figure 5-13. (Hey, I'm a software developer, not a graphic artist.)

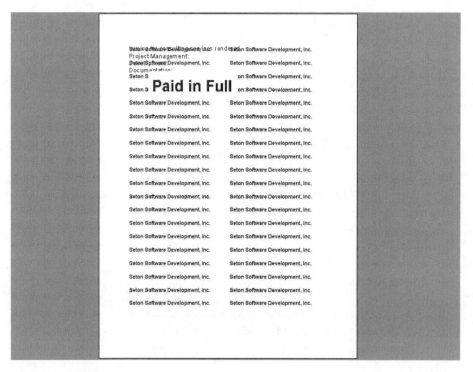

Figure 5-13. Rendering layers

Reports

You've already seen how Preview handles standard columnar reports. In the sections that follow, you'll be introduced to labels and free-form text reports. Cross tabs are studied in Chapter 8. Conceptually, the structure of Preview reports is very similar in approach and logic flow as VS-View. The similarities will become apparent as you read on.

Code for Printing Labels

Labels are a bit trickier than standard columnar reports, and your first time through you'll miss having a report writer's label creation wizard. However, once you have the layout working, it's a snap to reuse the code again and again. Essentially, you need to print each individual label as its own one-column table. The only question is how many columns per page you'll be printing and how many labels per column. Listing 5-18 prints labels that match Avery standard 5163, that is, two columns of five labels each.

Listing 5-18. Code for Printing Labels

```
Dim objLabel As New C1.C1PrintDocument.RenderTable(C1PDoc)
Dim oConn As New OleDb.OleDbConnection()
Dim objDR As OleDb.OleDbDataReader
Dim objCommand As New OleDb.OleDbCommand()
Dim cConnectString As String
Dim cSQL As String
Dim cCSZ As String
Dim iLabel As Integer
Dim iCol As Integer
Dim dblLeft As Double

cConnectString = "Provider=Microsoft.Jet.OLEDB.4.0;" & _
                 "Data Source=C:\Reports\SampleDatabase.mdb"

oConn.ConnectionString = cConnectString
oConn.Open()

cSQL = "SELECT * FROM Requester"
```

```
With objCommand
    .Connection = oConn
    .CommandText = cSQL
    .CommandType = CommandType.Text
    .CommandTimeout = 60
    objDR = .ExecuteReader()
End With

iLabel = 1
iCol = 1
dblLeft = 0

With C1PDoc

    .StartDoc()

    While objDR.Read

        objLabel = New C1.C1PrintDocument.RenderTable(C1PDoc)

        With objLabel
            .Columns.AddSome(1)
            .Columns(0).Width = 3.5
            .Style.Borders.AllEmpty = True
            .StyleTableCell.BorderTableHorz.Empty = True
            .StyleTableCell.BorderTableVert.Empty = True
        End With

        With objLabel.Body
            .Rows.AddSome(4)

            .Cell(0, 0).RenderText.Text = objDR.Item("FirstName") & " " & _
                                    objDR.Item("LastName")
            Cell(1, 0).RenderText.Text = "" & objDR.Item("Address1")

            cCSZ = objDR.Item("City") & ", " & _
                    objDR.Item("State") & " " & _
                    objDR.Item("Zip")

            If IsDBNull(objDR.Item("Address2")) Then
                .Cell(2, 0).RenderText.Text = cCSZ
            Else
```

```
                .Cell(2, 0).RenderText.Text = "" & objDR.Item("Address2")
                .Cell(3, 0).RenderText.Text = cCSZ
            End If

        End With

        .RenderDirect(dblLeft, ((iLabel - 1) * 1.9) + 0.3, objLabel)

        iLabel = iLabel + 1

        If iLabel > 5 Then

            iLabel = 1

            Select Case iCol

                Case 1
                    dblLeft = 4
                    iCol = iCol + 1

                Case 2
                    dblLeft = 0
                    iCol = 1
                    .NewPage()

            End Select

        End If

    End While

    .EndDoc()

End With
```

Free-Form Text

Preview allows you to work with free-form text to create mail merge documents or simply to print information anywhere you wish on a page. This functionality is accomplished via Render methods. The three main Render methods are RenderInlineText, RenderDirectText, and RenderBlockText. RenderInlineText displays text at the current print position without starting a new paragraph. When you need to start a new paragraph, invoke RenderInlineEnd. RenderBlockText renders text in the block flow. Finally, RenderDirectText prints a string at a specified position on the page. Take a look at the code in Listing 5-19, which illustrates how strings can be printed to the screen.

Listing 5-19. Render Methods

```
Dim objStyle As New C1DocStyle(Doc)

With objStyle
    .Font = New Font("Arial", 20, FontStyle.Bold)
End With

With Doc
    .StartDoc()

    .RenderInlineText("One thing that's really " & _
              "cool about this in-line text feature ")
    .RenderInlineText("is the ability to change fonts ", _
                   New Font("Arial", 24, FontStyle.Bold))
    .RenderInlineText("and text color", _
              New Font("Arial", 24, FontStyle.Regular), Color.Green)
    .RenderInlineEnd()
    .RenderInlineText("One thing that's really " & _
              "cool about this in-line text feature ")
    .RenderInlineText("is the ability to change fonts ", _
                   New Font("Arial", 24, FontStyle.Bold))
    .RenderInlineText("and text color", _
              New Font("Arial", 24, FontStyle.Regular), Color.Green)

    .RenderDirectText(1, 4, _
        "RenderDirectText is another cool feature", 20, 40, objStyle)
    .RenderDirectText(1.5, 4.5, _
        "that prints text exactly where you tell it to", 20, 40, objStyle)

    .RenderBlockText("RenderBlockText is another " & _
              "great method to print chunks of string data")

    .EndDoc()
End With
```

This code produces the output shown in Figure 5-14.

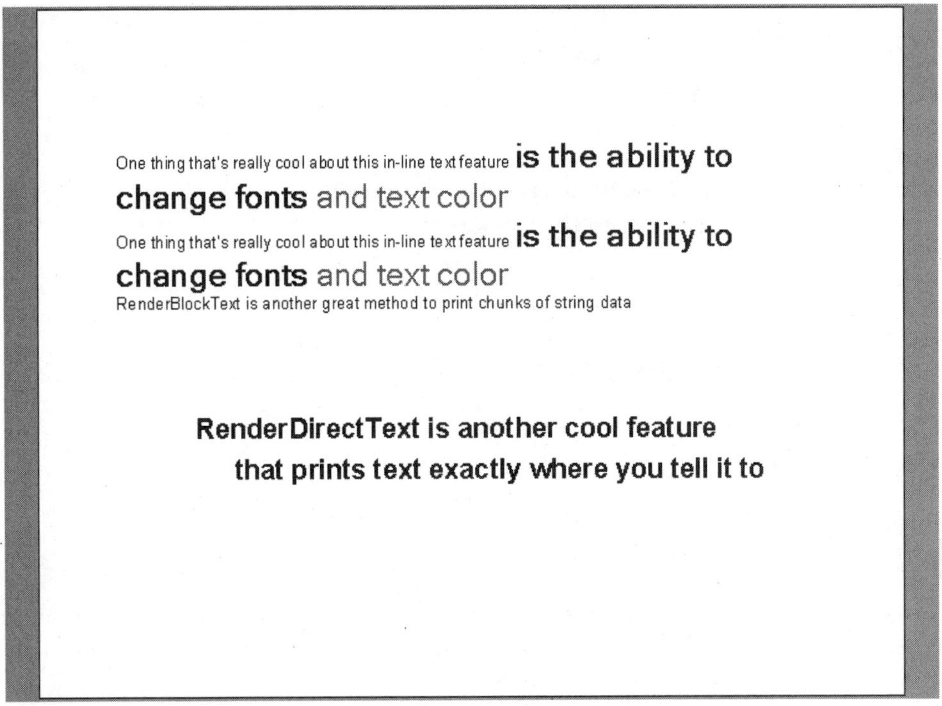

One thing that's really cool about this in-line text feature **is the ability to** **change fonts** and text color

One thing that's really cool about this in-line text feature **is the ability to** **change fonts** and text color

RenderBlockText is another great method to print chunks of string data

RenderDirectText is another cool feature **that prints text exactly where you tell it to**

Figure 5-14. Render methods output

The code in Listing 5-20 illustrates how to accomplish a mail merge. The code is very similar to its VS-View counterpart except that the RenderInlineText method is used to display the data rather than the VS-View Text property.

Listing 5-20. Mail Merge

```
Sub FreeFormText(ByVal oConn As OleDbConnection, ByVal iLetterType As Short)
    Dim objDR As OleDbDataReader
    Dim objCommand As OleDbCommand
    Dim cSQL As String
    Dim cName As String
    Dim cSalutation As String
    Dim cLastName As String
    Dim cAddress1 As String
    Dim cAddress2 As String
    Dim cCSZ As String
    Dim cCaseNumber As String
```

```
Dim cLetterText As String
Dim cText As String

cSQL = "SELECT LetterText " & _
       "FROM FormLetters " & _
       "WHERE ID = " & iLetterType

objCommand = New OleDbCommand(cSQL, oConn)
objDR = objCommand.ExecuteReader()


If objDR.Read Then
    cLetterText = objDR("LetterText")
Else
    Exit Sub
End If

objDR.Close()

cSQL = "SELECT ID, Salutation, LastName, FirstName, " & _
       "Address1, Address2, City, State, Zip " & _
       "FROM Requester " & _
       "WHERE Address1 IS NOT NULL " & _
       "ORDER BY LastName"

objCommand = New OleDbCommand(cSQL, oConn)
objDR = objCommand.ExecuteReader()

With Doc

    .Style.Font = New Font("Arial", 12)
    .Style.TextAlignHorz = AlignHorzEnum.Justify
    .Style.LineSpacing = 120

    .StartDoc()

    While objDR.Read

        cText = cLetterText

        cCaseNumber = objDR("id")
        cSalutation = "" & objDR("Salutation")
```

```
cLastName = "" & objDR("lastname")
cName = objDR("firstname") & " " & objDR("lastname")
cAddress1 = "" & objDR("Address1")
cAddress2 = "" & objDR("Address2")

If cAddress2 <> vbNullString Then
    cAddress1 = cAddress1 & vbCrLf & cAddress2
End If

cCSZ = ("" & objDR("city")) & ", " & _
            objDR("state") & " " & objDR("zip")

cText = Replace(cText, "%Name%", cName)
cText = Replace(cText, "%Address%", cAddress1)
cText = Replace(cText, "%CSZ%", cCSZ)
cText = Replace(cText, "%Salutation%", cSalutation)
cText = Replace(cText, "%LastName%", cLastName)
cText = Replace(cText, "%CaseNumber%", cCaseNumber)

.RenderInlineText(cText)

.NewPage()

End While

.EndDoc()

End With

objDR.Close()
objDR = Nothing

End Sub
```

Using Graphics

As you saw in the section on rendering layers, Preview can handle graphical images as well as text. Images are handled using the RenderDirectImage method. The following code prints an image stored in a JPG file 1 inch from the left margin and 7 inches from the top:

```
Private Sub Graphics()
    Dim cPath As String

    cPath = System.Reflection.Assembly.GetExecutingAssembly.Location
    cPath = Mid$(cPath, 1, InStrRev(cPath, "\"))

    With Doc

        .StartDoc()
        .RenderDirectImage(1, 7, Image.FromFile(cPath & "setonsoftware.jpg"))
        .EndDoc()

    End With

End Sub
```

Exporting Data

Preview handles exports to PDF files via the ExportToPDF method. At this writing, there is unfortunately no functionality to export data to either HTML or RTF, but an export method for these formats should be released in the near future. There are no plans to add export capability for ASCII or Excel. A function to export Preview Table objects to both ASCII and Excel can be found with the code for this book, available at the Apress Web site (http://www.apress.com).

Exporting a document to a PDF file is simply a matter of invoking the ExportToPDF method and passing the name of the output filename, as shown in the following code example. Two additional Boolean parameters have been added to this method: embedFonts and showProgressDialog. embedFonts indicates if the fonts should be embedded in the PDF file to make viewing of the document more consistent across systems. showProgressDialog will indicate if a progress bar should display when the PDF file is being created.

```
.ExportToPDF(cPath & "\mydoc.pdf", True)
```

Make sure you add the .PDF extension to the filename, as Preview will not do it for you.

Conclusion

By now you should have a comprehensive overview of how to create reports using VS-View for VB6 and Preview for .NET. Both of these products offer robust report development capabilities while giving you complete control via the source code. In the next chapter, you'll see how another popular product, ActiveReports, produces output.

ActiveReports for VB6 and .NET

Dᴀᴛᴀ Dʏɴᴀᴍɪᴄs' AᴄᴛɪᴠᴇRᴇᴘᴏʀᴛs (http://www.datadynamics.com/activereports) combines the visual interface of a report designer with the extensibility of the full Visual Basic programming language. Developers familiar with either Crystal Reports or VS-View will be very comfortable working with ActiveReports. If Crystal Reports doesn't fulfill your needs and you want the visual designer that the VS-View Classic Edition lacks, ActiveReports may be for you.

NOTE   *VS-View* does *offer the visual interface of a programmable report designer similar to ActiveReports. It is called the VS-View Reporting Edition. The only reason I am not devoting an entire chapter to this version of VS-View is that I covered a ComponentOne product in the previous chapter and wish to cover a Data Dynamics product here. This is **not** to be taken as an endorsement of one product over another as both are excellent development tools.*

ActiveReports

ActiveReports has been around since 1999 and is licensed in one of two versions—Standard ($499 per license) and Professional ($1299 per license). Three items are offered in the Professional version that do not come in the Standard version—the Runtime Designer, the WebCache service, and the Property List. Both the Runtime Designer and the Property List are explained later in this chapter and the WebCache service is covered in Chapter 9.

There are three ActiveReports components that you can add via the Project|Components dialog box in Visual Basic 6 as shown in Figure 6-1.

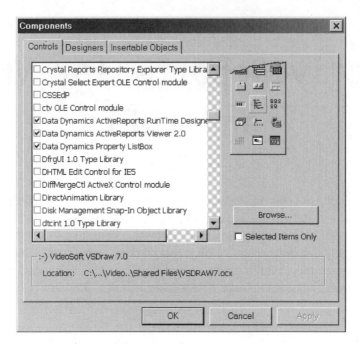

Figure 6-1. Components dialog box

These components consist of the Runtime Designer (Professional Edition only), the viewer, and the Property List, all of which will be discussed later in the chapter.

Using ActiveReports, new reports can be integrated into your applications by way of a designer or via a separate RPX file. An *RPX file* is an XML file that describes the positions, data bindings, and groupings of the fields and sections that comprise the report. Each report is a separate DSR file that is added to your application by selecting Project|Data Dynamics ActiveReports 2.0 and compiled into one EXE.

Getting Started

Often the hardest part of working with a new tool is simply knowing where to start. Fortunately, there is a wizard to help you get through the first few reports. Let's begin by connecting to a data source and creating a simple report. Open a new Visual Basic project and add a new designer to the project by selecting Project|Data Dynamics ActiveReports 2.0. Some versions of Windows will offer the designers under the Project|More ActiveX designers menu option. Drag an ActiveReports ADO data control to the Detail section and add the ReportStart event of the ActiveReport object as shown:

```
Private Sub ActiveReport_ReportStart()
    DataControl1.ConnectionString = "Provider=Microsoft.Jet.OLEDB.4.0;" & _
                              "Data Source=C:\BookCode\SampleDatabase.mdb;" & _
                              "Persist Security Info=False"

    DataControl1.Source = "SELECT * FROM Requester"
End Sub
```

Then, drag three TextBox objects to the Details section and three Label objects in the PageHeader section. Set the Caption properties of the Labels to Last Name, First Name, and State. Next, set the DataField property of each TextBox (to LastName, FirstName, and State). Finally, in the Form_Load event of the default Form1 in your main VB project, add the following line of code:

```
Private Sub Form_Load()
    ActiveReport1.Show
End Sub
```

and run the project. Voila! You've just created your first ActiveReport! Now that you understand the fundamentals, let's move on and do some real work.

> **NOTE**   *ActiveReports is well documented, with a variety of comprehensive samples. There is also a Knowledge Base available at* http://www.datadynamics.com/kb/default.htm. *If you don't already have a license for this product, you can download a 30-day trial version.*

Converting Microsoft Access and Crystal Reports

ActiveReports offers a utility to convert existing Microsoft Access and Crystal 7.0+ reports to the ActiveReports format. The tool isn't perfect but will save you a lot of layout work should you ever need to rebuild existing projects using ActiveReports. Note that if you are converting Crystal files, you'll need the Crystal Reports runtime installed on the same machine as the conversion utility. In both cases the conversion tool will produce an RPX file. Listing 6-1 shows some sample output from the conversion of one of the Access reports from Microsoft's Northwind sample database.

Listing 6-1. RPX Conversion File

```
<Section Type="Detail" Name="Detail"
    Height="270"
    ColumnDirection="1"
    ColumnSpacing="360"
    BackStyle="1"
    CanGrow="0"
>
    <Control
    Type="AR.Field"
    Name="ProductName"
    DataField="ProductName"
    Left="540"
    Top="30"
    Width="2790"
    Height="240"
    Text="ProductName"
    BackStyle="1"
    CanGrow="0"
    ClassName="Normal"
   Style="background-color: rgb(255,255,255); color: rgb(0,0,0); font-size: 8pt; "
    >
```

Unfortunately, the conversion utility does not recognize cross tab reports as ActiveReports does not directly support cross tab functionality. You can still produce cross tab reports using programming techniques explained in Chapter 8.

Data Connections

A report can be either bound directly to a "live" data source or "unbound," meaning that the data is connected to the source at runtime using code. Bound reports require a data connection. ActiveReports offers four types:

- ADO

- XML

- DAO (for backward compatibility)

- RDO (for backward compatibility)

To add a data source at design time, drag a data control icon from the toolbar to the Detail section of the report. Data controls are simply wrappers for the corresponding data controls offered by Visual Basic. You can set the properties of the control either in the property dialog box or in code. In most of the examples for this chapter, the properties will be set in code. If you have an existing ADO Recordset object already created in Visual Basic, you can pass it to the ActiveReports data control without needing to rerun the query. The code to accomplish this looks something like the following line. Here, *Me* refers to the report object itself as this code is run in the report object's code module.

```
Set Me.DataControl1.Recordset = oADORS
```

To connect to the data source when the report initializes, set the data connection in the ReportStart event of the ActiveReport object. If there's any data you need to have available during the processing of the report, this is the place where it should go. For example:

```
Private Sub ActiveReport_ReportStart()
    'Connect to Access Database using OLEDB provider
    DataControl1.ConnectionString = "Provider=Microsoft.Jet.OLEDB.4.0;" & _
                            "Data Source=C:\BookCode\SampleDatabase.mdb;" & _
                            "Persist Security Info=False"

    DataControl1.Source = "SELECT * FROM Requester"
End Sub
```

You could also add a data control dynamically as follows:

```
Private Sub ActiveReport_ReportStart()
    Dim objDataControl As DDActiveReports2.DataControl

  Set objDataControl = Me.Sections("Detail").Controls.Add("DDActiveReports2.DataControl")

    'Connect to Access Database using OLEDB provider
    objDataControl.ConnectionString = "Provider=Microsoft.Jet.OLEDB.4.0;" & _
                            "Data Source=C:\BookCode\SampleDatabase.mdb;" & _
                            "Persist Security Info=False"

    objDataControl.Source = "SELECT * FROM Requester"

End Sub
```

ActiveReports also connects to XML data sources. The XML data control handles the connectivity with the XML data file feeding the report. The two key properties of the XML data control are FileURL and RecordsetPattern. FileURL simply stores the location of the XML file, either as a URL or direct disk path. The RecordsetPattern property holds the Xpath that describes the node set to include in the results. To better explain this, refer to Figures 6-2 and 6-3.

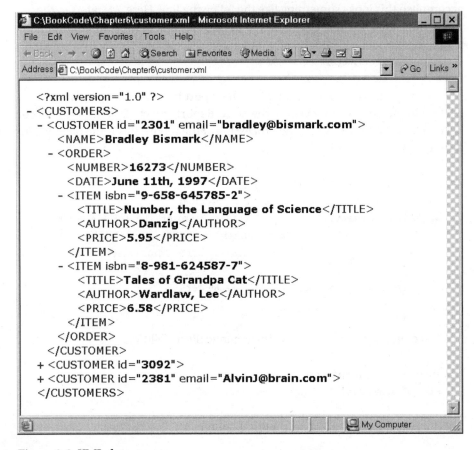

Figure 6-2. XML data source

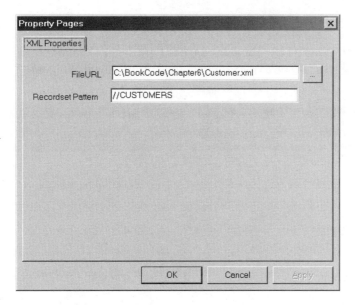

Figure 6-3. Property dialog box for XML data control

Note that the property dialog box has a RecordsetPattern property set to CUSTOMER, which refers to the CUSTOMER node in the XML file open in the browser. Remember that node names are case sensitive. By dropping a Field object in the Details section and setting the DataField to NAME, you'll end up with the output shown in Figure 6-4.

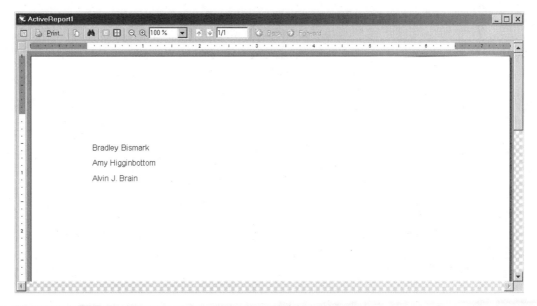

Figure 6-4. XML report

If you need to access other information deeper in the XML structure, you can set the Field object's DataField property to any valid XPath expression, like "ORDER/ITEM/TITLE". You don't have to type the full XPath, you can "shortcut" by setting it to "TITLE". This produces the output shown in Figure 6-5.

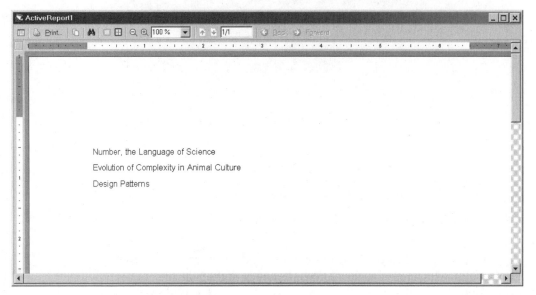

Figure 6-5. XML report, next node

NOTE *Xpath, short for XML Path Language, offers syntax for addressing parts of an XML document, specifically the path or node tree locations within XML documents. It allows the developer to reference the contents of XML documents separate of any markup. Moreover, it provides a standard library to manipulate strings, numbers, and Boolean expressions.*

Page and Print Settings

The PageSettings property group contains the page and paper setup properties for your report. These include the orientation, margins, paper bin, and paper size. Usually, you'll need to set these in the ActiveReport_ReportStart event as they will apply for the report in its entirety. The code in Listing 6-2 shows the setup of a report. The paper size is set to letter and the paper bin is set to the upper bin. The top and bottom margins are set at one inch (measured in twips at 1,440 twips to an inch). The left and right margins are set at half an inch. In the PageStart event, which is fired at the beginning of every page, the current page count is being checked. If any page other than the first is printing, the paper will come from the lower bin.

NOTE *If a report's PrintWidth is greater than the paper's width, a blank page will print after each report page.*

Listing 6-2. PageSettings Example

```
Private Sub ActiveReport_ReportStart()

    With Me.PageSettings
        .Orientation = ddOPortrait
        .PaperSize = 1
        .PaperBin = 1
        .BottomMargin = 1440
        .TopMargin = 1440
        .LeftMargin = 720
        .RightMargin = 720
    End With

End Sub


Private Sub ActiveReport_PageStart()
    If Me.Pages.Count > 0 Then
        Me.PageSettings.PaperBin = 2
    End If
End Sub
```

The complete list of paper bins is shown in Table 6-1, while the complete list of paper sizes is shown in Table 6-2. Note that not all printers use the same value for a given paper bin. Use the Paperbins property to determine if a printer supports a specific bin value.

Table 6-1. Paper Bins

VALUE	DESCRIPTION
1	Upper bin.
2	Lower bin.
3	Middle bin.
4	Wait for manual insertion of each sheet of paper.
5	Envelope feeder.
6	Use envelopes from feeder, but wait for manual insertion.
7	(Default) Current default bin.
8	Tractor feeder.
9	Small paper feeder.
10	Large paper bin.
11	Large capacity feeder.
14	Attached cassette cartridge.

Table 6-2. Paper Sizes

VALUE	DESCRIPTION	VALUE	DESCRIPTION
1	Letter, 8 1/2 × 11 in	13	B5, 182 × 257 mm
2	+A611Letter Small, 8 1/2 × 11 in	14	Folio, 8 1/2 × 13 in
3	Tabloid, 11 × 17 in	15	Quarto, 215 × 275 mm
4	Ledger, 17 × 11 in	16	10 × 14 in
5	Legal, 8 1/2 × 14 in	17	11 × 17 in
6	Statement, 5 1/2 × 8 1/2 in	18	Note, 8 1/2 × 11 in
7	Executive, 7 1/2 × 10 1/2 in	19	Envelope #9, 3 7/8 × 8 7/8 in
8	A3, 297 × 420 mm	20	Envelope #10, 4 1/8 × 9 1/2 in
9	A4, 210 × 297 mm	21	Envelope #11, 4 1/2 × 10 3/8 in
10	A4 Small, 210 × 297 mm	22	Envelope #12, 4 1/2 × 11 in
11	A5, 148 × 210 mm	23	Envelope #14, 5 × 11 1/2 in
12	B4, 250 × 354 mm	24	C size sheet

(continued)

Table 6-2. Paper Sizes (continued)

VALUE	DESCRIPTION	VALUE	DESCRIPTION
25	D size sheet	34	Envelope B5, 176 × 250 mm
26	E size sheet	35	Envelope B6, 176 × 125 mm
27	Envelope DL, 110 × 220 mm	36	Envelope, 110 × 230 mm
29	Envelope C3, 324 × 458 mm	37	Envelope Monarch, 3 7/8 × 7 1/2 in
30	Envelope C4, 229 × 324 mm	38	Envelope, 3 5/8 × 6 1/2 in
28	Envelope C5, 162 × 229 mm	39	U.S. Standard Fanfold, 14 7/8 × 11 in
31	Envelope C6, 114 × 162 mm	40	German Standard Fanfold, 8 1/2 × 12 in
32	Envelope C65, 114 × 229 mm	41	German Legal Fanfold, 8 1/2 × 13 in
33	Envelope B4, 250 × 353 mm	255	User Defined

You can use the Printer object to control such things as the target printer or even retrieve a list of the printers installed on the system. You can also bypass the PageSettings property described previously for those properties controlled by both the Printer object and PageSettings and address the Visual Basic Printer object directly. For example, the code in Listing 6-3 displays the available printers and ports.

Listing 6-3. Printer Object Example

```
Dim x As Integer
Dim cMsg As String

With Labels.Printer

    For x = 0 To .NDevices - 1
        cMsg = cMsg & .Devices(x) & vbCrLf
    Next

    cMsg = cMsg & vbCrLf
    cMsg = cMsg & "Current device: " & .DeviceName & vbCrLf
    cMsg = cMsg & "Current port: " & .Port & vbCrLf
    cMsg = cMsg & vbCrLf
```

```
For x = 0 To UBound(.PaperBinNames) - 1
    cMsg = cMsg & .PaperBinNames(x) & vbCrLf
Next

End With

MsgBox cMsg
```

This code produces the message box similar to the one shown in Figure 6-6.

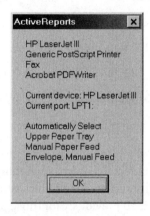

Figure 6-6. Printer object property settings

Printing in ranges is possible via the FromPage and ToPage properties. Once the report is run, you could execute the following code to print pages two through six:

```
Report.Printer.FromPage = 2
Report.Printer.ToPage = 6
Report.PrintReport
```

Sequence of Events

As a report is initialized and runs, a series of Events fire. You can include event handlers for each of these to provide precise control over report creation and formatting. Table 6-3 lists these events in the order in which they fire and the purpose they generally serve.

Table 6-3. Event Firing Sequence

EVENT	PURPOSE
Initialize	Triggers immediately when the report object is first instantiated.
Resize	Triggers immediately after Initialize and whenever the report window is resized.
DataInitialize	Used to add fields to the report's Field collection at runtime and to set up the data source.
ReportStart	Triggers just before the actual processing of the report. You can use this event to set the page size and other formatting attributes of the report.
FetchData	This event triggers whenever the data for the underlying report is accessed. If you need to store a variable that keeps track of a subtotal, for instance, this is the best place to increment it as this event is guaranteed to fire only once per row.
PageStart	Fires just before a page is rendered. Here you can change printer bins or paper orientations.
PageEnd	Fires immediately after a page is rendered. This event comes in handy with unbound reports. Here you can print page subtotals and reinitialize the total counter variable.
ReportEnd	Fires immediately after the report finishes processing. You can use this event to export the report data to one of the supported file formats, destroy recordset objects, and close any open database connections.

Grouping and Summary Fields

Structurally, the ActiveReports designer is very similar to that of Crystal Reports. Each report is organized into sections. There is one Report Header and one Report Footer section per report. Each of these sections prints only once at the top of the first page and the bottom of the last page, respectively. Each individual page has a header and footer section as well although these sections should neither contain bound controls nor be used to group data. There may be multiple groupings within a report, and each grouping also has a header and footer. Finally, within a grouping is the Detail section. You must always have a Detail section in the report, and you cannot have more than one. If you do not need this one Detail section to print, set its Visible property to False. The various sections of a report are illustrated in Figure 6-7.

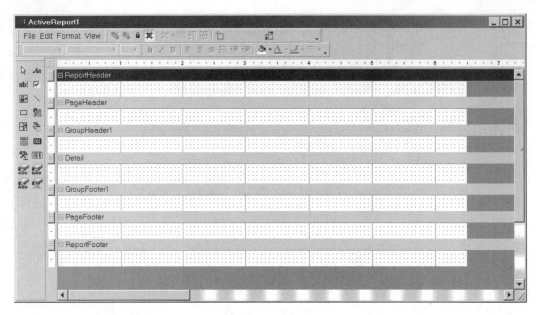

Figure 6-7. Report sections

Creating Groups

You can add group sections for the various summarization levels that you need and can have up to 32 nested groups in a report. Of course, if you use anywhere near this many you should be shot. To establish a grouping level, set the DataField property of the GroupHeader section to the name of a database field. Be sure to order the data to facilitate the grouping (order by the grouped field first, etc.). Since the group field is case-sensitive, take care that your grouping field is formatted in a single case. For example, if you are grouping on a Company Names field, data like "Seton Software" and "SETON SOFTWARE" will create two separate groups.

If you need to group on the combination of multiple fields, you'll need to get a little more creative. To handle this, create an unbound field in the DataInitialize event and update it in FetchData. For example:

```
Private Sub DataInitialize()
    Me.Fields.Add "GroupField"
End Sub

Private Sub ActiveReport_FetchData(EOF As Boolean)
    Me.Fields("GroupField").Value = _
    Me.Fields("CompanyName").Value & Me.Fields("MgrName").Value
End Sub
```

Since each section can contain controls, each section also has its own Control collection much like a Visual Basic form. To format every column header in a bold typeface, you could use the code in Listing 6-4.

Listing 6-4. Looping Through the Controls Collection

```
Dim iLabelCnt As Integer
Dim x As Integer

iLabelCnt = Me.Sections("PageHeader").Controls.Count - 1

For x = 0 To iLabelCnt
    Me.Sections("PageHeader").Controls(x).Font.Bold = True
Next x
```

Report Section Events

Each report section exposes three events—Format, BeforePrint, and AfterPrint. The Format event is the one you'll use most often. Format fires after the data is loaded to the fields but before the section actually prints. It is here that you can change the display of certain data elements based on specified conditions. For example, you could resize controls based on the data in their underlying fields. If you have CanGrow or CanShrink set to True, the growing or shrinking process occurs after this event triggers. Code in the AfterPrint event can be used for drawing on the canvas after the text has been rendered.

The Format event will always fire prior to BeforePrint and AfterPrint. However, you cannot be sure of the exact sequence. The events could trigger like this:

Record1—Format

Record1—BeforePrint

Record1—AfterPrint

Record2—Format

Record2—BeforePrint

Record2—AfterPrint

Or they could also fire like this:

Record1—Format

Record2—Format

Record1—BeforePrint

Record2—BeforePrint

Record1—AfterPrint

Record2—AfterPrint

Because you cannot be sure of the exact order of execution, these events are not a good place to put counters. Counters are best placed in the FetchData event.

The BeforePrint event of a particular section fires just before it is rendered to the canvas. Any final changes to the values of controls or fields should be written here. This event is also your last chance to perform any page-specific formatting. Once the section is rendered, AfterPrint fires.

You can control printing with the LayoutAction property. For each section of the report, ActiveReports first prints the section, then moves the layout (sets the next position for the rest of the report), and finally moves to the next record. By setting the LayoutAction property to one of the settings listed in Table 6-4, you can determine when or even if these steps occur. Bear in mind that LayoutAction should only be used in the Detail section.

Table 6-4. LayoutAction Constants

VALUE	CONSTANT	DESCRIPTION
1	ddLAPrintSection	Indicates whether a section should be printed
2	ddLAMoveLayout	Indicates whether ActiveReports should move to the next printing location on the page
4	ddLANextRecord	Indicates whether a section should advance to the next record

You can combine these constants when setting the LayoutAction property. For example, if for some reason you wanted to print the next record on top of the current record, you could do the following:

```
Me.LayoutAction = ddLAPrintSection + ddLANextRecord
```

One use of the LayoutAction property is in the printing of address labels. Suppose you wish to print multiple copies of the same record in a table as mailing labels. You can accomplish this by declaring a counter in the declarations section of the report designer and setting the counter to one in the ReportStart event. Then, set the LayoutAction property in the Detail_Format event as follows:

```
Private Sub Detail_Format()

    If iCopies < 10 Then
        Me.LayoutAction = ddLAMoveLayout + ddLAPrintSection
        iCopies = iCopies + 1
    End If

End Sub
```

Summary Fields

Summary fields are essentially counters that ActiveReports maintains and resets when appropriate. You would use a summary field to show, say, the subtotals for all sales grouped by individual company, and another summary field to show the grand total for all companies together. The former would appear in the Group Footer section and the latter in the Report Footer. To create a summary field, simply select one of the Summary properties of a Field object. The SummaryFunc property allows you to indicate if the field should display the sum, average, count, minimum or maximum value, or standard deviation of the values in the Detail section to which it refers. The SummaryType property allows you to specify a subtotal, grand total, page total, or page count.

Summary fields do not work on expressions. To accomplish this, you need to create an unbound field in the DataInitialize event, set its value in FetchData, and then use its name in the DataField property. For example:

```
Private Sub DataInitialize()
    Me.Fields.Add "NetAmount"
End Sub
```

```
Private Sub ActiveReport_FetchData(EOF As Boolean)
    Me.Fields("NetAmount").Value = _
    Me.Fields("Amount").Value - Me.Fields("Discount").Value
End Sub
```

Table of Contents

One way to make a long report more navigable for the user is to add a table of contents. A table of contents displays a list of the major report topics like group headings in a column down the left-hand side of the report as shown in Figure 6-8.

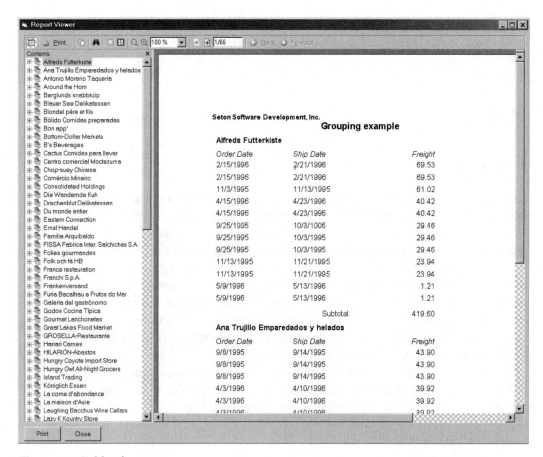

Figure 6-8. Table of contents

When a user selects one of the options in the table of contents, the body of the report advances the report viewer to display the information associated with the selected item. Creating this table of contents is very easy. Each report contains a TOC collection to which you can programmatically add, edit, and remove items as well as navigate the report. Tables of contents make the most sense for grouped reports. To add a table of contents to the grouping report example, you could do so with the following code:

```
Private Sub GroupHeader1_Format()
    Me.TOC.Add GroupHeader1.GroupValue
End Sub
```

Since the report is grouped, you may wish to use the table of contents to drill down to a sublevel, for example, the individual orders under each company. To create the order dates as nodes under each company name in the table of contents, simply add the following code to the Detail_Format event like so:

```
Private Sub Detail_Format()
    Me.TOC.Add GroupHeader1.GroupValue & "\" & fldOrderDate
End Sub
```

Doing so will produce the results shown in Figure 6-9.

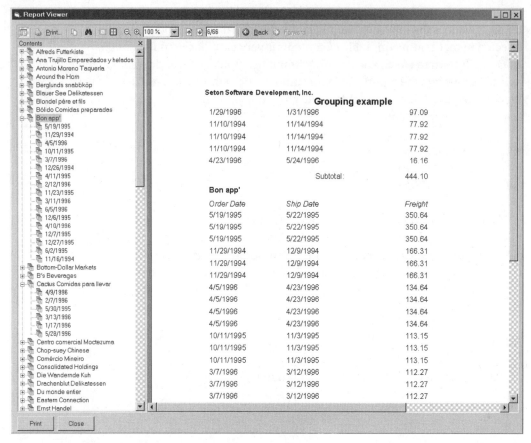

Figure 6-9. Table of contents with subnodes

Viewer Control

While the report designers will display your report to the screen simply by invoking the Show method, you can also display a report in a VB form using the ActiveReports Viewer. Using the viewer does require you to ship an additional OCX file (Arview2.ocx, weighing in at 476K) but you'll have much more control over how your viewer looks to the user. To display a report, simply set the ReportSource property to the report object you wish to view. For example:

```
Set ARViewer21.ReportSource = Grouping
```

Then you can control the appearance of the viewer such as determining if the toolbar will appear or not, controlling the table of contents browser, etc. The following code makes the table of contents visible and sets the width to 3500 twips:

```
ARViewer21.TOCVisible = True
ARViewer21.TOCWidth = 3500
ARViewer21.RulerVisible = False
```

If you wish to override the features of the toolbar with your own buttons, you can do that as well. To send the current report to the printer, simply add a button with the following code in the Click event:

```
ARViewer21.PrintReport
```

Property List

The Property List control allows you to create property windows much like the one used by Visual Basic to set the various properties for controls at design time (see Figure 6-10).

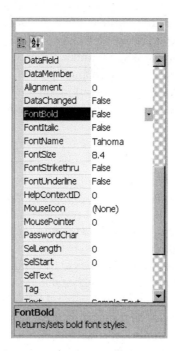

Figure 6-10. Property List dialog box

The control is similar to a tree view control in that it consists of nodes and subnodes arranged in a hierarchical fashion. ActiveReports ships with a demo of how the property list functions.

NOTE *Data Dynamics created the property list control because they needed to use it in the product. Since it was created as an ActiveX control they decided to make it available for free; however, they do not provide any support outside of newsgroups posts and they're not trying to push it as a useable supported control. Only the Professional Edition help file includes a complete reference to the control.*

Building Reports

Now that you understand the structure of reports and how to set up for them, let's examine the different types of reports that you can build using ActiveReports. In this section, particular emphasis is placed on creating these reports dynamically. One of the most powerful features of ActiveReports is that it can create reports at runtime, connect them to a data source, and render them to the screen or printer. If you're familiar with Crystal Reports' Report Creation API syntax, this approach will look very similar. Probably the biggest difference between the two products is the licensing costs. Whereas Crystal charges hefty per-seat license fees for its Report Creation API, ActiveReports includes this functionality as part of its standard user license with no additional costs involved.

Standard Columnar Report

You already saw how to create a simple columnar report in the "Getting Started" section using the visual designer. The previous section covered grouping and summary fields. Here, you'll see how to create a report dynamically with groupings and summary fields.

The true power of ActiveReports lies in its ability to create reports and modify them dynamically at runtime. Unlike Crystal Reports, there are no additional license fees for this functionality. As a general rule, anything that you can do in the visual designer you can do programmatically at runtime. Therefore, you can provide your users with the ability to select which columns appear on a report, or offer them choices as to how they would like the same report grouped, without having to prebuild a version of the same report with every possible permutation of user option.

Suppose you want to create a columnar report with one grouping level and subtotals for each group and a grand total of all groups. The first step is to establish the data connection by dynamically creating a data control and setting its properties as shown in Listing 6-5.

Listing 6-5. Dynamically Generated Group Report

```
With objDataControl
     .Name = "adoFreight"

     .ConnectionString = "Provider=Microsoft.Jet.OLEDB.4.0;" & _
     "Data Source=C:\Program Files\Microsoft Visual Studio\VB98\Nwind.mdb;" & _
     "Persist Security Info=False"

     .Source = "SELECT c.CompanyName, i.OrderDate, i.ShippedDate, i.Freight " & _
               "FROM Customers c LEFT JOIN Invoices I " & _
               "ON c.CustomerID = i.CustomerID " & _
               "ORDER BY c.CompanyName, i.Freight DESC"
End With
```

Next, you'll need to establish the report sections. By default, a report has a PageHeader, PageFooter, and Detail section so you'll need to add GroupHeader and GroupFooter as well as a ReportHeader/ReportFooter combination. When adding a header at any level you also have to make sure you add a matching footer or a runtime error will occur. You can use the ActiveReports standard for the default names of the sections, but if you had multiple groupings, then more descriptive names like GHState/GFState and GHCompany/GFCompany might be more appropriate.

Once the GroupHeader is in existence, set the DataField property of the section to the field name on which the data should be grouped, in this case CompanyName, as shown in Listing 6-6.

Listing 6-6. Create Report Sections

```
Call Me.Sections.Add("ReportHeader1", 1, ddSTReportHeader, 750)
Call Me.Sections.Add("GroupHeader1", 2, ddSTGroupHeader, 750)
Call Me.Sections.Add("GroupFooter1", 4, ddSTGroupFooter, 400)
Call Me.Sections.Add("ReportFooter1", 5, ddSTReportFooter, 400)

Me.Sections("GroupHeader1").DataField = "CompanyName"

Me.Sections("Detail").Height = 350
```

Now you're ready to add the fields. GroupHeader1 has one Field object that displays the company name, and three Label objects that contain the column headers. The code to create the Field object is shown in Listing 6-7.

Listing 6-7. Create Field Object in GroupHeader1

```
Set objField = Me.Sections("GroupHeader1").Controls.Add("DDActiveReports2.Field")

With objField
    .Name = "fldCompanyName"
    .DataField = "CompanyName"
    .Height = 300
    .Width = 3500
    .Top = 100
    .Left = 0
    .BackStyle = 0
    .Font.Bold = True
    .BackColor = vbWhite
    .ForeColor = vbBlack
    .Border.Shadow = False
End With
```

The code to create one of the label objects that serves as the column header is shown in Listing 6-8.

Listing 6-8. Create Label Object in GroupHeader1

```
Set objLabel = Me.Sections("GroupHeader1").Controls.Add("DDActiveReports2.Label")

With objLabel
    .Name = "lblLabel1"
    .Caption = "Order Date"
    .Font.Italic = True
    .Height = 500
    .Width = 1500
    .Top = 450
    .Left = 0
    .BackStyle = 0
    .BackColor = vbWhite
    .ForeColor = vbBlack
    .Border.Shadow = False
End With
```

The subtotal and grand total fields are Field objects as well. What makes them total is the settings for their various Summary properties. For example, the code in Listing 6-9 illustrates how the subtotal field works and how it differs from the grand total field.

Listing 6-9. Create Subtotal Field Object in GroupFooter1

```
Set objField = Me.Sections("GroupFooter1").Controls.Add("DDActiveReports2.Field")

With objField
    .Name = "fldSubTotal"
    .SummaryType = ddSMSubTotal
    .SummaryFunc = ddSFDSum
    .SummaryRunning = ddSRGroup
    .SummaryGroup = "GroupHeader1"
    .DataField = "Freight"
    .Alignment = ddTXRight
    .OutputFormat = "#,##0.00;(#,##0.00)"
    .Height = 300
    .Width = 1500
    .Top = 100
    .Left = 2600
    .BackStyle = 0
    .BackColor = vbWhite
    .ForeColor = vbBlack
    .Border.Shadow = False
End With

Set objField = Me.Sections("ReportFooter1").Controls.Add("DDActiveReports2.Field")

With objField
    .Name = "fldGrandTotal"
    .SummaryType = ddSMGrandTotal
    .SummaryFunc = ddSFDSum
    .SummaryRunning = ddSRAll
    .DataField = "Freight"
    .Alignment = ddTXRight
    .OutputFormat = "#,##0.00;(#,##0.00)"
    .Font.Bold = True
    .Height = 300
    .Width = 1500
    .Top = 100
    .Left = 2600
```

```
      .BackStyle = 0
      .BackColor = vbWhite
      .ForeColor = vbBlack
      .Border.Shadow = False
End With
```

Note that while this code is the correct way to dynamically create a subtotal, there is a bug in the current version that causes it to return zero. Data Dynamics expects to have a service release available by the time you are reading this, so if this problem occurs for you, please download the most recent version of ActiveReports.

Labels

ActiveReports makes it very easy to create mailing labels. Simply follow these steps:

1. Set the report width to the total width of the label sheet.

2. Set the Columns property of the Detail section to equal the number of label columns that print on a sheet.

3. Remove the Page Header and PageFooter sections from the report.

4. Set the height of the Detail section to the height of the label.

5. Set the CanGrow and CanShrink properties of the Detail section to false. But set the CanShrink property of the individual Field objects to True. CanShrink will allow controls that may have no data—like second address line—to close up so as not to leave visual gaps in the label.

6. Set the margins to match those of the label sheet.

7. Finally, paint the text and label controls in the Detail section.

Labels can also be created programmatically as shown in Listing 6-10.

Listing 6-10. Dynamic Mailing Labels

```
Dim objDataControl As DDActiveReports2.DataControl
Dim objNameField As DDActiveReports2.Field
Dim objContactField As DDActiveReports2.Field
Dim objAddressField As DDActiveReports2.Field
Dim objCSZField As DDActiveReports2.Field


Private Sub ActiveReport_DataInitialize()
    'These are custom fields whose value will be in FetchData
    Me.Fields.Add "Contact"
    Me.Fields.Add "CSZ"
End Sub


Private Sub ActiveReport_FetchData(EOF As Boolean)

    If EOF Then
        Exit Sub
    End If

    With objDataControl
        Me.Fields("Contact").Value = .Recordset("FirstName") _
                                        & " " & .Recordset("LastName")
        Me.Fields("CSZ").Value = .Recordset("City") _
                            & ", " & .Recordset("State") & " " &
.Recordset("Zip")
    End With

End Sub


Private Sub ActiveReport_ReportStart()

   Set objDataControl = Me.Sections("Detail").Controls.Add("DDActiveReports2.DataControl")
   objDataControl.Name = "adoRequester"

   objDataControl.ConnectionString = _
                        "Provider=Microsoft.Jet.OLEDB.4.0;" & _
                        "Data Source=C:\BookCode\SampleDatabase.mdb;" & _
                        "Persist Security Info=False"


   objDataControl.Source = "SELECT * FROM Requester"
```

```
If IsSection(Me, "PageHeader") Then
    Call Me.Sections.Remove("PageHeader")
End If

If IsSection(Me, "PageFooter") Then
    Call Me.Sections.Remove("PageFooter")
End If

With Me.Sections("Detail")
    .ColumnCount = 2
    .ColumnDirection = ddCDDownAcross
    .KeepTogether = True
    .Height = 1440
End With
```

The first step is to declare an object variable to hold each line in the label. You don't need an object for each field used as the lines of data are created by concatenating these fields at runtime. Since Contact and CSZ (city, state, zip) are created at runtime from multiple fields, their presence must be made known to ActiveReports in the DataInitialize event. Once ActiveReports knows about these Field objects, you can assign the concatenated values for each record printed in the FetchData event. In the ReportStart event, you can add the data control and establish the connectivity settings and record source. Since all the sections are in a Sections collection, the Remove method can get rid of the PageHeader and PageFooter. Finally, in the Detail section, you can indicate that there are two columns that must print each section down each column, followed by the next column to its right. The KeepTogether property is set to True as it is not at all appropriate for labels to print across columns or pages. Then, the height of each label is set to 1440 twips (one inch).

Once the labels have been set up, the individual fields can be added to the page. Listing 6-11 shows how this is done.

Listing 6-11. Add the Individual Fields

```
Set objContactField = _
        Me.Sections("Detail").Controls.Add("DDActiveReports2.Field")

With objContactField
    .Name = "fldContactName"
    .Height = 300
    .Width = 4500
    .Top = 300
    .Left = 0
```

```
        .BackStyle = 0
        .BackColor = vbWhite
        .ForeColor = vbBlack
        .DataField = "Contact"   'Custom Unbound Field
        .Border.Shadow = False
    End With



    Set objAddressField = _
        Me.Sections("Detail").Controls.Add("DDActiveReports2.Field")

    With objAddressField
        .Name = "fldAddress1"
        .Height = 300
        .Width = 4500
        .Top = 600
        .Left = 0
        .CanShrink = True
        .BackStyle = 0
        .BackColor = vbWhite
        .ForeColor = vbBlack
        .DataField = "Address1"
        .Border.Shadow = False
    End With



    Set objAddressField = _
        Me.Sections("Detail").Controls.Add("DDActiveReports2.Field")

    With objAddressField
        .Name = "fldAddress2"
        .Height = 300
        .Width = 4500
        .Top = 900
        .Left = 0
        .CanShrink = True
        .BackStyle = 0
        .BackColor = vbWhite
        .ForeColor = vbBlack
        .DataField = "Address2"
        .Border.Shadow = False
    End With
```

```
        Set objCSZField = _
            Me.Sections("Detail").Controls.Add("DDActiveReports2.Field")

    With objCSZField
        .Name = "fldCity"
        .Height = 300
        .Width = 4500
        .Top = 1200
        .Left = 0
        .BackStyle = 0
        .BackColor = vbWhite
        .ForeColor = vbBlack
        .Border.Shadow = False
        .DataField = "CSZ"   'Custom Unbound Field
    End With

End Sub

Function IsSection(objReport As Object, cSection As String) As Boolean
    Dim bResult As Boolean
    Dim iCnt As Integer
    Dim x As Integer

    iCnt = objReport.Sections.Count - 1
    bResult = False

    For x = 0 To iCnt

        If objReport.Sections(x).Name = cSection Then
            bResult = True
            Exit For
        End If

    Next x

    IsSection = bResult

End Function
```

Free-Form Text Report

Managing free-form text and mail-merge capability in ActiveReports centers around the use of the RichEdit control. This control recognizes RTF encoding and displays your document accordingly. You can open the RTF file at runtime using the following code:

```
RichEdit1.LoadFile App.Path & "\mailMergedoc.rtf", rtfRTF
```

The RichEdit control is similar to its VB counterpart control; however, it gets converted to the ActiveReports canvas format to support printing and exporting to PDF and such.

The RichEdit control can also read plain text files simply by passing rtfText as the second parameter of the LoadFile method. You can even save your merged document using the SaveFile method, likewise passing one of these two document types as the second parameter. You can also create your RTF document in Microsoft Word as shown in Figure 6.11 but note that ActiveReports does not support the same RTF specification as Word supports.

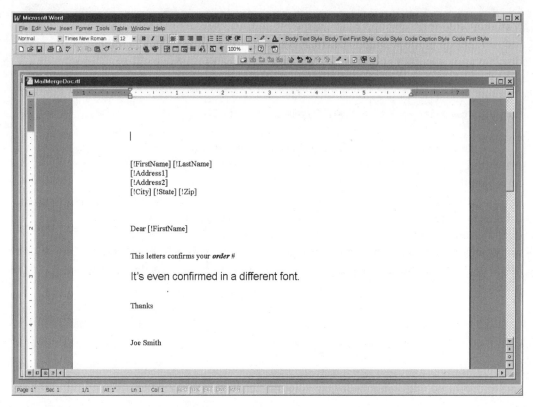

Figure 6-11. RTF document in Word

Note the layout of the name and address and the delimiters around each field as follows: [!LastName]. The presence of these delimiters makes this a merge field that you can replace with a value at runtime using the ReplaceField method as shown here:

```
With RichEdit1
    .ReplaceField "LastName", "Ganz"
    .ReplaceField "FirstName", "Carl"
    .ReplaceField "Address1", "3 Barbieri Court"
End With
```

Because ActiveReports is working with an RTF document and performing a simple text substitution, there is no equivalent to the CanShrink property. Therefore, if you have an option address field, the final merged document will show a blank space as illustrated in Figure 6-12.

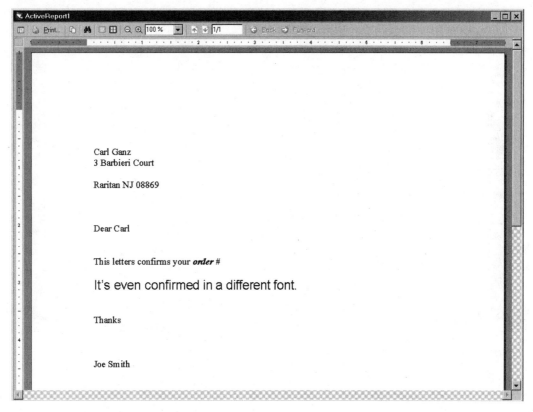

Figure 6-12. Optional field using merge

One technique to compensate for this problem is to display merge fields in the PageHeader and the RTF control in the Detail section. By placing the merge fields in the PageHeader section, one row of table data will merge per page. You'll need to set the font attributes for the merge fields to be the same settings as that of the text in the RichEdit control. The end result will look like Figure 6-13.

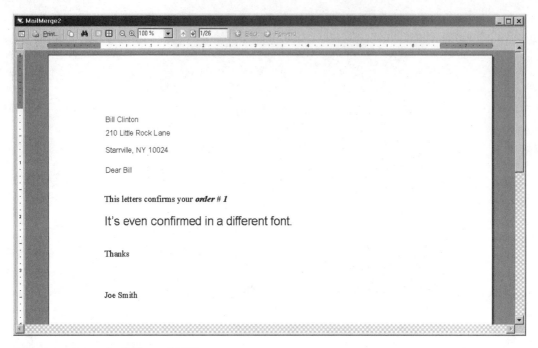

Figure 6-13. Merge fields and RTF text

Subreports

A subreport is simply a report that is displayed within another report. One report can have many subreports. Often a main report is really a collection of data that comes from a number of tables or databases and doesn't always fall into a columnar format. For example, one of my clients has an application that produces financial sales presentations. The report consists of some basic information about the client, a block of text with legal disclaimers, a columnar section displaying years and pension contributions, then some more explanatory text, and then another block of columnar data displaying ages and estimated payouts. The two columnar sections are implemented as subreports.

NOTE *The PageHeader/PageFooter and ReportHeader/ReportFooter sections do not display for subreports.*

ActiveReports offers a subreport control that simply serves as a container for another report built in another designer file. For example, suppose you wanted to create a report similar to the one in the preceding paragraph. You could paint four controls in the Details section of the designer—a label, a subreport container, another label, and then another subreport container. The CanGrow property defaults to True and you'll normally want it to stay that way. Otherwise, your report will most likely get cut off. Both subreport containers will contain the FirstReport example with a variation on the criteria. To create the subreport, examine the code in Listing 6-12.

Listing 6-12. Subreport Code

```
Private Sub ActiveReport_ReportStart()
    Dim objReport As FirstReport

    lblIntro.Caption = "This demo illustrates the cool things you can do with " & _
                "subreports. If this were a real report you would see some " & _
                " meaningfull text here."

    lblExplain.Caption = "Down here is the same subreport with a different " & _
                    "parameter passed to it "

    Set objReport = New FirstReport

    objReport.DataControl1.Source = "SELECT * FROM Requester WHERE State = 'CA'"
    Set SubReport1.object = objReport

    Set objReport = New FirstReport

    objReport.DataControl1.Source = "SELECT * FROM Requester WHERE State = 'NJ'"
    Set SubReport2.object = objReport


End Sub
```

Set the object variable objReport to an instance of FirstReport. Then, simply override the Source property of FirstReport's data control object by passing in a new SQL statement. Setting the Object property of the subreport container to the objReport variable will run FirstReport with the specified SQL statement filter. Then, by reinstantiating objReport as a New instance of FirstReport, the whole process occurs again using a different SQL statement as the filter. This example produces the report shown in Figure 6-14.

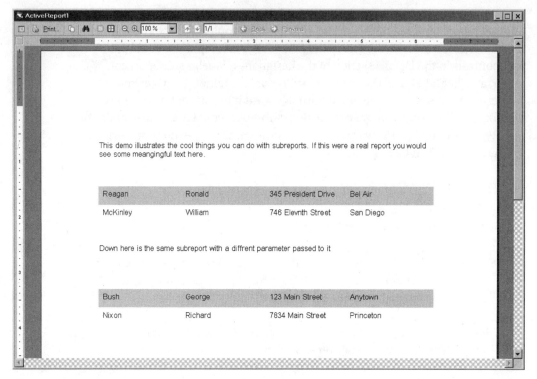

Figure 6-14. Subreport

You can also filter a subreport by passing parameters to the data source that populates it. These parameters are passed from the FetchData event in the main report. For example, to print a report listing all your vendors and under each vendor listing the products they supply in a subreport, you could pass the parameter as shown here:

```
Private Sub ActiveReport_FetchData(EOF As Boolean)
    Dim x As Integer

    If Not Me.DataControl1.Recordset.EOF Then
        x = Me.DataControl1.Recordset!vendorid
    End If
End Sub
```

Then, set the Source property of the data control in the subreport to the following:

```
SELECT * FROM products WHERE vendorid =<%vendorid %>
```

The <% %> delimiters—that's right, just like ASP—indicate that the value contained within is a parameter field. Make sure you set the subreport's ShowParameterUI to False, otherwise a dialog box will appear when the report is run. By default, this property is set to True.

Unbound Reports

Reports do not necessarily need to be bound to a data source. They can even have a combination of bound and unbound elements or all unbound elements. The data source for the rows can come from an array, a collection, or from a Recordset whose fields are accessed programmatically.

One of the most common instances where unbound fields are required is when derived information needs to be shown on a document. Derived data is that which can be deduced from component elements stored in a database. For example, the extended price on an invoice is simply the unit price multiplied by the quantity, and this product would not be stored in the database. You could always compute it in SQL like this:

```
SELECT price, quantity, price * quantity AS extendedprice
FROM invoicedetail
```

But this would involve pulling an extra column of data from the database server. Alternatively, you could create a report that has two columns bound to the price and quantity fields and a third that is computed at runtime. The report designer shown in Figure 6-15 shows an example of this approach.

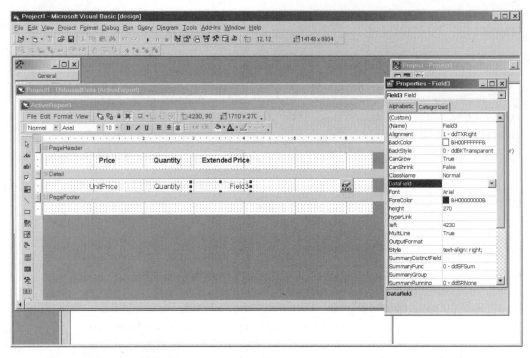

Figure 6-15. Unbound data field

The UnitPrice and Quantity fields shown in the Details section have their DataField properties set to UnitPrice and Quantity, respectively. The remaining field has its DataField property set to ExtendedPrice. Since there is no ExtendedPrice column in the Fields collection of the data source, its presence must be made known programmatically by adding it to the Fields collection of the report object. This can be accomplished in the DataInitialize event of the report object as shown here:

```
Private Sub ActiveReport_DataInitialize()
    Fields.Add "ExtendedPrice"
End Sub
```

Then, in the FetchData event, you can multiply the two data fields and set the product to the Value property of the unbound field.

```
Private Sub ActiveReport_FetchData(EOF As Boolean)

    If EOF Then
        Exit Sub
    End If
```

```
Fields("ExtendedPrice").Value = Fields("UnitPrice").Value * _
                            Fields("Quantity").Value


End Sub
```

Drill-Down

The ability to view a report listing—for example, all the customers who purchased product between a given range of dates—becomes much more useful if the user can click the name of a customer and see the details of those orders. This feature is called a drill-down, and ActiveReports allows you to implement this via the Hyperlink property of the Field object.

The first step is to select which field will contain the hyperlink. Since it is a Windows standard to display hyperlinks in blue forecolor with an underline, use the Font property dialog box to set these options for the field. Bear in mind that while this is appropriate for an on-screen hyperlink, the text will unfortunately print underlined and in blue. Since many users don't have color printers, you may want to skip the underline attribute so the printed version will appear properly.

Next, in the Detail_BeforePrint event you can set the Hyperlink property to the value of the customer ID that is stored in a hidden field. For example:

```
Private Sub Detail_BeforePrint()
    fldCompanyName.Hyperlink = fldCustomerID.Text
End Sub
```

Next, to activate the hyperlink, simply add code to the Hyperlink event of the report object as shown in Listing 6-13. In this event the Button parameter refers to the mouse button that was clicked to activate the hyperlink, whereas Link contains the value of the Hyperlink property of the control, in this case CustomerID.

Listing 6-13. Hyperlink Event

```
Private Sub ActiveReport_hyperLink(ByVal Button As Integer, link As String)
    Dim cSQL As String
    Dim objReport As DrillDownDetail

    Set objReport = New DrillDownDetail

    cSQL = "SELECT OrderDate, ShippedDate, Freight " & _
            "FROM orders " & _
            "WHERE customerid = " & Chr(39) & link & Chr(39)
```

```
objReport.DataControl1.Source = cSQL

objReport.Show

End Sub
```

Note that you can set the HyperLink property of more than one control in a report, but the HyperLink event cannot determine which control fired it. One workaround to this problem is to affix a character to the beginning of the HyperLink property's value like this:

```
Private Sub Detail_BeforePrint()
    fldCompanyName.Hyperlink = "1-" & fldCustomerID.Text
    fldCEOName.Hyperlink = "2-" & fldCEOID.Text
End Sub
```

Then, when the HyperLink event fires, you can simply check the initial characters to see which field fired it.

Shading and Graphics

One of the most common uses of graphics in a report is the alternate shading of lines. This can be accomplished via the Detail_Format event. As ActiveReports is moving through the record source, it needs to know the line count. A module variable called iLevel accomplishes this nicely. Then, you need only decode whether you want the odd or even numbered lines shaded and change the code in Listing 6-14 accordingly.

Listing 6-14. Shading Alternate Rows

```
Private Sub Detail_Format()

    If (iLine Mod 2) = 0 Then
        Detail.BackStyle = ddBKNormal
        Detail.BackColor = &H8000000F
    Else
        Detail.BackStyle = ddBKTransparent
    End If

    iLine = iLine + 1

End Sub
```

This code will produce the output shown in Figure 6-16.

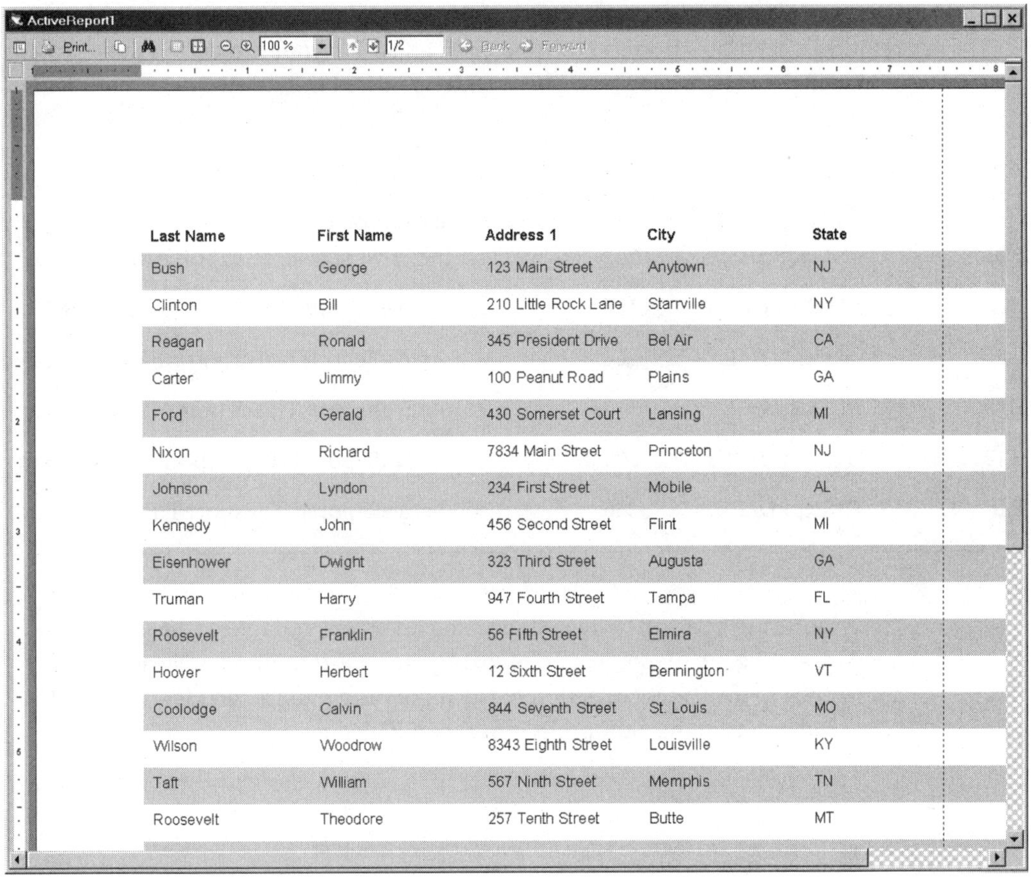

Figure 6-16. Shading alternate rows

Displaying graphical images is very straightforward. Simply use the Image control from the toolbar much as you would on a Visual Basic form. Then you can set the image control via the LoadPicture function as follows:

```
Image1.Picture = LoadPicture(App.Path & "\face02.ico")
Image1.Hyperlink ="www.apress.com"
```

The Hyperlink property makes the image an active link. Click it and your default browser will navigate you to the assigned URL. One very cool use of this is to display the company logo on the report header with an active link to the company Web site.

Exporting Data

ActiveReports offers export filters that dump your reports to RTF, PDF, Excel, HTML, TIFF, and delimited text files. Each export method that you use requires a separate support DLL that you can add to your project via the Project|References dialog box. These DLLs are listed in Table 6-5.

Table 6-5. Export DLLs

FILE TYPE	FILENAME	FILE SIZE (K)	OBJECT NAME
PDF	PDFExpt.DLL	252	ActiveReportsExcelExport.ARExportPDF
RTF	RTFExpt.DLL	128	ActiveReportsPDFExport.ARExportRTF
Excel	ExclExpt.DLL	264	ActiveReportsTextExport.ARExportExcel
Text	TextExpt.DLL	108	ActiveReportsTIFFExport.ARExportText
HTML	HTMLExpt.DLL	532	ActiveReportsHTMLExport.HTMLExport
Tiff	TiffExpt.DLL	256	ActiveReportsRTFExport.TIFFExport

Exports are performed by instantiating an object variable of the export type needed, setting the filename, and invoking the Export method while passing a reference to the Pages collection of the report as a parameter. Listing 6-15 illustrates the export of the Groupings report to a PDF file.

Listing 6-15. PDF Export

```
Dim objPDFExport As ActiveReportsPDFExport.ARExportPDF
Grouping.Run
Set objPDFExport = New ActiveReportsPDFExport.ARExportPDF
objPDFExport.FileName = App.Path & "\Grouping.PDF"
objPDFExport.Export Grouping.Pages
```

The various export objects all have different properties and methods that allow you to customize the export in ways appropriate to the format. In the example shown in Listing 6-16, both the GenPagebreaks and MultiSheet properties are set to True. This will break the data output after each pageful of information and create each page on a separate worksheet. The MinColumnwidth property will ensure that each column will be a specified number of twips wide. It is a good idea to explicitly set this property so as to prevent columns from closing up altogether and confusing users when they open the spreadsheet.

Listing 6-16. Excel Export

```
Dim objExcelExport As ActiveReportsExcelExport.ARExportExcel
Grouping.Run
Set objExcelExport = New ActiveReportsExcelExport.ARExportExcel
With objExcelExport
    .FileName = App.Path & "\Grouping.xls"
    .MinColumnwidth = 2000
    .GenPagebreaks = True
    .MultiSheet = True
    .Version = 8
    .Export Grouping.Pages
End With
```

For examples of the other export functionality, see the source code file, downloadable from the Apress Web site (http://www.apress.com).

SpreadBuilder

The Excel export component of ActiveReports contains a SpreadBuilder object. SpreadBuilder is a tool that allows you to create Microsoft Excel files, from 2.1 through 2000, without using ActiveX automation to instantiate an Excel object. SpreadBuilder creates XLS files (but cannot modify existing ones) using the Excel Binary File Format (BIFF) and offers properties and methods not just to write data but to do most of the formatting you'll need. SpreadBuilder's object model is nowhere near as rich as that of Excel, but for most report output purposes it doesn't need to be.

While using SpreadBuilder avoids the need to have Excel on a user's machine, SpreadBuilder provides a streamlined, server-friendly solution to generating Excel files. It's just not practical to instantiate the Excel application for each request on a server; the memory footprint of a single instance of Excel is daunting! Even if you're using another programmable reporting tool like VS-View, you can still take advantage of the SpreadBuilder component as it exists separately from the ActiveReports reports generation engine. Examine the code shown in Listing 6-17, which dumps the contents of a table into a spreadsheet.

Listing 6-17. SpreadBuilder Example

```
Dim objSpreadBuilder As New ActiveReportsExcelExport.SpreadBuilder
Dim oConn As New ADODB.Connection
Dim oRS As ADODB.Recordset
Dim cSQL As String
Dim rowIndex As Integer
Dim colIndex As Iinteger
```

```
oConn.ConnectionString = "Provider=Microsoft.Jet.OLEDB.4.0;" & _
"Data Source=" & GetPath & "SampleDatabase.mdb;" & _
"Persist Security Info=False"

oConn.Open

cSQL = "SELECT * FROM Requester"

Set oRS = oConn.Execute(cSQL)

objSpreadBuilder.Sheets.Add "Requesters"

'The zero element is the first ordinal value, or the first sheet in this case
With objSpreadBuilder.Sheets(0)

    ' set the first row's height (the rows collection is zero-based)
    .Rows(0).Height = 800

    For colIndex = 0 To 7
        .Columns(colIndex).Width = 1600

        ' Set style for column headers
        .Cell(0, colIndex).FontBold = True
        .Cell(0, colIndex).ForeColor = vbBlue
    Next colIndex

    rowIndex = 0 ' set to first row for column headers

    ' Write column header text
    .Cell(rowIndex, 0).Value = "Last Name"
    .Cell(rowIndex, 1).Value = "First Name"
    .Cell(rowIndex, 2).Value = "Address 1"
    .Cell(rowIndex, 3).Value = "Address 2"
    .Cell(rowIndex, 4).Value = "City"
    .Cell(rowIndex, 5).Value = "State"
    .Cell(rowIndex, 6).Value = "Zip"

    .Cell(rowIndex 7).Value = "Amount"
    .Cell(rowIndex, 7).Alignment = SBAlignRight

    rowIndex = 1
```

```
    Do While Not oRS.EOF


        .Cell(rowIndex, 0).Value = "" & oRS("LastName")
        .Cell(rowIndex, 1).Value = "" & oRS("FirstName")
        .Cell(rowIndex, 2).Value = "" & oRS("Address1")
        .Cell(rowIndex, 3).Value = "" & oRS("Address2")
        .Cell(rowIndex, 4).Value = "" & oRS("City")
        .Cell(rowIndex, 5).Value = "" & oRS("State")
        .Cell(rowIndex, 6).Value = "" & oRS("Zip")


        .Cell(rowIndex, 7).Type = SBNumber


        ' If an amount is null, set it to zero so calculations work properly
        If IsNull(oRS("Amount")) Then
            .Cell(rowIndex, 7).Value = 0
            .Cell(rowIndex, 7).NumberFormat = "###,##0.00"
        Else
            .Cell(rowIndex, 7).Value = oRS("Amount")
        End If


        rowIndex = rowIndex+1   ' increment to next row


        oRS.MoveNext


    Loop


End With


oRS.Close
Set oRS = Nothing


objSpreadBuilder.Save App.Path & "\myfile.xls"


Set objSpreadBuilder = Nothing
```

One negative is that in the current version you cannot write formulas into a cell. Thus, your subtotal numbers will need to remain as numbers and not @SUM() functions. Fortunately, Data Dynamics is planning to release SpreadBuilder as a separate product, which is why you will not find it in ActiveReports for .NET. This new version will include a complete Excel API that allows you to do everything that you can with Microsoft Excel including formulas, charts, pivot tables, and complete formatting.

Runtime Designer Control

ActiveReports provides a programmable runtime designer component for your applications that allows users to create their own reports. The designer is almost identical to that used by developers to create DSR files. To add this to your project, choose Components from the Projects menu, and click Data Dynamics ActiveReports RunTime Designer. The designer is encapsulated in an 892K DLL called Ardespro2.DLL. The report designer is shown in Figure 6-17.

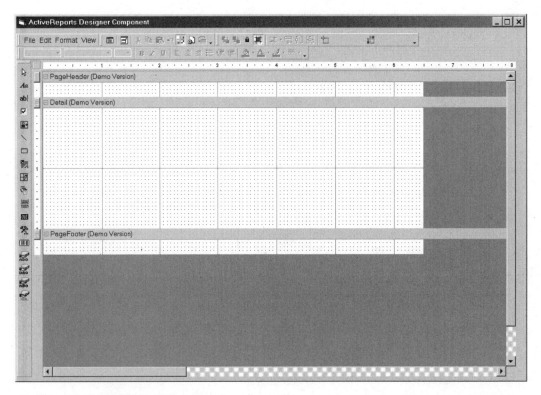

Figure 6-17. Runtime Designer control

User files are stored as XML-based RPX files that users can then edit and execute at any time. For an example of what these RPX files looks like, see Listing 6-1 in the section "Converting Microsoft Access and Crystal Reports."

Unlike the Crystal Reports Runtime Designer, that of ActiveReports offers a royalty-free distribution license. You can effectively give all your users a free report writer. Though it clearly does not have the power of Crystal Reports, it should serve the needs of most users.

ActiveReports for .NET

The .NET version of ActiveReports is remarkably similar to ActiveReports 2.0. The classes, methods, properties, and events all have names and syntax similar to their COM equivalents.

Take a look at the development environment shown in Figure 6-18.

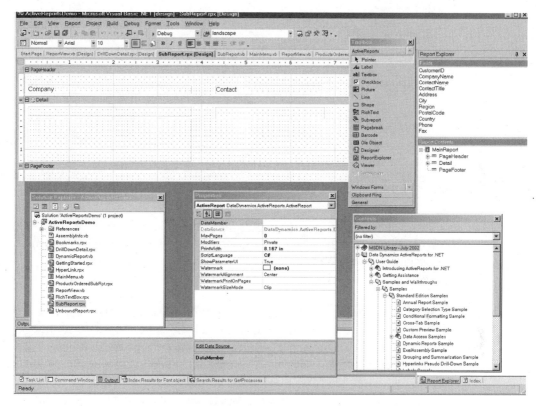

Figure 6-18. ActiveReports for .NET development environment

You can add the ActiveReports options to the toolbox by selecting Tools|Customize Toolbox as shown in Figure 6-19.

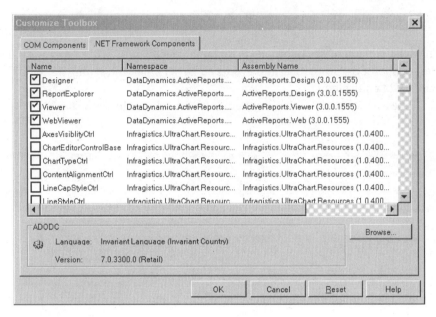

Figure 6-19. Customize toolbox

ActiveReports for .NET ships in both Standard and Professional versions. The professional version offers an end-user report designer and Web deployment technologies such as a Web viewer control and HTTP handlers. The end-user report designer is discussed later in the chapter, while the Web tools are discussed in Chapter 9.

While ActiveReports for .NET is a complete rewrite of the 2.0 version, the programming structure has remained very much the same. One of the more significant changes is that the ActiveReports class is no longer a Window class. This means that you cannot display reports via the ActiveReport.Show methods and must use the viewer control to preview the output of a report.

ActiveReports for .NET includes classes for each of the section types. The section classes include Detail, GroupHeader, GroupFooter, PageHeader, PageFooter, ReportHeader and ReportFooter. In addition, there is also a Stylesheet class that encapsulates the styles defined in the report and allows you to change the individual style item properties.

The data controls have been replaced by the OleDbDataSource, XmlDataSource, and SqlClientDataSource data source classes. The DAO and RDO data controls are no longer supported.

Getting Started

Let's begin by connecting to a data source and creating a simple report. Open a new VB .NET project and add a new designer to the project by selecting File|Add New Item and choosing ActiveReports File from the dialog box shown in Figure 6-20.

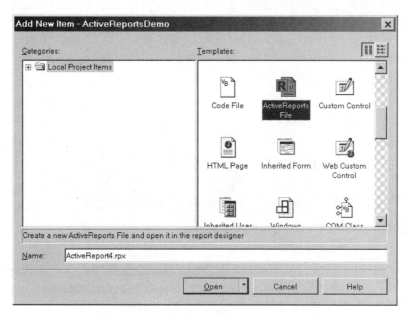

Figure 6-20. Add New Item dialog box

On the designer form, click the Details icon—specifically the yellow drum and not the word "Details"—and you'll be presented with a Report Data Source dialog box. Select SQLClient as the data source and build a query to attach to the SQL Server Northwind database. Then, enter the query as shown in Figure 6-21.

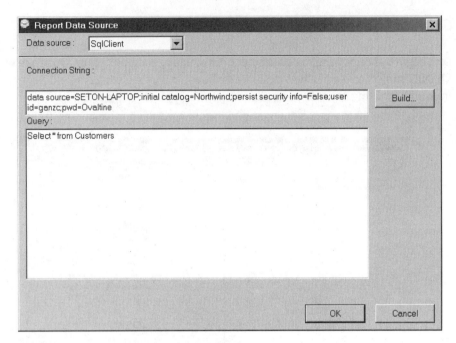

Figure 6-21. Report Data Source dialog box

Drag two TextBox objects into the Details section, set their DataField properties to CompanyName and ContactName, respectively, and then place the following code in the Load event of the Form containing the viewer:

```
Dim objAR As New ActiveReport1()

Viewer1.Document = objAR.Document
objAR.Run()
```

Then, drag two Label objects to the PageHeader section and set their Text properties appropriately to describe the TextBox objects. Press F5 and you'll get something like the output shown in Figure 6-22.

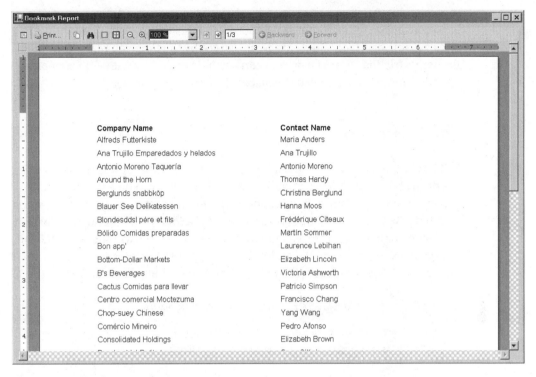

Figure 6-22. Basic report layout

That's it! You've just created your first report.

> **NOTE** *Often text boxes with borders show the data pushed up against the border. Unfortunately there is no property to control the padding. If you print the report, the letters should not appear pushed up against the border. And usually if you zoom in a bit, the problem doesn't show as well.*

Converting Microsoft Access and Crystal Reports

ActiveReports offers a utility that converts your existing Microsoft reports to the ActiveReports format. The tool is not perfect but will save you a lot of layout work should you ever need to rebuild existing projects using ActiveReports. There is no conversion utility for Crystal Reports as of this writing, but there should be one available on http://www.datadynamics.com by the time you read this. Due to license restrictions, Data Dynamics can't include the utility with ActiveReports for .NET, but the source will be available for download.

Data Connections

You have more flexibility in specifying data connectivity than was shown by using the dialog box in the "Getting Started" section. Reports can be either bound to a data source or unbound. Bound reports require some type of a data connection and ActiveReports offers three types—OleDbDataSource, SqlClientDataSource, XmlDataSource—which correspond to the three ADO.NET wrappers for OLE DB data sources, SQL Server 7.0+, and XML. Listing 6-18 illustrates how to instantiate an ADO.NET DataReader object and pass it to a report object at runtime.

Listing 6-18. Using ADO.NET DataReader as a Data Source

```
Private Sub Form1_Load(ByVal sender As System.Object, _
    ByVal e As System.EventArgs) Handles MyBase.Load

    Dim objAR As New ActiveReport1()
    Dim objSqlConnection As New SqlConnection()
    Dim objDR As SqlDataReader
    Dim objCommand As SqlCommand
    Dim cSQL As String

    objSqlConnection.ConnectionString = "Data Source=(local);" & _
                                        "Initial catalog=Northwind;" & _
                                        "Integrated security=SSPI;" & _
                                        "Persist security info=False"
    objSqlConnection.Open()

    cSQL = "SELECT CompanyName, ContactName " & _
           "FROM Customers "

    objCommand = New SqlCommand(cSQL, objSqlConnection)

    objDR = objCommand.ExecuteReader()

    objAR.DataSource = objDR
```

```
Viewer1.Document = objAR.Document

objAR.Run()
```

End Sub

Data Dynamics created these proprietary data source objects to give the ADO.NET data source an ActiveReports design time interface and eliminate the need to create Command and DataReader objects in code. Both methods are perfectly valid and which one you use is a matter of personal preference.

You can still use ADO Recordsets with ActiveReports for .NET using "unbound mode" by filling an ADO.NET DataSet object with the contents of an ADO Recordset and using that as the data source for your report. Just set the DataSet to ActiveReports' DataSource property, and set the ActiveReports' DataMember property to the name of the DataTable in the DataSet that you want the report to use. Unbound mode, however, is the fastest way to retrieve data from a non-ADO.NET data source such as an ADO Recordset.

Use of ActiveReports for .NET to access OLAP data sources is not possible. As of this writing, the provider for .NET is not yet released and Data Dynamics does not support the COM ADO-MD provider. One workaround is to use a stored procedure to copy the OLAP results to a temp table and treat that and your data source.

Page and Print Settings

The PageSettings class encapsulates the page and paper setup properties for your report. This class simply references the .NET class of the same name. These properties include the orientation, margins, paper bin, and paper size. Usually, you'll need to set these in the ActiveReport_ReportStart event, as they will apply for the report in its entirety. The code in Listing 6-19 shows the setup of a report. Here, the paper size is set to letter and the paper bin is set to the lower bin. The enumerators to designate these settings are supplied by .NET. The top and bottom margins are set at one and the left and right margins are set at half an inch.

Listing 6-19. PageSettings Example

```
Private Sub ActiveReport1_ReportStart(ByVal sender As Object, _
    ByVal e As System.EventArgs) Handles MyBase.ReportStart

    With PageSettings
        .Orientation = PageOrientation.Portrait
        .PaperSource = Drawing.Printing.PaperSourceKind.Lower
        .Margins.Bottom = 1
        .Margins.Top() = 1
```

```
        .Margins.Left() = 0.5
        .Margins.Right() = 0.5
        .PaperKind = Drawing.Printing.PaperKind.Letter
    End With

End Sub
```

ActiveReports does not provide class wrappers for every-printing related function. In some cases you'll need to access the .NET Framework directly in order to control such print-related functionality as listing the installed printers or specifying the page ranges to print. For example, the code in Listing 6-20 displays the available printers.

Listing 6-20. Printer Object Example

```
Imports System.Drawing.Printing
Dim objMsg As New System.Text.StringBuilder()
Dim cPrinter As String

For Each cPrinter In PrinterSettings.InstalledPrinters
    objMsg.Append (cPrinter)
    objMsg.Append (ControlChars.CrLf)
Next

MsgBox(objMsg.ToString, MsgBoxStyle.OKOnly, "Installed Printers")
```

This code produces the message box similar to the one shown in Figure 6-23.

Figure 6-23. Printer object property settings

Event Firing, Grouping, and Summary Fields

When a report executes, various events trigger in sequence. You can place code into the handlers for these events to further control what happens during the creation of the report. Fortunately, the event model for ActiveReports for .NET is the same as for the COM version. Please refer to the section "Sequence of Events" earlier in the chapter for full coverage of this topic.

Bookmarks (Table of Contents)

One way to make a long report more navigable for the user is to add a table of contents, referred to in ActiveReports for .NET as *bookmarks*. Bookmarks display a list of the major report topics like group headings in a hierarchical tree view column down the left-hand side of the report as shown in Figure 6-24.

 NOTE *Unlike ActiveReports 2.0, the Table of Contents tree control is now completely separate from the TOC collection. The TOC collection has been renamed to BookmarksCollection.*

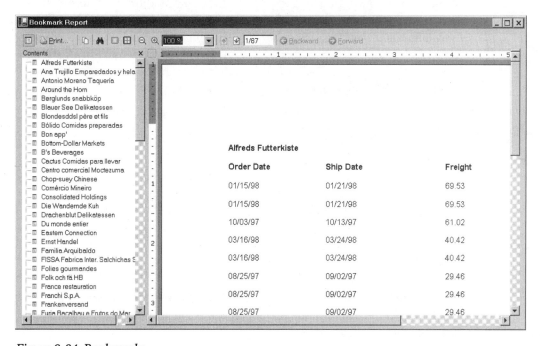

Figure 6-24. Bookmarks

When a user selects one of the bookmarks, the report viewer advances to display the information associated with the selected item. Creating bookmarks is very easy. Each report contains a Bookmark collection to which you can programmatically add, edit, and remove items as well as navigate the report. Bookmarks make the most sense for grouped reports. To add bookmarks to a report grouped on company name that lists individual orders in the Detail section, use the following code:

```
Private Sub Detail_Format(ByVal sender As Object, _
    ByVal e As System.EventArgs) Handles Detail.Format

    Me.Detail.AddBookmark(fldCompanyName.Text + "\" + fldOrderDate.Text)

End Sub
```

Viewer Control

ActiveReports for .NET no longer supports the Show method. Therefore, you must invoke your report objects and display them in a viewer. This viewer—ActiveReports.Viewer.DLL—is rather small, weighing in at only 328K. You'll want to set the Anchor property of this control to all sides of the owner form so it sizes along with the owner. To display a report, simply set the Document property to the report object you wish to view, for example:

```
Viewer1.Document = objReport.Document
objReport.Run()
```

Then you can control the appearance of the viewer such as the visibility of the toolbar, controlling the table of contents browser, etc. The following code makes the table of contents visible and sets the width to 200 pixels (two inches):

```
Viewer1.TableOfContents.Visible = True
Viewer1.TableOfContents.Width = 200
```

If you wish to override the features of the toolbar with your own buttons, you can do that as well. To send the current report to the printer, simply add a button with the following code in the Click event:

```
Viewer1.Document.Print()
```

Building Reports

Now that you understand the structure of reports and how to set up for them, let's examine the different types of reports that you can build using ActiveReports. One of the most powerful features of ActiveReports is that it can create reports at runtime, connect them to a data source, and render them to the screen or printer. As a general rule, anything that you can do in the visual designer you can do programmatically at runtime. Therefore, you can provide your users with the ability to select which columns appear on a report, or offer them choices as to how they would like the same report grouped, without having to prebuild a version of the same report with every possible permutation of user option. If you're familiar with Crystal Reports' Report Creation API syntax, this approach will look very similar. Probably the biggest difference between the two products is the licensing costs. Whereas Crystal charges hefty per-seat license fees for its Report Creation API, ActiveReports includes this functionality as part of its standard user license with no additional costs involved.

Standard Columnar

Suppose you want to create a simple columnar report. The first step is to establish the data connection by dynamically creating a data control and setting its properties as shown in Listing 6-21.

Listing 6-21. Establishing Data Connection

```
Dim objAR As New ActiveReport()
Dim objSqlConnection As New SqlConnection()
Dim objDR As SqlDataReader
Dim objCommand As SqlCommand
Dim cSQL As String
Dim objLabel As Label
Dim objTextBox As TextBox
Dim objSection As Section

'First, establish a data connection
objSqlConnection.ConnectionString = "Data Source=(local);" & _
                                    "Initial catalog=Northwind;" & _
                                    "Integrated security=SSPI;" & _
                                    "Persist security info=False"
objSqlConnection.Open()
```

```
cSQL = "SELECT CompanyName, ContactName " & _
       "FROM Customers "

objCommand = New SqlCommand(cSQL, objSqlConnection)

objDR = objCommand.ExecuteReader()
```

Now with the report object—objAR—instantiated, you can create and size the report sections and display and position the column headers and data fields. This is shown in Listing 6-22.

Listing 6-22. Dynamically Generated Columnar Report

```
'Next, create the various sections of the report object
With objAR.Sections
    .Add(SectionType.ReportHeader, "ReportHeader")
    .Add(SectionType.PageHeader, "PageHeader")
    .Add(SectionType.Detail, "Detail")
    .Add(SectionType.PageFooter, "PageFooter")
    .Add(SectionType.ReportFooter, "ReportFooter")
End With

'...and set the height of those sections measured in inches
objAR.Sections(0).Height = 0.5
objAR.Sections(1).Height = 0.3
objAR.Sections(2).Height = 0.3
objAR.Sections(3).Height = 0.3
objAR.Sections(4).Height = 0.5


'Create label objects for the column headers and add
'them to section 1, the PageHeader
objLabel = New Label()

With objLabel
    .Name = "Label1"
    .Text = "Company Name"
    .Width = 3
    .Left = 0.5
    .Height = 0.3
End With

objAR.Sections(1).Controls.Add (objLabel)
```

```
objLabel = New Label()

With objLabel
    .Name = "Label2"
    .Text = "Contact Name"
    .Width = 3
    .Left = 3.5
    .Height = 0.3
End With

objAR.Sections(1).Controls.Add (objLabel)

'Create TextBox objects for the data columns and add
'them to section 2, the Details
objTextBox = New TextBox()

With objTextBox
    .Name = "TextBox1"
    .DataField = "CompanyName"
    .Width = 3
    .Left = 0.5
    .Height = 0.3
End With

objAR.Sections(2).Controls.Add (objTextBox)

objTextBox = New TextBox()

With objTextBox
    .Name = "TextBox2"
    .DataField = "ContactName"
    .Width = 3
    .Left = 3.5
    .Height = 0.3
End With

objAR.Sections(2).Controls.Add (objTextBox)

'Finally, set the data source of the report
objAR.DataSource = objDR

'...set the document property of the viewer to
'that of the report object
Viewer1.Document = objAR.Document
```

```
'...and away you go
objAR.Run()
```

Labels

Labels can likewise be created programmatically as shown in Listing 6-23.

Listing 6-23. Dynamic Mailing Labels

```
Dim WithEvents objAR As New ActiveReport()
Dim objDR As SqlDataReader
Dim objCommand As SqlCommand

Private Sub Labels_DataInitialize(ByVal sender As Object, _
    ByVal e As System.EventArgs) _
    Handles objAR.DataInitialize

    objAR.Fields.Add("CSZ")

End Sub

Private Sub Labels_FetchData(ByVal sender As Object, _
    ByVal eArgs As DataDynamics.ActiveReports.ActiveReport.FetchEventArgs) _
    Handles objAR.FetchData

    If eArgs.EOF Then
        Exit Sub
    End If

    With objDR
        objAR.Fields("CSZ").Value = .Item("City") & ", " & _
                                    .Item("Region") & " " & _
                                    .Item("PostalCode")
    End With

End Sub
```

The first step is to declare an object variable to refer to the report itself using WithEvents. Since the CSZ (city, state, zip) TextBox is populated at runtime from a concatenation of multiple database columns, their presence must be made known to ActiveReports in the DataInitialize event. Once ActiveReports knows about these Field objects, you can assign the concatenated values for each record printed in the FetchData event.

Listing 6-24. Dynamic Mailing Labels (continued)

```
Dim objDetail As DataDynamics.ActiveReports.Detail
Dim objSqlConnection As New SqlConnection()
Dim cSQL As String
Dim objTextBox As TextBox

'First, establish a data connection
objSqlConnection.ConnectionString = "Data Source=(local);" & _
                                    "Initial catalog=Northwind;" & _
                                    "Integrated security=SSPI;" & _
                                    "Persist security info=False"
objSqlConnection.Open()

cSQL = "SELECT * " & _
       "FROM Customers "

objCommand = New SqlCommand(cSQL, objSqlConnection)

objDR = objCommand.ExecuteReader()

'Next, Detail section of the report object. No other
'sections are needed
objDetail = objAR.Sections.Add(SectionType.Detail, "Detail")

'Two columns of labels that snake down and across the page
With objDetail
    .ColumnCount = 2
    .ColumnDirection = ColumnDirection.DownAcross
    .KeepTogether = True
End With

'...and set the height of the detail section to one inch
objAR.Sections(0).Height = 1
```

In the Detail section, which is the only report section you'll need to create for labels, you can indicate that there are two columns that must print each label, snaking down the column and looping back to the next column to its right. The KeepTogether property is set to True as it is not at all appropriate for labels to print across columns or pages. Then, the height of the Detail section is set to one inch.

Once the labels have been set up, the individual fields can be added to the Details section as TextBox objects. Listing 6-25 shows how this is done.

Listing 6-25. Add the Individual Fields

```
'Create TextBox objects for the data columns and add
'them to section 0, the Details
objTextBox = New TextBox()

With objTextBox
    .Name = "fldCompanyName"
    .DataField = "CompanyName"
    .Width = 3
    .Left = 0.2
    .Height = 0.1
    .Top = 0
End With


objAR.Sections(0).Controls.Add (objTextBox)


objTextBox = New TextBox()

With objTextBox
    .Name = "fldContactName"
    .DataField = "ContactName"
    .Width = 3
    .Left = 0.2
    .Height = 0.1
    .Top = 0.13
End With


objAR.Sections(0).Controls.Add (objTextBox)


objTextBox = New TextBox()

With objTextBox
    .Name = "fldAddress"
    .DataField = "Address"
    .Width = 3
    .Left = 0.2
    .Height = 0.1
    .Top = 0.26
End With
```

```
objAR.Sections(0).Controls.Add (objTextBox)

objTextBox = New TextBox()

With objTextBox
    .Name = "fldCSZ"
    .DataField = "CSZ"
    .Width = 3
    .Left = 0.2
    .Height = 0.1
    .Top = 0.39
End With

objAR.Sections(0).Controls.Add (objTextBox)

objAR.DataSource = objDR

Viewer1.Document = objAR.Document

objAR.Run()
```

This label code is also an example of bound and unbound fields existing in the same report. A report's data fields can be bound to a data source via the DataField property of the TextBox or it can be assigned manually using the FetchData event.

Free-Form Text Reports

Managing free-form text and mail-merge capability in ActiveReports centers around the use of the RichTextBox control that has been greatly enhanced since its VB6 version. This control recognizes RTF encoding and displays your document accordingly. Listing 6-26 illustrates how the RichTextBox control can serve up a mail merge application.

Listing 6-26. Mail Merge Using the RichTextBox Control

```
Dim objDR As SqlDataReader
Dim cCompanyName As String
Dim cAddress As String
Dim cCSZ As String
```

```vb
Private Sub RichText_ReportStart(ByVal sender As Object, _
    ByVal e As System.EventArgs) Handles MyBase.ReportStart

    Dim objCommand As SqlCommand
    Dim objSqlConnection As New SqlConnection()
    Dim cSQL As String
    Dim objTextBox As TextBox

    'First, establish a data connection
    objSqlConnection.ConnectionString = "Data Source=(local);" & _
                                        "Initial catalog=Northwind;" & _
                                        "Integrated security=SSPI;" & _
                                        "Persist security info=False"
    objSqlConnection.Open()

    cSQL = "SELECT * " & _
            "FROM Customers "

    objCommand = New SqlCommand(cSQL, objSqlConnection)

    objDR = objCommand.ExecuteReader()
    objDR.Read()

    With RichTextBox1
        .RTF() = "{\rtf1\ansi\ansicpg1252\deff0\deflang1033" & _
                "{\fonttbl{\f0\fswiss\fcharset0 Arial;}" & _
                "{\f1\fswiss\fprq2\fcharset0 Univers;}}" & _
                "\viewkind4\uc1\pard\f0\fs20\par" & _
                "\b [!CompanyName]\par" & _
                "[!Address]\par" & _
                "[!CSZ]\b0\par" & _
                "\par" & _
                "\f1 This is the reminder letter for [!CompanyName]\f0\par}"

        'Indicate that the display control can size itself to
        'accommodate longer text
        .CanGrow = True
        .MultiLine = True
```

```
      End With

End Sub

Private Sub RichText_FetchData(ByVal sender As Object, _
    ByVal eArgs As DataDynamics.ActiveReports.ActiveReport.FetchEventArgs) _
    Handles MyBase.FetchData

    If eArgs.EOF Then
        Exit Sub
    End If

    cCompanyName = objDR.Item("CompanyName")
    cAddress = objDR.Item("Address")
    cCSZ = objDR.Item("City") & ", " & objDR.Item("Region") & " " & _
        objDR.Item("PostalCode")

End Sub

Private Sub RichText_Format(ByVal sender As Object, _
    ByVal e As System.EventArgs) Handles Detail.Format

    With RichTextBox1
        .ReplaceField("CompanyName", cCompanyName)
        .ReplaceField("Address", cAddress)
        .ReplaceField("CSZ", cCSZ)
    End With

End Sub
```

The first step is to establish a data connection and assign the RTF-encoded text to the RTF property of the RichTextBox object. In the FetchData event, you can assign the values of the CompanyName, Address, and CSZ variables from the DataReader object you created in the ReportStart event. The Format section is where you'll use the ReplaceField method to substitute the variable data for the field placeholder. The output of this operation is shown in Figure 6-25.

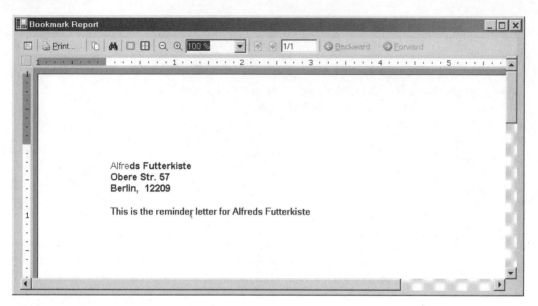

Figure 6-25. Mail merge

Subreports

A subreport is simply a report that is displayed within another report, and one report can have many subreports. Subreports are yet another of the many areas that are functionally the same between the 2.0 and .NET versions of ActiveReports. Read the section on subreports earlier in the chapter.

Drill-Down

Using hyperlinks to allow drill-down of data also functions in the same fashion as it did in ActiveReports 2.0. Suppose you want the user to view a list of customers and then by clicking the customer name, drill-down to a list of orders for that customer. First, you need to set the color of the customer name TextBox object to blue and the font attribute to underline as this is the traditional hyperlink indicator. Listing 6-27 shows how this is done.

Listing 6-27. Setting the Hyperlink Indicator

```
Private Sub Hyperlink_ReportStart(ByVal sender As Object, _
            ByVal e As System.EventArgs) _
            Handles MyBase.ReportStart
```

```
'Make the hyperlinked data element appear like a traditional hyperlink
Dim objFont As New Font("Arial", 10, FontStyle.Underline)

txtCompanyName.ForeColor = Color.Blue
txtCompanyName.Font = objFont

End Sub


Private Sub Detail_BeforePrint(ByVal sender As Object, _
    ByVal e As System.EventArgs) _
    Handles Detail.BeforePrint

    txtCompanyName.Hyperlink = txtCustomerID.Text

End Sub
```

Next, to activate the hyperlink, simply add code to the Hyperlink event of the report object as shown in Listing 6-28. In this event the Button parameter refers to the mouse button that was clicked to activate the hyperlink, whereas Link contains the value of the Hyperlink property of the control, in this case CustomerID.

Listing 6-28. Hyperlink Event

```
Private Sub Viewer1_HyperLink(ByVal sender As Object, _
        ByVal e As DataDynamics.ActiveReports.Viewer.HyperLinkEventArgs) _
        Handles Viewer1.HyperLink

    Dim objSqlConnection As New SqlConnection()
    Dim objCommand As SqlCommand
    Dim objDR As SqlDataReader
    Dim cSQL As String
    Dim objReport As New DrillDownDetail()

    objSqlConnection.ConnectionString = "Data Source=(local);" & _
                                        "Initial catalog=Northwind;" & _
                                        "Integrated security=SSPI;" & _
                                        "Persist security info=False"
    objSqlConnection.Open()

    cSQL = "SELECT OrderDate, ShippedDate, Freight " & _
            "FROM Orders " & _
            "WHERE CustomerID = " & Chr(39) & e.Hyperlink.ToString & Chr(39)
```

```
objCommand = New SqlCommand(cSQL, objSqlConnection)

objDR = objCommand.ExecuteReader()

objReport.DataSource = objDR

Viewer1.Document = objReport.Document

objReport.Run()

End Sub
```

Exporting Data

ActiveReports offers export filters that dump your reports to RTF, PDF, Excel, HTML, TIFF, and delimited text files. Each export method that you use requires a separate support DLL that you can add to your project via the Project|Add References dialog box and can reference through the Data Dynamics.ActiveReports.Export namespace. These DLLs are listed in Table 6-6.

Table 6-6. Export DLLs

FILE TYPE	FILENAME	FILE SIZE (K)	OBJECT NAME
PDF	ActiveReports.PdfExport.dll	268	Pdf.PdfExport()
RTF	ARExportRTF.DLL	380	Rtf.RtfExport()
Excel	ARExportExcel.DLL	552	Xls.ExcelExport()
Text	ARExportText.DLL	372	Text.TextExport()
HTML	ActiveReports.HtmlExport.dll	632	Html.HtmlExport()
Tiff	ARExportTiff.dll	540	Tiff.TiffExport()

Exports are performed by instantiating an object variable of the export type needed, setting the filename, and invoking the Export method while passing a reference to the Document object of the report as a parameter. Listing 6-29 illustrates the export of the Unbound report into selected file formats.

Listing 6-29. PDF Export

```vb
Dim objExcelExport As New Xls.ExcelExport()
Dim objPDFExport As New Pdf.PdfExport()
Dim objHTMLExport As New Html.HtmlExport()
Dim objRTFExport As New Rtf.RtfExport()
Dim objTextExport As New DataDynamics.ActiveReports.Export.Text.TextExport()
Dim objTIFFExport As New Tiff.TiffExport()
Dim cPath As String

cPath = Application.StartupPath

Select Case iExportOption

    Case ExportType.ExportExcel
        With objExcelExport
'Automatically create page breaks
            .GenPageBreaks = True
'Determines if the report will be generated as a single Excel sheet, or as a
'multiple sheet workbook. Each page in the report will be placed on its own
'Excel sheet.
            .MultiSheet = True
            .MinColumnWidth = 30
            .Export(Me.Document, cPath & "\export.xls")
        End With

    Case ExportType.ExportHTML
        With objHTMLExport
'Determines if the pages will be exported to one or multiple html pages.
            .MultiPage = True
            .Title = "HTML Export Document"
            .Export(Me.Document, cPath & "\export.html")
        End With

    Case ExportType.ExportPDF
        objPDFExport.Export(Me.Document, cPath & "\export.pdf")

    Case ExportType.ExportRTF
        objRTFExport.Export(Me.Document, cPath & "\export.rtf")

    Case ExportType.ExportText
        objTextExport.Export(Me.Document, cPath & "\export.txt")
```

```
Case ExportType.ExportTIFF
    objTIFFExport.Export(Me.Document, cPath & "\export.tif")

End Select
```

When selecting an export class, you may notice one named Internal. This is simply a shared public namespace used by the export filters internally and should not be called directly by your code.

Depending on the export format you choose, embedded graphics will export as well. ActiveReports for .NET and the new PDF export are optimized if you use JPEG source images in your picture controls on the report. Try using JPEG images instead of GIF images to optimize both quality and image size.

Runtime Designer Control

ActiveReports for .NET has a programmable and royalty-free runtime designer that allows users to create their own reports. Implementation of this designer is more complicated than in ActiveReports 2.0, but you have much more control over the functionality offered to the user. Fortunately, ActiveReports for .NET ships with a very complete sample program that illustrates how to programmatically access every feature of the designer. If you plan to distribute a report designer with your application, this demo is the place to start. You can copy the code into your application and customize it from there very quickly.

The designer, which is shown in Figure 6-26, is encapsulated in a 396K DLL called ActiveReports.Design.dll.

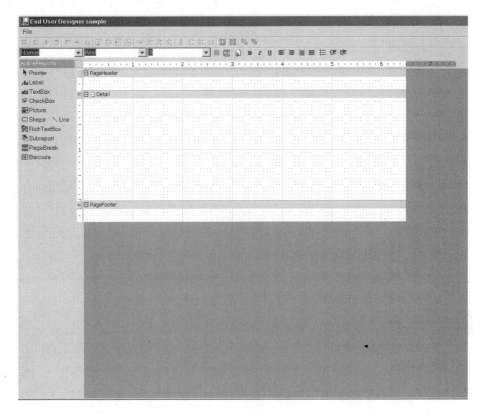

Figure 6-26. Runtime designer

User files are stored as XML-based RPX files that users can then edit and execute at any time.

Conclusion

ActiveReports for both VB and VB .NET has many rich features for creating all the report types you'll need. Its combination of visual designer and code-based structure complement one another well. In the next chapter, we'll examine how to create reports using the Microsoft Office suite.

Microsoft Office XP

THE MICROSOFT OFFICE suite is an immensely powerful developer's tool because of its Visual Basic for Applications (VBA) programming extensibility. Word, Excel, Outlook, and Access all have labyrinthine object models that offer features that quickly become indispensable when developing report output. In this chapter, we'll examine Word's MailMerge and Table objects; Excel's workbook, worksheet, and cell hierarchy, as well as its graphing functionality; Outlook's e-mail capability; and Access' report writer. In addition, you'll also see examples of such VBA-controlled applications as Lotus Notes and the Adobe Acrobat Writer.

Office XP as a Reporting Tool

Microsoft Word, Excel, and Access all offer functionality for reporting, and each could function as a report writing tool by itself. However, each tool has its relative strengths and weaknesses and needs to be used appropriately. Often where one product leaves off, one of the others picks up.

Select the Appropriate Reference

If you've never worked with ActiveX automation before, you must link the object model of the application you wish to program to your Application. In Visual Basic, this is done by selecting Project | References and then clicking the appropriate reference in the list presented, which is shown in Figure 7-1.

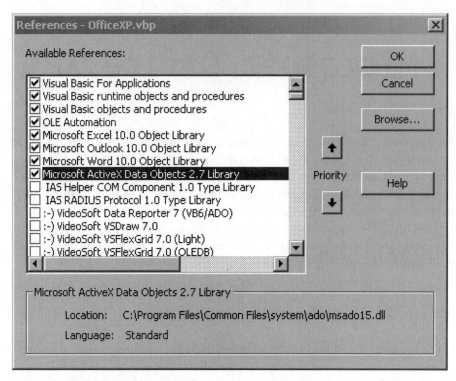

Figure 7-1. Visual Basic References dialog box

Doing so will make the object model you wish to program available to your application. To accomplish the same thing in VB .NET, select Project | Add Reference and choose the COM tab from the Add Reference dialog box as shown in Figure 7-2.

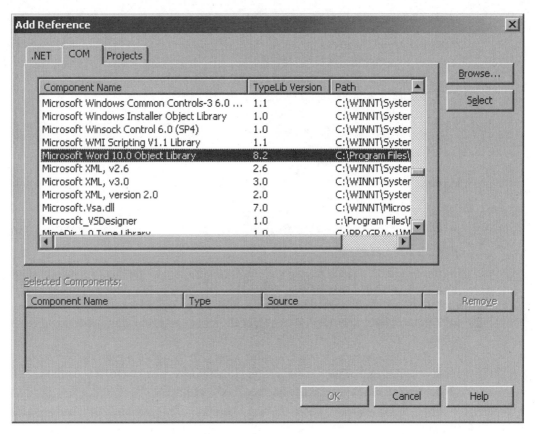

Figure 7-2. VB .NET References dialog box

When you've located the Microsoft product you wish to add, click the Select button and when finished click OK. This makes the object model available to you in VB .NET.

PageSetup

One important feature common to both Word and Excel is that they both offer PageSetup objects. PageSetup controls the format of the document itself and is vital to prepare it for printing. Using this object you can set margins, paper size, and orientation. These are properties that are common to the PageSetup objects in both Word and Excel. The PrintOut method of the Application object—named objWord and objExcel in the sample code—will send your document to the printer. The source code in Listing 7-1 illustrates these features.

Listing 7-1. PageSetup Options

```
With objDocument.PageSetup
    .LeftMargin = InchesToPoints(0.5)
    .RightMargin = InchesToPoints(0.5)
    .TopMargin = InchesToPoints(0.5)
    .BottomMargin = InchesToPoints(0.5)
    .Orientation = wdOrientPortrait
End With


objWord.PrintOut
```

Microsoft Word

Microsoft Word has two major areas that complement your report writing requirements. It offers mail merge features that make it an easy choice for sending out form letters, but its Table object allows you to create columnar reports as well.

First, let's review some of the main objects in the Word hierarchy. The topmost object is Application, which refers to Microsoft Word itself. It is from this object that all other objects are derived. For example:

```
Dim objWord As Word.Application
Dim objDocument As Word.Document

Set objWord = CreateObject("Word.Application")
Set objDocument = objWord.Documents.Add
```

The Document object refers to an individual open Word document. Each open Word document belongs to the Documents collection.

Portions of documents are represented by Selection, Range, Paragraphs, Sentences, Words, and Characters. Taken together, these objects and collections allow you to manipulate the smallest detail of a document. For example, given the text shown in Figure 7-3, examine the output in Listing 7-2.

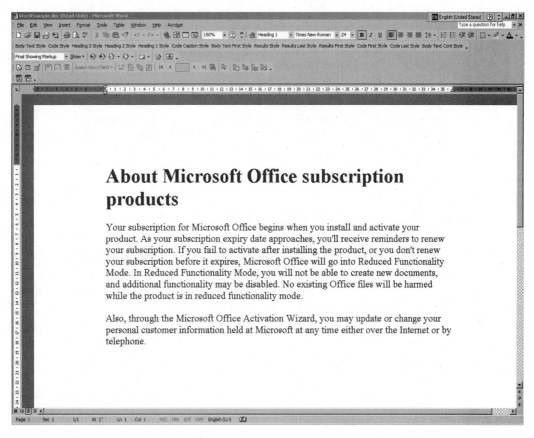

Figure 7-3. Word document example

Listing 7-2. Word Overview

```
Dim objWord As Word.Application
Dim objDocument As Word.Document
Dim cStats As String

Set objWord = CreateObject("Word.Application")
objWord.Visible = False

Set objDocument = objWord.Documents.Open(App.Path & "\WordExample.doc")

With objDocument
```

```
      cStats = "# paragraphs: " & .Paragraphs.Count & vbCrLf
      cStats = cStats & "# sentences: " & .Sentences.Count & vbCrLf
      cStats = cStats & "# words: " & .Words.Count & vbCrLf
      cStats = cStats & "# characters: " & .Characters.Count & vbCrLf & vbCrLf

      cStats = cStats & "First Paragraph: " & .Paragraphs(1).Range.Text & vbCrLf
      cStats = cStats & "Second Sentence: " & .Sentences(2) & vbCrLf
      cStats = cStats & "Third Word: " & .Words(3) & vbCrLf
      cStats = cStats & "Fourth Character: " & .Characters(4) & vbCrLf

End With

MsgBox cStats
```

A Selection object represents a highlighted area in the document. If no text is highlighted, it refers to the insertion point. A Range object refers to a defined starting and ending point in a document. The code in Listing 7-3 illustrates these objects. This example uses the text shown earlier in Figure 7-3.

Listing 7-3. Word Objects

```
Dim objWord As Word.Application
Dim objDocument As Word.Document
Dim objRange As Word.Range

Set objWord = CreateObject("Word.Application")
objWord.Visible = False

Set objDocument = objWord.Documents.Open(App.Path & "\WordExample.doc")

With objDocument

    Call objDocument.Sentences(3).Copy

    Set objRange = .Paragraphs(2).Range

End With
```

Style objects can make it easier to apply formatting to text. The code in Listing 7-4 illustrates how to create a Style object and then apply the formatting to text encapsulated in a Range object.

Listing 7-4. Style Object

```
Dim objWord As Word.Application
Dim objDocument As Word.Document
Dim objRange As Word.Range
Dim objStyle As Word.Style

Set objWord = CreateObject("Word.Application")
objWord.Visible = True

Set objDocument = objWord.Documents.Open(App.Path & "\WordExample.doc")

Set objStyle = objDocument.Styles.Add("Chapter Title 1")

With objStyle
    .Font.Name = "Arial"
    .Font.Size = 28
    .Font.Bold = True
    .Font.Color = wdColorDarkRed
End With

Set objRange = objDocument.Paragraphs(1).Range

objRange.Style = "Chapter Title 1"
```

Table Objects

Table objects are similar to spreadsheets in that they are composed of rows and columns. Each Word document may contain multiple Table objects. Syntactically, Word tables even operate in a fashion similar to Excel worksheets. However, they are not nearly as powerful. While you can use Table objects to output columnar reports, you're better off using Excel or one of the report writing alternatives discussed in this book. Excel is far more robust for working with columnar data. Word Table objects are useful when you are creating a document at runtime and you need to insert structured columnar text within the flow of the document. Of course, this is what Word is really intended for. As a word processor, it is designed for the manipulation of text and graphics. Outputting reports using Table objects in Word is rather slow, so don't use it unless you have a good reason.

Listing 7-5 illustrates some of the various features of Table objects.

Listing 7-5. Table Objects

```
Dim oRS As ADODB.Recordset
Dim objWord As Word.Application
Dim objDocument As Word.Document
Dim objTable As Word.Table
Dim objRange As Word.Range
Dim x As Integer
Dim iFieldCnt As Integer
Dim iRow As Integer
Dim cSQL As String

cSQL = "SELECT LastName, FirstName, State " & _
       "FROM Requester " & _
       "ORDER BY LastName"

Set oRS = oConn.Execute(cSQL)

iFieldCnt = oRS.Fields.Count
iRow = 1

Set objWord = CreateObject("Word.Application")
objWord.Visible = True

Set objDocument = objWord.Documents.Add

With objDocument.Sections(1).Headers(wdHeaderFooterPrimary).Range
    .InsertAfter "Status Report"
    .Paragraphs.Alignment = wdAlignParagraphLeft
End With

objDocument.Sections(1).Footers(wdHeaderFooterPrimary). _
    PageNumbers.Add.Alignment = wdAlignPageNumberCenter

With objDocument.PageSetup
    .LeftMargin = InchesToPoints(0.5)
    .RightMargin = InchesToPoints(0.5)
End With

Set objRange = objWord.ActiveDocument.Range(0, 0)

Set objTable = objDocument.Tables.Add(objRange, 1, iFieldCnt)
```

```
With objTable
     .Cell(iRow, 1).Range.InsertAfter "Last Name"
     .Cell(iRow, 1).Width = InchesToPoints(1.2)

     .Cell(iRow, 2).Range.InsertAfter "First Name"
     .Cell(iRow, 2).Width = InchesToPoints(1.2)

     .Cell(iRow, 3).Range.InsertAfter "State"
     .Cell(iRow, 3).Width = InchesToPoints(1.5)
     .Cell(iRow, 3).LeftPadding = PixelsToPoints(30)

     Call .Rows.Add

     iRow = iRow + 1

     Do While Not oRS.EOF

          .Cell(iRow, 1).Range.InsertAfter oRS("LastName")
          .Cell(iRow, 1).Width = InchesToPoints(1.2)

          .Cell(iRow, 2).Range.InsertAfter oRS("FirstName")
          .Cell(iRow, 2).Width = InchesToPoints(1.2)

          .Cell(iRow, 3).Range.InsertAfter oRS("State")
          .Cell(iRow, 3).Width = InchesToPoints(1.5)
          .Cell(iRow, 3).LeftPadding = PixelsToPoints(30)
          .Cell(iRow, 3).Shading.BackgroundPatternColorIndex = wdBrightGreen

          oRS.MoveNext

          If Not oRS.EOF Then
               Call .Rows.Add
          End If

          iRow = iRow + 1

     Loop

End With
```

This code produces the output in Figure 7-4.

Figure 7-4. Word Table object

Once you have instantiated a Word object using CreateObject, add a document to the Documents collection and set this new document to the objDocument object variable. By referring to the Headers property, you can use the InsertAfter method to create the header of the report. Then, by referring to the Footers property, you can set the page number to print automatically in the center.

After setting the document margins, create a Table object by adding to the Table collection of objDocument. You must indicate the number of cells and rows the new table will have, and a table must have at least one cell and one row. If you've ever done programming with Excel, the structure in Listing 7-4 will look very familiar to you. Each cell has a row and column offset. Invoking the Cells.Add method adds a blank row to the table. The Range.InsertAfter method will place text within the cell. You even have options to change the color of individual cells as well as pad the data with blank spaces.

TIP *When developing with VBA, use the Macro Recorder found under the Tools | Macro menu. Rather than trying to figure out how to map the Office object model to your application, you can choose to record a macro, perform your required functions using the menu options, stop the macro recording, and then examine the source code generated. Most of the code you'll need to link to your Visual Basic application can then simply be cut and pasted into your application. Since this code is intended to work as macros from within the Office product you're using, you'll need to make some modifications for it to work in VB. The Macro Recorder is available throughout the Microsoft Office suite.*

Mail Merge and Mailing Labels

Mail merge is probably the most common programmatic use of Microsoft Word in business applications. Word offers a powerful object hierarchy to manipulate its mail merge functionality to create customized letters for either printing, faxing, or e-mailing.

NOTE *Microsoft Publisher also has a similar object model as Word with respect to mail merge capabilities. If you need to produce a newsletter, for example, you could print it with the names and addresses merged into it. Or, if you need to customize the content of the newsletter to target specific audiences, you could, for example, replace a story about one topic with a story about another based on a field in a database. Because Word has such powerful support for graphics, text, and font styles, it makes a pretty good desktop publisher all by itself. Make sure you really need Publisher before you use it.*

Examine the code in Listing 7-6, which merges an existing merge document with a data source. Objects are created for both the application and the document, objWord and objDocument, respectively. Then, the OpenDataSource method of the MailMerge objects establishes a connection with the Access database and passes in a SQL statement to extract data for the merge. Once the database connection has been established, the Destination property is set to indicate the final form of the merge. In this example, the merged letters are going to a new document. Other options are fax, e-mail, or printer.

Listing 7-6. Mail Merge

```
Dim objWord As Word.Application
Dim objDocument As Word.Document
Dim objMailMerge As Word.MailMerge
Dim cConnection As String

cConnection = "Provider=Microsoft.Jet.OLEDB.4.0;" & _
              "Password="""";" & _
              "User ID=Admin;" & _
              "Data Source=C:\Reports\SampleDatabase.mdb;" & _
              "Mode=Read;" & _
              "Extended Properties="""";" & _
              "Jet OLEDB:System database="""";" & _
              "Jet OLEDB:Registry Path="""";" & _
              "Jet OLEDB:Database Password="""";" & _
              "Jet OLEDB:Engine Type=5;" & _
              "Jet OLEDB:"

Set objWord = CreateObject("Word.Application")
objWord.Visible = True

Set objDocument = objWord.Documents.Open(App.Path & "\mailmerge.doc")

Set objMailMerge = objDocument.MailMerge

Call objMailMerge.OpenDataSource( _
    "C:\Reports\SampleDatabase.mdb", ConfirmConversions:=False, ReadOnly:= _
    True, LinkToSource:=True, AddToRecentFiles:=False, PasswordDocument:="", _
     PasswordTemplate:="", WritePasswordDocument:="", WritePasswordTemplate:= _
    "", Revert:=False, Format:=wdOpenFormatAuto, Connection:= _
    cConnection _
    , SQLStatement:="SELECT * FROM Requester", SQLStatement1:="", SubType:= _
    wdMergeSubTypeAccess)

With objMailMerge
    .HighlightMergeFields = True
    .Destination = wdSendToNewDocument
    .Execute
End With
```

Word can produce mailing labels as well. The code in Listing 7-7 shows how the MailingLabel object can create labels based on any Avery number. Avery Dennison Corporation (http://www.avery.com) is the premier manufacturer of labels and other office supplies in the world. Their label numbers have become the de facto standard for indicating label size and dimensions. Even labels not manufactured by Avery adhere to the Avery numbering standard.

Listing 7-7. Mailing Labels

```
Dim objWord As Word.Application
Dim objDocument As Word.Document
Dim objAutoTextEntry As Word.AutoTextEntry
Dim cConnection As String

cConnection = "Provider=Microsoft.Jet.OLEDB.4.0;" & _
              "Password="""";" & _
              "User ID=Admin;" & _
              "Data Source=C:\Reports\SampleDatabase.mdb;" & _
              "Mode=Read;" & _
              "Extended Properties="""";" & _
              "Jet OLEDB:System database="""";" & _
              "Jet OLEDB:Registry Path="""";" & _
              "Jet OLEDB:Database Password="""";" & _
              "Jet OLEDB:Engine Type=5;" & _
              "Jet OLEDB:"

Set objWord = CreateObject("Word.Application")
objWord.Visible = True

Set objDocument = objWord.Documents.Add

With objDocument.MailMerge

    'Temporarily set up the merge fields required
    With .Fields
        .Add objWord.Selection.Range, "FirstName"
        objWord.Selection.TypeText " "
        .Add objWord.Selection.Range, "LastName"
        objWord.Selection.TypeParagraph
        .Add objWord.Selection.Range, "Address1"
        objWord.Selection.TypeParagraph
        .Add objWord.Selection.Range, "City"
        objWord.Selection.TypeText ", "
        .Add objWord.Selection.Range, "State"
        objWord.Selection.TypeText " "
```

```
            .Add objWord.Selection.Range, "Zip"
        End With

        'Create an AutoText entry encapsulating the
        'merge fields for the label
        Set objAutoTextEntry = objWord.NormalTemplate. _
            AutoTextEntries.Add("Labels", objDocument.Content)

        'Remove the merge fields from the document as
        'objAutoTextEntry now contains what we need
        objDocument.Content.Delete

        Call .OpenDataSource( _
        "C:\Reports\SampleDatabase.mdb", ConfirmConversions:=False, ReadOnly:= _
        True, LinkToSource:=True, AddToRecentFiles:=False, PasswordDocument:="", _
        PasswordTemplate:="", WritePasswordDocument:="", WritePasswordTemplate:= _
        "", Revert:=False, Format:=wdOpenFormatAuto, Connection:= _
        cConnection _
        , SQLStatement:="SELECT * FROM Requester", SQLStatement1:="", SubType:= _
        wdMergeSubTypeAccess)

        .MainDocumentType = wdMailingLabels

        Call objWord.MailingLabel.CreateNewDocument("5163", "", _
                "Labels", wdPrinterManualFeed)

        .Destination = wdSendToNewDocument
        .Execute

        objAutoTextEntry.Delete

        objWord.NormalTemplate.Saved = True

End With
```

The first step after creating both Application and Document objects is to temporarily set up the required mail merge fields. This is accomplished by adding the Range object of the current Selection and the specified field name to the Field connection of the MailMerge object as follows:

```
objDocument.MailMerge.Fields.Add objWord.Selection.Range, "FirstName"
```

If space is needed between fields as in the case of the first and last names, simply use the TypeText method of the Selection object like this:

```
objWord.Selection.TypeText " "
```

Once all the merge fields have been defined, they need to be set to an AutoTextEntry object. An AutoTextEntry is a section of text that is stored in an object along with all its formatting and can be used again in the document. Since at this point the document consists of nothing but these field definitions, the AutoTextEntry can be created from the Content property of the document as follows:

```
Set objAutoTextEntry = objWord.NormalTemplate.AutoTextEntries.Add("Labels", _
objDocument.Content)
```

Once this is accomplished, the Content property of the document is erased by invoking the Delete method, and the data source is set by invoking the OpenDataSource method. Finally, the CreateNewDocument method of the MailingLabel object creates the labels based on the Avery number passed in as a string.

The code in Listing 7-7 produces the output shown in Figure 7-5.

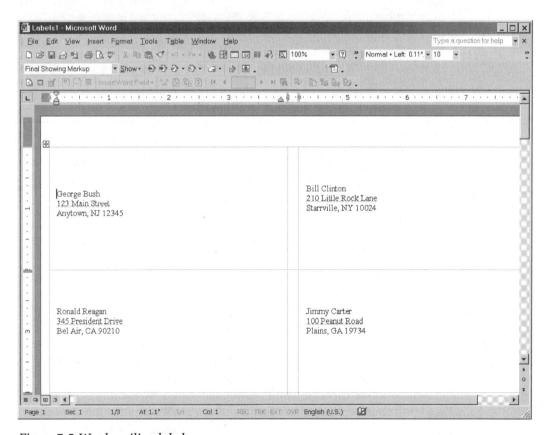

Figure 7-5. Word mailing labels

NOTE   *For more information on programming the Microsoft Word object model, check out* Word 2000 VBA Programmer's Reference, *by Duncan Mackenzie et al. (Wrox. ISBN: 1-86100-255-6).*

Microsoft Excel

Excel is a far more flexible choice for outputting data than Word. Excel stores data in rows and columns. Because it is an analysis tool, it has the functionality to perform different types of data manipulation and statistical summarization.

Spreadsheet Export

It is quite common for users to want their reports exported to Excel. Many of my clients *only* want their reports exported to Excel—no printed output is even necessary. These clients are normally Excel power users who can make any necessary changes to the output and print the report themselves. When they ask for this, find out what they plan to do with the data as there is more than one way to create an Excel dump.

TIP   *Exports to Excel should not be a requested feature. They should be available for every report whether requested or not. Even if users don't realize they need Excel dumps at specification time, they will down the road. Anticipate their needs and suggest it first. Better yet, just put it in the application as a standard feature. An Excel export on a report is like a horn in a car.*

There are two ways you can export data to Excel. One way is simply to dump the raw data to a spreadsheet to allow for further analysis. Crystal Reports will do this with a simple call to an Export method (see Chapter 4) and will respect the text formatting, but it will only include subtotals as formula fields that are in group headers and footers. Other reporting tools like VS-View and Preview require you to write a special export routine that either loops through the data source for the report or populates the spreadsheet as the report is being printed. In all cases, the result is a dump of the same data printed in the report. The only drawback to these export routines is that some or all of the totals and subtotals are simply numbers in the worksheet and not formulas. Therefore, if your user changes a detail number in the export spreadsheet, the total and subtotal will not recalculate.

Clients invariably need the spreadsheet to do further data analysis and run "what-if" scenarios. If you find that your users have these needs, you may wish to use Microsoft Excel as your report writer exclusively. Examine the code in Listing 7-8. This report is the Excel version of the Crystal report created program-matically in Chapter 4. The report extracts all the freight information for all customers and prints the details with a subtotal by customer and a grand total at the end. The result is shown in Figure 7-6.

Listing 7-8. Excel Output

```
Dim oConn As New ADODB.Connection
Dim oRS As ADODB.Recordset
Dim objExcel As Excel.Application
Dim objWB As Excel.Workbook
Dim objWS As Excel.Worksheet
Dim cSQL As String
Dim cConnectString As String
Dim cCompanyName As String
Dim cGrandTotal As String
Dim cFormula As String
Dim iRow As Integer
Dim iStartRow As Integer

cConnectString = "Provider=SQLOLEDB.1;Integrated Security=SSPI;" & _
                "Persist Security Info=False;" & _
                "Initial Catalog=EnterpriseReports;" & _
                "Data Source=SETON-VBNET"

oConn.ConnectionString = cConnectString
oConn.Open

cSQL = "SELECT Customers.CompanyName, Customers.ContactName, " & _
      "Orders.RequiredDate, Orders.Freight " & _
      "FROM { oj Northwind.dbo.Customers Customers " & _
      "INNER JOIN Northwind.dbo.Orders Orders ON " & _
      "Customers.CustomerID = Orders.CustomerID} " & _
      "ORDER BY Customers.CompanyName ASC"
```

```
Set oRS = oConn.Execute(cSQL)

Set objExcel = CreateObject("Excel.Application")
objExcel.Visible = True

Set objWB = objExcel.Workbooks.Add

Set objWS = objWB.Worksheets(1)

iRow = 1
cGrandTotal = "@SUM("

With objWS
    .Cells(iRow, "A").Value = "Company"
    .Cells(iRow, "B").Value = "Contact"
    .Cells(iRow, "C").Value = "RequiredDate"
    .Cells(iRow, "D").Value = "Freight"

    .Cells(iRow, "A").Font.Bold = True
    .Cells(iRow, "B").Font.Bold = True
    .Cells(iRow, "C").Font.Bold = True
    .Cells(iRow, "D").Font.Bold = True
End With

iRow = iRow + 1


Do While Not oRS.EOF

    If cCompanyName <> oRS("CompanyName") Then

        If cCompanyName <> vbNullString Then

            cFormula = "@SUM(D" & iStartRow & ":D" & iRow - 1 & ")"

            objWS.Cells(iRow, "E").Font.Bold = True
            objWS.Cells(iRow, "E").Value = cFormula
            iRow = iRow + 1
```

```
                    cGrandTotal = cGrandTotal & "E" & iRow - 1 & "+"

            End If

            iStartRow = iRow

            cCompanyName = oRS("CompanyName")

            objWS.Cells(iRow, "A").Value = cCompanyName
            objWS.Cells(iRow, "B").Value = oRS("ContactName")


        End If

        objWS.Cells(iRow, "C").Value = Format(oRS("RequiredDate"), "dd-mmm-yyyy")
        objWS.Cells(iRow, "D").Value = oRS("Freight")

        iRow = iRow + 1

        oRS.MoveNext

Loop

cGrandTotal = cGrandTotal & "E" & iRow & ")"
cFormula = "@SUM(D" & iStartRow & ":D" & iRow - 1 & ")"

With objWS
    .Cells(iRow, "E").Font.Bold = True
    .Cells(iRow, "E").Value = cFormula

    iRow = iRow + 1
    .Cells(iRow, "F").Font.Bold = True
    .Cells(iRow, "F").Value = cGrandTotal

    .Range("A1:F" & iRow).Columns.AutoFit
End With
```

	A	B	C	D	E	F	
890	White Clover Markets	Karl Jablonski	14-Aug-96	4.56			
891			29-Nov-96	23.29			
892			9-May-97	59.13			
893			21-Apr-97	15.28			
894			7-Apr-97	60.18			
895			11-Dec-97	81.88			
896			20-Oct-97	139.34			
897			19-Nov-97	102.55			
898			27-Nov-97	21.72			
899			8-Aug-97	16.34			
900			24-Mar-98	162.95			
901			27-Feb-98	14.93			
902			15-May-98	606.19			
903			29-May-98	44.72			
904					1353.06		
905	Wilman Kala	Matti Karttunen	5-May-98	0.75			
906			6-Mar-98	0.82			
907			10-Mar-98	8.5			
908			26-Mar-98	38.11			
909			27-Aug-97	0.75			
910			16-Oct-97	22.76			
911			18-Nov-97	16.72			
912					88.41		
913	Wolski Zajazd	Zbyszek Piestrzeniewicz	20-Jan-98	23.79			
914			22-Aug-97	80.65			
915			2-Jan-97	3.94			
916			11-Mar-98	26.29			
917			4-Mar-98	12.04			
918			17-Apr-98	20.31			
919			21-May-98	8.72			
920					175.74		
921						64942.69	

Sheet1 / Sheet2 / Sheet3 /

Figure 7-6. Excel report

Note that the individual freight details are in Column D, while the subtotals are in Column E and the grand total is in Column F. The reason for this organization is that financial professionals will often want to highlight ranges of numbers and see the total (or average, etc.) in the lower-right side of the Excel status bar. Keeping each subtotal number in a separate column prevents double counting of numbers.

NOTE   *Cross tab reports are often mapped to Excel PivotTable objects. For a discussion of PivotTables, see Chapter 8.*

Graphing

Excel has very powerful graphing capabilities that can be built into your application using VBA. The advantage of using Excel graphing is that you can export the summary data to the graph on one worksheet and then use that data for the generation of the graph on another worksheet. This way your power users have the underlying data for the graph available to them should they want to create their own graphs using the Chart Wizard. The code shown in Listing 7-9 illustrates how to create a bar graph using Excel.

Listing 7-9. Excel Graphing

```
Dim oConn As New ADODB.Connection
 Dim oRS As ADODB.Recordset
 Dim objExcel As Excel.Application
 Dim objWB As Excel.Workbook
 Dim objWS As Excel.Worksheet
 Dim objChartObj As Excel.Chart
 Dim objSourceRange As Excel.Range
 Dim cSQL As String
 Dim cConnectString As String
 Dim x As Integer

 Screen.MousePointer = vbHourglass

 cConnectString = "Provider=SQLOLEDB.1;Integrated Security=SSPI;" & _
                  "Persist Security Info=False;" & _
                  "Initial Catalog=Northwind;" & _
                  "Data Source=SETON-VBNET"
```

```
oConn.ConnectionString = cConnectString
oConn.Open

cSQL = "SELECT MONTH(Orders.RequiredDate) AS MonthYr, " & _
       "SUM(Orders.Freight) AS FreightTotal " & _
       "FROM Orders " & _
       "WHERE Year(Orders.RequiredDate) = 1997 " & _
       "GROUP BY MONTH(Orders.RequiredDate) " & _
       "ORDER BY MONTH(Orders.RequiredDate)"

Set oRS = oConn.Execute(cSQL)

x = 1

Set objExcel = CreateObject("Excel.Application")

Set objWB = objExcel.Workbooks.Add

Set objWS = objWB.Worksheets.Add

Do While Not oRS.EOF

    objWS.Cells(x, 1) = Chr(39) & Format(oRS("MonthYr") & "/01", "mmmm")
    objWS.Cells(x, 2) = Val(oRS("FreightTotal"))

    x = x + 1

    oRS.MoveNext
Loop


' Determine the size of the range and store it.
Set objSourceRange = objWS.Range("A1:B" & x - 1)

' Create a new chart.
Set objChartObj = objExcel.Charts.Add

With objChartObj
```

```
   .ChartType = xlColumnClustered

   ' Set the range of the chart.
   .SetSourceData Source:=objSourceRange, PlotBy:=xlColumns

   ' Specify that the chart is located on a new sheet.
   .Location Where:=xlLocationAsNewSheet

   ' Create and set the title; set title font.
   .HasTitle = True

   With .ChartTitle
       .Characters.Text = "Freight Charges by Month - 1997"
       .Characters.Font.Color = vbRed
       .Font.Size = 16
   End With

   ' Delete the legend.
   .HasLegend = False

   With .SeriesCollection(1)
       .ApplyDataLabels Type:=xlDataLabelsShowValue
       .DataLabels.NumberFormat = "#,##0"
   End With

   .Export App.Path & "\mychart.jpg", "JPEG"

End With

oRS.Close
Set oRS = Nothing

objExcel.Visible = True

Screen.MousePointer = vbDefault
```

This code produces the graph shown in Figure 7-7.

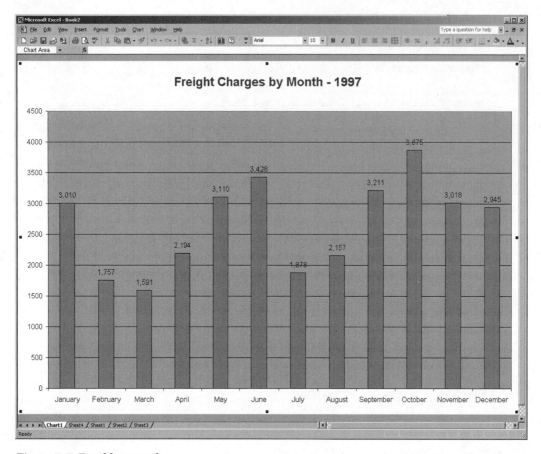

Figure 7-7. Excel bar graph

Note the Export method, which takes as parameters both a filename and a file type. Excel can export to GIF, JPEG, TIF, and PNG. Unfortunately, this doesn't seem to be documented anywhere.

Grid Dumping

Most applications display their data in one of the various grid controls that are on the market. Grid controls are useful for allowing users to first filter their data and then edit that data by selecting the record in the grid control and launching an edit form. It is helpful to users to add a generic print button for every grid control in the application. This way if a user has selected a group of records and sorted them in the grid, the ability to actually print out these records is a tremendous asset. Because the user may have sorted the records independent of the ORDER BY sort used in the underlying data object—assuming there is an underlying data object and the grid wasn't populated by an array—it's best to traverse the rows and column of the grid than to look toward a data source. The downside here is that you'll need a somewhat different routine for every brand of grid control you use, although some grid controls have export methods built in. Hopefully you'll have standardized on just one and won't change it very often. I've used the Janus grid (http://www.janusys.com) since mid-2001. The code shown in Listing 7-10 illustrates how a Janus grid control can be passed to a routine and its data exported to Excel.

Listing 7-10. Janus Grid Control Excel Dump

```
Sub ExportGrid(grGrid As GridEX)
    Dim objExcel As Excel.Application
    Dim objWB As Excel.Workbook
    Dim objWS As Excel.Worksheet
    Dim iRows As Integer
    Dim iCols As Integer
    Dim x As Integer
    Dim y As Integer
    Dim vntData As Variant

    Set objExcel = CreateObject("Excel.Application")

    Set objWB = objExcel.Workbooks.Add

    Set objWS = objWB.Worksheets(1)

    grGrid.Redraw = False

    iRows = grGrid.RowCount
    iCols = grGrid.Columns.Count

    For y = 1 To iCols

        vntData = grGrid.Columns(y).Caption

        objWS.Cells(1, y) = vntData

    Next y
```

```
For x = 1 To iRows

    For y = 1 To iCols

        grGrid.Row = x

        vntData = "" & grGrid.Value(y)

        If Not IsNull(vntData) Then

            If IsNumeric(vntData) And _
                vntData <> Empty And _
                InStr(vntData, ")") = 0 Then

                objWS.Cells(x + 1, y) = CDbl(vntData)

            Else

                If IsNumeric(Mid(vntData, 1, 1)) And _
                    Occurs(vntData, "/") = 2 Then

                    If IsDate(CStr("" & vntData)) Then
                        objWS.Cells(x + 1, y) = Format(CStr(vntData), _
                                "mm/dd/yyyy")
                    Else
                        objWS.Cells(x + 1, y) = Chr(39) & vntData
                    End If

                Else

                    objWS.Cells(x + 1, y) = Chr(39) & vntData

                End If

            End If

        End If

    Next y

Next x
```

```
grGrid.Redraw = True

objExcel.Columns.AutoFit

objExcel.Visible = True
```

End Sub

Because every grid works differently, you'll need to customize this code for your own grid's properties and methods. Most bound grids only retrieve records as they are needed for display. This means that if your grid is bound to a data source that contains 1,000 records, only a portion of those records may be present in the grid at any one time. Thus, the row count may only return 200 or 300 records. In these cases you'll need to make the grid access all the records in the data source before running the export. Usually, though, your grid should not be bound to a data source of more than a few hundred records, as anything more is an inefficient use of server resources.

TIP   *Like the Excel export for reports, grid exports are one of those features that you should just include in an application before a client realizes that they need it. Because the functionality exists in a generic routine, the addition of this feature simply involves the addition of an extra button and one line of code to invoke the export function. Clients will be impressed with your foresight when you demo this option to them.*

Third-Party Alternatives

While you could always use ActiveX Automation to create and write to spreadsheets, the restriction is that you'll need to have Excel installed in order to accomplish this. Since you cannot assume this for widely distributed systems, or perhaps you simply don't want to deal with the overhead of instantiating Excel objects, there is an alternative. ActiveReports has an object called SpreadBuilder that allows you to create Excel files without Excel. See the sidebar entitled "SpreadBuilder" in Chapter 6 for more details.

You can also turn to the third-party market for using Excel as a report writer. Active XL ReportPro from AfalinaSoft (http://www.afalinasoft.com) offers this functionality. Using Active XL ReportPro, you can create an Excel file as a template and determine what data elements fill what columns as well as specify grouping, sorting, and subtotaling. Crosstab (PivotTable) reports are supported as well.

Active XL ReportPro has an excellent demo project that you download along with the evaluation copy from their Web site. Runtime distribution requires only one OCX file weighing in at 495K.

NOTE *For more information on programming the Microsoft Excel object model, check out* Definitive Guide to Excel VBA *by Michael Kofler (Apress. ISBN: 1-89311-579-8) and* Excel 2002 VBA Programmer's Reference *by John Green et al. (Wrox. ISBN: 1-86100-570-9).*

Microsoft Offers Tools That Integrate Office XP with .NET

Microsoft is offering two tools that will help developers to integrate XML Web services with Office XP applications. The first tool is the Office XP Web Services Toolkit. The second tool is the Smart Tag Enterprise Resource Toolkit. You can use these tools to tie XML Web services data directly into Office XP to improve the amount and type of information available to users.

Microsoft is touting that incorporating XML Web services into popular Office applications is a key stage in the .NET rollout, as it brings Web services into everyday computing.

The Microsoft Office XP Web Services Toolkit lets you integrate Web services into Office XP applications using the VBA editor. According to Microsoft, the toolkit lets you link an Office XP application to a Web service with one click.

The Microsoft Smart Tag Enterprise Resource Toolkit works like a road map to help you plan, design, and launch smart tags within your company's computing environment. The download includes an example (complete with source code) that shows effective ways to work with smart tags and Web services. Also included is a set of white papers on planning and launching enterprise smart tags.

The Office XP Web Services Toolkit and the Smart Tag SDK are both available for free download from the Microsoft Web Site at
`http://msdn.microsoft.com/library/default.asp?url=/nhp/`
`Default.asp?contentid=28000550.`

The information for the Office XP Web Services Toolkit and the Smart Tag Enterprise Resource Toolkit can be found under the Essential Information heading on the right-hand side of the Web page.

Microsoft Access

Microsoft Access is one of the most commonly used Office development tools, and for very good reason. It includes a fairly robust database engine, form designers, macros, a VBA editor, support for linking to ODBC databases, and reporting tools. In fact, Access is so popular that it is often used to develop applications, and there are whole books dedicated to building applications in Access. Why am I mentioning this? Simple. Anything you can do with an Access database can be called from inside a Visual Basic (or .NET) application. That includes any object (tables, queries, reports, functions, etc.) that can be referenced via the Access Application object.

One of the more typical scenarios I run into is that a client has developed an application in Visual Basic that uses an Access database. The consumer who purchased the application from one such client has since developed a number of very nice reports and would like to have these reports integrated into the Visual Basic application. This leaves the developer with an interesting choice: Rewrite the reports using Crystal, Active Reports, VS View, or any of the other tools, or leave the reports in the database and call them from Visual Basic. While this is not an efficient solution, often the developer has to make use of such things to meet the client's wishes. Where possible it is best to avoid this scenario by presenting alternatives (such as rewriting).

I bet your head just spun around. That's right, I said "call them from Visual Basic." In truth, Access Reports can be called from any of the Office suite of applications. You simply need to add the reference "Microsoft Access 10.0 Object Library". With that you have access to all the objects within the Access database, including the reports. We'll talk more about this later on in this chapter.

For now let's focus on getting familiar with Access XP's report features and wizards. One of the nice features about Access is that you can create reports in it with very little effort thanks to the Report Wizard. You can even change the design of the report based on the set of templates provided.

To create an Access Report, you must first have a minimum of one table defined. You can then start building a report by selecting the Insert | Report menu option. This will open the New Reports dialog box. This dialog box, shown in Figure 7-8, displays a list of several choices:

- *Design View:* This option allows you to build a report yourself by selecting fields and controls and adding them to sections.

- *Report Wizard:* This option uses a wizard to help you build a fully functional report based on the design of one of the many templates.

- *AutoReport: Columnar:* This option automatically lays the fields out in a columnar fashion in a report view. Each field in this report appears on a separate line with a label.

- *AutoReport: Tabular:* This option automatically lays the fields out in a tabular fashion in a report view. Each field in this report is displayed as a single line with the field names printed at the top of the page.

- *Chart Wizard:* This option uses a wizard to help you build a fully functional chart report based on the fields selected from a specified table.

- *Label Wizard:* This option uses a wizard to help you build a fully functional label report.

Figure 7-8. Access Report Selection dialog box

Let's start by talking about the AutoReport features first. These features are designed to help get a novice up to speed with reports, and they require very little effort. These reports are also formatted as if they required very little effort. Traditionally you would use a report like this to dump data for quick display purposes or to cut and paste the fields from this report to another report. These reports are very simple and self-explanatory.

Next we'll cover the wizards, as these menu options actually help you produce a report that you could find useful. The Report Wizard begins by displaying a form that contains all the tables and queries (in Access you can generate a report using a query as well as table) in a combo box; below the combo box are two list boxes, one to display the available fields and the other to display the fields selected (see Figure 7-9). Once you have selected the fields to include in your report, you must now choose any grouping levels you wish to set.

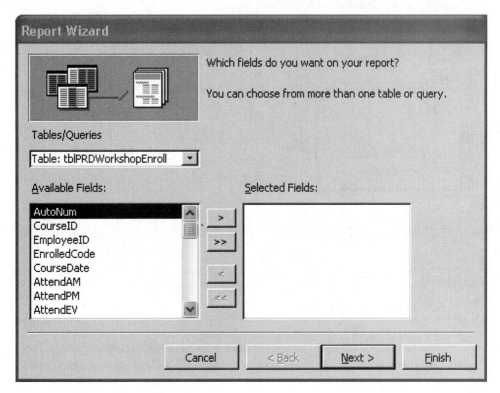

Figure 7-9. Access Report Wizard

Following the selection of any groupings, you must choose a sort order. If no sort order is specified, then the report will default to the current table sort. Next you must choose a report layout style. This means a Tabular, Columnar, or Justified report. After this selection, you must then choose a report style (see Figure 7-10).

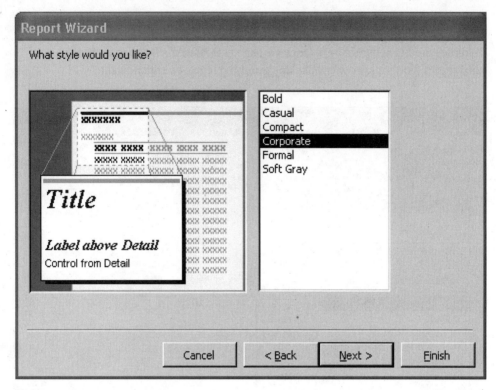

Figure 7-10. Report dialog box

The last step is to save the report under a name of your choosing and, if you wish, to preview the report. Once you have saved the report, you can call it from anywhere within the Access application.

The Label Wizard is another wizard that functions in much the same manner as the standard Report Wizard. This wizard is designed to create mailing labels based on industry standard sizes. The first form (see Figure 7-11) allows for selection of the label product, size, and number across information. What's very interesting about this is that you can also filter the list of available label formats by manufacturer.

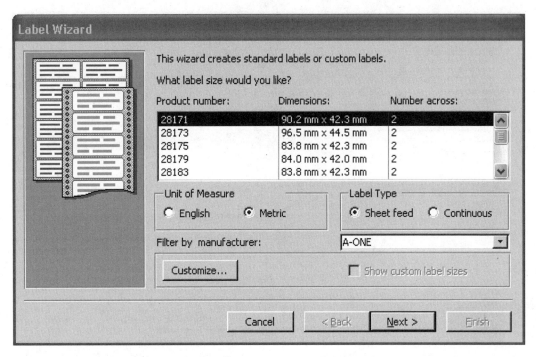

Figure 7-11. Access Label Report Wizard

Clicking the Next button will move you to the Font Selection screen. After selecting the font for your label, you can now move on to the field selection. Select the fields to appear on your mailing label. Fields are displayed in curly braces ({}) when you select them. You navigate rows by using the Enter key, and you can add punctuation (such as commas) between fields (see Figure 7-12).

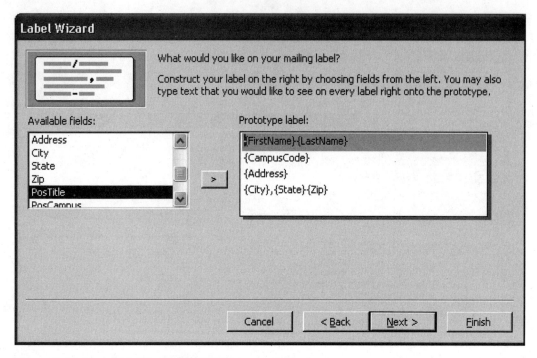

Figure 7-12. Access Mailing Label Field Layout dialog box

The final steps include selecting a field sort order, saving the report, and doing a preview.

Finally, we move on to the more common approach to designing reports, which is using the Access Report Design View. The Report Design View is the more common way of developing a report in Access (see Figure 7-13). Using the wizards can save you time, but eventually, like all tools designed to get us working faster, they fall down in their ability to be flexible.

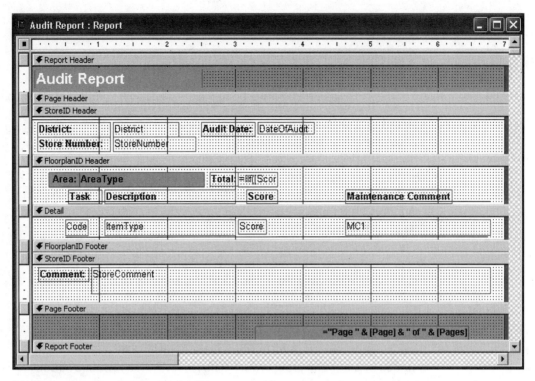

Figure 7-13. Access Report Design View

Now things are going to start getting interesting. Access Reports are designed much like any other form in Visual Basic. You have a toolbox (see Figure 7-14), which contains all the controls that may be added to a report.

Figure 7-14. Access Report Designer Toolbox

The controls you can place on a report are as follows:

- *Label:* Labels are the standard control used for displaying text. Generally a label is an unbound control.

- *Text box:* Text boxes are often used to represent data results pulled from a recordset. The contents of a text box control are often dynamic and will change as each record is iterated.

- *Option group:* Option groups are used to group controls (generally radio buttons, but any control can be used) that share a common meaning. For example, Gender makes an excellent option group, with radio buttons for "Male" and "Female".

- *Toggle button:* Toggle buttons are buttons that may appear in the up (unpressed) or down (pressed) position and are used to represent an on or off state.

- *Option button:* Option buttons are more commonly referred to by Visual Basic programmers as radio buttons. Option buttons are generally surrounded by an option group, which helps identify that only one option may be selected for this group.

- *Check box:* Check boxes are most commonly used to represent Boolean values on reports. While standard check boxes can have three states— on, off, or not selectable—in a report you will generally only use two states—on or off.

- *Combo box:* Combo boxes are most often used to select criteria. In Access you can use a combo box within a report to ultimately control the results.

- *List box:* List boxes work just like combo boxes, but with one notable exception: Within a list box you can have multiple selections.

- *Command button:* Command buttons are standard windows buttons.

- *Image:* Images can be used within the report or as a watermark (i.e., background image).

- *Unbound object frame:* Frame into which an object may be inserted; these objects are not tied to a database connection.

- *Bound object frame:* Frame into which an object may be inserted; these objects are tied to a database connection.

- *Page break:* Inserts a page break within a report.

- *Tab control:* This control allows you to group controls by tabs. Under each tab section, different controls will be displayed. These are common in many of the dialog boxes Office uses and were predominantly used in Access 97.

- *Subform/Subreport:* A subform or subreport control allows you to link another report inside the current report you are developing. By placing a subreport in the middle of a detail section, you can force a subreport to be run with different criteria passed from the master report for each row detail.

- *Line:* Graphic element for drawing lines. You can control the width and thickness for different effects.

- *Rectangle:* Graphic element for drawing rectangles. You can also control the width and thickness of a rectangle in a similar fashion to that of a line for different effects.

- *More controls:* This option will open a dialog box, which will display other installed and registered ActiveX controls for you to choose from. If you have Visual Basic installed on the same computer as Access, you may notice a number of Visual Basic controls in this window.

Now that you are familiar with the controls, you can begin to create your own reports. First, before you jump right into designing a report, you need to have a table or query that will serve as the basis for the report.

NOTE *Please note that in Access Reports the entire report can have a query, but each control that is present on the report may also have its own individual queries assigned to it.*

There are several ways to assign a query to a report. The first method is to click the New button from the Access Database window, which opens the New Reports dialog box described earlier in this section. This time, instead of using a wizard, however, you can select a table or query for the report and click the Design View option. This opens the Report Designer. The table or query results are displayed in a smaller window (see Figure 7-15) so you can choose which elements of the table or query to include in the report.

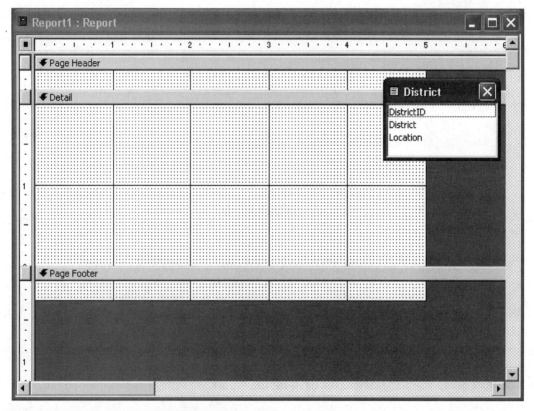

Figure 7-15. Access Report Designer with the table or query results

The source of the data behind a form or report is specified by the object's RecordSource property. The RecordSource property can be a table, a query, or a SQL statement. You can display subsets of the data contained in the object's RecordSource property by using the Filter property to filter the data or by using the wherecondition argument of the OpenReport method. When you have specified a record source for a report, you can use the field list (in Report Design View) to drag fields from the object's source of data to the report.

Subreport Controls

Reports can also contain a subreport control that contains another report. This control makes it possible for you to display related records from another form or report within a main report. A common example of this is a customer's report that includes a subreport containing customer orders. You use the SourceObject property of the subreport control to specify the report that you want displayed in the control.

The report in the subreport control can share a common field, known as the *linking field*, with the records displayed in the main report. The linking field is used to synchronize the records between the subreport and the main report. For example, if the record sources for an Orders subreport and a Customers main report both contain a CustomerID field, this would be the common field that links the two reports.

To specify the linking field, you use the LinkChildFields property of the subreport control and LinkMasterFields property of the main report. However, the easiest way to create a linked subreport is to open the main report in Design View, drag the appropriate report from the Database window to the main report, and then release the mouse button.

You use the Report property of a subreport control to refer to controls on a subreport. The following code illustrates how to get the value of a control on a subreport by using VBA. The RecordCount property gets the number of records contained in the recordset associated with a subreport control.

```
lngNumProducts = Reports!SuppliersAndProducts!SubReport1.Form.Recordset.RecordCount
```

Report Sections

Before you can begin building a report, it's a good idea to know about the sections that comprise a report. The three main sections of a report are Header, Detail, and Footer. Each section contains multiple areas. For example, the Header and Footer sections can include the following:

- *Report Header/Footer:* This is the header for the overall report and is printed only once.

- *Page Header/Footer:* This is the page header for the report and is printed on each page.

- *Grouping Header/Footer:* This is a grouping header and is printed when the grouping criteria changes.

The only report section that is not variable in the number of subsections it can include is the Report Detail section. This is the section where you place the controls that will display the report data in a repetitive format.

Sections are controlled by creating report grouping. You can have a group header without a corresponding group footer. To create a sort or group, you right-click the left-hand block, which denotes a section, and from the pop-up menu select Sorting and Grouping. This brings up a dialog box (see Figure 7-16) that allows you to sort and group based on fields within the report query.

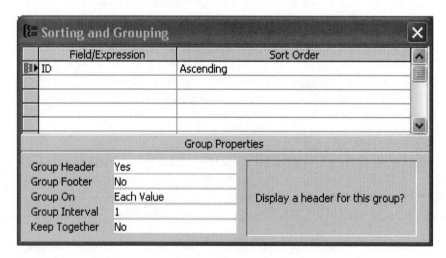

Figure 7-16. Access Sorting and Grouping dialog box

Report Events

Within each Access Report you create are also events that you can control:

- *Report_Activate:* Fired when the report first receives focus

- *Report_Deactivate:* Fired when the report loses focus

- *Report_Open:* Fired when the report is opened

- *Report_Close:* Fired when the report is being closed

- *Report_Error:* Fired when the report errors

- *Report_NoData:* Fired when a report has no data

- *Report_Page:* Fired during a page break

The most commonly used report method is Report_Open. This event is the first that occurs for a report, before the report begins printing or displaying. In fact, it happens even before the query underlying the report is run. When a report is opened in Access, a list of parameters is passed by default.

```
DoCmd.OpenReport cReport, acViewNormal, "", "", "[CustomerID]=19"
```

This list, named OpenArgs, is a read-only list that is passed to the called routine. Although in some cases it does not appear in the Intellisense feature, it's really there. Using our previous example of a customer and orders report, imagine that we wish to open a report filtered for a single customer. In the Report_Open method, we can do this by setting the Filter property:

```
Private Sub Report_Open(Cancel As Integer)
    Me.Filter = Me.OpenArgs ' [CustomerID] = 19
    Me.FilterOn = True
End Sub
```

The Report_Activate event is fired as the report is being displayed, much like Report_Deactivate is fired upon destruction of the report. Generally we have not worked with the Report_Activate or Report_Deactivate events. However, a good use of these events would be to create temporary working tables in Activate and destroy them in Deactivate.

The Report_Close event occurs as the report is closing, before the Deactivate event occurs. Generally, it is in this event that you would do any cleanup (such as closing another open form). For example, you may have created some temporary tables and wish to delete them before exiting the report.

```
Private Sub Report_Close()
    ' Drop Temporary Tables
    oADOConnection.Execute("DROP TABLE tmpWorking")
End Sub
```

The Report_Error event is fired when a report generates an error. You can handle runtime errors that trigger an Error event by adding code to a report's

Error event procedure. The Error event is triggered by any runtime error that is generated either in the Microsoft Access interface or by the Microsoft Jet database engine. The Error event won't trap errors in your Visual Basic code.

The Report_NoData event is fired if no records meet the criteria of the recordset underlying a report's record source. The report then prints without any data and displays #Error in the report's Detail section. To eliminate this problem, you can code the NoData event of the report as shown here:

```
Private Sub Report_NoData(Cancel As Integer)
    MsgBox "There is no data for this report. Canceling report..."
    Cancel = True
End Sub
```

The Page event gives you the opportunity to do something immediately before the formatted page is sent to the printer. An example of the use of the Page event would be to place a border around a page, as shown here:

```
Private Sub Report_Page()
    Me.Line (0, 0)-(Me.ScaleWidth, Me.ScaleHeight - 10), _
        RGB(255, 0, 0), B
End Sub
```

NOTE *You can use the Page event to do a variety of things including changing the paper bin.*

Access Report Events Within Report Sections

Just as a report has events, so do each of the sections of the report. The three sections all fire these events:

- *Format:* Allows for custom formatting of a report section

- *Print:* Allows for special print handling

- *Retreat:* Allows for moving back to a previous section

The Format event happens after Access has selected the data to be included in a report section, but before it formats or prints the data. Using the Format event, you can affect the layout of the section, calculate results of data in the section, and more before the section actually prints.

```
Private Sub Detail2_Format(Cancel As Integer, FormatCount As Integer)

    ' Determine whether to print detail record or "Continued."

    ' Show Continued text box if at maximum number of
    ' detail records for page.
    If (Me.txtRow > Me.txtRowsPerPage) Then _
        ' Set Continue Label Flag
        ' Using this flag we'll display a label with the
        ' words "Continued On Next Page" and hide
        ' the rest of the controls on this detail print ONLY
        Continue = True
    End If
    ' Check for Continue and if the Continue flag is set
    ' Then show page break and hide controls in detail record.
    If (Me.txtRow > Me.txtRowsPerPage) Then _
            ' Make Continue Label Visible
            Me.txtContinue.Visible = True

            ' Make Page Break Visible
            Me.txtDetailPageBreak.Visible = True

            ' Hide Controls
            txtCustomerID.Visible = False
            txtPaymentType.Visible = False
            txtAmountPd.Visible = False
            txtPymtType.Visible = False

            ' Don't move to Next Record in this print, will resume in next page.
            .NextRecord = False
    End If
End Sub
```

TIP   *By placing logic in the Format event of a report's Detail section, you can control what happens as each line of a Detail section is printed.*

The code in the Print event is executed when the data has been formatted to print in a section, but before it's actually printed. The Print event occurs at the following times for different sections of the report:

- *Detail section:* Just before the data is printed.

- *Group Header:* Just before the Group Header is printed; the Group Header's Print event has access to both the Group Header and the first row of data in the group.

- *Group Footer:* Just before the Group Footer is printed; the Print event of the Group Footer has access to both the Group Footer and the last row of data in the group.

NOTE   *People sometimes get confused about when to place code in the Format event versus when to place code in the Print event. Just remember that if you're doing something that doesn't affect the page layout, you should use the Print event. However, if you're doing something that affects the report's physical appearance (the layout), use the Format event.*

Occasionally with Access, it may be necessary to move back to a previous section before printing, such as when a group's Keep Together property is set to With First Detail or Whole in the Sorting and Grouping dialog box. Access needs to format the Group Header and the first detail record or, in the case of Whole, the entire group. It then determines whether it can fit the section on the current page. It "retreats" from the two sections, and then formats and prints them. The Retreat event occurs for each section. For example:

```
Private Sub Detail_Retreat()
    ' Move Recordset back to previous record when the detail section retreats
    rsTest.MovePrevious
End Sub
```

Use the Retreat event with caution. While very powerful, it can also make it very confusing for you if you're working with an unbound report. In cases like that, you need to be careful that the record pointer remains synchronized with the report. For example, if the record pointer has been advanced and the Retreat event occurs, the record pointer must be moved back to the previous record explicitly.

Changing an Access Report's Data Source

At times you might want to change a report's record source. Doing so allows your users to alter the conditions for your report and transparently modify the query on which the report is based. In some situations this can cause problems, most notably when the fields in the recordset do not match those fields being displayed on the report. In this instance, you would need special code to rebind the report control to the new data field:

```
Private Sub Report_Open(Cancel As Integer)
    ' Determine the Recordsource
    Select Case nReportType
        Case rptStandard
            Me.Recordsource = "SELECT * FROM Customer"
        Case rptPastDue
            Me.Recordsource = "SELECT * FROM Customer WHERE CustomerBalance > 0"
        Case rptCancelled
            Me.Recordsource = "SELECT * FROM Customer WHERE OrderCancelled = 1"
    End Select
End Sub
```

In this code, we use a variable (nReportType), and based on a value (say 1, 2, or 3) we change the SQL statement. In this instance, the SQL statement returns the same fields from the same database; no rebinding is required.

Report Filters

There are two properties within Access reports that are designed to aid the programmer in applying filter conditions to a report. This may sound funny, given that the user can control and filter reports in a variety of ways simply by changing the SQL statement associated with the data source, but there can be a number of reasons for needing a filter. This method works without changing the underlying record source. The properties are as follows:

- *Filter:* This is the filter criteria (such as salary < 10000). This option by itself does not apply the filter. You must set the FilterOn property to True for this filter condition to be applied to a report.

- *FilterOn:* This is a Boolean flag that sets the filter to active.

You can set filtering properties either at design time or at runtime:

```
Private Sub Report_Open(Cancel As Integer)
        'Evaluate which option button was selected
        'Set the Filter and FilterOn properties as appropriate
        Select Case  nReportType
            Case rptStandard
                Me.Filter = ""
                Me.FilterOn = False
            Case rptPastDue
                Me.Filter = "CustomerBalance > 0"
                Me.FilterOn = True
            Case rptCancelled
                Me.Filter = "OrderCancelled = 1"
                Me.FilterOn = True
        End Select
End Sub
```

> **NOTE**   *The code in the first example is much more efficient than the code in the filter listing. In a client/server environment, such as Microsoft SQL Server, with the code in the first listing, only the requested data comes over the network; in the case of the filter, the entire recordset is passed over the wire and the filter is applied when the data arrives at the target machine. The exception to this is a server-side filter. This type of filter is available with Access Data Projects (ADP files).*

Report Sort Orders

Reports may also be sorted in the same fashion that they can be filtered. There are two properties that can be used to control the report sort order:

- *OrderBy:* This is the order criteria (such as LastName). This option by itself does not apply the sort. You must set the OrderByOn property to True for this order condition to be applied to a report.

- *OrderByOn:* This is a Boolean flag that sets the sort order to active.

As with the Filter properties, you can set these report sort order properties at either design or runtime. The OrderBy property augments, rather than replaces, the existing sort order of the report. If the OrderBy property is in conflict with the sort order of the report, the OrderBy property is ignored. For example, if the sort order in the Sorting and Grouping window is set to CompanyName, and the OrderBy property is set to City combined with CompanyName, the OrderBy property is ignored.

```
Private Sub Report_Open(Cancel As Integer)
        'Evaluate which option button was selected
        'Set the OrderBy and OrderByOn properties as appropriate
        Select Case  nReportType
            Case rptStandard
                Me.OrderBy = "CustomerName"
                Me.OrderByOn = True
            Case rptPastDue
                Me.OrderBy = "CustomerName, CustomerBalance"
                Me.OrderByOn = True
            Case rptCancelled
                Me.OrderBy = "CustomerName, OrderCancelledDate"
                Me. OrderBy On = True
        End Select
End Sub
```

Using the Same Report for Summary and Detail Data

Many programmers often create multiple reports that serve to report the same basic information. An example would be creating one report that displays summary only, one that displays detail only, and another that displays both. This approach is rather long winded and totally unnecessary. Because report sections can be optionally hidden or displayed at runtime, you only need to create one report that encompasses all three needs.

For example, in my prepaid telecom billing package, customer service representatives accept payments for a variety of different phone-related services. These services range from home phone service to prepaid Internet access. The result is that any time money is accepted, it has to be deposited into a bank account. From that account the money is drawn to pay the providers. In order for this to work smoothly, the system must have reports that are broken down by payment type (e.g., cash, credit card, moneygram, money order) and which service they are for (e.g., home phone, Internet, cell phone, pager).

This main report combines both the summary (i.e., page and report totals by category) and the transaction detail in the daily deposit report. In the Report_Open event, we can determine the requested report type and then hide or show the sections as desired.

```
Private Sub Report_Open(Cancel As Integer)
        'Evaluate which report type was selected
        Select Case  nReportType
            Case rptFull
                ' Do Nothing, the report is built this way
            Case rptSummary
                Me.Detail.Visible = False
            Case rptDetail
                Me.GroupHeader0.Visible = False
                Me.GroupFooter1.Visible = False
        End Select
End Sub
```

The code begins by opening the report, and, based on the variable nReportType, determines which type of report to print. If Summary is selected, the Visible property of the Detail section is set to False. If the user selects Detail, the Visible property of the Group Header and Footer sections is set to False (it's in the header and footer sections that we calculate the summary information). When Both is selected as the level of detail, no sections are hidden.

Calling an Access Report from Visual Basic or VBA

I mentioned earlier that we can call Access reports from inside VBA or Visual Basic applications. The trick is to use the Access Application object. Once you have created the Access Application object, you have complete control over any features (such as reports) contained within that Access database. Listing 7-11 shows how to call an Access report from a Visual Basic application.

Listing 7-11. Code to Call an Access Report

```
' This example opens an Access database and launches a Report
' Requires that Access runtime files be installed
Sub PrintAccessReport(ByVal cReport As String, Optional cPath As String)
    Dim cPath     As String              ' Application Path
    Dim oApp      As Access.Application  ' Access Application

    ' Set Trap
    On Error Goto Trap

    ' Report Name
    cReport = "Your Report Name"
```

```vb
    ' If no Report Path and Database name we can't locate the report
    If Len(cPath) = 0 Then
        Exit Sub
    End If


    ' Toggle Mouse Pointer
    Screen.MousePointer = vbHourglass


    ' Create Access Application Object
    Set oApp = CreateObject("Access.Application")


    ' Define Path
    If cPath = vbNullString Then
        cPath = "c:\Program Files\Microsoft Office\Office\Samples\Northwind.mdb"
    End If


    With oApp
        ' Open the database
        .OpenCurrentDatabase (cPath)

        ' Open the requested Report
        .DoCmd.OpenReport cReport, acViewPreview

        ' Set the Application Visible (so we can see the report)
        .Application.Visible = True
    End With


    ' Reset Mouse Pointer
    Screen.MousePointer = vbNormal


    ' Quit Application
    oApp.Quit

Exit_Rtn:

    Exit Sub

Trap:
    MsgBox(Err.Description & vbCrlf & _
        "Error Code = " & Err.Number, vbExclamation, "Error")

    Goto Exit_Rtn
End Sub
```

First you must have added the Access Object 10.0 reference to your Visual Basic application. You can then call the PrintAccessReport subroutine with the report name and the full database path to the report. This results in a copy of the Access report being run and displayed.

ReportML

ReportML is an XML-based markup language that describes Access objects using a set of tags to present the object's properties, events, record source, and any other characteristics. The ReportML document is a well-formed XML document, meaning that the document conforms to the minimal set of criteria for an XML document (i.e., it contains a single root element, has opening and closing tags, has no tags that overlap, etc.).

NOTE *For more information on XML, well-formed XML documents, and XML Stylesheet Language Transformations (XSLT), please visit the Microsoft Developers Network (MSDN) Web site at* http://msdn.microsoft.com.

In previous versions of Microsoft Access, you could transform some Access objects into other Access objects by using the Save As dialog box (you could convert a form to a report, for example). You could also export Access objects into a wide variety of formats including text, HTML, Rich Text Format (RTF), and so on. The problem was that these objects weren't extensible, meaning you didn't have the ability to change or alter the properties and attributes of the objects.

Starting with Access XP, you can now export Access objects as a ReportML file, which makes them easier to share between applications. Access datasheets, forms, and reports can be exported using either one or two XML files:

- A ReportML file (specified as ObjectName_report.xml) for describing the properties, format, and other characteristics of the datasheet, form, or report

- Optionally, a data file (ObjectName.xml) if the option to associate data with the object is selected

In addition, by using an XML Stylesheet Language Transformation (XSLT) file with these XML files, you can programmatically transform the exported Access object into another presentation format, reorder the structure of the data or document, or dynamically sort and filter the data. This makes it easy to use these objects in other applications.

Currently, to allow other users to view your Access reports, they must either create a hard copy of the report, have Access installed locally, or use a product feature like the Snapshot Viewer. By using a ReportML version of the report and an XSLT file, you can save the report to the Web, and anyone using a browser (one that supports an XML Document Object Model, or DOM) can view the report as it originally appeared in Access.

In addition, you can use the ReportML file provided by Access as the starting point to further describe your object for use in other applications. Since it is written using XML syntax, you can extend and enhance the object by adding your own elements and attributes to the file to include more detail or granularity in the report.

Before we go much further, let's cover a few XML basics. I think of XML, which stands for Extensible Markup Language, as being HTML on serious steroids. If you've ever looked at HTML, you know what a tag is. For example, <body>, <head>, and <form> are all examples of tags. Tags are embedded in a document as a way of passing information to whatever program will process the document. HTML tags aren't part of the document's content. Instead, the program reading the document finds the tag, determines what that tag means, takes the appropriate action, and processes the content. For example, in a Web page, HTML tags tell a Web browser how the page is to be displayed.

Whereas HTML is about text, XML is about data. If HTML is used for displaying data, then XML is used for describing data. Case-sensitive XML is a metadata specification structure and describes data. In XML, not only can you define an unlimited set of tags, you can also decide on the naming conventions. Listing 7-12 is an example of a simple XML document.

Listing 7-12. A Simple XML Document

```
<?xml version="1.0"?>
    <VideoGame>
        <Players>
            <Player1>Jon Kilburn</Player1>
            <Player2>Carl Ganz</Player2>
        </Players>
    </VideoGame>
```

The first line of the document is the required XML version information. The second line is the document description; in this case it's something simple, "VideoGame". Next, I've created a grouping and named it Players. Within the Players group, I've created elements. As you can see, I'm using XML to "describe" what the document elements are about.

XML documents must be structured, and they contain several key elements made up by the following building blocks: elements, tags, attributes, entities, PCDATA, and CDATA.

Elements are the main building blocks of both XML and HTML documents. Examples of HTML elements are "body" and "table". Examples of XML elements could be "note" and "message". Elements can contain text, other elements, or even be empty.

Tags are used to mark up elements. A starting tag like <element_name> marks the beginning of an element, and an ending tag like </element_name> marks the end of an element. Common examples in HTML would be <html></html> and <form></form>.

Attributes provide extra information about elements. Attributes are a bit different from plain elements; they are actually placed inside the start tag of an element and must always come in name/value pairs. For example, in an HTML document you often use the <img> (or image) tag. A common attribute of the <img> tag is the src (or source) attribute. This attribute is used in conjunction with the image tag to point to the source location of the image to be displayed in the document.

PCDATA stands for *parsed character data.* PCDATA is text that will be parsed by a parser. Tags inside the text will be treated as markup and entities will be expanded. The best way to think of this is to think of the character data found between the start and end tags of an XML element.

CDATA means *character data* and is similar to PCDATA with one major exception: CDATA will not be parsed by a parser. Tags inside the text will not be treated as markup, and entities will not be expanded.

Entities are variables used to define common text. Entity references are references to entities. Most of you are familiar with the HTML entity reference that is used to insert an extra space in an HTML document. Entities are expanded when a document is parsed by an XML parser. Table 7-1 includes the predefined entities in XML.

Table 7-1. Predefined Entities in XML

ENTITY REFERENCE	CHARACTER
&lt;	<
&gt;	>
&amp;	&
&quot;	"
&apos;	'

There are two ways to define the structure of an XML document. The first method is known as a *document type definition* (DTD). The purpose of a DTD is to define the legal building blocks of an XML document. It defines the document structure with a list of legal elements, the order in which they can appear, the elements and attributes (more about these later) that can be used, and other document features. A DTD can be declared inline in your XML document or as an external reference. Listing 7-13 displays an internal DTD.

Listing 7-13. An Internal DTD

```
<?xml version="1.0"?>
<!DOCTYPE note [
  <!ELEMENT note    (to,from,heading,body)>
  <!ELEMENT to      (#PCDATA)>
  <!ELEMENT from    (#PCDATA)>
  <!ELEMENT heading (#PCDATA)>
  <!ELEMENT body    (#PCDATA)>
]>
<note>
<to>Carl Ganz</to>
<from>Jon Kilburn</from>
<heading>Reminder</heading>
<body>Chapter 7 is due this weekend!</body>
</note>
```

This may look complicated, but it is actually very simple to understand. The first line of this sample XML document contains the XML version information. The next line (line 2) defines the document type as "note". In the next line (line 3), !ELEMENT note defines the element "note" as having four elements: "to,from,heading,body". !ELEMENT to (in line 4) defines the "to" element to be of the type "PCDATA". !ELEMENT from (in line 5) defines the "from" element to be of the type "PCDATA" and so on.

Next, let's talk about schemas. An *XML schema* is an independent document that "describes" the data structure. Let's take the conference I attended as our document. If you want to create a conference schema, you need to decide where the schema will reside. Why? Because in the XML namespace of your data document, you have to "point to" the schema that defines each of the tags within the data document. The location of the schema can be anywhere—for example, on your local machine or on a Web site. The XML data document will locate it based on the path to the schema that you provide. Listing 7-14 includes two examples.

Listing 7-14. Schema Examples

```
<?xml version="1.0"?>
<! Schema on local drive>
<Schema xmlns="c:\Apress\ERBook\Chapter 7\ExampleSchema.xml">


<?xml version="1.0"?>
<! Schema on my site>
<Schema xmlns="http://www.VividSoftware/XML/ExampleSchema.xml">
```

Now that you understand a little bit about XML, let's talk about XSLT. During the development of the XML specification, the W3C working group realized that for XML to reach its full potential, a method of transforming XML documents into different formats needed to exist.

At some time or another, an application that has the capability to work with XML documents will need to display or structure the data in a different format than specified in the document. If the only method for accomplishing this task meant programmatically transforming the XML document into the appropriate format by using an XML parser and a programming language, then the power of cross-platform and language-independent XML would be lost.

To accommodate this transformation process, XSLT was created, and many XML parsers now provide full XSLT support. The .NET Framework provides 100 percent compliance with the XSLT version 1.0 specification.

XSLT provides the ability to transform XML documents into different formats that can be consumed by a variety of devices, including browsers, personal digital assistants (PDAs), Web-enabled phones, and other devices that will appear in the near future.

Transformations can also be useful in situations where an XML document's structure does not match up well with an application that will accept the data. An XML document may contain the appropriate data to be imported into a database, but may not be structured in a way that the application performing the import expects. For example, the application may be better prepared to handle element-based XML documents rather than ones with a lot of attributes. Listing 7-15 shows a sample XML document that includes recordset data.

Listing 7-15. Recordset Data in XML Format

```
<?xml version="1.0">
<root>
    <row id="1", fname="Jon", lname="Kilburn"/>
    <row id="2", fname="Carl", lname="Ganz"/>
    <row id="3", fname="Fred", lname="Seyffert"/>
</root>
```

Using XSLT, this document can be transformed into a structure that the application is better suited to work with (see Listing 7-16).

Listing 7-16. Transformed Recordset Data

```xml
<?xml version="1.0">
<root>
  <row>
    <id>1</id>
    <fname>Jon</fname>
    <lname>Kilburn</lname>
  </row>
  <row>
    <id>2</id>
    <fname>Carl</fname>
    <lname>Ganz</lname>
  </row>
  <row>
    <id>3</id>
    <fname>Fred</fname>
    <lname>Seyffert</lname>
  </row>
</root>
```

Suffice it to say that XSLT is very useful. Which brings us back around to ReportML documents. A ReportML document consists of two primary sections: a Prologue section and a Document Element section. The Prologue contains the XML declaration and the DTD, if one is used. The XML declaration is usually in the form <?xml version="1.0" encoding="UTF-8"?>.

NOTE *An XML Schema Definition (XSD) document can be used in place of a DTD to specify the schema or layout of your XML document. The advantage of using an XSD document instead of a DTD is that the XSD utilizes XML syntax. For more information on using document type definitions and XML Schema Definition files with your XML data, see the MSDN Web site (*http://msdn.microsoft.com*).*

The Document Element section begins with the <rptml> element (also called the root element); the root element indicates the start of the other elements, attributes, and data that describe the Access object.

Element and attribute tags provide information on such items as styles, group-level information, printing information, information on controls, and property values. A typical element consists of a start tag, the element data, and an end tag. An attribute is normally contained in the element start tag as a name-value pair and provides additional information about the element. The general form of an element and attribute tag is

```
<START-TAG attribute="value">element data<END-TAG>
```

Table 7-2 lists the type of tags usually used for items in a ReportML document.

Table 7-2. Types of Tags Used in a ReportML Document

OBJECTS	TAG TYPE	EXAMPLE
Form or report sections such as headers, footers	Element	<section>...</section>
Primary object properties such as visibility, can-grow, group-level	Element	<visibility>visible</visibility>
Supporting property information such as datatype	Attribute	<name type="last">Kilburn</name>
Object name ("id") or object types such as Orders_Subreport	Attribute	<report id="Orders_Subreport">

Whenever possible, the Access properties in ReportML have been mapped to similar HTML properties so someone familiar with the layout and elements of an HTML document should be able to understand a ReportML document. For example, ForeColor maps to Color and FontName equals FontFamily.

The ReportML file (ObjectName_report.xml) is created by default when you export a datasheet, form, or report to XML by using the ExportML method.

You can save or persist a ReportML file by setting the appropriate value in the Otherflags option in the ExportXML method. For example, the code in Listing 7-17 exports the table Customers in the current database as XML. The data and schema are exported as separate files, and the schema is in XSD format. The value 32 after the OtherFlags flag persists the ReportML file.

Listing 7-17. Exporting Report Data to a ReportML File

```
ExportML ObjectType:=acExportTable,  DataSource:="Customers", _
DataTarget:="Customers.xml", SchemaTarget:="CustomersSchema.xml", _
OtherFlags:="32"
```

As you can see, exporting your reports as ReportML files provides a consistent way of representing the properties and other attributes of these objects in XML. This can ease the work of moving these objects and the data they contain from one application to another. This can also provide additional options for viewing Access report data.

Report Snapshots

Once you have created an Access report, you can output it as a report snapshot (.snp) to allow users to view it online. A report snapshot contains an exact copy of each page of an Access report and preserves the two-dimensional layout, graphics, and other features of the report. You can then use Snapshot Viewer to view, print, mail, and distribute the report snapshot through Microsoft Internet Explorer.

You can create a report snapshot by using the Save As/Export command on the File menu. Additionally, you can send a report snapshot in electronic mail by using the Send command on the File menu in either Microsoft Access or Snapshot Viewer.

Using the Snapshot Viewer in this way doesn't require an Access license. You can install Snapshot Viewer not only from Access XP/2000, but also as a free download from the Microsoft Access Developer's Web site.

Creating PDF Reports

While Access doesn't natively create PDF reports, you can save them as PDFs if you have purchased a copy of Adobe Acrobat (http://www.Adobe.com). The saving of reports is handled through a special printer driver that converts printed output into PDF format. This is managed through the Adobe Distiller software. Because it is a printer driver, any software that can print can output to a PDF file.

Generally, Distiller will not be your default printer driver, so you have to select the printer driver manually. You can do this either through the menu or using the Printer dialog box. When you click the OK button (from Printer Selection), you are then prompted for the name of the PDF file that you want Distiller to create. The default name is the name of the Access report. If this is a report that you need to keep (such as a daily cash report), you need to manually enter a new filename or the report will be overwritten the next time you save the report.

> **NOTE**   *The Distiller printer driver is very smart in that it allows you to make a number of changes to the report before it is saved in PDF format. One alteration that is worth noting is the use of watermarks. If you wanted to, you could add a custom watermark to inform the customer that the invoice that you are sending them is overdue.*

Reporting Concepts Utilizing Access

For the most part, when you discuss Access as a reporting tool, you may first gravitate toward using the reporting elements such as the Report Designer. In many cases that may be only half the battle, especially when developing enterprise-level reports. A good example of this is that you can use Access as a lightweight database engine.

Consider this scenario: A salesman is traveling on an airplane or train and the trip will leave him disconnected from the corporate database. Yet the salesman is trying to do data analysis for the upcoming client meeting to discuss the sales figures of XYZ widgets in conjunction with the client's particular market niche. The salesman may need to perform more analysis, or perhaps build some bar graphs or any number of other things.

The trick now is to make that salesman's wishes come true. You can do this by dumping data from larger databases directly into Access tables. Using SQL Server the trick would be simple: a Data Transformation Script (DTS) could be run to produce the desired result. Sometimes this may not be available, or you may be interacting with a database back end that doesn't offer such a solution.

To extract a database, you simply need to create the table in the target Access database and then copy the fields over. You can do this with the SELECT INTO SQL statement. For example, if you have a table in a SQL Server database named Employees when you link the table to Access (using the Link Table Manager), the table name is prefaced with "dbo_", so the new name in the linked table is "dbo_Employees". Using this syntax, you could copy the database table over into a new one on the local Access database (see Listing 7-18).

Listing 7-18. Copying Tables from a Linked Database

```
Public Sub CopyTables()
    Dim oCn     As ADODB.Connection
    Dim cSQL    As String

    On Error GoTo Trap
```

```
    ' Get Connection
    Set oCn = CurrentProject.Connection

    ' Build Query
    cSQL = "SELECT dbo_Employees.* INTO Employees FROM dbo_Employees"

    ' Execute the copy
    oCn.Execute (cSQL)

Exit_Rtn:
    Exit Sub

Trap:
    MsgBox Err.Description & vbCrLf & _
        "Error Code = " & Err.Number, vbExclamation, "Error"

    GoTo Exit_Rtn
End Sub
```

This works quite well, and depending on what you may wish to do, you can always use the JOIN clause to create tables whose structures may be totally different from the master database. The SELECT clause also allows you to pick and choose the fields you wish to copy over. However, if you wish to append data to an existing Access database table from a linked table, you can do so by copying a record field by field. While the code in Listing 7-19 works, it is much slower than SELECT INTO.

Listing 7-19. Code to Copy a Recordset One Row and One Field at a Time

```
Sub CopyTable(oRsSource As ADODB.Recordset, oRsTarget As ADODB.Recordset)
    Do While Not oRsSource.EOF
        oRsTarget.AddNew
        ' Copy fields over
        For iLoop = 1 To (oRsSource.Fields.Count - 1)
            ' Ignore the User field
            oRsTarget (iLoop) = oRsSource(iLoop)
        Next iLoop
        oRsTarget.Update
        oRsSource.MoveNext
    Loop
End Sub
```

Another potential problem with this approach is that if the target table has an identity field (or more commonly an AutoNumber in Access), then this may not work either.

E-Mail Tools

E-mail is the foundation for a company's communication infrastructure. Interestingly enough, though, many programmers do not integrate it into their applications. Integrating e-mail functionality into applications for both event notification and reporting can take the usefulness of an application to an entirely new level. I am a strong believer in this technology and urge clients to integrate e-mail into applications instead of coding a proprietary communication or notification mechanism into the application.

One of the main ways e-mail can enhance an application's usefulness is to alert a client of an important event, such as the completion of a job or the failure of a system or process. For example, I have a client for whom I built a headcount system that tracks job applicants throughout the entire recruiting process. There are several dozen steps an applicant must take before coming on board with the organization. The individual steps are recorded as complete by entering the completion date. Depending on the different steps taken, e-mail notifications automatically go out to various individuals. For example, when an applicant successfully completes the background check, an alert e-mail goes out to the applicant, the agency who recruited that applicant, and the human resources department. By doing so, the applicant is kept abreast of his or her status, the recruiting agency is not constantly calling for progress reports of where their candidate stands, and users don't need to create a special e-mail to notify human resources. Everything is accomplished automatically behind the scenes.

The second area where e-mail is important is in the dissemination of reports throughout the enterprise. Reports that are exported to Adobe PDF, Excel, Word, or any other file format can be transmitted via e-mail as an attachment. Of course, it is often preferable for users to download reports rather than receive them as attachments. E-mail can notify them that a report is ready and provide a hyperlink to it. E-mail attachments have their downside as well. They can spread viruses and clog mail servers when users archive and forget them. Many companies scan attachments and block certain file types by default because of virus or Trojan horse problems. Check with your network security administrator before disseminating any reports via e-mail.

Exactly how these e-mails are implemented technically depends on the e-mail package that your client uses. The two most common are Microsoft Outlook and Lotus Notes.

Microsoft Outlook

Sending an e-mail in Outlook is a very simple process. Every e-mail can have a collection of primary recipients, a cc recipient, a subject, a body of text, and multiple attachments. These properties are mapped to the property assignments of the Outlook e-mail class shown in Listing 7-20. The complete code for this class is found with the downloadable source code for this book, available on the Apress Web site (http://www.apress.com).

Listing 7-20. Outlook E-Mail Class

```
Dim objOutlook As New Outlook.Application()
Dim objNameSpace As Outlook.NameSpace
Dim objEmail As Outlook.MailItem
Dim objAttachments As Outlook.Attachments
Dim cCC As String
Dim cSubject As String
Dim cBody As String


Public Property CC() As String
    Get
        CC = objEmail.CC
    End Get
    Set(ByVal Value As String)
        objEmail.CC = Value
    End Set
End Property


Public Property Subject() As String
    Get
        Subject = objEmail.Subject
    End Get
    Set(ByVal Value As String)
        objEmail.Subject = Value
    End Set
End Property


Public Property BodyText() As String
    Get
        BodyText = objEmail.Body
    End Get
    Set(ByVal Value As String)
        objEmail.BodyFormat = Outlook.OlBodyFormat.olFormatPlain
```

```
            objEmail.Body = Value
        End Set
End Property

Public Property BodyHTML() As String
    Get
            BodyHTML = objEmail.Body
        End Get
        Set(ByVal Value As String)
            objEmail.BodyFormat = Outlook.OlBodyFormat.olFormatHTML
            objEmail.Body = Value
        End Set
End Property
```

The AddRecipient method encapsulates Outlook's Recipient collection. As recipients are assigned via the AddRecipient property, they are added to the collection as well.

```
Public Function AddRecipient(ByVal cRecipient As String)
    objEmail.Recipients.Add (cRecipient)
End Function
```

Since it's quite possible to add invalid recipients, the ResolveAll property will reconcile all recipients to Outlook's contact dictionary to determine if they are valid. This rule applies only to those recipients who don't contain a server name. Therefore, Jon Kilburn will be checked against the contact database, whereas jkilburn@vividsoftware.com will not.

```
Public Function ResolveAll() As Boolean
    ResolveAll = objEmail.Recipients.ResolveAll
End Function
```

To begin, you'll first need to create an object reference to the Outlook application itself. Then you'll need a reference to the Messaging Application Programming Interface (MAPI) namespace. MAPI is a standard interface exposed by most mail servers. After that you'll need to create objects to encapsulate both the MailItem object and Attachments collection objects. The method StartOutlook instantiates all of these objects for you and its sister method, CloseOutlook, cleans them up when you're done.

```
Public Function StartOutlook()
    objEmail = objOutlook.CreateItem(Outlook.OlItemType.olMailItem)
```

```
    objNameSpace = objOutlook.GetNamespace("MAPI")
    objNameSpace.Logon(, , True, True)
End Function


Public Function CloseOutlook()

    objOutlook = Nothing
    objNameSpace = Nothing
    objEmail = Nothing
    objAttachments = Nothing

End Function
```

The Save and Send methods store the e-mail in the current user's outbox and then transmit it, respectively.

```
Public Function Save()
    objEmail.Save()
End Function


Public Function Send()
    CType(objEmail, Outlook._MailItem).Send()
End Function
```

Like the Recipient method, AddAttachment adds attachments to the Attachments collection. The Type parameter can have one of three values represented by internal constants: olByReference, which creates the attachment as a shortcut to the file; olByValue, which creates the attachment as a copy of the original item; and olEmbeddedItem, which creates the attachment as an Outlook item.

```
Public Function AddAttachments(ByVal cSource As String, _
                        ByVal iType As Outlook.OlAttachmentType)

    If Dir(cSource) <> String.Empty Then
        Call objEmail.Attachments.Add(cSource, iType)
    End If

End Function
```

Now that you know how the internals of the class work, let's take a look at how it is used from start to finish. Listing 7-21 shows how the e-mail class is instantiated and how its methods are invoked.

Listing 7-21. Outlook E-mail Class in Action

```
Dim objSendEmail As New SendEmail()

With objSendEmail
    .StartOutlook()
    .AddRecipient ("seton.software@verizon.net")
    .Subject = "Test Documents"
    .BodyText = "Attached are some sample documents"
    .AddAttachments("C:\DOCS\Reports\chapter9.doc", _
            Outlook.OlAttachmentType.olByValue)
    .AddAttachments("C:\DOCS\Reports\chapter8.doc", _
            Outlook.OlAttachmentType.olByValue)
    .Save()
    .Send()
    .CloseOutlook()
End With
```

> **NOTE**   *Outlook offers many other features like meeting planning, appointments, and contact management. Each of these options can be controlled via VBA but are beyond the scope of this book. There are several excellent books that explain Outlook VBA, most notably* Outlook 2000 VBA Programmers Reference, *by Dwayne Gifford (Wrox Press. ISBN: 1-86100-253-X).*

Lotus Notes

Lotus Notes is also a popular e-mail application, and about half my corporate clients use it. Its 5.0 release offers a far more powerful programmatic extensibility than its earlier incarnations. The function shown in Listing 7-22 shows how an e-mail is created with Notes.

Listing 7-22. Lotus Notes E-Mail Function

```
Public Function LotusNotesEmail(ByVal cRecipient As String, _
                        ByVal cCopyTo As String, _
                        ByVal cSubject As String, ByVal cBody As String, _
                        Optional vntAttachment As Variant, _
                        Optional vntSaveMessageOnSend As Variant) As Boolean
```

```
Dim objNotes As Object
Dim objNotesDB As Object
Dim objNotesMailDoc As Object
Dim objNotesRichText As Object
Dim objNotesEmbedded As Object
Dim objNotesDir As Object
Dim cPassword As String
Dim cMsg As String
Dim bResult As Boolean
Dim X As Integer
Dim aRecipient() As Variant
Dim aAttachment() As Variant
Dim ValueSALT As String


Const ERROR_NO_LOTUS_NOTES_PASSWORD = 1

ValueSALT = "SALTValue"

bResult = False

If cRecipient = vbNullString And _
   cCopyTo = vbNullString Then

    LotusNotesEmail = bResult

    Exit Function

End If

On Error GoTo ErrorHandler

If IsMissing(vntSaveMessageOnSend) Then
    vntSaveMessageOnSend = True
End If

aRecipient = Parse2Array(cRecipient, ";")


Set objNotes = GetObject("", "Lotus.NotesSession")

cPassword = GetSetting("LotusNotes", "AppInfo", "LotusNotesPassword")
```

```
cPassword = DecryptString(cPassword, ValueSALT)

If cPassword = vbNullString Then
    Err.Raise ERROR_NO_LOTUS_NOTES_PASSWORD
End If

'In order for this line of code not to prompt for a password
'every time it is invoked, the local installation of Lotus Notes
'needs to have the "Don't prompt for a password from
'other Notes-base programs" option checked under File|Tools|User ID
Call objNotes.Initialize(cPassword)


Call SaveSetting("LotusNotes", "AppInfo", "LotusNotesPassword", _
EncryptString(cPassword, ValueSALT))

Set objNotesDir = objNotes.GetDbDirectory("")
Set objNotesDB = objNotesDir.OpenMailDatabase

Set objNotesMailDoc = objNotesDB.CreateDocument

With objNotesMailDoc

    .SaveMessageOnSend = vntSaveMessageOnSend

    Call .AppendItemValue("Form", "Memo")
    Call .AppendItemValue("Subject", cSubject)
    Call .AppendItemValue("SendTo", aRecipient)

    If cCopyTo <> vbNullString Then
        Call .AppendItemValue("CopyTo", cCopyTo)
    End If

    If .HasItem("body") Then
        Set objNotesRichText = .GetFirstItem("body")
    Else
        Set objNotesRichText = .CreateRichTextItem("Body")
    End If

End With

Call objNotesRichText.AppendText(cBody)
Call objNotesRichText.AddNewLine(2)
```

```
    If Not IsMissing(vntAttachment) Then

        aAttachment = Parse2Array(vntAttachment, ";")

        For X = 0 To UBound(aAttachment)
            Set objNotesEmbedded = objNotesRichText.EmbedObject(1454, _
    "", aAttachment(X))
            objNotesMailDoc.CreateRichTextItem ("Attachment" & X)
        Next X

    End If

    Call objNotesMailDoc.Save(True, True)
    Call objNotesMailDoc.Send(True)

    bResult = True

    Set objNotes = Nothing
    Set objNotesDB = Nothing
    Set objNotesMailDoc = Nothing
    Set objNotesRichText = Nothing
    Set objNotesEmbedded = Nothing
    Set objNotesDir = Nothing

    LotusNotesEmail = bResult

Exit Function

ErrorHandler:

    Select Case Err.Number

        Case ERROR_NO_LOTUS_NOTES_PASSWORD
            cMsg = "There is no Lotus Notes password on " & _
                        "file with this application.  & vbCrLf & vbCrLf & _
                        "Please enter the correct password and press OK " & _
                        "to save and continue."

            cPassword = InputBox(cMsg, "Notes Password Invalid")

            Resume Next
```

```
      End Select

      LotusNotesEmail = bResult

End Function
```

This version of the Lotus e-mail routine stores the Lotus Notes password in the registry as an encrypted string. The lines

```
cPassword = GetSetting("LotusNotes", "AppInfo", "LotusNotesPassword")

cPassword = DecryptString(cPassword, ValueSALT)
```

retrieve the password and decrypt it. The DecryptString routine is not included with the downloadable source code (from the Apress Web site) as it uses a proprietary encryption algorithm along with the Windows Crypto API. Simply replace this with your own decryption routine if you use one.

SendEmail then instantiates the objNotesMailDoc object, which encapsulates the Recipient, CopyTo, Subject, Body, and Attachment properties. The Recipient parameter can be a series of e-mail addresses separated by a semicolon. The Parse2Array function (see the downloadable source code) returns an array where each e-mail address is an individual element. Likewise, the Attachments parameter may contain multiple attachments separated by a semicolon that are parsed into an array in the same fashion. The CreateRichTextItem method is then used to add each individual element to the objNotesMailDoc object. Finally, the Save method writes the e-mail to the Sent Box and the Send method sends the message.

Disclaimers

Disclaimers are often attached to each e-mail that is sent by an organization, and it is a good idea to attach disclaimers to every document, printed or electronic, that is produced by your system as well. One of my clients attaches the following text to every e-mail sent, in both English and German:

This message is confidential and may be privileged. It is intended solely for the named addressee. If you are not the intended recipient please inform us. Any unauthorized dissemination, distribution or copying hereof is prohibited.

*As we cannot guarantee the genuineness or completeness of the information con-
tained in this message, the statements set forth above are not legally binding. In
connection therewith, we also refer to our governing regulations of concerning sig-
natory authority published in the standard bank or company signature lists with
regard to the legally binding effect of statements made with the intent to obligate us.*

While there is clearly no way to enforce compliance with confidentiality
requirements, the presence of a disclaimer at least establishes a defense if the
information is used in an inappropriate manner. Check with your legal department regarding the necessity and wording of disclaimers.

E-Mail Setup Form

If you plan to offer e-mail functionality in your applications, you'll want to provide your users with some way of editing their own e-mail text and selecting
merge fields. Normally I include an e-mail editing form that gives users the
freedom to customize the body and subject line of the e-mail as well as select
a predefined set of recipients and optional attachments. While the merge fields
for every individual e-mail need to be custom programmed into the application,
this edit form will make maintenance of the e-mail text possible. The user is
given a defined set of merge fields appropriate to the situation. These merge
fields are displayed in a list box. Double-clicking the list box adds the merge field
to either the subject line or the body of the e-mail, depending on the field last vis-
ited, as shown in Figure 7-17.

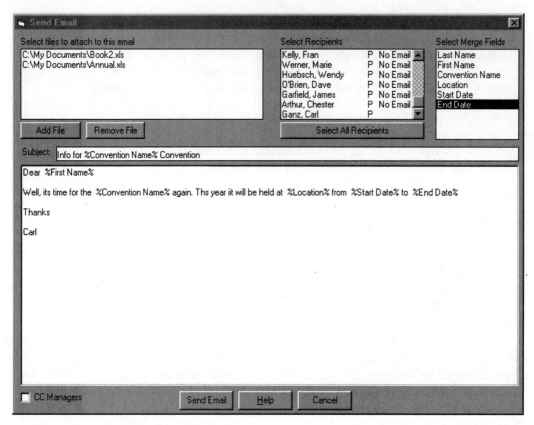

Figure 7-17. E-mail edit form

The text of the e-mail is stored in a memo field, and the merge fields are simply substituted at runtime with the Replace function as follows:

```
cEmail = Replace(cEmail, "%LastName%", oRS("LastName"))
```

I have included in the downloadable source code two e-mail forms I've used in production applications. They are self-contained FRM files and rather straightforward to understand. A detailed explanation of them here is beyond the scope of this book.

Adobe Acrobat

The now ubiquitous PDF files are one of the most popular formats for report and document distribution. Fortunately, most report development tools allow export to the PDF file format. The Adobe Acrobat Reader is free, and it is commonly found on most corporate desktops and part of the standard workstation build. Therefore, your clients should have no problems reading the PDF file format. Beginning with the 5.0 version, Acrobat offers the tagged PDF format. Tagged PDFs structure the PDF document in a logical fashion, differentiating titles, sections, subsections, etc. This is important for making PDF files that are easily readable on PDA devices.

Adobe offers a free Acrobat Software Developer Kit (SDK), as well an extensive supply of documentation, on their Web site at http://www.adobe.com. The SDK consists of all the sample code, documentation, and helpful utilities that will get you started in integrating Acrobat into your applications.

While almost all reporting packages themselves have PDF export ability, there is a separate license fee for the Acrobat Writer and Acrobat Distiller. The PDF writer adds itself as a separate Print option on the menu bar of certain installed applications such as Word and Excel. The base price of the Acrobat Writer and Distiller is $249. Using these tools, you can convert documents from Word, Excel, PowerPoint, RTF, WordPerfect, PageMaker, and Postscript, and such image formats as BMP, GIF, JPEG, PNG, RLE, and TIFF, directly into a PDF.

 NOTE *At this time Distiller cannot be used as an NT service nor can Acrobat be accessed in a multithreaded fashion.*

Adobe Licensing

In case you're thinking about creating a Web service or a report server that uses Distiller to perform automatic document conversion for the entire enterprise, you'll find that there are license restrictions to doing this. Using a single-user license you cannot, for example, create a conversion server that processes documents that are distributed to more than one person. Please note the following section of the Adobe Acrobat 5.0 end-user license agreement, as it applies to server distribution of the software.

> *Server Use. You may install one copy of the Software on your computer file server for the purpose of downloading and installing the Software onto other computers within your internal network up to the Permitted Number or you may install one copy of the Software on a computer file server within your internal network for the sole and exclusive purpose of using the Software through commands, data or instructions (e.g. scripts) from another computer on your internal network, provided that the total number of users that access or Use the Software on such computer file server, does not exceed the Permitted Number. No other network use is permitted, including but not limited to, using the Software either directly or through commands, data or instructions from or to a computer not part of your internal network, for internet or web hosting services or by any user not licensed to use this copy of the Software through a valid license from Adobe.*

> If you need to permit document conversion functionality for the entire enterprise, contact Adobe Systems for a multiuser license.

The two main reasons for integrating Adobe into your applications are to display existing PDF files and to convert existing documents into the PDF format. Let's start with the simpler option—converting existing documents to PDF.

Converting Existing Documents

Acrobat exposes its object model through ActiveX Automation via Acrobat Distiller. You can make the Distiller object model available to your application by selecting Acrobat Distiller from the Project | References menu. Distiller converts PostScript files into the PDF format. Therefore, you'll need to convert your documents to PostScript format as an intermediate stage before final conversion to PDF. This can be accomplished by installing the generic PostScript Printer Driver offered on Adobe's Web site as the target for printing. Then you invoke Distiller to perform the PS-to-PDF conversion. Listing 7-23 illustrates how the Adobe Writer can automatically convert a Word document into PDF and display a progress bar showing the results as the job is in progress.

Listing 7-23. Adobe Conversion for Microsoft Word

```
Dim WithEvents objAdobe As PdfDistiller

Private Sub ConvertDoc(cWordFileName As String)
    Dim objWord As Word.Application
    Dim objDocument As Word.Document
    Dim cCurrentPrinter As String
    Dim cTempPSDocName As String
    Dim cPDFDocName As String
```

```
Screen.MousePointer = vbHourglass

Set objAdobe = CreateObject("PdfDistiller.PdfDistiller.1")

Set objWord = CreateObject("Word.Application")

Set objDocument = objWord.Documents.Open(cWordFileName)

cTempPSDocName = Replace(cWordFileName, ".doc", ".ps")
cPDFDocName = Replace(cWordFileName, ".doc", ".pdf")

cCurrentPrinter = objWord.ActivePrinter

objWord.ActivePrinter = "Generic PostScript Printer"

Call objDocument.PrintOut(0, 0, 0, cTempPSDocName)

objWord.ActivePrinter = cCurrentPrinter

objDocument.Close False
Set objDocument = Nothing

If Dir(cPDFDocName) <> vbNullString Then
    Kill cPDFDocName
End If

Call objAdobe.FileToPDF(cTempPSDocName, cPDFDocName, 0)

If Dir(cTempPSDocName) <> vbNullString Then
    Kill cTempPSDocName
End If

objWord.Quit
Set objWord = Nothing

Set objAdobe = Nothing

Screen.MousePointer = vbDefault
```

```
End Sub

Private Sub objAdobe_OnPercentDone(ByVal nPercentDone As Long)
    ProgressBar1.Value = nPercentDone
End Sub

Private Sub objAdobe_OnJobDone(ByVal strInputPostScript As String, _
    ByVal strOutputPDF As String)
    MsgBox "All done!", vbOKOnly, Me.Caption
End Sub
```

The first step is to create both PdfDistiller and Microsoft Word objects. Then, you change the current printer setting in Word to Generic PostScript Printer. Output the Word document to this printer using the PrintOut method to create a PostScript file. By invoking the FileToPDF method of the Distiller object, this PostScript is then converted into a PDF document. You can pass a third parameter to the FileToPDF method that indicates the job option to be used in converting the document. Table 7-3 explains the various job options available. The OnPercentDone event is triggered as the document is in the conversion process. The nPercentDone parameter is set by Distiller and indicates the conversion job's completion percentage expressed as a whole number. When the conversion completes, Distiller triggers the OnJobDone event.

Table 7-3. Job Options

SETTING	DESCRIPTION
eBook	Intended for PDF files to be read on screen.
Press	Intended for PDF files to be produced as a printed product with high-quality final output.
Print	Intended for PDF files to be printed, digitally copied, published on a CD-ROM, or sent to a client as a publishing proof.
Screen	Intended for PDF files to be viewed on screen. The resulting PDF file has a resolution of 72 dpi. This job option file is provided for compatibility with the pre-5.0 Distiller ScreenOptimized job option file.

NOTE *Adobe also offers an online Web subscription service for PDF document conversion for $9.99 per month or $99.99 per year. Users can e-mail their documents to the Adobe Web site, and usually within a few minutes a PDF version of their document will be e-mailed back to them. If a large number of users need to produce PDFs only occasionally, this may be the most cost effective solution. The restriction here is that each subscription recognizes only one e-mail address. Therefore, you may need to configure your e-mail server to automatically route conversion requests through one registered e-mail address and then route response e-mails to the appropriate party. Note that the service requires a login, and the same user cannot have more than one simultaneous login.*

Displaying Documents in Your Application

Adobe offers an object model that allows you to integrate PDF documents within your applications. You can open documents, navigate to specific pages and bookmarks, search for text, and print all or specified pages. Unlike Distiller's rather simple and limited set of options, these API calls are quite voluminous. You can find the documentation for them in the Acrobat SDK.

The API is linked to your application by selecting Adobe Acrobat 5.0 Type Library from the Project | References menu. To illustrate a subset of this API, examine the code in Listing 7-24. Here, a user can select a PDF file from an open dialog box and display it in a defined region on the form itself.

Listing 7-24. Displaying a PDF File in an Application

```
Dim objAcroExchPDDoc As CAcroPDDoc
Dim objAcroExchAVDoc As CAcroAVDoc
Dim iPage As Integer
Dim cPDFFileName As String

Private Sub cmdOpenPDF_Click()
    Dim x As Integer

    iPage = 1

    With CommonDialog1
        .FileName = ""
        .DefaultExt = "pdf"
```

```
                    .Filter = "PDF Files (*.pdf)|*.pdf"
                    .ShowOpen
                    cPDFFileName = .FileName
            End With

            Me.Caption = cPDFFileName

            Set objAcroExchPDDoc = CreateObject("AcroExch.PDDoc")
            x = objAcroExchPDDoc.Open(cPDFFileName)

            Me.Refresh

        End Sub

        Private Sub Form_Paint()
            Dim objAcroExchPDPage As CAcroPDPage
            Dim objAcroRect As CAcroRect
            Dim x As Integer

            If cPDFFileName = vbNullString Then
                Exit Sub
            End If

            Cls

            Set objAcroExchPDPage = objAcroExchPDDoc.AcquirePage(iPage)
            Set objAcroRect = CreateObject("AcroExch.Rect")

            With objAcroRect
                .Top = 792
                .bottom = 0
                .Left = 0
                .Right = 612
            End With

            x = objAcroExchPDPage.DrawEx(hWnd, 0, objAcroRect, 0, 0, 100)

            Set objAcroExchPDPage = Nothing

        End Sub

        Private Sub Form_QueryUnload(Cancel As Integer, UnloadMode As Integer)
```

```
    Set objAcroExchPDDoc = Nothing
    Set objAcroExchAVDoc = Nothing

End Sub
```

The first step is to declare two module-wide objects—CAcroPDDoc and CAcroAVDoc. CAcroAVDoc represents the display of a PDF file in a window. By contrast, CAcroPDDoc refers to the underlying PDF representation of the same document. It is through CAcroPDDoc that actions such as page navigation can be performed against the PDF file. Once the user has selected a file from the open dialog box, that file is opened by the API and a reference is set to the objAcroExchPDDoc object variable.

Because the display of the document is made on the form itself and not in a container such as a graphic control, the code to display the document pages resides in the Paint method. Here a CAcroPDPage object is instantiated that holds the current page returned from the AcquirePage method. The number of the page desired is passed in as a parameter to this method. Then, a CAcroRect object is instantiated to reference an area of the screen to display the document. Finally, the DrawEx method of objAcroExchPDPage paints the requested page on the form.

When PDF files are created, they contain certain information in their headers that defines their title, who created them, and when. The code in Listing 7-25 shows how this data can be accessed via the GetInfo method of the objAcroExchPDDoc object.

Listing 7-25. Displaying Information About a PDF File

```
Private Sub cmdInfo_Click()
    Dim cMsg As String

    With objAcroExchPDDoc
        cMsg = "Title: " & .GetInfo("Title") & vbCrLf
        cMsg = cMsg & "Subject: " & .GetInfo("Subject") & vbCrLf
        cMsg = cMsg & "Author: " & .GetInfo("Author") & vbCrLf
        cMsg = cMsg & "Keywords: " & .GetInfo("Keywords") & vbCrLf
        cMsg = cMsg & "Creator: " & .GetInfo("Creator") & vbCrLf
        cMsg = cMsg & "Created: " & .GetInfo("Created") & vbCrLf
        cMsg = cMsg & "Modified: " & .GetInfo("Modified") & vbCrLf
        cMsg = cMsg & "Producer: " & .GetInfo("Producer")
    End With

    MsgBox cMsg

End Sub
```

You can find some excellent sample applications and technical articles on the programming extensibility of the Adobe Writer from the Adobe KnowledgeBase at `http://www.adobe.com`.

 NOTE *Three helpful references for PDF development are* Adobe Acrobat 5: The Professional User's Guide, *by Donna L. Baker (Apress. ISBN: 1-59059-023-6),* Adobe Acrobat 5 PDF Bible, *by Ted Padova (Hungry Minds, Inc. ISBN: 0-76453-577-3) and* Real World PDF with Adobe Acrobat 5, *by Anita Dennis and Tricia Gellman (Peachpit Press. ISBN: 0-20175-894-6).*

Adobe Alternatives

Though PDF is virtually the de facto standard for document distribution, Adobe is not the only company that produces software that creates PDF files. activePDF (`http://www.activepdf.com`) publishes a suite of software products that create and modify PDF file formats. They offer a server product as well as individual desktop licenses. Their products all offer a COM interface so you can access their functionality as easily as you can the Adobe products.

Amyuni Technologies (`http://www.amyuni.com`) publishes an ActiveX add-in called PDF Creator that allows you to view, edit, and print PDF files from within your application. They also publish PDF Converter, which serves as a printer driver to which you print your documents for conversion to PDF.

Conclusion

Through its Word, Excel, and Access components, the Microsoft Office Suite offers many options to complement your reporting requirements. Whether you need mail merge capability, data export functionality, or e-mails, Office XP and tools like Lotus Notes and the Adobe Acrobat Writer provide it.

So far we've covered largely desktop-based solutions for your reporting needs. In the remaining chapters, we'll look at distributing these reports over the Internet and via wireless devices.

CHAPTER 8

Crosstab Reports and OLAP

CROSSTAB REPORTS, also known as pivot tables, are a breed unto themselves, and each reporting tool handles them very differently. Likewise, each RDBMS has its own SQL approach for assembling crosstab data. In a similar fashion, each RDBMS has its own OLAP extensions (like SQL Server) or are OLAP databases unto themselves (like the Arbor/Essbase multidimensional OLAP engine that's also licensed by IBM as DB2's OLAP engine—see http://www.essbase.com for more information). In this chapter you'll learn how to assemble, query, and create crosstab data, and how OLAP databases differ from the traditional relational model.

Crosstab SQL

A crosstab report is one that shows summary information for cross-referenced data, and displays this information as row labels and column headers. The body of the report consists of a statistic—most commonly a count, sum, or average—that is located at the intersection of the individual row and column headers. Take a look at the following grid:

	SOURCE 1	SOURCE 2	SOURCE 3	TOTALS
Product 1	1	3	3	7
Product 2	1	4	4	9
Product 3	2	3	1	6
Totals	4	10	8	22

In this example, which shows the total number of inquiries received by product and source, you can see that four inquiries came in for Product 2 by Source 3.

Each database engine handles crosstab SQL differently, some better than others. Ideally, the DBMS should produce a result set that represents the exact crosstab layout, and does not require further manipulation by your reporting tool. In some cases this is rather straightforward, but in others it's easier to simply massage the data into a more suitable structure, such as an array or a collection that is physically structured like the crosstab report, and print that array or collection instead.

You need to adhere to certain formatting rules for crosstab reports to make such reports readable. If a crosstab report needs to span multiple pages in order to display an entire row's worth of data, the row description label that displays down the left side of the page should be repeated on each subsequent page. Also, the rows and the columns should all be summarized using the same statistic that comprises the body of the report—summation, average, minimum/maximum, etc. If it's really important to keep the row's data on one page, or if you wish to show multiple statistics for each intersection point, you could stack the rows so that each intersection contains two values under each column heading. The following grid shows a total and average unit sales for a given product in a given month:

	JAN	FEB	MAR	TOTALS
Product 1	2/3	2/3	4/1	8/7
Product 2	4/1	1/4	2/4	7/9
Product 3	1/2	2/3	1/1	4/6
Totals	7/6	5/10	7/6	19/22

Check this layout with your users first. It's not pretty, but it gets the job done.

As indicated previously, there are two types of crosstab reports: those where you know the number of columns in advance (static) and those whose number of columns vary (dynamic). As you may have guessed, the dynamic crosstabs are a lot harder to build than static ones are and they're generally the ones you'll be asked to deliver.

Excel

Microsoft Excel is a powerful tool for producing crosstab analysis reports. Excel can create a PivotTable, which allows you to take a set of normalized data (stored either in a spreadsheet or other data source) and produce a crosstab query from it. You can accomplish this seamlessly from your application using Excel VBA. By extracting the raw data using SQL, you can write your results to a worksheet. Then, using the PivotTable objects, you can create a crosstab report.

NOTE *Of course, you could always extract a Recordset using one of the SQL techniques described earlier. Then, by looping through the fields collection you could write the contents to an Excel spreadsheet. The code samples for Chapter 6 contain an example of how to dynamically dump an ADO Recordset to Excel.*

The code in Listing 8-1 illustrates how to create a PivotTable list of students, classes, and the tests taken by each student for each class.

Listing 8-1. Excel PivotTable

```
Dim oRS As ADODB.Recordset
Dim objExcel As Excel.Application
Dim objWorkBook As Excel.Workbook
Dim objWS As Excel.Worksheet
Dim objPivotWS As Excel.Worksheet
Dim iRow As Integer
Dim cSQL As String
Dim cRange As String

cConnectString = "Provider=SQLOLEDB.1;Integrated Security=SSPI;" & _
                 "Persist Security Info=False;" & _
                 "Initial Catalog=EnterpriseReports;" & _
                 "Data Source=(local)"

oConn.ConnectionString = cConnectString
oConn.Open

cSQL = "SELECT s.Last & ', ' & s.First AS name, p.Title, t.Score " & _
       "FROM Student s, Program p, Test t " & _
       "WHERE s.ID = t.Studnum " & _
       "AND p.ID = t.TestID"

Set oRS = oConn.Execute(cSQL)

Set objExcel = CreateObject("Excel.Application")
objExcel.Visible = True

'Eliminate screen flickering by not updating the screen after every change
objExcel.ScreenUpdating = False
```

```
Set objWorkBook = objExcel.Workbooks.Add
Set objWS = objExcel.Worksheets.Add

iRow = 1  ' Set index to header row

' Write header
objWS.Cells(iRow, 1) = "Student"
objWS.Cells(iRow, 2) = "Class"
objWS.Cells(iRow, 3) = "Average"

' Set index to first data row
iRow = 2


Do While Not oRS.EOF

    objWS.Cells(iRow, 1) = oRS("name")
    objWS.Cells(iRow, 2) = oRS("Title")
    objWS.Cells(iRow, 3) = oRS("Score")

    iRow = iRow + 1 ' go to next row

    oRS.MoveNext ' go to next row in recordset

Loop

iRow = iRow - 1

cRange = "Sheet4!R1C1:R" & iRow & "C3"

'Pass in the range to create the PivotTable
objWorkBook.PivotCaches.Add(xlDatabase, cRange).CreatePivotTable "", _
    "MyPivot", xlPivotTableVersion10

Set objPivotWS = objExcel.ActiveSheet

With objPivotWS.PivotTables("MyPivot").PivotFields("Student")
    .Orientation = xlRowField
    .Position = 1
End With

With objPivotWS.PivotTables("MyPivot").PivotFields("Class")
    .Orientation = xlColumnField
    .Position = 1
End With
```

The first step is to set Excel's ScreenUpdating property to False to avoid any visual noise while the spreadsheet is being populated. Of course, you could optionally set the Visible property of objExcel to False and avoid any screen interaction whatsoever. Next, loop through the ADO Recordset and write the field contents into individual cells of the Excel worksheet. Once you have populated the worksheet, create a PivotTable by invoking the Add method of the Pivot-Caches collection object. Then, establish the Student data as the row data and the Class data as the column data. You can accomplish this by referring to the PivotFields collection and setting the Orientation property to xlRowField and xlColumnField, respectively.

To create the summary information that displays at the row/column intersections, invoke the AddDataField method and indicate that it's the average of the data in which you're interested by passing the xlAverage constant. This is shown in Listing 8-2. Since users most likely will not need to see the PivotTable field list selector, set the ShowPivotTableFieldList property to False. Finally, to get rid of the PivotTable command bar, disable this option as well.

Listing 8-2. Completing the PivotTable

```
With objPivotWS.PivotTables("MyPivot")
    .AddDataField objPivotWS.PivotTables("MyPivot").PivotFields("Average"), _
        vbNullString, xlAverage
    .ColumnGrand = True
    .RowGrand = True
    .GrandTotalName = "Subject Averages"
    .EnableDrilldown = True
End With

objWorkBook.ShowPivotTableFieldList = False

objExcel.Application.CommandBars("PivotTable").Enabled = False

objExcel.ScreenUpdating = True
```

The final result of the PivotTable is shown in Figure 8-1.

Student	American History	Ancient Philosophy	Greek Literature	Modern European History	Nineteenth-century Americ	Subject Averages
Abdali, Mohammed			90			90
Able, Patricia	100					100
Abner, Susan	90				90	90
Conrad, Joseph		100				100
Donner, Brian	45				95	70
Engles, Laura	80	90		80		83.33333333
Garner, James			90			90
Heston, Eric			100			100
Monroe, Peter		100		70	100	90
O'Conner, Janet		75	95	85	100	88.75
Pavlov, Michael		95		85		90
Schmidt, Gerard		90				90
Smith, Claudette			100			100
Vaccuso, Linda			100		100	100
Subject Averages	78.75	91.42857143	95.83333333	80	97	89.80769231

Figure 8-1. PivotTable output

Note the use of the EnableDrilldown property. Setting this property to True allows the user to double-click a cell that contains data and see the underlying detail data that comprises the aggregate number. For example, clicking the intersection of Abner, Susan and American History will display the worksheet shown in Figure 8-2.

Student	Class	Average
Abner, Susan	American History	90

Figure 8-2. Drilldown output

NOTE *Automating Excel is not the most resource efficient approach to creating cross-tabs, especially if there is an alternative. In order to create a PivotTable in Excel, you have to instantiate the Excel application object, create a worksheet, and push the data to the sheet for processing. This can work for a single thread, but as you have multiple instances of Excel, you start having load problems.*

Microsoft Access

Microsoft Access has specific commands for creating crosstab reports—the TRANSFORM and PIVOT statements. TRANSFORM handles the aggregate function to summarize the data, while PIVOT establishes the column headings for the result set. The example that follows displays the average test scores for students across a variety of subjects. The statement

```
TRANSFORM AVG(test.score) AS AvgScore
SELECT student.id, student.last, student.first
FROM student INNER JOIN
(program INNER JOIN test
ON program.id = test.testid)
ON student.id = test.studnum
GROUP BY student.id, student.last, student.first
PIVOT program.title
```

returns the following results:

ID	LAST	FIRST	AMER. HIST.	ANCIENT PHIL.	GREEK LIT.	MODERN HIST.	19TH AMER. LIT.
45	Donner	Brian	45				95
47	Vaccuso	Linda			100		100
69	Conrad	Joseph		100			
70	Engles	Laura	80	90		80	
102	Able	Patricia	100				
110	Smith	Claudette			100		
127	Abdali	Mohammad			90		
136	Garner	James			90		
162	Abner	Susan	90				90
182	Monroe	Peter		100		70	100
192	Heston	Eric			100		
193	O'Conner	Janet		75	95	85	100
223	Schmidt	Gerard		90			
229	Pavlov	Michael		95		85	

Microsoft Access offers a wizard that will create the crosstab query for you. From the Database window, choose New from the Queries menu and pick the Crosstab Query Wizard.

MSDN Resources

Numerous MSDN articles and KnowledgeBase entries deal with crosstab reports using Access. Some of the highlights are listed here:

- "Programming PivotTable Reports in Microsoft Access 2002"

- 304458—"How to Create a Crosstab Query with Multiple Value Fields"

- 209141—"How to Group Column Headings in a Crosstab Query"

- 208556—"How to Group Row Headings in a Crosstab Query"

- 210004—"How to Use Code to Change Column Headings in a Crosstab Query"

- 208669—"How to Use IIf() in Crosstab to Limit Column Headings"

- 304348 HOW TO: Create a Crosstab Query in Microsoft Access 2000

- 304349 HOW TO: Create a Crosstab Query in Microsoft Access 2002

- 328320 HOW TO: Create a Dynamic Crosstab Report in Access 2002

- 207626 ACC2000: Access 2000 Sample Queries Available in Download Center

---

Microsoft SQL Server 2000

Surprisingly (since Access can do crosstabs), Microsoft SQL Server 2000 does *not* provide inherent crosstab functionality. Despite this, you can create both static and dynamic crosstabs with a few T-SQL tricks. To create a static crosstab, refer to Listing 8-3.

Listing 8-3. Static Crosstab

```
CREATE TABLE Inquiry
( Date smalldatetime,
  ProductID  integer,
```

```
  Gender    integer)
GO
INSERT INTO Inquiry VALUES ('01/01/2000', 1, 0)
INSERT INTO Inquiry VALUES ('02/01/2000', 2, 0)
INSERT INTO Inquiry VALUES ('03/01/2000', 2, 1)
INSERT INTO Inquiry VALUES ('04/01/2000', 3, 0)
INSERT INTO Inquiry VALUES ('05/01/2000', 4, 1)
INSERT INTO Inquiry VALUES ('05/01/2000', 4, 1)
INSERT INTO Inquiry VALUES ('06/01/2000', 3, 1)
INSERT INTO Inquiry VALUES ('06/01/2000', 4, 0)
INSERT INTO Inquiry VALUES ('06/01/2001', 3, 0)
INSERT INTO Inquiry VALUES ('01/01/2001', 3, 1)
INSERT INTO Inquiry VALUES ('02/01/2001', 2, 1)
INSERT INTO Inquiry VALUES ('03/01/2001', 1, 0)
INSERT INTO Inquiry VALUES ('03/01/2001', 2, 1)
INSERT INTO Inquiry VALUES ('01/01/2002', 1, 0)
```

Given that zero represents Male and one represents Female, the following SQL statement creates a crosstab result that counts up the number of inquiries made by year and gender and even shows the sum of both genders by year. The following statement

```
SELECT Year(Date),
    SUM(CASE Gender WHEN 0 THEN 1 ELSE 0 END) AS Male,
    SUM(CASE Gender WHEN 1 THEN 1 ELSE 0 END) AS Female,
    COUNT(*) AS GenderTotal
FROM Inquiry
GROUP BY Year(Date)
```

returns

	Male	Female	SubTotal
2000	4	4	8
2001	2	3	5
2002	1	0	1

This example uses a CASE...END statement that works in the same way a Select Case...End Case block works in Visual Basic. Here, the SQL statement is evaluating the Gender column for the values 1 and 0. If Gender contains a 0, then the first CASE statement uses the SUM aggregate function to increase the counter of the Male virtual column by 1; otherwise, the statement increments it by 0. The female virtual column is created the same way, except that the counter only increments by 1 if the Gender column contains a 1.

In the preceding example, there were only two possible columns, Male and Female, so this made creation of the SQL statement rather straightforward. Suppose you don't know how many columns you'll need, as is the case with the product inquiry example at the beginning of the chapter. You could always create the necessary SQL statement at runtime or dump your crosstab data into a temporary table via a stored procedure. Examine the code in Listing 8-4 to see how to dynamically create the crosstab SQL.

Listing 8-4. Crosstab SQL Builder

```
Sub CrossTabSQL()
    Dim oConn As New ADODB.Connection
    Dim oRS As ADODB.Recordset
    Dim cConnectString As String
    Dim cColumn As String
    Dim cSQL As String

    cConnectString = "Provider=SQLOLEDB.1;Password=Ovaltine" & _
                        ";Persist Security Info=True;User ID=sa" & _
                        ";Initial Catalog=EnterpriseReports" & _
                        ";Data Source=(local)"
    With oConn
        .ConnectionString = cConnectString
        .Open
    End With

    cSQL = "SELECT * FROM Source"

    Set oRS = oConn.Execute(cSQL)

    'Begin creation of the SQL statement
    cSQL = "SELECT p.Descr,"
    'Loop through each individual source in the table
    Do While Not oRS.EOF

        '...and get its name
        cColumn = oRS("descr")

        'Remove characters that would produce an invalid column name
        cColumn = Replace(cColumn, Space(1), vbNullString)
        cColumn = Replace(cColumn, "-", vbNullString)

        'and add the CASE statement to support this column
        cSQL = cSQL & "SUM(CASE SourceID WHEN " & oRS("id") & _
                    " THEN 1 ELSE 0 END) AS " & cColumn & ","
```

```
        oRS.MoveNext

    Loop

    cSQL = Mid$(cSQL, 1, Len(cSQL) - 1)

    'Now add the JOIN information and you're done
    cSQL = cSQL & " FROM Requester r, Product p " & _
                "WHERE r.ProductID = p.ID " & _
                "GROUP BY p.Descr"

End Sub
```

In this example, the code is looping through an ADO Recordset containing the contents of the Source table. The result is the following SQL statement:

```
SELECT p.Descr,
SUM(CASE SourceID WHEN 1 THEN 1 ELSE 0 END) AS Phone,
SUM(CASE SourceID WHEN 2 THEN 1 ELSE 0 END) AS Mail,
SUM(CASE SourceID WHEN 3 THEN 1 ELSE 0 END) AS EMail,
SUM(CASE SourceID WHEN 4 THEN 1 ELSE 0 END) AS Fax,
SUM(CASE SourceID WHEN 5 THEN 1 ELSE 0 END) AS Convention,
SUM(CASE SourceID WHEN 6 THEN 1 ELSE 0 END) AS WebSite,
SUM(CASE SourceID WHEN 7 THEN 1 ELSE 0 END) AS ReplyCard,
SUM(CASE SourceID WHEN 8 THEN 1 ELSE 0 END) AS ElectronicSubmission,
SUM(CASE SourceID WHEN 9 THEN 1 ELSE 0 END) AS SalesRep
FROM Requester r, Product p
WHERE r.ProductID = p.ID
GROUP BY p.Descr
```

Oracle

Oracle's crosstab functionality is similar to that of Microsoft SQL Server. Instead of using a CASE...END block, Oracle uses the DECODE function, which accomplishes the same thing. Take a look at the following example:

```
SELECT TRUNC(TO_CHAR(InqDate, 'YYYY')) AS InquiryDate,
    SUM(DECODE(Gender,0,1,0)) AS Male,
    SUM(DECODE(Gender,1,1,0)) AS Female,
    COUNT(Gender) AS Total
FROM Inquiry
GROUP BY TO_CHAR(InqDate, 'YYYY')
```

Here, the same summary data is being extracted as in the SQL Server example in the preceding section. The output of this statement is shown here:

```
INQUIRYDATE    MALE    FEMALE    TOTAL
-----------  --------  --------  --------
   2000         4        4         8
   2001         2        3         5
   2002         1        0         1
```

Of course, when you are dealing with an unknown number of columns in your crosstab, you could always build the SQL statement using the same technique as illustrated in Listing 8-4.

Printing Crosstab Reports

One of the biggest difficulties in printing crosstab reports is determining the number of rows and columns in the final result set of the crosstab query. The report may span multiple pages in both directions, and you'll likely need a total column after the rightmost column to sum all the rows and beneath the last row to sum all the columns. Moreover, row labels need to be printed on every page. The degree of difficulty of this task depends in no small way on your selection of reporting tool.

TIP *When planning a crosstab report for clients, ask if they would like the zero sum rows and columns to be suppressed. Most reporting tools easily allow you to suppress rows and columns that meet this criteria.*

VS-View/Preview

Creating crosstab reports in VS-View and Preview can be very difficult the first time. However, once you do the first one, it, like every other type of VS-View/Preview report, will serve as a template for the others that follow. The example presented in this section extracts the crosstab query results directly into an array. The report shows the number of inquiries that were sent into a pharmaceutical company's information department by product and source (phone, fax, e-mail, snail mail, etc.). All the products will print down the left side of the page (as row labels), while the different sources will print as column headers across the top. The complete code for this report can be found in the sample projects that are available from the Apress Web site (http://www.apress.com). I've only shown the highlights here.

The first step is to extract the needed data into an array. You could also use a collection or, in .NET, a DataTable object. I prefer arrays or collections, as it's rather easy and resource inexpensive to traverse them when calculating summary statistics on rows and columns. Listing 8-5 illustrates how both the product and source dictionaries are loaded into their own arrays while the array to contain the body of the report is dimensioned.

Listing 8-5. Extracting Data into an Array

```
'Should be defined so as to allow room for a totals
'column to the right of the last column in a row
Const COLS_PER_PAGE = 5


'Should be defined so as to allow room for a totals
'column below the last row
Const ROWS_PER_PAGE = 7



'Count the number of products

cSQL = "SELECT COUNT(*) " & _
        "FROM product "

Set oRS = oConn.Execute(cSQL)

iProdCnt = oRS.Fields(0)



'Count the number of sources

cSQL = "SELECT COUNT(*) " & _
        "FROM source"

Set oRS = oConn.Execute(cSQL)

iSourceCnt = oRS.Fields(0)



'Resize array to hold report data
ReDim aProduct(iProdCnt, 1)
ReDim aSource(iSourceCnt, 1)
ReDim aData(iProdCnt, iSourceCnt)
```

```
cSQL = "SELECT id, descr " & _
    "FROM product " & _
    "ORDER BY descr"

Set oRS = oConn.Execute(cSQL)

x = 1

Do While Not oRS.EOF

    aData(x, 0) = oRS("id")
    aProduct(x, 0) = oRS("id")
    aProduct(x, 1) = oRS("descr")

    x = x + 1

    oRS.MoveNext

Loop


'Load source ids and names into arrays

cSQL = "SELECT id, descr " & _
    "FROM source " & _
    "ORDER BY descr"

Set oRS = oConn.Execute(cSQL)

x = 1

Do While Not oRS.EOF

    aData(0, x) = oRS("id")
    aSource(x, 0) = oRS("id")
    aSource(x, 1) = oRS("descr")

    x = x + 1

    oRS.MoveNext

Loop
```

Once you build the array containing all the required data, you can now prepare the printing logic. The approach taken here is to print each page of the crosstab report as an individual table. The question is how many rows can a table have before a page break is required and how many columns can fit across a single page. Once these limits are determined, the appropriate rows and columns in the array are printed to fill the page. If you're either at the last column or the last row, the total column and row can then print. The code to accomplish this is rather involved. The pertinent code is shown in Listing 8-6.

Listing 8-6. VS-View Crosstab Source Code

```
With VSPrinter1
     .TableBorder = tbNone
     .PageBorder = pbNone
     .Orientation = orLandscape
     .FontName = "Arial"
     .FontSize = 10
     .StartDoc
End With


'How many pages are needed to print an entire row of data
iPagesPerRow = Int(iSourceCnt / COLS_PER_PAGE) + 1


'How many pages are needed to print a full set of products A through Z
iPagesPerDataSet = Int(iProdCnt / ROWS_PER_PAGE)

If iProdCnt Mod ROWS_PER_PAGE <> 0 Then
    iPagesPerDataSet = Int(iPagesPerDataSet + 1)
End If


'Which product array element are we on at the beginning of a given page
iProdAtPageStart = 1

'Of the number of pages it takes to print all the products,
'as indicated by iPagesPerDataSet, which pages are we currently on
iProdSet = 1


With VSPrinter1
```

```
'Row counter for the table on the page currently being
'printed. Reset after each page.
iRow = 1

'Page counter for rows that span multiple pages
iPageRow = 1

'Page counter for data sets that span multiple pages
iPageDataSet = 1

'Position in the array where the data should begin printing. The product
'description begins in column 1 on each page. Though it's a zero-based
'array, we are ignoring column zero
iColumnBegin = 2

'Which product of the entire list of products are we on
iProdRow = 1

'Print the header across the top of the page
Call CrossTabHdr(aSource(), iColumnBegin, iPageRow, COLS_PER_PAGE, iSourceCnt)


.StartTable

'Always one more than the COLS_PER_PAGE so as to display the product names
'down the left side of the page.
.TableCell(tcCols) = COLS_PER_PAGE + 2

Do While iProdRow <= iProdCnt

    'Insert row and fill with product name
    .TableCell(tcInsertRow) = iRow
    .TableCell(tcColWidth, iRow, 1) = "3400"
    .TableCell(tcText, iRow, 1) = aProduct(iProdRow, 1)


    'Calculate how many columns are being printed across this page
    iMaxCol = (COLS_PER_PAGE * iPageRow) + 1

    If iMaxCol > iSourceCnt Then
        iMaxCol = iSourceCnt + 1
    End If
```

```
If iPageRow = 1 Then
    iColumnBegin = 2
Else
    iColumnBegin = COLS_PER_PAGE * (iPageRow - 1) + 2
End If

'Now print those columns - one row's worth of data
iColPos = 1

For Z = iColumnBegin To iMaxCol

    iColPos = iColPos + 1

    .TableCell(tcColWidth, iRow, iColPos) = "1600"
    .TableCell(tcAlign, iRow, iColPos) = taRightMiddle
    .TableCell(tcText, iRow, iColPos) = aData(iProdRow, Z - 1)

    lGrandTotal = lGrandTotal + aData(iProdRow, Z - 1)

Next Z

'Go to the next row for this page
iRow = iRow + 1

'Go to the next product in this data set
iProdRow = iProdRow + 1

'If we have more rows than are allowed on a page or
'we've run out of products because we're on the last page
If iRow > ROWS_PER_PAGE Or iProdRow > iProdCnt Then

    'If it's the last part of the data set, then
    'print column totals across bottom of page
    If iPageDataSet = iPagesPerDataSet Then

        .TableCell(tcInsertRow) = iRow

        .TableCell(tcColWidth, iRow, 1) = "3400"
        .TableCell(tcText, iRow, 1) = "Totals"
        .TableCell(tcFontBold, iRow, 1) = True
        .TableCell(tcAlign, iRow, 1) = taLeftMiddle

        iColPos = 1
```

```
        If iPageRow = 1 Then
            iColumnBegin = 2
        Else
            iColumnBegin = COLS_PER_PAGE * (iPageRow - 1) + 2
        End If


        For Z = iColumnBegin To iMaxCol

            iColPos = iColPos + 1


            .TableCell(tcColWidth, iRow, iColPos) = "1600"
            .TableCell(tcAlign, iRow, iColPos) = taRightMiddle
            .TableCell(tcText, iRow, iColPos) = ASum(aData, 1, , Z - 1)


        Next Z

    End If



    'If we've printed one full row's worth of data for a data set
    If iPageRow = iPagesPerRow Then

        'Print total column for the row if this is the
        'last page on which a row prints
        If iSourceCnt Mod COLS_PER_PAGE = 0 Then
            iColPos = 2
        Else
            iColPos = (iSourceCnt Mod COLS_PER_PAGE) + 2
        End If

        iMaxRow = (iProdAtPageStart + ROWS_PER_PAGE) - 1

        If iMaxRow > iProdCnt Then
            iMaxRow = iProdCnt
        End If

        iRow = 1

        For Z = iProdAtPageStart To iMaxRow

            .TableCell(tcColWidth, iRow, iColPos) = "1600"
            .TableCell(tcAlign, iRow, iColPos) = taRightMiddle
            .TableCell(tcText, iRow, iColPos) = _
                    ASum(aData, 1, iSourceCnt, , Z)
```

```
        iRow = iRow + 1

    Next Z


    'If this is the very last page print the grand total
    If iProdRow >= iProdCnt And _
        iPageDataSet = iPagesPerDataSet Then


        .TableCell(tcColWidth, iRow, iColPos) = "1600"
        .TableCell(tcAlign, iRow, iColPos) = taRightMiddle
        .TableCell(tcText, iRow, iColPos) = lGrandTotal

    End If


    .EndTable


    'If this is the very last page then exit the
    'loop and close the Recordset
    If iProdRow >= iProdCnt And _
        iPageDataSet = iPagesPerDataSet Then
            Exit Do
    End If

    .NewPage

    iPageDataSet = iPageDataSet + 1
    iProdRow = iProdSet * ROWS_PER_PAGE
    iProdSet = iProdSet + 1
    iPageRow = 1
    iProdAtPageStart = iProdRow
    iColumnBegin = 2

Else

    .EndTable

    .NewPage

    iPageRow = iPageRow + 1
    iProdRow = iProdAtPageStart
    iColumnBegin = (COLS_PER_PAGE * (iPageRow - 1)) + 2

End If
```

```
            iRow = 1

            'Print the header
            Call CrossTabHdr(aSource(), iColumnBegin, _
                    iPageRow, COLS_PER_PAGE, iSourceCnt)

            .StartTable

            iMaxCol = iSourceCnt - (COLS_PER_PAGE * (iPageRow - 1))

            If iMaxCol > COLS_PER_PAGE Then
                iMaxCol = COLS_PER_PAGE
            End If

            .TableCell(tcCols) = COLS_PER_PAGE + 2

        End If

    Loop

    .EndDoc

End With
```

ActiveReports

ActiveReports is an ActiveX designer and as such works a bit differently from the other products you've seen so far in this chapter. ActiveReports uses sections for handling each printed area of a report. The example uses the Northwind database (installed by default in SQL Server). Even though crosstab reports can be done in ActiveReports, Data Dynamics openly admits that it isn't the best product for creating them. Instead, the company provides DynamiCube and ActiveCube, which can be used with ActiveReports. They have also stated that they intend to incorporate a subset of these controls to be implemented as a crosstab control in a fashion similar to that of Crystal Reports. As of the writing of this book, no definitive date for such a product release has been announced.

The report will walk through all records in the Orders table (in this case July 1996 through December 1997) and sum the freight charges by month for each column.

The first step is to create a SQL or T-SQL script to retrieve the data from the database. To accomplish this, do the following:

1. Combine the Product and Orders tables via a JOIN operation (by Product ID).

2. Calculate the SUM of...for each month.

3. Group the results by the product name (which will become the row header).

Once you've established the SQL connection and SQL query string to be executed, assign the contents to the ActiveReports Data Control. Listing 8-7 shows the basic SQL statement used for this report and how it's assigned to the data control.

Listing 8-7. SQL Statement for Northwinds Example Crosstab Report

```
' Build Connection String
cConn = "DSN=Northwind;UID=sa;Pwd=;"
On Error GoTo OpenConnectionError

' Dynamically create the Connection
oCn.ConnectionString = cConn
oCn.Open

On Error GoTo Trap

Set Me.dat.Connection = oCn

cSQL = "SELECT p.ProductName, "

cSQL = cSQL & "SUM(CASE WHEN OrderDate " & _
            "BETWEEN '7/1/1996' AND '7/31/1996' " & _
            "THEN Freight ELSE 0 END) As July96,"

'Here would go all the other SUM..CASE statements from
'8/96 through 11/97. This source code example is abbreviated
'to save space

cSQL = cSQL & "SUM(CASE WHEN OrderDate " & _
            "BETWEEN '12/1/1997' AND '&grave;12/31/1997' " & _
            "THEN Freight ELSE 0 END) As Dec97"
```

```
' Order and Grouping
cSQL = cSQL & "FROM Orders o, [Order Details] d, Products p "
cSQL = cSQL & "WHERE o.OrderID = d.OrderID "
cSQL = cSQL & "AND d.ProductID = p.ProductID "
cSQL = cSQL & "GROUP BY p.ProductName "

' Set Data Source
Me.dat.Source = cSQL
Me.dat.Refresh

Exit_Rtn:
    Exit Sub


OpenConnectionError:
    MsgBox "Unable to Open Database Connection!", vbExclamation, "Error"
    GoTo Exit_Rtn
```

....

Dynamic Date Ranges

For the purpose of this example, the date range was "hardwired." It's more likely that when developing a custom report, such as this crosstab example, a date range will not be specified. In these cases, the date range can be calculated using code similar to the following:

```
Public Sub BuildDateRange(ByVal dBegin As Date, ByVal dEnd As Date)
Dim dStartDate As Date
Dim dEndDate As Date
Dim iOffset As Integer
Dim aDates(0, 1) As Date

' Store Start Date
dStartDate = dBegin

' Using the beginning date and ending date, calculate the monthly pairs,
' then insert the pairs into the aDates Array
Do Until dEndDate > dEnd
    dEndDate = DateSerial(Year(dStartDate), Month(dStartDate) + 1, 0)

    ' Insert pairs
    iOffset = iOffset + 1
    ReDim Preserve aDates(iOffset, 1)
    aDates(iOffset, 0) = dStartDate
    aDates(iOffset, 1) = dEndDate
```

```
  ' Calculate new start date
    If Month(dStartDate) = 12 Then
       dStartDate = CDate("01/01/" & Year(dStartDate) + 1)
    Else
       dStartDate = Month(dStartDate) + 1 & "/01/" & Year(dStartDate)
    End If
Loop
```

This code will take a date range and produce an Array (aDates) of all the month beginning and ending dates.

Next, you'll create the columns (or in the case of ActiveReports, the field controls) dynamically. ActiveReports allows for the ability to create sections (such as groupings) and controls at runtime in much the same manner as Visual Basic permits runtime control creation.

ActiveReports uses Collection objects to hold sections, controls, pages, and other elements of a report. The sections are defined by the section report bands displayed in the ActiveReports Report Designer. For example, if the report bands indicate a PageHeader, Detail, and PageFooter, then the respective sections are "PageHeader", "Detail", and "PageFooter".

Once you have determined which section you wish to work in (such as the PageHeader for Labels, Detail for Fields, etc.), you can add controls to this section. In the case of the crosstab example, the ReportHeader section was filled out (using some labels and an image) and a Label control, which is to serve as a column header, was placed in the ReportHeader section. The Label controls could all be easily added at runtime, but this one was used as an example for copying formatting as well as other properties.

When a Label (or any control for that matter) is first added to a section, the new control does not "inherit" any characteristics. That means once a control is added, you must format and size the control. The code in Listing 8-8 shows how to dynamically create a Label in the PageHeader section at runtime.

Listing 8-8. Creating a Label Dynamically in the PageHeader Section at Runtime

```
Private Sub AddLabel(ByVal cCaption As String, ByVal nLeft As Integer, _
   Optional cName As String)
   '
   ' This subroutine dynamically creates a label at runtime.
   ' To call this function :
   '
   '   AddLabel("LabelName", 1350, "LabelHeader1")
   '
   Dim oLabel  As DDActiveReports2.Label    ' Label Object
```

```
            Set oLabel = Me.Sections("PageHeader").Controls.Add("DDActiveReports2.Label")
            ' Set label position, alignment, and other properties
            With oLabel
                .Caption = cCaption

                ' Set label position, alignment, and other properties
                .Left = nLeft
                .Top = Me.LabelCaption.Top
                .Height = Me.LabelCaption.Height
                .Width = 1260

                .BackStyle = Me.LabelCaption.BackStyle
                .BackColor = Me.LabelCaption.BackColor
                .Alignment = Me.LabelCaption.Alignment

                If cName <> vbNullString Then
                    .Name = cName
                End If
            End With
        End Sub
```

With this label creation routine developed, you can dynamically add fields to the report. Adding Field objects to the Detail section works in much the same manner as adding Label objects to the PageHeader. The basic differences are that Field controls are added to the Detail section and are bound to a data field in the report's data control. The code in Listing 8-9 shows how to dynamically create a Field control in the Detail section at runtime. Notice that there are several other properties that can be defined for a field, including the DataField property, which links it to the data control. Other properties can be used to set things like the format (in this example the formatting is for currency), alignment, and so on.

Listing 8-9. Code to Create Field Controls at Runtime in the Detail Section

```
Private Sub AddField(ByVal cField As String, ByVal nLeft As Integer, _
    Optional cName As String)

    Dim oField  As DDActiveReports2.field    ' Field

    ' Create the fields
    Set oField = Me.Sections("detail").Controls.Add("DDActiveReports2.Field")

    ' Set field, position, and other properties
```

```
    With oField
         .DataField = cField

         .Left = nLeft
         .Top = Me.field.Top
         .Height = Me.field.Height
         .Width = 1260

         .OutputFormat = Me.field.OutputFormat
         .Alignment = Me.field.Alignment

         If cName <> vbNullString Then
              .Name = cName
         End If
    End With
End Sub
```

Finally, to tie the whole report structure together, you need to calculate the columns and create them before the report runs. This is done in the ReportStart event. There are some known limitations when creating crosstab reports in ActiveReports. ActiveReports does not paginate the report horizontally. Rather, it will tell the printer that it has a very wide page to print and it will slice it horizontally to whatever fits on a sheet of paper. The maximum page width is 32,000 twips, or 22 inches. This means that if you have 50 columns of text (each column only 1 inch wide, or 1440 twips), then you would need 72,000 twips for display width. The results would be that only the first 32K worth of data would properly print and display.

 NOTE *The maximum print width for a PDF 5.0 file is 22 inches, so anything beyond two pages wide would not export to PDF.*

The code in Listing 8-10 is a subset of the Form_Load event. For the entire project, see the source code for this book, which you can download from the Apress Web site (http://www.apress.com). In this section of code a few things are happening. The PrintWidth is increased (although once it reaches 32K it's maxed out), and the Left offset of each label and control is calculated. This example uses both Labels and Fields with a width of 1260 (90 twips between controls for a total of 1350). However, for the purpose of reports, you may develop the font, spacing between labels, and control height, and many other features can be "tweaked" to better suit your report.

Listing 8-10. Code to Dynamically Create Both Labels and Fields

```
nLeft = 1350 ' Offset of Base Label

' Get first label contents
Me.LabelCaption.Caption = "Product"

' Get first data field
Me.field.DataField = "ProductName"

' Create the labels across the top
For iLoop = 1 To Me.dat.Recordset.Fields.Count - 1
    ' Increment position
    nLeft = nLeft + 1350

    ' Update print width
    If ((nLeft + 1350) > nWidth) Then
        ' Adjust width by one field and margin
        nWidth = nWidth + (1350 + Me.PageSettings.LeftMargin)
    End If

    ' Update print width
    If nWidth > Me.PrintWidth Then
        Me.PrintWidth = nWidth
    End If

    ' Add labels
    AddLabel Me.dat.Recordset(iLoop).Name, nLeft, "Lbl" & iLoop

    ' Add field
    AddField Me.dat.Recordset(iLoop).Name, nLeft, "fld" & iLoop
Next iLoop

' Adjust left
nLeft = nLeft + 1350

' Add Total label
AddLabel "Total", nLeft, "LabelTotal"

' Add field
AddField "", nLeft, "fieldTotal"
```

The final trick in this report demonstrates using the DetailFormat event. The code in Listing 8-11 shows how to calculate a row's total. While this total could easily be calculated in the SQL statement, the goal of this is to demonstrate using the DetailFormat event.

Listing 8-11. Code to Calculate a Row Total

```
Private Sub Detail_Format()
    Dim iLoop       As Integer      ' Loop counter
    Dim nTotal      As Currency     ' Row total

    nTotal = 0

    ' Sum this row
    For iLoop = 1 To (Me.dat.Recordset.Fields.Count - 1)
        nTotal = nTotal + Me.dat.Recordset(iLoop)
    Next iLoop

    ' Set the total for these columns
    Me.Sections("Detail").Controls("fieldTotal").Text = Format(nTotal, "$#,###.00")
End Sub
```

Another possible solution is to process the entire report from top to bottom, displaying the number of fields you can print in one pass and then restarting the report, resuming with the fields where you left off. This process has drawbacks in that the Preview screen becomes useless, as it will reset itself for each pass. The printed report, however, will come out correctly. Once you have reached the last set of pages, simply allow the report to terminate.

ActiveReports for .NET

ActiveReports is also available for .NET. In this section we're going to examine the crosstab report example that is included with the ActiveReports for .NET version. While Data Dynamics has done a great job with ActiveReports for .NET, they have done very little in the crosstab area. Sure, they provide an example, but there is little if not almost no documentation on how the crosstab example works, and for that matter there are almost no comments in the code.

 NOTE   *Unlike ActiveReports 2.0, the .NET version of ActiveReports ships with a crosstab example report.*

ActiveReports gives you complete control to bind reports to any type of data source, including arrays, through its programmable object model. You don't have to specify a data source when you create a report; you can do it dynamically. The Fields property, which allows data binding between the control and the runtime fields, can be set at runtime. It allows the control's DataField property to be set to any of the runtime-defined names. The DataInitialize and FetchData events are used to define the runtime fields and feed the data values of these fields so they can be used with unbound controls.

To create the crosstab report in this example, you'll create the fields and set the data source at runtime. This report shows weekly sales of products and the quantity sold of each. This example also performs some comparisons to prior years. This report is deceptively simple looking, but as you'll find out, things aren't always as they seem.

Let's begin by examining how the report is configured. Once you have opened the crosstab example solution, if you examine the ReportStart() section, you'll find the code shown in Listing 8-12.

Listing 8-12. The rptProductWeeklySales_ReportStart Code

```
Dim m_ds = New DataDynamics.ActiveReports.DataSources.OleDBDataSource()
m_ds.ConnectionString = "Provider=Microsoft.Jet.OLEDB.4.0; " & _
        "Persist Security Info=False;Data Source=" + _
        getDatabasePath() + "\nwind.mdb"

m_ds.SQL = "SELECT DISTINCTROW " & _
        "Categories.CategoryID, Categories.CategoryName, " & _
        "Products.ProductName, " & _
        "Orders.OrderDate, " & _
        "Sum([Order Details Extended].ExtendedPrice) AS ProductSales, " & _
        "Sum([Order Details Extended].Quantity) AS ProductUnits "

m_ds.SQL = m_ds.SQL & " FROM(Categories) " & _
        "INNER JOIN (Products " & _
        "INNER JOIN (Orders " & _
        "INNER JOIN [Order Details Extended] " & _
        "ON Orders.OrderID = [Order Details Extended].OrderID) " & _
        "ON Products.ProductID = [Order Details Extended].ProductID) " & _
        "ON Categories.CategoryID = Products.CategoryID "
```

```
        m_ds.SQL = m_ds.SQL & "GROUP BY " & _
            "Categories.CategoryID, Categories.CategoryName, " & _
            "Products.ProductName, Orders.OrderDate " & _
            "ORDER BY Categories.CategoryName, Products.ProductName"

        Me.DataSource = m_ds

        Me.PageSettings.Orientation = _
DataDynamics.ActiveReports.Document.PageOrientation.Landscape
        '//Set the report variables
        iCurrWk = 23
        iCurrMth = 6
        iCurrQtr = 2
        iCurrYr = 1996
        iLastYr = iCurrYr - 1
```

The first line declares the report data source. The next line configures the data source to connect to the Access Northwind example database that is shipped with ActiveReports. Now we get to the fun stuff. The SQL statement that is being prepared is designed to return a single row of product data while calculating the number of units sold and the dollar amount for that product on any order date.

The next step is to add the fields to the report. This is accomplished by using the DataInitialize event. However, once the fields have been added, if you examine the report designer, you will notice that the text fields on the report, such as txtWKUnits, are already bound to the fields, even though the data control was configured at design time. Listing 8-13 shows how the fields are created in the DataInitialize event.

Listing 8-13. The rptProductWeeklySales_DataInitialize Code

```
Private Sub rptProductWeeklySales_DataInitialize(ByVal sender As Object, _
    ByVal e As System.EventArgs) Handles MyBase.DataInitialize

        Me.Fields.Add("WkUnits")
        Me.Fields.Add("WkSales")
        Me.Fields.Add("MTDUnits")
        Me.Fields.Add("MTDSales")
        Me.Fields.Add("QTDUnits")
        Me.Fields.Add("QTDSales")
        Me.Fields.Add("PQTDSales")
        Me.Fields.Add("YTDUnits")
        Me.Fields.Add("YTDSales")

End Sub
```

Now what makes this interesting is that this crosstab report is far less dynamic than the one previously described and built for ActiveReports 2.0. While there are some fundamental differences between ActiveReports 2.0 and ActiveReports for .NET, the crosstab report built in the previous example can be done using ActiveReports for .NET with only a few modifications. This next section will examine what differences exist between the two and how to build the same crosstab report using ActiveReports for .NET.

To create the prior report, there are several things you must do in Visual Basic .NET. The first thing is to declare the ActiveReports Viewer form. Since ActiveReports for .NET does not support the .Show method of the report, you must first create a form, add the viewer, and then in the Form_Load event load and run the report. Listing 8-14 shows the code for the cmdReport_Click event, which declares the viewer and shows the report.

Listing 8-14. Code to Open the Viewer Window

```
Private Sub cmdReport_Click(ByVal sender As System.Object, _
    ByVal e As System.EventArgs) Handles cmdReport.Click

        ' Declare Report Viewer form
        Dim frm As New frmRptViewer()

        ' Show the Form
        frm.Show()


    End Sub
```

Now that the report viewer window is open, the report itself must be loaded. This is accomplished in the Form_Load event of the Viewer form. Listing 8-15 shows how to declare the report and load it into the viewer.

Listing 8-15. Code to Load the Crosstab Report

```
Private Sub frmRptViewer_Load(ByVal sender As Object, _
    ByVal e As System.EventArgs) Handles MyBase.Load
        ' Show the form
        Me.Show()

        ' Declare the report
        Dim rpt = New rptCrossTab()

        ' Set the Viewer document to the report
        Me.Viewer1.Document = rpt.Document
```

```
    ' Run the report
    rpt.Run(True)
End Sub
```

Now that we have the shell of code that will load the report into the viewer, let's examine the differences between the two reports. The first difference extends to making the actual database connection. In version 2.0, this is accomplished by a separate data control that you place on the report. With ActiveReports for .NET, there is already a data source object present on the Detail section. Listing 8-16 shows the code to create the data object and build the connection string. Finally, after building the SQL statement, the entire data source object is assigned to the Detail section data object.

Listing 8-16. Building the Data Source

```
' Declare data source
Dim oDs = New DataDynamics.ActiveReports.DataSources.OleDBDataSource()

' Build connection string
    oDs.ConnectionString = "Provider=SQLOLEDB;User ID=sa; " &_
    "password=poptart;Initial Catalog=Northwind;Data Source=VIVID_VIAO;"

...Code to build SQL Statement goes here

' Assign SQL back to data source
oDs.SQL = cSQL

' Open data source
Me.DataSource = oDs
```

Now that the data source is connected, you need to modify the loop that builds the dynamic Label and Textbox controls. Listing 8-17 shows the loop portion that has been modified to handle the change from twips to pixels.

Listing 8-17. The Modified Loop to Create the Controls

```
' Create the labels across the top
nFields = Me.Fields.Count

For iLoop = 1 To nFields - 1
    ' Increment position
    nLeft = nLeft + 0.75
```

```
' Update print width
' Adjust width by one field and margin
nWidth = nWidth + (0.75 + Me.PageSettings.Margins.Left)

' Update print width
Me.PrintWidth = nWidth

' Add labels
AddLabel(Me.Fields(iLoop).Name, nLeft, "Lbl" & iLoop)

' Add field
AddField(Me.Fields(iLoop).Name, nLeft, "fld" & iLoop)

Next iLoop

' Adjust left
nLeft = nLeft + 0.75

' Add Total label
AddLabel("Total", nLeft, "LabelTotal")

' Add field
AddField("", nLeft, "fieldTotal")
```

ActiveReports for .NET also incorporates a different approach for creating and adding controls. Under 2.0 you added controls to the controls array, and you still do that; however, in ActiveReports for .NET, you must first create the control and then add it directly to the controls array for the section. Listing 8-18 shows the modified AddLabel and AddField functions. The other major difference is that in ActiveReports for .NET the Textbox control has replaced the Field control in version 2.0.

Listing 8-18. AddLabel and AddField Functions

```
Private Sub AddLabel(ByVal cCaption As String, _
    ByVal nLeft As Integer, Optional ByVal cName As String = "")

    '

    ' This subroutine dynamically creates a label at runtime.
    ' To call this function :
    '
    '   AddLabel("LabelName", 1.53, "LabelHeader1")
    '
```

```
    Dim oLabel As DataDynamics.ActiveReports.Label = _
            New DataDynamics.ActiveReports.Label() ' Label Object

    Me.PageHeader.Controls.Add(oLabel)

    With oLabel
        .Text = cCaption

        ' Set label position, alignment, and other properties
        .Left = nLeft
        .Top = Me.LabelCaption.Top
        .Height = Me.LabelCaption.Height
        .Width = 0.75

        '.BackStyle = Me.LabelCaption.BackStyle
        .BackColor = Me.LabelCaption.BackColor
        .Alignment = Me.LabelCaption.Alignment

        If cName <> vbNullString Then
            .Name = cName
        End If

        .Visible = True
    End With

End Sub

Private Sub AddField(ByVal cField As String, ByVal nLeft As Integer, _
        Optional ByVal cName As String = "")

    Dim oField As DataDynamics.ActiveReports.TextBox = _
            New DataDynamics.ActiveReports.TextBox()

    ' Create the fields
    Me.Detail.Controls.Add(oField)

    ' Set field, position, and other properties
    With oField
        .DataField = cField

        .Left = nLeft
        .Top = Me.field.Top
        .Height = Me.field.Height
        .Width = 0.75
```

```
            .OutputFormat = Me.field.OutputFormat
            .Alignment = TextAlignment.Right 'Me.field.Alignment

            If cName <> vbNullString Then
                .Name = cName
            End If

            .Visible = True
        End With
    End Sub
```

The last minor changes (see Listing 8-19) involve converting the Field control in the Detail_Format event to a TextBox control and modifying the PageFooter_Format event to use the .Text property instead of the default property.

Listing 8-19. The Changes to Detail_Format and PageFooter_Format

```
Private Sub Detail_Format(ByVal sender As Object, _
    ByVal e As System.EventArgs) Handles Detail.Format
        Dim iLoop As Integer          ' Loop counter
        Dim nTotal As Double          ' Row total
        Dim oFld As DataDynamics.ActiveReports.TextBox

        oFld = Me.Detail.Controls("fieldTotal")
        nTotal = 0

        ' Sum this row
        For iLoop = 1 To (Me.Fields.Count - 1)
            nTotal = nTotal + Me.Fields(iLoop).Value
        Next iLoop

        ' Set the total for these columns
        oFld.Text = Format(nTotal, "$#,###.00")
    End Sub

Private Sub PageFooter_Format(ByVal sender As Object, _
            ByVal e As System.EventArgs) Handles PageFooter.Format
        ' Display page number
        Me.LabelPage.Text = "Page : " & CStr(nPage)

        ' Increment page count
        nPage = nPage + 1
    End Sub
```

Crystal Reports

Crystal Reports offers a wizard that allows you to create crosstabs reports very quickly. Even if you're not one to avail yourself of wizards, this is definitely one worth looking at. It will do almost all of the needed work for you.

Programming crosstabs using Crystal's Report Creation API is another story. Crystal offers the CrossTabObject and CrossTabGroup objects to allow you to create crosstab reports at runtime. If you aren't familiar with Crystal Developer tools like the Runtime Designer Components (RDC) or the Report Creation API, please read Chapter 4 as a prerequisite to this section.

To illustrate how to program crosstab reports using Crystal Reports, we'll look at an example from the Xtreme database that ships with Crystal's demo code. Here the objective is to show the total dollar value of all orders placed by product for a given region. The individual customer regions will print down the left side of the report, while the product names will print as the column headers across the top. The intersection of each region/product will be the total dollar amount sold for that product in that region. The final goal is a report like the one shown in Figure 8-3.

	Active Outdoors Crochet Glove	Active Outdoors Lycra Glove	Descent	Endorphin	Guardian "U" Lock
Abu Dhabi	$0.00	$0.00	$0.00	$0.00	$0.00
AL	$28,785.14	$12,833.15	$137,462.20	$40,320.53	$0.00
Alsace	$0.00	$0.00	$0.00	$899.85	$0.00
Ankara	$0.00	$0.00	$0.00	$0.00	$0.00
Aquitaine	$0.00	$0.00	$2,939.85	$0.00	$0.00
AR	$0.00	$0.00	$8,819.55	$0.00	$0.00
Auckland	$0.00	$0.00	$0.00	$0.00	$0.00
Auvergne	$0.00	$0.00	$0.00	$0.00	$0.00
Avon	$0.00	$0.00	$8,819.55	$0.00	$0.00
AZ	$0.00	$49.50	$0.00	$0.00	$0.00
Bangkok	$0.00	$0.00	$0.00	$0.00	$0.00
Basse Normandie	$0.00	$0.00	$0.00	$0.00	$0.00
Bayern	$0.00	$0.00	$0.00	$0.00	$0.00
BC	$2,189.51	$8,216.24	$131,782.93	$35,197.13	$35.00
Belo Horizonte	$0.00	$0.00	$0.00	$0.00	$0.00
Berkshire	$43.50	$0.00	$0.00	$0.00	$0.00

Figure 8-3. Crystal crosstab report (partial view)

Here, we'll limit ourselves to taking a look at the pertinent section of the source code used to create this report. The source in its entirety can be found with the downloadable code for this book (available from the Apress Web site at http://www.apress.com). The first step is to declare the appropriate Crystal objects as shown in Listing 8-20.

Listing 8-20. Crystal Object Declarations

```
Dim objApplication As CRAXDRT.Application
Dim objReport As CRAXDRT.Report
Dim objDBTables As CRAXDRT.DatabaseTables
Dim objSourceDBTable As CRAXDRT.DatabaseTable
Dim objDestDBTable As CRAXDRT.DatabaseTable
Dim objSourceDBField As CRAXDRT.DatabaseFieldDefinition
Dim objDestDBField As CRAXDRT.DatabaseFieldDefinition
Dim objDBlinks As CRAXDRT.TableLinks
Dim objDBLink As CRAXDRT.TableLink
Dim objCrossTabObject As CRAXDRT.CrossTabObject
Dim objCrossTabGroup As CRAXDRT.CrossTabGroup
Dim objFieldObject As CRAXDRT.FieldObject
```

Next, the database connection must be created and the various table links established. In this example, the report is connecting to an Access MDB file. objDBTables serves as an object reference to the table collection of the report object. Using the Add method of this object, each of the tables required to create the report—Customer, Orders, Orders Detail, Product—are added individually to the collection. The SetSessionInfo method passes in the user ID and password. The code to make this database connection appears in Listing 8-21.

Listing 8-21. Connecting the Crosstab Report to the Database

```
With objReport
    Set objDBTables = .Database.Tables

    .Database.Tables.Add cDatabasePath, "Customer"
    .Database.Tables(1).SetSessionInfo "Admin", ""

    .Database.Tables.Add cDatabasePath, "Orders"
    .Database.Tables(2).SetSessionInfo "Admin", ""

    .Database.Tables.Add cDatabasePath, "Orders Detail"
    .Database.Tables(3).SetSessionInfo "Admin", ""

    .Database.Tables.Add cDatabasePath, "Product"
    .Database.Tables(4).SetSessionInfo "Admin", ""
End With
```

Once the Tables collection has been populated, you can make the various relational links using the DBLink object. First, join the Orders Detail table to the Product table each on their common Product ID field. objSourceDBTable holds a reference to the Orders Detail table, while objDestDBTable refers to the Product table. Their common linked fields are referred to via the objSourceDBField and objDestDBField objects. Then, the Add method of the objDBLink object establishes the link between the two tables. As shown in the code in Listing 8-22, this linking occurs three times, once for each of the table links that must be established.

Listing 8-22. Creating the Table Joins

```
With objReport
    Set objSourceDBTable = .Database.Tables.Item(3) 'Orders Detail
    Set objDestDBTable = .Database.Tables.Item(4) 'Product
    Set objSourceDBField = .Database.Tables.Item(3).Fields.Item(2)
                                    '{Orders Detail.Product ID}
    Set objDestDBField = _
            .Database.Tables.Item(4).Fields.Item(1)
            '{Product.Product ID}
    Set objDBlinks = .Database.Links
    Set objDBLink = objDBlinks.Add(objSourceDBTable, objDestDBTable, _
            objSourceDBField,  objDestDBField, crJTEqual, _
            crLTLookupParallel, False, True)

    Set objSourceDBTable = .Database.Tables.Item(3) 'Orders Detail
    Set objDestDBTable = .Database.Tables.Item(2) 'Orders
    Set objSourceDBField = .Database.Tables.Item(3).Fields.Item(1)
            '{Orders Detail.Order ID}
    Set objDestDBField = .Database.Tables.Item(2).Fields.Item(1) '{Orders.Order ID}
    Set objDBlinks = .Database.Links
    Set objDBLink = objDBlinks.Add(objSourceDBTable, objDestDBTable, _
            objSourceDBField,  objDestDBField, crJTEqual, _
            crLTLookupParallel, False, True)

    Set objSourceDBTable = .Database.Tables.Item(2) 'Orders
    Set objDestDBTable = .Database.Tables.Item(1) 'Customer
    Set objSourceDBField = .Database.Tables.Item(2).Fields.Item(3)
            '{Orders.Customer ID}
    Set objDestDBField = .Database.Tables.Item(1).Fields.Item(1)
            '{Customer.Customer ID}
    Set objDBlinks = .Database.Links
    Set objDBLink = objDBlinks.Add(objSourceDBTable, objDestDBTable, _
```

```
                    objSourceDBField, objDestDBField, crJTEqual, _
                crLTLookupParallel, False, True)
End With
```

Listing 8-23 shows the key section of code to establish the crosstab rows and columns. First, you'll create a CrossTabObject, which adds the {Orders.Order Amount} field to the SummaryFields collection. Set the EnableRepeatRowLabels property to True in order to cause the region names that appear down the left side of the page to display on every page. It's rather difficult to read a crosstab report with many columns unless you repeat the row labels. The very poorly named EnableSuppressColumnGrandTotals and EnableSuppressRowGrandTotals properties will suppress column and row grand totals if set to True.

Listing 8-23. Creation of CrossTabObjects

```
Set objCrossTabObject = objReport.Sections("RHa").AddCrossTabObject(0, 0)

With objCrossTabObject
    .SummaryFields.Add "{Orders.Order Amount}"
    .EnableRepeatRowLabels = True
    .EnableSuppressColumnGrandTotals = False
    .EnableSuppressRowGrandTotals = False
    .RowGrandTotalColor = vbRed
    .ColumnGrandTotalColor = vbGreen
    .Suppress = False
    .KeepTogether = False
    .LeftLineStyle = crLSNoLine
    .RightLineStyle = crLSNoLine
    .TopLineStyle = crLSNoLine
    .BottomLineStyle = crLSNoLine
    .BackColor = vbWhite
End With

Set objCrossTabGroup = objCrossTabObject.RowGroups.Add("{Customer.Region}")

With objCrossTabGroup
    .BackColor = vbWhite
    .Condition = crGCAnyValue
    .SortDirection = crAscendingOrder
End With

Set objCrossTabGroup = objCrossTabObject.ColumnGroups.Add("{Product.Product Name}")
```

```
With objCrossTabGroup
    .BackColor = vbWhite
    .Condition = crGCAnyValue
    .SortDirection = crAscendingOrder
End With
```

NOTE *It isn't possible to change the size of the crosstab column or row captions programmatically in Crystal Reports.*

The CrossTabGroup object defines each of the fields that comprise the intersection of two database elements—in this example Regions and Product Names. These objects are then added to the RowGroups collection of the CrossTabObject.

After all that, your Crystal Reports crosstab is complete and you can save and run the RPT file.

Online Analytical Processing (OLAP)

All the database examples thus far used in this book are based on OLTP databases. OLTP—online transaction processing—stores the individual detail data records for all transactions. Summarization of this data is performed by executing queries that, at best, are optimized only with indices. In fact, storing presummarized data in an OLTP database constitutes "redundant data" and is *not* a recommended practice. By contrast, OLAP databases store presummarized data by design, against which you can run queries to track such things as trends and time series.

TIP *For an excellent overview of OLAP technology, check out the white papers at* http://www.olapreport.com *and* http://nds.nongshim.co.kr/nds/down/olap.html.

Therefore, calculation of the monthly sales by product from an OLAP database will happen almost instantaneously. Imagine the time it would take to compute the same numbers using several SUM()...WHERE...GROUP BY queries across ten million rows of data in an OLTP database.

NOTE *Both SQL Server and Oracle are traditional OLTP databases with OLAP support, whereas Essbase (Hyperion Solutions) is the most entrenched OLAP database on the market today.*

OLAP Usage

The majority of OLAP applications are financial in nature; for example, they are often used for budgeting, financial analysis, and marketing sales analysis. Another common use for an OLAP application is marketing research. This research can focus on sales and even promotional analysis to evaluate customer satisfaction with a given product.

Clearly, all of these applications provide managers with information that they can use to make business decisions. Because they consist of summarizations of vast quantities of data, OLAP applications are judged successful based on their ability to provide information to their users in a timely fashion. Data analysis that is performed using this model is referred to as "just in time" information.

Multidimensional Views

Before we can discuss multidimensional views, let's first define multidimensional data.

NOTE *It's important to make the distinction here between multidimensional views and views used in an OLTP database. In an OLTP RDBMS, a view is akin to a virtual table in a database, as criteria define what data is displayed. OLAP's multidimensional views, on the other hand, are organized around multiple tables and multiple data representations.*

RDBMSs contain individual rows (or records) of data. Each record stores related information that is organized into fields (or columns). For example, a contact table might contain the data shown in Table 8-1.

Table 8-1. Customer Database

CUSTOMER NUMBER	NAME	PHONE	ADDRESS
10192	Best Aeronet	972-555-0989	53 West Lane
10929	Westbrook Forms	469-555-0087	1019 Highline Drive
12309	New Connects	800-555-5656	8054 Sky Drive
13314	Johnson Controls	817-555-5645	3435 Legacy

Such tables are one dimensional because each piece of information relates to only one customer name. As you can see, looking at "Customer by Address" or "Address by Customer" only produces a one-for-one correspondence and is therefore not suitable for multidimensional representation.

Almost any OLTP financial application will contain a table where there is more than a one-for-one correspondence between the fields. For example, suppose you have sales data for each product in each country. Given three products (CPUs, Keyboards, and Monitors) that are sold in three countries (USA, Canada, and Mexico), the data could be loaded into a relational table as shown in Table 8-2.

Table 8-2. Product Data in Database

PRODUCT	COUNTRY	UNIT SALES
CPU	USA	1000
CPU	Canada	4000
Keyboard	Canada	1200
Keyboard	Mexico	2000
Monitor	USA	3000
Monitor	Mexico	500

Because this table has more than one product per country and more than one country per product, it's prime for multidimensional representation. A true multidimensional representation is shown in Table 8-3.

Table 8-3. Two-Dimensional Matrix View

PRODUCT	USA	CANADA	MEXICO
CPU		1000	4000
Monitor	3000		500
Keyboard		1200	2000

Multidimensional views not only enable users to slice and dice data down to the cell level, but also provide analytical processing and flexible access to stored data. The key to an OLAP database design model is that the same operation can be performed at many levels against any dimension, and should consistently return results in a timely fashion. This means that managers have the ability to access data that spans more than one dimension, and they can then analyze this data down to any level. Thus, a user can drill down from country, to region, to city, or from sales region, to district, to area, to individual sales rep.

Fast response times is a key element of OLAP databases, and the way that OLAP systems achieve this speed is through the use of consolidation. Response times in multidimensional databases still depend on the on-demand calculations. The numbers that have to be computed will affect the performance of the query. So using consolidation, which is a method of combining all the totals and sub-totals, OLAP databases can achieve superior performance. Since the data has been preconsolidated, totals can be retrieved from an OLAP system by accessing a single record.

Cubes and Dimensions

Cubes are the central concept to all OLAP analytical processing. A cube consists of a core or base "cuboid" to which is related multiple subcubes/subcuboids that represent the aggregation of the base cuboid across one or more dimensions. These aggregated dimensions are referred to as the *measure attribute*, while the other dimensions are called the *feature attributes*. Like a field in OLTP, a cube can be thought of as a cell of data that is the smallest building block. From this small cell, a row of cells is built, and on top of that a column of cells, and so on and so forth. The result is that the data is organized into a multidimensional (cube) structure. These cells contain summarized data from which complex queries may quickly return data.

The main elements of a cube are *dimension* and *measure*. Dimensions provide descriptions for each category by which the measures are separated for analysis. Measures are used to identify the numerical values of summarized analysis, such as price, cost, or quantity.

Each cube dimension can contain multiple levels known as a *hierarchy*. These hierarchies help to specify the available category breakdowns. For example, an oil company might have a Gas Station dimension that might include State, Zip Code, and City. Each level in a dimension is a finer grain of detail than that of the parent. Another way of conceptualizing this might be to think of how Windows Explorer browses files. At the top level you have the computer, within the computer you have drives, within the drives you have folders, and within each folder are files.

For a cube to synchronize itself with the underlying transaction data that it summarizes, it must be processed. Depending upon the frequency with which the underlying data is processed and the size of the database and the number of dimensions, this may or may not take a significant amount of time. Often large corporate databases are processed overnight so the dimensions are no more than 12 hours behind the latest updates to the underlying transaction tables. For most corporate analysis requirements this works just fine, but there may be a requirement for immediate updates to the cubes whenever the user makes a change to the data. This is called *real-time OLAP*. (See the sidebar "Real-Time OLAP" for more information.)

Real-Time OLAP

Real-time OLAP is typically implemented by cubes that utilize relational OLAP (ROLAP) dimensions. Normally, cubes are updated only when they are reprocessed, commonly overnight. With real-time cubes, the aggregate data updates when data in their underlying dimensions change. SQL Server's Analysis Services can periodically poll the SQL Server data source for notifications about updates to dimension or fact tables associated with specific ROLAP dimensions requiring real-time updates. If the Analysis Server determines that a change to a dimension or fact table has occurred, it flushes the Analysis Server cache and automatically reprocesses the associated ROLAP dimensions. Analysis Services accomplishes this feat via a "listener" thread that facilitates the notification process for all ROLAP dimensions that have a SQL Server 2000 data source.

Another type of hierarchy is a *time dimension*. Again, the unique properties of time define this dimension to include anything ranging from seconds to decades, but for most business requirements Month, Quarter, and Year are the most common. Of course, the finer the level of detail, the more preprocessing may be required to build the summaries. Plus, more than one hierarchy can exist for a single dimension. Using the Time dimensions as an example, let's further separate the hierarchies to be either a calendar or a fiscal period, both of which can exist in a single dimension. A Fiscal year includes a different 12 months of data than a Calendar year, yet both contain the levels of Year, Quarter, and Month.

A dimension is another level (or unit) that exists within an Analysis Services (OLAP) cube. There are two types of dimensions—Private dimensions (those created for an individual cube) and Shared dimensions (those that span multiple cubes). Dimensions are similar to columns in a relational database. In the example given earlier, there are columns called Product and Country. In the multidimensional database, Product and Country are both dimensions.

Think of it this way: A measure is the value you're tracking and a dimension is what you're measuring it by. Levels of a dimension are the hierarchy within a dimension.

The final OLAP concept is the *member*. A member is an item that exists within a dimension or measure, much like a file in the previous Windows Explorer example. There are two types of members—standard and calculated. Calculated members are dimension members whose value is calculated at runtime. When storing a calculated member, only the definition of the members is stored; the actual data is calculated when needed. One major advantage to calculated members is that they allow you to add members, and in some instances measures, to a cube without increasing the size of the cube. Calculated members can also be complex expressions that combine data with programming code. A standard member is simply a member whose data is stored within the dimension or measure.

Microsoft SQL Server ships with a demo FoodMart database, the OLAP/Analysis Services cousin to the SQL Server's Northwind and pubs databases. Because this has been used in most of the examples I've seen published, we'll use our own OLAP database from the more familiar Northwind structure. This database can be found with the code for this book on the Apress Web site (http://www.apress.com).

Setting Up the OLAP Database Example

Since OLAP data is derived from transactional data, let's start Analysis Manager under the SQL Server's Analysis Services option on your Start menu and connect to a relational data source. Since Analysis Manager doesn't automatically install with the standard SQL Server 2000 setup, you'll need to load it separately.

First create a new database called Northwind. Then, under the Northwind option, create a new data source using the Microsoft OLE DB Provider for SQL Server and establish a connection to the Northwind database.

When creating a cube, you need to first determine *what* you want to measure and *how.* Suppose you want to track orders geographically (by country and city) and chronologically (by year, quarter, month, etc.). These are the dimensions of the cube. Under the Shared Dimensions option, select New Dimension, and using the wizard create a Star Schema dimension using the Customers table.

Then, select Country and City as the levels of this dimension, and finally name the dimension Geography.

Using the Dimension Wizard again, create another dimension using a Start Schema called Time. Select Orders as the dimension table and OrderDate as the column. Realizing you are creating a time dimension, Analysis Manager will offer you options for time-specific levels. The default is Year, Quarter, Month, Day, so choose this option.

Now that you've created the Geography and Time dimensions, let's see how to create a new cube and select the fact table that will serve as the data source of your OLAP aggregations. Using the Cube Wizard, select Order Details as the fact table, and then choose Unit Price and Discount as the measures. Next, select both the Time and Geography dimensions, and finally name the new cube Sales.

To review what you just did: You chose to measure things by place and time. These are the dimensions. Then, you specified that it was Unit Price and Discount that you wanted to measure. Combining these dimensions and measures, you can do things like determine the quarterly sales made by country, or the monthly sales made across all cities within a given country. In the next section, we'll examine Microsoft ADO MD technology, which will allow you to do exactly that.

Microsoft and ADO MD Technologies

When Microsoft released SQL Server 7.0, they introduced an additional product known as SQL Server Analysis Services, which, at the time, was called OLAP Services. OLAP Services included tools for data mining and were designed to help programmers build basic OLAP functionality in SQL Server. To allow programmers to access these new structures programmatically, Microsoft created ADO MD.

Microsoft Multidimensional ActiveX Data Objects (ADO MDs) are designed to interact with OLE DB providers to allow developers access to multidimensional data using COM-based languages like Visual Basic or Visual C++, and using .NET via COM Interop. ADO MD is an extension of ADO that includes specific objects designed to manipulate multidimensional data so programmers can query cubes, retrieve results sets, and extract data out of single cells.

 NOTE *A cube in MDX is always represented by a DataSet object. The DataSet object is created with the OLE DB command object using the multidimensional expression objects (MDX) in the context of a multidimensional provider (MDP). The DataSet encapsulates the multidimensional result set returned by the MDP provider.*

Like ADO, ADO MD uses the underlying OLE DB provider to gain access to the data. There are two types of providers—multidimensional provider (MDP) and tabular data provider (TDP)—and both present data in a different fashion. MDPs supply the data in a multidimensional view, whereas TDPs supply data in a tabular view.

Rowset objects present data as a set of rows in tabular form. There are three types of rowsets:

- Schema rowsets, which return schema information

- Axis rowsets, which return information about the axes of a data set

- Range rowsets, where each cell in a data set is modeled as a row, and the collection of cells that can be updated by the application is presented as a range rowset

OLE DB for OLAP rowsets are usually much simpler than the typical OLE DB rowset. For example, they do not need to implement bookmarks or scrolling, and the axis rowsets and the schema rowsets need not be updatable.

Multidimensional Expressions (MDX)

Microsoft SQL Server OLAP Services provide a foundation upon which to build multidimensional data. MDX is syntactically similar to SQL in that it uses a SELECT statement that consists of all the standard SQL SELECT elements including FROM and WHERE. As with any SQL query, each MDX query utilizes SELECT, FROM, and WHERE clauses.

OLAP Services support the MDX functions, and there are MDX commands for manipulating cubes, dimensions, measures, and their subordinate objects as well as a full language with extensions for user-defined functions.

Getting Started with MDX

We'll begin our journey into the world of MDX by examining the simplest form of an MDX expression. This template uses a SELECT statement and will return a cube with two dimensions:

```
SELECT <axis> ON COLUMNS,
<axis> ON ROWS
FROM <cube>
WHERE <slicer>
```

The axis specification is used to define the dimensions that are returned. For a single dimension, the columns keyword must be returned. For more dimensions, the axes would be named pages, chapters, and, for the last dimension, sections.

The "slicer" specification (the WHERE clause) is optional. If no slicer condition is supplied, then the returned measure is assumed the default for the cube. Unless your query is directed against the Measures dimension, you should *always* use a WHERE clause to more accurately define the "slice" of data that is requested from the cube.

In the example that follows, the Unit price total across all dimensions of Time and Geography, that is, everything can be had by executing this query:

```
SELECT
{[Time].[All Time]}ON COLUMNS,
{[Geography].[All Geography]}  ON ROWS
FROM Sales
WHERE  ([Measures].[Unit Price])
```

This is functionally similar to running this SQL query against Northwind directly:

```
SELECT SUM(UnitPrice)
FROM [Order Details]
```

Either way, both statements return a single value: $56,500.91.

Suppose you want to break this $56,500.91 annual sales amount into subtotals for the years 1996, 1997, and 1998 across all geographic regions. Since Time is a dimension, you could specify each year as a level of this dimension as shown in the following query:

```
SELECT
{[Time].[1996], [Time].[1997], [Time].[1998]}ON COLUMNS,
{[Geography].[All Geography]}  ON ROWS
FROM Sales
WHERE  ([Measures].[Unit Price])
```

This is the same as running the following OLTP statement against Northwind directly:

```
SELECT YEAR(OrderDate), SUM(UnitPrice)
FROM [Order Details] od, Orders o
WHERE od.OrderID = o.OrderID
GROUP BY YEAR(OrderDate)
```

Either way, both queries return the same data, but while the SQL query displays the data in the more familiar vertical format, as follows:

```
1996    9410.20
1997    27615.08
1998    19475.63
```

the MDX query displays the results horizontally:

```
1996            1997            1998
9410.20        27615.08        19475.63
```

Suppose you want to see all the measures (in this case, UnitPrice and Discount) for all the countries in the Geography dimension. You need to use the MEMBERS keyword at the appropriate levels of aggregation as shown in the following statement:

```
SELECT Measures.MEMBERS ON COLUMNS,
[Country].MEMBERS ON ROWS
FROM [Sales]
```

To achieve the same result using Transact-SQL (T-SQL), you would use this statement:

```
SELECT c.Country, SUM(UnitPrice) AS UnitPrice, SUM(Discount) AS Discount
FROM [Order Details] od, Orders o, Customers c
WHERE od.OrderID = o.OrderID
AND o.CustomerID = c.CustomerID
GROUP BY c.Country
```

Both statements return the following results:

Country	UnitPrice	Discount
Argentina	1080.80	0.0
Austria	3469.95	8.60
Belgium	1341.98	2.15
Brazil	5324.64	13.50
Canada	1907.50	4.80
Denmark	1212.24	3.10
Finland	1293.79	2.00
France	4839.46	10.15
Germany	8544.84	20.70
Ireland	1719.86	6.25
Italy	1112.05	2.85
Mexico	1818.98	1.00
Norway	633.69	0.0
Poland	330.10	0.0
Portugal	740.89	2.85
Spain	1297.27	1.75
Sweden	2486.49	6.85
Switzerland	1331.69	2.55
UK	3116.87	3.10
USA	10462.91	20.94
Venezuela	2434.91	7.90

The following expression queries the measures for all orders from Germany and France. The CHILDREN keyword queries the actual members that make up the measures for both nations:

```
SELECT Measures.MEMBERS ON COLUMNS,
{[Geography].[Country].[Germany].CHILDREN,
    [Geography].[Country].[France].CHILDREN} ON ROWS
FROM [Sales]
```

Or, using the SQL equivalent like this:

```
SELECT c.City, SUM(UnitPrice) AS UnitPrice, SUM(Discount) AS Discount
FROM [Order Details] od, Orders o, Customers c
WHERE od.OrderID = o.OrderID
AND o.CustomerID = c.CustomerID
AND c.Country IN ('Germany', 'France')
GROUP BY c.City
```

you'll return the following results:

Aachen	191.08	0.0
Berlin	320.85	1.05
Brandenburg	1229.24	1.55
Cunewalde	2739.95	5.95
Frankfurt a.M.	1028.19	3.75
Köln	609.55	1.70
Leipzig	322.25	0.0
Lille	443.35	0.0
Lyon	510.45	2.30
Mannheim	347.05	0.0
Marseille	1061.40	3.20
München	982.98	3.15
Münster	212.45	1.25
Nantes	451.24	0.0
Paris	408.20	0.0
Reims	175.65	0.0
Strasbourg	848.75	0.75
Stuttgart	561.25	2.30
Toulouse	655.34	3.90
Versailles	285.03	0.0

The expression uses fully qualified, that is, unique, names. A fully qualified member name includes the dimension and the parent member of the given members at all levels. If the member names are uniquely identifiable, the fully qualified member names aren't necessary. Therefore, the use of unique names is preferred.

MEMBERS and CHILDREN do not have the ability to drill down to lower levels within the hierarchy. Since OLAP represents data hierarchies as well as aggregations, it should come as no surprise that this technology would use genealogical terms to describe relationships. To accomplish this, you need to use DESCENDANTS. When using the DESCENDANTS function, only members at the specified level are included. Thus it becomes possible to query specific items within the cube such as the individual store's city level, as well as the summary at the store's state level. By altering the value of the flags, you can include or exclude descendants or children both before and after the indicated level.

This next MDX statement retrieves first the aggregate totals across all Measures (UnitPrice and Discount) and across the entire Time dimension for Germany and for all cities that are DESCENDANTS of Germany on the city level:

```
SELECT Measures.MEMBERS ON COLUMNS,
{[Country].[Germany],
    DESCENDANTS([Country].[Germany], [City])} ON ROWS
FROM [Sales]
```

Note that is a mere four lines of code. Compare this to the rather extensive SQL statement that you would need to achieve the same results in OLTP:

```
SELECT c.Country, SUM(UnitPrice) AS UnitPrice,
SUM(Discount) AS Discount, 0 AS SortOrder
FROM [Order Details] od, Orders o, Customers c
WHERE od.OrderID = o.OrderID
AND o.CustomerID = c.CustomerID
AND c.Country = 'Germany'
GROUP BY c.Country
UNION
SELECT c.City, SUM(UnitPrice) AS UnitPrice,
SUM(Discount) AS Discount, 1 AS SortOrder
FROM [Order Details] od, Orders o, Customers c
WHERE od.OrderID = o.OrderID
AND o.CustomerID = c.CustomerID
AND c.Country = 'Germany'
GROUP BY c.City
ORDER BY SortOrder
```

Either way, both statements return the following results:

Country	UnitPrice	Discount
Germany	8544.84	20.70
Aachen	191.08	0.0
Berlin	320.85	1.05
Brandenburg	1229.24	1.55
Cunewalde	2739.95	5.95
Frankfurt a.M.	1028.19	3.75
Köln	609.55	1.70
Leipzig	322.25	0.0
Mannheim	347.05	0.0
München	982.98	3.15
Münster	212.45	1.25
Stuttgart	561.25	2.30

The possible values for the flag parameter are SELF (the default), BEFORE, AFTER, and BEFORE_AND_AFTER. So if you wished to return the level after the store cities (i.e., the actual store names), you could do so by modifying your query to look like this:

```
DESCENDANTS([Store].[Store State].[CA], [Store City], AFTER)
```

To return the information at the state level, you would use the BEFORE flag.

NOTE *Although I've been showing you the OLTP version of extracting the same data as the similar MDX expression, remember that this is simply for comparative purposes only. Each MDX command is extracting from a database of only a few records. The SQL statements by comparison could be traversing millions of rows.*

Additional MDX Functionality

While the basics of MDX are enough to provide simple queries against multidimensional data, there are many more enhanced features of the MDX implementation that make MDX a very powerful query tool such as the ability to use Visual Basic functions within the syntax. Coverage of the more advanced aspects of MDX is beyond the scope of this book. For the more advanced features and information on MDX, you should visit MSDN (`http://msdn.microsoft.com`), or read all of Russ Whitney's columns that are archived at `http://www.SQLMag.com`.

Connecting to an OLAP Database Using Visual Basic

Okay, so now you have some idea how to use MDX expressions, but that really doesn't help you except for running the queries. Connecting to the Analysis Server really isn't that different from building a standard connection in ADO. First, you must add the references for ADO and ADO MD to your project. Then you can simply use a Connection object and define the connection. Next, you create a Cellset object and set the Source property to the MDX Query expression. Finally, set the ActiveConnection property of the Cellset object to the ActiveConnection property of the Connection object, and use the Open method to retrieve the actual results (see Listing 8-24).

Listing 8-24. Code to Open an ADO MD Connection in Visual Basic

```
Public Sub OpenOLAPConnection()

    ' Set up the connection string to the server.
    objConn.ConnectionString = "Datasource=LocalHost; Provider=msolap; " & _
                        "Initial Catalog=Northwind;"


    objConn.Open
```

```
' Create the Cellset Active Connection object
Set objCellset.ActiveConnection = objConn

' Create the MDX query
objCellset.Source = "SELECT Measures.MEMBERS ON COLUMNS," & _
                    "{[Geography].[Country].[Germany].CHILDREN," & _
                    "[Geography].[Country].[France].CHILDREN} ON ROWS " & _
                    "From [Sales]"

' Open object
objCellset.Open

End Sub
```

Now that you've established a connection, display the data in a MSFlexGrid. For the results of an MDX query, there is one Axis collection for each dimension of the request. Listing 8-25 shows how to iterate through this Axis collection to build the column headers and populate the cells of the grid with data.

Listing 8-25. Building the Column Headers for the Axis Collection

```
Dim iCols As Integer
Dim iRows As Integer
Dim iColCount As Integer
Dim iRowCount As Integer
Dim oPos As ADOMD.Position
Dim x As Integer

With MSFlexGrid1

    iColCount = objCellset.Axes(0).Positions.Count
    iRowCount = objCellset.Axes(1).Positions.Count

    .Cols = iColCount + 1
    .Rows = iRowCount + 1

    .ColWidth(0) = 1500

    'Get the column headers and align numeric data to the right
    x = 1
```

```
        For Each oPos In objCellset.Axes(0).Positions
            .TextMatrix(0, x) = oPos.Members(0).Caption
            .ColAlignment(x) = flexAlignRightCenter
            x = x + 1
        Next

        'Get the row headers.
        x = 0

        For Each oPos In objCellset.Axes(1).Positions
            .TextMatrix(x + 1, 0) = oPos.Members(0).Caption
            x = x + 1
        Next

        'Populate the individual dollar values
        For iCols = 0 To iColCount - 1
            For iRows = 0 To iRowCount - 1
                .TextMatrix(iRows + 1, iCols + 1) = _
                    Format(objCellset(iCols, iRows).Value, "$#0.00")
            Next iRows
        Next iCols

    End With
```

Connecting to the Catalog object allows you to reference the cubes contained within the OLAP database. Once you have established a connection to the Catalog object, you can use the Cubes collection to retrieve whichever cube you wish to access. Listing 8-26 shows how to connect to the Catalog object using ADO.

Listing 8-26. Connecting to the Catalog Object

```
Dim objCubeDef As ADOMD.CubeDef
Dim objDimension As ADOMD.Dimension
Dim objCatalog As ADOMD.Catalog
Dim cMsg As String

'Create a Catalog object
Set objCatalog = New ADOMD.Catalog
Set objCatalog.ActiveConnection = objConn

'...and set a reference to the Sales Cube
Set objCubeDef = objCatalog.CubeDefs("Sales")
```

```
'Extract the names of the Sales cube dimensions
For Each objDimension In objCubeDef.Dimensions
    cMsg = cMsg & objDimension.Name & vbCrLf
Next objDimension

'...and show 'em to the user
MsgBox "Dimensions for the " & objCubeDef.Name & _
        " cube are: " & vbCrLf & cMsg
```

You can also access the hierarchies within the cube's Dimension object by referencing the name or offset:

```
Dim objHierachy As ADOMD.Hierarchy

For Each objHierachy In objDimension.Hierarchies
    cMsg = cMsg & objHierachy.Name
Next objHierachy
```

Connecting to an OLAP Database Using ADO.NET

Connecting to ADO MD in .NET is handled through the COM Interop. To make the connection, you must include the System.Data.OleDb namespace in your .NET application. Once you have done that, you then modify the provider string information to include the correct provider information for the ADO MD driver. Listing 8-27 shows how to make a connection to ADO MD using VB .NET.

Listing 8-27. Connecting to ADO MD Using VB .NET

```
Dim objDR As OleDbDataReader
Dim objConnection As New OleDbConnection()
Dim objCommand As New OleDbCommand()
Dim cConn As String
Dim cSQL As String

' Build the Provider string
 cConn = "Datasource=LocalHost; Provider=msolap; " & _
                "Initial Catalog=Northwind;"

objConnection.ConnectionString = cConn
objConnection.Open
```

```
cSQL = "SELECT Measures.MEMBERS ON COLUMNS," & _
            "{[Geography].[Country].[Germany].CHILDREN," & _
            "[Geography].[Country].[France].CHILDREN} ON ROWS " & _
            "From [Sales]"

    With objCommand
        .Connection = objConnection
        .CommandText = cSQL
        .CommandType = CommandType.Text
        .CommandTimeout = 60
        objDR = .ExecuteReader()
    End With
```

Conclusion

Crosstab queries can be quite a challenge regardless of the reporting tool you are using. Fortunately, they all have very similar characteristics, and once you've developed a template, you can reuse it again and again. Coming up, we'll examine how to deploy your reports to the Internet.

CHAPTER 9

Reports on the Web

THE INTERNET IS ONE OF THE greatest mediums for making reports available to a wide audience. In fact, given that there are many more users who wish to run an application's reports than need to run the application itself, making the reports Web-based can extend your audience without granting access to the application itself. By doing so, the application's report menu can simply link to the Web pages containing the criteria screens that drive the reports themselves. This all depends, of course, on your authentication method. In a secure system, you have to be authenticated before you can enter another system. If you are running a client application, you may have to take extra steps to link to the reports. This way, those users who only need to run the reports can simply have Web link shortcuts installed on their desktops.

Server-based applications make the most sense from almost every perspective. There are no client-side installations of DLLs or other runtime components to worry about, and therefore "DLL hell" doesn't rear its ugly head. Once a user is logged in to the network, adding a new user to the application is a snap as the user simply needs to navigate to a URL and log in. In fact, rather than providing the user with an application, you're really providing the application with a user. The application usually resides in only one place—or two places if you're working with larger multitiered systems. It's the users that come and go.

Because some reports can take more than two or three seconds to run—either due to complex stored procedures and business logic or simply the sheer volume of data—you don't want to tie up a user's machine and block him or her from using the application until the process completes. Since VB6 is a single-threaded development environment, your only viable alternative is to offload report processing to server-based components separate from your application. Granted, you could manipulate the WinAPI to create additional threads in VB6, but this can get rather complicated. Fortunately, the .NET architecture is another story. Because .NET allows you to create multithreaded applications, you can continue to run your report code while the user returns to doing other work with your application.

HTML browser compatibility has limited what you can do on the server, as HTML is not a very robust language for user interface development. Java developers have long chuckled at the crude user interfaces that we Microsoft developers have been stuck with for the past several years. Sure, we have ActiveX controls, but these are not supported cross-platform and, like ActiveX documents, they never really caught on for Web application development. Luckily, Web-based reporting is one of the few areas that is not made overtly difficult by the user interface limitations of HTML. The trickiest part of a report is a flexible criteria screen, and HTML is more than adequate to handle this. Since ASP.NET makes it much easier to create slick user interfaces than classic ASP—at least without performing various unnatural acts—we should all start seeing more and more server-based applications in the near future.

Web Criteria Screens

Like any other application, your Web-based reports will need criteria screens to allow the user to filter the data. In the next section we'll discuss how to dynamically create these screens and pass parameters to reports.

NOTE *In researching several Web-based reporting tools such as Crystal Enterprise (http://www.crystaldecisions.com), Actuate (http://www.actuate.com), and WebFocus (http://www.webfocus.com), we found that none have criteria screen creation tools. You are responsible for collecting criteria information from the user and passing it to the report objects on the server. Therefore, no matter what tool you use to distribute your reports over the Web you will need to develop your own criteria screens.*

Passing Parameters

Basic HTML offers all the necessary controls to display adequate report criteria screens—list boxes, combo boxes, check boxes, and text fields. While you can create criteria screens in ASP using the same fundamental techniques described in Chapter 3, there are a few ways to get the criteria to your report module. One way is to pass the parameters via the URL by redirecting the criteria page to the report's ASP module like this:

```
Response.Redirect ("myreport.asp?datefrom=01/01/01& _
                    dateto=01/31/01&deptid=(12345, 45678)")
```

The problem with this approach is that the user gets to see the entire URL call in the browser where it is available for editing. There is nothing stopping a curious user from changing one of the deptid parameters from 12345 to another value that could very well be a department to which he or she is not intended to have access. Most likely, you'll integrate a crude measure of security into your application by only displaying those departments (in this example) that this particular user is permitted to see.

To avoid this problem, you can set up the page as method=post in the FORM tag:

```
<form name=frmCriteria method="post" action="myreport.asp">
```

Then, in myreport.asp, you can retrieve the criteria parameters using the Request object's Form method like this:

```
cDateFrom = Request.Form("txtDateFrom")
cDateTo = Request.Form ("txtDateTo")
lDeptID = Request.Form ("txtDeptID")
```

However, this additional level of security is largely based on user ignorance. A computer-savvy user can save the criteria page, edit the source to include the forbidden parameters, and then resubmit the page. Of course, to do this he or she would need to hack into the server to put the page there.

NOTE   *There are limits to the length of the URL you can pass to a browser. The following is quoted from the Microsoft Knowledge Base article Q208427 and applies to IE 4-5.5:*

"Internet Explorer has a maximum uniform resource locator (URL) length of 2,083 characters, with a maximum path length of 2,048 characters. This limit applies to both POST and GET request URLs.

If you are using the GET method, you are limited to a maximum of 2,048 characters (minus the number of characters in the actual path, of course).

POST, however, is not limited by the size of the URL for submitting name/value pairs, because they are transferred in the header and not the URL."

Another commonly used security approach inserts a user ID and another key (such as a user's Session ID) into a table. When the user hits a page, all pages perform the session/user validation check, forcing the user back to the login page on a failure. This is how many Web sites prevent users from setting links directly to a page. Of course, Session variables do hog memory and you may wish to avoid these on high-volume sites. Moreover, there is a bug in IIS4 and 5 that causes Session variables to lose their values if the Global.asa file is empty. In fact, you shouldn't use Session variables at all when it can be avoided. The use of Session variables in small sites can create upgrade nightmares when you need to scale the site. Keep in mind that .NET uses the GET method in cookieless authentication mode. Note that it is also common practice to store flattened objects in hidden form fields.

Optionally, you could save the criteria to a database table—since you may need to have an audit trail anyway—and then launch the report ASP (or ASP.NET) page that knows to read these values.

Often, reports are transmitted to end users as URL links with the parameters—for example, their customer number—already on the URL line. One of my clients sends commission statements electronically to his sales associates. The Web link looks something like this:

```
www.companyname.com/commissionrpt.asp?id=6D738FT344H764EF2&checksum=87136487613
```

By clicking this URL, the sales associate can view his personal sales report for the current or any previous month. In order to avoid a user tampering with the associate ID parameter and seeing someone else's report, the ID is encrypted and the decryption key stored on the server. To further complicate matters for someone who wants to write a loop that tries various combinations of the alphanumeric encrypted user ID, a checksum value is added that corresponds to a server-based checksum algorithm. If the checksum does not match a valid user ID, access will not be granted. While this system is not foolproof, the odds of someone obtaining access this way are astronomical.

SQL Injection

One major security flaw in Web reporting is the problem of SQL injection. This nefarious practice usually occurs when a user enters a SQL statement into a criteria input field rather than the discrete value that is intended for the field. For example, suppose you have HTML text that receives as a parameter an employee number. This value is then posted to another page that concatenates the value to a SQL statement (using SQL Server syntax) such as

```
cSQL = "SELECT * FROM Employee WHERE ID = " & txtEmpID
```

Suppose the user enters a piece of another SQL statement for the txtEmpID value such as this one:

```
"0 UNION SELECT * FROM Employee"
```

The statement that gets executed is

```
SELECT * FROM Employee WHERE ID = 0
UNION
SELECT * FROM Employee
```

which effectively returns all the records. This is probably not what you intended. Users could also use the semicolon, which separates multiple SQL statements to do such nasty things as entering this line:

```
0; TRUNCATE TABLE Employee
```

Another security flaw lies in the use of the stored procedure sp_makewebtask, which produces an HTML document containing data returned by executed queries, and xp_cmdshell, which opens a command window. A user could easily inject the following, which produces a local copy of the entire employee table:

```
; EXEC makewebtask 'c:\\Inetpub\\wwwroot\\bendoverandsmile.html',
'SELECT * FROM Employee'
```

Using xp_cmdshell, he or she could easily execute the command to, say, reformat the hard disk.

To guard against SQL injection, you have a number of options. Because a user can modify the HTTP header of the page that posts non–free-form criteria to the server, most of these options are server based. First, you'll need to filter any criteria before they are concatenated to an in-line SQL statement or passed to a stored procedure to make sure nothing is amiss. You can use the IsNumeric() and IsDate() functions to make sure that the data types are not strings when strings are not expected. Likewise, the Len() function will indicate if discrete values are longer than they are expected to be. Also, the Instr() function will indicate if any unexpected keywords get passed in. The best defense is to restrict permissions to the tables so that the user created for the Web application has only the minimum rights necessary for SELECT, UPDATE, and DELETE on only those tables that are needed.

For more information on SQL injection as well as other Internet security topics, check out the following link: `http://www.nextgenss.com/research/papers.html`.

Dynamic Criteria Screens

Rather than build each report's criteria screens individually, you can apply the same concepts of dynamically created controls that are explained in Chapter 3. Basic HTML, that is, without Macromedia Flash or cascading style sheets (CSS), does not offer anything close to the slick user interface of a GUI front end. You could always use ActiveX controls or DHTML, but there are sometimes limitations to the browsers that support these technologies. IE supports both and as of this writing holds over 90 percent of the browser market. A significant number of people still use other browsers, however, and a growing number use special "lite" browsers with their PDAs. Therefore, when doing Web report development, it's sometimes best to aim for the lowest common denominator and make the best of it unless you are working in a controlled environment with a guaranteed browser brand and specific version number.

NOTE *The market has largely standardized on Internet Explorer. According to the statistics on the W3Schools Web site, as of October 2002, 90 percent of users have Internet Explorer 5.x and above. Only 2 percent use a Netscape browser and the rest use either Opera or one of the "obsolete" browsers like Mosaic. The following Web sites offer user browser statistics:*
`http://www.w3schools.com/browsers/browsers_stats.asp`
`http://www.webreference.com/stats/browser.html`
`http://www.soprano.com/browsstats.html.`

HTML has some controls familiar to Windows developers. Multiselect list boxes, combo boxes, and date ranges can all be implemented in a fashion similar to their desktop counterparts. Check boxes are a bit different. Because HTML check boxes have only two possible values—selected or unselected (that is, there is no "gray" state)—they have limited flexibility as criteria controls since there is then no way to make them optional. One way to overcome this limitation is to use a combo box instead. By filling the combo box with three values—Yes, No, and Ignore—you can achieve the same result as a three-state check box.

TIP *If you really have your heart set on check boxes, you can simulate a three-state check box via graphic images that show checked, unchecked, and grayed check box states. Then you can use JavaScript to toggle the three images.*

As anyone who has ever worked with HTML will tell you, there are many necessary kludges. When building list boxes or combo boxes, for example, you'll often need both the unique ID of the item(s) selected (to pass to a stored procedure) as well as the text description(s) (to display to the user). You could just send the unique IDs but to obtain the descriptions you'll need to hit the database again. When a user selects items in one of these controls and then posts the form with a submit button, only the unique IDs of the selected values are sent to the post page. For example, if three items are checked on a list box, the value of the code

```
cDepartment = Request.Form("lstDepartment")
```

would return a string containing, for example, this line:

```
1,2,4
```

However, you're going to need the text descriptions as well as the unique IDs if you wish to display the criteria selected on the report itself. To accomplish this, you could populate the list box in the fashion shown in Listing 9-1.

Listing 9-1. HTML List Box

```
<TABLE>

<TR><TD>Department</TD></TR>

<TR><TD>

<select name=lstDepartment multiple>

<option value="1,Department A">Department A
<option value="2,Department B">Department B
<option value="3,Department C">Department C
<option value="4,Department D">Department D

</select>

</TD></TR>

</TABLE>
```

Now, when lstDepartment is posted, the value of the code

```
cDepartment = Request.Form("lstDepartment")
```

would return

```
1, Department A, 2, Department B,4, Department D
```

Then, by using the Split function in ASP as follows:

```
aValues = Split(cValues, ",")
```

all of the values in this comma-delimited string are parsed into separate array elements like this:

```
aValues[0] = 1
aValues[1] = Department A
aValues[2] = 2
aValues[3] = Department B
aValues[4] = 4
aValues[5] = Department D
```

Since you know that zero and all the even-numbered elements contain the unique ID values and all the odd-numbered elements contain the descriptions, you can loop through the array accordingly, picking off the values you'll need like this:

```
For x = 0 to Ubound(aValues) Step 2
    cIDs = cIDs & aValues(x) & ", "
Next
```

and end up with a string containing the following value:

```
1,2,4
```

Likewise, you can loop through the same array starting at the second element and get the descriptions:

```
For x = 1 to Ubound(aValues) Step 2
    cNames = cNames & aValues(x) & ", "
Next
```

This code will give you a variable containing the following value:

```
Department A, Department B, Department D
```

Of course, this only works if your description data does not have commas. If so, you need to use some other delimiter such as a tilde.

Let's examine how a criteria collection page can be created dynamically. Due to space considerations, we'll look at the pertinent code for the list box routines, as they are the most complex. The remainder of the code can be found on the downloadable file available on the Apress Web site (http://www.apress.com).

The first step is to invoke the routines that create the individual controls we need for a particular report. The code shown in Listing 9-2 creates the page shown in Figure 9-1.

Listing 9-2. Control Creation Example

```
<%

Dim oConn
Dim iReport

iReport = Request.Form("Report")

Set oConn = Server.CreateObject("ADODB.Connection")

oConn.ConnectionString = "Provider=Microsoft.Jet.OLEDB.4.0;" & _
"Data Source=C:\Docs\Reports\SampleDatabase.mdb;" & _
"Persist Security Info=False"
oConn.Open

Select Case iReport

    Case 0
        Call CreateListBox(oConn, "Products", "lstProduct", _
            "Product", "ID", "Descr", 60, 120)
        Call CreateListBox(oConn, "Department", "lstDepartment", _
            "Department", "ID", "Descr", 60, 320)
        Call CreateComboBox(oConn, "Source:", "cboSource", _
            "Source", "ID", "Descr", 280, 120)
        Call CreateCheckBox("Closed Orders only:", "cboClosed", _
            "Ignore This", 320, 120)
        Call CreateDateRange("Range of Ship Dates:", _
```

```
                            "txtShip", 380, 120 )
               Call CreateDateRange("Range of Order Dates:", _
                    "txtOrder", 420, 120)
               Call DisplayButtons(480, 300)


         End Select


         %>


         <INPUT type="hidden"  id=text1 name=txtReport value=<%=iReport%>
```

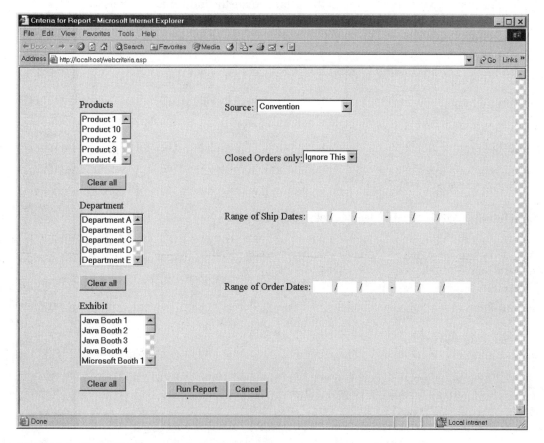

Figure 9-1. Dynamically generated criteria page

Listing 9-2 retrieves a report identifier (iReport) from the URL that invokes the page and then connects to a data source. Depending on the report chosen, a different set of criteria controls will display. The last line of the example creates a hidden control called txtReport that stores the iReport value so that you do not need to continue to pass it as a URL parameter.

The CreateListBox routine accepts an ADO Connection object, a caption, a control name, a table name, a unique ID column, a description column, and the top and left offset measured in pixels. This routine, shown in Listing 9-3, extracts the table information and, looping through the ADO Recordset, adds the individual items to the list box control.

Listing 9-3. CreateListBox Routine

```
Sub CreateListBox(oConn, cCaption, cName, cTable, cID, cDescr, iTop, iLeft)
    Dim oRS
    Dim cSQL

    cSQL = "SELECT " & cID & ", " & cDescr & _
            " FROM " & cTable & _
            " ORDER BY " & cDescr

    Set oRS = oConn.Execute(cSQL)

    With Response
        .Write("<DIV id=mydiv style='position:absolute; top:" & _
                iTop & "px; left:" & iLeft & "px;'>")

        .Write("<TABLE>")

        .Write("<TR>")
        .Write("<TD>")

        .Write(cCaption)

        .Write("</TD>")
        .Write("</TR>")

        .Write("<TR>")
        .Write("<TD>")

        .Write("<select name=" & cName & " multiple  style=height:120px>")

        Do While not oRS.EOF

                .Write("<option value=" & chr(39) & oRS(cID) & _
                    "," & oRS(cDescr) & chr(39) & ">" & oRS(cDescr))
```

```
                oRS.MoveNext

        Loop

        .Write("</select>")

        .Write("</TD>")
        .Write("</TR>")

        .Write("<TR>")
        .Write("<TD>")

        .Write("<INPUT type=button value='Clear all '" & cCaption & _
                " id=button1 name=button1 onclick=cmdClearAll_Click('" & _
                cName & "')>")

        .Write("</TD>")
        .Write("</TR>")

        .Write("</TABLE>")
        .Write("</DIV>")
    End With

    oRS.Close
    Set oRS = Nothing

End Sub
```

All of the controls invoked by these Create routines are wrapped in HTML table tags. Not only does this allow the top and left absolute positioning to be used, it also allows greater flexibility when a number of input elements are involved. In this case, you not only need a list box but also a label above to describe it and a button below to allow the user to clear the selections. Each of these component controls rests in its own table row. A full explanation of HTML tables is available later in the chapter.

Once the user has made all the needed criteria choices, he or she can post these selections by pressing the submit button labeled Run Report. Doing so will invoke the ASP page that extracts the selections from the dynamically created controls to create both a WHERE statement and a criteria description. The code for this ASP page is shown in Listing 9-4.

Listing 9-4. Posting ASP

```
<%

Dim iReport
Dim cSQL
Dim cCriteria
Dim cProduct
Dim cDept
Dim cSourceID
Dim iClosed
Dim cOrderDateFrom
Dim cOrderDateTo
Dim cShipDateFrom
Dim cShipDateTo

iReport = Request.Form("Report")

Select Case iReport

    Case 0

        With Request
            cProduct = .Form("lstProduct")
            cDept = .Form("lstDepartment")
            cSourceID = .Form("cboSource")
            iClosed = .Form("cboClosed")

            cOrderDateFrom = _
                .Form("txtShipMonthFrom") & "/" & _
                .Form("txtShipDayFrom") & "/" & _
                .Form("txtShipYearFrom")

            cOrderDateTo = _
                .Form("txtShipMonthTo") & "/" & _
                .Form("txtShipDayTo") & "/" & _
                .Form("txtShipYearTo")

            cShipDateFrom = _
                .Form("txtOrderMonthFrom") & "/" & _
                .Form("txtOrderDayFrom") & "/" & _
                .Form("txtOrderYearFrom")
```

```
                    cShipDateTo = _
                        .Form("txtOrderMonthTo") & "/" & _
                        .Form("txtOrderDayTo") & "/" & _
                        .Form("txtOrderYearTo")
            End With

            cSQL = GetListBoxSQL(cProduct, "productid")
            cSQL = cSQL & GetListBoxSQL(cDept, "deptid")
            cSQL = cSQL & GetComboBoxSQL(cSourceID, "sourceid")
            cSQL = cSQL & GetCheckBoxSQL(iClosed, "closed")
            cSQL = cSQL & GetDateSQL("orderdate", cOrderDateFrom, cOrderDateTo)
            cSQL = cSQL & GetDateSQL("shipdate", cShipDateFrom, cShipDateTo)

            cCriteria = GetListBoxCriteria(cProduct, "Product")
            cCriteria = cCriteria & GetListBoxCriteria(cDept, "Department")
            cCriteria = cCriteria & GetComboBoxCriteria(cSourceID, "Source")
            cCriteria = cCriteria & GetCheckBoxCriteria(iClosed, "Closed")
            cCriteria = cCriteria & GetDateCriteria("Order Date", _
                                    cOrderDateFrom, cOrderDateTo)
            cCriteria = cCriteria & GetDateCriteria("Ship Date", _
                                    cShipDateFrom, cShipDateTo)

End Select

If cSQL <> "" Then
    cSQL = Mid(cSQL, 1, Len(cSQL) - Len(" AND "))
End If

If cCriteria <> "" Then
    cCriteria = Mid(cCriteria, 1, Len(cCriteria) - Len(" AND "))
End If

Response.Write cSQL
Response.Write "<P>"
Response.Write cCriteria

%>
```

The code for both the GetListBoxSQL and GetComboBoxCriteria functions is very similar. Both receive a variable that contains a comma-delimited list of the unique IDs and descriptions of the values selected. Where GetListBoxSQL takes the column name as the second parameter, GetComboBoxCriteria takes

a column description. The code for both of these functions is shown in
Listing 9-5. You can find an explanation for parsing the cValues variable earlier
in the chapter.

Listing 9-5. GetListBoxSQL and GetComboBoxCriteria Functions

```
Function GetListBoxSQL(cValues, cColumn)
    Dim cSQL
    Dim aValues
    Dim x
    Dim cIDs

    aValues = Split(cValues, ",")

    For x = 0 to Ubound(aValues) Step 2
        cIDs = cIDs & aValues(x) & ", "
    Next

    cIDs = "(" & Mid(cIDs, 1, Len(cIDs) - 2) & ")"

    If cIDs <> "" Then
        cSQL = cColumn & " IN " & cIDs & " AND "
    End if

    GetListBoxSQL = cSQL

End Function

Function GetListBoxCriteria(cValues, cDescr)
    Dim cResult
    Dim cNames
    Dim aValues
    Dim x

    aValues = Split(cValues, ",")

    For x = 1 to Ubound(aValues) Step 2
        cNames = cNames & aValues(x) & ", "
    Next

    If cNames <> "" Then
      cNames = "(" & Mid(cNames, 1, Len(cNames) - 2) & ")"
```

```
        cResult = cResult & "the " & cDescr & _
            " is among " & cNames & " and "
    End if

    GetListBoxCriteria = cResult

End Function
```

At this point you have both a WHERE clause and a criteria string that you can pass into whatever report engine you are using on the back end.

HTML and Active Server Pages

One method of distributing reports via the Internet is to develop them using ASP and HTML. It is not at all difficult to do this but there are a number of plusses and minuses to this approach (see the sidebar "Pros and Cons of HTML/Classic ASP Report Delivery"). The rather versatile HTML table tag, <table>, will do most of the work for you in creating columnar and cross tab reports. It wouldn't make too much sense to create labels or free-form/mail merge documents for display in HTML.

....

Pros and Cons of HTML/Classic ASP Report Delivery

Before you get too excited about deploying ASP reports throughout your organization, be aware of the limitations of this approach. Since ASP reports ultimately appear as HTML output, you are limited by the restrictions of your browser. One of these limitations is the inability to control pagination easily, especially when looping through a Recordset and creating groupings and totals. When HTML is rendered to the browser, it displays one row after another with no concept of page breaks. Therefore, when you print a report from your browser, the data will print until your printer has filled up a page and only then will the printer issue a page break. You can force a page break in IE5 and higher using code like this:

```
<p style="page-break-before: always"> </p>
```

This tag issues a page break for printing that appears as a blank line in the browser display. Even using the page break tag, it becomes extremely difficult to display page headers such that they appear at the top of every page. To do so you would need to count the number of lines displayed and then print the header with a sufficiently comfortable margin of rows so that various printers won't display too many rows on a page. Sorry, no page events get triggered. Fortunately, the browser will at least number the pages for you as "Page x of y".

In addition, ASP is not fun to debug, but at least you can do some of the development in the Visual Basic IDE before moving it to the Web.

If you're using DHTML, things get a little easier, as you can specify pagination as shown in the following example, which defines a class mypage in a style sheet and employs it to set page breaks in the output:

```
<HTML>
<STYLE>
    P.page { page-break-after: always }
</STYLE>

<BODY>
    page 1 info
<P CLASS=mypage></P>
    page 2 info
</BODY>
</HTML>
```

ASP code is structured to facilitate HTML browser display and not for export to Excel or PDF. If you need an Excel dump, you'll need to create a routine to do this. Optionally, you could set the content type in the HTML page to application/excel, and the page will be rendered to Excel, roughly conforming to the layout of TABLE and table cell objects. Fortunately, generically dumping an ADO Recordset object to a worksheet is a relatively simple thing to accomplish. Chapter 7 explains how to accomplish it via ActiveX Automation, while Chapter 6 explains a utility called SpreadBuilder that allows you to create XLS files without Excel. For server-based applications, this latter choice is the far more viable option. PDF export is another matter entirely. Although Adobe publishes a PDF file specification, it is extremely complicated, and it is not realistic to build a converter utility. Doing so is actually a considerable undertaking.

Among the advantages of HTML/ASP reporting is the ability to display data as sets of hyperlinks to drill down to detail layers of additional data. Later in this chapter you'll see an example of a report that lists customers and the total freight charges they have incurred across all orders. By clicking the customer name, you can link to another report page and effectively drill down to the individual freight charge amounts that comprise this summary number.

HTML's <table> Tag

As you may have guessed, columnar reports are best formatted for display in a Web browser via tables. If you've done any work in HTML and ASP, you should be familiar with table tags as they are your lowest common denominator for performing positioning on a Web page. Absolute positioning, another option that involves specifying precise screen locations, is not supported in versions of HTML prior to 4.0. If you need to run your Web application in a wide variety of browsers, it is better to position elements by using paragraph alignment and tables. Even so, the page may render slightly differently in each browser. You should test your application in all browsers before deploying. While complete coverage of HTML is beyond the scope of this book, it is appropriate here to review the syntax rules for tables, as they are indispensable for ASP-based Web reporting. (Check out `http://www.htmlcompendium.org` for some excellent HTML documentation.)

Like other HTML tags, a table is enclosed in matching table tags as follows:

```
<TABLE>
</TABLE>
```

Column headers are designated by the <th> tag, whereas the <tr> tag indicates a row and the <td> tag—short for table data—defines a cell within a row. It is within these cells that the individual data elements are output. By default, all the cells in a given table will be the same size and adjusted to the width of the largest data element in its column. You can even create a caption for the entire table with the caption tag—<caption>.

There are other commands you should know that provide control over table formatting. BORDER determines the width of the table border and is expressed in terms of pixels. The larger the number, the thicker the border. Setting BORDER to zero removes borders altogether. CELLSPACING sets the amount of space between cells, whereas CELLPADDING determines the amount of space between the cell border and the cell contents. ALIGN will determine how the data is justified—"right", "left", or "center". Examine the code in Listing 9-6. It produces the tables shown in Figure 9-2.

Listing 9-6. Simple HTML Table

```
<TABLE BORDER="3" CELLSPACING="1" CELLPADDING="1">
<CAPTION>My Data</CAPTION>

<TR> <TD ALIGN = "right"> 100 </TD>
<TD ALIGN = "center"> Tom </TD>
<TD ALIGN = "center"> 01/01/60 </TD>
</TR>
```

```
<TR>
<TD ALIGN = "right"> 200 </TD>
<TD ALIGN = "center"> Dick </TD>
<TD ALIGN = "center"> 01/01/70 </TD>
</TR>

<TR>
<TD ALIGN = "right"> 300 </TD>
<TD ALIGN = "center"> Harry </TD>
<TD ALIGN = "center"> 01/01/80 </TD>
</TR>
<P>
</P>

</TABLE>

<TABLE CELLPADDING=5 BORDER=1 WIDTH=500>
      <CAPTION><B>Cell Alignment</B></CAPTION>

<TR>
      <TD HEIGHT=150 WIDTH=190 ALIGN="LEFT" VALIGN="TOP">VALIGN-Top
<BR>ALIGN-Left</TD>
      <TD WIDTH=200 ALIGN="CENTER" VALIGN="TOP"> VALIGN-Top<BR>ALIGN-Center</TD>
      <TD WIDTH=200 ALIGN="RIGHT" VALIGN="TOP">VALIGN-Top<BR>ALIGN-Right </TD>
</TR>
<TR>
      <TD HEIGHT=150 ALIGN="LEFT" VALIGN="MIDDLE">VALIGN-Middle<BR>ALIGN-Left</TD>
      <TD ALIGN="CENTER" VALIGN="MIDDLE"> VALIGN-Middle<BR>ALIGN-Center</TD>
      <TD ALIGN="RIGHT" VALIGN="MIDDLE">VALIGN-Middle<BR>ALIGN-Right </TD>
</TR>
<TR>
      <TD HEIGHT=150 ALIGN="LEFT" VALIGN="BOTTOM">VALIGN-Bottom<BR>ALIGN-Left</TD>
      <TD ALIGN="CENTER" VALIGN="BOTTOM">VALIGN-Bottom<BR>ALIGN-Center </TD>
      <TD ALIGN="RIGHT" VALIGN="BOTTOM">VALIGN-Bottom<BR>ALIGN-Right </TD>
</TR>
</TABLE>
```

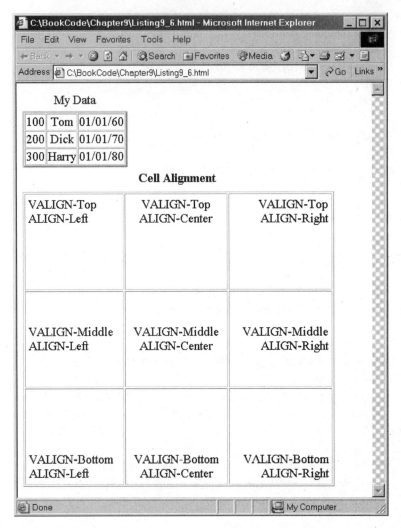

Figure 9-2. Simple HTML table

You can put more than just static text data in a table cell, however. If you look at the code in Listing 9-7 and its output in Figure 9-3, you'll see that the cell data can consist of hyperlinks and images as well. It can even consist of another table. To do this, simply use the appropriate HTML tag for an image or a hyperlink within the table cell in which you wish it to appear. When nesting tables, be sure to provide the proper matching tags, or you will have formatting and operation problems. If your forms are behaving strangely, this is a good item to check.

Listing 9-7. A Somewhat Cooler HTML Table

```
<TABLE BORDER="3" CELLSPACING="1" CELLPADDING="1">
<CAPTION>My Favorite Websites</CAPTION>

<TR>
    <TD ALIGN = "left">
        <A HREF="http://www.microsoft.com">Microsoft </A>
    </TD>
    <TD ALIGN = "center">
        <IMG SRC="C:\WINNT\Help\iisHelp\common\bestwith.gif">
    </TD>
</TR>

<TR>
    <TD ALIGN = "left">
        <A HREF="http://www.cnn.com">CNN </A>
    </TD>
    <TD ALIGN = "center">
        <IMG SRC="C:\WINNT\Help\iisHelp\common\bestwith.gif">
    </TD>
</TR>

<TR>
    <TD ALIGN = "left">
        <A HREF="http://www.nytimes.com">New York Times</A>
    </TD>
    <TD ALIGN = "center">
        <IMG SRC="C:\WINNT\Help\iisHelp\common\bestwith.gif">
    </TD>
</TR>

</TABLE>
```

Figure 9-3. A somewhat cooler HTML table

When you really need some more sophisticated formatting, you can use the COLSPAN and ROWSPAN commands as well as set the WIDTH of individual cells. COLSPAN allows a row to span multiple columns, whereas ROWSPAN allows a column to span multiple rows. WIDTH receives a value expressed either as pixels or as a percentage of the screen. Listing 9-8 illustrates how these commands work together and Figure 9-4 shows the output.

Listing 9-8. ROWSPAN and COLSPAN Commands

```
<TABLE BORDER=2>
    <TR>
        <TD>Family</TD>
        <TD COLSPAN=4 ALIGN="center">Young 'uns</TD>
        <TD ROWSPAN=5>Yeah, they're friends of mine <BR>
        but everyone gets a kick <BR>
        out of seeing the kids' names <BR>
        in a computer book <BR>
         (Hi, Mrs. Cavanagh)</TD>
    </TR>
```

```
<TR>
      <TD>Cavanagh</TD>
      <TD>Amanda</TD>
      <TD>Laura</TD>
      <TD>James</TD>
      <TD>John</TD>
</TR>

<TR>
      <TD>Grossman</TD>
      <TD>Alexandra</TD>
      <TD>Alton</TD>
</TR>

</TABLE>

<P>
</P>

<TABLE BORDER=2>

<TR>

        <TD ROWSPAN=2 WIDTH="200PX">
        Ronald Reagan
        </TD>

        <TD COLSPAN=3>
          <FONT FACE=ARIAL COLOR=GREEN SIZE=22>
          Term of Office
          </FONT>
        </TD>

</TR>

<TR>
      <TD ALIGN="center">1981</TD>
      <TD ALIGN="center">1989</TD>
</TR>

<TR>
      <TD ROWSPAN=2 WIDTH="200PX">George Bush</TD>
      <TD COLSPAN=3>Term of Office</TD>
```

```
    </TR>
    <TR>
        <TD ALIGN="center">1989</TD>
        <TD ALIGN="center">1992</TD>
    </TR>

</TABLE>
```

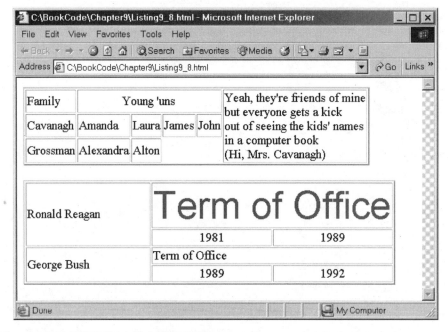

Figure 9-4. ROWSPAN and COLSPAN commands

NOTE *In case the end user doesn't have the font specified in your HTML code installed, you can list multiple fonts for the browser to try as shown in the following line:*

```
<FONT FACE=" Helvetica,Arial,Sans Serif">
```

The browser will try each font in the order they are listed. That last choice will automatically substitute a generic serif-less font on machines that lack any of the first two options.

Using the BGCOLOR command and the STYLE setting, you can produce multicolored output with different fonts and font attributes. Listing 9-9 shows how the visual appearance of a table can be changed using these commands. The output can be seen in Figure 9-5, but you'll need to run the code in order to see the actual colors displayed.

Listing 9-9. Color and Style Commands

```
<TABLE BORDER=2 style="FONT-WEIGHT: bold; FONT-SIZE: 24">

<TR BGCOLOR="red">
<TD ROWSPAN=2 WIDTH="200PX">Ronald Reagan</TD>
<TD COLSPAN=3>Term of Office</TD>
</TR>

<TR>
<TD ALIGN="center" BGCOLOR="cyan">1981</TD>
<TD ALIGN="center" BGCOLOR="yellow">1989</TD>
</TR>

<TR>
<TD ROWSPAN=2 WIDTH="200PX">George Bush</TD>
<TD COLSPAN=3>Term of Office</TD>
</TR>

<TR>
<TD ALIGN="center" style="FONT-SIZE: 12" BGCOLOR="cyan">1989</TD>
<TD ALIGN="center" BGCOLOR="yellow">1992</TD>
</TR>
```

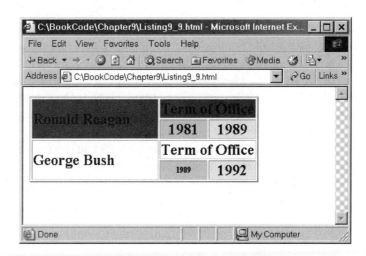

Figure 9-5. Color and style commands

JavaScript

JavaScript can create tables, or even alter existing elements of an HTML document. The code in Listing 9-10 creates a one-cell, one-row table that contains some sample text.

Listing 9-10. Code to Create a Table Using JavaScript

```
<body onload="JavaScriptTable();">

<script>

function JavaScriptTable() {
    var oTable = document.createElement('<table>');
    var oTBody = document.createElement('tbody');
    var oRow = document.createElement('tr');
    var oCell = document.createElement('td');
    var oText = document.createTextNode('This is a table of one cell created by JavaScript');

    oTable.appendChild(oTBody);
    oTBody.appendChild(oRow);
    oRow.appendChild(oCell);
    oCell.appendChild(oText);
    oCell.appendChild(oText);

    oTable.style.border = '2px double';
    document.body.appendChild(oTable);
}
</script>
```

Using the elements of the document and the onload event, this code inserts a table into the existing document. You may need to alter a table's appearance based on a selection or some other element. Do so by creating an id property for the table. The table can then be referenced by its ID. Using the id property you can effectively "name" a table object. (Note that ID is NOT the same as NAME. Other objects, such as FORM elements, can have an id property, but require a NAME if they are going to be referenced using FORM syntax (e.g., document.forms[0].txtMyTextbox) Using this table ID you can then alter the properties. By the same token, you can use the id property of a cell to produce a named element. A common naming convention for cells is to mimic the Row:Column Excel approach, naming each cell R[row]C[col]. Using this approach, you can alter the table or the contents of a particular cell.

Listing 9-11 demonstrates how to dynamically alter a table by adding rows. Note that it also names each cell accordingly. The results of clicking the Add Row button can be seen in Figure 9-6.

Listing 9-11. Code to Dynamically Add a Row to a Table

```
function tblInsertRow()
{

        var oTR;            // New Table Row Object
        var oTD;            // New Table Data Object
        var i;                  // Loop Counter

        // Using the Table ID (tblDemo) object we can
        // insert a new table row.  Doing this will
        // return a Table Row (TR) object
        oTR = tblDemo.insertRow();

        for (i = 1; i < 4; i++)
        {

                //Using the Table Row Object Insert a cell
                oTD = oTR.insertCell();
                oTD.align = "center"

                // Using the Rows calculate new cell information
                oTD.innerText="Element " + (tblDemo.rows.length -1) + ":" + i;


        }

}
```

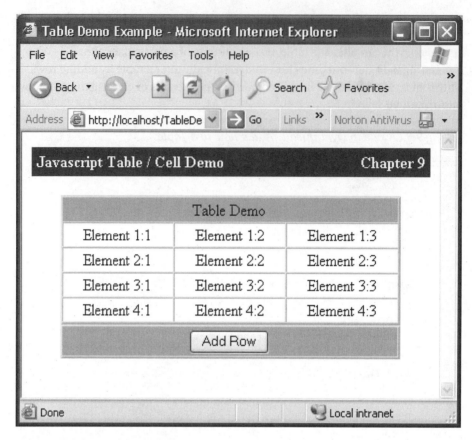

Figure 9-6. The HTML/JavaScript table demo

Cascading Style Sheets

Many of the report development tools examined in the preceding chapters allow you to create styles to control text formatting. By creating the definition, say, for a Chapter Title style as having a specific font, color, size, etc., you can apply the style to all chapter titles, and they will all look the same. If you then decide that chapter titles should be blue instead of red, you need only change the color property of the style and the change will apply automatically to all text using this style. The browser has the same style functionality that is implemented through cascading style sheets.

HTML tags were originally designed to define the content of a document. They were supposed to say "This is a header," "This is a paragraph," "This is a table," etc., by using tags like <h1>, <p>, <table>, and so on. The layout of the document was taken care of by the browser, without using any formatting tags. As the two major browsers—Netscape and Internet Explorer—continued to add new HTML tags and attributes (like the <font> tag and the color attribute) to the original HTML specification, it became more and more difficult to create Web sites where the content of HTML documents was clearly separated from the document's presentation layout.

To solve this problem, the World Wide Web Consortium (W3C)—the non-profit, standard-setting committee responsible for standardizing HTML—created STYLES simultaneously with their creation of HTML 4.0. Both Netscape 4.0 and Internet Explorer 4.0 support cascading style sheets, but at varying levels. Browser-based applications frequently need to be developed for a variety of browsers, including Netscape, Internet Explorer, and Opera. Each interprets stylesheets and script differently, making for a lengthy and tricky development process.

Styles in HTML 4.0 define how elements are displayed, just like the font tag and the color attribute define how text is formatted and displayed on a Web page. Styles are commonly saved in files external to your HTML documents (usually with a .css extension) when developing large Web sites. External style sheets enable you to change the appearance and layout of all the pages in your Web site, just by editing a single CSS document. (We'll explain internal and inline style sheets as well later in this chapter.) If you have ever tried to change the font or color of all the headings in all your Web pages, you understand how CSS can save you a lot of work.

Cascading style sheets are a breakthrough in Web design because they allow developers to control the style and layout of multiple Web pages all at once. This allows a Web developer to define a style for each HTML element and apply it to as many Web pages as he or she wishes. To make a global change, the developer simply changes the style, and all elements of the Web site are updated automatically.

Style sheets allow style information to be specified in many ways. Styles can be specified inside a single HTML element, inside the <head> element of an HTML page, or in an external CSS file. Even multiple external style sheets can be referenced inside a single HTML document.

The CSS syntax is relatively easy to understand. Each CSS element is made up of three parts: a selector, a property, and a value. The selector is normally the element (or tag) that you wish to define, and the property is the attribute you wish to change, and each property can take a value. The property and value are separated by a colon and surrounded by curly braces, like so:

```
Selector {property:value }
```

Using this syntax, if you wished to redefine the body tag so that all your Web pages had a black color, you would do it as follows:

```
body {color:black}
```

If the value is comprised of multiple words, you simply surround the words with quotes, like so:

```
p {font-family: "sans serif"}
```

If you wish to specify more than one property, separate each property with a semicolon. Here's how to define a center aligned paragraph, with a red text color:

```
p {text-align: center; color: red}
```

To make the style definitions more readable, you can describe one property on each line, like this:

```
p
{
text-align: center;
color: black;
font-family: arial
}
```

You can group selectors by separating each selector with a comma. If you want to apply specific styles to all the header elements, do it like so:

```
h1, h2, h3, h4, h5, h6 {color: green}
```

If you omit the tag name in the selector, then the style can be applied to any tag that supports that property, as shown in this example:

```
.center {text-align: center}
```

With the class attribute you can define different styles for the same element. Say that you would like to have two types of paragraphs in your document: one right-aligned paragraph, and one center-aligned paragraph. First you would define the styles, and then in your HTML code you would use the class attribute. The code in Listing 9-12 is a combination of the style (which would reside in an external stylesheet) and the HTML using the class attribute to define a paragraph.

Listing 9-12. CSS Example

```
p.right {text-align: right}
p.center {text-align: center}
...Code in HTML Page...
```

```
<p class="right">
This paragraph will be right-aligned.
</p>

<p class="center">
This paragraph will be center-aligned.
</p>
```

Lastly, let's talk about the id attribute. The id attribute can be defined in two ways. It can be defined to match one, many, or all elements with a particular ID. For example:

```
<p id="intro">
This paragraph will be right-aligned.
</p>
```

In this next example, the id attribute will match all elements with id="intro":

```
#intro
{
font-size:110%;
font-weight:bold;
color:#0000ff;
background-color:transparent
}
```

In this next example the id attribute will match only p elements with id="intro":

```
p#intro
{
font-size:110%;
font-weight:bold;
color:#0000ff;
background-color:transparent
}
```

When a browser reads a style sheet, it will format the document according to it. There are three ways of inserting a style sheet. The first way is to use an external style sheet.

An external style sheet is ideal when the style is applied to many pages. With an external style sheet, you can change the look of an entire Web site by changing one file. Each page must link to the style sheet using the <link> tag. The <link> tag goes inside the head section:

```
<head>
<link rel="stylesheet" type="text/css"
href="mystyle.css" />
</head>
```

The browser will read the style definitions from the file mystyle.css, located in the same folder as the page containing this LINK element, and format the document according to the style sheet.

An external style sheet can be written in any text editor, although Visual Interdev includes a style sheet editor, and you can also use FrontPage. The file should not contain any HTML tags. Your style sheet should be saved with a .css extension.

The next method is to use an internal style sheet. An internal style sheet should be used when a single document has a unique style. You define internal styles in the head section by using the <style> tag, like this:

```
<head>
<style type="text/css">
hr {color: sienna}
p {margin-left: 20px}
body {background-image: url("images/back40.gif")}
</style>
</head>
```

The browser will now read the style definitions, and format the document accordingly.

NOTE *A browser normally ignores unknown tags. This means that an old browser that does not support styles will ignore the <style> tag, but the content of the <style> tag will be displayed on the page. It is possible to prevent an old browser from displaying the content by hiding it in the HTML comment element.*

Lastly, you can also use inline styles. An inline style loses many of the advantages of style sheets by mixing content with presentation. Use this method sparingly, such as when a style is to be applied to a single occurrence of an element.

To use inline styles, you include the style attribute in the relevant tag. The style attribute can contain any CSS property. The following example shows how to change the color and the left margin of a paragraph:

```
<p style="color: sienna; margin-left: 20px">
This is a paragraph
</p>
```

CSS is important if you plan to do HTML reporting because it allows for a standard look and feel for all your HTML pages. Consistency enables the reader to focus on the report's content rather than sifting through erratic formatting. Many firms have published guidelines for the formatting of all browser-based content and other company publications. Quite a few of these same firms have created a CSS library to enforce these guidelines. Before attempting any Web project within a company, check with the Webmasters about obtaining a copy of the company's guidelines.

Active Server Pages

Once you've mastered the art of HTML tables, you can apply this knowledge to create Web-based reports using ASP. By connecting to a data source and extracting a data set using server-side script, you can loop through this result set and display the data line by line in an HTML table using the Response.Write method shown in Listing 9-13.

Listing 9-13. ASP Web Report

```
<html>
<title>Customer Freight Report</title>
<body bgcolor="#ffffff">



<%
Dim oConn
Dim oRS
Dim cnstr
Dim cSQL
Dim dblTotal
```

```
set oConn=server.createobject("ADODB.connection")
set oRS = Server.CreateObject("ADODB.Recordset")

cConnectString = "Provider=SQLOLEDB.1;" & _
                 "Password=Ovaltine;" & _
                 "Persist Security Info=True;" & _
                 "User ID=sa;" & _
                 "Initial Catalog=NorthWind;" & _
                 "Data Source=Y8P8P"


oConn.open cConnectString

cSQL = "SELECT c.CustomerID, c.CompanyName, c.ContactName, " & _
       "SUM(o.Freight) AS TotalFreight " & _
       "FROM Customers c, Orders o " & _
       "WHERE c.CustomerID = o.CustomerID " & _
       "GROUP BY c.CustomerID, c.CompanyName, c.ContactName  " & _
       "ORDER BY c.CompanyName"


Set oRS = oConn.Execute(cSQL)

With Response
     .Write("<font>")

     .Write("<table>")
     .Write("<tr>")
     .Write("<td width = ""350"" nowrap align=""left"">Seton Software</td>")
     .Write("<td width = ""140"" nowrap align=""right"">" & DATE & "</td>")
     .Write("</tr>")
     .Write("<tr>")
     .Write("</tr>")
     .Write("</table>")

     .Write("<table>")
     .Write("<tr>")
     .Write("<th width = ""500"" nowrap align=""center"">Freight Report </th>")
     .Write("</tr>")
     .Write("</table>")


     .Write("<html><body>")
     .Write("<table>")
     .Write("<tr>")
```

```
      .Write("<th nowrap align=""left"">Company Name</th>")
      .Write("<th nowrap align=""left"">Contact Name</th>")
      .Write("<th nowrap align=""right"">Total Freight</th>")
      .Write("</tr>")

   Do while not oRS.EOF
     .Write("<tr>")
     .Write("<td align=""left""><a href=customerdetails.asp?id=" & _
        oRS("CustomerID") & ">" & oRS("CompanyName") & "</a></td>" )
     .Write("<td align=""left"">" & oRS("ContactName") & "</td>" )
     .Write("<td align=""right"">" & FormatCurrency(0 & _
        oRS("TotalFreight"),2) & "</td>" )
     .Write("</tr>")

     dblTotal = dblTotal + CDbl((0 & oRS("TotalFreight")))

     oRS.movenext

   loop

     .Write("<tr>")
     .Write("</tr>")

     .Write("<tr>")
     .Write("<td></td>" )
     .Write("<td><b>Grand Total</b></td>" )
     .Write("<td align=""right""><b>" & dblTotal & "</b></td>" )
     .Write("</tr>")

     .Write("</table></body></html>")

End With

oRS.Close
oConn.Close

Set oRS = nothing
Set oConn = nothing
Set oCmd = nothing

%>
</body>
</html>
```

This code produces the output shown in Figure 9-7. Note how each customer name is a hyperlink. As you can see by looking at the lower-left corner of the browser window, this hyperlink invokes another ASP page that receives the customer ID as a URL parameter and displays the individual freight detail for each customer's order. This feature provides, in effect, a drilldown for your Web-based reports. The code for this detail Web page can be found on the source code file that you can download from the Apress Web site (http://www.apress.com).

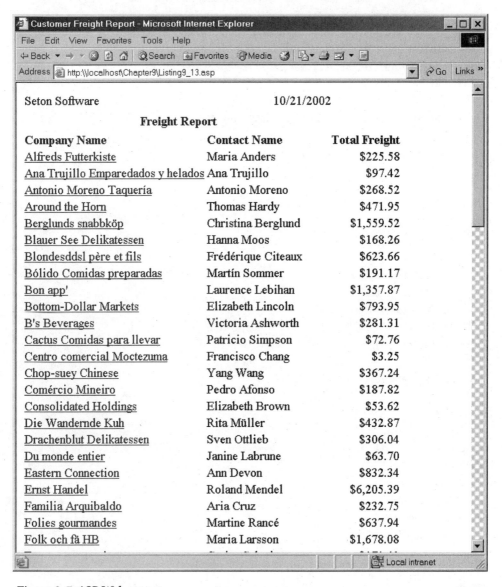

Figure 9-7. ASP Web report

NOTE *It is not possible to print table columns in HTML by moving from the top to the bottom and then right to the top of the next column. If you need to print a snaked column report, you'll need to store the report data in an array that matches the structure of the report and then print that array from left to right. This technique is explained in Chapter 5.*

HTML Table of Contents

Thanks to HTML's anchor tag, <A>, and the HREF attribute, you can easily add a table of contents to your reports. Tables of contents make the most sense when dealing with grouped reports. Suppose you want to display a report that shows a company name and grouped under each company the details of that company's orders with a subtotal at each group level. Since a report like this can get rather long and finding a particular company's data rather difficult, a table of contents at the top of the report will aid in navigation. Examine the code in Listing 9-14.

Listing 9-14. Table of Contents

```
<TABLE>

<TR><TD><A HREF=#101>Seton Software Development, Inc.</A></TD></TR>
<TR><TD><A HREF=#102>Vivid Software, Inc.</A></TD></TR>

<TR height=10></TR>

<TR><TD><A NAME="101"></A></TD></TR>

<TR><TD bgcolor=red>Seton Software Development, Inc.</TD></TR>

<TR><TD>This is the text for Seton Software Development, Inc.</TD></TR>
<TR><TD>This is the text for Seton Software Development, Inc.</TD></TR>
<TR><TD>This is the text for Seton Software Development, Inc.</TD></TR>

<TR height=10></TR>


<TR><TD><A NAME="102"></A></TD></TR>
```

```
<TR><TD bgcolor=red>Vivid Software, Inc.</TD></TR>

<TR><TD>This is the text for Vivid Software, Inc.</TD></TR>
<TR><TD>This is the text for Vivid Software, Inc.</TD></TR>
<TR><TD>This is the text for Vivid Software, Inc.</TD></TR>
<TR><TD>This is the text for Vivid Software, Inc.</TD></TR>

</TABLE>
```

Here, each company that has data is displayed at the top of the report as a hyperlink via an anchor tag. The HREF attribute is set to the company's unique ID. Just before the data for that company prints, another anchor tag appears whose NAME attribute is also set to the company's unique ID. By clicking a company name at the top of the report, the page will advance to that company's data (see Figure 9-8).

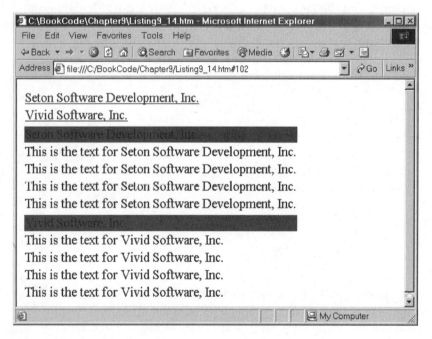

Figure 9-8. HTML table of contents

Because the company names appear at the top of the report, you'll hit the database twice in ASP when producing the report. The first pass is to retrieve the names of the companies that have data, and the second pass is to retrieve the data itself. You could do this in one Recordset and store the data in an array, but a large number of users on your site running lengthy reports could put a quick end to that plan. The two-pass ASP code is shown in Listings 9-15 and 9-16.

Listing 9-15. Create the Jumps at the Top of the Report

```
cSQL = "SELECT DISTINCT c.CustomerID, c.CompanyName " & _
        "FROM Customers c, Orders o " & _
        "WHERE c.CustomerID = o.CustomerID " & _
        "ORDER BY c.CompanyName"


Set oRS = oConn.Execute(cSQL)


Response.Write("<TABLE>")


Do While Not oRS.EOF


    Response.Write("<TR><TD><A HREF=#" & oRS("CustomerID") & ">" & _
        oRS("CompanyName") & "</A></TD></TR>")


    oRS.MoveNext
Loop


Response.Write("</TABLE>")
```

Listing 9-16. Print the Body of the Report

```
.Write("<html><body>")
.Write("<table>")


cCustomerID = oRS("CustomerID")


.Write("<TR><TD><A NAME=" & oRS("CustomerID") & "></A></TD></TR>")
.Write("<tr><td align=left colspan=2><B>" & _
    oRS("CompanyName") & "</B></td></tr>")


Do while not oRS.EOF


  .Write("</tr>")
  .Write("<td align=left>" & oRS("OrderDate") & "</td>")
```

```
.Write("<td align=right>" & oRS("Freight") & "</td>")
.Write("</tr>")

dblTotal = dblTotal + CDbl((0 & oRS("Freight")))
dblGrandTotal = dblGrandTotal + CDbl((0 & oRS("Freight")))

oRS.movenext

If oRS.EOF Then
    .Write("<tr height=10></tr>")
    .Write("<td align=right colspan=2>" & dblTotal & "</td>")
    Exit Do
End if


If cCustomerID <> oRS("CustomerID") Then

    cCustomerID = oRS("CustomerID")

    .Write("<tr height=10></tr>")
    .Write("<td align=right  colspan=2>" & dblTotal & "</td>")

    dblTotal = 0

    .Write("<tr height=10></tr>")
    .Write("<TR><TD><A NAME=" & oRS("CustomerID") & "></A></TD></TR>")
    .Write("<tr><td align=left colspan=2><B>" & _
        oRS("CompanyName") & "</B></td></tr>")

End If

loop

.Write("<tr>")
.Write("</tr>")

.Write("<tr>")
.Write("<td><b>Grand Total</b></td>" )
.Write("<td align=right><b>" & dblGrandTotal & "</b></td>" )
.Write("</tr>")

.Write("</table></body></html>")
```

Document Paging

One of the most common problems encountered when developing Web reports is how to display a subset of data on a page. Say that a customer wishes to run a report on equipment inventory. In the database is a table, tblEquipment, that contains all the equipment for this company. Using a criteria screen, users will fill out the parameters for their list of equipment.

Adding to the pain of this is that the results of the query could be one row or one million rows. The first problem is how to display the results. Just dumping a single Web page of data is not the answer if you are not certain how many rows will be returned. If your application pushes a million rows to the browser, they will be stored on the client PC, which may not have that capacity. Combined with slow loading times, this creates a nightmare. Dividing returned results into "pages" is a better solution Once you've decided to page the data, you have several options. You need to assess your application and environment to see which one will be the most efficient. When users are finished with their selections on the criteria screen, on the next Web page a series of strings is built, from which a dynamic stored procedure can be created. This stored procedure should be designed to get results and process (or page) them in small blocks for the purpose of speed and ease of navigation.

Until now most of the examples of Web site paging you've probably seen use client-side cursors to move to an absolute page position in the Recordset and then read *n* records forward from there. Although this works, there is one a disadvantage that most developers don't consider or often even know about. In many cases, the server that is running the database is a separate server from the Web server (sometimes it may even be running under a different operating system— for example, IIS on the Web server box, and Linux running Oracle on another). Whenever a request is made to the database server, it returns a Recordset to the Web server. Then the Web server uses the client-side cursor to select only the requested group of records for a given page.

While this doesn't seem like a big problem, consider what happens when you are working with large databases and multiple concurrent users. If you are only viewing 40 records at a time from a 50,000 record database table, and you have 10 people making the same request, you are now sending 500,000 records to the Web server for only 400 records of output to the client. To solve this problem, you can use a stored procedure that puts the burden on the RDBMS to return only the required number of records to the Web server, instead of the entire database table. This reduces the load on the Web server, or application server, as the case may be.

The first thing is to declare two integer values (@Page and @RecsPerPage). These values are supplied as parameters when calling the stored procedure. @Page is the page number to retrieve, and @RecsPerPage is the number of records to display each time the procedure is called.

Next create a temporary table named #TempEquipment. The key to making this stored procedure work is creating an auto-incrementing (identity) column named ID. This column is used to identify the record number of each record in the table, and is integral to making the paging code work. Then the temporary table is populated with records from the actual tblEquipment table using a SELECT statement.

Calculate the first and last record numbers requested from the temporary table, based on the number of records per page and the page number. The desired records from #TempEquipment (based on the value of ID) are then returned.

Finally, return a column that indicates how many records are left to iterate through. This information is useful when showing Next and Prev buttons dynamically. Listing 9-17 includes the entire procedure to "page" equipment records.

Listing 9-17. Stored Procedure to "Page" Records

```
CREATE PROCEDURE sp_PagedEquipment
    (
    @Page int,
    @RecsPerPage int
    )
AS

/*
We don't need the #\ of rows inserted
into our temporary table so turn off
the count
*/

SET NOCOUNT ON

/* Create a temporary table */
CREATE TABLE #TempEquipment
(
    ID int IDENTITY,
    EID int,
    INV_NUMBER int,
    Bldg varchar(5),
    Area varchar(5),
    OnHand int
)
```

```
/*
Insert the rows from tblEquipment into the temp table
by selecting from the master table
*/
INSERT INTO #TempEquipment (EID, INV_NUMBER, Bldg, Area, OnHand)
SELECT EID, INV_NUMBER, Bldg, Area, OnHand FROM tblEquipment ORDER BY INV_NUMBER


/* Find first and last records that we want to return */
DECLARE @FirstRec int, @LastRec int


/*
Calculate the starting record for this "page"
The way we calculate the page sets is quite simple.
use the page number, subtract 1 (which would position
your cursor at the end of the prior page, and then
multiply it by the number of records being returned
by this cursor.
*/
SELECT @FirstRec = (@Page - 1) * @RecsPerPage


/* Calculate the ending record for this "page" */
SELECT @LastRec = (@Page * @RecsPerPage + 1)


/*
Return the paged set of records including a column
which contains a Boolean indicating if there are more
records left
*/
SELECT *,
       MoreRecords =
     (
       SELECT COUNT(*)
       FROM #TempEquipment E
       WHERE E.ID >= @LastRec
     )
FROM #TempEquipment
WHERE ID > @FirstRec AND ID < @LastRec


/* Turn COUNT back on */
SET NOCOUNT OFF
```

Calling this procedure in ASP is very straightforward. Simply assign the results of the stored procedure callback to a Recordset variable as follows, where nPage is the current page you are on:

```
Set oRs = oCn.Execute("sp_PagedEquipment, " & nPage & ", 20")
```

So the first time you call the procedure, nPage should be 1. The next time iot should be 2, and so on.

ActiveX DLLs/EXEs

One of the fastest ways to deploy the reports for an existing desktop application over the Web is to create class wrappers for them. Except for the HTML/ASP interface, you can program your report logic in the VB environment with its debugging tools and superior IDE. If you compile the reports into server-based ActiveX EXEs and DLLs in COM-based VB6 or class libraries in VB .NET, you can easily allow access to their report functionality via an ASP front end.

TIP   *Microsoft has a Knowledge Base article (Q243548) that explains all the pitfalls of developing COM components to run under ASP. This one is a "must-read."*

While it's certainly possible to display the end result of your reports using HTML, you'll often find it better to avoid HTML entirely and use PDF files if at all possible. By exporting your report to a PDF file located on the client, the user's local copy of the Adobe Acrobat Reader can display the document within the browser itself. That way, because you are dealing with the Adobe document management technology, printing, pagination, and browser versioning issues are no longer a problem. If appropriate, Excel output is another Web delivery option. In both cases, the user will see the report in its native format, and by selecting the File | Save As option, can save the document to his or her local hard disk.

Examine the code in Listings 9-18 and 9-19. These code examples are the source for an ASP page and an ActiveX DLL using VS-View from ComponentOne. The ASP page instantiates an object of the Report class and passes parameters to it indicating the user ID and whether the report is being called from the Web. The reason for the IsWebReport property is that the same DLL will be used to support reports invoked from the desktop based application, and this Boolean property will indicate which one you're dealing with. Then, the report method is invoked and the report outputs to a PDF file. The name of the report file is returned to the ASP page and the Response.Redirect method displays the PDF in the client browser.

Listing 9-18. ASP Page

```
<%
Dim objReport
Dim cFileName
Dim cURL

Response.Buffer = "true"

Set objReport = CreateObject("Reports.Report")

With objReport
    .Destination = 0
    .UserID = 12
    .IsWebReport = True
    cFileName = .MyFirstWebReport
End With

Set objReport = Nothing

cURL = "http://myserver/" & cFileName

Response.Write("<script>" & vbCrLf)
Response.Write("window.open('" & cURL & "');" & vbCrLf)
    Response.Write("</script>")

%>
```

Listing 9-19. Report Class

```
Option Explicit

Dim objVSPrinter1 As New VSPrinter
Dim objVSPDF As New VSPDF

Dim bIsWebReport As Boolean
Dim lUserID As Long
```

```
Public Property Get UserID() As Variant
    UserID = lUserID
End Property

Public Property Let UserID(ByVal vNewValue As Variant)
    lUserID = vNewValue
End Property

Public Property Get IsWebReport() As Variant
    IsWebReport = bIsWebReport
End Property

Public Property Let IsWebReport(ByVal vNewValue As Variant)
    bIsWebReport = vNewValue
End Property

Public Function MyFirstWebReport() As String
    Dim cFileName As String
    Dim x As Integer

    cFileName = "c:\temp\" & GetTempFileName(lUserID, "pdf")

    With objVSPrinter1

        .StartDoc

        .Preview = True

        .StartTable

        .TableCell(tcCols) = 2
        .TableCell(tcColWidth, , 1) = 3900
        .TableCell(tcColWidth, , 2) = 3900

        For x = 1 To 1000

            .TableCell(tcInsertRow) = x
            .TableCell(tcText, x, 1) = "Column 1 - Data Element " & x
            .TableCell(tcText, x, 2) = "Column 2 - Data Element " & x

        Next x
```

```
        .EndTable

        .EndDoc

        If bIsWebReport Then
            objVSPDF.ConvertDocument objVSPrinter1, cFileName
        End If

    End With

    Set objVSPrinter1 = Nothing
    Set objVSPDF = Nothing

    MyFirstWebReport = cFileName

End Function

Private Sub VSPrinter1_NewPage()

    objVSPrinter1.AddTable "3900|3900", _
        "Header 1|Header 2", vbNullString

End Sub

Function GetTempFileName(lUserID As Long, _
    cExtension As String) As String
    Dim cResult As String

    cResult = Month(Now) & _
            Day(Now) & _
            Year(Now) & _
            Hour(Now) & _
            Minute(Now) & _
            Second(Now) & "_" & _
            lUserID & "." & cExtension

    GetTempFileName = cResult

End Function
```

NOTE *Often you'll need to create temporary filenames. Since you may be writing these filenames to the same directory, they will clearly need to be unique. The Windows API offers a function, called GetTempFileName, that can return a unique name, but unfortunately invoking this function actually creates the file. You may wish to use a function like the GetTempFileName function shown in Listing 9-19. This version of GetTempFileName uses the date and time values down to the second plus the unique user ID to return a filename with the extension you pass to it.*

PDF and Internet Explorer

While PDF files are an excellent way to distribute reports via the Web, there are a few issues with using them under certain versions of Microsoft Internet Explorer of which you should be aware. Please reference the following Knowledge Base documents if you are experiencing any of the following problems:

- Unable to print PDF files in Internet Explorer (Q258915)

- Adobe Acrobat PDF files appear as a blank window or frame (Q177321)

- PDF file is displayed as a blank page on redirects (Q247663)

- Internet Explorer opens a blank window loading a PDF file by using name destinations (Q296207)

- Internet Explorer may not open a small document (Q276436)

- Internet Explorer opens a blank page with a placeholder icon instead of a PDF file in Adobe Acrobat Reader (Q305153)

- PRB: active documents appear blank in Internet Explorer when they are not cached (Q297822)

For more information about Adobe Acrobat Web solutions, check out Adobe's partners' and developers' Web page at http://partners.adobe.com/.

ActiveReports

Both the COM and .NET versions of ActiveReports offer a number of Web deployment options. In both cases you can still build the ActiveReports functionality into a Web-based DLL and use Response.Redirect to direct the browser to the chosen export format as shown in the VS-View section earlier in the chapter. However, there are additional options for Web deployment as shown in the sections that follow.

ActiveReports 2.0 (Visual Basic 6)

ActiveReports can produce Web reports in a variety of different ways. There are three traditional methods—ActiveX viewer, Java Applet Viewer, and the PDF—or you can build ActiveX DLL components that include integrated reports, such as a report server. Each of the viewers can interact with a Web browser and server (the PDF file is a result of saving a report as a PDF). These controls are included in both editions, and a complete example of each is included in the Web Examples selection of the Data Dynamics Active Reports menu option.

The output that each viewer creates to HTML, Excel, or PDF can easily be sent to the client browser by a simple call to the Response.Redirect method.

```
Response.Redirect("myExportedHTMLReport.html")
```

However, ActiveReports does offer other Web functionality via an ActiveX viewer control and a Java applet. Note that no additional licensing costs are required for using these tools regardless of the number of end users. There are some limitations, of course, to using these approaches. The first is that only Microsoft Internet Explorer natively supports ActiveX controls (OCXs). Netscape only supports ActiveX controls via a plug-in. Even in strictly IE environments, ActiveX controls have never really caught on. Many browsers have security settings that will prevent their download to the desktop unless they are from a specified trusted source. Java applets are supported in both IE and Netscape but tend to be a bit slow in loading, especially if the client machine does not have the Java Virtual Machine (VM) already installed on it.

ActiveReports supports saving and loading of reports in their own standard format, known as Report Document Format (RDF). Once you have saved a report as an RDF file, you can load this report quickly and easily into the report viewer.

NOTE *RDFs are similar to Access Report Snapshot Viewer in that the displayed reports are a static representation. They are not dynamic and therefore need to be re-created whenever the report criteria changes.*

If you wish to provide these static reports to your users in a timely fashion (so they accurately reflect current information, such as weekly sales figures), you should consider creating them in batch mode and uploading them to your server, or using ASP to build the report on the fly and then properly setting the datapath to the report. An example of doing this might be to post daily sales figures. You could create a Visual Basic application that generates each of the reports, one right after the other for, say, a total of ten reports. After the generation of ten RDF files is complete, these ten files would then be posted to your Web site. Hence, these reports are static "moment in time" representations of daily sales figures. Once you have posted the sales reports using code similar to that in Listing 9-20, you would load an RDF document into the AR Viewer control.

Listing 9-20. Code to Load an RDF Document

```
<script language="VBScript">
    'Set the data path
    Sub Window_OnLoad()
        ARViewCtrl.DataPath = "samplereport.rdf"
    End Sub
</script>
```

There are two important items to note here. The first is that you should always use the Window_OnLoad event of an ASP page to set the datapath. If you do not set the datapath, then the report will not properly load. The reason for this is that the datapath is how the ARViewer downloads the pages to your browser. Use of the name "datapath" is a bit confusing, as it really represents both the path and the report.

The next viewer control is the Java Viewer control. The ActiveReports Java Viewer control can be used for browsers that do not support ActiveX controls (such as Netscape, as we mentioned earlier), or it may simply be your method of choice for displaying reports. The Java Viewer is quite involved and includes a full set of documentation in the \help\Java Viewer directory. The ActiveReports Java Applet consists of a single JAR file. The main Applet class file in the JAR file is com.datadynamics.activereports.ActiveReportsViewer.class. All of the other classes are merely used by the ActiveReportsViewer class.

If you intend to use the Java Viewer, you should review the HTML help file documentation thoroughly, as there are some items to be aware of—for example, since the Java Viewer employs the printing features available only in Java 2 (Java version 1.2) or higher, you must take several special steps to use the plug-in.

If you have a license for the Professional edition of ActiveReports, you can use the WebCache feature to stream data to the client browser. Each of the report export options (which we explain fully in Chapter 6) has an ExportStream method that writes the data to a byte array for this purpose. In its most simple example, the WebCache allows for programmers to stream reports straight to client browsers in PDF, HTML, or RDF format without having to save any files to the hard drive of the Web server.

The WebCache service and the ISAPI DLL (more on this in a moment) manage report delivery to the client by caching the output. The WebCache contains two pieces: a service (WebCache) and an ISAPI DLL. Both pieces work together to manage report output on Web servers running Microsoft Internet Information Server (IIS). The caching service is a COM component that runs as a service on the Web server and caches the report's output. The ISAPI DLL receives requests for cached items, retrieves the items from the caching service, and delivers them to client browsers.

Using the CacheContent method of the WebCache service, you can direct the service to cache any type of content, including report output (RDF) and export filters byte array output. The CacheContent method specifies the content type, and the ISAPI filter serves the cached items with the content and headers specified in this method.

You can call the ExportWebCache method from the Excel or PDF export filters, which allow a direct export into the WebCache service objects and return the proper cache item IDs to redirect the client browser. This process is illustrated in Listing 9-21.

Listing 9-21. Sample WebCache Report

```
Function ExportReport() As Long
    ' Sample WebCache Report

    Dim rpt          As New ActiveReport
    Dim oWebCache    As New WebCache
    Dim oPDF         As New ActiveReportsPDFExport.ARExportPDF
    Dim aByteArray   As Variant
    Dim lReturnID    As Long

    ' Load the Report
    rpt.LoadLayout ("\Test.RPX")

    ' Run the Report
    rpt.Run

    ' Export the Report to a Byte Array
    Call oPDF.ExportStream(rpt.Pages, aByteArray)

    ' Now Cache the Byte Array
    lReturnID = oWebCache.CacheContent("Application/PDF", aByteArray)
```

```
      ' Return the Cached Report ID, which is how you can later
      ' retrieve this Cached report document
      ExportReport = lReturnID
End Function
```

As you can see, this is a fairly straightforward process. The report is loaded and run, and then the pages are passed to a byte array. This byte array is then cached by the WebCache service and given an ID (similar to inserting a row into a database table and retrieving the new row ID). Using this ID you can now call up the cached report.

```
nWebCacheID = ExportReport()
' Load Report
Response.Redirect "webcache.dll?" & nWebCacheID & "?"
```

Let's move on to reviewing a more advanced example, starting with the example WebCache application provided by Data Dynamics. This sample can be found on their Web site. The sample contains several pieces and requires IIS to be installed on the developer's machine. The purpose for reviewing this example is to help you more clearly understand what is required to use and distribute reports through the WebCache mechanism.

Two samples are included in the download: One is a Visual Basic application that uses a report server, and the other is a series of DLLs and ASP pages designed to run on a Web server. This sample demonstrates how to place PDF, HTML, and RDF files into the WebCache and stream the reports to client browsers that are accessing your server. The sample also demonstrates streaming reports directly to the client browser using the ExportStream() method of the PDF and HTML export filters without the WebCache as byte arrays.

The first step in the process is to unzip the WebCache demo. This creates several folders, the two main folders being ddWebProject and WebCacheSample. The WebCacheSample folder contains all the Visual Basic code (including the report server), whereas the ddWebProject folder contains the several subfolders that represent how to organize a WebCache report.

In creating your own WebCache reports, you will find that you can reuse several of the components presented in this sample. The first folder created is the bin folder. In the bin folder are all the ActiveReports runtime files, the PDF and HTML export filters, and the WebCache ISAPI DLL. Also included in the bin directory is an ActiveX DLL report server created in Visual Basic (the source is in the WebCacheSample folder). The second folder is the RPXfiles folder. This folder is where all the "Streamed" RPX files are placed.

To view the sample, simply share the ddWebProject folder (right-click the folder, and select Sharing and Security, and then select Web Sharing and share the folder). Once you have shared this folder, you should now be able to view it using IIS (see Figure 9-9). However, at this stage the report is not completely set up. The next step is to register four of the five DLLs (ARPro2.dll, htmlexpt.dll, pdf-expt.dll, reportserver.dll, and webcache.dll) located in the bin folder (to do this you can use Start | Run regsvr32 *path*\ddlname). Of the five DLLs, you can actually register only four (although the documentation tells you to register all five). The webcache.dll will not register if the machine you are using it on is in fact a development box that already includes a copy of ActiveReports.

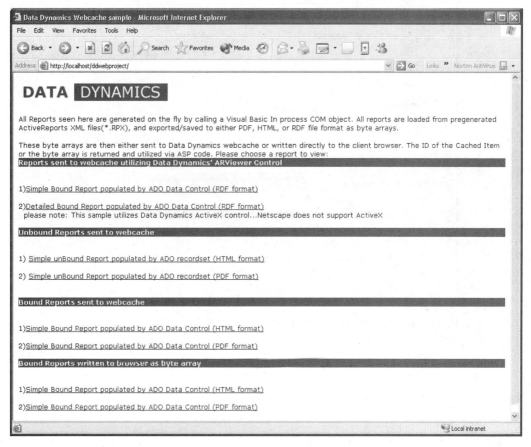

Figure 9-9. The WebCache sample

Once the DLLs are registered, you now need to enable the in-process server so that it can be executed. To do this, open IIS and select the ddWebProject folder. Under the ddWebProject folder you will find the bin directory. Right-click the bin folder in IIS and select Properties. Next, select the execute permissions and change them from Scripts only to Scripts and Executables (see Figure 9-10).

Figure 9-10. Changing bin properties

Now you are ready to run the example (see Figure 9-11).

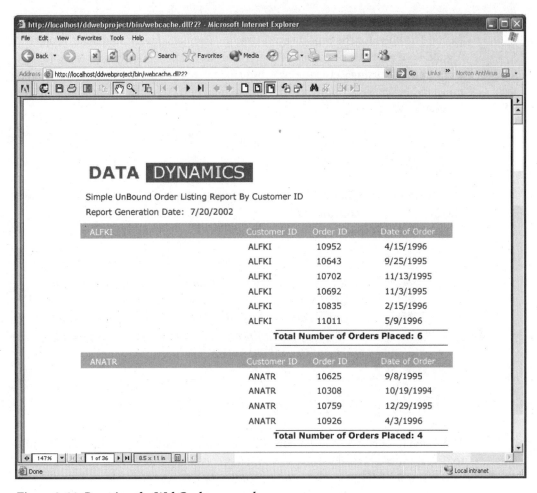

Figure 9-11. Running the WebCache example

The two functions that really do most of the work are ExportToWebCache and ExportToByteArray. The basic premises behind the workings of a WebCache are that you will generate an output document (be that HTML or PDF) and then pass it to the cache using the ExportStream() method.

Another example using Visual Basic is also located in the WebCacheSample folder. The code for the report server is in the ReportServer Visual Basic Project. A good review of this code will help you to understand not only how to build a report server using ActiveReports, but also how to utilize the WebCache. We recommend looking over both sets of code to help you gain a clearer understanding of how the WebCache features work.

ActiveReports for .NET

The .NET version of ActiveReports allows you to display output over the Internet via the WebViewer control and HTTP handlers. You can also transfer data via MemoryStream objects.

 NOTE *Data Dynamics has not yet produced an end-user report designer for the Web. This feature is in the discussion stage only and may be included in a future release of the product. If you require a Web-delivered report design tool, check out Crystal Enterprise.*

ActiveReports WebViewer Control

The ActiveReports WebViewer control is a programmable object that allows you to display your server-based reports via a browser. Accomplishing this task is rather simple. Set the Report property of the WebViewer control to an ActiveReports object and then indicate the ViewerType property as AcrobatReader, ActiveXViewer, HTMLViewer, or RawHTML. Executing the Web page produces output similar to that shown in Figure 9-12.

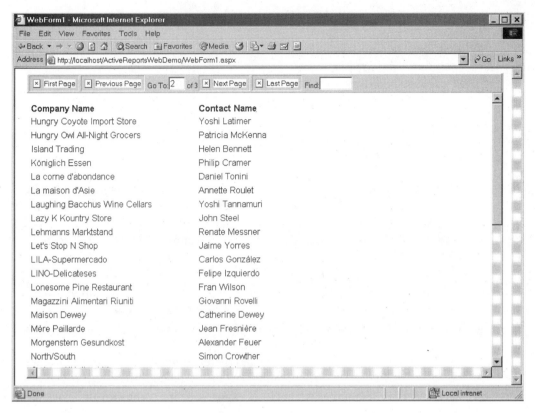

Figure 9-12. WebView HTMLViewer output

As Figure 9-12 illustrates, HTMLViewer is a navigable report display that divides the output into multiple pages, each with its own page header. By contrast, a ViewerType of RawHTML would display the output in one continuous stream of HTML navigable only by the browser scrollbar. The ActiveXViewer option, functional only with Internet Explorer, will push the arview2.cab file to the client desktop to install the ActiveX viewer. You should only select this option if you are certain that the client machines will accept ActiveX controls or if your Web site is at least registered as a trusted site on the client. Finally, the AcrobatReader option will display the output in PDF format on the client with all the navigation and printing options afforded by the local copy of Acrobat.

The code that follows instantiates a report object, assigns it to the WebViewer control's Report property, and displays it using the HTMLViewer option:

```
Dim objReport As New WebReport()

WebViewer1.Report = objReport

WebViewer1.ViewerType = WebViewer1.ViewerType.HtmlViewer
```

HTTP Handlers

Whereas the WebViewer control is used within ASP Web form pages so it can be sized and positioned relative to other content on the page, HTTP handlers simply run the report from the RPX file (it does not have to be compiled within the Web application) and takes over the whole page, returning PDF or HTML. You can directly link to the RPX file just like you link to any other ASP or HTML page. Internally, both approaches work the same.

Currently the PDF and HTML export filters are the only ones supported by the HTTP handler. The main difference between the HTTP handler's export method and the manual method is that the HTTP handler exports to a stream and the other writes the stream to the file.

HTTP handlers do not allow any parameters other than the export format to be passed in. In order to pass parameters, you would need to do so through a DLL. You can set up the DLL to either export the report and stream it back to the Web page, or export the output to disk and redirect the browser to the exported file.

MemoryStream Objects

MemoryStream objects creates data streams encapsulated as unsigned byte arrays that are directly accessible in memory. Use of memory streams can reduce the need for temporary buffers and files and can speed data transfer. The code shown in Listing 9-22 illustrates how an ActiveReport Document object is exported to a MemoryStream object and transferred to the client machine via the BinaryWrite method of the Response object.

Listing 9-22. MemoryStream Object

```
Dim objWebReport As New WebReport()
Dim objPDF As New Pdf.PdfExport()
Dim objMemoryStream As System.IO.MemoryStream = _
    New System.IO.MemoryStream()
```

```
objWebReport.Run()

objPDF.Export(objWebReport.Document, objMemoryStream)

Response.BinaryWrite (objMemoryStream.ToArray())

Response.End()
```

ASP.NET

ASP.NET is in many ways leagues beyond the comparatively crude classic ASP technology. ASP.NET still produces HTML output that will run on a client browser. It is the browser that interprets the output. The same restrictions apply as discussed previously in the chapter in the sidebar "Pros and Cons of HTML/ASP Report Delivery." However, ASP.NET still makes it much easier to program Web reports, collect criteria, and deliver them to the desktop.

Since you're ultimately delivering browser-compatible HTML, your existing ASP code will work just fine in the ASP.NET environment. Simply change the extension on your ASP files to.aspx, run them under ASP.NET, and see what happens.

DataGrid

Server-side Web controls are one of the most powerful new features in ASP.NET, and arguably the most powerful of the server-side Web controls is the DataGrid. If you've ever worked with any of the third-party OCX grid controls in VB6, DataGrid will look very familiar. Simply drag and drop a DataGrid on your design window and you can begin setting the properties. Because grids display data in a row and column format, they are an obvious choice for delivering reports over the Internet. In many respects a DataGrid is a visual object wrapper for the HTML table tag, and the output delivered to the browser is wrapped in the various table tags—<tr>, <td>, etc. However, DataGrid is far more powerful than the static table tags ever were. Because the DataGrid is an object with methods and properties, it can be programmed as such with code added to event handlers, and changes are easily made to the visual display once the page is delivered to the browser.

Examine the code in Listing 9-23. This example prints a simple columnar report where the first column is a hyperlink to another page providing more information. To illustrate the various formatting features, this report displays with a rather garish-looking appearance.

Listing 9-23. DataGrid Report

```vb
Dim objCol1 As New HyperLinkColumn()
Dim objCol2 As New BoundColumn()
Dim objCol3 As New BoundColumn()
Dim objCol4 As New BoundColumn()
Dim objStyle As New Style()

With objCol1
    .DataTextField = "ConventionName"
    .HeaderText = "Convention"
    .DataNavigateUrlField = "ID"
    .DataNavigateUrlFormatString = "convinfo.aspx?id={0}"
    .SortExpression = "ConventionName"
End With

With objCol2
    .DataField = "StartDate"
    .HeaderText = "Start Date"
    .DataFormatString = "{0:MM/dd/yyyy}"
    .SortExpression = "StartDate"
End With

With objCol3
    .DataField = "City"
    .HeaderText = "City"
    .SortExpression = "City"
End With

With objCol4
    .DataField = "State"
    .HeaderText = "State"
    .SortExpression = "State"
End With

With DataGrid1
    .AllowPaging = True
    .PageSize = 5
    .AllowSorting = True
    .AutoGenerateColumns = False
    .Columns.Add (objCol1)
    .Columns.Add (objCol2)
    .Columns.Add (objCol3)
```

```
      .Columns.Add (objCol4)
      .BackColor = objStyle.BackColor.Gray
      .ForeColor = objStyle.BackColor.Black
      .GridLines = GridLines.None
      .Width = Unit.Pixel(600)
      .GridLines = GridLines.None
      .CellPadding = 5
      .CellSpacing = 5
      .BorderWidth = Unit.Point(10)
      .BorderColor = Color.Red
End With

Call BindToDataSource
```

This DataGrid has four columns. The first, a HyperLinkColumn object, displays a hyperlink that allows you to drill down to another Web page to see more information. To create a URL parameter for this hyperlink, set the DataNavigateUrlField and DataNavigateUrlFormatString properties. DataNavigateUrlFormatString contains the part of the URL that remains the same regardless of what parameter is being passed, while DataNavigateUrlField contains the field name that supplies the value identifying the record to be retrieved. The "{0}" placeholder in the DataNavigateUrlFormatString settings indicates the first replaceable parameter value. The remainder of the columns are created individually as BoundColumn objects by setting the DataField, HeaderText, and SortExpression properties. The result is the Web page shown in Figure 9-13.

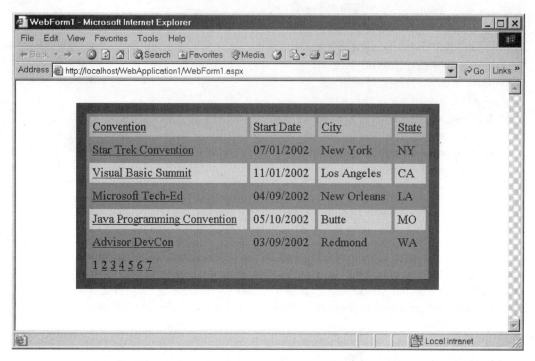

Figure 9-13. DataGrid report

Sorting

Because the AllowSorting property of our DataGrid is set to True, the headers to
each column are set to hyperlinks as well. When you click any one of these headers, the SortCommand event shown next gets triggered.

```
Private Sub DataGrid1_SortCommand(ByVal source As Object, _
    ByVal e As System.Web.UI.WebControls.DataGridSortCommandEventArgs) _
    Handles DataGrid1.SortCommand

    ViewState("SortOrder") = e.SortExpression
    BindToDataSource

End Sub
```

Within SortCommand, you can add the code that stores the SortExpression property of the column that was clicked to a ViewState variable. ViewState variables maintain their values even after the page is posted back to itself, as will happen when the link is clicked. They are much better than using Session variables as they don't consume precious server memory resources. Then you can invoke the routine that binds the DataGrid to the data source (see Listing 9-24) and pass the sort expression from the ViewState variable to the Sort property of the DataView object, and the result is a sorted grid.

Listing 9-24. BindToDataSource

```
Private Sub BindToDataSource()
    Dim oConn As New OleDb.OleDbConnection()
    Dim objDA As New OleDb.OleDbDataAdapter()
    Dim objCommand As New OleDb.OleDbCommand()
    Dim objDS As New DataSet()
    Dim objDV As New DataView()
    Dim cConnectString As String
    Dim cSQL As String

    cConnectString = "Provider=Microsoft.Jet.OLEDB.4.0;" & _
    "Data Source=C:\\BookCode\\SampleDatabase.mdb"

    oConn.ConnectionString = cConnectString
    oConn.Open()

    cSQL = "SELECT ID, ConventionName, StartDate, City, State " & _
           "FROM Convention"

    With objCommand
        .Connection = oConn
        .CommandText = cSQL
    End With

    objDA.SelectCommand = objCommand
    objDA.Fill(objDS, "Convention")

    objDV.Table = objDS.Tables("Convention")
    objDV.Sort = ViewState("SortOrder")

    DataGrid1.DataSource = objDV
    DataGrid1.DataBind()
End Sub
```

Paging

One of the biggest annoyances when displaying reports using classic ASP was the inherent difficulties in paging. You needed to use a technique similar to the one shown earlier in this chapter. ASP.NET makes it much easy to page DataGrid information. Simply set the AllowPaging property to True and then indicate how many records should show per page via the PageSize property. By default, previous and next arrows will appear to allow navigation, but you can display page numbers instead by setting the value of the PagerStyle.Mode property to PagerMode.NumericPages. Then, add a PageIndexChanged event handler to handle the click on the arrows as follows:

```
Private Sub DataGrid1_PageIndexChanged(ByVal source As Object, _
    ByVal e As System.Web.UI.WebControls.DataGridPageChangedEventArgs) _
        Handles DataGrid1.PageIndexChanged

    DataGrid1.CurrentPageIndex = e.NewPageIndex
    BindToDataSource()

End Sub
```

Criteria Screens

Before you can run any report, you'll need to collect criteria from the user to filter the information delivered. Earlier in this chapter you saw how to dynamically create criteria screens using ASP and HTML. Here, you'll learn how the same approach works with ASP.NET.

Because server-based Web controls are object-oriented, you can program them in a fashion similar to WinForm controls. Thus, the difference between the approach taken in ASP.NET versus VB .NET is minimal, whereas the approach taken by VB6 versus classic ASP is radically different. It's a good idea to read Chapter 3 as a background for this ASP.NET section to see how it's done in VB .NET. There you'll also see the sidebar "Data-Driven Programming with VB .NET."

Suppose you need to create a criteria page similar to the one shown in Figure 9-14, which is designed for a pharmaceutical inquiry system. Here, users can enter a range of dates, indicate if they only want the complex questions to display, and filter by one department only but by any number of sources and products. If they wish, users may skip any or all of these criteria.

Because check box Web controls have only two possible values—checked or unchecked (that is, there is no "gray" state)—they have limited flexibility as criteria controls since there is then no easy way to make them optional. One way to overcome this limitation is to use a combo box instead. By filling the combo box with three values—Yes, No, and Ignore—you can achieve the same result as a three-state check box. If you really have your heart set on check boxes, you can simulate a three-state check box via graphic images that show checked, unchecked, and grayed check box states. Then you can use JavaScript to toggle the three images.

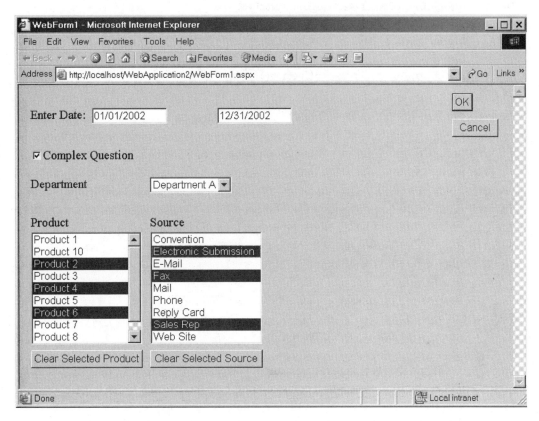

Figure 9-14. ASP.NET criteria page

Rather than building each Web page customized for each report, you can create this criteria page by dynamically creating Web controls and reading the selections made by users when they click the OK button. You'll only need to invoke a set of control display routines each for the different types of controls used so as to create this screen with only a few lines of code.

The first step in accomplishing this is to instantiate Collection objects to hold and manage the dynamically created controls. In addition, you'll need constant values to make references to the elements of these Collection objects so as to identify the individual criteria controls. The setup is shown in Listing 9-25.

Listing 9-25. Setup for Dynamic Criteria Controls

```
Dim objListBoxLabelColl As New Collection()
Dim objListBoxColl As New Collection()
Dim objListBoxButtonColl As New Collection()

Dim objComboBoxLabelColl As New Collection()
Dim objComboBoxColl As New Collection()

Dim objDateRangeLabelColl As New Collection()
Dim objDateFromColl As New Collection()
Dim objDateToColl As New Collection()

Dim objCheckBoxColl As New Collection()

Const SELECT_PRODUCT = 1
Const SELECT_SOURCE = 2

Const SELECT_ENTER_DATE = 1
Const SELECT_RECEIVE_DATE = 2

Const SELECT_FIRST_NAME = 1
Const SELECT_LAST_NAME = 2

Const SELECT_DEPARTMENT = 1

Const SELECT_COMPLEX_QUESTION = 1
```

When the Web page is first loaded, you can connect to your data source and invoke the subroutines that create various criteria controls. Once these controls are created, you can then populate the data-bound ones. Note that you only need to populate the controls from the database during the initial load of the page and not during any subsequent page loads triggered as the result of a postback. Fortunately, the ASP.NET Page object has an IsPostBack property that indicates if the page is loading as the result of a postback. Listing 9-26 shows the Load event in its entirety.

Listing 9-26. Page_Load Event

```
Private Sub Page_Load(ByVal sender As System.Object, _
    ByVal e As System.EventArgs) Handles MyBase.Load

    Dim oConn As New OleDb.OleDbConnection()
    Dim objDR As OleDb.OleDbDataReader
    Dim cConnectString As String
```

```
'Connect to data source
cConnectString = "Provider=Microsoft.Jet.OLEDB.4.0;" & _
"Data Source=C:\\BookCode\\SampleDatabase.mdb"

oConn.ConnectionString = cConnectString
oConn.Open()

'Invoke routines which display web controls
ShowDateRange(SELECT_ENTER_DATE, 8, 32, 20, "Enter Date:")
ShowCheckBox(SELECT_COMPLEX_QUESTION, 8, 95, 20, "Complex Question")
ShowComboBox(SELECT_DEPARTMENT, 8, 140, 180, 20, "Department")
ShowListBox(SELECT_PRODUCT, 8, 200, 180, 20, "Product")
ShowListBox(SELECT_SOURCE, 200, 200, 180, 20, "Source")

'Populate data bound web controls (list and combo boxes) with data
If Not Page.IsPostBack Then
    LoadTable(oConn, objComboBoxColl(SELECT_DEPARTMENT), _
        "Department", "ID", "Descr")
    LoadTable(oConn, objListBoxColl(SELECT_PRODUCT), _
        "Product", "ID", "Descr")
    LoadTable(oConn, objListBoxColl(SELECT_SOURCE), _
        "Source", "ID", "Descr")
End If

PositionButtons()

End Sub 'Page_Load
```

The various Show subroutines create the individual controls that display on the page. We'll examine the ListBox control routines to illustrate how the data-driven techniques are implemented. Listing 9-27 shows the ShowListBox routine, and as you can see it simply invokes three other routines that display the three elements needed to display a ListBox criteria in good form: a caption, a Clear All button, and the ListBox control itself, each displayed one over the other on the page.

Listing 9-27. ShowListBox Routine

```
Private Sub ShowListBox(ByVal iIndex As Short, ByVal iLeft As Short, _
    ByVal iTop As Short, ByVal iWidth As Short, ByVal iHeight As Short, _
    ByVal cCaption As String)

    Dim iListBoxHeight As Short
```

```
Call AddDynamicListBoxLabel(iIndex, iLeft, iTop, iWidth, cCaption)

Call AddDynamicListBox(iIndex, iLeft, iTop + iHeight + 5, iWidth, 180)

iListBoxHeight = _
    Replace(objListBoxColl(iIndex).style("height"), "px", String.Empty)

Call AddDynamicListBoxButton(iIndex, iLeft, (iTop + iHeight + 5) + _
        iListBoxHeight + 5, iWidth, cCaption)

End Sub
```

The fundamentals of creating a control dynamically in ASP.NET are illustrated in any one of the three AddDynamicListBox routines invoked by the ShowListBox routine. These routines all receive the parameters first passed to the ShowListBox routine. Examine the code in Listing 9-28, which dynamically creates a ListBox object, sets its properties, and adds it to both the objListBoxColl collection and the Controls collection of the owner Panel object.

Listing 9-28. AddDynamicListBox Routine

```
Private Sub AddDynamicListBox(ByVal iIndex As Short, ByVal iLeft As Short, _
    ByVal iTop As Short, ByVal iWidth As Short, ByVal iHeight As Short)

    Dim objListBox As New ListBox()

    With objListBox
        .Style("position") = "absolute"
        .Style("left") = iLeft & "px"
        .Style("top") = iTop & "px"
        .Style("height") = iHeight & "px"
        .Style("width") = iWidth & "px"
        .SelectionMode = ListSelectionMode.Multiple
    End With

    objListBoxColl.Add (objListBox)

    Panel1.Controls.Add (objListBox)

End Sub
```

In the AddDynamicListBox routine, you first declare an object of type ListBox. Then, you'll need to set its various (absolute) positioning attributes as expressed in pixels. Finally, set the SelectionMode property to Multiple and add the new control to the objListBoxColl collection and also to the Controls collection of the owner Panel.

One display problem manifests itself in displaying controls dynamically on a Web page. It occurs when you need to display controls side by side, as in the case of a combo box. Since you'll want to display the combo box control immediately to the right of the label that describes it, you'll naturally need to know the width of the label. Unfortunately, you can never precisely know this width as, unlike a desktop application, the font settings for the page vary based on the user settings in the browser. Therefore, you can only approximate based on the length of the label text, but this approach won't be perfect.

Because users may select multiple values from a ListBox, they will also need a way to clear those selections should they change their minds. To accomplish this feat in one routine for an undetermined number of ListBox objects, create a Click event handler that invokes the ClearSelection method for the ListBox object passed to it as the sender parameter. Listing 9-29 illustrates this event handler.

Listing 9-29. Click Event Handler

```vb
Private Sub objListBox_Click(ByVal sender As Object, ByVal e As System.EventArgs)
    Dim objListbox As ListBox
    Dim objButton As Button
    Dim iIndex As Integer

    For Each objButton In objListBoxButtonColl

        iIndex += 1

        If objButton Is sender Then
            Exit For
        End If

    Next

    objListbox = CType(objListBoxColl(iIndex), ListBox)

    objListbox.ClearSelection()

End Sub
```

By iterating through the objListBoxButtonColl button collection, you can determine to which ListBox the Click event belonged. Then, by invoking the ClearSelection method, the selected items are immediately deselected.

Once the user has selected his or her criteria, he or she is ready to run the report. By clicking the OK button, a postback will occur and you can extract both the values needed to form a SQL WHERE clause as well as a human-readable explanation of the options chosen. Listing 9-30 shows the extraction process for the Web controls.

Listing 9-30. OK Button

```
Private Sub cmdOK_Click(ByVal sender As System.Object, _
    ByVal e As System.EventArgs) Handles cmdOK.Click

    Dim objSQL As New StringBuilder()
    Dim cSQL As String
    Dim objCriteria As New StringBuilder()
    Dim cCriteria As String
    Dim cDateFrom As String
    Dim cDateTo As String

    cDateFrom = objDateFromColl(SELECT_ENTER_DATE).Text
    cDateTo = objDateToColl(SELECT_ENTER_DATE).Text

    With objSQL
        .AppendFormat (GetDateSQL("createdate", cDateFrom, cDateTo))
        .AppendFormat (GetListBoxSQL(objListBoxColl(SELECT_PRODUCT), "ProductID"))
        .AppendFormat (GetListBoxSQL(objListBoxColl(SELECT_SOURCE), "SourceID"))
        .AppendFormat (GetComboBoxSQL(SELECT_DEPARTMENT, "deptid"))
        .AppendFormat (GetCheckBoxSQL(SELECT_COMPLEX_QUESTION, "questiontype"))
    End With

    With objCriteria
        .AppendFormat (GetDateCriteria("Create Date", cDateFrom, cDateTo))
        .AppendFormat (GetListBoxCriteria(objListBoxColl(SELECT_PRODUCT), _
                                "Product"))
        .AppendFormat (GetListBoxCriteria(objListBoxColl(SELECT_SOURCE), "Source"))
        .AppendFormat (GetComboBoxCriteria(SELECT_DEPARTMENT, "Department"))
        .AppendFormat (GetCheckBoxCriteria(SELECT_COMPLEX_QUESTION, _
                                "Complex Question"))
    End With
```

```
cSQL = objSQL.ToString
cCriteria = objCriteria.ToString

If objSQL.ToString <> String.Empty Then
    cSQL = cSQL.Substring(0, cSQL.Length - 5)
End If

If objCriteria.ToString <> String.Empty Then
    cCriteria = cCriteria.Substring(0, cCriteria.Length - 5)
End If

End Sub
```

The various Get routines retrieve the values (for a SQL statement) or the text descriptions (for a criteria explanation) of the options selected. The goal is to produce a WHERE clause that looks like this:

```
createdate BETWEEN '01/01/02' AND '12/31/02'
AND ProductID IN (1,3,6)
AND SourceID IN (8,4,2)
AND deptid = 4
AND questiontype = -1
```

and a criteria explanation that looks like this:

```
the Create Date is between 01/01/02 and 12/31/02 and
the Product is among (Product 1,Product 3,Product 6) and
the Source is among (Electronic Submission,Fax,Mail) and
the Department is Department D and the Complex Question is True
```

Listing 9-31 illustrates the code used to extract the selected values from a ListBox object.

Listing 9-31. GetListBoxSQL Function

```
Function GetListBoxSQL(ByRef objListBox As ListBox, _
    ByVal cColumn As String) As String

    Dim cSQL As String = String.Empty
    Dim cList As String

    cList = ParseIt(objListBox, True, False, 0)
```

```
    If cList <> String.Empty Then
        cSQL = cColumn & " IN " & cList & " AND "
    End If


    GetListBoxSQL = cSQL

End Function
```

GetListBoxSQL receives as parameters a reference to the ListBox object and the table column name. GetListBoxSQL calls the ParseIt function, which does most of the work. ParseIt loops through the ListBox object and returns a list of the selected items—or all items depending on the parameter settings—in the format similar to the string "(32, 321, 672)". The purpose is to use this string in an IN clause as shown in the preceding SQL statements. The code for the ParseIt function is shown in Listing 9-32.

Listing 9-32. ParseIt Function

```
Function ParseIt(ByVal oList As ListBox, ByVal bTagged As Boolean, _
    ByVal bQuotes As Boolean, ByVal iCol As Short) As String

    Dim objResult As New StringBuilder("(")
    Dim cResult As String = String.Empty
    Dim cQuotes As String
    Dim cData As String
    Dim oTemp As ListItem
    Dim oCollection As Object

    If bQuotes Then
        cQuotes = ControlChars.Quote
    Else
        cQuotes = String.Empty
    End If

    If bTagged Then

        For Each oTemp In oList.Items

            If oTemp.Selected Then

                If iCol = 0 Then
                    cData = oTemp.Value
                Else
```

```
                    cData = oTemp.Text
            End If

            objResult.AppendFormat (cQuotes & cData & cQuotes & ",")

        End If

    Next

Else

    For Each oTemp In oList.Items

        If iCol = 0 Then
            cData = oTemp.Value
        Else
            cData = oTemp.Text
        End If

        objResult.AppendFormat (cQuotes & cData & cQuotes & ",")

    Next

End If

cResult = objResult.ToString

If bQuotes Then
    cResult = Mid$(cResult, 1, Len(cResult) - 2) & cQuotes & ")"
Else
    cResult = Mid$(cResult, 1, Len(cResult)) & cQuotes & ")"
End If

cResult = Replace(cResult, ",)", ")")

cResult = Replace(cResult, ",,", String.Empty)

If cResult = "()" Then
    cResult = String.Empty
End If

ParseIt = cResult

End Function
```

Similarly, GetListBoxCriteria extracts the text descriptions of the selected items and returns them as a string in the format "(Electronic Submission,Fax,Mail)". The iCol parameter determines which property of the ListBox object is read, either Value or Text.

Web Services

Web services are probably the single greatest technological leap offered in the .NET platform. Because they use HTTP as their communication protocol and transmit all data as XML, you can truly achieve the cross-platform interoperability between systems that is not possible with either COM or CORBA. If ever there were a killer app for XML, Web services are it. Fortunately, they are not only perfect for report delivery, but disarmingly simple to implement.

To deliver reports as Web services, you'll need to create a minimum of two Web methods: one that receives the criteria that filters the report and another that delivers the requested output. The first method is very simple to create, the second one a bit more difficult.

Web methods are created just like any other method except that the tag <WebMethod()> gets placed before the declaration as shown in Listing 9-33. In this example, the Web method extracts the data needed for the report and runs whatever reporting tool you select.

Listing 9-33. WebMethod to Run Report

```
Public Enum ExportFormats
    Excel = 0
    PDF = 1
    HTML = 2
    RTF = 3
    ASCII = 4
    XML = 5
End Enum

<WebMethod()> Public Sub EmployeeRpt(ByVal cWhere As String, _
    ByVal iExport As ExportFormats)

    Dim objSQL As New System.Text.StringBuilder()

    objSQL.Append ("SELECT * " & _
                   "FROM Employee " & _
                   "WHERE ")
```

```
objSQL.Append (cWhere)

'Execute report code using your reporting tool and
'dump the output to the export format of choice

End Sub
```

Once you have run the report and dumped the output to a file, the real fun can begin. Because Web services only transmit ASCII data in an XML wrapper, you cannot directly send a PDF or an XLS file, for example, as these are both binary objects. Therefore, you'll need to convert these files into an ASCII format that can receive this XML wrapper—a feat you can achieve with Base64 encoding. Base64 encoding converts binary data into printable characters. The main drawback to this approach is that the resulting encoded data can be up to one-third larger than the original file.

Fortunately, VB .NET provides a method of the System namespace that handles Base64 encoding for you. This method receives as parameters an array of integers, an offset, and the length of the integer array. The final output is a text string that looks something like this:

```
JVBERi0xLjINJeLjz9MNCjEzMiAwIG9iago8PCANLOxpbmVhcml6Z...
```

You can create this string by using the Web method shown in Listing 9-34.

Listing 9-34. Base64 Encoding

```
<WebMethod()> Public Function SendReportToUser(ByVal cFileName As String) As String

    SendReportToUser = Base64Encode(cFileName)

End Function

Private Function Base64Encode(ByVal cFileName As String) As String
    Dim objFileStream As System.IO.FileStream
    Dim aData() As Byte
    Dim lBytes As Long
    Dim cResult As String

    objFileStream = New System.IO.FileStream(cFileName, _
        IO.FileMode.Open, IO.FileAccess.Read)

    ReDim aData(objFileStream.Length)
```

```
lBytes = objFileStream.Read(aData, 0, objFileStream.Length)

objFileStream.Close()

cResult = System.Convert.ToBase64String(aData, 0, aData.Length)

Base64Encode = cResult
```

End Function

The idea is to return this encoded string to the consumer of the Web server where it can be decoded and rendered as a readable file. The Button Click event in Listing 9-35 shows the invocation of the reporting Web service in its entirety. First, it passes a filter statement to the report generation method that will run the report on the server and return the encoded string representing the output file. This encoded string is then passed to the Base64Decode function along with an output filename where it is re-created on the client machine simply by reversing the process done on the server.

Listing 9-35. Retrieving Encoded String and Re-creating Output File

```
Private Sub Button1_Click(ByVal sender As System.Object, _
    ByVal e As System.EventArgs) _
    Handles Button1.Click

    Dim objRunReport As New localhost1.Service1()
    Dim cWhere As String
    Dim cEncodedFile As String

    Cursor.Current = System.Windows.Forms.Cursors.WaitCursor

    cWhere = "State = 'NJ'"

    objRunReport.EmployeeRpt(cWhere, localhost1.ExportFormats.PDF)

    cEncodedFile = objRunReport.SendReportToUser("c:\docs\reports\chapter4.pdf")

    Call Base64Decode(cEncodedFile, "c:\docs\myreportdoc.pdf")

    Cursor.Current = System.Windows.Forms.Cursors.Default

End Sub
```

```
Sub Base64Decode(ByVal cData As String, ByVal cFileName As String)
    Dim aData() As Byte
    Dim objFileStream As System.IO.FileStream

    aData = System.Convert.FromBase64String(cData)

    objFileStream = New System.IO.FileStream(cFileName, _
        IO.FileMode.Create, IO.FileAccess.Write)

    objFileStream.Write(aData, 0, aData.Length - 1)

    objFileStream.Close()

End Sub
```

Crystal Reports

Many companies have standardized on Crystal Reports over the years and have a vast collection of legacy reports in this format. As the need arises to make these reports available over the Web, some strategic decision making needs to be done. Crystal's Web licensing is rather expensive, and you'll need to weigh whether it's worth obtaining Crystal Enterprise, or changing reporting tools altogether in favor of development platforms that do not have any restrictive licensing.

Crystal Reports 9 Web Services

Crystal Reports allows you to publish reports as Web services, thereby making the objects and data in the report available as XML over the Internet. The basics of exposing a Crystal Report as a Web service is rather simple. Simply create a Web services project and add the RPT file via Project | Add Existing Item. Then, right-click the RPT file in the Solution Explorer and select Publish as Web Service. Doing so will create an ASMX file to match the RPT. In your client application, create a form that contains a Crystal Reports viewer control and issue the following lines of code:

```
CrystalReportViewer1.DisplayGroupTree = False
CrystalReportViewer1.ReportSource = _
http://localhost/CrystalReportsWebService/RequestorService.asmx
```

If you're using the Advanced edition of Crystal Reports 9, you're in luck. For Web reports, you get three simultaneous active licenses for a given report. When the report is complete, the process is available for someone else to use. Crystal Reports 9 ships with a cache server that offers unlimited queuing ability. Therefore, if more than three users are simultaneously running the same report, their request will wait in a queue until a process becomes available, and they won't receive a "All Licenses Used" message.

Crystal Enterprise 8.5

Crystal Enterprise (CE) is, essentially, Crystal Decisions' report server. Of course, that is only one part of what Crystal Enterprise offers. Not only does Crystal Enterprise allow you to distribute your existing Crystal reports over the Internet, it provides users with report creation ability. In addition, Crystal Enterprise includes the Crystal Analysis tool, which allows you to drill into your OLAP databases to develop reports and charts, and make your results available on the Web. Crystal Enterprise offers three licensing models: named user, concurrent users, or processor.

 NOTE   *Although Crystal Decisions released Crystal Reports 9 in August 2002, this version is not compatible with Crystal Enterprise 8.5. Crystal Reports 9 reports can be used with Crystal Enterprise 9.0, which is scheduled for release by the end of the first quarter of 2003.*

Running Reports

The essence of the report server functionality is found in the Automated Process Server (APS). The APS handles security and user rights, and manages the various folders, reports, and servers. The APS database is created during the installation process. If you have Microsoft SQL Server installed on the same machine as Crystal Enterprise, the APS will use this as its database. Otherwise, Crystal Enterprise will create a Microsoft Data Engine (MSDE) database. This database should not be queried via a direct data access layer such as ADO. System information should only be retrieved through the objects exposed by the Crystal Enterprise SDK.

NOTE *The APS stores the InfoObjects that encapsulate the reports published to CE. The RPT files themselves are stored in the File Repository Service (FRS).*

You can access the APS information using CE's SQL-based query language. The data that drives all of CE's functionality can be found in two categories: CI_INFOOBJECTS, which handles reports, folders, shortcuts, etc., and SI_SYSTEMOBJECTS, which handles the administrative tasks relating to users, groups, and servers. For example, to extract all the Crystal Reports registered with CE, use the following statement:

```
SELECT SI_ID, SI_NAME
FROM CI_INFOOBJECTS
WHERE SI_PROGID = 'CrystalEnterprise.Report'
```

The Crystal eBusiness Framework is the key to Crystal Enterprises architecture. It manages communication and data exchange between all components installed in the Crystal Enterprise system. The Crystal Enterprise SDK is the API for this framework. The SDK consists of a series of COM DLLs that are designed to act as a programmable interface between the client applications and the Crystal Enterprise servers. This interface handles all user and server functionality, as well as a series of plug-ins that control the behavior of the various Crystal Enterprise objects themselves. The main structure of the SDK is comprised of the following DLLs:

- *CrystalEnterpriseLib (EnterpriseFramework.DLL):* CrystalEnterpriseLib is responsible for most client-server communication. This DLL provides the ability to log on to the APS and access the rest of Crystal Enterprise's functionality.

- *CrystalPluginManager (PluginManager.DLL):* The Crystal Enterprise system stores object information in the form of InfoObjects. These InfoObjects are represented by a series of plug-ins that are simply server-based COM DLLs. There are four categories of plug-ins: desktop, authentication, administration, and destination. Through these plug-ins you can set report parameters and change various report attributes.

- *CrystalInfoStoreLib (InfoStor.DLL):* The CrystalInfoStoreLib manages such InfoObjects as Folders, Reports, and Report Instances. Though every InfoObject is represented by a separate COM DLL or plug-in, these objects must still be managed by the APS. InfoStor.DLL allows you to read, write, and schedule InfoObjects on the APS.

Now that you understand the overall purpose and general object architecture of Crystal Enterprise, let's see how the objects can be programmed in ASP. The code shown in Listing 9-36 illustrates how a report that has been published to Crystal Enterprise can be displayed in the browser. This is only a small sample of the functionality of Crystal Enterprise. A full explanation of its features is way beyond the scope of this book.

Listing 9-36. ASP Code to Display Report

```
<%

Option Explicit

Dim objSessionMgr, objEnterpriseSession, objService
Dim objInfoObjects, objReportObject, objLogonTokenMgr
Dim lReportID, cToken, cSQL, cRedirect

lReportID = 250

Set objSessionMgr = CreateObject("CrystalEnterprise.SessionMgr")

Set objEnterpriseSession = _
objSessionMgr.Logon("administrator","","nydwetl3","secEnterprise")

Set objService = objEnterpriseSession.Service("", "InfoStore")

Set objLogonTokenMgr = objEnterpriseSession.LogonTokenMgr
cToken = objLogonTokenMgr.CreateLogonToken("", 1, 100)

cSQL = "SELECT * " & _
    "FROM CI_INFOOBJECTS " & _
    "WHERE SI_ID = " & lReportID & " AND " & _
    "SI_PROGID = 'CrystalEnterprise.Report'"

Set objInfoObjects = objService.Query(cSQL)

Set objReportObject = objInfoObjects.Item(1).PluginInterface
```

```
With objReportObject.ReportParameters.Item(1).CurrentValues.Item(1)
    .Value = 6164
End With

With objReportObject.ReportLogons.Item(1)
    .ServerName="MYSERVER"
    .Databasename="testdb"
    .UserName="myUID"
    .Password="mypass"
End With

objService.Commit objInfoObjects

cRedirect = "http://nydwetl3/crystal/enterprise/" & _
"admin/en/viewrpt.cwr?id=" & lReportID & _
"&apstoken=" & cToken

Response.Redirect(cRedirect)

set objSessionMgr = nothing
set objEnterpriseSession = nothing
set objService = nothing
set objInfoObjects = nothing
set objReportObject = nothing
set objLogonTokenMgr = nothing

%>
```

Each report is represented in the APS database by a unique number which you can retrieve from the ePortfolio report screen. In this example, that unique ID is 250. The first step is to create an instance of the CrystalEnterprise SessionMgr object, here called objSessionMgr. Then, create an EnterpriseSession object by logging to the APS and passing the user name, password, APS name, and authorization type. Passing the string "secEnterprise" as the authorization type will validate passwords against the Crystal Enterprise security database, whereas passing "secWindowsNT" will use Windows NT authentication.

The Service method of the EnterpriseSession object returns a reference to the service on the APS. This method takes two parameters, the name of the server and the service requested. If the server name is left blank, the APS server is used. The LogonTokenMgr manages the number of concurrent users and tracks the number of licenses currently in use. The CreateLogonToken method returns a string value that names the token. The parameters are the server name, which, if left blank, indicates the APS, the number of days the token is valid, and the number of times the token may be used. The Query method executes a SQL statement against the APS database. The result of this query is an InfoObject that encapsulates an object (report) registered with Crystal Enterprise.

objReportObject refers to the PluginInterface of the report represented by Item(1) of the InfoObjects collection. In this example, only one report's information is returned from the SQL statement executed since we're specifying only one unique ID in the WHERE clause. Plug-in objects encapsulate the interface to the specific properties of individual reports.

Through the plug-ins, you can reference the report's parameter collection. In this example there is only one parameter—6164—and this parameter can be either a single value or a range. Note that unlike the ReportParameters collection used in the RDC model, the Crystal Enterprise ReportParameters collection will only recognize parameters created in the RPT file itself and not the parameters retrieved from the stored procedure to which the RPT is bound. The next step is to set the database information for this report. Refer to the Enterprise viewer and pass in the report ID and the token created earlier by the CreateLogonToken method.

> **NOTE** *If you wish, you can pass all the information in the preceding code—login data, parameters, etc.—to the Crystal viewer on a URL. The URL interface is documented in the file8_urlcommands.pdf found on the Crystal support Web site (*`http://support.crystaldecisions.com/docs`*).*

Finally, using the Response.Redirect method, you can display the report in the browser.

Scheduling Reports

Crystal Enterprises also exposes its report scheduling functionality through the SchedulingInfo object. Using SchedulingInfo you can determine how frequently a report is run and the start and end dates for this automatic run. The code in Listing 9-37 displays the name and description of the report, as well as the begin date, end date, and frequency of the report.

Listing 9-37. ASP Code to Report Properties

```
<%

Option Explicit
```

```
Dim objSessionMgr, objEnterpriseSession, objService
Dim objSchedulingInfo, objInfoObjects
Dim lReportID, cSQL

lReportID = 250

Set objSessionMgr = CreateObject("CrystalEnterprise.SessionMgr")

Set objEnterpriseSession = _
   objSessionMgr.Logon("administrator","","nydwetl3","secEnterprise")

Set objService = objEnterpriseSession.Service("", "InfoStore")

cSQL = "SELECT * " & _
        "FROM CI_INFOOBJECTS " & _
        "WHERE SI_ID = " & lReportID & " AND " & _
        "SI_PROGID = 'CrystalEnterprise.Report'"

Set objInfoObjects = objService.Query(cSQL)

Set objSchedulingInfo = objInfoObjects.Item(1).SchedulingInfo

With Response
    .Write "<P> Report Name: " & objInfoObjects.Item(1).Properties("SI_NAME")
    .Write "<P> Report Description: " & objInfoObjects.Item(1).Description
    .Write "<P> Schedule Begin: " & objSchedulingInfo.BeginDate
    .Write "<P> Schedule End: " & objSchedulingInfo.EndDate
    .Write "<P> Frequency: " & objSchedulingInfo.Type
End With

%>
```

Licensing and Crystal Enterprise

Before you go too far in planning the distribution of your existing Crystal Reports via the Web or using a report server, you need to fully understand the licensing issues involved. The developer license allows you to distribute your existing reports to as many desktop installations as you wish. This license includes the runtime engine, the report viewer, and all the data export support files. However, a very expensive problem arises if you wish to distribute reports to the enterprise as a whole. The reason is that Crystal is very restrictive about licensing their report engine for use by multiple users.

NOTE   *These licensing restrictions only apply to version 8.0 and later. If you wish to use the Crystal Reports version 7.x or earlier for your report server or Web-based system, you may do so without incurring any additional licensing costs.*

Server-Based Applications

If you create a Web-application in ASP, ASP.NET, Java, or one of the other Web development tools, you'll find that using Crystal Reports in these environments can be a rather complex legal process. Crystal Decisions defines server-based and Web-based applications, as well as server environments, as follows in their 8.5 licensing agreement:

"Server/Web-based Application" means a purpose-specific software program that utilizes the Runtime Software and allows multiple users to Access the Runtime Software. Software programs consisting of more than one related module(s) or components shall be considered one Server/Web-based Application.

"Server Environment" is defined as any server system, licensed from Crystal or any other entity, that consists of one or more server software processes, operating independently or otherwise, including but not limited to report servers, Web servers, database servers, terminal servers, mail servers, application servers, or transaction servers, facilitated by an Internet, intranet, "xtranet", client/server network, wide-area network, or any other multiuser network.

This rule is further clarified by the definition of "deployment" below. The 8.x license only permits five concurrent users to access Web-based Crystal Reports at any one time. As you can see, even the purchase of additional licenses will not allow you to increase the number of concurrent users.

> *Deployment. You have the right to Deploy each Server/Web-based Application for Access by up to, but not to exceed, 5 Concurrent Users. If you want to exceed the 5 Concurrent Users authorized to Access each Server/Web-based Application, you just acquire additional Access Licenses as a stand-alone offering. Under no circumstances may the 5 Concurrent Users you are authorized to allow Access to each Server/Web-based Application be exceeded by combining additional Software licenses, other Crystal products that include Access Licenses, promotional offers of any kind, or by any other means, other than through the purchase of additional Access Licenses as stand-alone offering.*

These concurrent users are counted by tracking the number of application object—oSession("oApp")—instances active at any one time. Since you'll need one application instance for the administrator and since many users may have more than one report, and therefore Application objects, open simultaneously, the five-user license is quickly used up. The costs mount in that a single additional license costs $1,495, but there's a ten license minimum, so the moment you go over five licenses you've just made a $15,000 purchase. To compound the issue, this is an annual license fee. As you can imagine, long-time Crystal users are screaming about this.

Report Servers

If you wish to utilize a report server or as Crystal terms it, a "report distribution system," you'll need to purchase the Crystal Broadcast license. Crystal defines a "report distribution system" as follows:

> *"Report Distribution System" means any process or system or combination of processes or systems that is or are used to automatically and/or regularly deliver, share or distribute Reports, without providing any Access to a Server/Web-based Application: (a) to greater than fifty (50) end users directly, or (b) to a location that is accessible to greater than fifty (50) end users, who are reasonably likely to view or use the Reports. A Report Distribution System shall not include: (a) distribution of Reports in hard copy form; (b) manual distribution on a one-time or ad hoc basis; or (c) distribution of Client Applications created using the Royalty Free Runtime Software. For purposes of calculating the number of end users, you do not need to include any end user who otherwise has a valid license to use the Software or any of Crystal's other products (other than any product offered free of charge).*

This means that you cannot use a broadcast license to allow multiple users to select their own criteria and run or schedule reports themselves. It means that an administrator can set up criteria and scheduling information for a report and have the output made available to a defined set of users. You do not have the right to use the Crystal ActiveX or Java report viewers when using a broadcast license.

Broadcast licenses are not cheap. A license for 500 users will cost you $10,000 per year, 1500 users will cost you $25,000 per year, and more than 1500 users will cost you $50,000 per year. A user is any individual who during the course of the year utilizes the report server at least once.

Crystal provides the ePortfolio product as an open source report server. ePortfolio is written in ASP and JavaScript (there is no word yet from Crystal Decisions on an ASP.NET version) and will allow you to do most of the scheduling and publishing of reports to the enterprise. Figure 9-15 shows the management page that allows you to select an existing RPT file and publish it to the server.

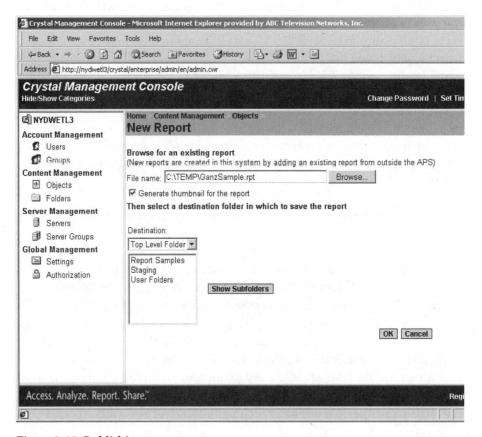

Figure 9-15. Publishing a new report

Once a report has been published, you can set the properties for user access, database connectivity, parameters, and record selection. Figure 9-16 shows the settings page.

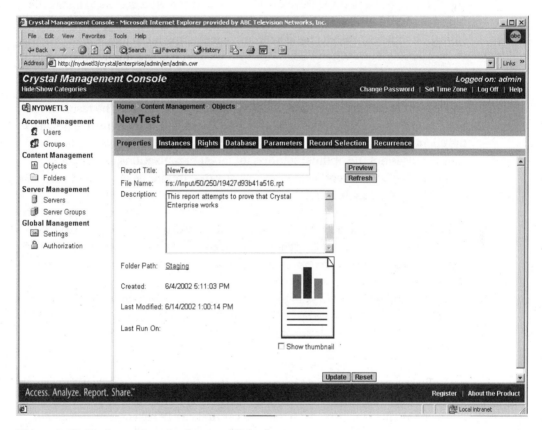

Figure 9-16. Setting properties for a published report

While ePortfolio is open source, is has a drawback: It is entirely optimized to distribute only Crystal reports to the enterprise. If you have reports created in other tools, Crystal Enterprise falls short. While the open source allows you to add in this flexibility, this is still additional work you'll need to undertake.

Alternatives

The main goal of Crystal Decisions' licensing structure is to prohibit you from making your 8.x+ reports available to the enterprise without purchasing a rather expensive Crystal Enterprise license. We've read various posts to Internet newsgroups that refer to Crystal's licensing scheme as "extortionate" and "gouging." The key to the licensing is the location of the report engine itself. Crystal owns the report engine but not the RPT files and certainly not the data. With only one copy of the Crystal Reports Developer's Edition, you have a license to install the report engine on every desktop in the enterprise as part of a compiled application. Therefore, you can create a report viewer application that is installed on every user's desktop. When a user wants to run a report, this application points a Web browser to a server-based ASP page that allows the user to find and select the report to run and enter the criteria. A server-based COM component then creates and executes a SQL statement from this criteria screen. The result of this SQL statement, in the form of an XML-based Recordset, is then pushed down to the client machine along with the RPT file and displayed in the viewer application. This is not the optimal solution for larger organizations, as you must maintain the Crystal Reports Engine on every desktop in the enterprise.

The bottom line here is this: Unless you select another reporting tool like VS-View or ActiveReports or freeze all your Crystal development with version 7.x, you'll end up paying a similar amount in licensing fees plus the cost of writing or licensing your own report server as you would by licensing Crystal Enterprise. If Crystal Reports is entrenched as a development tool in your organization, then, as expensive as it is, Crystal Enterprise may be your only financially viable solution.

For a solid review of Crystal Enterprises features, check out *Crystal Reports 8.5: The Complete Reference* by George Peck (McGraw-Hill Osborne Media. ISBN: 0-07219-327-1). There is also an edition available covering Crystal Reports 9.0.

Using an XML File as a Data Source for Reports

Since XML files are character based and can, unlike ADO Recordsets, exist independently of your application's runtime, they make an excellent source for persistence of report data. Because of their character-based nature, they can easily be passed through firewalls via HTTP and are an excellent interchange format between heterogeneous platforms and applications.

ADO offers the Save method to export your Recordset-encapsulated data to an XML file. Simply pass the export filename and the format as follows:

```
oRS.Save "c:\temp\data.xml",adPersistXML
```

You could also write your data to a stream as shown here:

```
Dim objStream As ADODB.Stream

Set oRS = New ADODB.Recordset
```

```
Set objStream = New ADODB.Stream
oRS.Save objStream, adPersistXML
```

XML is far superior to plain text, as it is marked up and "processible" for further usage such as electronic publishing or formatting for paper printing. One of XML's strengths is that it's technology neutral and nonproprietary. Another is its extensibility; the developer can define custom tag sets as needed. The related eXtensible Style Language (XSL) is used to transform XML-based data into HTML or other presentation formats. XSL offers a superset of the cascading style sheets (CSS) language and allows developers to create presentation structures different from the underlying data structure. For example, you can use XSL to convert an XML-based Social Security Number into a bulleted list item in one HTML view and into a table cell entry in another HTML view. In other words, you can harness XML to target different devices.

See Soo Mee Foo and Wei Meng Lee's XML Programming Using the Microsoft XML Parser (Apress, ISBN: 1-893115-42-9) for more on XML.

ReCrystallize Pro

ReCrystallize Pro from ReCrystallize Software (http://www.recrystallize.com) consists of a wizard that examines your Crystal Reports RPT file and produces an ASP wrapper for delivery of your existing reports over the Web. Recrystallize Pro examines the RPT file to determine what database connections are needed, what parameters must be passed in, etc. For each parameter, the ReCrystallize Pro Wizard provides options for supplying the required value(s). Finally, you'll determine how the user can view the report (ActiveX viewer, PDF, Word, etc.) in his or her browser. ReCrystallize Pro then creates Web pages specific to the individual RPT that prompt the user for parameter values and allow the report to be run/viewed on the Web using the options selected in the wizard.

> **NOTE** *The Crystal Reports runtime DLLs are required for the Web pages, and this triggers the licensing issues introduced in version 8x. However, Crystal Enterprise is not required.*
>
> *Crystal Reports version 7 is also supported with no licensing issues.*

There are three data retrieval options you can set in the wizard when creating Web pages for a report:

1. You may indicate whether the report will use information that was saved at design time (from the Crystal menu choose File | Save Data with Report) as opposed to retrieving data from the RDBMS at runtime. This Static option is appropriate for information that does not change frequently and when all users will see the same information. This dramatically speeds up delivery of your report content and reduces the load on the server.

2. The Dynamic option retrieves new data from the RDBMS each time the report is run. It is used when a report has data that changes frequently, uses parameters to control the data that is included in the report, or shows different data depending on the user's identity.

3. The Automatic option is similar to the Dynamic option, but can improve performance and decrease the need for recurring database access. The first time an Automatic report is requested, data is retrieved from the database and the report is presented to the user. The report and its data, specific to the criteria entered, are saved to the Web server. If the same report is requested again within the time period you specify, as measured in hours and minutes, it can be retrieved from the Web server without requerying the database. If the specified time period has elapsed, the report data is refreshed from the RDBMS.

Listing 9-38 shows the abridged sample output for Orders.rpt with the PDF format set as the view option.

Listing 9-38. Recrystallize Pro Output

```
<%@ Language=VBScript %>
<%

basePath = Request.ServerVariables("PATH_TRANSLATED")
While (Right(basePath, 1) <> "\" And Len(basePath) <> 0)
    iLen = Len(basePath) - 1
    basePath = Left(basePath, iLen)
Wend

baseVirtualPath = Request.ServerVariables("PATH_INFO")
While (Right(baseVirtualPath, 1) <> "/" And Len(baseVirtualPath) <> 0)
    iLen = Len(baseVirtualPath) - 1
```

```
        baseVirtualPath = Left(baseVirtualPath, iLen)
Wend


If Not IsObject(session("oApp")) Then
    Set session("oApp") = Server.CreateObject("CrystalRuntime.Application")
    If Not IsObject(session("oApp")) Then
        response.write "Error:  Could not instantiate the Crystal Reports..."
        response.end
    End If
End If


If IsObject(session("oRpt")) then
     set session("oRpt") = nothing
End If


reportFileName = "Orders.rpt"


Set session("oRpt") = session("oApp").OpenReport(basepath & reportFileName, 1)
If Err.Number <> 0 Then
  Response.Write "Error Occurred creating Report Object: " & Err.Description
  Set Session("oRpt") = Nothing
  Set Session("oApp") = Nothing
  Session.Abandon
  Response.End
End If


if not session("oRpt").HasSavedData then
    Response.Write "<strong>ReCrystallize</strong><br><br>You are...</b><br>"
    Response.End
end if


session("oRpt").MorePrintEngineErrorMessages = False
session("oRpt").EnableParameterPrompting = False


If IsObject (session("oPageEngine")) Then
   set session("oPageEngine") = nothing
End If


set session("oPageEngine") = session("oRpt").PageEngine
%>
<% viewer = "PDF" %>
<%
if viewer = "PDF" then
```

```
        exporttype = "31"
        fileextension = ".pdf"
end if
%>
<%
set crystalExportOptions = Session("oRpt").ExportOptions
ExportFileName = "Orders report-" & CStr(Session.SessionID) & fileextension
ExportDirectory = basePath

crystalExportOptions.DiskFileName = basepath & ExportFileName
crystalExportOptions.FormatType = CInt(exporttype)
crystalExportOptions.DestinationType = 1
Session("oRpt").Export False

Set Session("oPageEngine") = Nothing
Set Session("oRpt") = Nothing
'Set Session("oApp") = Nothing

response.write "<META http-equiv=" & Chr(34) & "Refresh" & Chr(34) & _
" content=" & Chr(34) & "0; url=" & basevirtualpath & _
exportfilename & Chr(34) & ">"
'clean up files that are more than 1 day old

set objFS = CreateObject("Scripting.FileSystemObject")
set objFC = objFS.GetFolder( Left( basePath, ( len( basePath ) - 1) ) )
set objF = objFC.Files
for each Item in objF
 testfilename = UCase(Item.Name)
 testextension = UCase(right(testfilename,4))
 if UCase(left( testfilename, len( "Orders report"))) = _
    UCase("Orders report") and _
    testextension=UCase(fileextension) and _
    right(testfilename, 15) <> "-PARAMETERS.HTM" then
    if Item.DateCreated < Now - 1 then
        on error resume next
        Item.Delete
    end if
 end if
next
set  objF = Nothing
set objFC = Nothing
set objFS = Nothing
%>
```

Conclusion

Now that we have demystified Web report creation, it should not be a difficult thing for you to do, and you have a myriad venues by which to accomplish this. Depending on the tools you're using, licensing costs may have a major effect on your deployment strategy. Now that you understand the Internet as a medium for report distribution, let's take a look at how it's done on wireless devices.

CHAPTER 10

Reporting for Palm Users

DELIVERING REPORTS TO PDAs and other devices poses unique challenges to the developer. Your first problem is figuring out how and what to display on a small screen. Does your report delivery system have to be flexible enough to target multiple types of devices? Are the browsers compatible? How much memory do the devices have? Do they have color or monochrome displays? What kind of connectivity can you assume? As Palms legitimized the market for handheld devices, and as everyone from CEOs to field reps wanted to receive timely information on their device, developers have had to wrestle with problems such as these. In this chapter, we'll look at devices powered by the Palm operating system. First we'll examine Palm hardware and then software, including Web Clipping, which displays HTML pages. Finally, I'll show how you can use this technology for report delivery. In the next chapter, we'll look at delivering reports to Pocket PC devices.

The Palm OS Platform

The first Palm, the Pilot 1000, shipped in March 1996, and since then, the platform has evolved and expanded. (By "platform," I mean the underlying hardware design, the published interface for extending the hardware with add-on hardware components, the Palm OS and its SDK, and the data synchronization via Palm's HotSync.) Aside from "pure" Palms (see Table 10-1), there are a host of Palm-powered devices from other vendors.

Table 10-1. Palms Through the Ages

PALM PILOT	OS	MEMORY	EXPANDABILITY
Pilot 1000	1.0	128KB	Limited to memory
Pilot 5000	1.0	512KB	Limited to memory
PalmPilot Personal	2.0	512KB	Limited to memory
PalmPilot Professional	2.0	1MB	Limited to memory
Palm III	3.0	2MB	Limited to memory
Palm IIIx	3.1	4MB	Connector slot
Palm V	3.1	2MB	N/A
Palm VII	3.2	2MB	N/A
TRG Pro	3.3	8MB	Compact flash slot
Palm IIIe	3.1	2MB	N/A
Palm Vx	3.3	8MB	N/A
Palm IIIc	3.5	8MB	Connector slot
Palm VIIx	3.5	8MB	N/A
Palm m100	3.5.1	2MB	N/A
Palm m105	3.5	8MB	N/A
Palm m125	4.0	8MB	Connector slot, expansion card slot
Palm m130	4.1	8MB	Connector slot, expansion card slot
Palm m500	4.0	8MB	Connector slot, expansion card slot, flash ROM
Palm i705	4.1	8MB	Connector slot, expansion card slot, flash ROM
Palm m515	4.1	16MB	Connector slot, expansion card slot, flash ROM
Palm Zire	4.1	2MB	N/A
Palm Tungsten T	5.0	16MB	Connector slot, expansion card slot, flash ROM
Palm Tungsten W	4.1.1	16MB	Connector slot, expansion card slot, flash ROM

You can obtain more information at `http://www.palmos.com/dev/tech/hardware/compare.html` (updated only through the end of 2002) and `http://www.palm.com/products/family.epl`.

The Palm CPU has evolved as well: The original Motorola DragonBall MC68328 shipped with all Palms until Palm IIIx, which used the MC68EZ328, and subsequent Palms ship with Motorola DragonBall EZ or VZ chips. All of these CPUs are essentially derived from the Motorola 68000, a mixed 16/32-bit processor. DragonBall EZ and earlier CPUs can only address 8MB of memory at a time, a limit imposed by the CPU's DRAM controller. The newer DragonBall VZ chip supports up to 32MB of memory. The Palm Tungsten W launches a new era for Palm, one based on the more powerful ARM CPUs.

As this book goes to press, Palm claims to have sold well over 20 million units, and created a programmer community with more than 200,000 registered developers, who have spawned tens of thousands of commercial applications.

Emulators and Simulators

Before you can begin to write programs for the Palm (or any other OS, for that matter), you need a platform to test on. If you have a device, that's fine. But what if you don't—or if you just want to reduce your development and testing time? The Palm Operating System Emulator (POSE) is essentially a program that lets you have a "virtual" Palm on your desktop—Mac and Unix desktops included. Thanks to POSE, you can write, debug, and run the programs you develop on your computer, instead of performing a HotSync (sending the code to the device to run) every time you make a new build. (You definitely need the emulator unless you enjoy resetting your Palm device several times a day while writing your software.) You can download POSE, including "legacy" versions, from `http://www.palmos.com/dev/tools/emulator/`.

NOTE *POSE was based on Copilot, a program that was originally written by several different developers, principally Greg Hewgill (`http://www.hewgill.com/pilot/copilot/index-old.html`). Palm enhanced it with new features, debugging support, and support for more recent ROMs. The core of the Copilot emulator, in fact, is still available as open source and is a central piece of many other emulators available on the Web.*

After you download POSE, you'll need to join one of Palm's developer communities in order to download ROM images. What, you ask, are ROM images? Well, they're the software that's built into each type of device. Palm IIIs have different ROM images than Palm IIIxs or Palm VIIxs, for example, and they work with POSE to let you test your programs with virtual ROMs against any number of different "virtual" devices. If you don't want to read the documentation that comes with POSE (I highly recommend that you do), click the Help button the first time you run it to find out how to get and install the ROM images. (If you have a device, you can HotSync it to POSE.) You'll also need the *skins* (JPEGs) for the different devices you want to run from POSE. Figure 10-1 illustrates POSE and its right-click menu.

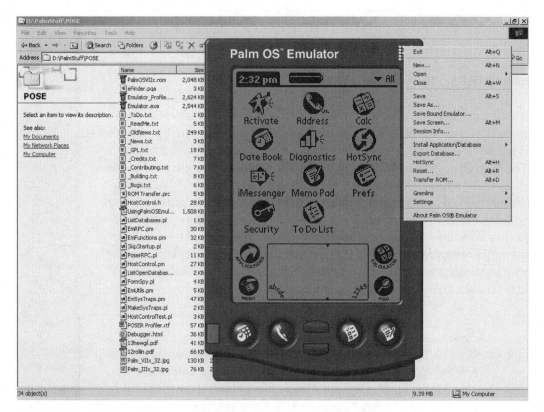

Figure 10-1. POSE running on a PC with Explorer in the background

If you're interested in developing applications that will run on Palm OS 5 devices, you need to use the Palm OS 5 Simulator—a 7.5MB (debug version) download available from `http://www.palmos.com/dev/tools/simulator/`. So what's the Simulator and how does it differ from POSE?

The Palm OS Simulator (see Figure 10-2) is the Palm OS 5.0 system compiled to run as a native application under Windows. In other words, it's not a hardware emulation like POSE, but rather the "real" OS running on top of the Windows Device Application Layer (DAL). The Simulator runs from within Windows DLLs and includes the Palm Application Compatibility Environment (PACE, which emulates the 68KB PRCs, effectively simulating the functionality supported by Palm OS 4.1) and Palm's various default PRCs such as Datebook and Memopad.

NOTE *PRCs, or Palm resource files, are basically Palm executables that are created on the desktop using tools such as Metrowerks' CodeWarrior (*http://www.metrowerks.com*), NS Basic's NSBasic/Palm (*http://www.nsbasic.com/palm*), or AppForge's MobileVB (*http://www.appforge.com*) and then transferred to the Palm device via HotSync. PRCs contain all the elements of the application, including code and UI elements.*

Figure 10-2. Palm's Simulator for Palm OS 5.0

Unlike earlier versions of Palm OS, which only run on Motorola DragonBall CPUs, Palm OS 5.0 was written for the ARM architecture, which includes Intel's StrongArm chips as well as the newer XScale and Texas Instruments' Omap chips. This presents two major enhancements to OS target wireless users: 1) built-in support for *both* 802.11b (WiFi) and Bluetooth networks, and 2) strong data encryption and Secure Sockets Layer (SSL) services for secure e-mail, browsing, and online transactions. Palm OS 5.0 also features an enhanced UI that sports higher-resolution icons and fonts.

Beginning with Palm OS 5.1, Web Browser 2.0 *replaces* Clipper. Web Browser 2.0 is proxy-less (doesn't require Palm.Net and, indeed, won't work with Web Clipping) and supports HTML 4.01, SSL 3.0, JavaScript 1.5, cHTML, and other Internet standards. Because Web Browser 2.0 doesn't require a proxy server (and doesn't use the Palm.Net infrastructure), you don't have to test your wireless apps against proxies. The new browser also supports wireless download and installation of Palm applications (these are apps sporting .prc, .pdb, .vcf, or any other application extensions that are registered with Exchange Manager) with a simple <a href> tag, but the palm and palmcall URL schemes are still supported, allowing for the new browser to interface with other Palm apps.

To develop using Web Browser 2.0, download the Web Browser 2.0 SDK. In it, you'll find a doc that describes strategies for converting your Palm Query Applications (PQAs) to content for Web Browser 2.0. Palm has stated that it will support Web Clipping in all 3.5 and 4.x platforms.

Web Clipping

Palms have been able to communicate wirelessly via infrared (IrDA) from the beginning, but it didn't take long before users started clamoring for wireless Internet connectivity. That, of course, is easier said than done. For starters, you need either wireless modems (and a port to plug them into) or devices that have them built in. Second, you need a solid WLAN infrastructure—ideally one that works nationally, if not globally. Finally, if you've ever used a PDA to do Web browsing, you're probably aware of the fact that handheld devices in general have a *very* hard time rendering standard Web pages due to the length of time required to download the HTML and any embedded graphics and the fact that typical Web pages are not designed for such a small screen size.

Palm tackled the problem of wireless connectivity to the Internet by inventing a proprietary technology called *Web Clipping* (vendors as diverse as IBM and Oracle have their own versions of Web Clipping now, too). The concept is simple. Imagine that you saw a recipe or article in the newspaper that you want to send to your mom. You want to send her just a clipping, not the entire newspaper, so you tear out just the article. Web Clipping works the same way, delivering only the content you want (and compiled/compressed at that), reducing the number of bytes that have to be transmitted.

Palm's Web Clipping relies on Palm's proprietary subscription network, Palm.Net, and its proxy servers. As of Spring 2003, Palm.Net advertised itself as providing links to 600+ wireless-ready sites. By exploring these, you can get an idea of the standard "look and feel" of PQA apps.

PQAs are really only special Palm database files (PDBs) that contain compressed and specially tagged HTML pages instead of "normal" records. On a Palm device, all PQAs are associated automatically with the Web Clipping Application

Viewer. When a user opens a PQA file for viewing, the Applications Launcher starts the Viewer, which in turn displays the contents of the selected PQA.

> **NOTE** *Palm file formats are as follows: PDBs are Palm database files. PRCs are Palm resource files that contain resources instead of records, but have structures that are almost identical to PDB files. Palm Query Application (PQA) files are special PDBs that contain compressed and specially tagged HTML pages instead of "normal" records. Read more details about the Palm file formats at* `http://www.palmos.com/dev/support/docs/fileformats/Intro.html#939356.`

Figure 10-3 shows POSE running a shareware eFinder PQA (downloaded from `http://www.freewarepalm.com/internetpqa/efinder.shtml`). The easiest way to run a PQA in POSE is to drag and drop it onto the POSE image.

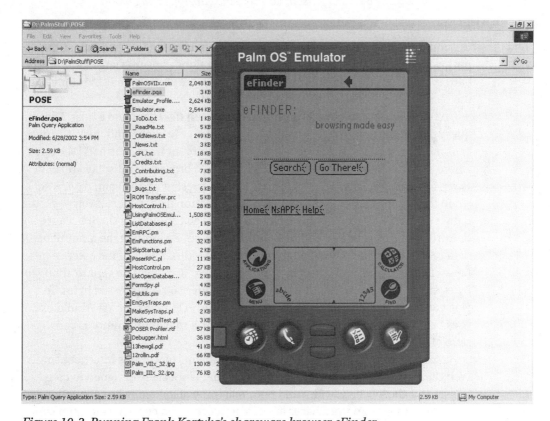

Figure 10-3. Running Frank Kortyka's shareware browser eFinder

As you know, HTML isn't executable code; it's simply a series of tags used to "describe" a formatting action associated with a piece of content. On a PC, your browser (typically Microsoft's Internet Explorer) interprets the HTML codes and displays the requested content in a readable format. But because you really can't do general purpose browsing on a Palm, you need a way to interpret HTML codes on the Palm OS device.

That's why Palm developed Clipper. Think of Clipper as Palm's proprietary browser for Palm OS 3.x and 4.x devices whose job it is to load, decompress, and render the HTML stored in a PQA database. Clipper is free with the purchase of any Palm VII device and will run on other Palm devices such as a Palm V—even Palm IIIcs, for example (see http://www.golddave.com/palm/howto/using_pqas_on_a_non_palm_vii.html). However, for those devices, you'll have to purchase Clipper (which costs about $15).

NOTE *Some of you may remember the DOS programming language Clipper, which was a dBase language compiler. This is* not *the same Clipper. See* http://www.clipx.net/dbf.php *for some links to that disappearing world.*

Although it was the bandwidth and display issues that inspired Palm Computing to develop Web Clipping (lengthy connections consume large amounts of battery power, so that was another driving force), the client-side PQA is only half the picture. There's also a server-side component.

A Web Clipping solution is partitioned between the client and a host. The query part of the application (the PQA) is stored on the client, and the Web application is stored on the host Web server. This is different from "normal" Web apps where a form might be downloaded into your PC's browser for display and data entry, for example. In a PQA, the form is already present on the Palm device, so when the user has entered the requested information into the local Web page, the data is sent off. The result of the query, called a Web Clipping, is small because it doesn't contain formatting and display information. By limiting the amount of data sent in both directions, you minimize bandwidth. Size is of the essence here—Palm recommends that the query sent up to the server be kept to about 40 bytes and that the Web Clipping sent back be under 360 compressed bytes. To give you an idea of its compression efficiency, the PQA compiler, WCABuild.exe, uses Lz77 compression for Palm OS 4.x—yielding a maximum compression ratio of 9.

A key element in Palm's solution to the problems of wireless Internet using Web Clipping is to use a special architecture that is specially designed to compensate for the low bandwidth and poor reliability of Palm device connections. Also, the content that the devices are able to receive and correctly interpret simply isn't as rich (read complex) as that included in most Web pages.

The architecture used by the Web Clipping system is a bit more complex than simply connecting a Palm directly to the Web sites that you want to browse. Instead, it involves the use of special, intermediate servers called *Web Clipping proxies*. The proxy receives a query request from the handheld device via the User Datagram Protocol (UDP).[1] Next, the proxy communicates with the HTML server via an Internet standard protocol—typically HTTP—to retrieve the information requested by the query. Then the proxy server *compresses* the data and sends it back to the handheld over the wireless network.

Understanding Web Clipping Security

Web Clipping has been designed to be secure enough to perform online banking or Internet shopping. Secure connections between a Palm OS handheld and the wireless network are protected using Certicom's elliptic curve encryption. This is a small, but highly efficient, secure public key encryption-based system.

For a complete tutorial on elliptic curve encryption, you can visit Certicom's Web site and read their online tutorial at `http://www.certicom.com/resources/ecc_tutorial/ecc_tut_1_0.html`.

Messages sent over the wireless network are also protected using a message integrity check (MIC). MICs can detect both transmission errors and message tampering. This helps to ensure that the data you send in a secure transmission is untouched on its journey from your handheld device to the wireless network.

Once a Palm proxy server has received a secure query, the connection between the proxy server and the server that contains the requested query information is protected using standard SSL encryption and authentication. To perform authentication, the Web Clipping application should request a user name and password when submitting a secured query. Each Web Clipping–enabled Palm device has a unique identifier embedded in the ROM, which may also be sent with the query to enhance the level of security. (For more on Palm's security in general, you may want to download `http://www.palmsource.com/includes/security.pdf`.)

HTML Features That Are Missing from Web Clipping

One of the most important things that the Web Clipping proxy servers do is to strip unsupported content out of target Web sites. So, before you get too excited about Web Clipping, you'd better steel yourself for its limitations.

---

1. Use of the simple UDP on the wireless network means that only two small packets are exchanged between the handheld and the proxy—one for the query, and one for the clipping.

To begin with, Clipper expects any links within a page to come in the form of simple anchor tags. For example:

```
<a href="http://www.apress.com">A Berkeley-Based Publisher</a>
```

This means you can't use image maps. Any image maps that are included in the requested Web pages will either be converted to a standard image or, more likely, simply be removed. What Web Clipping offers instead is a BUTTON attribute for the anchor tag, allowing you to create button-style links on the fly with no image work necessary. For example:

```
<a href="http://www.apress.com" button>Books4Geeks</a>
```

would display the preceding link as a button instead of the standard underlined text.

Unlike a standard Internet browser, Clipper isn't equipped to interpret scripts and binaries that are downloaded onto the Palm client. For this reason, JavaScript and VBScript on Web pages are completely ignored, as are Java applets and ActiveX controls.

Other HTML features that aren't supported:

- Frames

- Nested tables

- Cascading style sheets (CSSs)

- Animated GIFs

- Layers

- Named typefaces

- Cookies

In general, it's safe for you to assume that you can't use any complex HTML features. Of all the unsupported features just listed, cookies will probably be the hardest for most programmers to live without. As you know, cookies are often used to speed up a user's navigation of a Web site by offering to "remember" key elements of the user's profile. So, if your site uses cookies to remember from one page to the next if a user has already logged in, then it simply won't work with Clipper. Users will be prompted to log in on every page, because the cookies that identify them will get lost after each visit. This represents a serious functionality loss, as cookies are used frequently in Web sites to control navigation, customize content, and hold hidden page variables.

Special Web Clipping <meta> Tags

The good news is that there are also some features supported by Clipper that are otherwise unknown to the world of HTML. You can build a Web Clipping application that exists entirely on the Palm OS device and never have it call out to the Web. In fact, some of the features offered by Web Clipping make this a very real scenario.

Consider, for example, how you can use a special <meta> tag to reference client-side images from your HTML pages. These pages may be located either on the client or the server. For example:

```
<meta name="LocalIcon" content="CarlMug.gif">
```

This command tells Clipper to load an image of yours truly called CarlMug.gif from the local device rather than from whatever server this current page is located on. This improves the display of pages in Clipper. Since the image is retained locally, Clipper won't have to wait for the image to be transferred over the wireless network.

There are four important <meta> tags you'll want to learn and become familiar with when building Web Clipping applications:

- *PalmComputingPlatform:* This tag identifies your page as a "Palm-friendly" page. When you include this tag, images will be rendered and the entire text will be displayed on the device. If you don't use this tag, then images will be stripped out, and only the first 1024 bytes of your page will display. You should use this <meta> tag on all of your local pages and clippings.

  ```
  <meta name="PalmComputingPlatform" content="true">
  ```

- *HistoryListText:* This tag specifies the user-visible string for each clipping displayed in the history pop-up menu. Use this tag on all of your Web Clipping apps if you want them to be added to the history pop-up menu.

  ```
  <meta name="HistoryListText" content="true">
  ```

- *LocalIcon:* This tag identifies to your Web Clipping application HTML documents and graphic images that should be stored locally within your Web Clipping app. LocalIcon is for use in local pages only, and recommended practice is to put them in the root page of your Web Clipping apps.

  ```
  <meta name="LocalIcon" content="CarlPicture.gif">
  ```

- *PalmLauncherRevision:* This tag sets the version string for your Web Clipping application. Use it on the main index (or root) page of your Web Clipping app.

```
<meta name="PalmLauncherRevision" content="1.0">
```

Another way in which Clipper improves the display of pages is by allowing Web site designers to specify portions of their pages that should not be displayed by Clipper. In this way, a single page may be used both for PQA and for other normal Web browsers. If there is content on this page that shouldn't be sent to Clipper, the Web designer can tell Clipper to skip content by enclosing it in a <smallscreenignore> tag.

Web Clipping also includes a set of internal constants that the developer can use. For example, there's a Web Clipping application available from Starbucks that can tell a Palm user where the nearest Starbucks is. How does it work? By using the special value %ZIPCODE. If you embedded this value in your page, the Web Clipping proxy server will replace the code with the zip code from the region settings of the Palm accessing the page.

Another cool addition is the ability to link to "real" Palm applications directly from Web Clipping pages. Using special tags, you can launch and interact with other applications (those resident on your Palm device); these applications can be another PQA, or another application, such as the Address book, or even an action such as sending mail. There are three special tags for this: <file:>, <palm:>, and <mailto:>.

For example, let's say you have a Web page where users must agree to certain terms before they can enter your site. Rather than require users to click an "Agree" button every time they visit your site, by including the following link in your page, you could call an application stored on their Palm device to check the Preferences database on their device to see if the page should be skipped.

```
<A HREF="PALM:CHECKPREF.APPL"></A>
```

What if I needed to check the weather from my current PQA application? I could launch another PQA application, such as the Weather Channel:

```
<A HREF="FILE:WEATHER.PQA"></A>
```

Or suppose I needed to send an e-mail from inside my PQA application (we've all seen these pages on Web sites for sending mail). I can simulate the same process from inside the PQA by invoking the iMessenger application:

```
<A HREF="MAILTO:SETON.SOFTWARE@VERIZON.NET"></A>
```

Steps to Create a PQA

Creating a PQA application is really quite simple. There are just a few simple (and free, I might add) tools that you need to do the job:

- *An HTML editor:* You can always use NotePad if you don't have anything else. A pure text editor generally works best in this situation.

- *Query Application Builder(QAB):* This is provided in the Palm SDK, but it's also available from the Palm developer site at `http://www.palmos.com/dev/tech/webclipping/gettingstarted.html` as a separate download. This product, also known as WCA Builder (see Figure 10-4), converts one or more HTML files along with any linked images into a PQA. I like to think of the Query Application Builder as a compiler that takes source HTML and compiles it to a source form that Clipper (which I suppose could be thought of as a Virtual Machine) can recognize and display.[2]

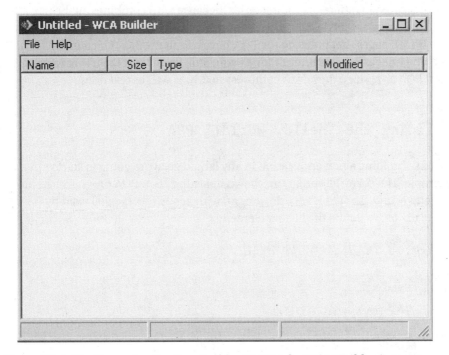

Figure 10-4. The Query Application Builder (QAB), aka WCA Builder, is pretty Spartan.

---

2. The Query Application Builder also compresses the PQA data content to anywhere between 5 and 60 percent depending on the actual number of images and the content of the HTML pages.

Now we're ready (finally, I know) to begin building a PQA. The process of building the application begins with organizing the HTML files. A PQA can be composed of multiple pages, each of which is defined as a single .htm or .html file. The best way to organize a PQA is to have a central index page to which all subcontent links.

 TIP *It's best to try and give users simple and direct access to the most used sections of the PQA. In this way, users only need to launch the PQA to start querying for information rather than clicking through a bunch of pages to find what they want.*

All of the pages that make up a PQA must fall under the same root directory (subdirectories are okay). Keep in mind that from within the PQA, links to pages and images must be *relative* paths that include whatever subdirectories the information may reside under. It's also a good idea to keep filenames unique, even if they're stored in different subdirectories, because QAB combines all the pages and images into a single Palm OS database.

HTML pages that make up the PQA have a limit of 63KB. Of course, 63KB of text and images is a fair amount for a Palm. Still, try to limit the use of images in your PQA app, since they don't compress nearly as well as text does.

Building the "Hello, World!" PQA

Just like building a first application in any language, we're going to start with a simple "Hello, World!" program, shown in Listing 10-1. PQA programs should start, like any standard HTML document, with an <html> tag, followed by a <head> tag to define the header elements.

Listing 10-1. The "Hello, World!" HTML

```
<HTML>
<HEAD>
    <TITLE>PQA Sample!</TITLE>
    <META NAME="palmcomputingplatform" CONTENT="TRUE">
    <META NAME="palmlauncherrevision" CONTENT="1.0">
</HEAD>
<BODY>Hello, World!</BODY>
</HTML>
```

The text that's contained in the page's <title> tag will appear in the title bar of the Clipper application (see Figure 10-5). This title string should be fairly small, because if it's too long, it will just be truncated.

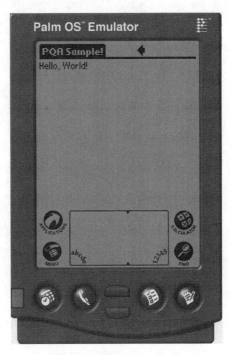

Figure 10-5. "Hello, World!" running in POSE

Building the "Hello, World!" app is easy. Start by typing in Listing 10-1 and save it as Hello.htm.

Next, run Query Application Builder and select the File I Open Index option. Don't be confused by the use of the term "Index". Remember that PQAs are special versions of PDB files, and HTML pages are considered index pages. Select the Hello.htm file you just created. The newly opened index page will now be displayed in the body of the Query Application Builder. If this index page had contained other pages and images, they would also have appeared in the list.

Now select the File I Build option. When the Build PQA window opens, you'll have the opportunity to supply an icon image. Select an icon and then press the Build button. Now in the same directory as the Hello.htm file you created, you should see a file named Hello.pqa. Run POSE, drag the file onto the emulator, and you'll see your PQA application as a program icon (see Figure 10-6).

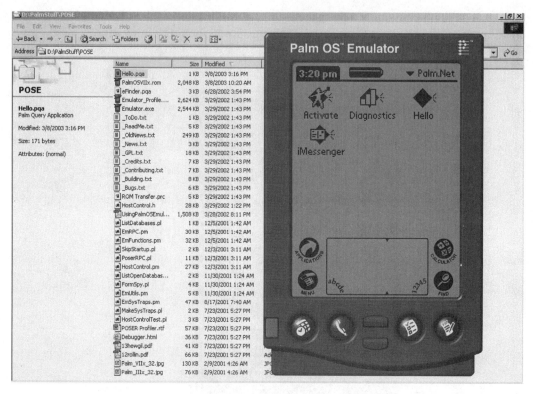

Figure 10-6. Identifying a PQA application with its characteristic "broadcast" or "over-the-air" icon

Formatting Text

You may have noticed that Clipper will display HTML pages using its own type-face, which is called Palm TD. When displayed in normal size, Palm TD looks just like the standard Palm font. Clipper does not, however, support bold, italic, bold italic, or monospaced fonts.

The sizes available range from 7 to 12, and only certain sizes are available for the <small>, <big>, or <font size=n> HTML tags. Allowable font sizes depend on what other formatting is applied to the text.

Nuts, Bolts, and PQA Applications

Okay, now you've developed your first PQA application, but it doesn't do a whole lot. So now let's begin to explore the other options you have available to you for developing PQA applications. The first thing we're going to look at is linking pages together. Using the standard HTML <a> (anchor) tag, you can define links within a local PQA as well as links to other online content.

TIP *You can also use hyperlinks to launch other PQAs—and even other Palm applications.*

To mark a specific location in a document, you use the <a> tag in association with a name link. You can also link to a specific location within the page by prefixing the link with the pound (#) symbol:

```
<a name="target page">Link to Another Page</a>
<a name="currentpage.html#target">Link inside the current page</a>
```

By combining the <a> tag with the hyperlink reference marker, you can also create links to other pages:

```
<a href="localpage.html">Link to Local Page</a>
```

Pages located in a subdirectory on the PC can also be referenced by including the subdirectory in the hyperlink reference:

```
<a href="subdirectory/localpage.html">Link to Local Page</a>
```

The only difference between linking to a local page and a remote Web hosted page is that you need to include the complete URL in your link. For all remote links, Clipper automatically appends the over-the-air icon to the end of the link's text.

```
<a href="http://www.amazon.com">Link to Amazon.com</a>
```

If you need a secured connection via SSL, you can use the same approach, just remember to use the HTTPS prefix. In the same fashion as standard remote links, if you're using a secured server link, then Clipper will append the secure over-the-air icon.

```
<a href="https://www.amazon.com/purchase.asp">Secure Link to Amazon.com</a>
```

 NOTE *If you use images for links, you should include the appropriate icons. This will help your pages to maintain the same consistent "look and feel" of all the other pages.*

If you want the link to appear as a button instead of underlined text, type the word **button** immediately after the terminating URL quote. Clipper will automatically surround the link text with a Palm OS button, adding the appropriate over-the-air icons to any remote links.

```
<a href="http://www.amazon.com" button>Amazon</a>
```

Linking to Other Applications

As I mentioned earlier, you can also link to other applications using a PQA, and those other applications can be one of two types:

- Another Palm Query Application

- Another application stored on the Palm or Palm-powered device

To jump to another PQA application, you simply use the file: prefix and supply the name of the PQA.

```
<a href="file:Another.PQA">Launch another PQA</a>
```

NOTE *Be sure to include the .pqa extension after the name of the PQA. Without the extension, Clipper will return an error.*

To link to a page within a PQA, use the following syntax:

```
<a href="file:Another.PQA/subpage.html">Launch another PQA</a>
```

Because you're linking to another page within a compiled PQA, any subdirectory information has been removed, so you should code your calls to another PQA as if all the pages were in the original root directory of the application.

There are two supported keywords for launching an application on the current device: palm and palmcall. The differences between the two aren't apparent in the syntax for calling them—it's at the OS level that the differences occur. Using the palm syntax will cause Clipper to quit before it launches the requested application, whereas the use of palmcall will cause Clipper to remain open and running in the background.

```
<a href="palm:memo.appl">Launch Memo Pad</a>
<a href="palmcall:writeprefs.appl">Write Preferences</a>
```

The final piece of information on linking that I'm going to cover is mail. You can send mail by using the keyword mailto in your supplied URL.

```
<a href="mailto:Seton.Software@Verizon.net">Email Carl Ganz</a>
```

When a user selects a mailto-type link, Clipper will automatically launch the iMessenger application to open and display a new mail message. Unfortunately, the iMessenger application does not automatically send the e-mail. The user must complete the sending mail task.

Building Forms

Collecting data in a PQA is as simple as coding a standard HTML <form> tag. One of the most commonly used forms is a user login form. Such a form consists of (usually) two elements: a username and a password. In this example, I'm going to add another common feature, a selection combo. When users log into this example page, they'll be prompted for a user name and password, and to select the property code that they are associated with. To accept these inputs in a PQA application, you can construct a simple form (see Listing 10-2).

Listing 10-2. The Sample Login Page

```
<HTML>
<HEAD>
    <TITLE>Login</TITLE>
    <META NAME="palmcomputingplatform" CONTENT="TRUE">
    <META NAME="palmlauncherrevision" CONTENT="1.0">
</HEAD>

<BODY>
    <FORM ACTION="http://www.gosomewhere.com" METHOD="GET">
        <TABLE>
            <TR>
                <TD ALIGN="RIGHT">User Name :</TD>
                <TD><INPUT TYPE="TEXT" NAME="USERID" SIZE="15" MAXLENGTH="7"></TD>
            </TR>

            <TR>
                <TD ALIGN="RIGHT">Password :</TD>
                <TD><INPUT TYPE="TEXT" NAME="PWD" SIZE="15" MAXLENGTH="10"></TD>
            </TR>
```

```
        <TR>
            <TD ALIGN="RIGHT">Property :</TD>
            <TD>
                <SELECT NAME="PROPERTY_CODE">
                <OPTION SELECTED VALUE ="101">AMLI
                <OPTION VALUE="102">TRAM
                <OPTION VALUE="103">AMCO
                </SELECT>
            </TD>
        </TR>


    <TR>
        <TD ALIGN="CENTER" COLSPAN="2">
        <INPUT TYPE="SUBMIT" VALUE="Login">
        </TD>
    </TR>
    </TABLE>
    </FORM>
</BODY>
</HTML>
```

 NOTE *HTML comments can sometimes cause a PQA to fail. Until this bug is resolved, avoid using them. Also, comments will not compile to run under Palm OS 5.0 Simulator.*

Special Variables In Web Clipping Forms

In Palm OS 4.0 and later, it's possible to take advantage of some special variables which, when passed through the Web Clipping proxy server, will return values providing information about the device that's accessing the Web Clipping app. You can use these variables to customize your returned data. The most relevant variable to our discussion is

```
%WCDevCaps
```

This variable will return information regarding the Web Clipping device's capabilities. For example:

```
<INPUT TYPE="Hidden" NAME="cap" VALUE="%WCDevCaps">
```

The Web Clipping proxy server will replace this value with a hexadecimal string of undefined length encoded as shown in Table 10-2.

Table 10-2. Hexadecimal String Encoding as Returned by Web Clipping Server for %WCDevCaps

CAPACITY	BITS USED	DESCRIPTION
Screen	0 = 1 bit monochrome	The bit-depth supported by the handheld device.
	1 = 2 bit monochrome	Note that this setting does *not* determine the bit depth of what gets downloaded.
	2 = 4 bit monochrome 3 = 8 bit color 4 = 16 bit color 5 and 6 are reserved	
Lz77 Available	7	Defines if the Lz77 library is available in the installed version of the Palm OS.
Communications bandwidth	8 to 11	Values: 0 = unknown 1 = Mobitex Other values are currently undefined.
OS free memory	12 to 15	Values: $0 = 2^{16}$ (<64 KB) $1 = 2^{17}$ $2 = 2^{18}$ ... $14 = 2^{30}$ $15 = 2^{31}$ For example, if the value is 2, then 128 KB <= size <= 256 KB.
Palm OS Version	16 to 20	Values: 0 = unknown 1 = 3.2 2 = 3.3 3 = 3.5 4 = 4.0
OS heap size	21 to 23	Values: 0 = > 256KB 1 = 64KB 2 = 96KB 3 = 128KB 4 = 256KB

The next most likely to be used variable is

```
%Zipcode
```

You may want to develop location-based apps that require you to know the user's location. When you include the following input object:

```
<INPUT TYPE="hidden" NAME="zip" value="%zipcode">
```

the "zip" variable's value will be replaced with the zip code of the base station with which the user is currently communicating. A returned value of "00000" indicates that either the device is communicating with a base station for which no zip code has been entered, or the form was submitted by an emulated device (which, clearly, is not communicating with a base station).

Once you have saved the HTML file (login.htm), go ahead and run Query Application Builder. Select the login file and build the PQA application as before.

Running PQA from the Command Line

You can also run PQA from the command line (select Start | Run, and type in your command line). Here's the syntax:

```
wcabuild html-filename [commands] [options]
```

The commands are as follows:

```
/pqa
```

builds the PQA file directly, without user intervention.

```
/h
```

displays wcabuild help (WCABuild.exe is the compiler that generates PQAs).

Options (which must have double quotes around their values) for these commands are listed here:

```
/d <value>
```

specifies the bit depth to use for images (default is "2"). The <meta> tag for this option is PalmPQABitDepth.

```
/e <value>
```

specifies the HTML encoding format cp1252 (the default) or shift_jis.

`/l  "largeicon.gif "`

specifies the graphic to use as large icon. Use a BMP, GIF, or JPEG file. The default value is the large Web Clipping icon that WCA displays in the Build PQA dialog box.

`/n  "appname"`

specifies the application name to be displayed in Applications Launcher.

`/o "output.pqa"`

specifies the output filename for your Web Clipping application.

`/p <value>`

specifies the POST encoding format to use for your application. You can specify one of the following values, with case and punctuation ignored:

```
"us-ascii"
"iso-8859-1"
"cp1252"
"shift_jis"
"EUC-JP"
"iso-2022-jp"
```

The default value is "1".

`/q <value>`

specifies which version of the Viewer your application requires. You can specify either "1" or "2". The <meta> tag for this option is PalmPQAVersion.

`/r <value>`

specifies the version of your application, which is displayed in the Applications Launcher Info display. The <meta> tag for this option is PalmLauncherRevision.

`/s "smallicon.gif"`

specifies the graphic to use as small icon.

`/u "username"`

specifies user folder into which to install the application.

`/v`

tells WCA Builder to run in verbose mode (displays error strings).

See WCABuild.hlp for more options.

The final application will return an error because you didn't supply a real URL, but if you look at Figure 10-7 closely, you'll see that it behaves just like a normal form. Bear in mind, however, that no validation can be performed on this page until the Login button has been pressed.

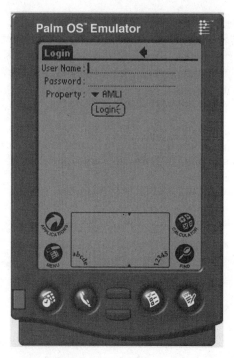

Figure 10-7. The Login PQA application

Using the Built-In Palm OS Date and Time Pickers

Clipper has the ability to handle two special form input types: a date picker and a time picker. These open the standard Palm OS date and time picker dialog boxes. To insert the date picker, use this syntax:

```
<input type="datepicker" name="DatePick" value="YYYY-MM-DD">
```

The date picker will display the date using whatever system preferences have been defined. If you omit the value attribute, the date picker will display the current system date as defined by the Palm device.

Inserting the time picker is similar:

```
<input type="timepicker" name="TimePick" value="HH:MM">
```

Like the date picker, the time picker will display the time using whatever system preferences have been set by the current user. If you omit the value attribute, then the time picker will display the current system time as defined by the Palm device's internal system clock.

Building Web Clipping Apps

The major difference between a local PQA application and a Web Clipping application really occurs on the server end. On the server, an application (generally a CGI type application) runs to generate on the fly the Web Clipping content. That content can be in the form of data or HTML pages.

Server-Side HTML Considerations

The only requirement for server-side code is that it generate proper Clipper-compliant HTML. Don't forget to keep in mind the following Palm limitations when designing your server-side application's HTML output.

A serious limitation to the size and functionality of PQAs is the "per-byte" billing rates associated with the Palm VII, VIIx, i705, and clip-on CDPD modems. Many Palm devices have 8, 16, or even more megabytes of memory—leaving plenty of room for even large PQAs. But, a poorly designed PQA and associated server-side applications can require over 1000KB of data transfer, costing the user plenty! Even with the advent of "all you can eat" data services, the slow transmission speed of these devices (no higher than 14 kbps, and often much slower) can seriously damage the user-friendliness of your PQA. (Imagine the user's chagrin when they must wait over a minute to see your logo on each screen!)

Therefore, you should reduce the load time and associated user cost of your returned HTML pages by identifying images you intend to use in return HTML and including them in your PQA. When the QAB compiles your PQA, it binds all image files directly into the PQA. You are not limited to including only images that display in HTML local to the PQA. Therefore, it's possible to include additional images for display in your server-side–generated HTML responses. This is easy.

First, make sure your images are included in the PQA when you compile. The WCA Builder will automatically bind any images referred to in your local (compiled) HTML pages. If you're intending to use an image solely by reference in response (server-generated) HTML, you'll need to use the LocalIcon <meta> tag to indicate that you'd like the image bound into the PQA.

Then, in your return HTML, you simply refer to the local image in the same way you would refer to a local HTML name. For example:

```
<IMG SRC="file:myapp.pqa/image.gif">
```

Remember that directory hierarchies are lost during the PQA compile process. For example, if you had placed your image in an images subdirectory and referred to it as such in your PQA (client-side) HTML as

```
<IMG SRC="images/image.gif">
```

you wouldn't need to reference the images/ directory. When the WCA builder binds your image file, it removes any directory hierarchies (and, incidentally, adjusts any links to local content in the compiled HTML).

In fact, this method can be used to include entire HTML response pages to further decrease load time. For example, you might wish to include multiple response pages using the server-side application only to select which local page users are sent to based on their form submission. Or, you might include help or descriptive pages that will only be referenced by your return HTML.

Furthermore, images should be restricted to Web Clipping's limit of 153 pixels. Horizontal scroll bars weren't introduced into the Web Clipping application until the release of Palm OS 4.0, and even then they are hard to use as they are very small and available only via Palm's touch screen (unlike vertical scroll bars, which can be accessed via physical buttons on the Palm). The 153-pixel width limitation also applies to tables, which are automatically sized to "best fit" unless the WIDTH attribute is used.

Starting with Palm OS 4.0, you can use 16-bit color images in your Web Clipping apps. However, it's important to note that Palm's proxy servers automatically convert your 16-bit color images to 2-bit or 4-bit grayscale images automatically to accommodate older Palms that can't do color, and the conversion isn't always particularly friendly. Therefore, you may wish to produce color and grayscale versions of your PQA if you intend to use color, allowing you to make the grayscale conversions and provide the best looking and most legible images possible.

When using images with the Palm, it's critical that you use the PalmComputingPlatform <meta> tag (see the section "Special Web Clipping <meta> Tags" earlier in this chapter). Without this tag, many images won't display correctly on the Palm platform.

Color selection for text and other HTML objects depends on the type of Palm devices you wish to support. Color devices are capable of displaying the full Netscape Web-safe color palette, while 4-bit grayscale devices can only display the hex values #000000, #101010, #202020, and so on up to #F0F0F0. 2-bit grayscale devices can only display four colors:

- *Black:* #000000

- *Silver:* #C0C0C0

- *Gray:* #808080

- *White:* #FFFFFF

Testing Your PQA

To test an actual PQA Web Clipping application, you have to make a small adjustment to the POSE. Once you have installed one of the wireless supporting ROMs (such as the Palm VII), you need to set up the POSE for PQA testing. Start POSE and then select the Prefs application. From the menu (see Figure 10-8), select the Wireless option (depending on the emulator or version of Palm OS you're using, you may see the option Web Clipping instead).

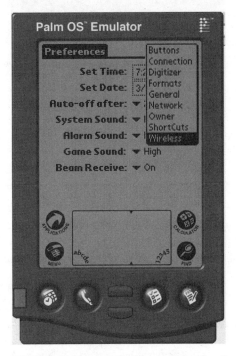

Figure 10-8. Selecting the Wireless (or Web Clipping) option from the menu

Once you've selected the Wireless (or Web Clipping) option, the proxy selection screen should appear (see Figure 10-9). The proxy selector trigger in the center of the screen should contain the specific address of a proxy server that Palm.Net has set up for testing purposes.

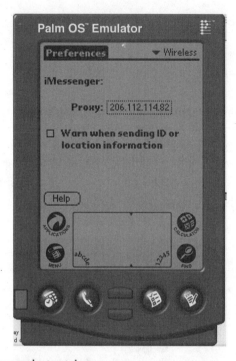

Figure 10-9. The proxy selector trigger

 NOTE *The proxy address displayed in Figure 10-9 may or may not be the address that Palm is currently using. Go to the Palm Web site and confirm this address by visiting the Web Clipping section of the developer's zone.*

Once you've verified the proxy address, right-click the POSE and select the Settings | Properties menu options. This will bring up a dialog box (see Figure 10-10) that contains a very important setting. You *must* select the "Redirect NetLib calls to host TCP/IP" option. Once this is checked, POSE will redirect all the network library calls to your desktop PC's network connection.

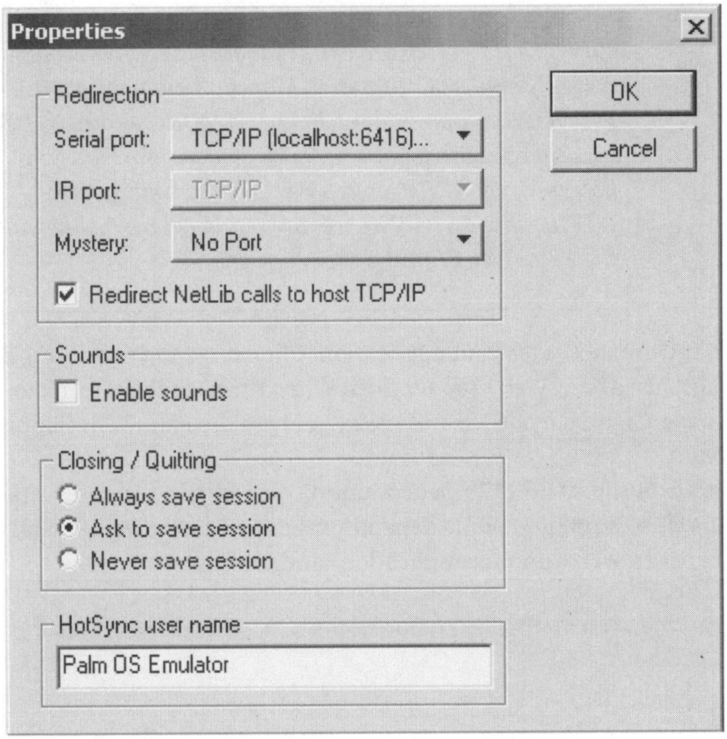

Figure 10-10. The POSE property settings

Once you have the proxy address and the POSE properly configured, PQAs running in POSE should connect to remote Internet servers as if they were real devices.

Big Picture Review

By now, you've seen that a Palm Query Application is an application that can be installed on a Palm in the same way as any other application. It's basically a special mini Web application that consists of a set of pages and images stored locally on the client side. It can send a "query" to a Web server that will send back a page in the form of a Web Clipping, which is translated by the Palm device's Clipper browser.

For the definition of a Web Clipping, just reverse the order of the preceding sentence: A Web Clipping is a page sent by a Web server in response to a query from a PQA. Web Clipping pages and PQA pages are HTML pages—or, more precisely, HTML pages that are compiled. The local PQA pages are compiled by the Query Application Builder tool before the application is installed on the device, whereas Web Clipping pages are compiled on the fly by a Palm.Net proxy.

> **NOTE** *Desktop Web browsers render HTML. The Viewer actually renders Compressed Markup Language (CML), which is a compressed version of HTML developed by Palm, Inc., for use with low-bandwidth connections. You can, however, regard Viewer as a Web browser that renders HTML, since any differences are managed by Viewer and the Palm Web Clipping proxy servers.*

When the user activates your application, Clipper displays your top-level (index) page, just as any Web browser does. When the user clicks a link to a remote page, Clipper sends a compressed query to the Palm Web Clipping proxy servers.

Figure 10-11 shows how Clipper communicates with Internet servers. As you can see, the Web Clipping scheme depends upon the Palm proxy servers, which mediate between Web Clipping applications and Internet servers.

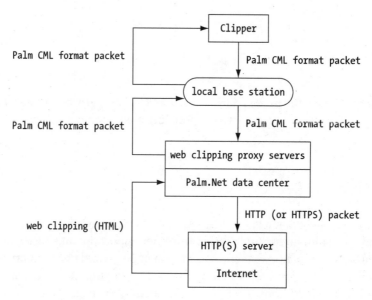

Figure 10-11. The physical architecture of a Web Clipping application

Flow of the Web Clipping application works like this:

1. The PQA requires a page that is *not* stored locally. To retrieve the information, the PQA sends a query via the wireless network to which the Palm is connected. The packet containing the query is compressed to save on transfer time. This query is relayed to the base station that's closest to the user.

2. The local base station relays the compressed query to the Palm proxy servers that are located at the Palm.Net address. The Web Clipping proxy translates the compressed packet into an HTTP (or HTTPS) query, which it can then pass to the requested Web server.

3. When the Web server responds and sends back an HTML response, this response page (which may be either static or dynamic) is passed once again to the Palm proxy servers.

4. The Palm proxy servers compress the HTTP response and send it to the Palm client.

Reportings

By now you should have a good grasp of what it takes to build a PQA and generate a simple query request back to a Web server. The resulting page (or pages) that are returned can, in turn, be used for any number of things—including reports, which, of course, are the focus of this book. Consider this simple report request: I have a software package that handles phone service billing. What makes the system rather unique is that if customers go online to the company's Web site (let's use ABC Communications, for example) using their Palm device, they can enter the zip code of the area they are currently located in, and the Web Server will fire back a report of all the locations within that area where ABC Communications customers can make payments.

To accomplish this, I first built a simple zip code search page in HTML (Listing 10-3) and compiled it using the PQA compiler tools.

Listing 10-3. The Zip Code Search HTML

```
<HTML>
<HEAD>
    <TITLE>ABC Communications Payment Finder</TITLE>
    <META NAME="palmcomputingplatform" CONTENT="TRUE">
    <META NAME="palmlauncherrevision" CONTENT="1.0">
</HEAD>
```

```
<BODY>
    <H1 ALIGN=center>Payment Center Finder by Zip Code</H1>
    <P>Enter a Zip Code to find the address of our nearest payment service
location.</P><BR>
    <FORM METHOD="post" ACTION="http://www.abcWebserver.com/palmreq/storefinder.asp">
        <B>Zip Code: </B>  <INPUT TYPE="text" NAME="zipcode" value="">
            <BR><BR>
                <INPUT TYPE="submit" VALUE="Find">
                <INPUT TYPE="reset" VALUE="Clear">
    </FORM>
</BODY>
</HTML>
```

The resulting HTML search page can be seen in Figure 10-12.

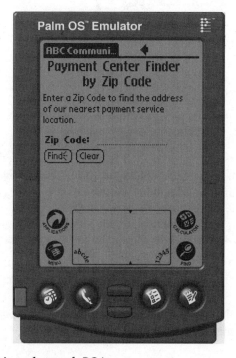

Figure 10-12. The zip code search PQA

Once the HTML code posts its requests, then the Web server will launch the zip code search page (see Listing 10-4), which will generate the content to be returned to the Palm device. The content returned from the Web server (which could also be done using a CGI-compatible scripting language such as PHP,

PERL, JAVA, etc.) should be a very "tight" listing of all the stores with a matching zip code (see Listing 10-5 for the returned HTML).

Listing 10-4. The ASP Zip Code Search

```
<HTML>
<HEAD>
    <TITLE>ABC Communications Payment Finder Results</TITLE>
    <META NAME="palmcomputingplatform" CONTENT="TRUE">
    <META NAME="palmlauncherrevision" CONTENT="1.0">
</HEAD>
<BODY>
<H1 ALIGN=center>Search Results</H1>
<TABLE WIDTH=100% BORDER=0>
<%

Dim cZip      ' Zip Code
Dim oCn       ' Database Connection
Dim oRs       ' Recordset Object
Dim cSQL      ' SQL Statement

' Open Database Connection - change for your own database
Set oCn = Server.CreateObject("ADODB.Connection")
oCn.Open "DSN=MyDSN;pwd=nopass;"

' Get the Requested ZipCode
cZip = Request.Form("ZipCode")

' Find the Exact Match
cSQL = "SELECT * FROM ZipCity WHERE ZipCode ='" & cZip & "'"
Set oRs = oCn.Execute(cSQL)

' Return Table
Do While Not oRs.EOF
%>
    <TR>
        <TD><%=oRs("Name")%></TD>
    </TR>
    <TR>
        <TD><%=oRs("Address")%></TD>
    </TR>
    <TR>
        <TD><%=Trim(oRs("City")) & "," & oRs("State") & " " & oRs("Zip")%> <TD>
    </TR>
```

```
        <TR>
            <TD><%=oRs("Phone")%></TD>
        </TR>
        <TR>
            <TD> </TD>
        </TR>
<%
Loop

' Close Recordset
oRs.Close
Set oRs = Nothing

' Close Connection
oCn.Close
%>
        </TABLE>
</BODY>
</HTML>
```

Listing 10-5. Resulting Payment Centers by Zip Code HTML

```
<HTML>
<HEAD>
    <TITLE>ABC Communications Payment Finder Results</TITLE>
    <META NAME="palmcomputingplatform" CONTENT="TRUE">
    <META NAME="palmlauncherrevision" CONTENT="1.0">
</HEAD>
<BODY>
<H1 ALIGN=center>Search Results</H1>
<TABLE WIDTH=100% BORDER=0>
    <TR>
        <TD>Tony's Cash Express</TD>
    </TR>
    <TR>
        <TD>123 Hampton Lane</TD>
    </TR>
    <TR>
        <TD>Allen, TX 75002<TD>
    </TR>
    <TR>
        <TD>(469)555-2938</TD>
    </TR>
    <TR>
```

```
      <TD> </TD>
   </TR>

   <TR>
      <TD>A1-Cash Express</TD>
   </TR>
   <TR>
    <TD>123 Main Street</TD>
   </TR>
   <TR>
      <TD>McKinney, TX 75002<TD>
   </TR>
   <TR>
      <TD>(972)555-4797</TD>
   </TR>
   <TR>
   <TD> </TD>
   </TR>
</TABLE>
</BODY>
</HTML>
```

The resulting list can then be used by the customer to locate the closest payment center. You could also make the system even more dynamic by allowing the user to select a payment center and then retrieve driving instructions. However, it's best to use the KISS (keep it simple, stupid) principal when building a Web Clipping app.

Given the restraints of bandwidth, the size restrictions imposed by the Palm Screen (160×160), and the lack of JavaScript for doing any client-side manipulations, it's better to keep the resulting reports simple in design and format.

 NOTE *Remember that Web Clipping apps running on Palm OS prior to version 4.0 don't support horizontal scrolling.*

Differences in Report Results

As you develop large, complex Web-based reporting systems, think in terms of creating summary or subset reports that could be delivered to Palm-powered devices. There are several options available to you the programmer to perform such tasks.

You could start by using the same Web page and embedding a value in either a hidden field or the query string, which would identify to the Web server the type of report request to process. Since Web Clipping applications support only a subset of HTML, this would allow the ASP (or other script language) component to make logical determinations on formatting (such as what to do with embedded tables, which aren't supported in Web Clipping).

Another possibility would be to use only those tags supported by Web Clipping, but this wouldn't solve the screen resolution issues. For these instances, you could limit the table widths; this would, of course, make many reports appear to be formatted in a strange manner. Note that this table-width issue is only relevant to those Palm-powered devices running pre–OS 4.0.

Real-World Reporting

So far we've seen the theory behind the Web Clipping delivery mechanisms and we've even done a small sample. This next section will introduce a more complex example.

Consider that you have a traveling salesman for a company (for this example, we'll use the name WeSellAutoParts) that sells automotive shop repair gear. While on the road, the salesman needs current product and quantity information from the warehouse. With this information, the salesperson can make orders based on current inventory quantities, and provide the customer with up-to-date information. The first step is to build a client-side (Palm-based) Web query page. Let's assume that the inventory list is refreshed by hand periodically, but that it's stable enough to be stored locally on the device as hard-coded HTML (in a SELECT list). Listing 10-6 shows the code for this application.

Listing 10-6. The Code to Generate the Inventory Quantity Report Request

```
<HTML>
<HEAD>
   <TITLE>WeSellAutoParts</TITLE>
   <META NAME="palmcomputingplatform" CONTENT="True">
   <META NAME="palmlaunchrevision" CONTENT="1.0">
</HEAD>
```

```
<BODY>
    <H1 ALIGN=center>Inventory On Hand Report</H1>
    <P>Please Select Inventory Item</P><BR>

    <FORM METHOD="post" ACTION="GenReport.asp">
    <TABLE WIDTH=100%>
    <TR>
        <TD>Product:</TD>
        <TD><SELECT Name="PRODUCT">
                <OPTION Selected VALUE=1>All Products</OPTION>
                <OPTION VALUE=2>Torque Wrench</OPTION>
                <OPTION VALUE=3>Air Compressior</OPTION>
                <OPTION VALUE=4>Hose Assembly</OPTION>
                <OPTION VALUE=5>Belt Assembly</OPTION>
                <OPTION VALUE=6>Lift Arm Assembly</OPTION>
                <OPTION VALUE=7>Winch Cables</OPTION>
                <OPTION VALUE=8>Mounting Brackets</OPTION>
                <OPTION VALUE=9>Filter Kit</OPTION>
                <OPTION VALUE=10>Drain Pipe Extension</OPTION>
            </SELECT>
        </TD>
    </TD>
    </TABLE>
    <P>
    <INPUT TYPE="Submit" VALUE="View">
    </P>
    </FORM>
</BODY>
</HTML>
```

When the salesperson chooses an item and presses the View button, the selected value in the Product list is posted to the server. If the salesperson picks All Products (see Figure 10-13), then all selected product information is displayed (see Figure 10-14). Be sure to test the response time for all products and consider the impact of a growing product list. One way to mitigate a large response time is to notify the user if a large amount of data will be returned and provide an option to cancel or continue.

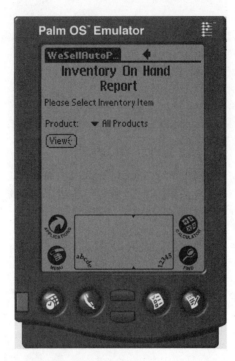

Figure 10-13. Inventory list Web Clipping app

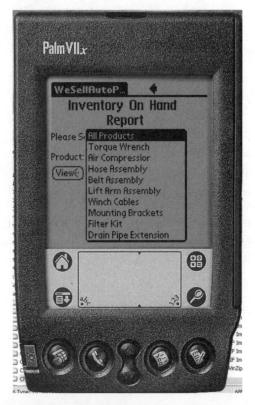

Figure 10-14. The inventory list selection list

> **TIP** *The maximum rate at which data can be transmitted or received is 14K baud. This is once again dependent on your physical location from the closest transmitter, weather, and any number of other factors. The report size itself is only half the issue you can potentially face when delivering a report to a wireless device.*

The report results are generated via an ASP page that processes the requested inventory item (by using Request.Form to retrieve the ID value of the inventory item) and returns the results (see Listing 10-7).

Listing 10-7. The Code to Generate the Inventory On Hand Report

```
<HTML>
<HEAD>
    <TITLE>WeSellAutoParts: Results</TITLE>
    <META NAME="palmcomputingplatform" CONTENT="TRUE">
    <META NAME="palmlauncherrevision" CONTENT="1.0">
</HEAD>
<BODY>
    <H1 ALIGN=center>Inventory On Hand Report</H1>
    <P>
    <TABLE WIDTH=100% BORDER=1>
        <TR>
            <TD>Name</TD>
            <TD>Qty</TD>
            <TD>On Order</TD>
        </TR>

<%


Dim nItem      ' Inventory Item ID
Dim oCn         ' Database Connection
Dim oRs         ' Recordset Object
Dim cSQL       ' SQL Statement
```

```
' Open Database Connection
Set oCn = Server.CreateObject("ADODB.Connection")
oCn.Open "DSN=MyDSN;pwd=nopass;"

' Get the Requested Inventory Item
nItem = Request.Form("PRODUCT")

' Find the Exact Match
cSQL = "SELECT * FROM Inventory WHERE ProductID = " & nItem
Set oRs = oCn.Execute(cSQL)

' Return Table
Do While Not oRs.EOF
%>
    <TR>
        <TD><%=oRs("Name")%></TD>
        <TD><%=oRs("Qty")%></TD>
        <TD><%=oRs("OnOrder")%></TD>
      </TR>
<%
Loop

' Close Recordset
oRs.Close
Set oRs = Nothing

' Close Connection
oCn.Close
%>
    </TABLE>
    </P>
</BODY>
</HTML>
```

When the ASP code is executed on the server, it returns HTML to the requesting Palm device (see Figure 10-15). This code is shown in Listing 10-8.

Figure 10-15. Inventory report results

Listing 10-8. The HTML Produced by the Inventory Report

```
<HTML>
<HEAD>
    <TITLE>WeSellAutoParts: Select Product</TITLE>
    <META NAME="palmcomputingplatform" CONTENT="True">
    <META NAME="palmlaunchrevision" CONTENT="1.0">
</HEAD>
<BODY>
    <H1 ALIGN=center>Inventory On Hand Report</H1>
    <P>
    <TABLE WIDTH=100% BORDER=1>
       <TR>
           <TD>Name</TD>
           <TD>Qty</TD>
           <TD>On Order</TD>
       </TR>
```

```
<TR>
    <TD>Torque Wrench</TD>
    <TD>4</TD>
    <TD>1</TD>
</TR>
<TR>
    <TD>Air Compressor</TD>
    <TD>3</TD>
    <TD>0</TD>
</TR>
<TR>
    <TD>Hose Assembly</TD>
    <TD>14</TD>
    <TD>9</TD>
</TR>

<TR>
    <TD>Belt Assembly</TD>
    <TD>11</TD>
    <TD>21</TD>
</TR>
<TR>
    <TD>Lift Arm Assembly</TD>
    <TD>2</TD>
    <TD>1</TD>
</TR>
<TR>
    <TD>Winch Cables</TD>
    <TD>5</TD>
    <TD>4</TD>
</TR>
<TR>
    <TD>Mounting Brackets</TD>
    <TD>114</TD>
    <TD>25</TD>
</TR>
<TR>
    <TD>Filter Kit</TD>
    <TD>4</TD>
    <TD>25</TD>
</TR>
```

```
    <TR>
        <TD>Drain Pipe Extension</TD>
        <TD>11</TD>
        <TD>4</TD>
    </TR>
  </TABLE>
    </P>
</BODY>
</HTML>
```

Conclusion

In this chapter, I've shown you how you can build Palm Query Applications to run as Web Clipping apps on Palm OS 4.1 and earlier devices. While much more sophisticated applications are possible, I've demonstrated that with little effort (and a bit of knowledge of HTML), you can develop PQA applications quickly and easily. A Web Clipping application is relatively straightforward to set up.

Design your Web Clipping apps to limit round-trips to the server, and to reduce the amount of data sent with each query. Do so by using static content when appropriate. Web Clipping is, overall, a simple and effective technology, but one that's subject to certain limitations:

- The technology only works on Palm-powered devices that are compatible with Clipper. Remember that devices running Palm OS 5.0 and above don't run Web Clipping apps.

- The programming language is a subset of HTML 3.2 and contains no support for client-side scripting languages such as JavaScript or VBScript.

As long as you keep these limitations in mind while designing and creating a Web Clipping report, you should have little difficulty with developing simple, yet robust, handheld reporting solutions for Palm-powered devices.

There are a host of other tools VB programmers can use to create applications that can deliver reports to Palm devices. See the book *Palm Programming in Basic,* by Jon Kilburn (Apress. ISBN: 1-893115-49-6) for step-by-step instructions on building VB apps using products from AppForge, CASL, and NS Basic, and visit those vendors' sites. Rumor has it that a .NET version of AppForge is imminent.

On the other hand, if you want to target Palm OS 5.0 devices, enroll as a Palm developer, download the Simulator, and learn all you can about Browser 2.0. The technology is too new for me to have covered it here.

Now let's see how to deliver reports to Pocket PCs.

CHAPTER 11

Reporting from the Pocket PC[1]

WHEN MICROSOFT INTRODUCED Pocket PCs, the concept of mobile computing took a tremendous leap forward. Suddenly, Windows developers had a powerful portable environment within which they could extend enterprise solutions. The Pocket PC's hardware prowess combined with the common Windows look-and-feel of the interface was appealing to both developers and users alike.

Developing applications for Pocket PCs forces desktop developers to revisit, reconsider, and adjust their programming practices. Not least among these adjustments is the limited support offered through the Pocket PC operating system and the Pocket PC development tools for reporting and printing.

In this chapter, I'll introduce you to the reporting and printing limitations facing mobile developers. I'll show you the following:

- The basics of generating reports through the .NET CF

- How your mobile application can retrieve data from Pocket Access, SQL Server CE, and SQL Server databases

- How to create HTML-based reports and display those reports

- PrinterCE.NetCF, a third-party component that enables your applications to send output to both network and portable printers

- Report CE, a report formatting and generation utility for the Pocket PC

The .NET Compact Framework

If you're a developer who's already familiar with Visual Studio .NET, then you'll be right at home creating applications for the Pocket PC. Microsoft has created

---

1. This chapter was written by Larry Roof and is adapted from his forthcoming book, *The Definitive Guide to the .NET Compact Framework* (Apress. ISBN 1-59059-095-3), coauthored by Dan Fergus.

a scaled-down version of the .NET Framework, called the .NET Compact Framework (.NET CF). The .NET CF simplifies application development on smart devices. A *smart device* is Microsoft's generic category name for any device that has, well, smarts. Currently this includes the Pocket PC, Pocket PC 2002, Pocket PC Phone Edition, Smartphone, and other devices running Windows CE .NET 4.1 or later. Microsoft has already announced plans to release smart watches in the fall of 2003 that will utilize Smart Personal Objects Technology (SPOT) and will include a scaled-down version of .NET CF.

The .NET CF has two main components: the common language runtime, or CLR, and the .NET CF class library.

The CLR is the foundation of the .NET CF. It's responsible for managing code at execution time, providing core services such as memory management and thread management, while enforcing code safety and accuracy. Code that targets the runtime is known as *managed code*; code that does not target the runtime, as is the case with eMbedded Visual C++, is known as *unmanaged*, or *native*, code.

The .NET CF class library is a collection of reusable classes that you can use to quickly and easily develop applications. This framework was designed with porting in mind, whether that is to Microsoft or other third-party platforms. What does this mean to you? Simply that the coding techniques and the applications you create today to run on a Pocket PC could run on other platforms, such as a cell phone or another vendor's PDA, if a version of the .NET CF was created for that platform.

Limitations of the .NET CF

While it would be nice to be able to leverage the complete .NET Framework with your mobile applications, the limitations of the Pocket PC prohibits that. While the .NET Framework tops out at just over 30MB in size, .NET CF is a diminutive 1.5MB. Obviously, more than a few features and functions needed to be trimmed as part of this compression. While it's outside of the scope of this chapter to list all of the limitations, two notable absences demand mentioning: reporting and printing. Simply stated, whatever built-in reporting or printing functionality you've been using in the .NET Framework you won't find in the .NET CF.

NOTE *At publication time, ComponentOne had announced that a ComponentOne Studio for Mobile Devices was scheduled for release in Q2 2003, and I think it's a safe bet that DataDynamics and Crystal Decisions will follow suit. Hewlett-Packard is also shipping a Mobile Printing for Pocket PC SDK (*http://www.hp.com/go/pocketpcprint*).*

Throughout the remainder of this chapter, I'll show you how to work around these limitations to produce and print reports. We'll start with a brief overview of what Visual Studio .NET 2003 offers mobile developers. Next, we'll look at how to retrieve data from a variety of data sources used within the Pocket PC environment. Finally, we'll address the process of producing reports.

Using VS .NET to Create Mobile Solutions

Visual Studio .NET 2003 provides a robust development environment for creating applications that target the .NET CF. It offers mobile developers a rich, powerful development environment from which to work.

Visual Studio .NET 2003 includes a set of prebuilt device profiles. A *device profile* contains information necessary to build applications that target specific devices including both the Pocket PC and the Pocket PC 2002. These profiles allow you to create applications that include WinForms and ADO.NET and offer the ability to consume XML Web services. In the future, other profiles will be added, including a profile that will allow you to create applications for Smartphones (http://www.microsoft.com/mobile/smartphone).

In addition to all of the features found natively in Visual Studio .NET 2003, you'll find the following device-specific features:

- *Templates:* Predefined configurations for common project types. Templates are provided for both Pocket PC and Pocket PC 2002 devices.

- *Device-specific controls:* Controls specifically designed for use with the Pocket PC. The interface, resource consumption, and functionality have been tailored for the Pocket PC environment.

- *Device emulators:* Testing environments that simulate specific devices. Emulators run on the developer's PC, allowing for testing without the presence of a device.

- *Automatic deployment of applications:* Allows you to easily test on either an emulator or a device, providing developers with a seamless testing environment.

- *Remote debugging:* Allows you to leverage the debugging tools offered through the VS .NET IDE with your Pocket PC applications. All of the debugging tools can be used with applications running either in an emulator or on a device.

Creating a Pocket PC Project

You initiate Pocket PC projects from the Visual Studio .NET 2003 Start Page.
Simply click the New Project button to begin the process. The New Project dialog
box appears, as shown in Figure 11-1. From this dialog box, you can select a tem-
plate to create a wide variety of project types, including two that target the .NET
CF. Visual Studio .NET 2003 includes a project template named Smart Device
Application under both the Visual Basic and Visual C# project folders.

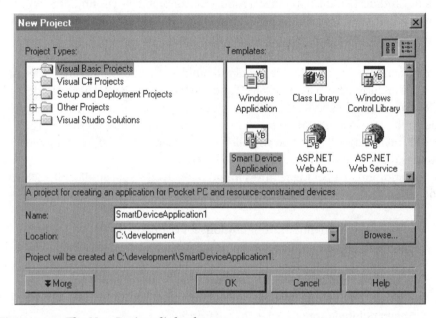

Figure 11-1. The New Project dialog box

Selecting the Smart Device Application template will result in loading the
Smart Device Application Wizard, as shown in Figure 11-2. This wizard walks you
through the process of further selecting the project type for your application.

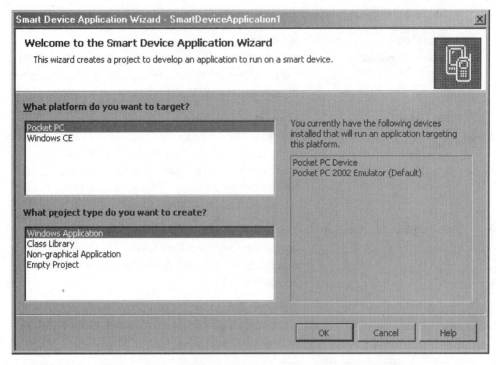

Figure 11-2. The Smart Device Application Wizard

The interface of this wizard has two list boxes. The top list box allows you to select the target platform. It contains two options, Pocket PC and Windows CE. Whereas Pocket PC targets a specific device platform, the Windows CE template creates a more general-purpose application that could run on a variety of devices running that operating system.

The lower list box displays the project types that are available for the target (Pocket PC or Windows CE) you selected. Four project types target the Pocket PC and Pocket PC 2002 platforms, as shown in Figure 11-2: Windows Application, Class Library, Non-graphical Application, and Empty Project. A description of each of these project types is provided in Table 11-1.

Table 11-1. Pocket PC Project Types

PROJECT TYPE	DESCRIPTION
Windows Application	WinForm-based project including Pocket PC–specific controls. This is the most commonly used template as it generates typical Windows-based applications.
Class Library	Class libraries allow you to package related components in a single file. You can use class libraries to develop other applications or as a base for inheritance for other components. This project type is best suited for creating modules of code that will be reused with multiple applications.
Non-graphical Application	This type is used to create executables that will *not* have a user interface. Best used for background and maintenance applications that do not require user interaction.
Empty Project	This type defines a project with no predefined components, allowing you to custom build everything from the ground up.

These project types can be used to create applications that target Pocket PC devices running SH3, MIPS, or ARM processors and Pocket PC 2002 devices with ARM or XScale processors. Starting with the PPC 2002, Microsoft has restricted PPC CPUs to the ARM architecture.

Designing a Form

If you are already an experienced Visual Studio .NET developer, you'll probably require little orientation to begin creating user interfaces for Pocket PC applications. Figure 11-3 shows a new project based upon the Windows Application template.

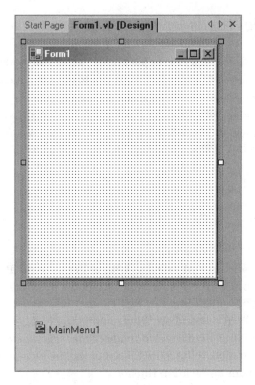

Figure 11-3. An empty Pocket PC form

In this example, the project type is a Windows Application that will target the Pocket PC. The template for this type of application includes a form that's correctly sized for the Pocket PC platform. A menu control, shown below the form, is included with the form, as most Pocket PC applications include menus.

To add a control to your user interface, simply select the control in the Toolbox and then draw the control on your form, just as you would for any other Visual Studio .NET application.

Controls Provided with the .NET CF

The .NET CF includes a subset of the controls that can be used to construct a desktop Windows application. For the most part, you'll find that these controls offer less functionality than their counterparts provided through the .NET Framework. This difference has to do with resource limitations imposed by the target platforms.

Adding Code to an Application

You add code to your Pocket PC applications just as you would to a desktop application. You use the Code window to create both event and general-purpose procedures. Since you are working inside of the Visual Studio .NET IDE, you have all of the functionality and features available with your Pocket PC development as you have come to depend upon when developing desktop applications. Features such as IntelliSense, online help, automatic syntax verification, and debugging are available for use with your Pocket PC projects.

Testing Your Application

Visual Studio .NET 2003 offers two methods for testing Pocket PC applications: through an emulator and on a device. With either the emulator or a device, VS .NET handles deploying both your application and all of the components your application requires, including the .NET CF and SQL Server CE.

Here's how all this is handled: When you test a .NET CF application from within Visual Studio .NET, a check is made of the target platform to confirm that the .NET CF is installed. If the .NET CF is missing, it's automatically copied and installed before your application runs.

A similar process applies if your application uses SQL Server CE. The target platform is checked to confirm that the SQL Server CE components are installed. If they aren't, they are automatically copied and installed before running your application.

After Visual Studio .NET confirms that all of the components required by your application are present, it will copy your application to the target platform, place it in the directory you specified in your project configurations, and finally launch your application.

Running a Test

There are several ways to run a test of your application:

- From the Visual Studio .NET toolbar, click the Start button.

- From the Debug menu, select Start or Start without Debugging.

- Press the F5 key (start with debugging) or Ctrl+F5 (start without debugging).

Testing in the Emulator

The emulator provides an environment within your desktop PC that mimics the functionality and operation of the device platform you are targeting with your application. The emulator is useful in situations where you do not have a device or when your device is not available.

Be forewarned: Testing in the emulator has its shortcomings. First and foremost is that the emulator runs on a desktop PC, which has far more processing resources than the target device. This can give you a false sense of how well your application performs. In addition, input for the emulator is provided through a keyboard and a mouse rather than the stylus the end user will be forced to use. If you aren't consciously aware of this difference, you may end up creating an application that's easy to use in the emulator and a pain to use on the device. Finally, the emulator offers a "close" representation of a device, not an exact match. There are subtle differences in all emulators.

There can be several types of emulators on a development PC, each of which represents a specific device. When you choose to test your application in the emulator, Visual Studio .NET uses your project configurations to determine the appropriate emulator.

Deploying to the Emulator

You can elect to deploy to the emulator using any of the following methods:

- On the Smart Device Extensions toolbar, select Pocket PC Emulator from the Deployment Device combo box as shown in Figure 11-4.

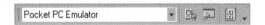

Figure 11-4. Selecting the emulator for deployment

- Under the Device page of the Project Property Pages dialog box, select Pocket PC Emulator from the Deployment Device combo box.

- From the Property window, set the Deployment Device property of your project to Pocket PC Emulator.

Testing on a Device

Testing on a device allows you to get first-hand experience for how your applications perform. From within Visual Studio .NET you can test on devices connected to your development PC via USB, serial connection, or Ethernet.

 TIP *Use Ethernet to connect your device to your development PC. This is by far the quickest and easiest method for testing and debugging.*

Deploying to a Device

You can deploy to a device using any of the following ways:

- On the Smart Device Extensions toolbar, select Pocket PC Device from the Deployment Device combo box as shown in Figure 11-5.

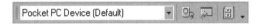

Figure 11-5. Selecting the device for deployment

- Under the Device page of the Project Property Pages dialog box, select Pocket PC Device from the Deployment Device combo box.

- From the Property window, set the Deployment Device property of your project to Pocket PC Device.

Debugging an Application

Assuming you are a typical developer, your development process hinges on at least a bit of debugging. This is one area where Visual Studio .NET can help you out tremendously. The debugging environment provided through the VS .NET IDE is robust. It allows you to pause your application, look about its inner workings, modify code, examine values, and step through your application in a systematic manner.

The core of the debugging functionality can be found under the Debug menu. From this menu, you can start and stop a debugging session, set breakpoints, and navigate about your application while in debug mode.

> **NOTE**   *Breakpoints identify a line of code within your application where you want to pause or interrupt the execution of your application.*

Visual Studio .NET enables you to remotely debug applications that are running on a device or in an emulator from the comfort of your development PC. You can use the Command window to enter statements, query and set variables, execute lines of code, and other similar tasks.

Now that you have a general understanding of what Visual Studio .NET offers in the way of Pocket PC application development, let's turn our attention to the task of retrieving the data you'll need to produce mobile reports.

Accessing Data

The .NET CF uses a special version of ADO.NET. .NET Framework's ADO.NET offers you a wide variety of functionality for you to construct data-enabled applications including the following:

- Access to both local and remote data provides you with options on how to incorporate data into your mobile applications.

- Support for disconnected data is especially useful with mobile applications. Data can be loaded, updated, and viewed without requiring an active connection to its data source.

- Integrated support for XML makes it easy for you to pass data over the Internet and to persist data on the device.

- The ability to assemble data from a variety of sources including local and network based, and over the Internet.

- Robust error handling that provides a comprehensive way to address problems that may occur when working with data.

The implementation of ADO.NET under the .NET CF is like everything else under .NET CF, a subset of the version provided with the .NET Framework. Even so, it's an incredible improvement over earlier versions of Pocket PC programming tools. What makes ADO.NET even more useful to you is that you can leverage your ADO.NET skills between the server, desktop, and device.

NOTE *Remember, ADO.NET for .NET CF is different from the old ADOCE you may have used in the past. For more about ADOCE, see* `http://msdn.microsoft.com/library/default.asp?url=/library/en-us/adoce31/html/adowlcm.asp` *and* `http://msdn.microsoft.com/library/default.asp?url=/library/en-us/sqlce/htm/_lce_adoce.asp?frame=true`.

Anxious to get your hands on a .NET CF provider for Analysis Services cubes? Don't hold your breath. The provider for .NET Framework is still in beta at press time.

System.Data Namespace

We'll start our discussion of ADO.NET with the namespace through which much of the functionality is provided: System.Data. If you're a VB .NET developer, you should already be familiar with this namespace. Like other .NET CF namespaces, System.Data is limited, providing only the most commonly used functionality of the .NET Framework version.

The System.Data namespace includes two relational data sources: SQL Server and SQL Server CE. This support is delivered through two providers: SqlClient and SqlServerCE. Both of these providers are similar in functionality, differing primarily in the source that they work with. It's through these providers that your Pocket PC applications access data.

SQL Server Provider

The SQL Server provider is implemented through the System.Data.SqlClient namespace. Through this provider, you can access SQL Server from your mobile applications, allowing you to directly query and modify enterprise databases over a wireless connection. For all practical purposes, with this provider you can create mobile applications that function identically to desktop applications in the way that they work with data. The commonly used classes of this namespace are listed in Table 11-2.

Table 11-2. Key Classes of the System.Data.SqlClient Namespace

CLASS	DESCRIPTION
SqlCommand	Transact-SQL statement or stored procedure that will be executed against the target SQL Server database
SqlConnection	Connection to a SQL Server database
SqlDataAdapter	Class used to fill DataSets and update SQL Server databases
SqlDataReader	Forward-only stream of rows
SqlError	Class that contains a warning or error returned by the SQL Server provider
SqlErrorCollection	Collection of warnings and errors returned by the SQL Server provider
SqlParameter	Parameter for use with a SqlCommand
SqlParameterCollection	Collection of parameters used with a SqlCommand
SqlTransaction	SQL transaction to be made against a SQL Server database

SQL Server CE Provider

The SQL Server CE provider is implemented through the System.Data.SqlServerCe namespaces. This provider enables you to access SQL Server CE databases that are resident on your device. Table 11-3 lists the commonly used classes of this namespace.

Table 11-3. Key Classes of the System.Data.SqlServerCe Namespace

CLASS	DESCRIPTION
SqlCeCommand	Transact-SQL statement that will be executed against the target SQL Server CE database
SqlCeConnection	Connection to a SQL Server CE database
SqlCeDataAdapter	Class used to fill DataSets and update SQL Server CE databases
SqlCeDataReader	Forward-only stream of rows
SqlCeEngine	Properties, methods, and other objects that represent a SQL Server CE database
SqlCeError	Class that contains a warning or error returned by the SQL Server CE provider
SqlCeErrorCollection	Collection of warnings and errors returned by the SQL Server CE provider
SqlCeParameter	Parameter for use with a SqlCeCommand
SqlCeParameterCollection	Collection of parameters used with a SqlCeCommand
SqlCeRemoteDataAccess	Instance of the SqlCeRemoteDataAccess object
SqlCeReplication	Instance of the SqlCeReplication object
SqlCeTransaction	SQL transaction to be made against a SQL Server CE database

The Connection Classes

When it comes to accessing databases, whether locally from SQL Server CE or remotely from SQL Server, everything starts with a connection. Both the System.Data.SqlClient and System.Data.SqlServerCe namespaces include Connection classes.

The SqlConnection Class

The Connection class for the System.Data.SqlClient namespace is SqlConnection. You'll use this class to establish a connection to a SQL Server database directly from your device. I list the commonly used methods of the SqlConnection class in Table 11-4 and show the commonly used properties of this class in Table 11-5.

Table 11-4. Methods of the SqlConnection Class

METHOD	DESCRIPTION
BeginTransaction	Starts a database transaction. You'll use the SqlTransaction object to commit or roll back a transaction.
Close	Closes the connection to a database.
CreateCommand	Creates and returns a SQLCommand object.
Open	Opens a connection to a database.

Table 11-5. Properties of the SqlConnection Class

PROPERTY	DESCRIPTION
ConnectionString	String that defines how a SQL Server database will be opened
ConnectionTimeout	Amount of time to wait when opening a connection before generating an error
Database	Name of the database to open
DataSource	Instance of SQL Server to connect to
State	Current state of the connection to the SQL Server database

Opening a Connection to SQL Server

Listing 11-1 shows an example of opening a connection to a SQL Server database. In this example, the server name is being provided as an IP address, and the database being used is the infamous NorthWind database.

Listing 11-1. Opening a Connection to a SQL Server Database

```
Dim cn As System.Data.SqlClient.SqlConnection

' Open the connection.
  cn = New System.Data.SqlClient.SqlConnection( _
    "user id=sa;password=;database=Northwind;server=192.168.1.101")
```

The SqlCeConnection Class

The Connection class for the System.Data.SqlServerCe namespace is SqlCeConnection. This class is used to connect to a SQL Server CE database (.sdf filename extension) that's located on your device. Table 11-6 lists the commonly used methods of the SqlCeConnection class and Table 11-7 shows the commonly used properties of this class.

Table 11-6. Methods of the SqlCeConnection Class

METHOD	DESCRIPTION
BeginTransaction	Starts a database transaction. You'll use the SqlCeTransaction object to commit or roll back a transaction.
Close	Closes the connection to a database.
CreateCommand	Creates and returns a SQLCeCommand object.
Open	Opens a connection to a database.

Table 11-7. Properties of the SqlCeConnection Class

PROPERTY	DESCRIPTION
ConnectionString	String that defines how a SQL Server CE database will be opened
ConnectionTimeout	Time to wait when opening a connection before generating an error
Database	Name of the database to open
DataSource	Path and filename of the SQL Server CE database
State	Current state of the connection to the SQL Server CE database

Opening a Connection to SQL Server CE

Listing 11-2 shows an example of opening a connection to a SQL Server CE database. In this example, it's the Northwind database located in the My Documents folder. SQL Server CE databases make use of the .sdf extension as shown in Listing 11-2.

Listing 11-2. Opening a Connection to a SQL Server CE Database

```
Dim cn As System.Data.SqlServerCe.SqlCeConnection

' Open the connection.
  cn = New _
    System.Data.SqlServerCe.SqlCeConnection( _
      "Data Source=\My Documents\NorthwindDemo.sdf")
' .sdf = SQL Server 2000 for CE database filename extension
```

The Command Classes

Now that we've discussed connections, we're ready for the next topic: Commands. Commands are used to define, query, and modify databases and their contents. As with connections, both the System.Data.SqlClient and System.Data.SqlServerCe namespaces include Command classes.

The SqlCommand Class

The Command class for the System.Data.SqlClient namespace is SqlCommand. This class is used to execute commands against your SQL Server enterprise databases. This approach is frequently used in wireless deployments, where your Pocket PC application directly accesses the server. Table 11-8 lists the commonly used methods of the SqlCommand class. Table 11-9 lists the commonly used properties.

Table 11-8. Methods of the SqlCommand Class

METHOD	DESCRIPTION
Cancel	Cancels the execution of a command.
CreateParameter	Creates a parameter object, SqlParameter, for use with a command.
ExecuteNonQuery	Executes a SQL command and returns the number of rows affected. This is commonly used for bulk updates and deletions.
ExecuteReader	Executes a command and returns a SqlDataReader object.
ExecuteScalar	Executes a command and returns the first column in the first row of the query results. Used to obtain summary information from a database.
ExecuteXmlReader	Executes a command and returns an XmlReader object.

One of the cool features of the SqlCommand class is the quartet of Execute methods that offer you a variety of ways to receive data back from a command.

Table 11-9. Properties of the SqlCommand Class

PROPERTY	DESCRIPTION
CommandText	Command that will be executed. This can be either a SQL statement or the name of a stored procedure.
CommandTimeout	Amount of time to wait when executing a command before generating an error.
CommandType	Property that defines whether CommandText is a SQL command, the name of a table, or the name of a stored procedure.
Connection	Connection to use when executing this command.
Parameters	Collection of parameters to pass when calling a stored procedure.
Transaction	SqlTransaction used when executing this command.

Executing a Command Against SQL Server

Listing 11-3 shows an example of executing a command against a SQL Server database. This example starts by opening a connection to the Northwind database. Next, a command with two arguments is defined. The first argument is a SQL statement that specifies what the command will do. The second argument is the connection to the database. Finally, the command is executed. In this example, the command is a SQL SELECT statement that returns a DataReader object.

Listing 11-3. Executing a Command Against SQL Server

```
Dim cn As System.Data.SqlClient.SqlConnection
Dim cmd As System.Data.SqlClient.SqlCommand
Dim dr As System.Data.SqlClient.SqlDataReader

' Open the connection. Modify the cn string for your own environment
cn = New System.Data.SqlClient.SqlConnection( _
    "user id=sa;password=;database=Northwind;server=192.168.1.101")

' Configure and execute the command.
cmd.CommandText = "SELECT * FROM Customers"
cmd.Connection = cn
dr = cmd.ExecuteReader
```

The SqlCeCommand Class

The Command class for the System.Data.SqlServerCe namespace is
SqlCeCommand. This class is used to execute commands against a SQL Server
CE database, a local database that will reside on your Pocket PC. Table 11-10
shows the commonly used methods of this class, and in Table 11-11, you'll find
commonly used properties of this class.

Table 11-10. Methods of the SqlCECommand Class

METHOD	DESCRIPTION
Cancel	Cancels the execution of a command
CreateParameter	Creates a parameter object, SqlCeParameter, for use with a command
ExecuteNonQuery	Executes a SQL command and returns the number of rows affected
ExecuteReader	Executes a command and returns a SqlCeDataReader
ExecuteScalar	Executes a command and returns the first column in the first row of the query results

Table 11-11. Properties of the SqlCeCommand Class

PROPERTY	DESCRIPTION
CommandText	SQL command that will be executed.
CommandTimeout	Amount of time to wait when executing a command before generating an error. Note that timing out a command is of less concern when working with a SQL Server CE database as 1) the data is not usually being shared, and 2) there is no network connection involved.
CommandType	Property that defines whether CommandText is a SQL command or the name of a table. Note that the value of StoredProcedure is not supported by this property.
Connection	Connection to use when executing this command.
Parameters	Collection of parameters to pass with this command.
Transaction	SqlCeTransaction to use when executing this command.

Executing a Command Against SQL Server CE

Listing 11-4 shows an example of executing a command against a SQL Server CE database. This example begins by opening a connection to a local copy of the Northwind database. The command then uses this connection to retrieve all of the records from the Customers table into a DataReader.

Listing 11-4. Executing a Command Against SQL Server CE

```
Dim cn As System.Data.SqlServerCe.SqlCeConnection
Dim cmd As System.Data.SqlServerCe.SqlCeCommand
Dim dr As System.Data.SqlServerCe.SqlCeDataReader

' Open the connection.
cn = New _
    System.Data.SqlServerCe.SqlCeConnection( _
        "Data Source=\My Documents\NorthwindDemo.sdf")

' Configure and execute the command.
cmd.CommandText = "SELECT * FROM Customers"
cmd.Connection = cn
dr = cmd.ExecuteReader
```

The DataReader Classes

In the previous section, we looked at how the SqlCommand and SqlCeCommand objects return the results of a query in a DataReader object. A DataReader is a set of records that are read-only and can only be navigated through in a forward motion, which is perfectly suited for your reporting needs.

The System.Data.SqlClient and System.Data.SqlServerCe namespaces each include DataReader classes. There are two commonly used methods of these namespaces: The Close method closes the reader, and the Read method moves the reader to the next record.

The SqlDataReader Class

The DataReader class for the System.Data.SqlClient namespace is SqlDataReader. You'll use this class to receive the results of a query made against a SQL Server database.

Listing 11-5 shows how to loop through a SqlDataReader object loading a ListBox with the contents of the CompanyName field from each record.

Listing 11-5. Looping Through a SqlDataReader Object

```
Sub ReadSqlDataReader()
   Dim cn As System.Data.SqlClient.SqlConnection
   Dim cmd As System.Data.SqlClient.SqlCommand
   Dim dr As System.Data.SqlClient.SqlDataReader
Try
' Open the connection.
   cn = New System.Data.SqlClient.SqlConnection( _
      "user id=sa;password=;database=Northwind;server=192.168.1.101")

' Configure and execute the command.
   cmd.CommandText = "SELECT * FROM Customers"
   cmd.Connection = cn
   dr = cmd.ExecuteReader

' Loop through the data.
   While dr.Read()
      ListBox1.Items.Add(dr("CompanyName"))
   End While
Catch
Finally
' Clean up.
   dr.Close()
   cn.Close()
End Try
```

SqlCeDataReader

The DataReader class for the System.Data.SqlServerCe namespace is
SqlCeDataReader. This class is used to receive the results from a query that's
made against a SQL Server CE database.

The example shown in Listing 11-6 demonstrates how to loop through
a SqlDataReader object to load a ListBox with the contents of the CompanyName
field from each record.

Listing 11-6. Looping Through a SqlCeDataReader Object

```
   Dim cn As System.Data.SqlServerCe.SqlCeConnection
   Dim cmd As System.Data.SqlServerCe.SqlCeCommand
   Dim dr As System.Data.SqlServerCe.SqlCeDataReader
```

```
' Open the connection.
    cn = New _
      System.Data.SqlServerCe.SqlCeConnection( _
        "Data Source=\My Documents\NorthwindDemo.sdf")
    cn.Open()

' Configure and execute the command.
    cmd.CommandText = "SELECT * FROM Customers"
    cmd.Connection = cn
    dr = cmd.ExecuteReader

' Loop through the data.
    While dr.Read()
      ListBox1.Items.Add(dr("CompanyName"))
    End While

' Clean up.
  dr.Close()
  cn.Close()
```

Working with Pocket Access Data

Although Pocket Access shipped with the original Pocket PCs, it's not included in Pocket PC 2002 or higher. Developers of mobile applications who relied on Pocket Access because of its ease of use and the synchronization options provided through ActiveSync have to either write their own wrapper (a challenge, as .NET CF doesn't support COM Interop) or buy a third-party tool such as the ADOCE .NET wrapper from InTheHand Software (http://www.inthehand.com).

Producing Reports

Now that you have an understanding of how to retrieve data into your Pocket PC application, let's turn our attention to the second task at hand, producing a report. As I mentioned at the start of this chapter, the .NET CF offers nothing in the form of reporting tools. There is no compact equivalent to Crystal Reports, nor any printing functionality provided.

In addressing these shortcomings, developers have two options: 1) to code around the limitation, or 2) to purchase a third-party solution. In the remainder of this chapter, we'll look at both approaches. First, using the roll-your-own code approach, we'll see how you can combine HTML and the .NET CF to produce reports that users will view on their Pocket PC devices. Next, we'll look at a printer component from Field Software that allows you to create and send print content to both mobile and network-based printers. Finally, we'll look at a report generation tool, Report CE, that can be leveraged from your Pocket PC applications. While it's not Crystal Reports, it certainly goes a long way in making up for .NET CF's absence of reporting capabilities.

Producing HTML Reports

If you have ever worked with ASP or ASP.NET, you'll be right at home with this form of Pocket PC reporting. Simply stated, it uses HTML to format reports. This HTML content can in turn be displayed either in Pocket IE or within your application through a third-party HTML viewer control.

This approach to reporting is simple. It's a three-step process:

1. Retrieve the data that will appear in your report from the data source.

2. Format the report by combining your data with HTML tags.

3. Display the HTML content to the user.

The HTML report approach is best suited for situations where you want to provide a rich, device-based report. Note that I'm not talking about printing here—this is an on-device approach. That's just one of the limitations of HTML reports. The other has to do with the viewing limitation imposed by the Pocket PC itself. Developing HTML content that displays well on its small screen is at best a challenge. The key to this whole approach is creating HTML content that's easy to view on a screen that's 240×320 pixels.

The following section walks you through the complete process of HTML reporting, from retrieving the data, to producing the HTML content, and finally to displaying the content.

The HTML Reporting Sample

You'll find the HTML reporting sample application in this book's downloadable source code (available from the Apress Web site at http://www.apress.com). Figure 11-6 shows the report output produced by this application.

Figure 11-6. The HTML-based report as it's displayed within Pocket IE

NOTE *If you are not familiar with developing applications that target the Pocket PC, you should be aware that the process of building, deploying, and launching an application takes longer than it does for a desktop application. It's not unusual for that delay to be a minute or longer.*

Examining the HTML Reporting Sample

The key to the HTML reporting sample application is the click event procedure for the Display Report button. Listing 11-7 displays the contents of this procedure. As you can see, the procedure is nothing more than a series of subroutine and function calls as listed here:

- *RetrieveData:* Gathers the data

- *ProductReport:* Formats the report

- *SaveReport:* Saves the report to a file

- *DisplayReport:* Displays the report in Pocket IE

Listing 11-7. The Contents of the Display Report Button Click Event

```
Private Sub btnDisplayReport_Click(ByVal sender As System.Object, _
  ByVal e As System.EventArgs) Handles btnDisplayReport.Click

  Dim ReportFile As String = "\Windows\Start Menu\Programs\Apress\report.html"
  Dim ReportHtml As String

' Retrieve the data.
  RetrieveData()

' Generate the report.
  ReportHtml = ProduceReport()

' Save the report.
  SaveReport(ReportHtml, ReportFile)

' Display the report.
  DisplayReport(ReportFile)

End Sub
```

Gathering the Data

The HTML reporting sample application gets its data from a SQL Server CE database. In this case, a SQLServerCE DataReader is loaded with the contents of the Customers table from the NorthwindDemo database. Listing 11-8 shows the code used to accomplish this task.

Listing 11-8. Retrieving Customer Data from the Database

```
Sub RetrieveData()

' Open the connection.
  cn = New _
    System.Data.SqlServerCe.SqlCeConnection( _
    "Data Source=\Windows\Start Menu\Programs\Apress\NorthwindDemo.sdf")
  cn.Open()

' Configure and execute the command.
  cmd.CommandText = "SELECT * FROM Customers"
  cmd.Connection = cn
  dr = cmd.ExecuteReader

End Sub
```

The process used to retrieve the data is straightforward. A SqlCeCommand selects all of the records from the customers table. The DataReader in turn is loaded with these records.

Formatting the Report

The data that's held within the DataReader is in turn used to produce the HTML content of your report. As I mentioned earlier in this chapter, the HTML reporting option is very similar to ASP or ASP.NET development in that you're using HTML tags combined with your data to create an HTML document.

Listing 11-9 demonstrates this process. The ProduceReport routine shown in this listing has three sections. The first section produces the document header, that's to say the opening HTML tags. This includes tags for the document itself, the body, a header, a table, and the table's header row.

Listing 11-9. Generating the HTML Content

```
Function ProduceReport() As String
    Dim HTML As String

' Build the report header.
    HTML = "<HTML>"
    HTML += "<BODY>"
    HTML += "<H1><FONT COLOR=Blue>Customer List</FONT></H1>"
    HTML += "<TABLE>"
    HTML += "<TR>"
    HTML += "<TD><B>COMPANY</B></TD>"
    HTML += "<TD><B>CONTACT</B></TD>"
    HTML += "<TD><B>PHONE</B></TD>"

' Loop through the data.
    While dr.Read()
        HTML += "<TR>"
        HTML += "<TD><FONT SIZE=-2>" & dr("CompanyName") & "</TD>"
        HTML += "<TD><FONT SIZE=-2>" & dr("ContactName") & "</TD>"
        HTML += "<TD><FONT SIZE=-2>" & dr("Phone") & "</TD>"
        HTML += "</TR>"
    End While
```

```
' Add the report footer.
  HTML += "</TABLE>"
  HTML += "</BODY>"
  HTML += "</HTML>"

' Return the report.
  Return HTML

End Function
```

In the middle of Listing 11-9 you'll find the code that combines the customer's data taken from the DataReader with some simple HTML formatting. By looping through the DataReader, you can generate the body of your report with a few lines of code.

Finally, at the bottom of the listing a footer is added to the report. At this point, the report is complete. Next, the report is saved to file before it's displayed within Pocket IE.

Saving the Report

Before the report can be displayed within Pocket IE, you need to save it to a file. Listing 11-10 demonstrates how this is accomplished. Using a System.IO.StreamWriter object, you open the report file, write out your HTML content, and then close the report file. As you can see, it's a simple process to save the report.

Listing 11-10. Storing the Report in a File

```
Sub SaveReport(ByVal ReportHtml As String, ByVal ReportFile As String)
 Dim sw As System.IO.StreamWriter

' Open the file.
  sw = New System.IO.StreamWriter(ReportFile)

' Write the report.
  sw.Write(ReportHtml)

' Close the file.
  sw.Close()

End Sub
```

Displaying the Report

Finally, you're ready to display the report to the user. This is accomplished by launching Pocket IE programmatically from within the sample application, passing your report file as a command line argument. Listing 11-11 shows the code for this.

Listing 11-11. Launching Pocket IE and Displaying the Report

```
Sub DisplayReport(ByVal ReportFile As String)
   Dim pi As ProcessInfo
   Dim si() As Byte
   Dim intResult As Int32

' Launch Pocket IE to display the report.
   intResult = LaunchApplication("\Windows\iexplore.exe", ReportFile, Nothing, _
      Nothing, 0, 0, Nothing, Nothing, si, pi)

End Sub
```

Don't be misled by the simplicity of the DisplayReport routine. What allows this routine to be so simple is the CreateProcess module that's part of the HTML reporting project. Within the CreateProcess module, you'll find the declaration for the Windows CE API function CreateProcess and the wrapper routine LaunchApplication, which is shown in Listing 11-11.

The Windows CE CreateProcess API function allows you to launch another executable from within your application. In this case, it's Pocket IE.

TIP *Pocket IE, like other versions of Microsoft's browsers, does not refresh a document unless forced to. What that means in the case of this example is that if you use a single filename to output your reports, then the user will have to tap the refresh button on Pocket IE to see the report after each generation. A simple workaround to this problem is to create each report in a temporary file that has a unique name.*

Summary of Producing HTML Reports

As this section demonstrates, producing HTML reports is simple and straight-forward. If you have any background in ASP or ASP.NET, you'll have no trouble embracing this method of reporting. The primary downside of this reporting approach is that it doesn't allow you to produce a printed version of your reports. If your mobile applications absolutely need printed output, read on.

Producing Printed Reports

If your application needs to print a report rather than just view the report on the device, you have two good options. The first option is to use the PrinterCE.NetCF component from Field Software Products (http://www.fieldsoftware.com/). This component enables applications written to the .NET CF to print to a wide variety of mobile and network printing devices. The second option is to use the Report CE product from SYWARE (http://www.syware.com). Field Software offers a trial version of its software; SYWARE doesn't.

Some developers may argue that there's a third approach, one in which you write code to handle communicating to a specific printer. I'm not fond of this old-school approach to printing for the following reasons:

- It is incredibly labor intensive.

- It is printer specific, often limiting your application to a single printer or family of printers.

- It requires a solid understanding of how a specific type of printer communicates and the format of the print language it supports.

It's because of these limitations that I'll limit the discussion of printing options to the first two choices: the PrinterCE.NetCF component and Report CE.

Producing Printed Reports with PrinterCE.NetCF

The PrinterCE.NetCF component offers developers tremendous printing flexibility, but requires a fair bit of coding and formatting to produce the desired results. It provides a wide variety of functionality including the following:

- It includes support for both VB .NET and C# .NET under the .NET CF.

- It's easy to use. You don't have to worry about device contexts, bit-blits, or other complexities.

- You have complete control over the appearance of text including the font, size, style, color, rotation, and page position (or you can have PrinterCE.NetCF automatically position multiple rows of text for you).

- Both auto-word wrap and page feed options are available.

- It provides a wide-variety of drawing objects including lines, ellipses, rectangles, and rounded rectangles. You can select size, location, line width, color, and fill.

- It supports printing of images including bitmaps, JPEGs, and GIFs. You can control the size, aspect ratio, and rotation of the printed image.

- Full color printing is available.

- You can print using infrared, Bluetooth, serial, and network connections.

- Custom printer support is provided for a variety of commercial and industrial printers.

- Fast text-only printing to any ASCII printer is available.

A trial version of the PrinterCE.NetCF component is available online at `http://www.fieldsoftware.com/PrinterCE_NetCF.htm`. To help you get started with the PrinterCE.NetCF component, I've created a sample application called PrinterCE .NET Demo. You'll find this project in this book's downloadable source code (available from the Apress Web site at `http://www.apress.com`).

NOTE *If you are not familiar with developing applications that target the Pocket PC, you should be aware that the process of building, deploying, and launching an application takes longer than it does for a desktop application. It's not unusual for that delay to be a minute or longer.*

Examining the PrinterCE .NET Demo

The purpose behind this demo isn't as much to show you how to create a robust report as to show the process behind working with the PrinterCE.NetCF component. The process for incorporating the PrinterCE.NetCF component into your Pocket PC applications is as follows:

1. Add a reference to the PrinterCE.NetCF component to your project.

2. Add the FieldSoftware.PrinterCE_NetCF Imports statement to your form's code module.

3. Dimension a variable as a PrinterCE type.

4. Create a new instance of the PrinterCE object.

5. Configure the instance of the PrinterCE object.

6. Use the various Draw methods of the PrinterCE object to produce output.

7. Use the EndDoc method to complete your printing output.

Step 1: Adding a Reference to the PrinterCE.NetCF Component

To work with the PrinterCE.NetCF component, you need to add a reference to the component to your Pocket PC project. To add this reference, perform the following steps:

1. In the Solution Explorer window, right-click the References folder. A pop-up menu displays.

2. From the menu, select Add Reference.

3. The Add Reference dialog box appears. Select the PrinterCE.NetCF component.

4. Click the OK button to add the selected components to your project.

Step 2: Importing FieldSoftware.PrinterCE

To simplify the process of working with the PrinterCE.NetCF component, you should add an Imports statement to the top of your form module. The syntax of this statement is

```
Imports FieldSoftware.PrinterCE_NetCF
```

Step 3: Dimension the PrinterCE Variable

All of your printing work will be carried out through a PrinterCE object. To accomplish this, you must first dimension a variable as this type:

```
Dim prce As PrinterCE
```

Step 4: Create an Instance of the PrinterCE Object

Next, you're ready to use this variable to create a new instance of the PrinterCE object. When creating the object, you can specify an exception level at which printing terminates. You must also specify your developer license to enable the product for commercial use.

```
prce = New PrinterCE(PrinterCE.EXCEPTION_LEVEL.ABORT_JOB, "YourLicense")
```

Step 5: Configure the PrinterCE Object

At this point, you're almost ready to begin output of your report. Before proceeding onto that, this is a good time to configure the settings for the PrinterCE object. In the example that follows, I've specified that the user will be prompted to select the desired printer:

```
prce.SelectPrinter(True)
```

NOTE *PrinterCE.NetCF allows you either to specify a printer or to request the user to select a printer. This flexibility allows you to specify a particular type of printer for some applications while enabling your application to support a wide variety of printers in other instances.*

In your application, you may want to specify the margins, size of the paper, orientation, and scale, among other options.

Step 6: Produce Your Report

You're now ready to begin producing output. PrinterCE.NetCF provides a number of Draw methods that you can use to produce your report. Following is a simple example of outputting plain text:

```
prce.DrawText("The PrinterCE .NET Demo")
```

NOTE *More on the PrinterCE.NetCF Draw methods can be found later in this section.*

Step 7: Send Your Report

Finally, the report is ready to send. To complete the process and submit the print job, you call the EndDoc method of the PrinterCE object:

```
prce.EndDoc()
```

Bringing It All Together

Listing 11-12 shows how the preceding examples fit together. Here, the simple phrase "The PrinterCE .NET Demo" is sent to a printer.

Listing 11-12. A Simple Example of the PrinterCE.NetCF Component

```
Private Sub Button1_Click(ByVal sender As System.Object, _
   ByVal e As System.EventArgs) Handles Button1.Click
   Dim prce As PrinterCE

   Try
' Create an instance of the PrinterCE component.
      prce = New PrinterCE(PrinterCE.EXCEPTION_LEVEL.ABORT_JOB, "YourLicense")

' Prompt the user for the target printer.
      prce.SelectPrinter(True)

' Print out a simple message.
      prce.DrawText("The PrinterCE .NET Demo")

' Complete the print document, which in turn submits the print job.
      prce.EndDoc()

' Handle any errors that occur.
   Catch exc As PrinterCEException
      MessageBox.Show("PrinterCE Exception", "Exception")

' Clean up.
   Finally
      prce.ShutDown()
   End Try

End Sub
```

The PrinterCE Object

Now that you have a general understanding of the process of working with the PrinterCE.NetCF component, let's look at another sample application that demonstrates more of the functionality offered by this product.

The Northwind Mobile Application

The Northwind Mobile application allows the user to view customer orders and print invoices. Figure 11-7 provides an example of how a customer's order appears to the user. Figure 11-8 shows a sample invoice produced by the application. You'll find this project in this book's downloadable source code (available from the Apress Web site at `http://www.apress.com`).

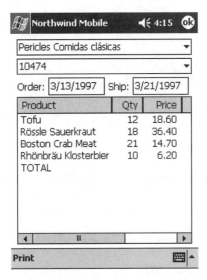

Figure 11-7. Examining an order with the Northwind Mobile application

 NOTE *If you are not familiar with developing applications that target the Pocket PC, you should be aware that the process of building, deploying, and launching an application takes longer than it does for a desktop application. It's not unusual for that delay to be a minute or longer.*

Account Number	Order Number	Payment Due By	PLEASE PAY THIS AMOUNT
06-036171-408	R52581782D-AB	4/15/2003	**$1,249.10**

Pericles Comidas clásicas
1217 5th Avenue
New York, NY 10010

> To avoid Late Payment charge,
> full payment must be received by
> 4/15/2003

THANK YOU FOR YOUR PROMPT PAYMENT

PLEASE RETURN THIS STUB WITH PAYMENT   TO ENSURE PROPER CREDIT, PLEASE WRITE YOUR ACCOUNT NUMBER ON YOU CHECK.

Product	Quantity	Unit Price	Item Total
Tofu	12	18.60	$223.20
Rössle Sauerkraut	18	36.40	$655.20
Boston Crab Meat	21	14.70	$308.70
Rhönbräu Klosterbier	10	6.20	$62.00

Figure 11-8. A sample invoice produced by the Northwind Mobile application

Examining the Northwind Mobile Application

A detailed discussion of this application is outside of the scope of this chapter. Instead, I'm going to focus on the module that produces the invoice. Listing 11-13 contains that code, which is called when the user taps the Print menu. What you should immediately notice is that this is a lengthy routine. As I already mentioned, what PrinterCE.NetCF offers in the way of printing functionality and flexibility it exacts as cost the length of code.

Listing 11-13. Producing a Customer's Invoice

```
Private Sub PrintInvoice()
   Dim curItemTotal As Single
   Dim curTotalAmount As Single
   Dim intCounter As Integer
   Dim prce As PrinterCE

' Create an instance of the printer object.
   prce = New PrinterCE(PrinterCE.EXCEPTION_LEVEL.ABORT_JOB, "YourLicense")

' Prompt the user to select printing attributes.
   prce.SelectPrinter(True)
```

```
' Setup the layout and margins.
  With prce
      .PrOrientation = PrinterCE_Base.ORIENTATION.PORTRAIT ' Portrait mode
      .ScaleMode = PrinterCE_Base.MEASUREMENT_UNITS.INCHES ' Work in inches
      .PrLeftMargin = 0.5
      .PrTopMargin = 0.7
      .PrRightMargin = 0.5
      .PrBottomMargin = 0.7
      .DrawWidth = 0.02

' Begin to draw the invoice starting with the top rectangle.
      .DrawRect(0, 0, 5.7, 0.5)
```

Looking through Listing 11-13, you'll see at the top of this module the exact same setup code found in the previous example, where you saw how to create an instance of the PrinterCE object and then configure that instance. You should note that here, the configuration is more involved as you define margins, page orientation, and other items.

Next is the code used to generate the invoice. Here you'll find examples of a variety of the capabilities offered through the PrinterCE.NetCF component, including the quartet of Draw methods: DrawText, DrawLine, DrawRect, and DrawRoundedRect. As you can see by the output shown in Figure 11-8, these four methods can be combined to create some truly powerful results.

You can leverage rectangles, lines, and shading to spice up your reports, giving them a preprinted appearance. This is very different from single font, no-graphic reporting that's frequently associated with mobile printing.

```
' Add a shaded rectangle.
      .FillColor = System.Drawing.Color.LightGray
      .FillStyle = PrinterCE.FILL_STYLE.SOLID
      .DrawRect(0, 0, 5.7, 0.25)
      .DrawLine(2, 0, 2, 0.5)
      .DrawLine(3.8, 0, 3.8, 0.5)

' Add the top headers.
      .FontSize = 12
      .FontBold = True
      .ForeColor = System.Drawing.Color.Black
      .JustifyHoriz = PrinterCE_Base.JUSTIFY_HORIZ.CENTER
      .JustifyVert = PrinterCE_Base.JUSTIFY_VERT.CENTER

      .DrawText("Account Number", 1, 0.125)
      .DrawText("Order Number", 2.9, 0.125)
      .DrawText("Payment Due By", 4.75, 0.125)
```

Shading can be used to enhance the appearance of your printed output. Following is the code used to create the total amount box found in the upper-left corner of the invoice:

```
' Add the total amount box. This is accomplished by drawing a
' black box with a smaller white box over top of it.
    .FillColor = System.Drawing.Color.DarkGray
    .DrawRect(5.7, 0, 7.5, 0.7)
    .ForeColor = System.Drawing.Color.White
    .FontSize = 9
    .FontBoldVal = 1000        ' Set to maximum value.
    .DrawText("PLEASE PAY THIS AMOUNT", 6.6, 0.1)
    .FillColor = System.Drawing.Color.White
    .DrawRoundedRect(5.8, 0.2, 7.4, 0.6, 0.15, 0.15)

' Set the drawing color back to black after finishing the white box.
    .ForeColor = System.Drawing.Color.Black

' Add late payment box.
    .FontSize = 12
    .FontBold = False
    .DrawRect(5, 1.9, 7.5, 2.6)
    .DrawText("To avoid Late Payment charge,", 6.25, 2.05)
    .DrawText("full payment must be received by", 6.25, 2.25)

' Add invoice footer.
    .JustifyHoriz = PrinterCE_Base.JUSTIFY_HORIZ.LEFT
    .FontSize = 8
    .DrawText("PLEASE RETURN THIS STUB WITH PAYMENT", 0, 2.8)
    .JustifyHoriz = PrinterCE_Base.JUSTIFY_HORIZ.RIGHT
    .DrawText("TO ENSURE PROPER CREDIT, PLEASE WRITE YOUR " & _
        "ACCOUNT NUMBER ON YOU CHECK.", 7.5, 2.8)
    .FontSize = 14
    .FontBold = True
    .FontItalic = True
    .JustifyHoriz = PrinterCE_Base.JUSTIFY_HORIZ.CENTER
    .DrawText("THANK YOU FOR YOUR PROMPT PAYMENT", 2.5, 2.5)

' Add the item header bar.
    .FillColor = System.Drawing.Color.LightGray
    .FillStyle = PrinterCE.FILL_STYLE.SOLID
    .DrawRect(0, 3.1, 7.5, 3.35)
    .DrawLine(2, 3.1, 2, 3.35)
    .DrawLine(3.8, 3.1, 3.8, 3.35)
    .DrawLine(5.7, 3.1, 5.7, 3.35)
```

You have complete control of the size and type of font that you use with your reports. You can alter and combine fonts to produce any desired appearance.

```
' Add the item header titles.
    .FontSize = 12
    .FontBold = True
    .FontItalic = False
    .ForeColor = System.Drawing.Color.Black
    .JustifyHoriz = PrinterCE_Base.JUSTIFY_HORIZ.CENTER
    .JustifyVert = PrinterCE_Base.JUSTIFY_VERT.CENTER

    .DrawText("Product", 1, 3.225)
    .DrawText("Quantity", 2.9, 3.225)
    .DrawText("Unit Price", 4.75, 3.225)
    .DrawText("Item Total", 6.75, 3.225)

' Fill in data component of the invoice. Some of the content
' is hardcoded, but could just as easily be retrieved from a
' database.
    .FontBold = False
    .FontItalic = False
    .FillStyle = PrinterCE.FILL_STYLE.TRANSPARENT

' Print the account number and order number.
    .DrawText("06-036171-408", 1, 0.375)
    .DrawText("R52581782D-AB", 2.9, 0.375)

' Add the due dates.
    .DrawText(DateAdd(DateInterval.Day, 30, Date.Today), 4.75, 0.375)
    .FontSize = 12
    .DrawText(DateAdd(DateInterval.Day, 30, Date.Today), 6.25, 2.45)
```

Here, in the middle of the invoice generation routine, you find the code used to extract line items from the user interface and insert them into the output. You could just as well be retrieving these values from a DataReader object as shown in the HTML example.

```
' Add the line items.
    .FontSize = 14
    For intCounter = 0 To lvwOrder.Items.Count - 2
      .JustifyHoriz = PrinterCE_Base.JUSTIFY_HORIZ.LEFT
      .DrawText(lvwOrder.Items(intCounter).Text, 0, _
          3.5 + (intCounter * 0.25))
```

```
            .JustifyHoriz = PrinterCE_Base.JUSTIFY_HORIZ.RIGHT
            .DrawText(lvwOrder.Items(intCounter).SubItems(1).Text, _
                2.9, 3.5 + (intCounter * 0.25))
            .DrawText(lvwOrder.Items(intCounter).SubItems(2).Text, _
                5.0, 3.5 + (intCounter * 0.25))

' Calculate and print the total of this line item.
            curItemTotal = (CSng(lvwOrder.Items(intCounter).SubItems(1).Text) * _
                CSng(lvwOrder.Items(intCounter).SubItems(2).Text))
            .DrawText(FormatCurrency(curItemTotal.ToString), 7, 3.5 + _
                (intCounter * 0.25))

' Add the amount of this line item to the running total.
            curTotalAmount = curTotalAmount + curItemTotal
        Next intCounter
```

One of the cool features offered through the PrinterCE.NetCF component is the ability to produce your output in any order. In the following code, you see how to add the total amount of the invoice to the upper-left corner of the invoice. This is easily accomplished even though you print the box in which this value is placed far earlier in this routine.

```
' Add the total amount.
        .JustifyHoriz = PrinterCE_Base.JUSTIFY_HORIZ.CENTER
        .FontSize = 16
        .FontBold = True
        .DrawText(FormatCurrency(curTotalAmount), 6.6, 0.4)

        .JustifyHoriz = PrinterCE_Base.JUSTIFY_HORIZ.LEFT
        .FontSize = 16
        .FontBold = False
        .DrawText(cmbCustomers.Items(cmbCustomers.SelectedIndex), _
            0.5, 1.2)
        .DrawText("1217 5th Avenue")
        .DrawText("New York, NY 10010")

' Add line between header and order content.
        .DrawWidth = 0.01
        .DrawLine(0, 3, 7.5, 3)

' Complete the print document.
        .EndDoc()
    End With
End Sub
```

At the end of Listing 11-13, you see where the EndDoc method is called to send the invoice to your printer, just as was done in the simple example shown earlier in this chapter.

TIP *Since PrinterCE.NetCF does not include a graphical design component, designing and implementing complex printed output is frequently a tedious task. To simplify this process, I would suggest sending output to a network printer rather than your target mobile printer. Network printers, with their Ethernet connections and high-speed print capabilities, make the process far more tolerable than the slow printing speed and IR and Bluetooth interfaces found in most mobile printers.*

Summary of Printing with PrinterCE.NetCF

PrinterCE.NetCF offers mobile application developers a vibrant toolkit of printing functionality. Simply stated, with PrinterCE.NetCF you can produce any report that you have the imagination to conceive and the time to code. This component offers the powerful combination of support for industry-standard printers, communication methods, and printing functionality. I recommend that you visit the Field Software Web site for further details on the capabilities and uses for PrinterCE.NetCF.

Now that you've seen the longhand approach at printing reports, let's look at a far more development-friendly method provided by Report CE from SYWARE.

Pocket PC Report Generation with Report CE

Report CE from SYWARE offers mobile application developers the closest thing available to a report generation tool. It provides a scaled-down version of what you have come to expect to find in products such as Crystal Reports.

Report CE allows you to create report templates, which you can subsequently call to produce reports from your mobile applications. You can either print via the IR port, Bluetooth, or to a network printer. Optionally, you can send your report through e-mail or save it as text to a file. Report CE supports producing color reports.

The data that you use within a report can come from both enterprise and local data sources. Reports can include a header, footer, data, and calculated data. Report CE's filtering capabilities allow you to control the data shown within a report. For more information on Report CE, visit SYWARE's Web site at http://www.syware.com/prodlib/win_ce/rpt_ce/rpt_ce.htm.

While SYWARE does not offer a trial version of Report CE, it does offer a 30-day money back guarantee. You can purchase Report CE online from SYWARE's Web site at http://www.syware.com/olstore/olstore.htm.

The Report CE Demo

To give you a flavor of what Report CE has to offer, I've created a sample application called Report CE Demo. You'll find this project in this book's downloadable source code (available from the Apress Web site at http://www.apress.com).

 NOTE *If you are not familiar with developing applications that target the Pocket PC you should be aware that the process of building, deploying, and launching an application takes longer than it does for a desktop application. It's not unusual for that delay to be a minute or longer.*

Examining the Report CE Demo

The process of leveraging Report CE for your mobile application's printing needs involves very little in the way of code. Most of the real work is done within the Report CE design interface. Figure 11-9 shows an example of this interface.

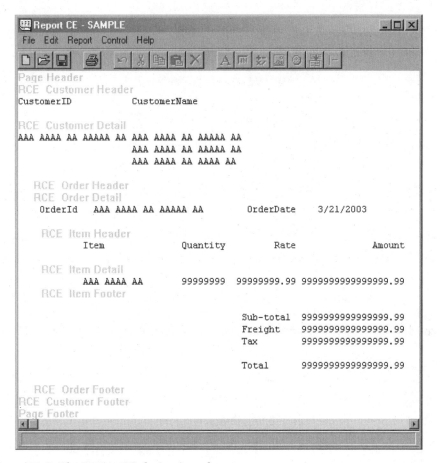

Figure 11-9. The Report CE design interface

As you can see, the report is divided into sections—header, detail, and footer—just as you would expect to find in the larger desktop report generation tools. Each section can in turn be divided into subsections as required by your reporting needs. Sections can be configured to automatically calculate and insert totals. Values can be retrieved from databases. Spots, or fields for values, can be reserved. You can define the type of data to insert into each field as well as the font to use, the size of the font, and its color.

Your reports can include filters as shown in Figure 11-10. This enables you to selectively restrict the data included in your reports.

Figure 11-10. The Filter dialog box shown when a report runs

Figure 11-11 shows the output produced from the template that appears in Figure 11-9. You should note that this is a simple example, using a single font type and size. You can easily enhance your reports by varying your fonts.

```
CustomerID          CustomerName

C04                 ABC Books
                    57 Ocean Drive
                    Lincoln RI

    OrderId   R41                       OrderDate   5/15/1999

            Item            Quantity        Rate            Amount

            Paper                 10        2.85             28.50
            Pencil                50        0.05              2.50

                                        Sub-total            31.00
                                        Freight              10.00
                                        Tax                   0.00

                                        Total                41.00

    OrderId   R42                       OrderDate   9/1/1999

            Item            Quantity        Rate            Amount

            Pen                  100        0.25             25.00
            Paper                  5        2.85             14.25

                                        Sub-total            39.25
                                        Freight               5.00
                                        Tax                   0.00

                                        Total                44.25
```

Figure 11-11. Sample output produced by Report CE

Adding a Report to Your Mobile Application

As I've already stated, the coding part of working with Report CE is minimal. All that you need to do is launch the Report CE application, passing the name of the report as a command-line argument.

You use the same approach to accomplish this as was demonstrated with the HTML report example. Adding the CreateProcess module to the demonstration project makes starting the Report CE executable easy, as shown in Listing 11-14.

Listing 11-14. Printing a Report Through Report CE

```
Private Sub btnRunReport_Click(ByVal sender As System.Object, _
  ByVal e As System.EventArgs) Handles btnRunReport.Click
  Dim pi As ProcessInfo
  Dim si() As Byte
  Dim intResult As Int32

' Launch the Report CE engine, passing to it the sample report.
  intResult = LaunchApplication("\Program Files\Report CE\ReportCE.exe", _
    "\Windows\Start Menu\Programs\Sample.rce", Nothing, Nothing, 0, _
    0, Nothing, Nothing, si, pi)

End Sub
```

NOTE *You could also specify the criteria for the filter as part of the command line, enabling you to programmatically control the data included in the report.*

Figure 11-12 shows how the report appears to the user before it's printed. Report CE offers the user the option to print, save, or e-mail the report.

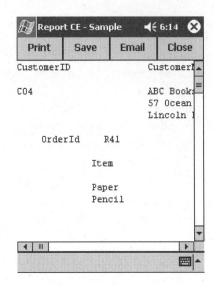

Figure 11-12. A sample report within Report CE

Selecting to print the report presents the user with the dialog interface shown in Figure 11-13. From this dialog interface, the user can select the target printer, the method to communicate, and even control the configuration and appearance of the print job.

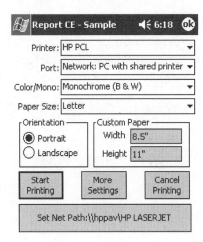

Figure 11-13. The print dialog interface of Report CE

If users desire, they can send the report via e-mail simply by tapping on the Email button from within the Report CE interface. Doing so will cause the Email dialog interface to display as shown in Figure 11-14. From this dialog interface, the user can select the recipient of the e-mail from a list of names drawn from the

Pocket PC's contact list. The report is placed into the Outbox on the device, and will be sent the next time users synchronize their device.

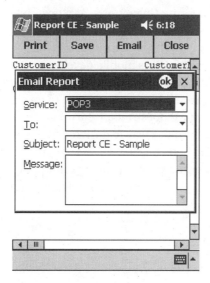

Figure 11-14. The Email dialog interface of Report CE

Summary of Printing with Report CE

While Report CE doesn't offer the flexibility of the PrinterCE.NetCF component, it does offer both ease of design and use. With Report CE, you can create reports that group and summarize data without requiring any code. As you saw in the demo included with this section, incorporating a Report CE report into your mobile application involves nothing more than the few lines of code required to launch an application.

The combination of its price, royalty-free use, ease of design, and ability to produce output to printers, files, and e-mail make Report CE a viable reporting tool for every mobile developer.

Summary

While neither printing nor report generation are natively supported by either the Pocket PC or the .NET CF, that doesn't mean you have do without. There are several good reporting options available to mobile application developers.

HTML-based reports provide a flexible option in situations where your reports do not need to be printed. This approach is similar to both ASP and ASP.NET in that it's based on formatting data using HTML tags.

The PrinterCE.NetCF component from Field Software offers developers a printing option with support for a wide-variety of mobile and network printers. On the plus side, this component is flexible and provides developers with nearly limitless possibilities for formatting reports. As a negative, working with PrinterCE.NetCF usually requires a fair bit of coding to accomplish the desired effects.

Report CE from SYWARE offers mobile developers the closest thing to a report generation utility. Its graphical design environment enables you to easily construct reports. It's reasonably priced and easy to incorporate into applications written with .NET CF. While it doesn't offer the range of flexibility found in PrinterCE.NetCF, it offers a quick way to design and deploy reports.

Regardless of the method you choose, this chapter demonstrates that the Pocket PC can be a powerful extension of your enterprise reporting functionality.

The .NET Compact Framework

Adapted from Larry Roof's forthcoming Apress book,
The Definitive Guide to the .NET Compact Framework (ISBN 1-59059-095-3).

MICROSOFT DEVELOPED the .NET Compact Framework (.NET CF) with one intention in mind: to build applications. By applications, I do not mean drivers, COM components, ActiveX controls, or Today screen plug-ins. I am talking about applications that display, gather, process, and forward information—those applications that give users a reason to carry a device. While they typically will have an interface, they do not have to have one. The data that they are working with might be local, remote, or some combination of the two.

The .NET Compact Framework simplifies application development on smart devices. Presently this includes the Pocket PC, Pocket PC 2002, Pocket PC Phone Edition, Smartphone, and other devices running Windows CE .NET 4.1 or later.

 NOTE *Currently you cannot use the .NET Compact Framework to develop applications that target the SmartPhone. There will be a Smartphone software development kit (SDK) released later. This SDK will install on top of Visual Studio .NET and will include a Smartphone emulator.*

You will need Visual Studio .NET 2003 to build applications that target the .NET Compact Framework. You can build applications using either Visual C# .NET, Visual Basic .NET, or both.

The .NET Compact Framework has two main components: the common language runtime, or CLR, and the .NET Compact Framework class library.

The CLR is the foundation of the .NET Compact Framework. It is responsible for managing code at execution time, providing core services such as memory management and thread management while enforcing code safety and accuracy.

Code that targets the runtime is known as managed code; code that does not target the runtime, as is the case with eMbedded Visual C++, is known as unmanaged, or native, code.

The .NET Compact Framework class library is a collection of reusable classes that you can use to quickly and easily develop applications. This framework was designed with porting in mind, whether to Microsoft or other third-party platforms. What does this mean to you? Simply that the coding techniques and the applications you create today to run on a Pocket PC could run on other platforms, such as a cell phone or another vendor's PDA, if a version of the .NET Compact Framework was created for that platform.

Common Language Runtime

The common language runtime provides a code-execution environment that manages code targeting the .NET Framework. Code management can take the form of memory management, thread management, security management, code verification and compilation, and other system services.

The CLR is designed to enhance performance. It makes use of Just-In-Time (JIT) compiling, which enables managed code to run in the native machine language of your application's platform. This allows you to create applications that can target a variety of platforms and not have to worry about recompiling or generating executables that target each specific platform.

Even though your mobile application is written in VB .NET or C# .NET, and as such is managed code, you are still able to incorporate functions and subroutines stored externally in dynamic link libraries (DLLs), including the Windows CE APIs. The .NET Compact Framework provides the data types and support for structures to allow you to easily incorporate functions from the Windows CE APIs into your application.

.NET Compact Framework Class Library

The .NET Compact Framework class library is a collection of reusable classes that tightly integrate with the common language runtime. Your applications leverage these libraries to derive functionality.

As you would expect from an object-oriented class library, the .NET Compact Framework types enable you to accomplish a range of common programming tasks, including tasks such as interface design, leveraging XML, database access, thread management, and file I/O.

The following sections describe the common functionality available through .NET CF.

Form-Related Classes

The .NET Compact Framework implements a subset of the System.Windows.Forms and System.Drawing classes, which allow you to construct rich Windows CE–based user interfaces for your device applications. The Form Designer within Visual Studio .NET manages much of the interaction with these classes for you.

The implementation of WinForms under the .NET Compact Framework includes support for forms, most controls found in the .NET Framework, hosting of third-party controls, bitmaps, and menus. Table A-1 lists the controls included with the .NET Compact Framework.

Table A-1. Controls Included with the .NET Compact Framework

CONTROL	DESCRIPTION
Button	Simple command button
CheckBox	Common check box
ComboBox	Drop-down list of times
ContextMenu	Context-sensitive menu for association with another object
DataGrid	Grid that can be bound to a data source
DomainUpDown	List of items that the user can navigate using scroll bars
HScrollBar	Horizontal scroll bar
ImageList	Container used to store images, which in turn will be used with other controls such as the ToolBar, ListView, and TreeView
InputPanel	Controls the Soft Input Panel (SIP) on Windows CE devices
Label	Simple control that allows you to display text
ListBox	List of items from which the user can pick
ListView	Provides four views for displaying data: large icon, small icon, list, and details
MainMenu	Menu with a form
NumericUpDown	Numeric input field that allows both manual entry as well as scroll bars
OpenFileDialog	Interfaces with the standard Windows CE open file dialog box
Panel	Container used to hold other controls
PictureBox	Used to display images of a variety of formats

(continued)

Table A-1. Controls Included with the .NET Compact Framework (Continued)

CONTROL	DESCRIPTION
ProgressBar	Visual indicator of a task's progress
RadioButton	Common radio button
SaveFileDialog	Interfaces with the standard Windows CE save file dialog box
StatusBar	Simple panel for displaying text
TabControl	Tabbed interface for an application
TextBox	Standard text input field
Timer	Basic timing component
ToolBar	Implements a toolbar on a form
TrackBar	Slider interface used with numeric data
TreeView	Presents data in a hierarchical layout
VScrollBar	Vertical scroll bar

Like everything that is part of the .NET Compact Framework, the controls included with .NET CF have limited functionality. They are missing properties, methods, and events found in their .NET Framework counterparts. A little coding can correct these shortcomings. That is because .NET CF allows you to create your own controls by inheriting from the base control class. From this foundation, you can add your own properties, methods, and events to create just the control you need.

Data and XML Classes

The .NET Compact Framework includes a set of classes that allow you to easily incorporate data, whether it is from a relational or nonrelational data source, and XML content into your mobile applications. These classes are defined under the System.Data and System.Xml namespaces. The implementation of both data and XML classes under .NET CF is a subset of those found in the .NET Framework.

Web Services

The .NET Framework is much about Web services. In the .NET Compact Framework System.Web namespace, you have a scaled-down version of the capabilities and functionality offered in the corresponding .NET Framework namespace. Most significantly, you can create Web service clients, but you cannot host Web services under the .NET Compact Framework.

These Web service clients can be either synchronous or asynchronous. Creating a Web service client that targets the .NET Compact Framework is easy. The Visual Studio .NET IDE does much of the work for you.

GDI Support

The .NET Compact Framework provides support for the basic GDI drawing elements including bitmaps, brushes, fonts, icons, and pens through the System.Drawing namespace.

Base Classes

The .NET Compact Framework provides a robust set of base classes that expose a wide range of functionality for use by developers. This underlying infrastructure enables you to write rich .NET applications, including being able to create multithreaded applications (System.Threading), leveraging networking resources (System.Net), and working with files (System.IO).

IrDA Support

Windows CE devices, such as the Pocket PC and Pocket PC 2002, include infrared (IR) communication capabilities. In support of this, the .NET Compact Framework includes classes that allow you to leverage IR communication from within your application. These classes are part of the System.Net.IrDA namespace. You can use IR to communicate to Pocket PCs, printers, and other IR-enabled devices.

Bluetooth Support

The .NET Compact Framework does not natively provide support for Bluetooth. You can access most third-party Pocket PC implementations of Bluetooth via either serial port communications or a provider's API.

Visual Basic Support

Visual Basic .NET makes liberal use of helper functions that are located in a VB Helper library. The .NET Compact Framework includes a subset of these functions as well. These functions are considered by VB developers to be a core part of the language, which is the reason for their inclusion.

If you are an existing Visual Basic or eMbedded Visual Basic developer converting over to .NET CF, what this means is that many of the VB language functions you are used to working with will be available to you in Visual Basic .NET.

A La Carte Features

To conserve resources on the target device, Microsoft divided the .NET Compact Framework into logical components. By delivering components as separate DLLs, or, as they are referred to within the .NET Compact Framework, assemblies, Microsoft gives you the option of picking and choosing the features you need, and only those features that your target device has the space to hold.

An example of this is the System.SR assembly, which contains error message strings. Including this assembly with your application allows access to detailed descriptions of any errors encountered, which is certainly helpful during a debugging session, but infrequently needed in an application once it is released to production. Excluding this assembly does not affect the performance or functionality of your application; it simply means you will not have access to detailed error messages.

Another example of the .NET CF a la carte approach is the SQL Server CE components, delivered in a set of DLLs totaling slightly over 1MB in size. Unless you explicitly add a reference to the System.Data.SqlServerCe assemblies, these DLLs will not be included with your application.

Features Missing from the .NET Compact Framework

Some serious trimming had to be made to the .NET Framework so that it could fit into the operating constraints of Windows CE. The most notable .NET Framework features that did not make it into the .NET Compact Framework are the subject of this section.

Method Overloads

Overloading a method provides alternative ways to call that method. It also increases the size of a framework. Because of this, the .NET Compact Framework trimmed the overloads from almost all methods.

What this means to you is twofold. First, there is a good chance that a particular method overload you used with a desktop application will not be available under .NET CF. Second, when you read the documentation, pay close attention to whether or not a method is supported by .NET CF.

Missing Controls

A number of .NET controls did not make their way into the .NET Compact Framework. The absence of most of these controls is insignificant to mobile developers. Since printing has such a limited role in mobile applications, removing the whole family of print-related controls is not an issue. That takes care of the CrystalReportViewer, PageSetupDialog, PrintDialog, PrintDocument, PrintPreviewControl, and PrintPreviewDialog controls. You can replace many of the missing dialog boxes with your own or by accessing system dialog boxes directly using the Windows CE API.

XML Functionality

As much as the .NET Compact Framework offers in the way of XML, an equal amount of functionality was trimmed. The key missing XML-related component is the System.Xml.XPath namespace. The XPath namespace made XML parsing far easier than the methods offered under .NET CF. In its absence, you can use a combination of recursive and iterative searches against the Document Object Model (DOM).

The .NET Compact Framework is missing another key XML component, Extensible Stylesheet Language Transformation, or XSLT. With XSLT, you can convert an XML document into different formats.

On an XML-related note, .NET CF does not provide support for developing device-based Web services.

Database Support

While the .NET Compact Framework offers a robust set of data-related tools, it is not without shortcomings. Support is provided for a single database, SQL Server CE. The .NET Compact Framework does not provide support for Pocket Access databases or other third-party device-based databases.

On the server side, the .NET Compact Framework provides support for only SQL Server. The key missing namespace is System.Data.OleDb.

Binary Serialization

Both the BinaryFormatter and SoapFormatter classes are absent from the .NET Compact Framework, severely limiting serializing and deserializing objects.

Access to the Windows Registry

The .NET Framework has the Microsoft.Win32.Registry namespace, which makes it easy to work with the Windows registry from an application. Obviously, this namespace was not included in .NET CF, as it has to do with Win32, not Windows CE. Unfortunately, no Windows CE equivalent of this namespace was included in .NET CF. As a result, you are forced to turn to the Windows API if your application requires access to the Windows CE registry.

Leveraging COM Components

The absence of the COM interop is one of the most debated limitations of the .NET Compact Framework. This is particularly true for developers who are switching over from eMbedded Visual Basic, where they were accustom to leveraging COM objects, including ActiveX controls, to extend their development capabilities.

Incorporating COM objects into a .NET CF application is a two-step process. First, you must write an unmanaged (that is to say, eMbedded Visual C++) DLL wrapper that exposes the COM object. Depending upon the complexity of the COM object, this may be anything from a simple to extremely complicated process. Second, you must use PInvoke to access your DLL wrapper. Luckily, the development community has already begun work on accessing the more commonly used COM components, several of which are included in the references at the end of this appendix.

Security

The .NET Compact Framework does not secure access to unmanaged code. Any application can call any system or nonsystem API.

There is no role-based security with the .NET Compact Framework. The principal object has no understanding of known identity or known role.

Web Services

The most notable exclusion from the .NET Compact Framework Web service capabilities is the inability to use cookies. Cookies are widely used to maintain state on the server between calls from a client. While the use of cookies in Web services is not as prevalent as their use on Web sites, they are still in use.

The .NET Compact Framework offers limited cryptographic abilities in respect to Web services.

Printing

The .NET Compact Framework provides no support for printing. There is no easy way to interact with either network printers or external printers via IR.

The workaround for accessing network printers is to build a server-based application that accepts and prints jobs submitted by your mobile application.

You can send output through the IR port directly to IR-enabled printers. You use the System.Net.IrDA namespace to access the IR port of your device. The difficult part is that your application needs to control everything sent to the printer, including any control characters that the printer supports.

GDI+

Windows CE natively does not support GDI+, so GDI+-related functionality was removed from .NET Compact Framework.

Remoting

Remoting, that wonderful feature of the .NET Framework that allows you to easily build distributed applications, is, sad to say, missing from the .NET Compact Framework. Now, one could make the case that mobile applications are ideal candidates for remoting. To make matters worse, there is not a good way to code around this limitation.

Additional Resources

Following is a list of resources for further information on .NET CF:

- Larry Roof's *MSDN Magazine* article "Develop Handheld Apps for the .NET Compact Framework with Visual Studio .NET" at `http://msdn.microsoft.com/msdnmag/issues/02/03/NETCF/default.aspx`

- Larry Roof's "Smart Device Extensions, SQL Server CE, and Me" at `http://msdn.microsoft.com/library/default.asp?url=/library/en-us/dnroad/html/road05222002.asp`

- John Kennedy's "Taking Control with C#" at `http://msdn.microsoft.com/library/default.asp?url=/library/en-us/dnroad/html/road01082003.asp` (and other "Two for the Road" columns at MSDN Online)

- Microsoft Newsgroups:

  `microsoft.public.dotnet.framework.compactframework`

  `microsoft.public.dotnet.framework.aspnet.mobile`

  `microsoft.public.in.dotnet.compactframework`

  `microsoft.public.smartphone.developer`

  `microsoft.public.pocketpc.developer`

  `microsoft.public.pocketpc` (and lots of others such as `microsoft.public.pocketpc.wireless`)

....

Focus on SQL Server CE 2.0

Microsoft SQL Server CE 2.0 is downloadable from `http://www.microsoft.com/sql/ce/downloads/20readme.asp`. (Free registration is required—the download is 47.6MB.) Note that it requires Windows XP or 2000 or higher for development. More specifically, you need

- An IIS system running under NT4/SP5 or later or Windows 2000 to do an RDA or replication

- Windows 2000 or Windows XP for the development system

- A Windows CE–based device running Windows CE 4.1 for deployment (though you can develop and test apps using the emulators that are included both in Microsoft's free eMbedded Visual Tools 3.0 or the not free Visual Studio .NET and the .NET Compact Framework)

For unmanaged (native) applications (which can run on Pocket PC 2000, Pocket PC 2002, Pocket PC Phone Edition, Handheld PC 2000 [HP/C 2000], and certain other embedded devices that use Windows CE 4.1), you'll use Microsoft eMbedded Visual Tools 3.0 installed with at least one of the following software development kits: Palm-size PC SDK, Handheld PC Pro SDK, or Pocket PC SDK for native (unmanaged) application development.

To create Microsoft .NET Compact Framework (managed) applications (which can run on Pocket PC 2000, Pocket PC 2002, Pocket PC Phone Edition, and certain other embedded devices that use Windows CE 4.1), you'll need Visual Studio .NET and the .NET Compact Framework (ideally, the just-released 1.1 "Everett" edition). Both development environments have emulators in case you don't have a physical device running CE 4.1.

Side-by-side installations of this release of SQL Server CE 2.0 with earlier versions of SQL Server CE are supported.

Download the documentation from `http://www.microsoft.com/sql/ce/techinfo/20bol.asp`.

If you use SQL Server CE, you must update the server replication components on servers running Internet Information Services (IIS) when you install SQL Server 2000 Service Pack 2 (SP2). Download this package to make sure your operating environment is up to date.

SQL Server CE 2.0 Readme (`http://support.microsoft.com/default.aspx?scid=kb;en-us;Q327957`) describes additional info that didn't make it into the SQL Server CE 2.0 documentation. For example, Pocket PC 2000 Service Pack 1 (`http://support.microsoft.com/default.aspx?scid=http://www.microsoft.com/mobile/pocketpc/downloads/servicepack1.asp` or `http://www.compaq.com/support/files/handhelds/us/download/9820.html` for iPAQ users) is required for Integrated Security.

Index